New Perspectives on

MICROSOFT®
EXCEL 2002

Comprehensive

COURSE TECHNOLOGY

THOMSON LEARNING

New Perspectives on Microsoft® Excel 2002—Comprehensive

is published by Course Technology.

Managing Editor: Greg Donald	**Technology Product Manager:** Amanda Young	**Production Editor:** Aimee Poirier
Senior Editor: Donna Gridley	**Editorial Assistant:** Jessica Engstrom	**Composition:** GEX Publishing Services
Senior Product Manager: Kathy Finnegan	**Marketing Manager:** Sean Teare	**Text Designer:** Meral Dabcovich
Product Manager: Melissa Hathaway	**Developmental Editor:** Jane Pedicini	**Cover Designer:** Efrat Reis

New Perspectives on

MICROSOFT®
EXCEL 2002

Comprehensive

JUNE JAMRICH PARSONS

DAN OJA

ROY AGELOFF
University of Rhode Island

PATRICK CAREY
Carey Associates, Inc.

**COURSE
TECHNOLOGY**
™
THOMSON LEARNING

Australia • Canada • Mexico • Singapore • Spain • United Kingdom • United States

APPROVED COURSEWARE

What does this logo mean?

It means this courseware has been approved by the Microsoft® Office User Specialist Program to be among the finest available for learning Microsoft Excel 2002. It also means that upon completion of this courseware, you may be prepared to become a Microsoft Office User Specialist.

What is a Microsoft Office User Specialist?

A Microsoft Office User Specialist is an individual who has certified his or her skills in one or more of the Microsoft Office desktop applications of Microsoft Word, Microsoft Excel, Microsoft PowerPoint®, Microsoft Outlook® or Microsoft Access, or in Microsoft Project. The Microsoft Office User Specialist Program typically offers certification exams at the "Core" and "Expert" skill levels.* The Microsoft Office User Specialist Program is the only Microsoft approved program in the world for certifying proficiency in Microsoft Office desktop applications and Microsoft Project. This certification can be a valuable asset in any job search or career advancement.

More Information:

To learn more about becoming a Microsoft Office User Specialist, visit www.mous.net

To purchase a Microsoft Office User Specialist certification exam, visit www.DesktopIQ.com

To learn about other Microsoft Office User Specialist approved courseware from Course Technology, visit www.course.com/NewPerspectives/TeachersLounge/mous.cfm

Preface

Course Technology is the world leader in information technology education. The New Perspectives Series is an integral part of Course Technology's success. Visit our Web site to see a whole new perspective on teaching and learning solutions.

New Perspectives—Building Computer Skills Has Never Been This Real

Why New Perspectives will work for you.

Critical thinking and **problem solving**—without them, computer skills are learned but soon forgotten. With its **case-based** approach, the New Perspectives Series challenges students to apply what they've learned to real-life situations. Become a member of the New Perspectives community and watch your students not only **master** computer skills, but also **retain** and carry this **knowledge** into the world.

New Perspectives catalog
Our online catalog is never out of date! Go to the Catalog button on our Web site to check out our available titles, request a desk copy, download a book preview, or locate online files.

Complete system of offerings
Whether you're looking for a Brief book, an Advanced book, or something in between, we've got you covered. Go to the Catalog button on our Web site to find the level of coverage that's right for you.

Instructor materials
We have all the tools you need—data files, solution files, figure files, a sample syllabus, and ExamView, our powerful testing software package.

How well do your students know Microsoft Office?
Find out with performance-based testing software that measures your students' proficiency in the application. Click the Tech Center button to learn more.

Get certified
If you want to get certified, we have the titles for you. Find out more by clicking the Teacher's Lounge button.

Interested in online learning?
Enhance your course with any one of our online learning platforms. Go to the Teacher's Lounge to find the platform that's right for you.

Your link to the future is at
www.course.com/NewPerspectives

What you need to know about this book.

- Student Online Companion takes students to the Web for additional work.

- ExamView testing software gives you the option of generating a printed test, LAN-based test, or test over the Internet.

- New Perspectives Labs provide students with self-paced practice on computer-related topics.

- All tutorial cases are NEW to this edition!

- Our coverage of functions is more extensive and complete than that of other texts. Students work with financial functions to calculate the cost of mortgages and loans; calculate a payments schedule using Excel's financial and logical functions; and work with text and date functions.

- Students will appreciate the in-depth explanation of cells and cell references, as they learn about absolute, relative, and mixed references and how to correctly apply them in formulas.

- Our coverage of macros emphasizes the importance of rehearsing macros before recording them, and provides ample opportunity for students to reinforce learning by creating a variety of macros.

- The tutorial on using Solver goes into great detail to explain how to solve a complex problem using the tools that Excel provides. The examples used will help students understand and master these tools.

- The PivotTable tool can be one of the hardest for a new student to learn. Our explanation of PivotTables and real-world context helps students to realize their power and value.

- The tutorial on VBA provides both the basic concepts and principles of VBA programming and broadens students' experience with VBA, as they create and modify interactive macros using VBA.

- This book is certified at the MOUS Expert level for Excel 2002!

CASE	TROUBLE?	SESSION 1.1	QUICK CHECK	RW
Tutorial Case Each tutorial begins with a problem presented in a case that is meaningful to students. The case sets the scene to help students understand what they will do in the tutorial.	**TROUBLE? Paragraphs** These paragraphs anticipate the mistakes or problems that students may have and help them continue with the tutorial.	**Sessions** Each tutorial is divided into sessions designed to be completed in about 45 minutes each. Students should take as much time as they need and take a break between sessions.	**Quick Check Questions** Each session concludes with conceptual Quick Check questions that test students' understanding of what they learned in the session.	**Reference Windows** Reference Windows are succinct summaries of the most important tasks covered in a tutorial. They preview actions students will perform in the steps to follow.

BRIEF CONTENTS

TABLE OF CONTENTS

Tutorial 1   WIN 2000 1.03

Exploring the Basics

Investigating the Windows 2000 Operating System

Tutorial 2   WIN 2000 2.01

Working with Files

Creating, Saving, and Managing Files

Tutorial 3   EX 3.01

Developing a Professional-Looking Worksheet

Formatting a Sales Report

Tutorial 4   EX 4.01

Working with Charts and Graphics

Charting Sales Data for Vega Telescopes

Tutorial 6 — EX 6.01

Working with Multiple Worksheets and Workbooks

Tracking Cash Flow for the Lakeland Boychoir

Microsoft Excel 2002

Tutorial 9 EX 9.03

Data Tables and Scenario Management

Performing a Cost-Volume-Profit Analysis for Front Range Rafting

Tutorial 10   EX 10.01

Using Solver for Complex Problems

Determining the Optimal Product Mix for GrillRite Grills

Tutorial 11   EX 11.01

Importing Data Into Excel

Working with a Stock Portfolio for Davis & Larson

Additional Case 1   EX AC1.01

Sales Invoicing for Island Dreamz Shoppe

Additional Case 2   EX AC2.01

Performance Reporting for Biodeck, Inc.

Additional Case 3   EX AC3.01

Negotiating Salaries for the National Basketball Association

Additional Case 4   EX AC4.01

Analyzing Product Mix for Stardust Telescopes

Appendix 1   EX A1.01

Working with Logical Functions

Recording Employee Financial Data

Appendix 2   EX A2.01

Integrating Excel with Other Windows Programs

Creating Integrated Documents for The Lighthouse

Appendix 3   EX A3.01

Creating Custom Formats

Formatting Stock Market Data

Appendix 4   EX A4.01

Saving PivotTables in HTML Format

Creating Interactive PivotTables for the Web

Acknowledgments

We would like to thank the many people whose invaluable contributions made this book possible. First, thanks go to our reviewers: Rory DeSimone, University of Florida; Michael Feiler, Merritt College; Eric Johnston, Vatterott College; Mary McIntosh, Red River College; and Donna Occhifinto, County College of Morris. At Course Technology we would like to thank Greg Donald, Managing Editor; Donna Gridley, Senior Editor; Kathy Finnegan, Senior Product Manager; Jessica Engstrom, Editorial Assistant; Aimee Poirier, Production Editor; John Bosco, Quality Assurance Project Leader; and Marianne Broughey, Harris Bierhoff, and John Freitas, Quality Assurance Testers. A special thanks to Jane Pedicini, Developmental Editor, for her dedication and hard work in completing this text.

June Jamrich Parsons

Dan Oja

Roy Ageloff

Patrick Carey

New Perspectives on

MICROSOFT®
WINDOWS® 2000
PROFESSIONAL

Read This Before You Begin

To the Student

Make Data Disk Program

To complete the Level I tutorials, Review Assignments, and Projects, you need three Data Disks. Your instructor will either provide you with Data Disks or ask you to make your own.

If you are making your own Data Disks you will need three blank, formatted high-density disks and access to the Make Data Disk program. If you want to install the Make Data Disk program to your home computer, you can obtain it from your instructor or from the Web. To download the Make Data Disk program from the Web, go to www.course.com, click Data Disks, and follow the instructions on the screen.

To install the Make Data Disk program, select and click the file you just downloaded from www.course.com, 6548-9.exe. Follow the onscreen instructions to complete the installation. If you have any trouble obtaining or installing the Make Data Disk program, ask your instructor or technical support person for assistance.

Once you have obtained and installed the Make Data Disk program, you can use it to create your Data Disks according to the steps in the tutorials.

Course Labs

The Level I tutorials in this book feature three interactive Course Labs to help you understand Using a Keyboard, Using a Mouse, and Using Files concepts. There are Lab Assignments at the end of Tutorials 1 and 2 that relate to these Labs. To start a Lab, click the **Start** button on the Windows 2000 taskbar, point to **Programs**, point to

Course Labs, point to New Perspectives Course Labs, and click the name of the Lab you want to use.

Using Your Own Computer

If you are going to work through this book using your own computer, you need:

- **Computer System** Microsoft Windows 2000 Professional must be installed on a local hard drive or on a network drive. This book is about Windows 2000 Professional—for those who have Windows 2000 Millennium, you might notice some differences.

- **Data Disks** You will not be able to complete the tutorials or exercises in this book using your own computer until you have your Data Disks. See "Make Data Disk Program" above for details on obtaining your Data Disks.

- **Course Labs** See your instructor or technical support person to obtain the Course Lab software for use on your own computer.

Visit Our World Wide Web Site

Additional materials designed especially for you are available on the World Wide Web. Go to http://www.course.com.

To the Instructor

The Make Data Disk Program and Course Labs for this title are available in the Instructor's Resource Kit for this title. Follow the instructions in the Help file on the CD-ROM to install the programs to your network or standalone computer. For information on using the Make Data Disk Program or the Course Labs, see the "To the Student" section above. Students will be switching the default installation settings to Web style in Tutorial 2. You are granted a license to copy the Data Files and Course Labs to any computer or computer network used by students who have purchased this book.

In this tutorial you will:

■ Start and shut down Windows 2000

■ Identify the objects on the Windows 2000 desktop

■ Practice mouse functions

■ Run software programs, switch between them, and close them

■ Identify and use the controls in a window

■ Use Windows 2000 controls such as menus, toolbars, list boxes, scroll bars, option buttons, tabs, and check boxes

■ Explore the Windows 2000 Help system

LABS

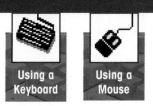

EXPLORING THE BASICS

Investigating the Windows 2000 Operating System

CASE

Your First Day on the Computer

You walk into the computer lab and sit down at a desk. There's a computer in front of you, and you find yourself staring dubiously at the screen. Where to start? As if in answer to your question, your friend Steve Laslow appears.

"You start with the operating system," says Steve. Noticing your puzzled look, Steve explains that the **operating system** is software that helps the computer carry out operating tasks such as displaying information on the computer screen and saving data on your disks. (Software refers to the **programs**, or **applications**, that a computer uses to perform tasks.) Your computer uses the **Microsoft Windows 2000 Professional** operating system—Windows 2000, for short.

Steve explains that much of the software available for Windows 2000 has a standard graphical user interface. This means that once you have learned how to use one Windows program, such as Microsoft Word word-processing software, you are well on your way to understanding how to use other Windows software. Windows 2000 lets you use more than one program at a time, so you can easily switch between them—between your word-processing software and your appointment book software, for example. Finally, Windows 2000 makes it very easy to access the **Internet**, the worldwide collection of computers connected to one another to enable communication. All in all, Windows 2000 makes your computer effective and easy to use.

Steve recommends that you get started right away by starting Microsoft Windows 2000 and practicing some basic skills.

<table>
<tr><td>

SESSION 1.1

</td><td>

In this session, in addition to learning basic Windows terminology, you will learn how to use a pointing device, how to start and close a program, and how to use more than one program at a time.

</td></tr>
</table>

Starting Windows 2000

Using a Keyboard

Windows 2000 automatically starts when you turn on the computer. Depending on the way your computer is set up, you might be asked to enter your username and password.

> *To start Windows 2000:*
>
> **1.** Turn on your computer.
>
> TROUBLE? If you are asked to select an operating system, do not take action. Windows 2000 will start automatically after a designated number of seconds. If it does not, ask your technical support person for help.
>
> TROUBLE? If prompted to do so, type your assigned username and press the Tab key. Then type your password and press the Enter key to continue.
>
> TROUBLE? If this is the first time you have started your computer with Windows 2000, messages might appear on your screen informing you that Windows is setting up components of your computer. If the Getting Started with Windows 2000 box appears, press and hold down the Alt key on your keyboard and then, while you hold down the Alt key, press the F4 key. The box closes.

After a moment, Windows 2000 starts. Windows 2000 has a **graphical user interface** (**GUI,** pronounced "gooey"), which uses **icons,** or pictures of familiar objects, such as file folders and documents, to represent items in your computer such as programs or files. Microsoft Windows 2000 gets its name from the rectangular work areas, called "windows," that appear on your screen as you work (although no windows should be open right now).

The Windows 2000 Desktop

In Windows terminology, the area displayed on your screen when Windows 2000 starts represents a **desktop**—a workspace for projects and the tools needed to manipulate those projects. When you first start a computer, it uses **default** settings, those preset by the operating system. The default desktop, for example, has a plain blue background. However, Microsoft designed Windows 2000 so that you can easily change the appearance of the desktop. You can, for example, add color, patterns, images, and text to the desktop background.

Many institutions design customized desktops for their computers. Figure 1-1 shows the default Windows 2000 desktop and two other examples of desktops, one designed for a business, North Pole Novelties, and one designed for a school, the University of Colorado. Although your desktop might not look exactly like any of the examples in Figure 1-1, you should be able to locate objects on your screen similar to those in Figure 1-1. Look at your screen and locate the objects labeled in Figure 1-1. The objects on your screen might appear larger or smaller than those in Figure 1-1, depending on your monitor's settings.

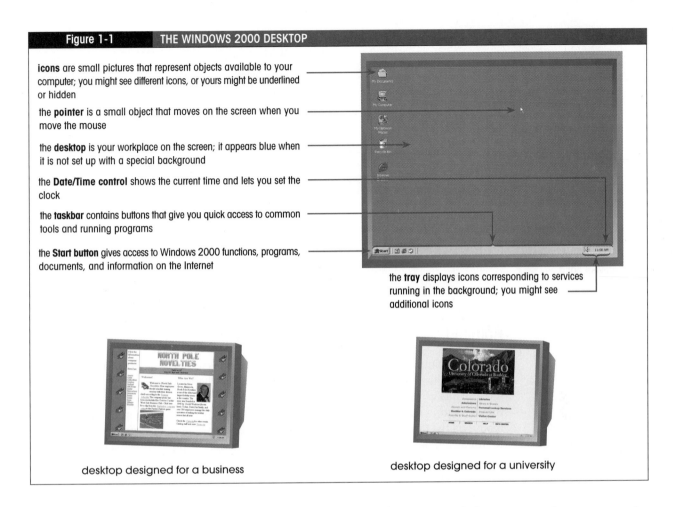

| Figure 1-1 | THE WINDOWS 2000 DESKTOP |

icons are small pictures that represent objects available to your computer; you might see different icons, or yours might be underlined or hidden

the **pointer** is a small object that moves on the screen when you move the mouse

the **desktop** is your workplace on the screen; it appears blue when it is not set up with a special background

the **Date/Time control** shows the current time and lets you set the clock

the **taskbar** contains buttons that give you quick access to common tools and running programs

the **Start button** gives access to Windows 2000 functions, programs, documents, and information on the Internet

the **tray** displays icons corresponding to services running in the background; you might see additional icons

desktop designed for a business

desktop designed for a university

If the screen goes blank or starts to display a moving design, press any key to restore the Windows 2000 desktop.

Using a Pointing Device

Using a Mouse

A **pointing device** helps you interact with objects on the screen. Pointing devices come in many shapes and sizes; some are designed to ensure that your hand won't suffer fatigue while using them. Some are directly attached to your computer via a cable, whereas others function like a TV remote control and allow you to access your computer without being right next to it. Figure 1-2 shows examples of common pointing devices.

The most common pointing device is called a **mouse**, so this book uses that term. If you are using a different pointing device, such as a trackball, substitute that device whenever you see the term "mouse." Because Windows 2000 uses a graphical user interface, you need to know how to use the mouse to manipulate the objects on the screen. In this session you will learn about pointing and clicking. In Session 1.2 you will learn how to use the mouse to drag objects.

You can also interact with objects by using the keyboard; however, the mouse is more convenient for most tasks, so the tutorials in this book assume you are using one.

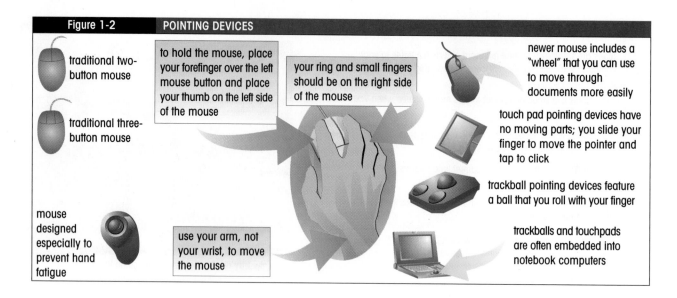

Figure 1-2   POINTING DEVICES

traditional two-button mouse

to hold the mouse, place your forefinger over the left mouse button and place your thumb on the left side of the mouse

your ring and small fingers should be on the right side of the mouse

newer mouse includes a "wheel" that you can use to move through documents more easily

traditional three-button mouse

touch pad pointing devices have no moving parts; you slide your finger to move the pointer and tap to click

trackball pointing devices feature a ball that you roll with your finger

mouse designed especially to prevent hand fatigue

use your arm, not your wrist, to move the mouse

trackballs and touchpads are often embedded into notebook computers

Pointing

You use a pointing device to move the pointer over objects on the desktop. The pointer is usually shaped like an arrow , although it can change shape depending on where it is on the screen and on what tasks you are performing. Most computer users place the mouse on a **mouse pad**, a flat piece of rubber that helps the mouse move smoothly. As you move the mouse on the mouse pad, the pointer on the screen moves in a corresponding direction.

You begin most Windows operations by positioning the pointer over a specific part of the screen. This is called **pointing**.

To move the pointer:

1. Position your right index finger over the left mouse button, as shown in Figure 1-2, but don't click yet. Lightly grasp the sides of the mouse with your thumb and little fingers.

   TROUBLE? If you want to use the mouse with your left hand, ask your instructor or technical support person to help you use the Control Panel to swap the functions of the left and right mouse buttons. Be sure to find out how to change back to the right-handed mouse setting, so that you can reset the mouse each time you are finished in the lab.

2. Place the mouse on the mouse pad and then move the mouse. Watch the movement of the pointer.

   TROUBLE? If you run out of room to move your mouse, lift the mouse and place it in the middle of the mouse pad. Notice that the pointer does not move when the mouse is not in contact with the mouse pad.

When you position the mouse pointer over certain objects, such as the objects on the taskbar, a "tip" appears. These "tips" are called **ScreenTips**, and they tell you the purpose or function of an object.

To view ScreenTips:

1. Use the mouse to point to the **Start** button ![Start], but don't click it. After a few seconds, you see the tip "Click here to begin," as shown in Figure 1-3.

   TROUBLE? If the Start button and taskbar don't appear, point to the bottom of the screen. They will then appear.

Figure 1-3	VIEWING SCREENTIPS

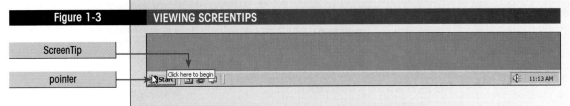

ScreenTip

pointer

2. Point to the time on the right end of the taskbar. Notice that today's date (or the date to which your computer's time clock is set) appears.

Clicking

Clicking is when you press a mouse button and immediately release it. Clicking sends a signal to your computer that you want to perform an action on the object you click. In Windows 2000 most actions are performed using the left mouse button. If you are told to click an object, click it with the left mouse button, unless instructed otherwise.

When you click the Start button, the Start menu appears. A **menu** is a list of options that you use to complete tasks. The **Start menu** provides you with access to programs, documents, and much more. Try clicking the Start button to open the Start menu.

To open the Start menu:

1. Point to the **Start** button ![Start].

2. Click the left mouse button. An arrow ▶ following an option on the Start menu indicates that you can view additional choices by navigating a **submenu**, a menu extending from the main menu. See Figure 1-4.

Figure 1-4	START MENU

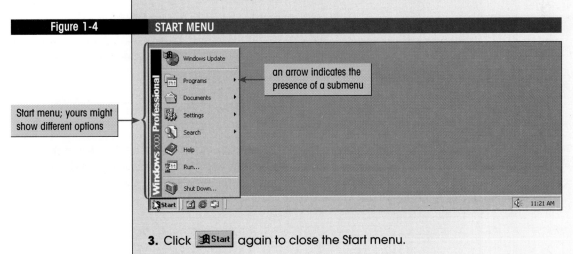

Start menu; yours might show different options

3. Click ![Start] again to close the Start menu.

Next you'll learn how to select items on a submenu.

Selecting

In Windows 2000, pointing and clicking are often used to **select** an object, in other words, to choose it as the object you want to work with. Windows 2000 shows you which object is selected by highlighting it, usually by changing the object's color, putting a box around it, or making the object appear to be pushed in, as shown in Figure 1-5.

Figure 1-5	SELECTED OBJECTS

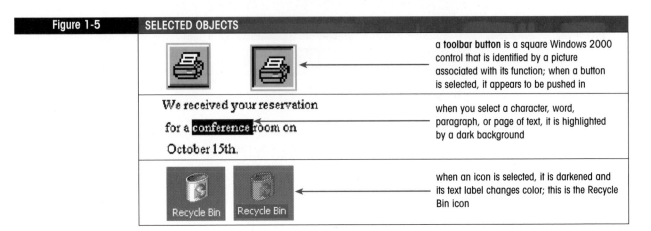

a **toolbar button** is a square Windows 2000 control that is identified by a picture associated with its function; when a button is selected, it appears to be pushed in

when you select a character, word, paragraph, or page of text, it is highlighted by a dark background

when an icon is selected, it is darkened and its text label changes color; this is the Recycle Bin icon

In Windows 2000, depending on your computer's settings, some objects are selected when you simply point to them, others when you click them. Practice selecting the Programs option on the Start menu to open the Programs submenu.

To select an option on a menu:

1. Click the **Start** button  and notice how it appears to be pushed in, indicating it is selected.

2. Point to (but don't click) the **Programs** option. After a short pause, the Programs submenu opens, and the Programs option is highlighted to indicate it is selected. See Figure 1-6.

Figure 1-6	PROGRAMS SUBMENU

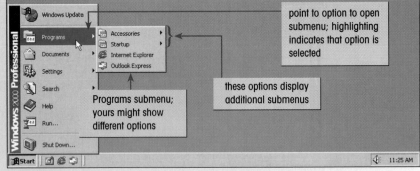

point to option to open submenu; highlighting indicates that option is selected

these options display additional submenus

Programs submenu; yours might show different options

TROUBLE? If a submenu other than the Programs menu opens, you selected the wrong option. Move the mouse so that the pointer points to Programs.

TROUBLE? If the Programs option doesn't appear, your Start menu might have too many options to fit on the screen. If that is the case, a double arrow ⱱ appears at the top or bottom of the Start menu. Click first the top and then the bottom arrow to view additional Start menu options until you locate the Programs menu option, and then point to it.

3. Now close the Start menu by clicking **Start** again.

You return to the desktop.

Right-Clicking

Pointing devices were originally designed with a single button, so the term "clicking" had only one meaning: you pressed that button. Innovations in technology, however, led to the addition of a second and even a third button (and more recently, options such as a wheel) that expanded the pointing device's capability. More recent software—especially that designed for Windows 2000—takes advantage of the additional buttons, especially the right button. However, the term "clicking" continues to refer to the left button; clicking an object with the *right* button is called **right-clicking**.

In Windows 2000, right-clicking both selects an object and opens its **shortcut menu**, a list of options directly related to the object you right-clicked. You can right-click practically any object—the Start button, a desktop icon, the taskbar, and even the desktop itself—to view options associated with that object. For example, the first desktop shown in Figure 1-7 illustrates what happens when you click the Start button with the left mouse button to open the Start menu. Clicking the Start button with the right button, however, opens the Start button's shortcut menu, as shown in the second desktop.

Figure 1-7	CLICKING WITH THE LEFT AND RIGHT MOUSE BUTTONS

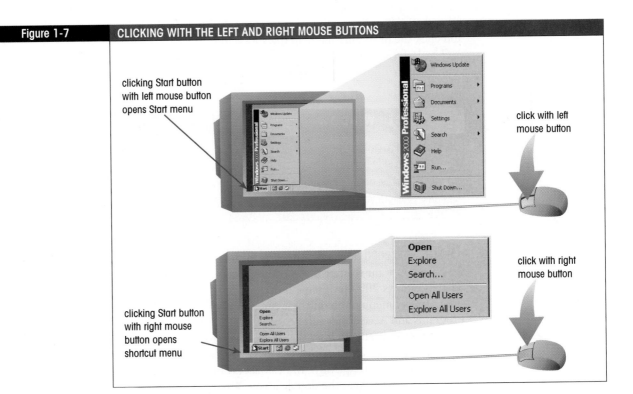

Try using right-clicking to open the shortcut menu for the Start button.

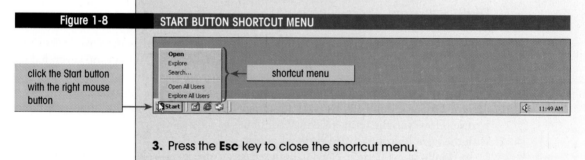

To right-click an object:

1. Position the pointer over the Start button.

2. Right-click the **Start** button [Start]. The shortcut menu that opens offers a list of options available to the Start button.

   TROUBLE? If you are using a trackball or a mouse with three buttons or a wheel, make sure you click the button on the far right, not the one in the middle.

   TROUBLE? If your menu looks slightly different from the one in Figure 1-8, don't worry. Different systems will have different options.

Figure 1-8	START BUTTON SHORTCUT MENU

click the Start button with the right mouse button

Open
Explore
Search...
Open All Users
Explore All Users

← shortcut menu

Start   11:49 AM

3. Press the **Esc** key to close the shortcut menu.

You again return to the desktop.

Starting and Closing a Program

To use a program, such as a word-processing program, you must first start it. With Windows 2000 you usually start a program by clicking the Start button and then you locate and click the program's name in the submenus.

The Reference Window below explains how to start a program. Don't do the steps in the Reference Windows as you go through the tutorials; they are for your later reference.

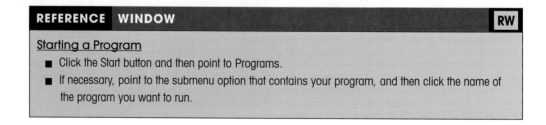

REFERENCE WINDOW   RW

Starting a Program
- Click the Start button and then point to Programs.
- If necessary, point to the submenu option that contains your program, and then click the name of the program you want to run.

Windows 2000 includes an easy-to-use word-processing program called WordPad. Suppose you want to start the WordPad program and use it to write a letter or report. You open Windows 2000 programs from the Start menu. Programs are usually located on the Programs submenu or on one of its submenus. To start WordPad, for example, you select the Programs and Accessories submenus.

If you can't locate an item that is supposed to be on a menu, it is most likely temporarily hidden. Windows 2000 menus use a feature called **Personalized Menus** that hides menu options you use infrequently. You can access hidden menu options by pointing to the menu name and then clicking the double arrow ⮟ (sometimes called a "chevron") at the bottom of the menu. You can also access the hidden options by holding the pointer over the menu name.

To start the WordPad program from the Start menu:

1. Click the **Start** button [Start] to open the Start menu.

2. Point to **Programs**. The Programs submenu appears.

3. Point to **Accessories**. The Accessories submenu appears. Figure 1-9 shows the open menus.

   TROUBLE? If a different menu opens, you might have moved the mouse diagonally so that a different submenu opened. Move the pointer to the right across the Programs option, and then move it up or down to point to Accessories. Once you're more comfortable moving the mouse, you'll find that you can eliminate this problem by moving the mouse quickly.

   TROUBLE? If WordPad doesn't appear on the Accessories submenu, continue to point to Accessories until WordPad appears.

Figure 1-9	START MENU

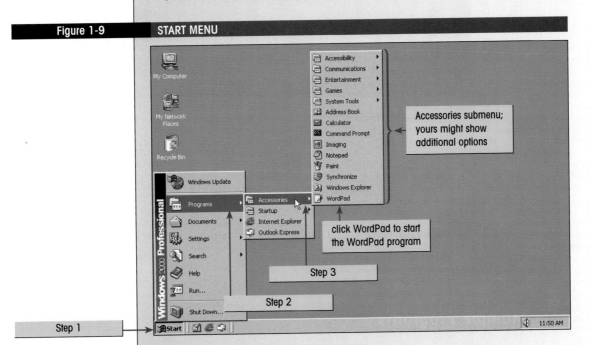

4. Click **WordPad**. The WordPad program opens, as shown in Figure 1-10. If the WordPad window fills the entire screen, don't worry. You will learn how to manipulate windows in Session 1.2.

Figure 1-10   THE WORDPAD PROGRAM

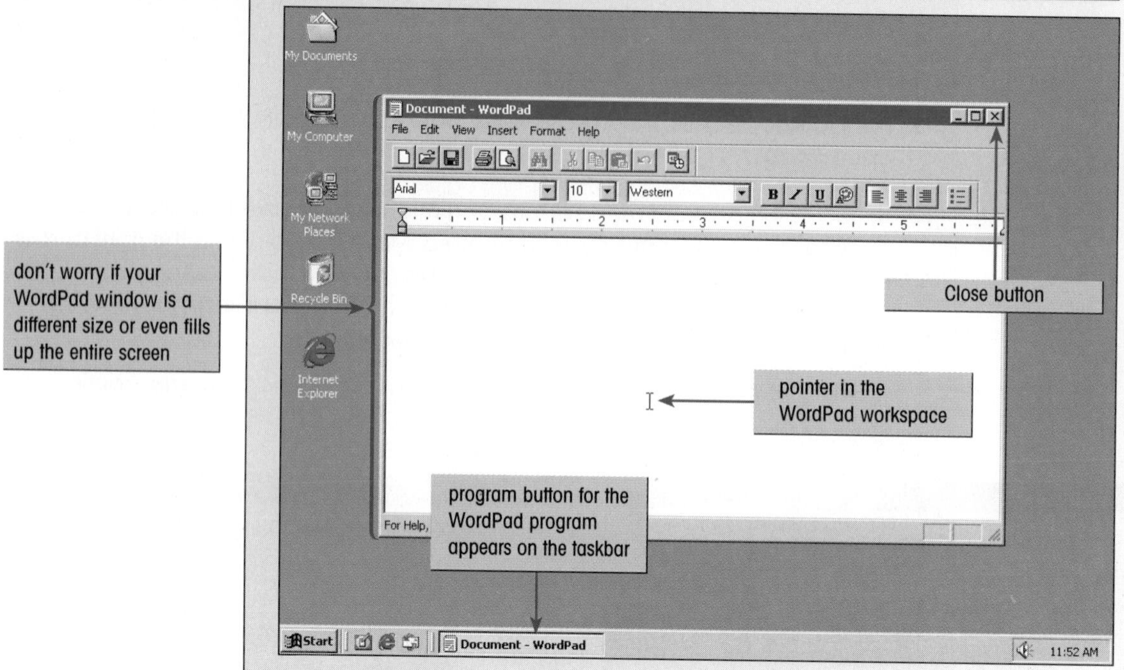

don't worry if your WordPad window is a different size or even fills up the entire screen

Close button

pointer in the WordPad workspace

program button for the WordPad program appears on the taskbar

When a program is started, it is said to be **open** or **running**. A **program button** appears on the taskbar for each open program. You click program buttons to switch between open programs. When you are finished using a program, click the Close button ☒.

To exit the WordPad program:

1. Click the **Close** button ☒. See Figure 1-10. You return to the Windows 2000 desktop.

Running **Multiple Programs**

One of the most useful features of Windows 2000 is its ability to run multiple programs at the same time. This feature, known as **multitasking**, allows you to work on more than one project at a time and to switch quickly between projects. For example, you can start WordPad and leave it running while you then start the Paint program.

To run WordPad and Paint at the same time:

1. Start WordPad again and then click the **Start** button 🏁Start again.

2. Point to **Programs** and then point to **Accessories**.

3. Click **Paint**. The Paint program opens, as shown in Figure 1-11. Now two programs are running at the same time.

   TROUBLE? If the Paint program fills the entire screen, don't worry. You will learn how to manipulate windows in Session 1.2.

Figure 1-11 | **THE PAINT PROGRAM**

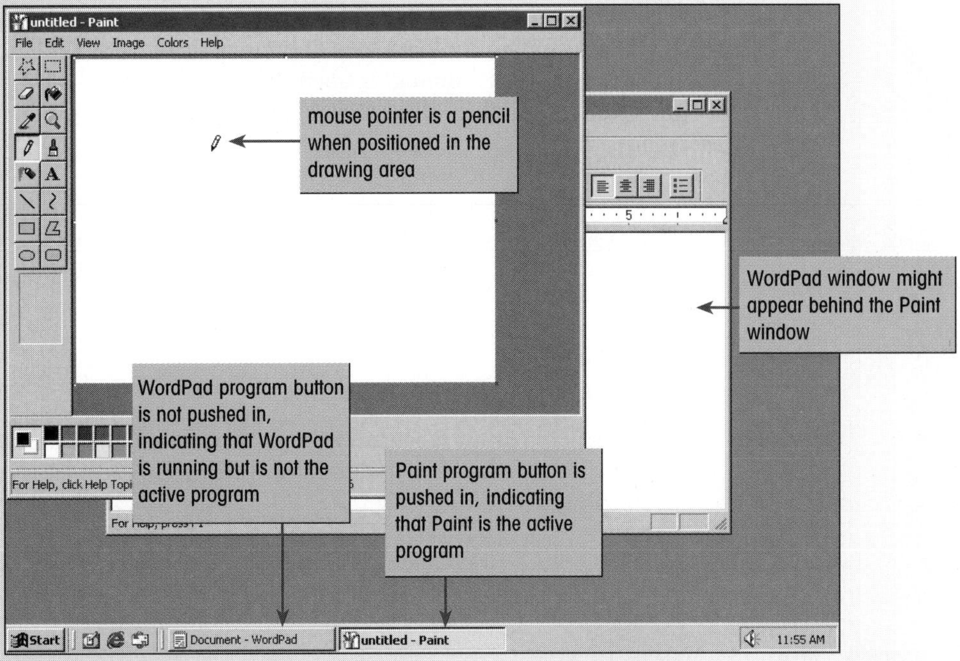

untitled - Paint

File   Edit   View   Image   Colors   Help

mouse pointer is a pencil when positioned in the drawing area

WordPad window might appear behind the Paint window

WordPad program button is not pushed in, indicating that WordPad is running but is not the active program

Paint program button is pushed in, indicating that Paint is the active program

For Help, click Help Topi

For help, press F1

Start | Document - WordPad | untitled - Paint | 11:55 AM

What happened to WordPad? The WordPad program button is still on the taskbar, so even if you can't see it, WordPad is still running. You can imagine that it is stacked behind the Paint program, as shown in Figure 1-12. Paint is the active program because it is the one with which you are currently working.

Figure 1-12 | **PROJECTS STACKED ON A DESK**

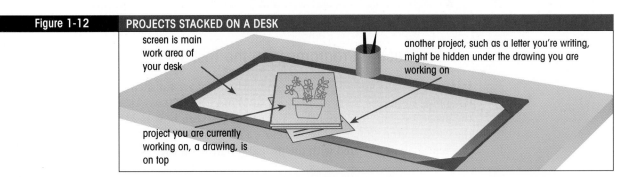

screen is main work area of your desk

another project, such as a letter you're writing, might be hidden under the drawing you are working on

project you are currently working on, a drawing, is on top

Switching Between Programs

The easiest way to switch between programs is to use the buttons on the taskbar.

To switch between WordPad and Paint:

1. Click the button labeled **Document - WordPad** on the taskbar. The Document - WordPad button now looks as if it has been pushed in, to indicate that it is the active program, and WordPad moves to the front.
2. Next, click the button labeled **untitled - Paint** on the taskbar to switch to the Paint program.

The Paint program is again the active program.

Accessing the Desktop from the Quick Launch Toolbar

The Windows 2000 taskbar, as you've seen, displays buttons for programs currently running. It also can contain **toolbars**, sets of buttons that give single-click access to programs or documents that aren't running or open. In its default state, the Windows 2000 taskbar displays the **Quick Launch toolbar**, which gives quick access to Web programs and to the desktop. Your taskbar might contain additional toolbars, or none at all.

When you are running more than one program but you want to return to the desktop, perhaps to use one of the desktop icons such as My Computer, you can do so by using one of the Quick Launch toolbar buttons. Clicking the Show Desktop button ☑ returns you to the desktop. The open programs are not closed; they are simply made inactive and reduced to buttons on the taskbar.

To return to the desktop:

1. Click the **Show Desktop** button ☑ on the Quick Launch toolbar. The desktop appears, and both the Paint and WordPad programs are temporarily inactive. See Figure 1-13.

   TROUBLE? If the Quick Launch toolbar doesn't appear on your taskbar, right-click the taskbar, point to Toolbars, and then click Quick Launch and try Step 1 again.

Figure 1-13	ACCESSING THE DESKTOP

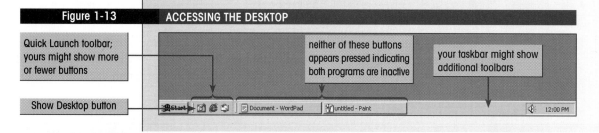

Quick Launch toolbar; yours might show more or fewer buttons

neither of these buttons appears pressed indicating both programs are inactive

your taskbar might show additional toolbars

Show Desktop button

Closing Inactive Programs from the Taskbar

It is good practice to close each program when you are finished using it. Each program uses computer resources, such as memory, so Windows 2000 works more efficiently when only the programs you need are open. You've already seen how to close an open program using the Close button ☒. You can also close a program, whether active or inactive, by using the shortcut menu associated with the program button on the taskbar.

To close WordPad and Paint using the program button shortcut menus:

1. Right-click the **untitled - Paint** button on the taskbar. To right-click something, remember that you click it with the right mouse button. The shortcut menu for that program button opens. See Figure 1-14.

2. Click **Close**. The button labeled "untitled - Paint" disappears from the taskbar, indicating that the Paint program is closed.

3. Right-click the **Document - WordPad** button on the taskbar, and then click **Close**. The WordPad button disappears from the taskbar.

Figure 1-14   PROGRAM BUTTON SHORTCUT MENU

shortcut menu opens
when you right-click
program button

Restore
Move
Size
Minimize
Maximize
Close   Alt+F4

click to close
inactive program

Start   Document - WordPad   untitled - Paint   12:01 PM

Shutting Down Windows 2000

It is very important to shut down Windows 2000 before you turn off the computer. If you turn off your computer without correctly shutting down, you might lose data and damage your files.

You should typically use the "Shut Down" option when you want to turn off your computer. However, your school might prefer that you select the Log Off option in the Shut Down Windows dialog box. This option logs you out of Windows 2000, leaves the computer turned on, and allows another user to log on without restarting the computer. Check with your instructor or technical support person for the preferred method at your lab.

To shut down Windows 2000:

1. Click the **Start** button Start on the taskbar to display the Start menu.

2. Click the **Shut Down** menu option. A box titled "Shut Down Windows" opens.

   TROUBLE? If you can't see the Shut Down menu option, your Start menu has more options than your screen can display. A double arrow ⚭ appears at the bottom of the Start menu. Click this button until the Shut Down menu option appears, and then click Shut Down.

   TROUBLE? If you are supposed to log off rather than shut down, click the Log Off option instead and follow your school's logoff procedure.

3. Make sure the **Shut Down** option appears in the box shown in Figure 1-15.

   TROUBLE? If "Shut down" does not appear, click the arrow to the right of the box. A list of options appears. Click Shut Down.

Figure 1-15   SHUTTING DOWN

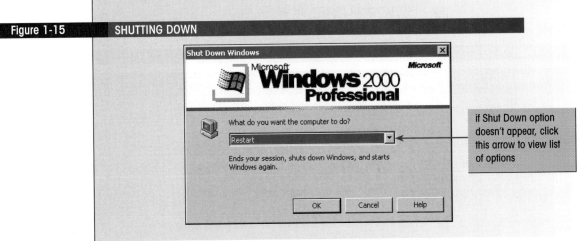

if Shut Down option
doesn't appear, click
this arrow to view list
of options

4. Click the **OK** button.

5. Wait until you see a message indicating it is safe to turn off your computer. If your lab staff has requested you to switch off your computer after shutting down, do so now. Otherwise leave the computer running. Some computers turn themselves off automatically.

Session 1.1 QUICK | CHECK

1. What is the purpose of the taskbar?

2. The _____ feature of Windows 2000 allows you to run more than one program at a time.

3. The _____ is a list of options that provides you with access to programs, documents, submenus, and more.

4. What should you do if you are trying to move the pointer to the left edge of your screen, but your mouse bumps into the keyboard?

5. Even if you can't see an open program on your desktop, the program might be running. How can you tell if a program is running?

6. Why is it good practice to close each program when you are finished using it?

7. Why should you shut down Windows 2000 before you turn off your computer?

SESSION 1.2

In this session you will learn how to use many of the Windows 2000 controls to manipulate windows and programs. You will also learn how to change the size and shape of a window; how to move a window; and how to use menus, dialog boxes, tabs, buttons, and lists to specify how you want a program to carry out a task.

Anatomy of a Window

When you run a program in Windows 2000, it appears in a window. A **window** is a rectangular area of the screen that contains a program or data. Windows, spelled with an uppercase "W," is the name of the Microsoft operating system. The word "window" with a lowercase "w" refers to one of the rectangular areas on the screen. A window also contains controls for manipulating the window and for using the program. Figure 1-16 describes the controls you are likely to see in most windows.

Figure 1-16	WINDOW CONTROLS
CONTROL	**DESCRIPTION**
Menu bar	Contains the titles of menus, such as File, Edit, and Help
Sizing buttons	Let you enlarge, shrink, or close a window
Status bar	Provides you with messages relevant to the task you are performing
Title bar	Contains the window title and basic window control buttons
Toolbar	Contains buttons that provide you with shortcuts to common menu commands
Window title	Identifies the program and document contained in the window
Workspace	Part of the window you use to enter your work—to enter text, draw pictures, set up calculations, and so on

WordPad is a good example of a typical window, so try starting WordPad and identifying these controls in the WordPad window.

To look at window controls:

1. Make sure Windows 2000 is running and you are at the Windows 2000 desktop.

2. Start WordPad.

   TROUBLE? To start WordPad, click the Start button, point to Programs, point to Accessories, and then click WordPad.

3. On your screen, identify the controls labeled in Figure 1-17. Don't worry if your window fills the entire screen or is a different size. You'll learn to change window size shortly.

| Figure 1-17 | WORDPAD WINDOW CONTROLS |

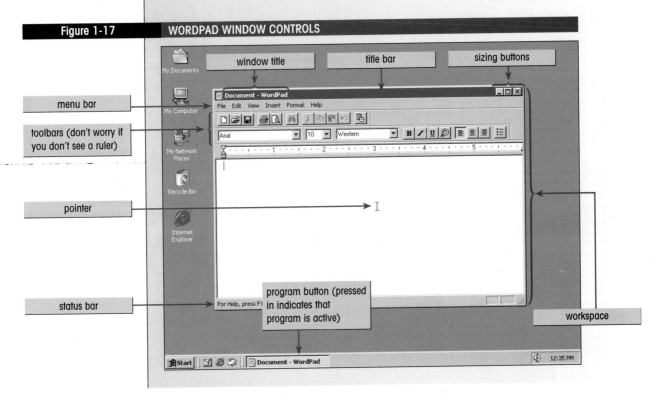

Manipulating a Window

There are three buttons located on the right side of the title bar. You are already familiar with the Close button. The Minimize button ▬ hides the window so that only its program button is visible on the taskbar. The other button changes name and function depending on the status of the window (it either maximizes the window or restores it to a predefined size). Figure 1-18 shows how these buttons work.

Minimizing a Window

The Minimize button hides a window so that only the button on the taskbar remains visible. You can use the Minimize button when you want to temporarily hide a window but keep the program running.

Figure 1-18   WINDOW BUTTONS

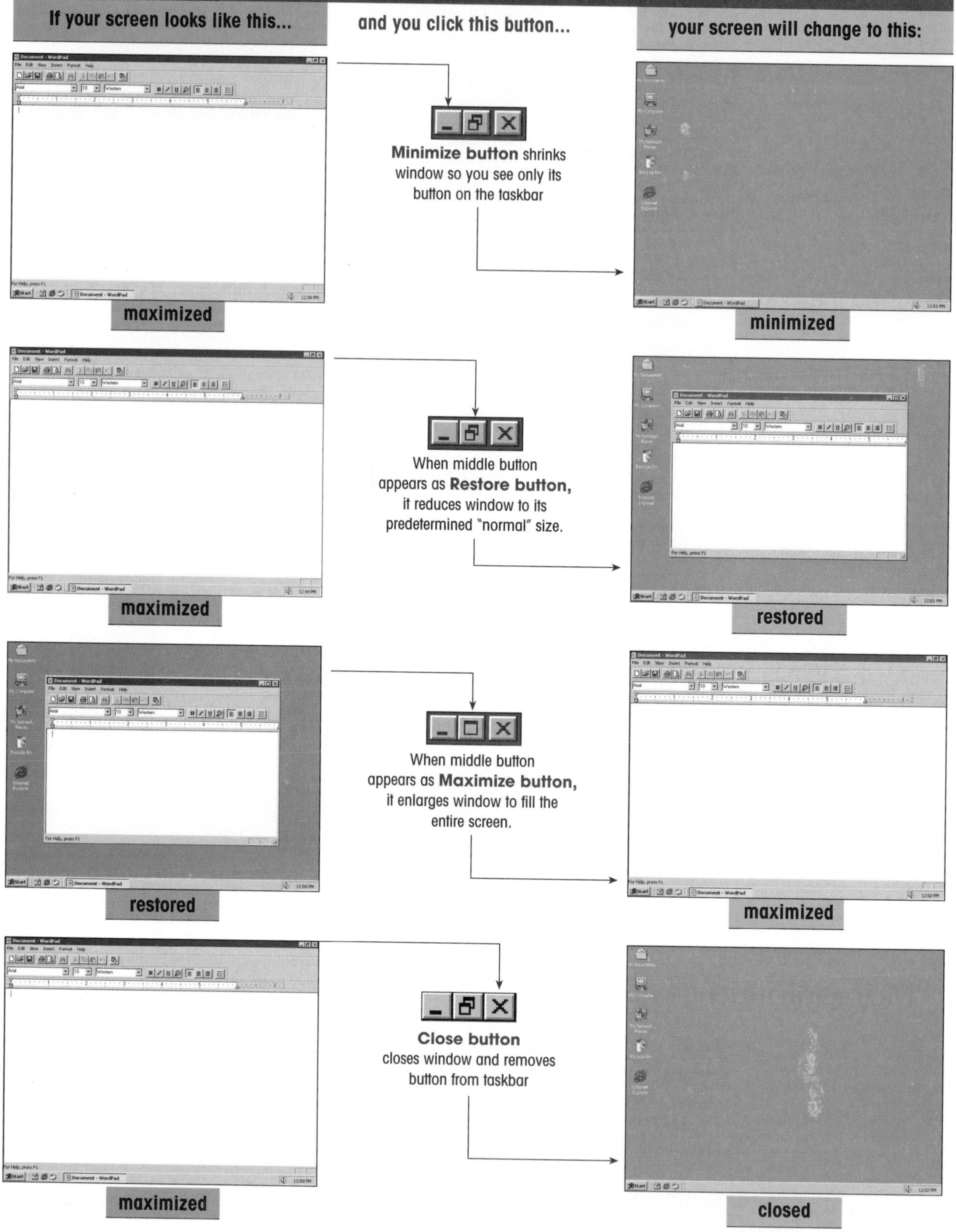

If your screen looks like this...	and you click this button...	your screen will change to this:

maximized

Minimize button shrinks window so you see only its button on the taskbar

minimized

maximized

When middle button appears as **Restore button,** it reduces window to its predetermined "normal" size.

restored

restored

When middle button appears as **Maximize button,** it enlarges window to fill the entire screen.

maximized

maximized

Close button closes window and removes button from taskbar

closed

To minimize the WordPad window:

1. Click the **Minimize** button ⬛. The WordPad window shrinks so that only the Document - WordPad button on the taskbar is visible.

TROUBLE? If you accidentally clicked the Close button and closed the window, use the Start button to start WordPad again.

Redisplaying a Window

You can redisplay a minimized window by clicking the program's button on the taskbar. When you redisplay a window, it becomes the active window.

To redisplay the WordPad window:

1. Click the **Document - WordPad** button on the taskbar. The WordPad window is restored to its previous size. The Document - WordPad button looks pushed in as a visual clue that WordPad is now the active window.

2. The taskbar button provides another means of switching a window between its minimized and active state: Click the **Document - WordPad** button on the taskbar again to minimize the window.

3. Click the **Document - WordPad** button once more to redisplay the window.

Maximizing a Window

The Maximize button enlarges a window so that it fills the entire screen. You will probably do most of your work using maximized windows because they allow you to see more of your program and data.

To maximize the WordPad window:

1. Click the **Maximize** button ⬜ on the WordPad title bar.

TROUBLE? If the window is already maximized, it will fill the entire screen, and the Maximize button won't appear. Instead, you'll see the Restore button ⬜. Skip Step 1.

Restoring a Window

The Restore button ⬜ reduces the window so it is smaller than the entire screen. This is useful if you want to see more than one window at a time. Also, because of its smaller size, you can drag the window to another location on the screen or change its dimensions.

To restore a window:

1. Click the **Restore** button ⬜ on the WordPad title bar. Notice that once a window is restored, ⬜ changes to the Maximize button ⬜.

Moving a Window

You can use the mouse to move a window to a new position on the screen. When you click an object and hold down the mouse button while moving the mouse, you are said to be **dragging** the object. You can move objects on the screen by dragging them to a new location. If you want to move a window, you drag its title bar. You cannot move a maximized window.

To drag the WordPad window to a new location:

1. Position the mouse pointer on the WordPad window title bar.
2. While you hold down the left mouse button, move the mouse to drag the window. A rectangle representing the window moves as you move the mouse.
3. Position the rectangle anywhere on the screen, then release the left mouse button. The WordPad window appears in the new location.
4. Now drag the WordPad window to the upper-left corner of the screen.

Changing the Size of a Window

You can also use the mouse to change the size of a window. Notice the sizing handle [//] at the lower-right corner of the window. The **sizing handle** provides a visible control for changing the size of a window.

To change the size of the WordPad window:

1. Position the pointer over the sizing handle [//]. The pointer changes to a diagonal arrow ⬉ .
2. While holding down the mouse button, drag the sizing handle down and to the right.
3. Release the mouse button. Now the window is larger.
4. Practice using the sizing handle to make the WordPad window larger or smaller, and then maximize the WordPad window.

You can also drag the window borders left, right, up, or down to change a window's size.

Using **Program Menus**

Most Windows programs use menus to organize the program's menu options. The menu bar is typically located at the top of the program window and shows the titles of menus such as File, Edit, and Help.

Windows menus are relatively standardized—most Windows programs include similar menu options. It's easy to learn new programs, because you can make a pretty good guess about which menu contains the option you want.

Selecting Options from a Menu

When you click any menu title, choices for that menu appear below the menu bar. These choices are referred to as **menu options** or **commands**. To select a menu option, you click it. For example, the File menu is a standard feature in most Windows programs and contains the options typically related to working with a file: creating, opening, saving, and printing a file or document.

To select the Print Preview menu option on the File menu:

1. Click **File** on the WordPad menu bar to display the File menu. See Figure 1-19.

TROUBLE? If you open a menu but decide not to select any of the menu options, you can close the menu by clicking its title again.

Figure 1-19	FILE MENU

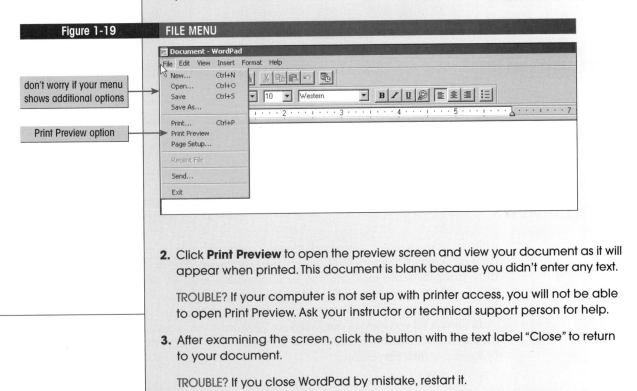

don't worry if your menu shows additional options

Print Preview option

2. Click **Print Preview** to open the preview screen and view your document as it will appear when printed. This document is blank because you didn't enter any text.

TROUBLE? If your computer is not set up with printer access, you will not be able to open Print Preview. Ask your instructor or technical support person for help.

3. After examining the screen, click the button with the text label "Close" to return to your document.

TROUBLE? If you close WordPad by mistake, restart it.

Not all menu options immediately carry out an action—some show submenus or ask you for more information about what you want to do. The menu gives you hints about what to expect when you select an option. These hints are sometimes referred to as **menu conventions**. Figure 1-20 describes the Windows 2000 menu conventions.

Figure 1-20	MENU CONVENTIONS

CONVENTION	DESCRIPTION
Check mark	Indicates a toggle, or "on-off" switch (like a light switch) that is either checked (turned on) or not checked (turned off)
Ellipsis	Three dots that indicate you must make additional selections after you select that option. Options without dots do not require additional choices—they take effect as soon as you click them. If an option is followed by an ellipsis, a dialog box opens that allows you to enter specifications for how you want a task carried out.
Triangular arrow	Indicates the presence of a submenu. When you point at a menu option that has a triangular arrow, a sub-menu automatically appears.
Grayed-out option	Option that is not available. For example, a graphics program might display the Text Toolbar option in gray if there is no text in the graphic to work with.
Keyboard shortcut	A key or combination of keys that you can press to activate the menu option without actually opening the menu
Double arrow	Indicates that additional menu options are available; click the double arrow to access them

Figure 1-21 shows examples of these menu conventions.

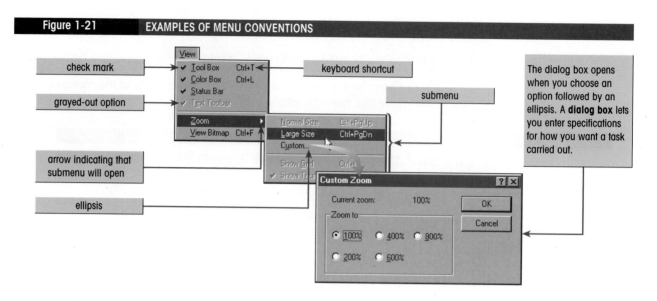

Figure 1-21   EXAMPLES OF MENU CONVENTIONS

Using Toolbars

Although you can usually perform all program commands using menus, toolbar buttons provide convenient one-click access to frequently used commands. For most Windows 2000 functions, there is usually more than one way to accomplish a task. To simplify your introduction to Windows 2000 in this tutorial, we will usually show you only one method for performing a task. As you become more accomplished at using Windows 2000, you can explore alternate methods.

In Session 1.1 you learned that Windows 2000 programs include ScreenTips, which indicate the purpose and function of a tool. Now is a good time to explore the WordPad toolbar buttons by looking at their ScreenTips.

To find out a toolbar button's function:

1. Position the pointer over any button on the toolbar, such as the Print Preview button. After a short pause, the name of the button appears in a box near the button, and a description of the button appears in the status bar just above the Start button. See Figure 1-22.

Figure 1-22   TOOLBAR BUTTON AIDS

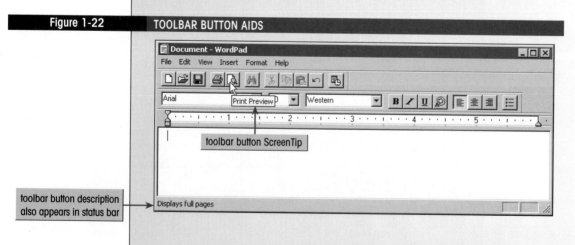

2. Move the pointer over each button on the toolbar to see its name and purpose.

You select a toolbar button by clicking it.

To select the Print Preview toolbar button:

1. Click the **Print Preview** button 🔍. The Print Preview screen appears. This is the same screen that appeared when you selected Print Preview from the File menu.

2. After examining the screen, click the button with the text label "Close" to return to your document.

Using **List Boxes and Scroll Bars**

As you might guess from the name, a **list box** displays a list of choices. In WordPad, date and time formats are shown in the Date/Time list box. List box controls usually include arrow buttons, a scroll bar, and a scroll box, as shown in Figure 1-23.

To use the Date/Time list box:

1. Click the **Date/Time** button 📅 to display the Date and Time dialog box. See Figure 1-23.

| Figure 1-23 | LIST BOX |

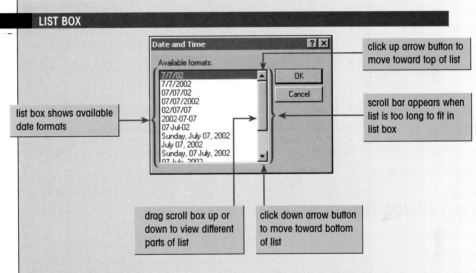

2. To scroll down the list, click the **down arrow** button ▼. See Figure 1-23.

3. Find the scroll box on your screen. See Figure 1-23.

4. Drag the **scroll box** to the top of the scroll bar. Notice how the list scrolls back to the beginning.

   TROUBLE? You learned how to drag when you learned to move a window. To drag the scroll box up, point to the scroll box, press and hold down the mouse button, and then move the mouse up.

5. Find a date in the format "July 07, 2002." Click that date format to select it.

6. Click the **OK** button to close the Date and Time dialog box. This inserts the current date in your document.

You can access some list boxes directly from the toolbar. When a list box is on the toolbar, only the current option appears in the list box. A **list arrow** appears on the right of the box and you can click it to view additional options.

To use the Font Size list box:

1. Click the **Font Size** list arrow, as shown in Figure 1-24.

Figure 1-24	FONT SIZE LIST ARROW

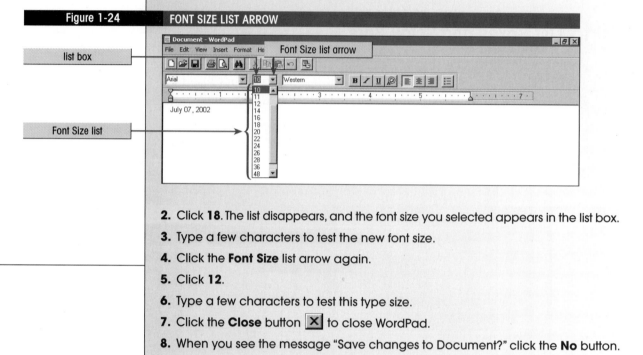

2. Click **18**. The list disappears, and the font size you selected appears in the list box.

3. Type a few characters to test the new font size.

4. Click the **Font Size** list arrow again.

5. Click **12**.

6. Type a few characters to test this type size.

7. Click the **Close** button ☒ to close WordPad.

8. When you see the message "Save changes to Document?" click the **No** button.

Using **Dialog Box Controls**

Recall that when you select a menu option or button followed by an ellipsis, a dialog box opens that allows you to provide more information about how a program should carry out a task. Some dialog boxes group different kinds of information into bordered rectangular areas called **panes**. Within these panes, you will usually find tabs, option buttons, check boxes, and other controls that the program uses to collect information about how you want it to perform a task. Figure 1-25 describes common dialog box controls.

Figure 1-25	DIALOG BOX CONTROLS

CONTROL	DESCRIPTION
Tabs	Modeled after the tabs on file folders, tab controls are often used as containers for other Windows 2000 controls such as list boxes, radio buttons, and check boxes. Click the appropriate tabs to view different pages of information or choices.
Option buttons	Also called **radio buttons**, option buttons allow you to select a single option from among one or more options.
Check boxes	Click a check box to select or deselect it; when it is selected, a check mark appears, indicating that the option is turned on; when deselected, the check box is blank and the option is off. When check boxes appear in groups, you can select or deselect as many as you want; they are not mutually exclusive, as option buttons are.
Spin boxes	Allow you to scroll easily through a set of numbers to choose the setting you want
Text boxes	Boxes into which you type additional information

Figure 1-26 displays examples of these controls.

| Figure 1-26 | EXAMPLES OF DIALOG BOX CONTROLS |

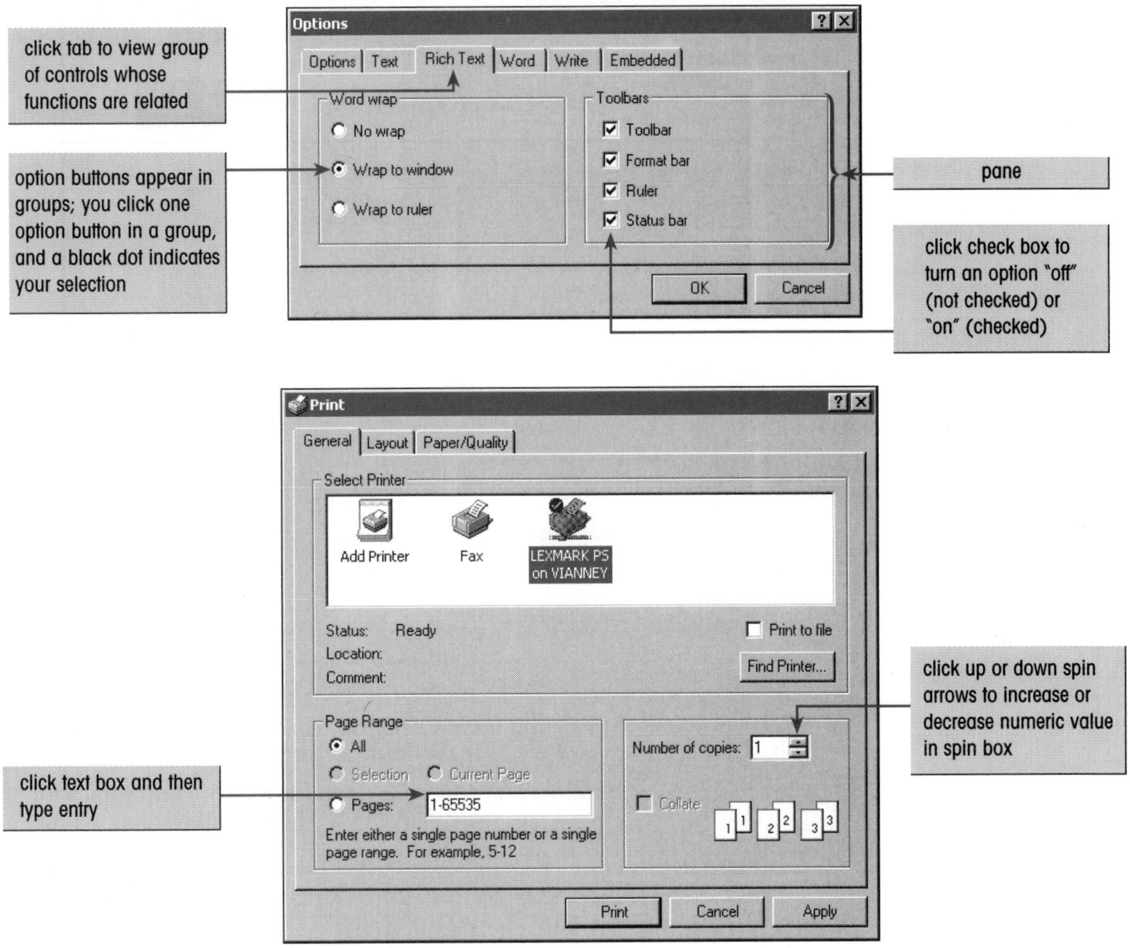

click tab to view group of controls whose functions are related

option buttons appear in groups; you click one option button in a group, and a black dot indicates your selection

pane

click check box to turn an option "off" (not checked) or "on" (checked)

click up or down spin arrows to increase or decrease numeric value in spin box

click text box and then type entry

Using **Help**

Windows 2000 **Help** provides on-screen information about the program you are using. Help for the Windows 2000 operating system is available by clicking the Start button on the taskbar, then selecting Help from the Start menu. If you want Help for a program, such as WordPad, you must first start the program, then click Help on the menu bar.

When you start Help, a Windows Help window opens, which gives you access to help files stored on your computer as well as help information stored on Microsoft's Web site. If you are not connected to the Web, you have access only to the help files stored on your computer.

To start Windows 2000 Help:

1. Click the **Start** button.

2. Click **Help**. The Windows 2000 window opens to the Contents tab. See Figure 1-27.

TROUBLE? If the Contents tab is not in front, click the Contents tab to view the table of contents.

| Figure 1-27 | WINDOWS 2000 HELP |

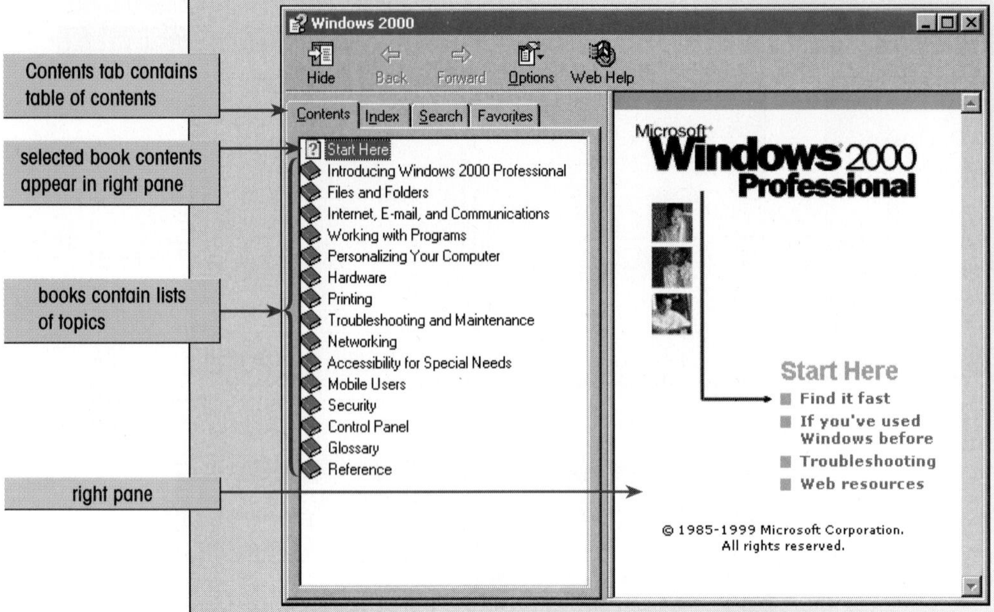

Contents tab contains table of contents

selected book contents appear in right pane

books contain lists of topics

right pane

Help uses tabs for the four sections of Help: Contents, Index, Search, and Favorites. The **Contents tab** groups Help topics into a series of books. You select a book 📖 by clicking it. The book opens, and a list of related topics appears from which you can choose. Individual topics are designated with the ? icon. Overview topics are designated with the 🖼 icon.

The **Index tab** displays an alphabetical list of all the Help topics from which you can choose. The **Search tab** allows you to search the entire set of Help topics for all topics that contain a word or words you specify. The **Favorites tab** allows you to save your favorite Help topics for quick reference.

Viewing Topics from the Contents Tab

You know that Windows 2000 gives you easy access to the Internet. Suppose you're wondering how to connect to the Internet from your computer. You can use the Contents tab to find more information on a specific topic.

To use the Contents tab:

1. Click the **Internet, E-mail, and Communications** book icon 📖. A list of topics and an overview appear below the book title.

2. Click the **Connect to the Internet** topic icon ?. Information about connecting to the Internet appears in the right pane. See Figure 1-28.

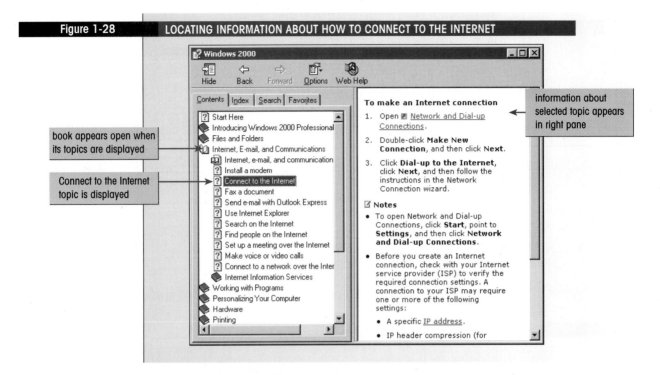

Figure 1-28 | LOCATING INFORMATION ABOUT HOW TO CONNECT TO THE INTERNET

Selecting a Topic from the Index

The Index tab allows you to jump to a Help topic by selecting a topic from an indexed list. For example, you can use the Index tab to learn more about the Internet.

To find a Help topic using the Index tab:

1. Click the **Index** tab. A long list of indexed Help topics appears.

   TROUBLE? If this is the first time you've used Help on your computer, Windows 2000 needs to set up the Index. This takes just a few moments. Wait until you see the list of index entries in the left pane, and then proceed to Step 2.

2. Drag the scroll box down to view additional topics.

3. You can quickly jump to any part of the list by typing the first few characters of a word or phrase in the box above the Index list. Click the box and then type **Internet**.

4. Click the topic **searching the Internet** (you might have to scroll to see it) and then click the **Display** button. When there is just one topic, it appears immediately in the right pane; otherwise, the Topics Found window opens, listing all topics indexed under the entry you're interested in. In this case, there are four choices.

5. Click **Using Internet Explorer** and then click the **Display** button. The information you requested appears in the right pane. See Figure 1-29. Notice in this topic that there are a few underlined words. You can click underlined words to view definitions or additional information.

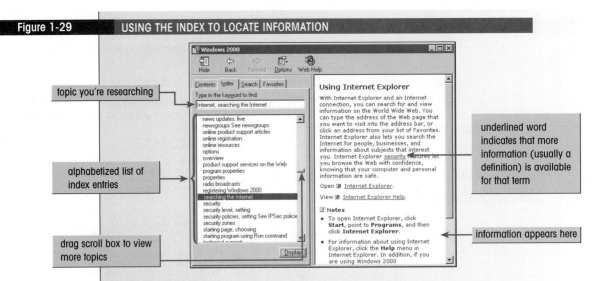

Figure 1-29   USING THE INDEX TO LOCATE INFORMATION

topic you're researching

alphabetized list of index entries

drag scroll box to view more topics

underlined word indicates that more information (usually a definition) is available for that term

information appears here

6. Click **security**. A small box appears that defines the term "security." See Figure 1-30.

Figure 1-30   VIEWING ADDITIONAL INFORMATION

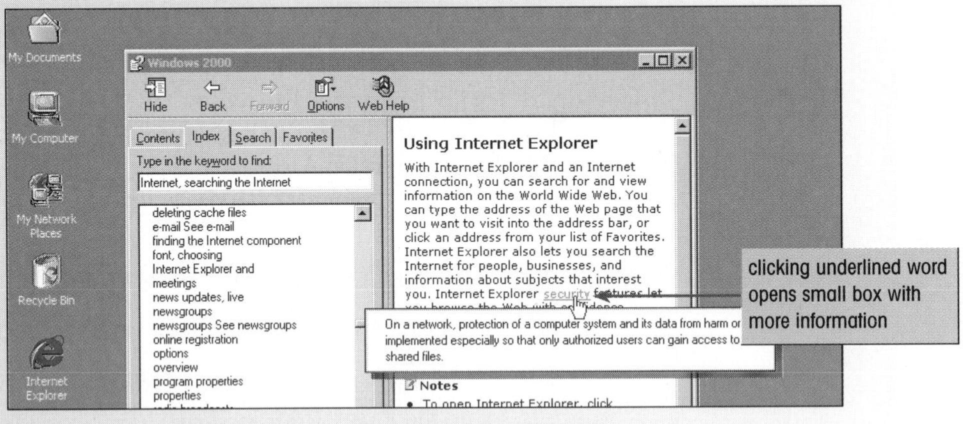

clicking underlined word opens small box with more information

7. Click a blank area of the Windows 2000 window to close the box.

The third tab, the Search tab, works similarly to the Index tab, except that you type a word, and then the Help system searches for topics containing that word. You'll get a chance to experiment with the Search and Favorites tabs in the Review Assignments.

Returning to a Previous Help Topic

You've looked at a few topics now. Suppose you want to return to the one you just saw. The Help window includes a toolbar of buttons that help you navigate the Help system. One of these buttons is the **Back** button, which returns you to topics you've already viewed. Try returning to the help topic on connecting to the Internet.

To return to a Help topic:

1. Click the **Back** button. The Internet topic appears.

2. Click the **Close** button ☒ to close the Windows 2000 window.

3. Log off or shut down Windows 2000, depending on your lab's requirements.

Now that you know how Windows 2000 Help works, don't forget to use it! Use Help when you need to perform a new task or when you forget how to complete a procedure.

You've finished the tutorial, and as you shut down Windows 2000, Steve Laslow returns from class. You take a moment to tell him all you've learned: you know how to start and close programs and how to use multiple programs at the same time. You have learned how to work with windows and the controls they employ. Finally, you've learned how to get help when you need it. Steve is pleased that you are well on your way to mastering the fundamentals of using the Windows 2000 operating system.

Session 1.2 QUICK CHECK

1. What is the difference between the title bar and a toolbar?

2. Provide the name and purpose of each button:
   a. ▬ b. ▢ c. ⧉ d. ✕

3. Describe what is indicated by each of the following menu conventions:
   a. Ellipsis... b. Grayed-out c. ▶ d. ✔

4. A(n) _____ consists of a group of buttons, each of which provides one-click access to important program functions.

5. What is the purpose of the scroll bar? What is the purpose of the scroll box?

6. Option buttons allow you to select _____ option(s) at a time.

7. It is a good idea to use _____ when you need to learn how to perform new tasks.

REVIEW ASSIGNMENTS

1. **Running Two Programs and Switching Between Them** In this tutorial you learned how to run more than one program at a time, using WordPad and Paint. You can run other programs at the same time, too. Complete the following steps and write out your answers to questions b through f:
   a. Start the computer. Enter your username and password if prompted to do so.
   b. Click the Start button. How many menu options are on the Start menu?
   c. Run the Calculator program located on the Accessories menu. How many program buttons are now on the taskbar (don't count toolbar buttons or items in the tray)?
   d. Run the Paint program and maximize the Paint window. How many programs are running now?
   e. Switch to Calculator. What are two visual clues that tell you that Calculator is the active program?
   f. Multiply 576 by 1457 using the Calculator accessory. What is the result?
   g. Close Calculator, then close Paint.

Explore 2. **WordPad Help** In Tutorial 1 you learned how to use Windows 2000 Help. Almost every Windows 2000 program has a Help feature. Many users can learn to use a program just by using Help. To use Help, start the program, then click the Help menu at the top of the screen. Try using WordPad Help:
   a. Start WordPad.
   b. Click Help on the WordPad menu bar, and then click Help Topics.
   c. Using WordPad Help, write out your answers to questions 1 through 4.
      1. How do you create a bulleted list?
      2. How do you set the margins in a document?
      3. How do you undo a mistake?
      4. How do you change the font style of a block of text?
   d. Close WordPad.

Explore

3. **The Search Tab** In addition to the Contents and Index tabs you worked with in this tutorial, Windows 2000 Help also includes a Search tab. Windows 2000 makes it possible to use a microphone to record sound on your computer. You could browse through the Contents tab, although you might not know where to find information about microphones. You could also use the Index tab to search through the indexed entry. Or you could use the Search tab to find all Help topics that mention microphones.

   a. Start Windows 2000 Help and use the Index tab to find information about microphones. How many topics are listed?

   b. Now use the Search tab to find information about microphones. Type "microphone" in the box on the Search tab, and then click the List Topics button.

   c. Write a paragraph comparing the two lists of topics. You don't have to view them all, but indicate which tab seems to yield more information, and why. Close Help.

4. **Getting Started** Windows 2000 includes Getting Started, an online "book" that helps you discover more about your computer and the Windows 2000 operating system. You can use this book to review what you learned in this tutorial and pick up some tips for using Windows 2000. Complete the following steps and write out your answers to questions d–j.

   a. Start Help, click the Contents tab, click Introducing Windows 2000 Professional, and then click Getting Started online book. Read the information and then click Windows 2000 Professional Getting Started.

   b. In the right pane, click New to Windows? Notice the book icons in the upper-right and upper-left corners of the right pane.

   c. Read each screen, and then click the right book icon to proceed through the Help topics. Alternately, you can view specific Getting Started Help topics by clicking them on the Contents tab. To answer the following questions, locate the information on the relevant Help topic. All the information for these questions is located in Chapter 4—"Windows Basics." When you are done, close Help.

   d. If your computer's desktop style uses the single-click option, how do you select a file? How do you open a file?

   e. What features are almost always available on your desktop, regardless of how many windows you have open?

   f. How can you get information about a dialog box or an area of the dialog box?

   g. How does the Getting Started online book define the word "disk"?

   h. If your computer is connected to a network, what Windows 2000 feature can you use to browse network resources?

   i. Why shouldn't you turn off your computer without shutting it down properly?

5. **Favorite Help Topics** You learned in this tutorial that you can save a list of your favorite Help topics on the Favorites tab. Try adding a topic to your list of favorites.

   a. Open a Help topic in the Help system. For this assignment, click the Contents tab, click Personalizing Your Computer, and then click Personalizing your workspace overview.

   b. Click the Favorites tab. The topic you selected appears on the right, and the topic name appears in the lower-left corner.

   c. Click the Add button. The topic appears in the box on the Favorites tab. This provides you an easy way to return to this topic.

   d. Click the Remove button to remove the topic from the Favorites list.

PROJECTS

1. There are many types of pointing devices on the market today. Go to the library and research the types of devices available. Consider what devices are appropriate for these situations: desktop or laptop computers, connected or remote devices, and ergonomic or standard designs (look up the word "ergonomic").

Use up-to-date computer books, trade computer magazines such as *PC Computing* and *PC Magazine*, or the Internet (if you know how) to locate information. Your instructor might suggest specific resources you can use. Write a one-page report describing the types of devices available, the differing needs of users, special features that make pointing devices more useful, price comparisons, and what you would choose if you needed to buy a pointing device.

2. Using the resources available to you, either through your library or the Internet (if you know how), locate information about the release of Windows 2000. Computing trade magazines are an excellent source of information about software. Read several articles about Windows 2000 and then write a one-page essay that discusses the features that are most important to the people who evaluated the software. If you find reviews of the software, mention the features that reviewers had the strongest reaction to, pro or con.

3. Upgrading is the process of placing a more recent version of a product onto your computer. When Windows 2000 first came out, people had to decide whether or not they wanted to upgrade to Windows 2000. Interview several people you know who are well-informed Windows computer users. Ask them whether they are using Windows 2000 or an older version of Windows. If they are using an older version, ask why they have chosen not to upgrade. If they are using Windows 2000, ask them why they chose to upgrade. Ask such questions as:

   a. What features convinced you to upgrade or made you decide to wait?
   b. What role did the price of the upgrade play?
   c. Would you have had (or did you have) to purchase new hardware to make the upgrade? How did this affect your decision?
   d. If you did upgrade, are you happy with that decision? If you didn't, do you intend to upgrade in the near future? Why, or why not?

   Write a single-page essay summarizing what you learned from these interviews.

4. Choose a topic to research using the Windows 2000 online Help system. Look for information on your topic using three tabs: the Contents tab, the Index tab, and the Search tab. Once you've found all the information you can, compare the three methods (Contents, Index, Search) of looking for information. Write a paragraph that discusses which tab proved the most useful. Did you reach the same information topics using all three methods? In a second paragraph, summarize what you learned about your topic. Finally, in a third paragraph, indicate under what circumstances you'd use which tab.

LAB ASSIGNMENTS

Using a Keyboard

Using a Keyboard To become an effective computer user, you must be familiar with your primary input device—the keyboard. See the Read This Before You Begin page for information on installing and starting the lab.

1. The Steps for the Using a Keyboard Lab provide you with a structured introduction to the keyboard layout and the function of special computer keys. Click the Steps button and begin the Steps. As you work through the Steps, answer all of the Quick Check questions that appear. When you complete the Steps, you will see a Summary Report that summarizes your performance on the Quick Checks. Follow the directions on the screen to print the Summary Report.

2. In Explore, start the typing tutor. You can develop your typing skills using the typing tutor in Explore. Take the typing test and print out your results.

3. In Explore, try to improve your typing speed by 10 words per minute. For example, if you currently type 20 words per minute, your goal will be 30 words per minute. Practice each typing lesson until you see a message that indicates that you can proceed to the next lesson.

Create a Practice Record, as shown here, to keep track of how much you practice. When you have reached your goal, print out the results of a typing test to verify your results.

Practice Record
Name:
Section:
Start Date: Start Typing Speed: wpm
End Date: End Typing Speed: wpm
Lesson #:   Date Practiced/Time Practiced

Using a Mouse A mouse is a standard input device on most of today's computers. You need to know how to use a mouse to manipulate graphical user interfaces and to use the rest of the Labs. See the Read This Before You Begin page for information on installing and starting the lab.

1. The Steps for the Using a Mouse Lab show you how to click, double-click, and drag objects using the mouse. Click the Steps button and begin the Steps. As you work through the Steps, answer all of the Quick Check questions that appear. When you complete the Steps, you will see a Summary Report that summarizes your performance on the Quick Checks. Follow the directions on the screen to print the Summary Report.

2. In Explore, create a poster to demonstrate your ability to use a mouse and to control a Windows program. To create a poster for an upcoming sports event, select a graphic, type the caption for the poster, then select a font, font styles, and a border. Print your completed poster.

QUICK | CHECK ANSWERS

Session 1.1

1. The taskbar contains buttons that give you access to tools and programs.
2. multitasking
3. Start menu
4. Lift the mouse up and move it to the right.
5. Its button appears on the taskbar.
6. To conserve computer resources such as memory.
7. To ensure you don't lose data and damage your files.

Session 1.2

1. The title bar identifies the window and contains window controls; toolbars contain buttons that provide you with shortcuts to common menu commands.
2. a. Minimize button shrinks window so you see button on taskbar
   b. Maximize button enlarges window to fill entire screen
   c. Restore button reduces window to predetermined size
   d. Close button closes window and removes button from taskbar
3. a. ellipsis indicates a dialog box will open
   b. grayed-out indicates option is not currently available
   c. arrow indicates a submenu will open
   d. check mark indicates a toggle option
4. toolbar
5. Scroll bars appear when the contents of a box or window are too long to fit; you drag the scroll box to view different parts of the contents.
6. one
7. online Help

OBJECTIVES

In this tutorial you will:

- Format a disk

- Enter, select, insert, and delete text

- Create and save a file

- Open, edit, and print a file

- Create and make a copy of your Data Disk

- View the list of files on your disk and change view options

- Move, copy, delete, and rename a file

- Navigate a hierarchy of folders

LABS

Using Files

WORKING WITH FILES

Creating, Saving, and Managing Files

CASE

Distance Education

You recently purchased a computer in order to gain new skills so you can stay competitive in the job market. You hope to use the computer to enroll in a few distance education courses. **Distance education** is formalized learning that typically takes place using a computer and the Internet, replacing normal classroom interaction with modern communications technology. Distance education teachers often make their course material available on the **World Wide Web**, a popular service on the Internet that makes information readily accessible.

Your computer came loaded with Windows 2000. Your friend Shannon suggests that before you enroll in any online courses, you should get more comfortable with your computer and with Windows 2000. Knowing how to save, locate, and organize your files will make your time spent at the computer much more productive. A **file**, often referred to as a **document**, is a collection of data that has a name and is stored in a computer. Once you create a file, you can open it, edit its contents, print it, and save it again—usually using the same program you used to create it.

Shannon suggests that you become familiar with how to perform these tasks in Windows 2000 programs. Then she'll show you how to choose different ways of viewing information on your computer. Finally, you'll spend time learning how to organize your files.

SESSION 2.1

In Session 2.1, you will learn how to format a disk so it can store files. You will create, save, open, and print a file. You will find out how the insertion point differs from the mouse pointer, and you will learn the basic skills for Windows 2000 text entry, such as entering, selecting, inserting, and deleting. For the steps of this tutorial you will need two blank 3½-inch disks.

Formatting a Disk

Before you can save files on a floppy disk, the disk must be formatted. When the computer **formats** a disk, the magnetic particles on the disk surface are arranged so that data can be stored on the disk. Today, many disks are sold preformatted and can be used right out of the box. However, if you purchase an unformatted disk, or if you have an old disk you want to completely erase and reuse, you can format the disk using the Windows 2000 Format command. This command is available through the **My Computer window**, a feature of Windows 2000 that you use to view, organize, and access the programs, files, drives and folders on your computer. You open My Computer by using its icon on the desktop. You'll learn more about the My Computer window later in this tutorial.

The following steps tell you how to format a 3½-inch high-density disk, using drive A. Your instructor will tell you how to revise the instructions given in these steps if the procedure is different for your lab.

Make sure you are using a blank disk (or one that contains data you no longer need) before you perform these steps.

To format a disk:

1. Start Windows 2000, if necessary.

2. Write your name on the label of a 3½-inch disk and insert your disk in drive A. See Figure 2-1.

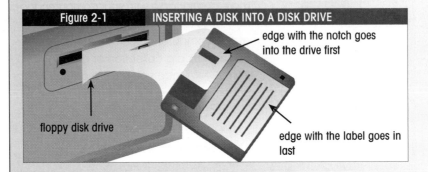

| Figure 2-1 | INSERTING A DISK INTO A DISK DRIVE |

edge with the notch goes into the drive first

floppy disk drive

edge with the label goes in last

TROUBLE? If your disk does not fit in drive A, put it in drive B and substitute drive B for drive A in all of the steps for the rest of the tutorial.

3. Click the **My Computer** icon on the desktop. The icon is selected. Figure 2-2 shows this icon on your desktop.

TROUBLE? If the My Computer window opens, skip Step 4. Your computer is using different settings, which you'll learn to change in Session 2.2.

4. Press the **Enter** key to open the My Computer window. See Figure 2-2 (don't worry if your window opens maximized).

TROUBLE? If you see a list of items instead of icons like those in Figure 2-2, click View, and then click Large Icons. Don't worry if your toolbars don't exactly match those in Figure 2-2.

TROUBLE? If you see additional information or a graphic image on the left side of the My Computer window, Web view is enabled on your computer. Don't worry. You will learn how to return to the default Windows 2000 settings in Session 2.2.

Figure 2-2	MY COMPUTER WINDOW

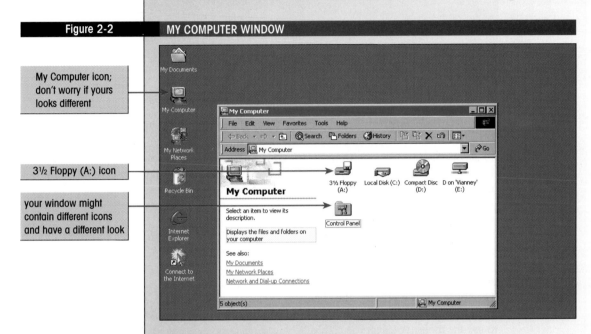

My Computer icon; don't worry if yours looks different

3½ Floppy (A:) icon

your window might contain different icons and have a different look

5. Right-click the **3½ Floppy (A:)** icon to open its shortcut menu, and then click **Format**. The Format dialog box opens.

6. Make sure the dialog box settings on your screen match those in Figure 2-3.

Figure 2-3	FORMATTING A FLOPPY DISK

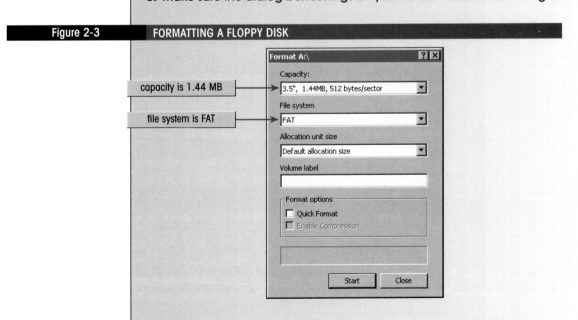

capacity is 1.44 MB

file system is FAT

By default, Windows 2000 uses the FAT (File Allocation Table) file system for floppy disks. A **file system** is the way files are organized on the disk. Windows 2000 supports other file systems such as FAT32 and NTFS, but this is a more advanced topic.

7. Click the **Start** button to start formatting the disk.

8. Click the **OK** button to confirm that you want to format the disk (the actual formatting will take a minute to perform). Click the **OK** button again when the formatting is complete.

9. Click the **Close** button.

10. Click the **Close** button [X] to close the My Computer window.

Now that you have a formatted disk, you can create a document and save it on your disk. First you need to learn how to enter text into a document.

Working **with** Text

To accomplish many computing tasks, you need to enter text in documents and text boxes. This involves learning how to move the pointer so the text will appear where you want it, how to insert new text between existing words or sentences, how to select text, and how to delete text. When you type sentences of text, do not press the Enter key when you reach the right margin of the page. Most software contains a feature called **word wrap**, which automatically continues your text on the next line. Therefore, you should press Enter only when you have completed a paragraph.

If you type the wrong character, press the Backspace key to back up and delete the character. You can also use the Delete key. What's the difference between the Backspace and Delete keys? The **Backspace** key deletes the character to the left, while the **Delete** key deletes the character to the right. If you want to delete text that is not next to where you are currently typing, you need to use the mouse to select the text; then you can use either the Delete key or the Backspace key.

Now you will type some text, using WordPad, to practice text entry. When you first start WordPad, notice the flashing vertical bar, called the **insertion point**, in the upper-left corner of the document window. The insertion point indicates where the characters you type will appear.

To type text in WordPad:

1. Start WordPad and locate the insertion point.

TROUBLE? If the WordPad window does not fill the screen, click the Maximize button [□].

TROUBLE? If you can't find the insertion point, click in the WordPad **document window**, the white area below the toolbars and ruler.

2. Type your name, pressing the Shift key at the same time as the appropriate letter to type uppercase letters and using the Spacebar to type spaces, just as on a typewriter.

3. Press the **Enter** key to move the insertion point down to the next line.

4. As you type the following sentences, watch what happens when the insertion point reaches the right edge of the page:

This is a sample typed in WordPad. See what happens when the insertion point reaches the right edge of the page. Note how the text wraps automatically to the next line.

TROUBLE? If you make a mistake, delete the incorrect character(s) by pressing the Backspace key on your keyboard. Then type the correct character(s).

TROUBLE? If your text doesn't wrap, your screen might be set up to display more information than the screen used for the figures in this tutorial, or your WordPad program might not be set to use Word Wrap. Click View, click Options, make sure the Rich Text tab is selected, click the Wrap to window option button, and then click the OK button.

The Insertion Point Versus the Pointer

The insertion point is not the same as the mouse pointer. When the mouse pointer is in the text-entry area, it is called the **I-beam pointer** and looks like $\lceil$. Figure 2-4 explains the difference between the insertion point and the I-beam pointer.

| Figure 2-4 | THE INSERTION POINT VS. THE POINTER |

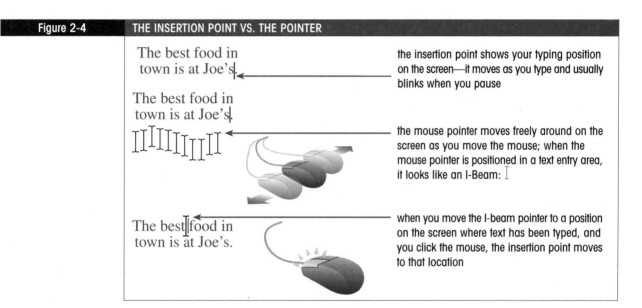

When you enter text, the insertion point moves as you type. If you want to enter text in a location other than where the mouse pointer is currently positioned, you move the I-beam pointer to the location where you want to type, and then click. The insertion point jumps to the location you clicked. In most programs, the insertion point blinks, making it easier for you to locate it on a screen filled with text.

To move the insertion point:

1. Check the locations of the insertion point and the I-beam pointer. The insertion point should be at the end of the sentence you typed in the last set of steps. The easiest way to locate the I-beam pointer is to move your mouse gently until you see the pointer. Remember that it will look like ⬚ until you move the pointer into the document window.

2. Use the mouse to move the I-beam pointer just to the left of the word "sample" and then click the mouse button. The insertion point should be just to the left of the "s."

TROUBLE? If you have trouble clicking just to the left of the "s," try clicking in the word and then using the arrow keys to move the insertion point one character at a time.

3. Move the I-beam pointer to a blank area near the bottom of the workspace and then click. Notice the insertion point does not jump to the location of the I-beam pointer. Instead the insertion point jumps to the end of the last sentence or to the point in the bottom line directly above where you clicked. The insertion point can move only within existing text. It cannot be moved out of the existing text area.

Selecting Text

Many text operations are performed on a **block** of text, which is one or more consecutive characters, words, sentences, or paragraphs. Once you select a block of text, you can delete it, move it, replace it, underline it, and so on. To deselect a block of text, click anywhere outside the selected block.

If you want to delete the phrase "See what happens" in the text you just typed and replace it with the phrase "You can watch word wrap in action," you do not have to delete the first phrase one character at a time. Instead, you can select the entire phrase and then type the replacement phrase.

To select and replace a block of text:

1. Move the I-beam pointer just to the left of the word "See."

2. While holding down the mouse button, drag the I-beam pointer over the text to the end of the word "happens." The phrase "See what happens" should now be highlighted. See Figure 2-5.

TROUBLE? If the space to the right of the word "happens" is also selected, don't worry. Your computer is set up to select spaces in addition to words. After completing Step 4, simply press the Spacebar to type an extra space if required.

Figure 2-5	SELECTING TEXT

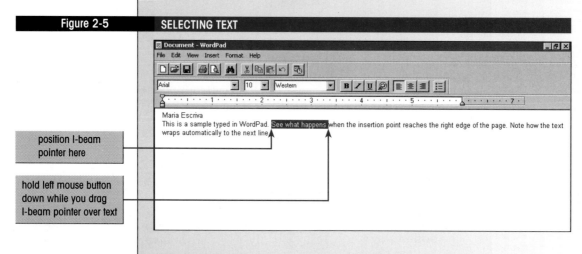

position I-beam pointer here

hold left mouse button down while you drag I-beam pointer over text

3. Release the mouse button.

TROUBLE? If the phrase is not highlighted correctly, repeat Steps 1 through 3.

4. Type **You can watch word wrap in action**

The text you typed replaces the highlighted text. Notice that you did not need to delete the selected text before you typed the replacement text.

Inserting a Character

Windows 2000 programs usually operate in **insert mode**—when you type a new character, all characters to the right of the insertion point are pushed over to make room.

Suppose you want to insert the word "page" before the word "typed" in your practice sentences.

To insert text:

1. Move the I-beam pointer just before the word "typed" and then click to position the insertion point.

2. Type **page**

3. Press the **Spacebar**.

Notice how the letters in the first line are pushed to the right to make room for the new characters. When a word gets pushed past the right margin, the word-wrap feature moves it down to the beginning of the next line.

Saving a File

As you type text, it is held temporarily in the computer's memory, which is erased when you turn off the computer. For permanent storage, you need to save your work on a disk. In the computer lab, you will probably save your work on a floppy disk in drive A.

When you save a file, you must give it a name, called a **filename**. Windows 2000 allows you to use up to 255 characters in a filename—this gives you plenty of room to name your file accurately enough so that you'll know the contents of the file by just looking at the filename. You may use spaces and certain punctuation symbols in your filenames. You cannot use the symbols \ / ? : * " < > | in a filename, because Windows uses those for designating the location and type of the file, but other symbols such as & ; - and $ are allowed.

Another thing to consider is whether you might use your files on a computer running older programs. Programs designed for the Windows 3.1 and DOS operating systems (which were created before 1995) require that files be eight characters or less with no spaces. Thus when you save a file with a long filename in Windows 2000, Windows 2000 also creates an eight-character filename that can be used by older programs. The eight-character filename is created from the first six nonspace characters in the long filename, with the addition of a tilde (~) and a number. For example, the filename Car Sales for 1999 would be converted to Carsal~1.

Most filenames have an extension. An **extension** (a set of no more than three characters at the end of a filename, separated from the filename by a period) is used by the operating system to identify and categorize the file. In the filename Car Sales for 1999.doc, for example, the file extension "doc" identifies the file as one created with Microsoft Word. You might also have a file called Car Sales for 1999.xls—"xls" identifies the file as one created with Microsoft Excel, a spreadsheet program. When pronouncing filenames with extensions, say "dot" for the period, so that the file Resume.doc is pronounced "Resume dot doc."

You usually do not need to add extensions to your filenames because the program you use to create the file does this automatically. Also, Windows 2000 keeps track of file extensions, but not all computers are set to display them. The steps in these tutorials refer to files by using the filename without its extension. So if you see the filename Practice Text in the steps, but "Practice Text.doc" appears on your screen, don't worry—these refer to the same file. Also don't worry if you don't use consistent lowercase and uppercase letters when saving files. Usually the operating system doesn't distinguish between them. Be aware, however, that some programs are "case-sensitive"—they check for case in filenames.

Now you can save the WordPad document you typed.

To start saving a document:

1. Click the **Save** button 💾 on the toolbar. The Save As dialog box opens, as shown in Figure 2-6.

| Figure 2-6 | SAVING A FILE |

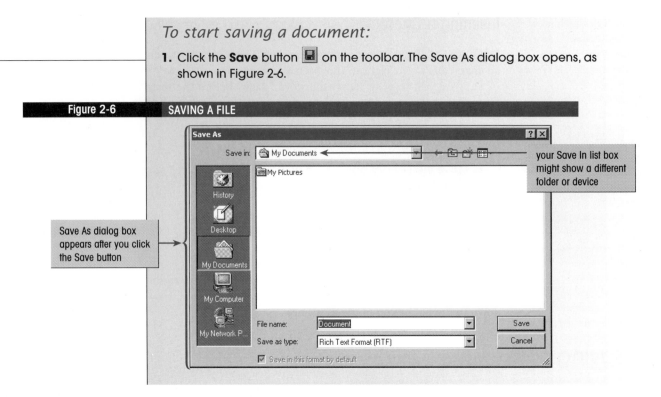

Save As dialog box appears after you click the Save button

your Save In list box might show a different folder or device

You use the Save As dialog box to specify where you want to save your file (on the hard drive or on a floppy disk, in a folder or not, and so on). Before going further with the process of saving a file, let's examine some of the features of the Save As dialog box so that you learn to save your files exactly where you want them.

Specifying the File Location

In the Save As dialog box, Windows 2000 provides the **Places Bar**, a list of important locations on your computer. When you click the different icons in the Places Bar, the contents of those locations will be displayed in the white area of the Save As dialog box. You can then save your document directly to those locations. Figure 2-7 displays the icons in the Places Bar and gives their function.

| Figure 2-7 | ICONS IN THE PLACES BAR |

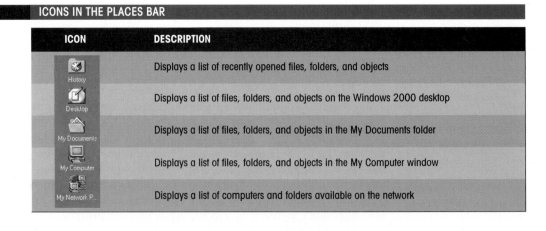

ICON	DESCRIPTION
History	Displays a list of recently opened files, folders, and objects
Desktop	Displays a list of files, folders, and objects on the Windows 2000 desktop
My Documents	Displays a list of files, folders, and objects in the My Documents folder
My Computer	Displays a list of files, folders, and objects in the My Computer window
My Network P...	Displays a list of computers and folders available on the network

To see this in action, try displaying different locations in the dialog box.

To use the Places Bar:

1. Click the **Desktop** icon in the Places Bar.

2. The Save As dialog box now displays the contents of the Windows 2000 desktop. See Figure 2-8.

Figure 2-8	USING THE PLACES BAR

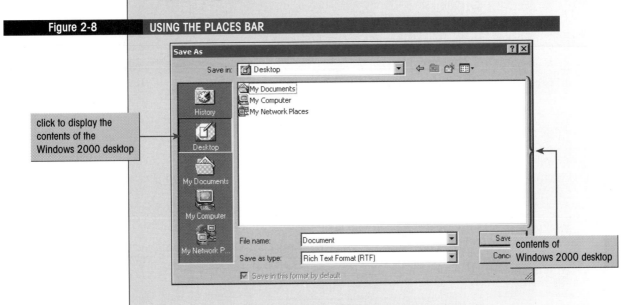

click to display the contents of the Windows 2000 desktop

contents of Windows 2000 desktop

3. Click the **My Documents** icon to display the contents of the My Documents folder.

Once you've clicked an icon in the Places Bar, you can open any file displayed in that location, and you can save a file into that location. The Places Bar doesn't have an icon for every location on your computer, however. The **Save in** list box (located at the top of the dialog box) does. Use the Save in list box now to save your document to your floppy disk.

To use the Save in list box:

1. Click the **Save in** list arrow to display a list of drives.

2. Click **3½ Floppy (A:)**.

Now that you've specified where you want to save your file, you can specify a name and type for the file.

Specifying the File Name and Type

After choosing the location for your document, you have to specify the name of the file. You should also specify (or at least check) the file's format. A file's **format** determines what type of information you can place in the document, the document's appearance, and what kind of programs can work with the document. There are five file formats available in WordPad: Word for Windows 6.0, Rich Text Format (RTF), Text, Text for MS-DOS, and Unicode Text. The Word and RTF formats allow you to create documents with text that can use bold-faced or italicized fonts as well as documents containing graphic images and scanned photos. However, only word-processing programs like WordPad or Microsoft Word can work with those files. The three text formats allow only simple text with no graphics or special formatting, but such documents are readable by a wider range of programs. The default format for WordPad documents is RTF, but you can change that, as you'll see shortly.

Continue saving the document, using the name "Practice Text" and the file type Word 6.0.

To finish saving your document:

1. Select the text **Document** in the File name text box and then type **Practice Text** in the File name text box. The new text replaces "Document."

2. Click the **Save as type** list arrow and then click **Word for Windows 6.0** in the list. See Figure 2-9.

| Figure 2-9 | COMPLETED SAVE AS DIALOG BOX |

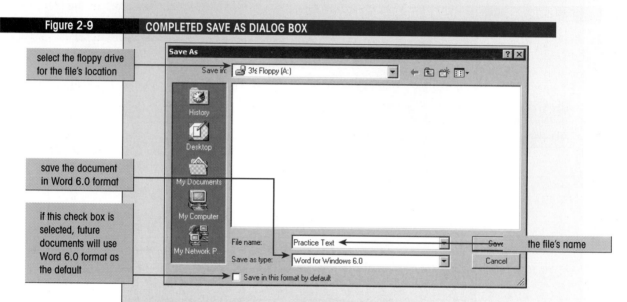

select the floppy drive for the file's location

save the document in Word 6.0 format

if this check box is selected, future documents will use Word 6.0 format as the default

the file's name

Note that if you want all future documents saved by WordPad to use the Word 6.0 format as the default format rather than RTF, you can select the Save in this format by default check box. If you select it, the next time you save a document in WordPad, this format will be the initial choice, so you won't have to specify it.

3. Click the **Save** button in the lower-right corner of the dialog box.

4. If you are asked whether you are sure that you want to save the document in this format, click the **Yes** button.

Your file is saved on your Data Disk, and the document title, "Practice Text," appears on the WordPad title bar.

Note that after you save the file the document appears a little different. What has changed? By saving the document in Word 6.0 format rather than RTF, you've changed the format of the document slightly. One change is that the text is wrapped differently in Word 6.0 format. A Word 6.0 file will use the right margin and, in this case, limit the length of a single line of text to 6 inches.

What if you try to close WordPad before you save your file? Windows 2000 will display a message—"Save changes to Document?" If you answer "Yes," Windows will display the Save As dialog box so you can give the document a name. If you answer "No," Windows 2000 will close WordPad without saving the document. Any changes you made to the document will be lost, so when you are asked if you want to save a file, answer "Yes," unless you are absolutely sure you don't need to keep the work you just did.

After you save a file, you can work on another document or close WordPad. Since you have already saved your Practice Text document, you'll continue this tutorial by closing WordPad.

To close WordPad:

1. Click the **Close** button ⊠ to close the WordPad window.

Opening a File

Suppose you save and close the Practice Text file, then later you want to revise it. To revise a file you must first open it. When you open a file, its contents are copied into the computer's memory. If you revise the file, you need to save the changes before you close the program. If you close a revised file without saving your changes, you will lose them.

There are several methods to open a file. You can select the file from the Documents list (available through the Start menu) if you have opened the file recently, since the Documents list contains the 15 most recently opened documents. This list is very handy to use on your own computer, but in a lab, other student's files quickly replace your own. You can also locate the file in the My Computer window (or in **Windows Explorer**, another file management tool) and then open it. And finally, you can start a program and then use the Open button within that program to locate and open the file. Each method has advantages and disadvantages.

The first two methods for opening the Practice Text file simply require you to select the file from the Documents list or locate and select it from My Computer or Windows Explorer. With these methods the document, not the program, is central to the task; hence, this method is sometimes referred to as **document-centric**. You need only to remember the name of your file—you do not need to remember which program you used to create it.

Opening a File from the My Computer Window

If your file is not in the Documents list, you can open the file by selecting it from the My Computer window. Either way, Windows 2000 uses the file extension (whether it is displayed or not) to determine which program to start so you can manipulate the file. It starts the program, and then automatically opens the file. The advantage of both methods is simplicity. The disadvantage is that Windows 2000 might not start the program you expect. For example, when you select Practice Text, you might expect Windows 2000 to start WordPad because you used WordPad to create it. Depending on the programs installed on your computer system, however, Windows 2000 might start Microsoft Word instead. Usually this is not a problem. Although the program might not be the one you expect, you can still use it to revise your file.

To open the Practice Text file by selecting it from My Computer:

1. Open the **My Computer** window, located on the desktop.

2. Click the **3½ Floppy (A:)** icon in the My Computer window.

   TROUBLE? If the 3½ Floppy (A:) window opens, skip Step 3.

3. Press the **Enter** key. The 3½ Floppy (A:) window opens.

4. Click the **Practice Text** file icon.

   TROUBLE? If the Practice Text document opens, skip Step 5.

5. Press the **Enter** key. Windows 2000 starts a program, and then automatically opens the Practice Text file. You could make revisions to the document at this point, but instead, you'll close all the windows on your desktop so you can try the other method for opening files.

   TROUBLE? If Windows 2000 starts Microsoft Word or another word-processing program instead of WordPad, don't worry. You can use Microsoft Word to revise the Practice Text document.

6. Close all open windows on the desktop.

Opening a File from Within a Program

The third method for opening the Practice Text file requires you to open WordPad, and then use the Open button to select the Practice Text file. The advantage of this method is that you can specify the program you want to use—WordPad, in this case. This method, however, involves more steps than the method you tried previously.

You can take advantage of the Places Bar to reduce the number of steps it takes to open a file from within a program. Recall that one of the icons in the Places Bar is the History icon, which displays a list of recently opened files or objects. One of the most recently opened files was the Practice Text file, so it should appear in the list.

To start WordPad and open the Practice Text file:

1. Start **WordPad** and, if necessary, maximize the WordPad window.

2. Click the **Open** button 📂 on the toolbar.

3. Click **History** in the Places Bar.

The Practice Text file doesn't appear in the list. Why not? Look at the Files of Type list box. The selected entry is "Rich Text Format (*.rtf)". What this means is that the Open dialog box will display only RTF files (as well as drives). This frees you from having to deal with the clutter of unwanted or irrelevant files. The downside is that unless you're aware of how the Open dialog box will filter the list of files, you may mistakenly think that the file you're looking for doesn't exist. You can change how the Open dialog box filters this file list. Try this now by changing the filter to show only Word documents.

To change the types of files displayed:

1. Click the **Files of type** list arrow and then click **Word for Windows (*.doc)**

   The Practice Text file now appears in the list.

2. Click **Practice Text** in the list of files. See Figure 2-10.

Figure 2-10	THE OPEN DIALOG BOX

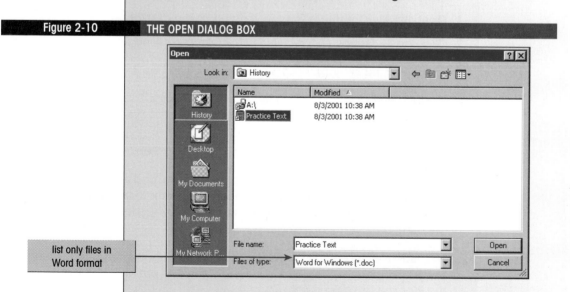

list only files in Word format

3. Click the **Open** button. The document should once again appear in the WordPad window.

Now that the Practice Text file is open, you can print it.

Printing a File

Windows 2000 provides easy access to your printer or printers. You can choose which printer to use, you can control how the document is printed, and you can control the order in which documents will be printed.

Previewing your Document Before Printing

It is a good idea to use Print Preview before you send your document to the printer. **Print Preview** shows on the screen exactly how your document will appear on paper. You can check your page layout so that you don't waste time and paper printing a document that is not quite the way you want it. Your instructor might supply you with additional instructions for printing in your school's computer lab.

> ### To preview, then print, the Practice Text file:
>
> **1.** Click the **Print Preview** button 🔲 on the toolbar.
>
>   TROUBLE? If an error message appears, printing capabilities might not be set up on your computer. Ask your instructor or technical support person for help, or skip this set of steps.
>
> **2.** Look at your document in the Print Preview window. Before you print the document, you should make sure the font, margins, and other document features look the way you want them to.
>
>   TROUBLE? If you can't read the document text on screen, click the Zoom In button as many times as needed to view the text.
>
> **3.** Click the **Close** button to close Print Preview and return to the document.

Now that you've verified that the document looks the way you want, you can print it.

Sending the Document to the Printer

There are three ways to send your document to the printer. The first approach is to print the document directly from the Print Preview window by clicking the Print button. Thus once you are satisfied with the document's appearance, you can quickly move to printing it.

Another way is to click the Print button 🖨 on your program's toolbar. This method will send the document directly to your printer without any further action on your part. It's the quickest and easiest way to print a document, but it does not allow you to change settings such as margins and layout. What if you have access to more than one printer? In that case, Windows 2000 sends the document to the default printer, the printer that has been set up to handle most print jobs.

If you want to select a different printer, or if you want to control how the printer prints your document, you can opt for a third method—selecting the Print command from the File menu. Using this approach, your program will open the Print dialog box, allowing you to choose which printer to use and how that printer will operate. Note that clicking the Print button from within the Print Preview window will also open the Print dialog box so you can verify or change settings.

To open the Print dialog box:

1. Click **File** on the WordPad menu bar and then click **Print**.

2. The Print dialog box opens, as displayed in Figure 2-11. Familiarize yourself with the controls in the Print dialog box.

Figure 2-11	THE PRINT DIALOG BOX

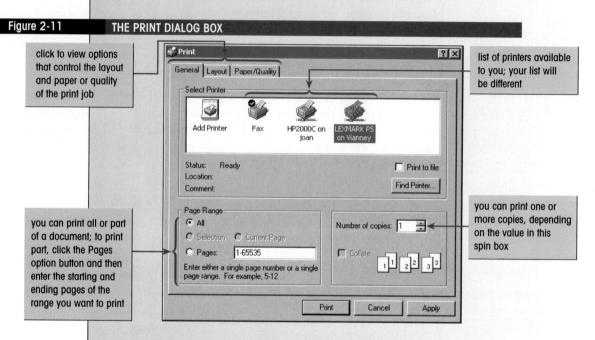

click to view options that control the layout and paper or quality of the print job

list of printers available to you; your list will be different

you can print all or part of a document; to print part, click the Pages option button and then enter the starting and ending pages of the range you want to print

you can print one or more copies, depending on the value in this spin box

3. Make sure your Print dialog box shows the Print range set to "All" and the Number of copies set to "1."

4. Select one of the printers in the list (your instructor may indicate which one you should select) and then click the **Print** button. The document is printed.

5. Close WordPad.

TROUBLE? If you see the message "Save changes to Document?" click the No button.

You've now learned how to create, save, open, and print word-processed files—essential skills for students in distance education courses that rely on word-processed reports transmitted across the Internet. Shannon assures you that the techniques you've just learned apply to most Windows 2000 programs.

Session 2.1 QUICK CHECK

1. A(n) _____ is a collection of data that has a name and is stored on a disk or other storage medium.

2. _____ erases all the data on a disk and arranges the magnetic particles on the disk surface so that the disk can store data.

3. True or False: When you move the mouse pointer over a text entry area, the pointer shape changes to an I-beam.

4. What indicates where each character you type will appear?

5. What does the History icon in the Places Bar display?

6. A file that you saved does not appear in the Open dialog box. Assuming that the file is still in the same location, what could be the reason that the Open dialog box doesn't display it?

7. What are the three ways to print from within a Windows 2000 application? If you want to print multiple copies of your document, which method(s) should you use and why?

SESSION 2.2

In this session, you will learn how to change settings in the My Computer window to control its appearance and the appearance of desktop objects. You will then learn how to use My Computer to manage the files on your disk; view information about the files on your disk; organize the files into folders; and move, delete, copy, and rename files. For this session you will use a second blank 3½-inch disk.

Creating Your Data Disk

Starting with this session, you must create a Data Disk that contains some practice files. You can use the disk you formatted in the previous session.

If you are using your own computer, the NP on Microsoft Windows 2000 menu option will not be available. Before you proceed, you must go to your school's computer lab and find a computer that has the NP on Microsoft Windows 2000 program installed. If you cannot get the files from the lab, ask your instructor or technical support person for help. Once you have made your own Data Disk, you can use it to complete this tutorial on any computer running Windows 2000.

To add the practice files to your Data Disk:

1. Write "Disk 1 - Windows 2000 Tutorial 2 Data Disk" on the label of your formatted disk (the same disk you used to save your Practice Text file).

2. Place the disk in drive A.

3. Click the **Start** button 📁 Start .

4. Point to **Programs**.

5. Point to **NP on Microsoft Windows 2000 – Level I**.

   TROUBLE? If NP on Microsoft Windows 2000 - Level I is not listed, ask your instructor or technical support person for help.

6. Click **Disk 1 (Tutorial 2)**. A message box opens, asking you to place your disk in drive A (which you already did, in Step 2).

7. Click the **OK** button. Wait while the program copies the practice files to your formatted disk. When all the files have been copied, the program closes.

Your Data Disk now contains practice files you'll use throughout the rest of this tutorial.

My Computer

The My Computer icon, as you have seen, represents your computer, with its storage devices, printers, and other objects. The My Computer icon opens into the My Computer window, which contains an icon for each of the storage devices on your computer. My Computer also gives you access to the **Control Panel**, a feature of Windows 2000 that controls the behavior of other devices and programs installed on your computer. Figure 2-12 shows how the My Computer window relates to your computer's hardware.

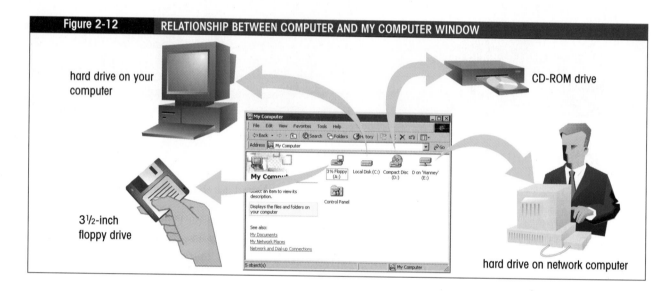

Figure 2-12   RELATIONSHIP BETWEEN COMPUTER AND MY COMPUTER WINDOW

hard drive on your computer

CD-ROM drive

3½-inch floppy drive

hard drive on network computer

Each storage device that you have access to has a letter associated with it. The first floppy drive on a computer is usually designated as drive A (if you add a second floppy drive, it is usually designated as drive B), and the first hard drive is usually designated drive C. Additional hard drives will have letters D, E, F and so forth. If you have a CD-ROM drive, it will usually have the next letter in the alphabetic sequence. If you have access to hard drives located on other computers on a network, those drives will sometimes (though not always) have letters associated with them. In the example shown in Figure 2-12, the network drive has the drive letter E.

You can use the My Computer window to organize your files. In this section of the tutorial, you'll use the My Computer window to move and delete files on your Data Disk, which is assumed to be in drive A. If you use your own computer at home or work, you will probably store your files on drive C instead of drive A. In a school lab environment, you can't always save your files to drive C, so you need to carry your files with you on a floppy disk. Most of what you learn about working on the floppy drive will also work on your home or work computer when you use drive C (or other hard drives).

Now you'll open the My Computer window.

To open the My Computer window and explore the contents of your Data Disk:

1. Open the My Computer window.

2. Click the **3½ Floppy (A:)** icon and then press the **Enter** key. A window appears showing the contents of drive A; maximize this window if necessary. See Figure 2-13.

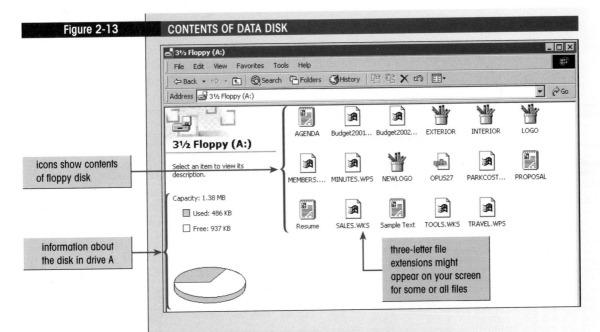

Figure 2-13   CONTENTS OF DATA DISK

icons show contents
of floppy disk

information about
the disk in drive A

three-letter file
extensions might
appear on your screen
for some or all files

TROUBLE? If the window appears before you press the Enter key, don't worry. Windows 2000 can be configured to use different keyboard and mouse combinations to open windows. You'll learn about these configuration issues shortly.

TROUBLE? If you see a list of filenames instead of icons, click View on the menu bar and then click Large Icons on the menu.

Changing the Appearance of the My Computer Window

Windows 2000 offers several different options that control how toolbars, icons, and buttons appear in the My Computer window. To make the My Computer window look the same as it does in the figures in this book, you need to ensure three things: that only the Address and Standard toolbars are visible, that files and other objects are displayed using large icons, and that the configuration of Windows 2000 uses the default setting. Setting your computer to match the figures will make it easier for you to follow the steps.

Controlling the Toolbar Display

The My Computer window, in addition to displaying a Standard toolbar, allows you to display the same toolbars that can appear on the Windows 2000 taskbar, such as the Address toolbar or the Links toolbar. These toolbars make it easy to access the Web from the My Computer window. In this tutorial, however, you need to see only the Address and Standard toolbars.

To display only the Address and Standard toolbars:

1. Click **View**, point to **Toolbars**, and then examine the Toolbars submenu. The Standard Buttons and Address Bar options should be preceded by a check mark. The Links and Radio options should not be checked. Follow the steps below to ensure that you have check marks next to the correct options.

2. If the Standard Buttons and Address Bar options *are not checked*, then click them to select them (you will have to repeat Step 1 to view the Toolbars submenu to do this for each option).

3. If the Links or Radio options *are checked*, then click them to deselect them (you will have to repeat Step 1 to view the Toolbars submenu to do this for each option).

4. Click **View** and then point to **Toolbars** one last time and verify that your Toolbars submenu and the toolbar display look like Figure 2-14.

| Figure 2-14 | CHECKING VIEW OPTIONS |

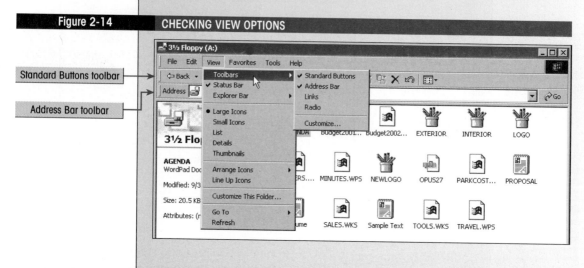

TROUBLE? If the check marks are distributed differently than in Figure 2-14, repeat Steps 1–4 until the correct options are checked.

TROUBLE? If your toolbars are not displayed as shown in Figure 2-14 (for example, both the Standard and Address toolbars might be on the same line, or the Standard toolbar might be above the Address toolbar), you can easily rearrange them. To move a toolbar, drag the vertical bar at the far left of the toolbar. By dragging that vertical bar, you can drag the toolbar left, right, up, or down.

Changing the Icon Display

Windows 2000 provides five ways to view the contents of a disk—Large Icons, Small Icons, List, Details, and Thumbnails. Figure 2-15 shows examples of these five styles.

| Figure 2-15 | VIEWING STYLES |

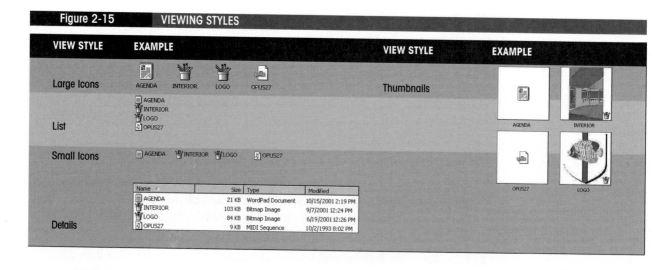

The default view, **Large Icons view**, displays a large icon and title for each file. The icon provides a visual cue to the type of the file, as Figure 2-16 illustrates. You can also get this same information with the smaller icons displayed in the **Small Icons** and **List** views, but in less screen space. In Small Icons and List views, you can see more files and folders at one time, which is helpful when you have many files in one location.

Figure 2-16	TYPICAL ICONS IN WINDOWS 2000
FILE AND FOLDER ICONS	
	Text documents that you can open using the Notepad accessory are represented by notepad icons.
	Graphic image documents that you can open using the Paint accessory are represented by drawing instruments.
	Word-processed documents that you can open using the WordPad accessory are represented by a formatted notepad icon, unless your computer designates a different word-processing program to open files created with WordPad.
	Word-processed documents that you can open using a program such as Microsoft Word are represented by formatted document icons.
	Files created by programs that Windows does not recognize are represented by the Windows logo.
	A folder icon represents folders.
	Certain folders created by Windows 2000 have a special icon design related to the folder's purpose.
PROGRAM ICONS	
	Icons for programs usually depict an object related to the function of the program. For example, an icon that looks like a calculator represents the Calculator accessory.
	Non-Windows programs are represented by the icon of a blank window.

All of the three icon views (Large Icons, Small Icons, and List) help you quickly identify a file and its type, but what if you want more information about a set of files? **Details view** shows more information than the Large Icon, Small Icon, and List views. Details view shows the file icon, the filename, the file size, the program you used to create the file, and the date and time the file was created or last modified.

Finally, if you have graphic files, you may want to use **Thumbnails view**, which displays a small "preview" image of the graphic, so that you can quickly see not only the filename, but also which picture or drawing the file contains. Thumbnails view is great for browsing a large collection of graphic files, but switching to this view can be time-consuming, since Windows 2000 has to create all of the preview images.

To see how easy it is to switch from one view to another, try displaying the contents of drive A in Details view.

To view a detailed list of files:

1. Click **View** and then click **Details** to display details for the files on your disk, as shown in Figure 2-17. Your files might be listed in a different order.

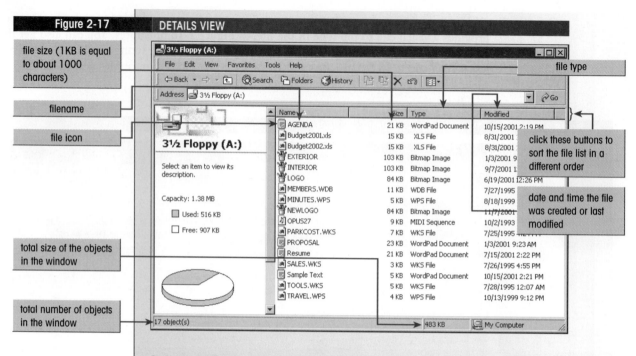

Figure 2-17   DETAILS VIEW

file size (1KB is equal to about 1000 characters)

file type

filename

file icon

click these buttons to sort the file list in a different order

date and time the file was created or last modified

total size of the objects in the window

total number of objects in the window

2. Look at the file sizes. Do you see that Exterior and Interior are the largest files?

3. Look at the dates and times the files were modified. Which is the oldest file?

One of the advantages that Details view has over other views is that you can sort the file list by filename, size, type, or the date the file was last modified. This helps if you're working with a large file list and you're trying to locate a specific file.

To sort the file list by type:

1. Click the **Type** button at the top of the list of files.

The files are now sorted in alphabetical order by type, starting with the "Bitmap Image" files and ending with the "XLS File" files. This would be useful if, for example, you were looking for all the .doc files (those created with Microsoft Word), because they would all be grouped together under "M" for "Microsoft Word."

2. Click the **Type** button again.

The sort order is reversed with the "XLS File" files now at the top of the list.

3. Click the **Name** button at the top of the file list.

The files are now sorted in alphabetical order by filename.

Now that you have looked at the file details, switch back to Large Icon view.

To switch to Large Icon view:

1. Click **View** and then click **Large Icons** to return to the large icon display.

Restoring the My Computer Default Settings

Windows 2000 provides other options in working with your files and windows. These options fall into two general categories: Classic style and Web style. **Classic style** is a mode of working with windows and files that resembles earlier versions of the Windows operating system. **Web style** allows you to work with your windows and files in the same way you work with Web pages on the World Wide Web. For example, to open a file in Classic style, you can double-click the file icon (a **double-click** is clicking the left mouse button twice quickly) or click the file icon once and press the Enter key. To open a file in Web style, you would simply click the file icon once, and the file would open. You could also create your own style, choosing elements of both the Classic and Web styles, and add in a few customized features of your own.

In order to simplify matters, this book will assume that you're working in the Default style, that is the configuration that Windows 2000 uses when it is initially installed. No matter what changes you make to the configuration of Windows 2000, you can always revert back to the Default style. Try switching back to Default style now.

To switch to the Default style:

1. Click **Tools** and then click **Folder Options** on the menu.

2. If it is not already selected, click the **General** tab.

   The General sheet displays general options for working with files and windows. Take some time to look over the list of options available.

3. Click the **Restore Defaults** button.

4. Click the **View** tab.

   The View sheet displays options that control the appearance of files and other objects. You should set these options to their default values as well.

5. Click the **Restore Defaults** button.

6. Click the **OK** button to close the Folder Options dialog box.

Working with Folders and Directories

Up to now, you've done a little work with files and windows, but before going further you should look at some of the terminology used to describe these tasks. Any location where you can store files on a computer is referred to as a **directory**. The main directory of a disk is sometimes called the **root directory**, or the **top-level directory**. All of the files on your Data Disk are currently in the root directory of your floppy disk.

If too many files are stored in a directory, the list of files becomes very long and difficult to manage. You can divide a directory into **subdirectories,** also called **folders**. The number of files for each folder then becomes much fewer and easier to manage. A folder within a folder is called a **subfolder**. The folder that contains another folder is called the **parent folder**.

All of these objects exist in a **hierarchy**, which begins with your desktop and extends down to each subfolder. Figure 2-18 shows part of a typical hierarchy of Windows 2000 objects.

| Figure 2-18 | PART OF A TYPICAL HIERARCHY OF WINDOWS 2000 OBJECTS |

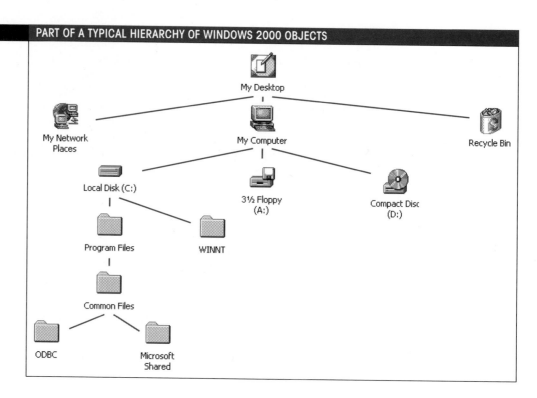

Creating a Folder

You've already seen folder icons in the various windows you've previously opened. Now, you'll create your own folder called Practice to hold your documents.

> ### To create a Practice folder:
>
> 1. Click **File** and then point to **New** to display the submenu.
>
> 2. Click **Folder**. A folder icon with the label "New Folder" appears.
>
> 3. Type **Practice** as the name of the folder.
>
>   TROUBLE? If nothing happens when you type the folder name, it's possible that the folder name is no longer selected. Right-click the Practice folder, click Rename, and then repeat Step 3.
>
> 4. Press the **Enter** key.
>
>   The folder is now named "Practice" and is the selected item on your Data Disk.
>
> 5. Click a blank area next to the Practice folder to deselect it.

Navigating Through the Windows 2000 Hierarchy

Now that you've created a subfolder, how do you move into it? You've seen that to view the contents of a file, you open it. To move into a subfolder, you open it in the same way.

> ### To view the contents of the Practice folder:
>
> **1.** Click the **Practice** folder and press the **Enter** key.
>
> **2.** The Practice folder opens. Because there are no files in the folder, there are no items to display. You'll change that shortly.

You've seen that to navigate through the devices and folders on your computer, you open My Computer and then click the icons representing the objects you want to explore. But what if you want to move back to the root directory? The Standard toolbar, which stays the same regardless of which folder or object is open, includes buttons that help you navigate through the hierarchy of drives, directories, folders, subfolders and other objects in your computer. Figure 2-19 summarizes the navigation buttons on the Standard toolbar.

Figure 2-19		NAVIGATION BUTTONS
BUTTON	**ICON**	**DESCRIPTION**
Back	⇐	Returns you to the folder, drive, directory, or object you were most recently viewing. The button is active only when you have viewed more than one window in the current session.
Forward	⇒	Reverses the effect of the Back button.
Up	⬆	Moves you up one level in the hierarchy of directories, drives, folders, and other objects on your computer.

You can return to your floppy's root directory by using the Back or the Up button. Try both of these techniques now.

> ### To move up to the root directory:
>
> **1.** Click the **Back** button ⇐.
>
> Windows 2000 moves you back to the previous window, in this case the root directory of your Data Disk.
>
> **2.** Click the **Forward** button ⇒.
>
> The Forward button reverses the effect of the Back button and takes you to the Practice folder.
>
> **3.** Click the **Up** button ⬆.
>
> You move up one level in hierarchy of Windows 2000 objects, going to the root directory of the Data Disk.

Another way of moving around in the Windows 2000 hierarchy is through the Address toolbar. By clicking the Address list arrow, you can view a list of the objects in the top part of the Windows 2000 hierarchy (see Figure 2-20). This gives you a quick way of moving to the top without having to navigate through the intermediate levels.

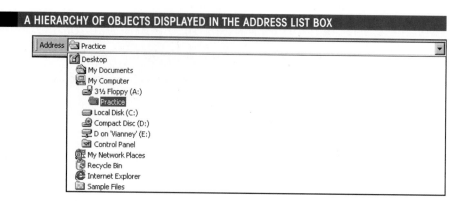

Figure 2-20 | **A HIERARCHY OF OBJECTS DISPLAYED IN THE ADDRESS LIST BOX**

Now that you know how to move among the folders and devices on your computer, you can practice manipulating files. The better you are at working with the hierarchy of files and folders on your computer, the more organized the hierarchy will be, and the easier it will be to find the files you need.

Working with Files

As you've seen, the Practice folder doesn't contain any files. In the next set of steps, you will place a file from the root directory into it.

Moving and Copying a File

If you want to place a file into a folder from another location, you can either move the file or copy it. **Moving** a file takes it out of its current location and places it in the new location. **Copying** places the file in both locations. Windows 2000 provides several different techniques for moving and copying files. One way is to make sure that both the current and the new location are visible on your screen and then hold down the right mouse button and drag the file from the old location to the new location. A menu will then appear, and you can then select whether you want to move the file to the new location or make a copy in the new location. The advantage of this technique is that you are never confused as to whether you copied the file or merely moved it. Try this technique now by placing a copy of the Agenda file in the Practice folder.

To copy the Agenda file:

1. Point to the **Agenda** file in the root directory of your Data Disk and press the *right* mouse button.

2. With the right mouse button still pressed down, drag the **Agenda** file icon to the **Practice** folder icon; when the Practice folder icon turns blue, release the button.

3. A menu appears, as shown in Figure 2-21. Click **Copy Here**.

| Figure 2-21 | COPYING A FILE |

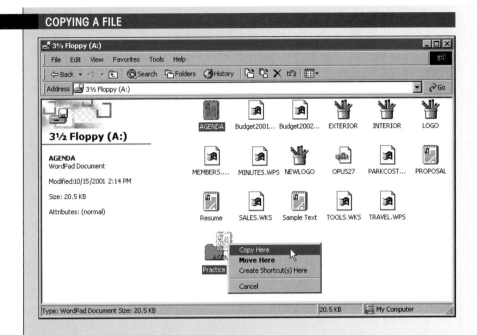

TROUBLE? If you release the mouse button by mistake before dragging the Agenda icon to the Practice folder, the Agenda shortcut menu opens. Press the Esc key and then repeat Steps 1 and 2.

4. Double-click the **Practice** folder.

The Agenda file should now appear in the Practice folder.

Note that the "Move Here" command was also part of the menu. In fact, the command was in boldface, indicating that it is the default command whenever you drag a document from one location to another on the same drive. This means that if you were to drag a file from one location to another on the same drive using the left mouse button (instead of the right), the file would be moved and not copied.

Renaming a File

You will often find that you want to change the name of files as you change their content or as you create other files. You can easily rename a file by using the Rename option on the file's shortcut menu or by using the file's label.

Practice using this feature by renaming the Agenda file "Practice Agenda," since it is now in the Practice folder.

To rename the Agenda file:

1. Right-click the **Agenda** icon.

2. Click **Rename**. After a moment the filename is highlighted and a box appears around it.

3. Type **Practice Agenda** and press the **Enter** key.

> TROUBLE? If you make a mistake while typing and you haven't pressed the Enter key yet, you can press the Backspace key until you delete the mistake, then complete Step 3. If you've already pressed the Enter key, repeat Steps 1-3 to rename the file a second time.
>
> The file appears with a new name.

Deleting a File

You should periodically delete files you no longer need so that your folders and disks don't get cluttered. You delete a file or folder by deleting its icon. Be careful when you delete a folder, because you also delete all the files it contains! When you delete a file from a hard drive on your computer, the filename is deleted from the directory but the file contents are held in the Recycle Bin. The Recycle Bin is an area on your hard drive that holds deleted files until you remove them permanently; an icon on the desktop allows you easy access to the Recycle Bin. If you change your mind and want to retrieve a file deleted from your hard drive, you can recover it by using the Recycle Bin. However, once you've emptied the Recycle Bin, you can no longer recover the files that were in it.

When you delete a file from a floppy disk or a disk that exists on another computer on your network, it does not go into the Recycle Bin. Instead, it is deleted as soon as its icon disappears—and you can't recover it.

Try deleting the Practice Agenda file from your Data Disk. Because this file is on a floppy disk and not on the hard disk, it will not go into the Recycle Bin, and if you change your mind you won't be able to get it back.

To delete the Practice Agenda file:

1. Right-click the icon for the Practice Agenda file.

2. Click **Delete** on the menu that appears.

3. Windows 2000 asks if you're sure that you want to delete this file. Click the **Yes** button.

4. Click the **Close** button ⊠ to close the My Computer window.

If you like using your mouse, another way of deleting a file is to drag its icon to the Recycle Bin on the desktop. Be aware that if you're dragging a file from your floppy disk or a network disk, the file will *not* be placed in the Recycle Bin—it will still be permanently deleted.

Other Copying and Moving Techniques

As was noted earlier, there are several ways of moving and copying. As you become more familiar with Windows 2000, you will no doubt settle on the technique you like best. Figure 2-22 describes some of the other ways of moving and copying files.

Figure 2-22	METHODS FOR MOVING AND COPYING FILES	
METHOD	**TO MOVE**	**TO COPY**
Cut, copy, and paste	Select the file icon. Click **Edit** on the menu bar and **Cut** on the menu bar. Move to the new location. Click **Edit** and **Paste**.	Select the file icon. Click **Edit** on the menu bar and **Copy** on the menu bar. Move to the new location. Click **Edit** and **Paste**.
Drag and drop	Click the file icon. Drag and drop the icon in the new location.	Click the file icon. Hold down the Ctrl key and drag and drop the icon in the new location.
Right-click, drag and drop	With the right mouse button pressed down, drag the file icon to the new location. Release the mouse button and click **Move Here** on the menu.	With the right mouse button pressed down, drag the file icon to the new location. Release the mouse button and click **Copy Here** on the menu.
Move to folder and copy to folder	Click the file icon. Click **Edit** on the menu bar and **Move to Folder** on the menu bar. Select the new location in the Browse for Folder dialog box.	Click the file icon. Click **Edit** on the menu bar and **Copy to Folder** on the menu bar. Select the new location in the Browse for Folder dialog box.

The techniques shown in Figure 2-22 are primarily for document files. Because a program might not work correctly if moved into a new location, the techniques for moving program files are slightly different. See the Windows 2000 online Help for more information on moving or copying a program file.

Copying an Entire Floppy Disk

You can have trouble accessing the data on your floppy disk if the disk is damaged, is exposed to magnetic fields, or picks up a computer virus. To avoid losing all your data, it is a good idea to make a copy of your floppy disk.

If you wanted to make a copy of an audiocassette, your cassette player would need two cassette drives. You might wonder, therefore, how your computer can make a copy of your disk if you have only one floppy disk drive. Figure 2-23 illustrates how the computer uses only one disk drive to make a copy of a disk.

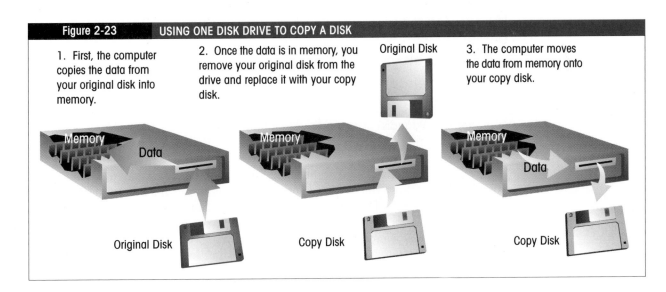

Figure 2-23	USING ONE DISK DRIVE TO COPY A DISK

1. First, the computer copies the data from your original disk into memory.

2. Once the data is in memory, you remove your original disk from the drive and replace it with your copy disk.

3. The computer moves the data from memory onto your copy disk.

REFERENCE WINDOW RW

<u>Copying a Disk</u>
- Insert the disk you want to copy in drive A.
- In My Computer, right-click the 3½ Floppy (A:) icon, and then click Copy Disk.
- Click Start to begin the copy process.
- When prompted, remove the disk you want to copy, place your second disk in drive A, and then click OK.

If you have an extra floppy disk, you can make a copy of your Data Disk now. Make sure you copy the disk regularly so that as you work through the tutorials in this book it will stay updated.

To copy your Data Disk:

1. Write your name and "Windows 2000 Disk 1 Data Disk Copy" on the label of your second disk. Make sure the disk is blank and formatted.

   TROUBLE? If you aren't sure if the disk is blank, place it in the disk drive and open the 3½ Floppy (A:) window to view its contents. If the disk contains files you need, get a different disk. If it contains files you don't need, you could format the disk now, using the steps you learned at the beginning of this tutorial.

2. Make sure your original Data Disk is in drive A and the My Computer window is open.

3. Right-click the **3½ Floppy (A:)** icon, and then click **Copy Disk**. The Copy Disk dialog box opens.

4. Click the **Start** button and then the **OK** button to begin the copy process.

5. When the message "Insert the disk you want to copy to (destination disk)..." appears, remove your Data Disk and insert your Windows 2000 Disk 1 Data Disk Copy in drive A.

6. Click the **OK** button. When the copy is complete, you will see the message "Copy completed successfully." Click the **Close** button.

7. Close the My Computer window.

8. Remove your disk from the drive.

As you finish copying your disk, Shannon emphasizes the importance of making copies of your files frequently, so you won't risk losing important documents for your distance learning course. If your original Data Disk were damaged, you could use the copy you just made to access the files.

Keeping copies of your files is so important that Windows 2000 includes a program called Backup that automates the process of duplicating and storing data. In the Projects at the end of the tutorial you'll have an opportunity to explore the difference between what you just did in copying a disk and the way in which a program such as the Windows 2000 Backup program helps you safeguard data.

Session 2.2 QUICK CHECK

1. If you want to find out about the storage devices and printers connected to your computer, what window could you open?

2. If you have only one floppy disk drive on your computer, it is usually identified by the letter _____.

3. The letter C is typically used for the _____ drive of a computer.

4. What information does Details view supply about a list of folders and files?

5. The main directory of a disk is referred to as the _____ directory.

6. What is the topmost object in the hierarchy of Windows 2000 objects?

7. If you have one floppy disk drive, but you have two disks, can you copy the files on one floppy disk to the other?

REVIEW ASSIGNMENTS

1. **Opening, Editing, and Printing a Document** In this tutorial you learned how to create a document using WordPad. You also learned how to save, open, and print a document. Practice these skills by copying the document called **Resume** into the Practice folder on your Data Disk. Rename the file **Woods Resume**. This document is a resume for Jamie Woods. Make the changes shown in Figure 2-24. Save your revisions in Word for Windows 6.0 format, preview, and then print the document. Close WordPad.

Figure 2-24

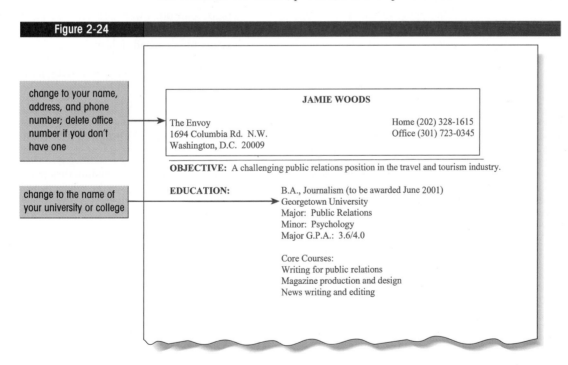

change to your name, address, and phone number; delete office number if you don't have one

change to the name of your university or college

JAMIE WOODS

The Envoy
1694 Columbia Rd. N.W.
Washington, D.C. 20009

Home (202) 328-1615
Office (301) 723-0345

OBJECTIVE: A challenging public relations position in the travel and tourism industry.

EDUCATION: B.A., Journalism (to be awarded June 2001)
Georgetown University
Major: Public Relations
Minor: Psychology
Major G.P.A.: 3.6/4.0

Core Courses:
Writing for public relations
Magazine production and design
News writing and editing

2. **Creating, Saving, and Printing a Letter** Use WordPad to write a one-page letter to a relative or a friend. Save the document in the Practice folder on your Data Disk with the name **Letter**. Use the Print Preview feature to look at the format of your finished letter, then print it, and be sure to sign it. Close WordPad.

3. **Managing Files and Folders** Using the copy of the disk you made at the end of the tutorial, complete steps a through f below to practice your file-management skills, and then answer the questions below.

   a. Create a folder called Spreadsheets on your Data Disk.
   b. Move the files **Parkcost**, **Budget2001**, **Budget2002**, and **Sales** into the Spreadsheets folder.
   c. Create a folder called Park Project.
   d. Move the files **Proposal**, **Members**, **Tools**, **Logo**, and **Newlogo** into the Park Project folder.
   e. Delete the file called **Travel**.
   f. Switch to the Details view and write out your answers to Questions 1 through 5:
       1. What is the largest file or files in the Park Project folder?
       2. What is the newest file or files in the Spreadsheets folder?
       3. How many files (don't include folders) are in the root directory of your Data Disk?
       4. How are the Opus and Exterior icons different? Judging from the appearance of the icons, what would you guess these two files contain?
       5. Which file in the root directory has the most recent date?

4. **More Practice with Files and Folders** For this assignment, you need a third blank disk. Complete steps a through g below to practice your file-management skills.

   a. Write "Windows 2000 Tutorial 2 Assignment 4" on the label of the blank disk, and then format the disk if necessary.
   b. Create another copy of your original Data Disk, using the Assignment 4 disk. Refer to the section "Creating Your Data Disk" in Session 2.2.
   c. Create three folders on the Assignment 4 Data Disk you just created: Documents, Budgets, and Graphics.
   d. Move the files **Interior**, **Exterior**, **Logo**, and **Newlogo** to the Graphics folder.
   e. Move the files **Travel**, **Members**, and **Minutes** to the Documents folder.
   f. Move **Budget2001** and **Budget2002** to the Budgets folder.
   g. Switch to Details view and write out your answers to Questions 1 through 6:
       1. What is the largest file or files in the Graphics folder?
       2. How many word-processed documents are in the root directory? *Hint*: These documents will appear with the WordPad, Microsoft Word, or some other word-processing icon, depending on what software you have installed.
       3. What is the newest file or files in the root directory (don't include folders)?
       4. How many files in all folders are 5 KB in size?
       5. How many files in the root directory are WKS files? *Hint*: Look in the Type column to identify WKS files.
       6. Do all the files in the Graphics folder have the same icon? What type are they?

5. **Searching for a File** Windows 2000 Help includes a topic that discusses how to search for files on a disk without looking through all the folders. Start Windows Help, then locate this topic, and answer Questions a through c:

   a. To display the Search dialog box, you must click the _____ button, then point to _____ on the menu, and finally click _____ on the submenu.
   b. Do you need to type in the entire filename to find the file?
   c. How do you perform a case-sensitive search?

6. **Help with Files and Folders** In Tutorial 2 you learned how to work with Windows 2000 files and folders. What additional information on this topic does Windows 2000 Help provide? Use the Start button to access Help. Use the Index tab to locate topics related to files and folders. Find at least two tips or procedures for working with files and folders that were not covered in the tutorial. Write out the tip in your own words and include the title of the Help screen that contains the information.

7. **Formatting Text** You can use a word processor such as WordPad to format text, that is, to give it a specific look and feel by using bold, italics, and different fonts, and by applying other features. Using WordPad, type the title and words to one of your favorite songs and

then save the document on your Data Disk (make sure you use your original Data Disk) with the filename Song.

  a. Select the title, and then click the Center ▤ , Bold **B** , and Italic *I* buttons on the toolbar.

  b. Click the Font list arrow and select a different font. Repeat this step several times with different fonts until you locate a font that is appropriate for the song.

  c. Experiment with other formatting options until you find a look you like for your document. Save and print the final version.

PROJECTS

1. Formatting a floppy disk removes all the data on a disk. Answer the following questions using full sentences:

  a. What other method did you learn in this tutorial for removing data from a disk?

  b. If you wanted to remove all data from a disk, which method would you use? Why?

  c. What method would you use if you wanted to remove only one file? Why?

2. A friend who is new to computers is trying to learn how to enter text into WordPad. She has just finished typing her first paragraph when she notices a mistake in the first sentence. She can't remember how to fix a mistake, so she asks you for help. Write the set of steps she should try.

3. Computer users usually develop habits about how they access their files and programs. Follow the steps below to practice methods of opening a file, and then evaluate which method you would be likely to use and why.

  a. Using WordPad, create a document containing the words to a favorite poem, and save it on your Data Disk with the name Poem.

  b. Close WordPad and return to the desktop.

  c. Open the document using a document-centric approach.

  d. After a successful completion of step c, close the program and reopen the same document using another approach.

  e. Write the steps you used to complete steps c and d of this assignment. Then write a paragraph discussing which approach is most convenient when you are starting from the desktop, and indicate what habits you would develop if you owned your own computer and used it regularly.

Explore   4. The My Computer window gives you access to the objects on your computer. In this tutorial you used My Computer to access your floppy drive so you could view the contents of your Data Disk. The My Computer window gives you access to other objects too. Open My Computer and write a list of the objects you see, including folders. Then open each icon and write a two-sentence description of the contents of each window that opens.

Explore   5. In this tutorial you learned how to copy a disk to protect yourself in the event of data loss. If you had your own computer with an 80 MB hard drive that was being used to capacity, it would take many 1.44 MB floppy disks to copy the contents of the entire hard drive. Is copying to floppy disks a reasonable method to use for protecting the data on your hard disk? Why, or why not?

  a. As mentioned at the end of the tutorial, Windows 2000 also includes an accessory called Backup that helps you safeguard your data. Backup doesn't just copy the data—it organizes it so that it takes up much less space than if you simply copied it. This program might not be installed on your computer, but if it is, try starting it (click the Start button, point to Programs, point to Accessories, point to System Tools, and then click Backup) and opening the Help files to learn what you can about how it functions. If it is not installed, skip Part a.

  b. Look up the topic of backups in a computer concepts textbook or in computer trade magazines. You could also interview experienced computer owners to find out which method they use to protect their data. When you have finished researching the concept of the backup, write a single-page essay that explains the difference between copying and backing up files, and evaluates which method is preferable for backing up large amounts of data, and why.

LAB ASSIGNMENTS

Using Files In this Lab you manipulate a simulated computer to view what happens in memory and on disk when you create, save, open, revise, and delete files. Understanding what goes on "inside the box" will help you quickly grasp how to perform basic file operations with most application software. See the Read This Before You Begin page for instructions on starting the Using Files Course Lab.

1. Click the Steps button to learn how to use the simulated computer to view the contents of memory and disk when you perform basic file operations. As you proceed through the Steps, answer all of the Quick Check questions that appear. After you complete the Steps, you will see a Quick Check Summary Report. Follow the instructions on the screen to print this report.

2. Click the Explore button and use the simulated computer to perform the following tasks:
   a. Create a document containing your name and the city in which you were born. Save this document as NAME.
   b. Create another document containing two of your favorite foods. Save this document as FOODS.
   c. Create another file containing your two favorite classes. Call this file CLASSES.
   d. Open the FOOD file and add another one of your favorite foods. Save this file without changing its name.
   e. Open the NAME file. Change this document so that it contains your name and the name of your school. Save this as a new document called SCHOOL.
   f. Write down how many files are on the simulated disk and the exact contents of each file.
   g. Delete all the files.

3. In Explore, use the simulated computer to perform the following tasks.
   a. Create a file called MUSIC that contains the name of your favorite CD.
   b. Create another document that contains eight numbers and call this file LOTTERY.
   c. You didn't win the lottery this week. Revise the contents of the LOTTERY file, but save the revision as LOTTERY2.
   d. Revise the MUSIC file so that it also contains the name of your favorite musician or composer, and save this file as MUSIC2.
   e. Delete the MUSIC file.
   f. Write down how many files are on the simulated disk and the exact contents of each file.

QUICK | CHECK ANSWERS

Session 2.1
   1. file
   2. Formatting
   3. True
   4. insertion point
   5. a list of recently opened files and objects
   6. The Files of Type list box could be set to display files of a different type than the one you're looking for.
   7. From the Print Preview window, using the Print button on the toolbar, and using the Print command from the File menu. If you want to print multiple copies of a file, use either the Print button from the Print Preview window or the Print command from the File menu—both of these techniques will display the Print dialog box containing the options you need to set.

Session 2.2
   1. My Computer
   2. A
   3. hard
   4. filename, size, type, and date modified
   5. root or top-level
   6. the Desktop
   7. yes

New Perspectives on

MICROSOFT®
OFFICE XP

TUTORIAL 1   OFF 3

Introducing Microsoft Office XP

Read This Before You Begin

To the Student

Data Disks

To complete this tutorial and the Review Assignments, you need one Data Disk. Your instructor will either provide you with the Data Disk or ask you to make your own.

If you are making your own Data Disk, you will need **one** blank, formatted high-density disk. You will need to copy a set of files and/or folders from a file server, standalone computer, or the Web onto your disk. Your instructor will tell you which computer, drive letter, and folder contain the files you need. You could also download the files by going to www.course.com and following the instructions on the screen.

The information below shows you which folder goes on your disk, so that you will have enough disk space to complete the tutorial and Review Assignments:

Data Disk 1

Write this on the disk label:
Data Disk 1: Introducing Office XP

Put this folder on the disk:
Tutorial.01

When you begin the tutorial, be sure you are using the correct Data Disk. Refer to the "File Finder" chart at the back of this text for more detailed information on which files are used in the tutorial. See the inside front or inside back cover of this book for more information on Data Disk files, or ask your instructor or technical support person for assistance.

Using Your Own Computer

If you are going to work through this tutorial using your own computer, you need:

- **Computer System** Microsoft Windows 98, NT, 2000 Professional, or higher must be installed on your computer. This book assumes a typical installation of Microsoft Office XP.

- **Data Disk** You will not be able to complete this tutorial or Review Assignments using your own computer until you have your Data Disk.

Visit Our World Wide Web Site

Additional materials designed especially for you are available on the World Wide Web.
Go to www.course.com/NewPerspectives.

To the Instructor

The Data Disk Files are available on the Instructor's Resource Kit for this title. Follow the instructions in the Help file on the CD-ROM to install the programs to your network or standalone computer. For information on creating the Data Disk, see the "To the Student" section above.

You are granted a license to copy the Data Disk Files to any computer or computer network used by students who have purchased this book.

OBJECTIVES

In this tutorial you will:

- Explore the programs that comprise Microsoft Office

- Explore the benefits of integrating data between programs

- Start programs and switch between them

- Use personalized menus and toolbars

- Save and close a file

- Open an existing file

- Print a file

- Get Help

- Close files and exit programs

INTRODUCING MICROSOFT OFFICE XP

Preparing Promotional Materials for Delmar Office Supplies

CASE

Delmar Office Supplies

Delmar Office Supplies, a company in Wisconsin founded by Nicole Delmar in 1996, sells recycled office supplies to businesses and home-based offices around the world. The demand for quality recycled papers, reconditioned toner cartridges, and renovated office furniture has been growing each year. Nicole and all her employees use Microsoft Office XP, which provides everyone in the company the power and flexibility to store a variety of information, create consistent documents, and share data. In this tutorial, you'll review some of the latest documents the company's employees have created using Microsoft Office XP.

Exploring Microsoft Office XP

Microsoft Office XP, or simply **Office**, is a collection of the most popular Microsoft programs: Word, Excel, PowerPoint, Access, and Outlook. Each Office program contains valuable tools to help you accomplish many tasks, such as composing reports, analyzing data, preparing presentations, and compiling information.

Microsoft Word 2002, or simply **Word**, is a **word processing program** you use to create text documents. The files you create in Word are called **documents**. Word offers many special features that help you compose and update all types of documents, ranging from letters and newsletters to reports, fliers, faxes, and even books—all in attractive and readable formats. You also can use Word to create, insert, and position figures, tables, and other graphics to enhance the look of your documents. Figure 1 shows a business letter that a sales representative composed with Word.

Figure 1   **LETTER COMPOSED IN A WORD DOCUMENT**

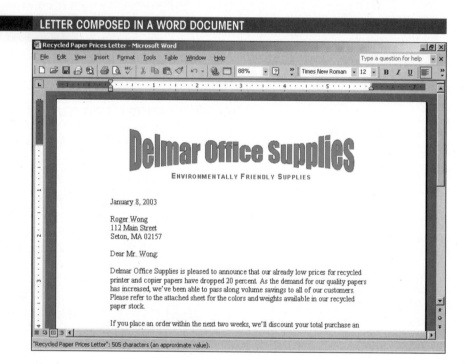

Microsoft Excel 2002, or simply **Excel**, is a **spreadsheet program** you use to display, organize, and analyze numerical information. You can do some of this in Word with tables, but Excel provides many more tools for performing calculations than Word does. Its graphics capabilities also enable you to display data visually. You might, for example, generate a pie chart or bar chart to help readers quickly see the significance of and the connections between information. The files you create in Excel are called **workbooks**. Figure 2 shows an Excel workbook with a line chart that the Operations Department uses to track the company's financial performance.

Figure 2 FINANCIAL DATA IN AN EXCEL WORKBOOK

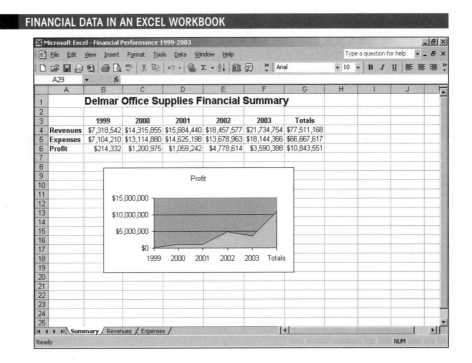

Microsoft PowerPoint 2002, or simply **PowerPoint**, is a **presentation graphics program** you use to create a collection of "slides" that can contain text, charts, pictures, and so on. The files you create in PowerPoint are called **presentations**. You can show these presentations on your computer monitor, project them onto a screen as a slide show, print them, share them over the Internet, or display them on the World Wide Web. You also can use PowerPoint to generate presentation-related documents such as audience handouts, outlines, and speakers' notes. Figure 3 shows an effective slide presentation the Sales Department created with PowerPoint to promote the latest product line.

Figure 3 SLIDE PRESENTATION CREATED IN POWERPOINT

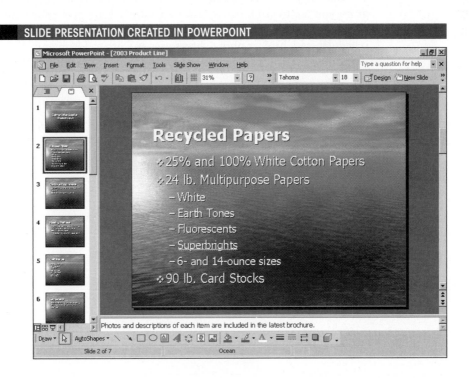

Microsoft Access 2002, or simply **Access**, is a **database program** you use to enter, organize, display, and retrieve related information. The files you create in Access are called **databases**. With Access you can create data entry forms to make data entry easier, and you can create professional reports to improve the readability of your data. Figure 4 shows a table in an Access database with customer names and addresses compiled by the Sales Department.

Figure 4	CUSTOMER ADDRESSES COMPILED IN AN ACCESS DATABASE

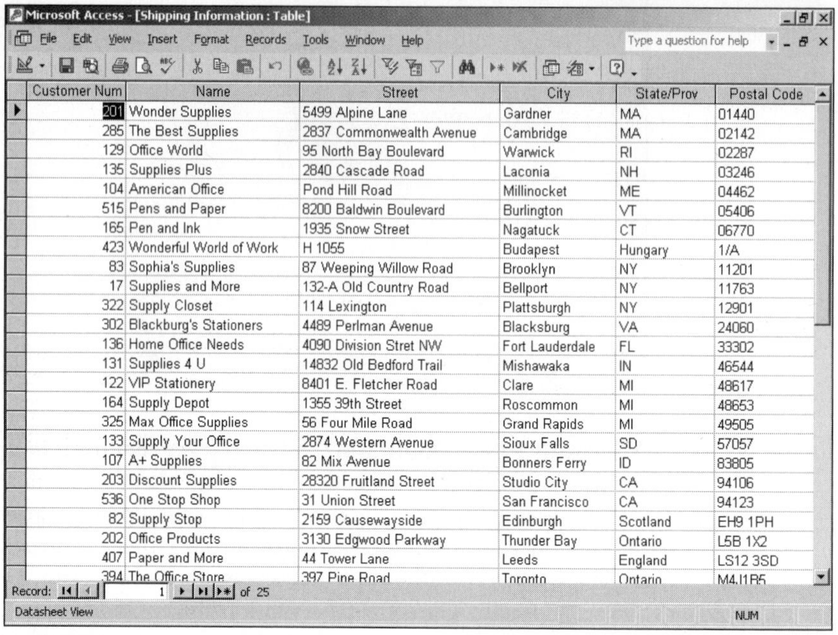

Microsoft Outlook 2002, or simply **Outlook**, is an **information management program** you use to send, receive, and organize e-mail; plan your schedule; arrange meetings; organize contacts; create a to-do list; and jot down notes. You also can use Outlook to print schedules, task lists, or phone directories and other documents. Figure 5 shows how Nicole Delmar uses Outlook to plan her schedule and create a to-do list.

Figure 5   CALENDAR AND TASKS IN OUTLOOK

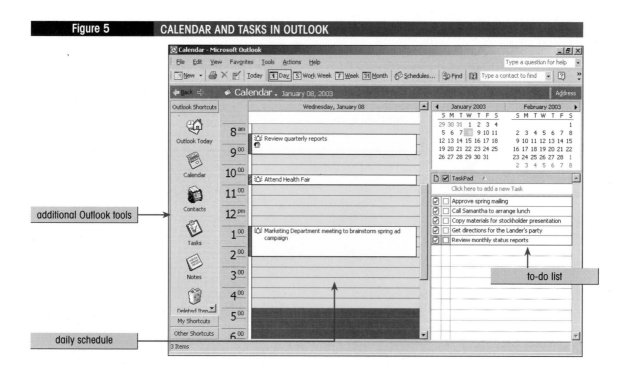

additional Outlook tools

to-do list

daily schedule

Although each Office program individually is a strong tool, their potential is even greater when used together.

Integrating Programs

One of the main advantages of Office is **integration**, the ability to share information between programs. Integration ensures consistency and accuracy, and it saves time because you don't have to re-enter the same information in several Office programs. The staff at Delmar Office Supplies uses the integration features of Office daily, including the following examples:

■ The Accounting Department created an Excel bar chart on the last two years' fourth-quarter results, which they inserted into the quarterly financial report, created in Word. They added a hyperlink to the Word report that employees can click to open the Excel workbook and view the original data. See Figure 6.

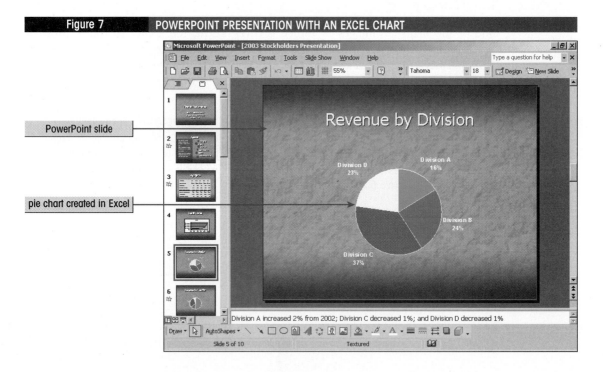

Figure 6   WORD DOCUMENT WITH AN EXCEL CHART

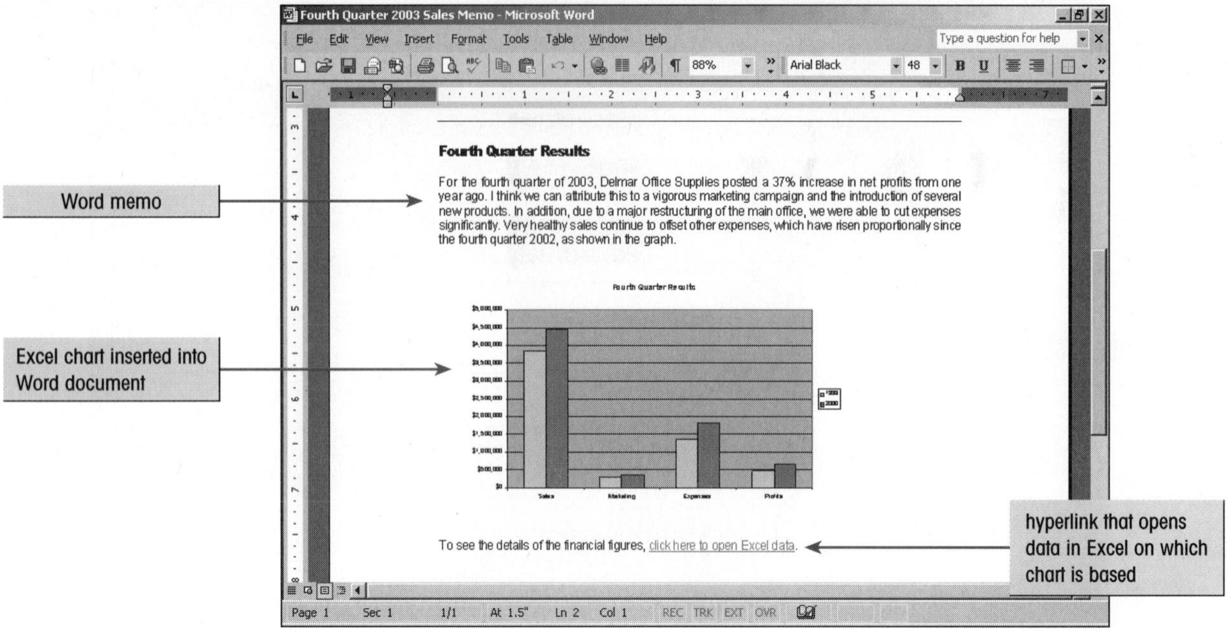

Word memo

Excel chart inserted into Word document

hyperlink that opens data in Excel on which chart is based

■ An Excel pie chart of sales percentages by divisions of Delmar Office Supplies can be duplicated on a PowerPoint slide. The slide is part of the Operations Department's presentation to stockholders. See Figure 7.

Figure 7   POWERPOINT PRESENTATION WITH AN EXCEL CHART

PowerPoint slide

pie chart created in Excel

■ An Access database or an Outlook contact list that stores the names and addresses of customers can be combined with a form letter that the Marketing Department created in Word, to produce a mailing promoting the company's newest products. See Figure 8.

Figure 8	WORD LETTER WITH ACCESS OR OUTLOOK DATA

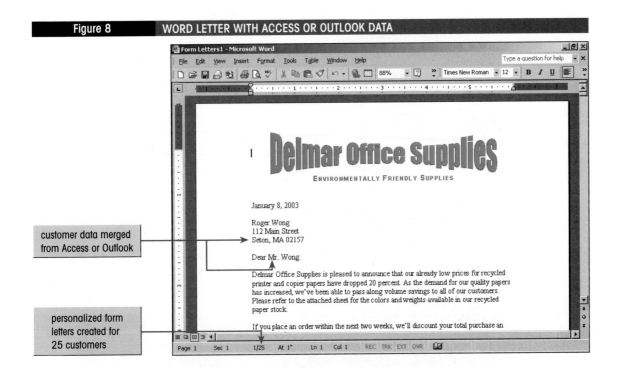

customer data merged from Access or Outlook

personalized form letters created for 25 customers

These are just a few examples of how you can take information from one Office program and integrate it into another.

Starting **Office Programs**

All Office programs start the same way—from the Programs menu on the Start button. You select the program you want, and then the program starts so you can immediately begin to create new files or work with existing ones.

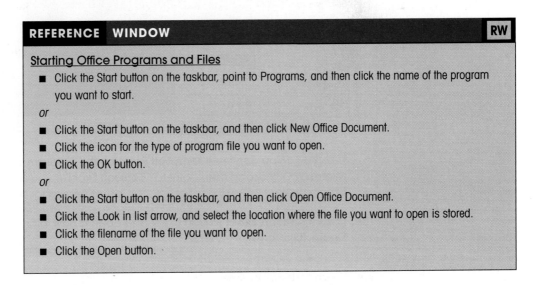

REFERENCE   WINDOW   RW

Starting Office Programs and Files
- Click the Start button on the taskbar, point to Programs, and then click the name of the program you want to start.

or
- Click the Start button on the taskbar, and then click New Office Document.
- Click the icon for the type of program file you want to open.
- Click the OK button.

or
- Click the Start button on the taskbar, and then click Open Office Document.
- Click the Look in list arrow, and select the location where the file you want to open is stored.
- Click the filename of the file you want to open.
- Click the Open button.

You'll start Excel using the Start button.

To start Excel and open a new, blank workbook from the Start menu:

1. Make sure your computer is on and the Windows desktop appears on your screen.

   TROUBLE? Don't worry if your screen differs slightly from those shown in the figures. The figures in this book were created while running Windows 2000 in its default settings, but Office runs equally well using Windows 98 or later or Windows NT 4 with Service Pack 5. These operating systems share the same basic user interface.

2. Click the **Start** button on the taskbar, and then point to **Programs** to display the Programs menu.

3. Point to **Microsoft Excel** on the Programs menu. See Figure 9. Depending on how your computer is set up, your desktop and menu might contain different icons and commands.

| Figure 9 | START MENU WITH PROGRAMS MENU DISPLAYED |

other ways to open Office programs and files

click to start Excel

Office programs

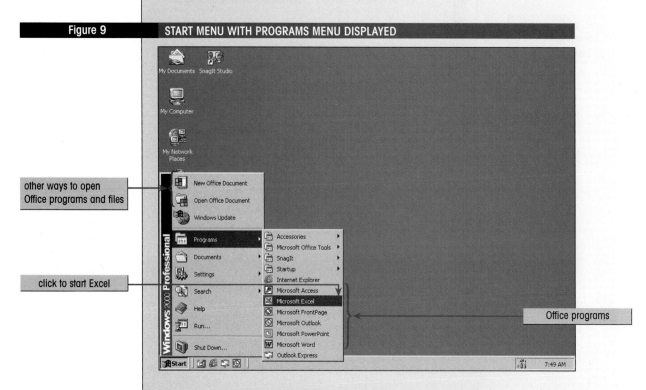

   TROUBLE? If you don't see Microsoft Excel on the Programs menu, point to Microsoft Office, and then point to Microsoft Excel. If you still don't see Microsoft Excel, ask your instructor or technical support person for help.

4. Click **Microsoft Excel** to start Excel and open a new, blank workbook. See Figure 10.

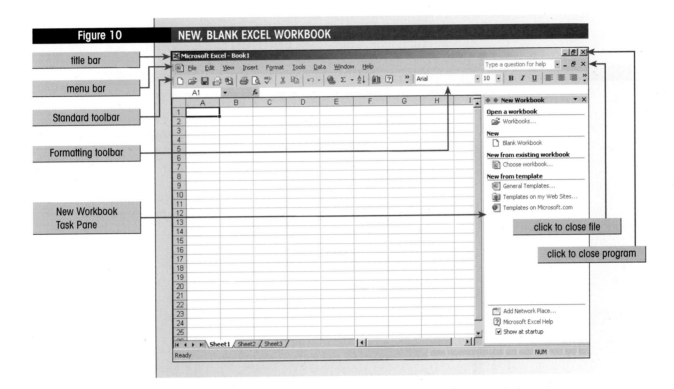

| Figure 10 | NEW, BLANK EXCEL WORKBOOK |

title bar

menu bar

Standard toolbar

Formatting toolbar

New Workbook
Task Pane

click to close file

click to close program

An alternate method for starting programs with a blank file is to click the New Office Document command on the Start menu; the kind of file you choose determines which program opens. You'll use this method to start Word and open a new, blank document.

To start Word and open a new, blank document with the New Office Document command:

1. Leaving Excel open, click the **Start** button on the taskbar, and then click **New Office Document**. The New Office Document dialog box opens, providing another way to start Office programs. See Figure 11.

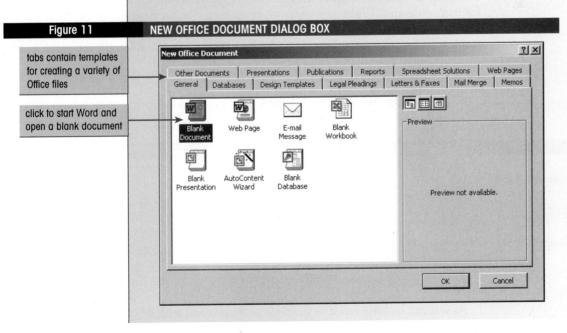

| Figure 11 | NEW OFFICE DOCUMENT DIALOG BOX |

tabs contain templates
for creating a variety of
Office files

click to start Word and
open a blank document

2. If necessary, click the **General** tab, click the **Blank Document** icon, and then click the **OK** button. Word opens with a new, blank document. See Figure 12.

| Figure 12 | NEW, BLANK DOCUMENT IN WORD |

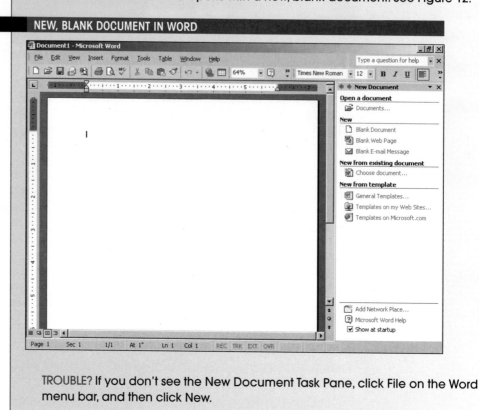

TROUBLE? If you don't see the New Document Task Pane, click File on the Word menu bar, and then click New.

You've tried two ways to start a program. There are several methods for performing most tasks in Office. This flexibility enables you to use Office in the way that fits how you like to work.

Switching Between Open Programs and Files

Two programs are running at the same time—Excel and Word. The taskbar contains buttons for both programs. When you have two or more programs running, or two files within the same program open, you can use the taskbar buttons to switch from one program or file to another. The employees at Delmar Office Supplies often work in several programs at once.

To switch between Word and Excel:

1. Click the **Microsoft Excel – Book1** button on the taskbar to switch from Word to Excel. See Figure 13.

| Figure 13 | EXCEL AND WORD PROGRAMS OPENED |

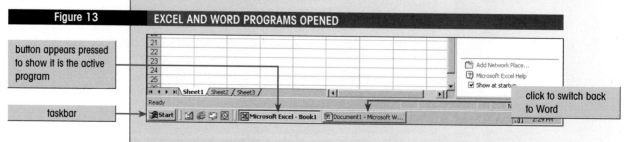

2. Click the **Document1 – Microsoft Word** button on the taskbar to return to Word.

As you can see, you can start multiple programs and switch between them in seconds.

The Office programs also share many features, so once you've learned one program, it's easy to learn the others. One of the most visible similarities among all the programs is the "personalized" menus and toolbars.

Using **Personalized Menus and Toolbars**

In each Office program, you perform tasks using a menu command, a toolbar button, or a keyboard shortcut. A **menu command** is a word on a menu that you click to execute a task; a **menu** is a group of related commands. For example, the File menu contains commands for managing files, such as the Open command and the Save command. A **toolbar** is a collection of **buttons** that correspond to commonly used menu commands. For example, the Standard toolbar contains an Open button and a Save button. **Keyboard shortcuts** are combinations of keys you press to perform a command. For example, Ctrl+S is the keyboard shortcut for the Save command (you hold down the Ctrl key while you press the S key). Keyboard shortcuts are displayed to the right of many menu commands.

When you first use a newly installed Office program, the menus and toolbars display only the basic and most commonly used commands and buttons, streamlining the program window. The other commands and buttons are available, but you have to click an extra button to see them (the double-arrow button on a menu and the Toolbar Options button on a toolbar). As you select commands and click buttons, the ones you use often are put on the short, personalized menu and on the visible part of the toolbars. The ones you don't use remain available on the full menus and toolbars. This means that the Office menus and toolbars might display different commands and buttons on each person's computer.

To view a personalized and full menu:

1. Click **Insert** on the Word menu bar to display the short, personalized menu. See Figure 14. The Bookmark command, for example, does not appear on the short menu.

Figure 14	SHORT, PERSONALIZED MENU

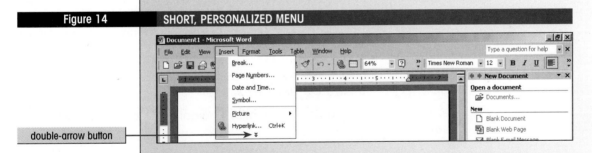

double-arrow button

TROUBLE? If the Insert menu displays different commands than shown in Figure 14, you need to reset the menus. Click Tools on the menu bar, click Customize (you might need to pause until the full menu appears to see that command), and then click the Options tab in the Customize dialog box. Click the Always show full menus check box to remove the check mark if necessary, and then click the Show full menus after a short delay check box to insert a check mark if necessary. Click the Reset my usage data button, and then click the Yes button to confirm that you want to reset the commands. Click the Close button. Repeat Step 1.

You can display the full menu in one of three ways: (1) pause until the full menu appears, which might happen as you read this; (2) click the double-arrow button at the bottom of the menu; or (3) double-click the menu name on the menu bar.

2. Pause until the full Insert menu appears, as shown in Figure 15. The Bookmark command and other commands are now visible.

Figure 15   **EXPANDED, FULL MENU**

commands with light border appear on short menu

commands with dark border appear only on full menu

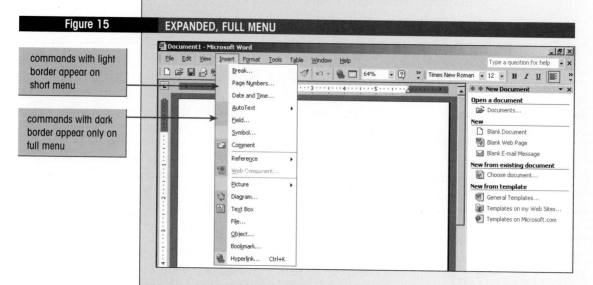

3. Click the **Bookmark** command. A dialog box opens when you click a command whose name is followed by an ellipsis (...). In this case, the Bookmark dialog box opens.

4. Click the **Cancel** button to close the Bookmark dialog box.

5. Click **Insert** on the menu bar again to display the short, personalized menu. The Bookmark command appears on the short, personalized menu because you used it.

6. Press the **Esc** key to close the menu.

As you can see, the menu changed based on your actions. Over time, only the commands you use frequently will appear on the personalized menu. The toolbars work similarly.

To use the personalized toolbars:

1. Observe that the Standard and Formatting toolbars appear side by side below the menu bar.

TROUBLE? If the toolbars appear on two rows, you need to reset them. Click Tools on the menu bar, click Customize, and then click the Options tab in the Customize dialog box. Click the Show Standard and Formatting toolbars on two rows check box to remove the check mark. Click the Reset my data usage button, and then click the Yes button to confirm you want to reset the commands. Click the Close button. Repeat Step 1.

The Formatting toolbar sits to the right of the Standard toolbar. You can see most of the Standard toolbar buttons, but only a few Formatting toolbar buttons.

2. Click the **Toolbar Options** button ⟫ at the right side of the Standard toolbar. See Figure 16.

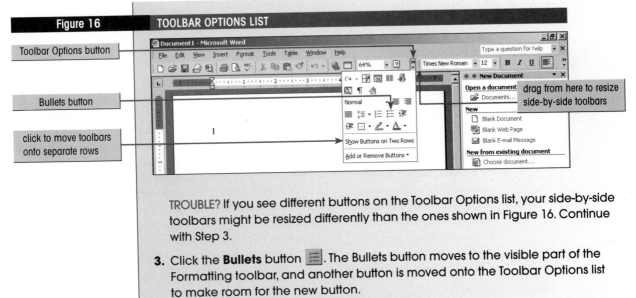

Figure 16   TOOLBAR OPTIONS LIST

Toolbar Options button

Bullets button

click to move toolbars onto separate rows

drag from here to resize side-by-side toolbars

TROUBLE? If you see different buttons on the Toolbar Options list, your side-by-side toolbars might be resized differently than the ones shown in Figure 16. Continue with Step 3.

3. Click the **Bullets** button. The Bullets button moves to the visible part of the Formatting toolbar, and another button is moved onto the Toolbar Options list to make room for the new button.

TROUBLE? If the Bullets button already appears on the Formatting toolbar, click another button on the Toolbar Options list. Then click that same button again in Step 4 to turn off that formatting.

4. Click again to turn off the Bullets formatting.

Some people like that the menus and toolbars change to meet their work habits. Others prefer to see all the menu commands or to display the toolbars on different rows so that all the buttons are always visible. You'll change the toolbar setting now.

To turn off the personalized toolbars:

1. Click the **Toolbar Options** button at the right side of the Standard toolbar.

2. Click the **Show Buttons on Two Rows command**. The toolbars move to separate rows (the Standard toolbar on top) and you can see all the buttons on each toolbar.

You can easily access any button on the toolbars with one mouse click. The drawback is that the toolbars take up more space in the program window.

Using Speech Recognition

Another way to perform tasks in Office is with your voice. Office's **speech recognition technology** enables you to say the names of the toolbar buttons, menus, menu commands, dialog box items, and so forth, rather than clicking the mouse or pressing keys to select them. The Language toolbar includes the Speech Balloon, which displays the voice command equivalents of a selected button or command. If you switch from Voice mode to Dictation mode, you can dictate the contents of your files rather than typing the text or numbers. For better accuracy, complete the Training Wizard, which helps Office learn your vocal quality, rate of talking, and speech patterns. To start using speech recognition, click Tools on the menu bar in any Office program, and then click Speech. The first time you start this feature, the Training Wizard guides you through the setup process.

Saving and Closing a File

As you create and modify Office files, your work is stored only in the computer's temporary memory, not on disk. If you were to exit the programs, turn off your computer, or experience a power failure, your work would be lost. To prevent losing work, frequently save your file to a disk—at least every ten minutes. You can save files to the hard disk located inside your computer or to portable storage disks, such as CD-ROMs, Zip disks, or floppy disks.

The first time you save a file, you need to name it. This name is called a **filename**. When you choose a filename, select a descriptive one that accurately reflects the content of the document, workbook, presentation, or database, such as "Shipping Options Letter" or "Fourth Quarter Financial Analysis." Filenames can include a maximum of 255 letters, numbers, hyphens, or spaces in any combination. Office appends a **file extension** to the filename, which identifies the program in which that file was created. The file extensions are .doc for Word, .xls for Excel, .ppt for PowerPoint, and .mdb for Access. Whether you see file extensions depends on how Windows is set up for your computer.

You also need to decide where you'll save the file—on which disk and in what folder. Choose a logical location that you'll remember whenever you want to use the file again.

REFERENCE WINDOW RW

Saving a File

- Click the Save button on the Standard toolbar (*or* click File on the menu bar, and then click Save or Save As).
- Click the Save in list arrow, and then select the location where you want to save the file.
- Type a filename in the File name text box.
- Click the Save button.
- To resave the named file to the same location, click the Save button on the Standard toolbar (*or* click File on the menu bar, and then click Save).

Nicole has asked you to start working on the agenda for the stockholder meeting. You enter text in a Word document by typing. After you type some text, you'll save the file.

To enter text in a document:

1. Type **Delmar Office Supplies**, and then press the **Enter** key. The text you typed appears on one line in the Word document.

   TROUBLE? If you make a typing error, press the Backspace key to delete the incorrect letters, and then retype the text.

2. Type **Stockholder Meeting Agenda**, and then press the **Enter** key. The text you typed appears on the second line.

The two lines of text you typed are not yet saved on disk. You'll do that now.

To save a file for the first time:

1. Insert your Data Disk in the appropriate drive.

> TROUBLE? If you don't have a Data Disk, you need to get one before you can proceed. Your instructor or technical support person will either give you one or ask you to make your own by following the instructions on the "Read This Before You Begin" page at the beginning of this tutorial. See your instructor or technical support person for more information.

2. Click the **Save** button 🖫 on the Standard toolbar. The Save As dialog box opens. See Figure 17. The first few words of the first line appear in the File name text box, as a suggested filename. You'll replace this with a more descriptive filename.

Figure 17	SAVE AS DIALOG BOX

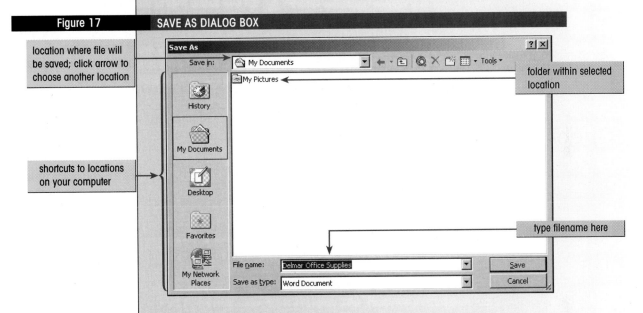

location where file will be saved; click arrow to choose another location

folder within selected location

shortcuts to locations on your computer

type filename here

> TROUBLE? If the .doc file extension appears after the filename, then your computer is configured to show file extensions. Just continue with Step 3.

3. Type **Stockholder Meeting Agenda** in the File name text box.

4. Click the **Save in** list arrow, and then click the drive that contains your Data Disk.

5. Double-click the **Tutorial.01** folder in the list box, and then double-click the **Tutorial** folder. This is the location where you want to save the document.

6. Click the **Save** button. The Save As dialog box closes, and the name of your file appears in the program window title bar.

The saved file includes everything in the document at the time you saved. Any edits or additions you then make to the document exist only in the computer's memory and are not saved in the file on the disk. As you work, remember to save frequently so that the file is updated to reflect the latest content of the document.

Because you already named the document and selected a storage location, the second and subsequent times you save, the Save As dialog box doesn't open. If you wanted to save a copy of the file with a different filename or to a different location, you would reopen the Save As dialog box by clicking File on the menu bar, and then clicking Save As. The previous version of the file remains on your disk as well.

You need to add your name to the agenda. Then you'll save your changes and close the file. You can close a file by clicking the Close command on the File menu or by clicking the Close Window button in the upper-right corner of the menu bar.

To modify, save, and close a file:

1. Type your name, and then press the **Enter** key. The text you typed appears on the next line.

2. Click the **Save** button 🖫 on the Standard toolbar.

   The updated document is saved to the file. When you're done with a file, you can close it. Although you can keep multiple files open at one time, you should close any file you are no longer working on to conserve system resources.

3. Click the **Close Window** button ☒ on the Word menu bar to close the document. Word is still running, but no documents are open.

   TROUBLE? If a dialog box opens and asks whether you want to save the changes you made to the document, you modified the document since you last saved. Click the Yes button to save the current version and close it.

Opening a File

Once you have a program open, you can create additional new files for the open programs or you can open previously created and saved files. You can do both of these from the New Task Pane. The New Task Pane enables you to create new files and open existing ones. The name of the Task Pane varies, depending on the program you are using: Word has the New Document Task Pane, Excel has the New Workbook Task Pane, PowerPoint has the New Presentation Task Pane, and Access has the New File Task Pane.

When you want to work on a previously created file, you must open it first. Opening a file transfers a copy of the file from the storage disk (either a hard disk or a portable disk) to the computer's memory and displays it on your screen. The file is then in your computer's memory and on the disk.

REFERENCE   WINDOW   **RW**

Opening an Existing or New File

- Click File on the menu bar, click New, and then (depending on the program) click the More documents, More workbooks, More presentations, or More files link in the New Task Pane (*or* click the Open button on the Standard toolbar *or* click File on the menu bar, and then click Open).
- Click the Look in list arrow, and then select the storage location of the file you want to open.
- Click the filename of the file you want to open.
- Click the Open button.

or

- Click File on the menu bar, click New, and then (depending on the program) click the Blank Document, Blank Workbook, Blank Presentation, or Blank Database link in the New Task Pane (*or* click the New button on the Standard toolbar).

Nicole asks you to print the agenda. To do that, you'll reopen the file. Because Word is still open, you'll use the New Document Task Pane.

To open an existing file:

1. If necessary, click **File** on the menu bar, and then click **New** to display the New Document Task Pane. See Figure 18.

Figure 18	NEW DOCUMENT TASK PANE

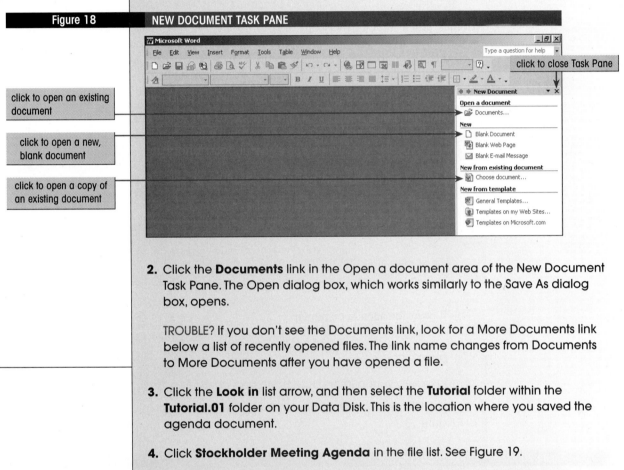

click to open an existing document

click to open a new, blank document

click to open a copy of an existing document

click to close Task Pane

2. Click the **Documents** link in the Open a document area of the New Document Task Pane. The Open dialog box, which works similarly to the Save As dialog box, opens.

   TROUBLE? If you don't see the Documents link, look for a More Documents link below a list of recently opened files. The link name changes from Documents to More Documents after you have opened a file.

3. Click the **Look in** list arrow, and then select the **Tutorial** folder within the **Tutorial.01** folder on your Data Disk. This is the location where you saved the agenda document.

4. Click **Stockholder Meeting Agenda** in the file list. See Figure 19.

Figure 19	OPEN DIALOG BOX

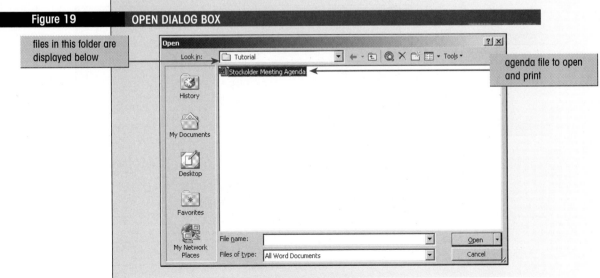

files in this folder are displayed below

agenda file to open and print

5. Click the **Open** button. The file you saved earlier reopens in the Word program window, and the New Document Task Pane closes.

After the file is open, you can view, edit, print, or resave it.

Printing a File

At times, you'll want a paper copy of your Office file. The first time you print during each computer session, you should use the Print menu command to open the Print dialog box so you can verify or adjust the printing settings. You can select a printer, the number of copies to print, the portion of the file to print, and so forth; the printing settings vary slightly from program to program. For subsequent print jobs you can use the Print button to print without opening the dialog box, if you want to use the same default settings.

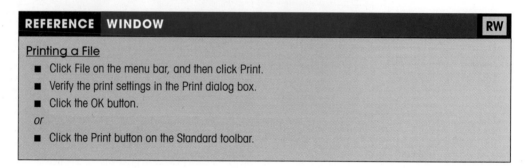

REFERENCE WINDOW   **RW**

Printing a File
- Click File on the menu bar, and then click Print.
- Verify the print settings in the Print dialog box.
- Click the OK button.

or

- Click the Print button on the Standard toolbar.

You'll print the agenda document.

To print a file:

1. Make sure your printer is turned on and contains paper.

2. Click **File** on the menu bar, and then click **Print**. The Print dialog box opens. See Figure 20.

Figure 20	PRINT DIALOG BOX

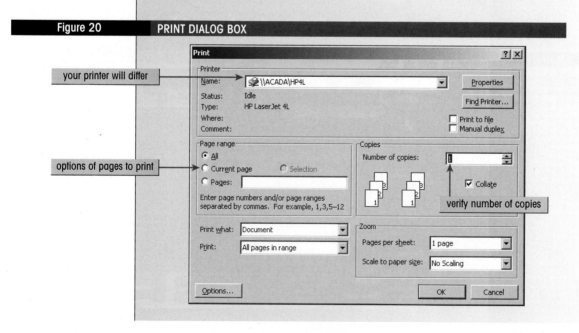

3. Verify that the correct printer appears in the Name list box. If the wrong printer appears, click the **Name** list arrow, and then click the correct printer from the list of available printers.

4. Verify that **1** appears in the Number of copies text box.

5. Click the **OK** button to print the document. See Figure 21.

Figure 21	PRINTED STOCKHOLDER MEETING AGENDA DOCUMENT

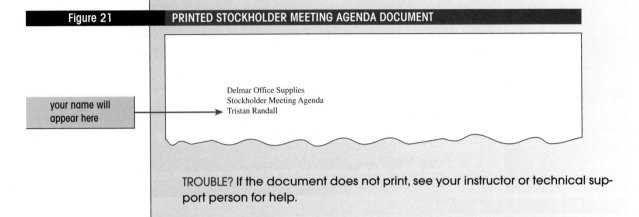

your name will appear here

Delmar Office Supplies
Stockholder Meeting Agenda
Tristan Randall

TROUBLE? If the document does not print, see your instructor or technical support person for help.

Another important aspect of Office is the ability to get help right from your computer.

Getting **Help**

If you don't know how to perform a task or want more information about a feature, you can turn to Office itself for information on how to use it. This information, referred to simply as **Help**, is like a huge encyclopedia stored on your computer. You can access it in a variety of ways.

There are two fast and simple methods you can use to get Help about objects you see on the screen. First, you can position the mouse pointer over a toolbar button to view its **ScreenTip**, a yellow box with the button's name. Second, you can click the **What's This?** command on the Help menu to change the pointer to ⤵**?**, which you can click on any toolbar button, menu command, dialog box option, worksheet cell, or anything else you can see on your screen to view a brief description of that item.

For more in-depth help, you can use the **Ask a Question** box, located on the menu bar of every Office program, to find information in the Help system. You simply type a question using everyday language about a task you want to perform or a topic you need help with, and then press the Enter key to search the Help system. The Ask a Question box expands to show Help topics related to your query. You click a topic to open a Help window with step-by-step instructions that guide you through a specific procedure and explanations of difficult concepts in clear, easy-to-understand language. For example, you might ask how to format a cell in an Excel worksheet; a list of Help topics related to the words you typed will appear. The Help window also has Contents, Answer Wizard, and Index tabs, which you can use to look up information directly from the Help window.

If you prefer, you can ask questions of the **Office Assistant**, an interactive guide to finding information from the Help system. In addition, the Office Assistant can provide Help topics and tips on tasks as you work. For example, it might offer a tip when you select a menu command instead of clicking the corresponding toolbar button. You can turn on or off the tips, depending on your personal preference.

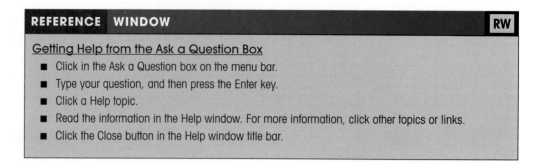

REFERENCE WINDOW   **RW**

Getting Help from the Ask a Question Box
- Click in the Ask a Question box on the menu bar.
- Type your question, and then press the Enter key.
- Click a Help topic.
- Read the information in the Help window. For more information, click other topics or links.
- Click the Close button in the Help window title bar.

You'll use the Ask a Question box to obtain more information about Help.

To use the Ask a Question box:

1. Click in the **Ask a Question** box on the menu bar, and then type **How do I search help?**.

2. Press the **Enter** key to retrieve a list of topics, as shown in Figure 22.

Figure 22   ASK A QUESTION BOX WITH HELP TOPICS

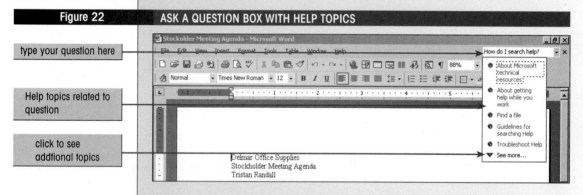

type your question here

Help topics related to question

click to see addtional topics

3. Click the **See more** link, review the additional Help topics, and then click the **See previous** link.

4. Click **About getting help while you work** to open the Help window and learn more about the various ways to obtain assistance in Office. See Figure 23.

Figure 23   HELP WINDOW

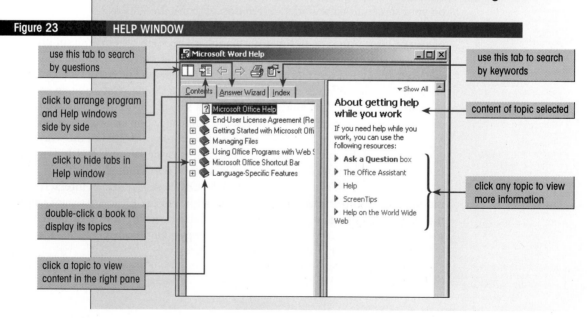

use this tab to search by questions

click to arrange program and Help windows side by side

click to hide tabs in Help window

double-click a book to display its topics

click a topic to view content in the right pane

use this tab to search by keywords

content of topic selected

click any topic to view more information

5. Click **Help** in the right pane to display information about that topic.

6. Click the other links about Help features and read the information.

7. When you're done, click the **Close** button ☒ in the Help window title bar to return to the Word window.

The Help features enable the staff at Delmar Office Supplies to get answers to questions they have about any task or procedure when they need it. The more you practice getting information from the Help system, the more effective you will be at using Office to its full potential.

Exiting Programs

Whenever you finish working with a program, you should exit it. As with many other aspects of Office, you can exit programs with a button or from a menu. You'll use both methods to close Word and Excel.

To exit a program:

1. Click the **Close** button ☒ in the upper-right corner of the screen to exit Word. Word exits, and the Excel window is visible again on your screen.

   TROUBLE? If a dialog box opens, asking whether you want to save the document, you may have inadvertently made a change to the document. Click the No button.

2. Click **File** on the menu bar, and then click **Exit**. The Excel program exits.

Exiting programs after you are done using them keeps your Windows desktop uncluttered for the next person using the computer, frees up your system's resources, and prevents data from being lost accidentally.

QUICK CHECK

1. Which Office program would you use to write a letter?
2. Which Office programs could you use to store customer names and addresses?
3. What is integration?
4. Explain the difference between Save As and Save.
5. What is the purpose of the New Task Pane?
6. When would you use the Ask a Question box?

REVIEW ASSIGNMENTS

Before the stockholders meeting at Delmar Office Supplies, you'll open and print documents for the upcoming presentation.

1. Start PowerPoint using the Start button and the Programs menu.

2. Use the Ask a Question box to learn how to change the toolbar buttons from small to large, and then do it. Use the same procedure to change the buttons back to regular size. Close the Help window when you're done.

3. Open a blank Excel workbook using the New Office Document command on the Start menu.

Explore

4. Switch to the PowerPoint window using the taskbar, and then close the presentation but leave open the PowerPoint program. (*Hint:* Click the Close Window button in the menu bar.)

Explore

5. Open a new, blank PowerPoint presentation from the New Presentation Task Pane. (*Hint:* Click Blank Presentation in the New area of the New Presentation Task Pane.)

6. Close the PowerPoint presentation and program using the Close button in the PowerPoint title bar; do not save changes if asked.

Explore

7. Open a copy of the Excel **Finances** workbook located in the **Review** folder within the **Tutorial.01** folder on your Data Disk using the New Workbook Task Pane. (*Hint:* Click File on the Excel menu bar and then click New to open the Task Pane. Click Choose Workbook in the New from existing workbook area of the New Workbook Task Pane; the dialog box functions similarly to the Open dialog box.)

8. Type your name, and then press the Enter key to insert your name at the top of the worksheet.

9. Save the worksheet as **Delmar Finances** in the **Review** folder within the **Tutorial.01** folder on your Data Disk.

10. Print one copy of the worksheet using the Print command on the File menu.

11. Exit Excel using the File menu.

Explore

12. Open the **Letter** document located in the **Review** folder within the **Tutorial.01** folder on your Data Disk using the Open Office Document command on the Start menu.

13. Use the Save As command to save the document with the filename **Delmar Letter** in the **Review** folder within the **Tutorial.01** folder on your Data Disk.

Explore

14. Press and hold the Ctrl key, press the End key, and then release both keys to move the insertion point to the end of the letter, and then type your name.

15. Use the Save button on the Standard toolbar to save the change to the Delmar Letter document.

16. Print one copy of the document, and then close the document.

17. Exit the Word program using the Close button on the title bar.

QUICK | CHECK ANSWERS

1. Word
2. Access or Outlook
3. the ability to share information between programs
4. Save As enables you to change the filename and save location of a file. Save updates a file to reflect its latest contents using its current filename and location.
5. enables you to create new files and open existing files
6. when you don't know how to perform a task or want more information about a feature

New Perspectives on

MICROSOFT®
EXCEL 2002

Read This Before You Begin

To the Student

Data Disks

To complete the Level 1 tutorials, Review Assignments, and Case Problems, you need two Data Disks. Your instructor will either provide you with these Data Disks or ask you to make your own.

If you are making your own Data Disks, you will need **two** blank, formatted high-density disks. You will need to copy a set of files and/or folders from a file server, standalone computer, or the Web onto your disks. Your instructor will tell you which computer, drive letter, and folders contain the files you need. You could also download the files by going to **www.course.com** and following the instructions on the screen.

The information below shows you which folders go on each of your disks, so that you will have enough disk space to complete all the tutorials, Review Assignments, and Case Problems:

Data Disk 1

Write this on the disk label:
Data Disk 1: Excel Tutorials 1 and 2

Put these folders on the disk:
Tutorial.01
Tutorial.02

Data Disk 2

Write this on the disk label:
Data Disk 2: Excel Tutorials 3 and 4

Put these folders on the disk:
Tutorial.03
Tutorial.04

When you begin each tutorial, be sure you are using the correct Data Disk. Refer to the "File Finder" chart at the back of this text for more detailed information on which files are used in which tutorials. See the inside front or inside back cover of this book for more information on Data Disk files, or ask your instructor or technical support person for assistance.

Course Labs

The Excel Level I tutorials feature an interactive Course Lab to help you understand spreadsheet concepts. There are Lab Assignments at the end of Tutorial 1 that relate to this Lab.

To start a Lab, click the **Start** button on the Windows taskbar, point to **Programs**, point to **Course Labs**, point to **New Perspectives Course Labs**, and then click the name of the Lab you want to use.

Using Your Own Computer

If you are going to work through this book using your own computer, you need:

- **Computer System** Microsoft Windows 98, NT, 2000 Professional, or higher must be installed on your computer. This book assumes a typical installation of Microsoft Excel.

- **Data Disks** You will not be able to complete the tutorials or exercises in this book using your own computer until you have your Data Disks.

- **Course Labs** See your instructor or technical support person to obtain the Course Lab software for use on your own computer.

Visit Our World Wide Web Site

Additional materials designed especially for you are available on the World Wide Web.
Go to **www.course.com/NewPerspectives**.

To the Instructor

The Data Disk Files and Course Labs are available on the Instructor's Resource Kit for this title. Follow the instructions in the Help file on the CD-ROM to install the programs to your network or standalone computer. For information on creating Data Disks or the Course Labs, see the "To the Student" section above.

You are granted a license to copy the Data Files and Course Labs to any computer or computer network used by students who have purchased this book.

USING EXCEL TO MANAGE FINANCIAL DATA

Creating an Income Statement

Spreadsheets

CASE

Lawn Wizards

Lawn Wizards is a small company that specializes in lawn, bush, and tree care. The company started out as a two-person operation, but in recent years the service has gained in popularity. In the last few months, Lawn Wizards has added three employees—two of them full-time workers. The sudden growth in his small business has caught the owner of the company, Mike Bennett, by surprise. Up to now, he has been entering his financial records using a paper financial ledger. However, he realizes that with the growth of his business he needs to store his documents in electronic form.

Mike has just purchased Microsoft Excel 2002 for the business. He has come to you for help. He has many projects for you to work on, but first he needs help with electronic spreadsheets so he can prepare his income figures. Mike needs to know what electronic spreadsheets can do, and he needs to become familiar with the basics of Excel.

In this tutorial you will use Excel to help Mike understand electronic spreadsheets. You will explain the different parts of the Excel document window and show him how to move around an Excel worksheet. You will show him how Excel works by modifying an Excel workbook that contains some of the monthly income figures for Mike's lawn service business.

SESSION 1.1

In this session, you will learn about electronic spreadsheets and how they can be used in business. You will explore the components of the Excel window and learn how to move around within an Excel worksheet. Finally, you will select cells and cell ranges and move the selections to a new location within the worksheet.

Introducing Excel

Mike has just purchased Excel and has loaded it on one of his computers. Before working with his financial records, you and Mike sit down to learn about the fundamental parts of Excel. Understanding why electronic spreadsheets such as Excel have become an essential tool for businesses will help Mike to use Excel more fully and help him run his business efficiently.

Understanding Spreadsheets

Excel is a computerized spreadsheet. A **spreadsheet** is an important business tool that helps you report and analyze information. Spreadsheets are often used for cash flow analysis, budgeting, inventory management, market forecasts, and decision making. For example, an accountant might use a spreadsheet like the one shown in Figure 1-1 to record budget information.

Figure 1-1 | **BUDGET SPREADSHEET**

Cash Budget Forecast

	January Estimated	January Actual
Cash in Bank (Start of Month)	$1,400.00	$1,400.00
Cash in Register (Start of Month)	100.00	100.00
Total Cash	$1,500.00	$1,500.00
Expected Cash Sales	$1,200.00	$1,420.00
Expected Collections	400.00	380.00
Other Money Expected	100.00	52.00
Total Income	$1,700.00	$1,852.00
Total Cash and Income	$3,200.00	$3,352.00
All Expenses (for Month)	$1,200.00	$1,192.00
Cash Balance at End of Month	$2,000.00	$2,160.00

In this spreadsheet, the accountant has recorded predicted and observed income and expenses for the month of January. Each line, or row, in this spreadsheet displays a different income or expense. Each column contains the predicted or observed values or text that describes those values. The accountant has also entered the income and expense totals, perhaps having used a calculator to do the calculations.

Figure 1-2 shows the same spreadsheet in Excel. The spreadsheet is now laid out in a grid in which the rows and columns are easily apparent. As you will see later, calculations are also part of this electronic spreadsheet, so that the expense and income totals are calculated automatically rather than entered manually. If an entry in the spreadsheet is changed, the spreadsheet will automatically update any calculated values based on that entry. Thus an electronic spreadsheet provides more flexibility in entering and analyzing your data than the paper version.

Figure 1-2	BUDGET SPREADSHEET IN EXCEL

Excel stores electronic spreadsheets in documents called **workbooks**. Each workbook is made up of individual **worksheets**, or **sheets**, just as Mike's spiral-bound ledger is made up of sheets of paper. You will learn more about multiple worksheets later in this tutorial. For now, just keep in mind that the terms *worksheet* and *sheet* are used interchangeably.

Parts of the Excel Window

Excel displays workbooks within a window that contains many tools for entering, editing, and viewing the data. You will view some of these tools after starting Excel. By default, Excel will open with a blank workbook.

To start Excel:

1. Make sure Windows is running on your computer and the Windows desktop appears on your screen.

2. Click the **Start** button on the taskbar to display the Start menu, and then point to **Programs** to display the Programs menu.

3. Point to **Microsoft Excel** on the Programs menu. See Figure 1-3.

Figure 1-3	STARTING EXCEL

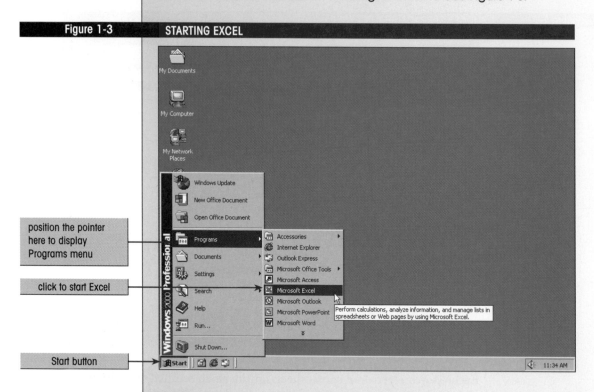

position the pointer here to display Programs menu

click to start Excel

Start button

TROUBLE? Do not worry if your screen differs slightly. Although the figures in this book were created while running Windows 2000 in its default settings, the Windows 98 and Windows NT operating systems share the same basic user interface as Windows 2000, and Excel runs equally well using any of these.

TROUBLE? Depending on how your system was set up, the menu entry for Excel may appear in a different location on the Programs menu. If you cannot locate Excel, ask your instructor for assistance.

4. Click **Microsoft Excel**. After a short pause, the Excel program window and a blank workbook appear. See Figure 1-4.

Figure 1-4	PARTS OF THE EXCEL WINDOW

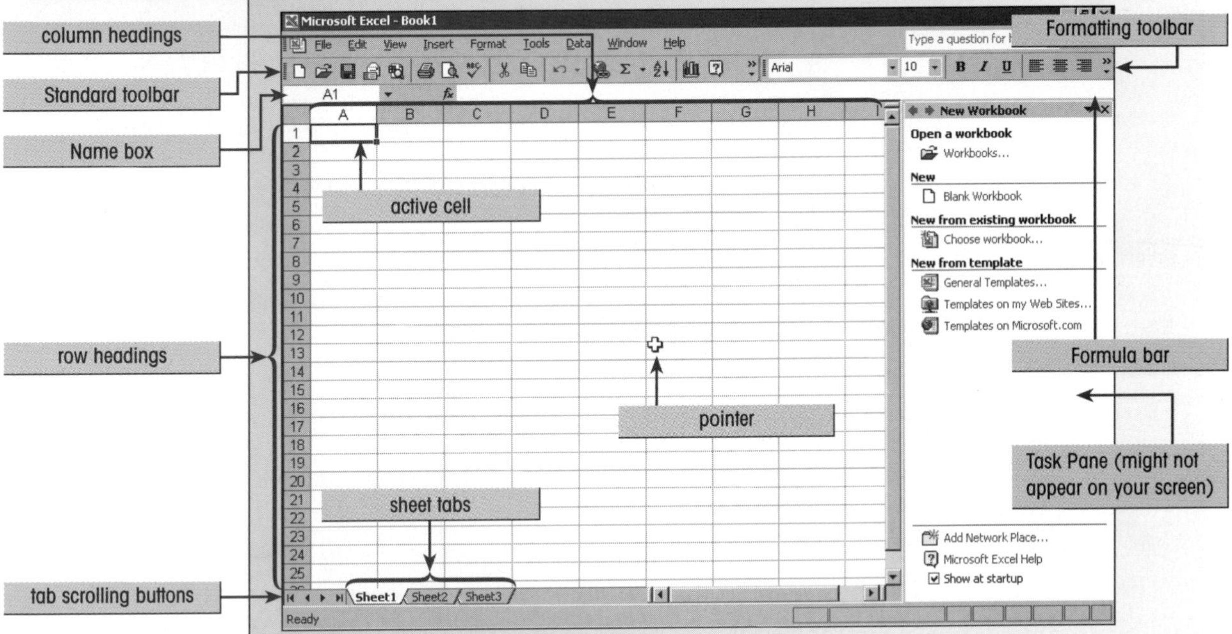

- column headings
- Standard toolbar
- Name box
- active cell
- row headings
- pointer
- sheet tabs
- tab scrolling buttons
- Formatting toolbar
- Formula bar
- Task Pane (might not appear on your screen)

Microsoft Excel - Book1

File   Edit   View   Insert   Format   Tools   Data   Window   Help

Type a question for h

Arial   ▾   10   ▾   **B** *I* U

A1

New Workbook

Open a workbook
- Workbooks...

New
- Blank Workbook

New from existing workbook
- Choose workbook...

New from template
- General Templates...
- Templates on my Web Sites...
- Templates on Microsoft.com

- Add Network Place...
- Microsoft Excel Help
- ☑ Show at startup

Sheet1 Sheet2 Sheet3

Ready

TROUBLE? Depending on your Excel configuration, the Task Pane might not appear in the Excel window. To display the Task Pane, click View on the menu bar, and then click Task Pane.

The Excel window has features similar to other Windows programs. It contains a title bar, menu bar, scroll bars, and a status bar. The Excel window also contains features that are unique to the program itself. Within the Excel program window is the document window, which is also referred to as the **workbook window** or **worksheet window**. The worksheet window provides a grid of columns and rows in which the intersection of a column and row is called a **cell**. Figure 1-4 identifies many of the other components of the Excel window. Take a look at each of these components so you are familiar with their location and purpose. Figure 1-5 summarizes the properties of each of these components.

Figure 1-5	EXCEL WINDOW COMPONENTS
FEATURE	**DESCRIPTION**
Active cell	The **active cell** is the cell in which you are currently working. A dark border outlining the cell identifies the active cell.
Column headings	**Column headings** list the columns in the worksheet. Columns are listed alphabetically from A to IV (a total of 256 possible columns).
Formula bar	The **Formula bar**, which is located immediately below the toolbars, displays the contents of the active cell. As you type or edit data, the changes appear in the Formula bar.
Name box	The **Name box** displays the location of the currently active cell in the workbook window.
Pointer	The **pointer** indicates the current location of your mouse pointer. The pointer changes shape to reflect the type of task you can perform at a particular location in the Excel window.
Row headings	**Row headings** list the rows in the worksheet. Rows are numbered consecutively from 1 up to 65,536.
Sheet tabs	Each worksheet in the workbook has a **sheet tab** that identifies the sheet's name. To move between worksheets, click the appropriate sheet tab.
Task Pane	The **Task Pane** appears when you initially start Excel, and it displays a list of commonly used tasks. The Task Pane will disappear once you open a workbook.
Tab scrolling buttons	The **tab scrolling buttons** are used to move between worksheets in the workbook.
Toolbars	**Toolbars** provide quick access to the most commonly used Excel menu commands. The **Standard toolbar** contains buttons for Excel commands such as Save and Open. The **Formatting toolbar** contains buttons used to format the appearance of the workbook. Additional toolbars are available.

Now that you are familiar with the basic layout of an Excel workbook, you can try moving around within the workbook.

Navigating in a Workbook

You can navigate in a workbook by moving from worksheet to worksheet or in a worksheet by moving from cell to cell. Each cell is identified by a **cell reference**, which indicates its row and column location. For example, the cell reference B6 indicates that the cell is located where column B and row 6 intersect. The column letter is always first in the cell reference. B6 is a correct cell reference; 6B is not. One cell in the worksheet, called the **active cell**, is always selected and ready for receiving data. Excel identifies the active cell with a dark border outlining it. In Figure 1-4, cell A1 is the active cell. Notice that the cell reference for the active cell appears in the Name box next to the Formula bar. You can change the active cell by selecting another cell in the worksheet.

Navigating Within a Worksheet

Excel provides several ways of moving around in the worksheet. The most direct way is to use your mouse. To change the active cell, move the mouse pointer over a different cell and click anywhere within the cell with your left mouse button. If you need to move to a cell that is not currently displayed in the workbook window, use the vertical and horizontal scroll bars to display the area of the worksheet containing the cell.

The second way of moving around the worksheet is through your keyboard. Excel provides you with many keyboard shortcuts for moving to different cells within the worksheet. Figure 1-6 describes some of these keyboard shortcuts.

Figure 1-6	KEYS FOR NAVIGATING WITHIN A WORKSHEET
KEYSTROKE	**ACTION**
↑, ↓, ←, →	Moves the active cell up, down, left, or right one cell
Enter	Moves the active cell down one cell
Tab	Moves the active cell to the right one cell
Page Up	Moves the active cell up one full screen
Page Down	Moves the active cell down one full screen
Home	Moves the active cell to column A of the current row
Ctrl + Home	Moves the active cell to cell A1
F5 (function key)	Opens the Go To dialog box in which you can enter the cell address of the cell that you want to make active

Finally, you can enter a cell reference in the Name box to move directly to that cell in the worksheet.

Explore these techniques by moving around the worksheet using your keyboard and mouse.

To move around the worksheet:

1. Position the mouse pointer over cell E8, and then click the left mouse button to make cell E8 the active cell.

   Notice that cell E8 is surrounded by a black border, indicating it is the active cell, and that the Name box displays the cell reference "E8." Note also that the row and column headings for row 8 and column E are highlighted, giving another visual indication about the location of the active cell.

2. Click cell **B4** to make it the active cell.

3. Press the → key on your keyboard to make cell C4 the active cell.

4. Press the ↓ key to make cell C5 the active cell. See Figure 1-7.

Figure 1-7	MAKING CELL C5 THE ACTIVE CELL

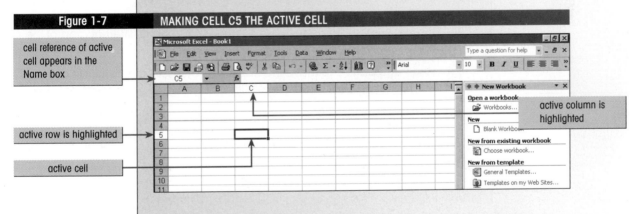

5. Press the **Home** key to move to cell A5, the first cell in the current row.

6. Press **Ctrl + Home** to make cell A1 the active cell.

So far you have moved around the portion of the worksheet displayed in the workbook window. The content of many worksheets will not fit into the workbook window, so you may have to move to cells that are not currently displayed by Excel. You can do this using your keyboard or the scroll bars.

To bring other parts of the worksheet into view:

1. Press the **Page Down** key on your keyboard to move the display down one screen. The active cell is now A26 (the active cell on your screen may be different). Notice that the row numbers on the left side of the worksheet indicate you have moved to a different area of the worksheet. See Figure 1-8.

Figure 1-8	MOVING TO A DIFFERENT AREA OF THE WORKSHEET

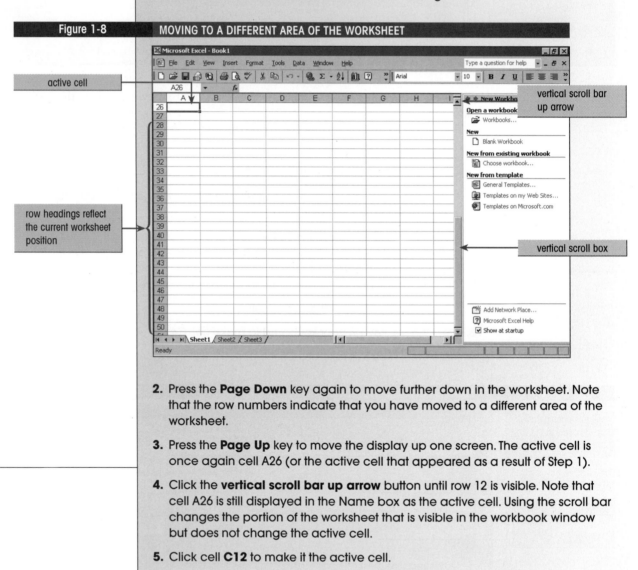

2. Press the **Page Down** key again to move further down in the worksheet. Note that the row numbers indicate that you have moved to a different area of the worksheet.

3. Press the **Page Up** key to move the display up one screen. The active cell is once again cell A26 (or the active cell that appeared as a result of Step 1).

4. Click the **vertical scroll bar up arrow** button until row 12 is visible. Note that cell A26 is still displayed in the Name box as the active cell. Using the scroll bar changes the portion of the worksheet that is visible in the workbook window but does not change the active cell.

5. Click cell **C12** to make it the active cell.

6. Click the blank area above the vertical scroll box to move up one full screen, and then click the blank area below the vertical scroll box to move down a full screen.

7. Click the **vertical scroll box** and drag it to the top of the scroll bar to again change the area of the worksheet being displayed in the window.

You can also use the Go To dialog box and the Name box to jump directly to a specific cell in the worksheet, whether the cell is currently visible in the workbook window or not. Try this now.

To use the Go To dialog box and Name box:

1. Press the **F5** key to open the Go To dialog box.

2. Type **K55** in the Reference text box, and then click the **OK** button. Cell K55 is now the active cell.

3. Click the **Name** box, type **E6**, and then press the **Enter** key. Cell E6 becomes the active cell.

4. Press **Ctrl + Home** to make cell A1 the active cell.

Navigating Between Worksheets

A workbook is usually composed of several worksheets. The workbook shown in Figure 1-8 contains three worksheets (this is the default for new blank workbooks) labeled Sheet1, Sheet2, and Sheet3. To move between the worksheets, you click the sheet tab of the worksheet you want to display.

To move between worksheets:

1. Click the **Sheet2** tab. Sheet2, which is blank, appears in the workbook window. Notice that the Sheet2 tab is now white with the name "Sheet2" in a bold font. This is a visual indicator that Sheet2 is the active worksheet.

2. Click the **Sheet1** tab to return to the first sheet in the workbook.

Some workbooks will contain so many worksheets that some sheet tabs will be hidden from view. If that is the case, you can use the tab scrolling buttons located in the lower-left corner of the workbook window to scroll through the list of sheet tabs. Figure 1-9 describes the actions of the four tab scrolling buttons. Note that clicking the tab scrolling buttons does not change the active sheet; clicking the tab scrolling buttons allows you to view the other sheet tabs in the workbook. To change the active sheet, you must click the sheet tab itself.

Figure 1-9	TAB SCROLLING BUTTONS

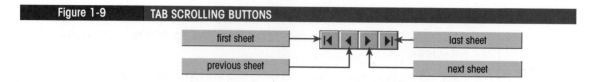

Now that you have some basic skills navigating through a worksheet and a workbook, you can begin working with Mike's financial records. Some of the figures from the Lawn Wizards' April income statement have already been entered in an Excel workbook.

Opening **and Saving a Workbook**

There are several ways of accessing a saved workbook. To open a workbook, you can click the Open command on Excel's File menu or you can click the Open button found on the Standard toolbar. You can also click the Workbooks link found in the Task Pane (if the Task Pane is visible to you). Any of these methods will display the Open dialog box. Once the Open dialog box is displayed, you have to navigate through the hierarchy of folders and drives on your computer or network to locate the workbook file.

Mike has saved the income statement with the filename "Lawn1." Locate and open this file now.

To open the Lawn1 workbook:

1. Place your Excel Data Disk in the appropriate drive.

   TROUBLE? If you don't have a Data Disk, you need to contact your instructor or technical support person who will either give you one or give you instructions for creating your own. You can also review the instructions on the Read This Before You Begin page located at the front of this book.

2. Click the **Open** button 📂 on the Standard toolbar. The Open dialog box is displayed. See Figure 1-10.

Figure 1-10	OPEN DIALOG BOX

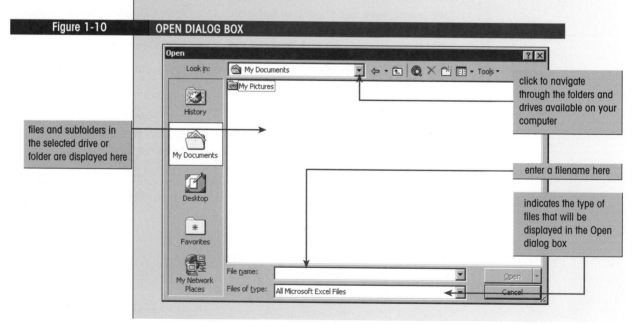

3. Click the **Look in** list arrow to display the list of available drives. Locate the drive that contains your Data Disk. This text assumes your Data Disk is a 3½-inch disk in drive A.

4. Click the drive that contains your Data Disk. A list of documents and folders on your Data Disk appears in the list box.

5. In the list of file and folder names, double-click **Tutorial.01**, double-click **Tutorial** to display the contents of the folder, and then click **Lawn1**.

6. Click the **Open** button (you could also have double-clicked Lawn1 to open the file). The workbook opens, displaying the income figures in the Sheet1 worksheet. Note that if the Task Pane was previously visible, it has now disappeared. See Figure 1-11.

Figure 1-11	LAWN1 WORKBOOK

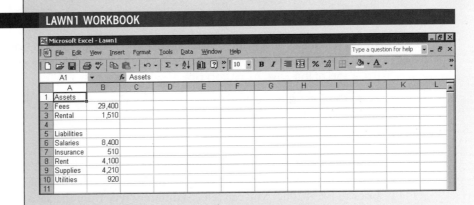

Sometimes you will want to open a new blank workbook. Excel allows you to have several workbooks open at the same time. To create a new blank workbook, you can click the New button on the Standard toolbar.

Before going further in the Lawn1 workbook, you should make a copy of the file with a new name. This will allow you to go back to the original version of the file if necessary.

Mike suggests that you save the file with the name "Lawn2."

To save the workbook with a different name:

1. Click **File** on the menu bar, and then click **Save As**. The Save As dialog box opens with the current workbook name in the File name text box. Note that the Tutorial folder on your Data Disk is automatically opened, so you do not have to navigate through your computer's hierarchy of folders and drives.

2. Click immediately to the right of "Lawn1" in the File name text box, press the **Backspace** key, and then type **2**.

3. Make sure that "Microsoft Excel Workbook" is displayed in the Save as type list box. See Figure 1-12.

Figure 1-12	SAVE AS DIALOG BOX

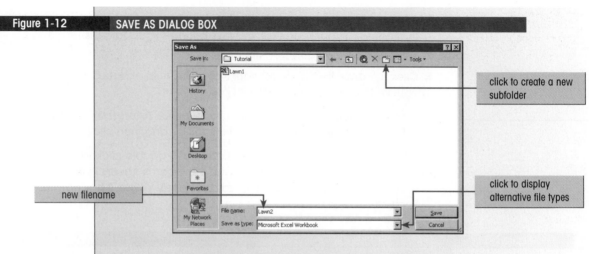

click to create a new subfolder

new filename

click to display alternative file types

Note that if you want to save the file to a new folder, you can create a new folder "on the fly" by clicking the Create New Folder button located at the top of the Save As dialog box.

4. Click the **Save** button. Excel saves the workbook under the new name and closes the Save As dialog box.

By default, Excel saves the workbooks in Microsoft Excel Workbook format. If you are creating a report that will be read by applications other than Excel (or versions of Excel prior to Excel 2002), you can select a different type from the Save as type list box in the Save (or Save As) dialog box.

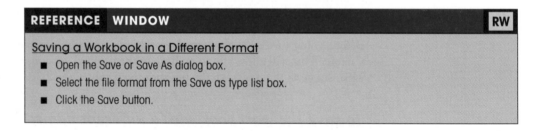

REFERENCE   WINDOW   **RW**

Saving a Workbook in a Different Format
- Open the Save or Save As dialog box.
- Select the file format from the Save as type list box.
- Click the Save button.

Figure 1-13 displays a partial list of the other formats you can save your workbook as. You can add other formats by running the Excel 2002 or Office XP installation program. Note that some of the formats described in Figure 1-13 save only the active worksheet, not the entire workbook.

Figure 1-13	SOME OF THE FILE FORMATS SUPPORTED BY EXCEL
FORMAT	**DESCRIPTION**
CSV (Comma delimited)	Saves the active worksheet as a text file with columns separated by commas
DBF2, DBF3, DBF4	Saves the active worksheet as a dBASE table in the different versions of dBASE
Formatted Text (Space delimited)	Saves the active worksheet as a text file with columns separated by spaces
Microsoft Excel 2.1, 3.0, 4.0 Worksheet	Saves the workbook in the earliest versions of Excel
Microsoft Excel 5.0, 95, 97, 2000 Workbook	Saves the workbook in an earlier version of Excel
Text (Tab delimited)	Saves the active worksheet as a text file with columns separated by tabs
Web Archive	Saves the workbook as a Web site, enclosed within a single file
Web Page	Saves the workbook in HTML format, suitable for use as a Web page
WK1, WK2, WK3	Saves the active worksheet as a Lotus 1-2-3 spreadsheet
WK4 (1-2-3)	Saves the workbook as a Lotus 1-2-3 document
WQ1	Saves the active worksheet as a Quattro Pro spreadsheet
XML Spreadsheet	Saves the workbook in XML format, suitable for use in Web queries

In this text you will use only the Microsoft Excel Workbook format.

Working with Ranges

The data in the Lawn2 workbook contains the assets and liabilities for Lawn Wizards during the month of April, 2003. Mike would like to include this information in a title at the top of the worksheet. To make room for the title, you have to move the current content down a few rows. To move a group of cells in a worksheet, you have to first understand how Excel handles cells.

A group of worksheet cells is called a **cell range**, or **range**. Ranges can be either adjacent or nonadjacent. An **adjacent range** is a single rectangular block such as all of the data entered in cells A1 through B10 of the Lawn2 workbook. A **nonadjacent range** is comprised of two or more separate adjacent ranges. You could view the Lawn2 workbook as containing two non-adjacent ranges: the first range, cell A1 through cell B3, contains the company's assets, and the second range, cell A5 through cell B10, displays the company's liabilities.

Just as a cell reference indicates the location of the cell on the worksheet, a range reference indicates the location and size of the range. For adjacent ranges, the range reference identifies the cells in the upper-left and lower-right corners of the rectangle, with the individual cell references separated by a colon. For example, the range reference for Mike's income statement is A1:B10. If the range is nonadjacent, a semicolon separates the rectangular blocks, such as A1:B3;A5:B10, which refers to data in Mike's income statement, but does not include the blank row (row 4), which separates the assets from the liabilities.

Selecting Ranges

Working with ranges of cells makes working with the data in a worksheet easier. Once you know how to select ranges of cells, you can move and copy the data anywhere in the worksheet or workbook.

REFERENCE WINDOW   **RW**

Selecting Adjacent or Nonadjacent Ranges of Cells
To select an adjacent range of cells:
- Click a cell in the corner of the rectangle that comprises the adjacent range.
- Press and hold down the left mouse button, and drag the pointer through the cells you want selected.
- Release the mouse button.
To select a nonadjacent range of cells:
- Select an adjacent range of cells.
- Press and hold down the Ctrl key, and then select another adjacent cell range.
- With the Ctrl key still pressed, continue to select other cell ranges until all of the ranges are selected.
- Release the mouse button and the Ctrl key.

Next you'll select the adjacent range A1 through B10.

To select the range A1:B10:

1. Click cell **A1** (if necessary) to make it the active cell, and then press and hold down the left mouse button.

2. With the mouse button still pressed, drag the pointer to cell **B10**.

3. Release the mouse button. All of the cells in the range A1:B10 are now highlighted, indicating that they are selected. See Figure 1-14.

Figure 1-14   SELECTING RANGE A1:B10

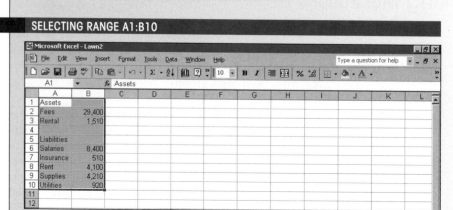

To deselect the range, you can click any cell in the worksheet.

4. Click cell **C1** to deselect the range.

To select a nonadjacent range, you begin by selecting an adjacent range, and then you press and hold down the Ctrl key and select other adjacent ranges. Release the Ctrl key and the mouse button when you are finished. Next you'll select the assets and then select the liabilities in the income statement.

To select the nonadjacent range A1:B3;A5:B10:

1. Select the range **A1:B3**.

2. Press and hold down the **Ctrl** key.

3. Select the range **A5:B10**. See Figure 1-15.

Figure 1-15	SELECTING THE NONADJACENT RANGE A1:B3;A5:B10

4. Click any cell in the worksheet to deselect the range.

Other Selection Techniques

To select a large range of data, Excel will automatically scroll horizontally or vertically to display additional cells in the worksheet. Selecting a large range of cells using the mouse drag technique can be slow and frustrating. For this reason, Excel provides keyboard short-cuts to quickly select large blocks of data without having to drag through the worksheet to select the necessary cells. Figure 1-16 describes some of these selection techniques.

Figure 1-16	OTHER RANGE SELECTION TECHNIQUES

TO SELECT...	ACTION
A large range of cells	Click the first cell in the range, press and hold down the Shift key, and then click the last cell in the range. All of the cells between the first and last cell are selected.
All cells on the worksheet	Click the Select All button, the gray rectangle in the upper-left corner of the worksheet where the row and column headings meet.
All cells in an entire row or column	Click the row or column heading.
A range of cells containing data	Click the first cell in the range, press and hold down the Shift key, and then double-click the side of the active cell in which you want to extend the selection. Excel extends the selection up to the first empty cell.

Try some of the techniques described in Figure 1-16 using the income statement.

To select large ranges of cells:

1. Click cell **A1** to make it the active cell.

2. Press and hold down the **Shift** key, and then click cell **B10**. Note that all of the cells between A1 and B10 are selected.

TROUBLE? If the range A1:B10 is not selected, try again, but make sure you hold down the Shift key while you click cell B10.

3. Release the Shift key.

4. Click cell **A1** to remove the selection.

5. Press and hold down the **Shift** key, and move the pointer to the bottom edge of cell A1 until the mouse pointer changes to ⇕.

6. Double-click the bottom edge of cell **A1**. The selection extends to cell A3, the last cell before the blank cell A4.

7. With the Shift key still pressed, move the pointer to the right edge of the selection until, once again, the pointer changes to ⇕.

8. Double-click the right edge of the selection. The selection extends to the last non-blank column in the worksheet.

9. Click the **A** column heading. All of the cells in column A are selected.

10. Click the **1** row heading. All of the cells in the first row are selected.

Moving a Selection of Cells

Now that you know various ways to select a range of cells, you can move the income statement data to another location in the worksheet. To move a cell range, you first select it and then position the pointer over the selection border and drag the selection to a new location. Copying a range of cells is similar to moving a range. The only difference is that you must press the Ctrl key while you drag the selection to its new location. A copy of the original data appears at the location of the pointer when you release the mouse button.

You can also move a selection to a new worksheet in the current workbook. To do this, you press and hold down the Alt key and then drag the selection over the sheet tab of the new worksheet. Excel will automatically make that worksheet the active sheet, so you can drag the selection into its new location on the worksheet.

Next you'll move the cells in the range A1:B10 to a new location, beginning at cell A5.

To move the range A1:B10 down four rows:

1. Select the range **A1:B10**.

2. Move the pointer over the bottom border of the selection until the pointer changes to ⇕.

3. Press and hold down the left mouse button, and then drag the selection down four rows. A ScreenTip appears indicating the new range reference of the selection. See Figure 1-17.

Figure 1-17	MOVING A SELECTION TO THE RANGE A5:B14

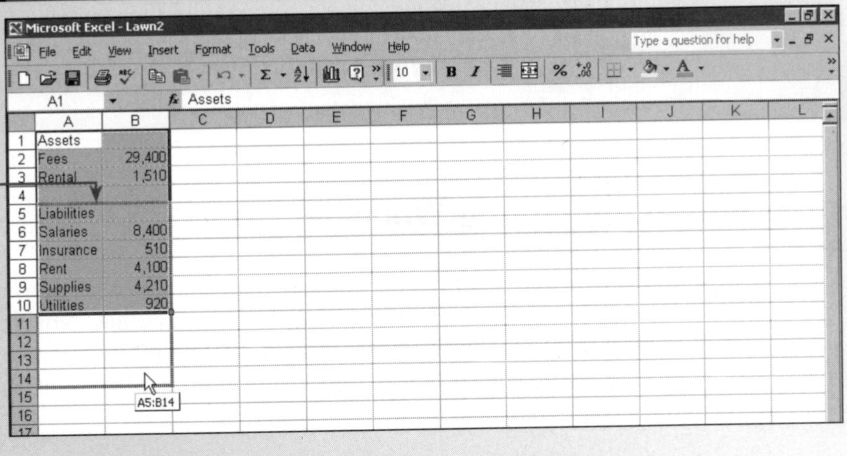

outline indicates new location

4. When the ScreenTip displays "A5:B14", release the left mouse button. The income statement is now moved to range A5:B14.

5. Click cell **A1** to remove the selection.

At this point, you have made space for a title and other information to be placed above the income statement. In the next session you will learn how to enter the new text into the worksheet, as well as how to edit the contents already there.

To exit Excel:

1. Click **File** on the menu bar, and then click **Exit**.

2. When Excel prompts you to save your changes, click the **Yes** button. Excel saves the changes to the workbook and closes.

Session 1.1 QUICK CHECK

1. A(n) _____ is the place on the worksheet where a column and row intersect.

2. Cell _____ refers to the intersection of the fourth column and second row.

3. What combination of keys can you press to make A1 the active cell in the worksheet?

4. To make Sheet2 the active worksheet, you _____.

5. Describe the two types of cell ranges in Excel.

6. What is the cell reference for the rectangular group of cells that extends from cell A5 down to cell F8?

7. Describe how you move a cell range from the Sheet1 worksheet to the Sheet2 worksheet.

SESSION 1.2

In this session, you will enter text and values into a worksheet. You will also enter formulas using basic arithmetic operators. You will use Excel's edit mode to change the value in a cell. You will insert rows and columns into a worksheet and modify the width of a column. You will insert, delete, and move worksheets, and you will rename sheet tabs. Finally, you will create a hard copy of your workbook by sending its contents to a printer.

Entering Information into a Worksheet

In the previous session, you learned about the different parts of Excel's workbook window, and you learned how to work with cells and cell ranges. Now you will enter some new information in Mike's April income statement. The information that you enter in the cells of a worksheet can consist of text, values, or formulas. Mike wants you to enter text that describes the income statement located on Sheet1.

Entering Text

Text entries include any combination of letters, symbols, numbers, and spaces. Although text is sometimes used as data, text is more often used to describe the data contained in the workbook. For example, the range A5:A14 of the income statement indicates the various asset and liability categories.

To enter text in a worksheet, you click the cell in which you want the text placed and then type the text you want entered. Excel automatically aligns text with the left edge of the cell. Mike wants you to enter the text labels "Lawn Wizards" in cell A1 and "Income Statement" in cell A2.

To enter labels in cell A1 and A2:

1. If you took a break after the previous session, make sure Excel is running and the Lawn2 workbook is open.

2. Verify that Sheet1 is the active worksheet in the Lawn2 workbook.

3. Click cell **A1** if necessary to make it the active cell.

4. Type **Lawn Wizards** and then press the **Enter** key.

5. In cell A2, type **Income Statement** and then press the **Enter** key. See Figure 1-18.

   TROUBLE? If you make a mistake as you type, you can correct the error with the Backspace key. If you realize you made an error after pressing the Enter key, reenter the text by repeating Steps 3 through 5.

Figure 1-18

Figure 1-18 | **ADDING NEW TEXT TO THE INCOME STATEMENT**

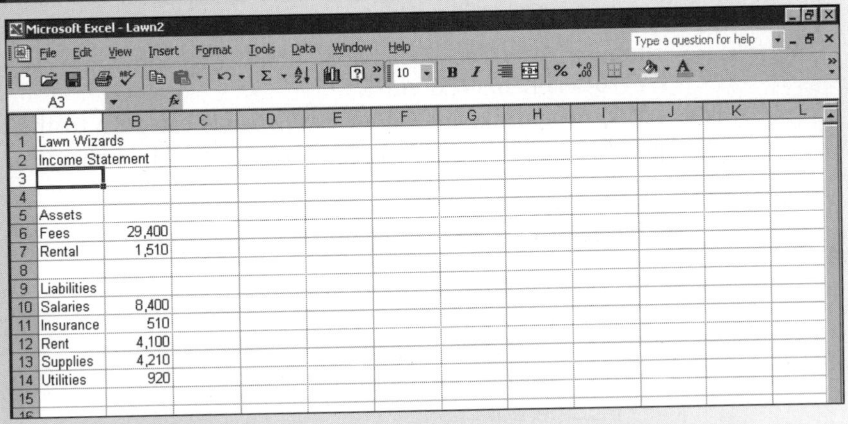

Note that even though you entered text in cells A1 and A2, the text appears to flow into cells B1 and B2. When you enter a text string longer than the width of the active cell, Excel will display the additional text if the cells to the right of the active cell are blank. If those cells are not blank, then Excel will truncate the display (though the entire text is still present in the cell). As you will see later, you can increase the width of the column if the text is cut off.

Entering Dates

Dates are treated as separate from text in Excel. As you will learn later, Excel includes several special functions and commands to work with dates. For example, you can insert a function that will calculate the number of days between two dates (you will learn more about this in the next tutorial). To enter a date, separate the parts of the date with a slash or hyphen. For example, the date April 1, 2003 can be entered as either "4/1/2003" or "1-Apr-2003".

You can also enter the date as the text string "April 1, 2003", in which case Excel might automatically convert the text to "1-Apr-2003". You can change the format used by Excel to display dates by changing the cell's format. You will learn about date formats in Tutorial 3.

Mike wants the date "4/1/2003" to appear in cell A3.

To insert the date in cell A3:

1. Verify that cell A3 is the active cell.

2. Type **4/1/2003** and then press the **Enter** key.

TROUBLE? Your system may be set up to display dates using the mm/dd/yy format; therefore, you may see the date displayed as 4/1/03 rather than 4/1/2003.

Entering Values

Values are numbers that represent a quantity of some type: the number of units in an inventory, stock prices, an exam score, and so on. Values can be numbers such as 378 and 25.275, or negative numbers such as –55.208. Values can also be expressed as currency ($4,571.25) or percentages (7.5%). Dates and times are also values, though that fact is hidden from you by the way Excel displays date information.

As you type information into a cell, Excel determines whether the information you have entered can be treated as a value. If so, Excel will automatically recognize the value type and right-align the value within the cell. Not all numbers are treated as values. For example, Excel treats a telephone number (1-800-555-8010) or a Social Security number (372-70-9654) as a text entry.

Mike would like to add a miscellaneous category to the list of monthly liabilities. In April, the total miscellaneous expenses incurred by Lawn Wizards totaled $351.

To add the miscellaneous expenses:

1. Click cell **A15** and then type **Misc** as the category.

2. Press the **Tab** key to move to the next column.

3. Type **351** and then press the **Enter** key. Figure 1-19 shows the new entry in the income statement.

| Figure 1-19 | ADDING A NEW CATEGORY AND VALUE TO THE INCOME STATEMENT |

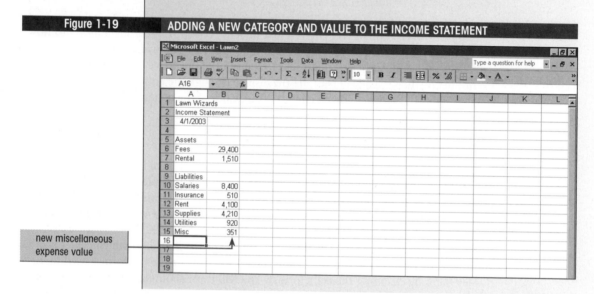

new miscellaneous expense value

Entering Formulas

A **formula** is an expression that is used to calculate a value. You can enter a formula by typing the expression into the active cell, or in special cases Excel will automatically insert the formula for you. Excel formulas always begin with an equal sign (=) followed by an expression that calculates a value. If you do not start with an equal sign, Excel will treat the expression you enter as text. The expression can contain one or more **arithmetic operators**, such as +, −, *, or /, that are applied to either values or cells in the workbook. Figure 1-20 gives some examples of Excel formulas.

Figure 1-20	ARITHMETIC OPERATORS USED IN FORMULAS		
ARITHMETIC OPERATION	**ARITHMETIC OPERATOR**	**EXAMPLE**	**DESCRIPTION**
Addition	+	=10+A5	Adds 10 to the value in cell A5
		=B1+B2+B3	Adds the values of cells B1, B2, and B3
Subtraction	–	=C9–B2	Subtracts the value in B2 from the value in cell C9
		=1–D2	Subtracts the value in cell D2 from 1
Multiplication	*	=C9*B9	Multiplies the value in cell C9 by the value in cell B9
		=E5*0.06	Multiplies the value in cell E5 by 0.06
Division	/	=C9/B9	Divides the value in cell C9 by the value in cell B9
		=D15/12	Divides the value in cell D15 by 12
Exponentiation	^	=B5^3	Raises the value in cell B5 to the third power
		=3^B5	Raises 3 to the power specified in cell B5

REFERENCE   WINDOW   RW

Entering a Formula

- Click the cell where you want the formula value to appear.
- Type = and then type the expression that calculates the value you want.
- For formulas that include cell references, such as B2 or D78, you can type the cell reference or you can use the mouse or arrow keys to select each cell.
- When the formula is complete, press the Enter key.

If an expression contains more than one arithmetic operator, Excel performs the calculation in the order of precedence. The **order of precedence** is a set of predefined rules that Excel follows to unambiguously calculate a formula by determining which operator is applied first, which operator is applied second, and so forth. First, Excel performs exponentiation (^). Second, Excel performs multiplication (*) or division (/). Third, Excel performs addition (+) or subtraction (-).

For example, because multiplication has precedence over addition, the formula =3+4*5 has the value 23. If the expression contains two or more operators with the same level of precedence, Excel applies them going from left to right in the expression. In the formula =4*10/8, Excel first multiplies 4 by 10 and then divides the product by 8 to return the value 5.

You can add parentheses to a formula to make it easier to interpret or to change the order of operations. Excel will calculate any expression contained within the parentheses before any other part of the formula. The formula =(3+4)*5 first calculates the value of 3+4 and then multiplies the total by 5 to return the value 35 (note that without the parentheses, Excel would return a value of 23 as noted in the previous paragraph). Figure 1-21 shows other examples of Excel formulas in which the precedence order is applied to return a value.

Figure 1-21	EXAMPLES ILLUSTRATING ORDER OF PRECEDENCE RULES	
FORMULA VALUE A1=10, B1=20, C1=3	**ORDER OF PRECEDENCE RULE**	**RESULT**
=A1+B1*C1	Multiplication before addition	70
=(A1+B1)*C1	Expression inside parentheses executed before expression outside	90
=A1/B1+C1	Division before addition	3.5
=A1/(B1+C1)	Expression inside parentheses executed before expression outside	.435
=A1/B1*C1	Two operators at same precedence level, leftmost operator evaluated first	1.5
=A1/(B1*C1)	Expression inside parentheses executed before expression outside	.166667

The Lawn2 workbook contains the asset and liability values for various categories, but it doesn't include the total assets and liabilities, nor does it display Lawn Wizards' net income (assets minus liabilities) for the month of April. Mike suggests that you add formulas to calculate these values now.

To calculate the total assets for the month of April:

1. Click cell **A8** to make it the active cell.

2. Type **Total** and then press the **Tab** key twice.

3. In cell C8, type **=B6+B7** (the income from fees and rental for the month).

   Note that as you type in the cell reference, Excel surrounds each cell with a different colored border that matches the color of the cell reference in the formula. As shown in Figure 1-22, Excel surrounds cell B6 with a blue border matching the blue used for the cell reference. Green is used for the B7 cell border and cell reference.

Figure 1-22	TYPING A FORMULA INTO A CELL

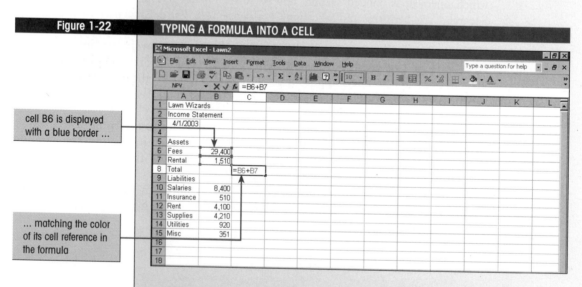

cell B6 is displayed with a blue border ...

... matching the color of its cell reference in the formula

4. Press the **Enter** key.

   The total assets value displayed in cell C8 is 30,910.

You can also enter formulas interactively by clicking each cell in the formula rather than typing in the cell reference. Using this approach reduces the possibility of error caused by typing in an incorrect cell reference.

To enter a formula by pointing and clicking:

1. Click cell **A16** to make it the active cell.
2. Type **Total** and then press the **Tab** key twice.

   TROUBLE? Note that when you started to type the word "Total" in cell A16, Excel automatically completed it for you. Since some worksheets will repeat the same word or phrase several times within a row or column, this AutoComplete feature can save you time.

3. In cell C16, type = and then click cell **B10**. Excel automatically inserts the reference to cell B10 into your formula.
4. Type **+** and then click cell **B11**.
5. Type **+** and then click cell **B12**.
6. Continue to select the rest of the liabilities in the range B13:B15, so that the formula in cell C16 reads **=B10+B11+B12+B13+B14+B15**. Do not type an equal sign after you click cell B15.
7. Press the **Enter** key. The total liabilities value "18,491" appears in cell C16.

   Now you can calculate the net income for the month of April.

8. In cell A18, enter **Net Income** and then press the **Tab** key twice.
9. In cell C18, enter the formula **=C8-C16** by clicking to select the cell references, and then press the **Enter** key. Figure 1-23 shows the completed formulas in the income statement.

Figure 1-23 TOTAL ASSETS, LIABILITIES, AND NET INCOME

	A	B	C
1	Lawn Wizards		
2	Income Statement		
3	4/1/2003		
4			
5	Assets		
6	Fees	29,400	
7	Rental	1,510	
8	Total		30,910
9	Liabilities		
10	Salaries	8,400	
11	Insurance	510	
12	Rent	4,100	
13	Supplies	4,210	
14	Utilities	920	
15	Misc	351	
16	Total		18,491
17			
18	Net Income		12,419
19			
20			

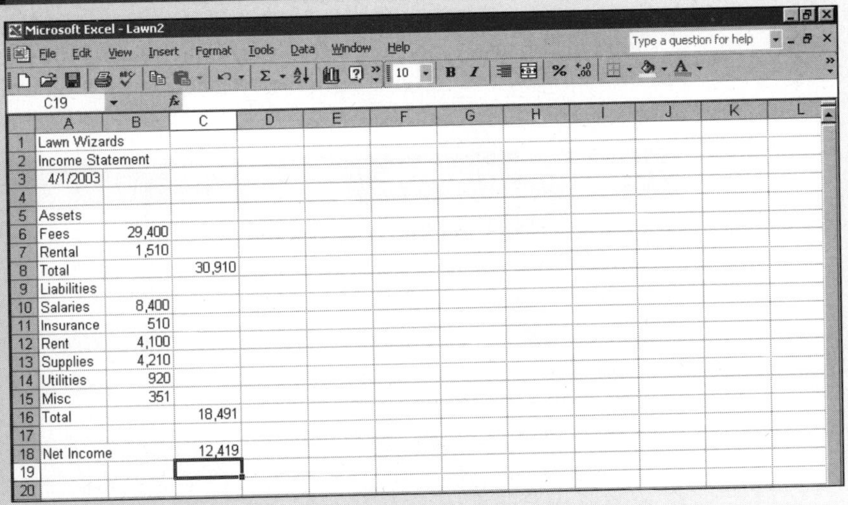

Working **with Rows and Columns**

Mike examines the worksheet and points out that it is difficult to separate the assets from the liabilities. He would like you to insert a blank row between row 8 and row 9. You could do this by moving the cell range A9:C18 down one row, but there is another way. Excel allows you to insert rows or columns into your worksheet.

Inserting a Row or Column

To insert a new row, you select a cell in the row where you want the new row placed. You then select Rows from the Insert menu. Excel will shift that row down, inserting a new blank row in its place. Inserting a new column follows the same process. Select a cell in the column where you want the new column inserted, and click Columns on the Insert menu. Excel will shift that column to the right, inserting a new blank column in its place.

To insert multiple rows or columns, select multiple cells before applying the Insert command. For example, to insert two new blank rows, select two adjacent cells in the same column, and click Rows on the Insert menu. To insert three new blank columns, select three adjacent cells in the same row, and click Columns on the Insert menu.

You can also insert individual cells within a row or column (rather than an entire row or column). To do this, select the range where you want the new cells placed, and click Cells on the Insert menu. Excel provides four options:

- **Shift cells right**   Inserts new blank cells into the selected region, and moves the selected cells to the right. The new cells will have the same number of rows and columns as the selected cells.

- **Shift cells down**   Inserts new blank cells into the selected region, and moves the selected cells down. The new cells will have the same number of rows and columns as the selected cells.

- **Entire row**   Inserts an entire blank row.
- **Entire column**   Inserts an entire blank column.

You can also insert rows and columns by right-clicking the selected cells and choosing Insert on the shortcut menu. This is equivalent to clicking the Cells command on the Insert menu.

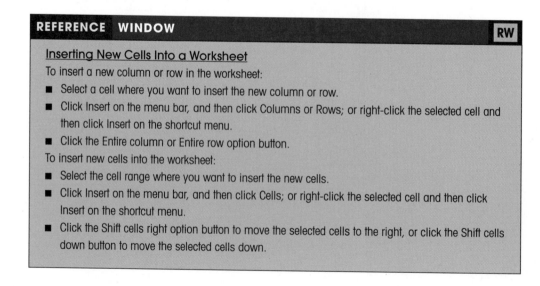

REFERENCE WINDOW   **RW**

Inserting New Cells Into a Worksheet

To insert a new column or row in the worksheet:

- Select a cell where you want to insert the new column or row.
- Click Insert on the menu bar, and then click Columns or Rows; or right-click the selected cell and then click Insert on the shortcut menu.
- Click the Entire column or Entire row option button.

To insert new cells into the worksheet:

- Select the cell range where you want to insert the new cells.
- Click Insert on the menu bar, and then click Cells; or right-click the selected cell and then click Insert on the shortcut menu.
- Click the Shift cells right option button to move the selected cells to the right, or click the Shift cells down button to move the selected cells down.

Now that you have seen how to insert new cells into your worksheet, you'll insert three new blank cells into the range A9:C9.

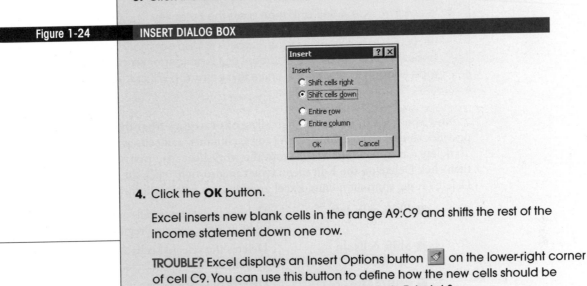

To insert three new cells into the worksheet:

1. Select the range **A9:C9**.

2. Click **Insert** on the menu bar, and then click **Cells**.

3. Click the **Shift cells down** option button, if necessary. See Figure 1-24.

Figure 1-24	INSERT DIALOG BOX

4. Click the **OK** button.

Excel inserts new blank cells in the range A9:C9 and shifts the rest of the income statement down one row.

TROUBLE? Excel displays an Insert Options button ⬛ on the lower-right corner of cell C9. You can use this button to define how the new cells should be formatted. You will learn about formatting in Tutorial 3.

When you insert a new row, the formulas in the worksheet are automatically updated to reflect the changing position. For example, the formula for Net Income has changed from *=C8–C16* to *=C8–C17* to reflect the new location of the total liabilities cell. You will learn more about how formulas are adjusted in Tutorial 2.

Clearing or Deleting a Row or Column

Mike wants to make one further change to the income statement. He wants to consolidate the supplies and miscellaneous categories into one entry. Your first task will be to remove the current contents of the range A14:B14 (the supplies category). Excel provides two ways of removing data. One way, called **clearing**, simply deletes the contents of the cells. To clear the contents of a cell, you use either the Delete key or the Clear command on the Edit menu. Clearing the contents of a cell does not change the structure of the workbook; that is, the row is not removed from the worksheet. Do not press the spacebar to enter a blank character in an attempt to clear a cell's content. Excel treats a blank character as text, so even though the cell appears to be empty, it is not.

To remove the supplies category data:

1. Select the range **A14:B14**.

2. Press the **Delete** key. The text and values in the range A14:B14 are cleared.

   Now you can enter the text for the supplies and miscellaneous category.

3. In cell A14, type **Supplies & Misc.** and then press the **Tab** key.

   Now enter the total for the new category.

4. In cell B14, type **4,561** and then press the **Enter** key.

   TROUBLE? Do not worry that the Supplies & Misc category label in cell A14 appears to be cut off. The adjacent cell is no longer empty, and cell A14 is not wide enough to display the entire text entry. You will correct this problem shortly.

Now you need to delete the miscellaneous category from the income statement. Excel provides similar options for deleting rows, columns, and cells as it does for inserting them. To delete a row, column, or cell from the worksheet, you first select the cell or range and then click Delete on the Edit menu (you can also right-click the selected range and choose Delete on the shortcut menu). Excel provides you with the following delete options:

■ **Shift cells left**	Deletes the selected cells and shifts cells from the right into the selected region
■ **Shift cells up**	Deletes the selected cells and shifts cells from the bottom up into the selected region
■ **Entire row**	Deletes the entire row
■ **Entire column**	Deletes the entire column

Because you no longer need the miscellaneous category, you will delete the cell range A16:C16.

To delete the cell range A16:C16:

1. Select the range **A16:C16**.

2. Click **Edit** on the menu bar, and then click **Delete**.

3. Select the **Shift cells up** option button if necessary, and then click the **OK** button. Excel deletes the contents of the cell range and moves the cells below up one row. See Figure 1-25.

Figure 1-25   **DELETING THE MISCELLANEOUS CATEGORY FROM THE INCOME STATEMENT**

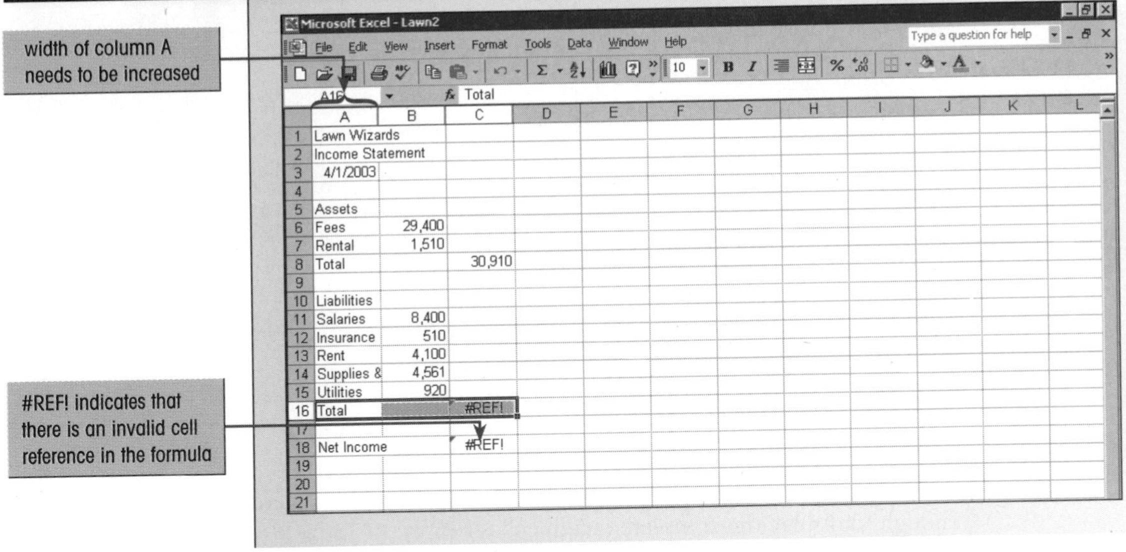

width of column A
needs to be increased

#REF! indicates that
there is an invalid cell
reference in the formula

	A	B	C
1	Lawn Wizards		
2	Income Statement		
3	4/1/2003		
4			
5	Assets		
6	Fees	29,400	
7	Rental	1,510	
8	Total		30,910
9			
10	Liabilities		
11	Salaries	8,400	
12	Insurance	510	
13	Rent	4,100	
14	Supplies &	4,561	
15	Utilities	920	
16	Total		#REF!
17			
18	Net Income		#REF!
19			
20			
21			

Mike immediately sees two problems. One problem is that the text entry in cell A14 is cut off. The second is that the liabilities total in cell C16 and the net income in cell C18 have been replaced with *#REF!* The *#REF!* entry is Excel's way of indicating that there is an invalid cell reference in a formula. Because Excel cannot calculate the formula's value, Excel displays this text as a warning. The invalid cell reference occurred when the miscellaneous total was deleted. Since that cell no longer exists, any formula that is based on that cell, such as the formula that calculates the liability, will return an error message, and since the total liability now returns an error message, the formula for the net income on which the total liability value is based also returns an error.

So you need to do two things: 1) increase the width of column A so that no text is truncated, and 2) revise the formula in cell C16 to remove the error message. First you will change the width of column A.

Increasing the Width of a Column or the Height of a Row

Excel provides several methods for changing the width of a column or the height of a row. You can click the dividing line of the column or row, or you can drag the dividing line to change the width of the column or the height of the row. You can also double-click the border of a column heading, and the column will increase in width to match the length of the longest entry in the column. Widths are expressed either in terms of the number of characters or the number of screen pixels.

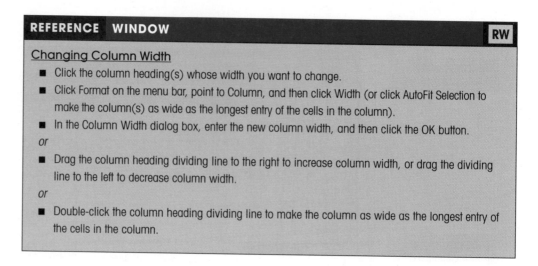

<u>Changing Column Width</u>

- Click the column heading(s) whose width you want to change.
- Click Format on the menu bar, point to Column, and then click Width (or click AutoFit Selection to make the column(s) as wide as the longest entry of the cells in the column).
- In the Column Width dialog box, enter the new column width, and then click the OK button.

or

- Drag the column heading dividing line to the right to increase column width, or drag the dividing line to the left to decrease column width.

or

- Double-click the column heading dividing line to make the column as wide as the longest entry of the cells in the column.

You'll drag the dividing line between columns A and B to increase the width of column A enough to display the complete text in cell A14.

To increase the width of column A:

1. Move the mouse pointer to the dividing line between the column A and column B headings until the pointer changes to ↔.

2. Click and drag the pointer to the right to a length of about **15** characters (or 110 pixels).

3. Release the mouse button. The entire text in cell A14 should now be visible. See Figure 1-26.

Figure 1-26	INCREASING THE WIDTH OF COLUMN A

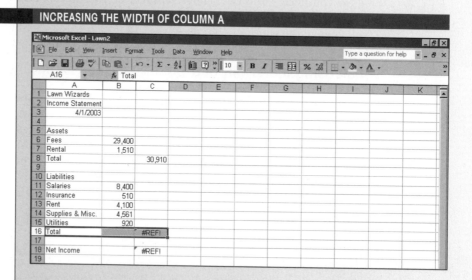

TROUBLE? If the text in cell A14 is still truncated, drag the dividing line further to the right.

Editing **Your Worksheet**

When you work in Excel you might make mistakes that you want to correct or undo. You have an error in the Lawn2 workbook of an invalid cell reference in cell C16. You could simply delete the formula in cell C16 and reenter the formula from scratch. However, there may be times when you will not want to change the entire contents of a cell, but merely edit a portion of the entry. For example, if a cell contains a large block of text or a complicated formula, you might not want to retype the text or formula completely. Instead, you can edit a cell by either selecting the cell and then clicking in the Formula bar to make the changes or by double-clicking the cell to open the cell in **edit mode**.

Working in Edit Mode

When you are working in edit mode or editing the cell using the Formula bar, some of the keys on your keyboard act differently than they do when you are not editing the content of a cell. For example, the Home, Delete, Backspace, and End keys do not move the insertion point to different cells in the worksheet; rather they move the insertion point to different locations within the cell. The Home key, for example, moves the insertion point to the beginning of whatever text has been entered into the cell. The End key moves the insertion point to the end of the cell's text. The left and right arrow keys move the insertion point backward and forward through the text in the cell. The Backspace key deletes the character immediately to the left of the insertion point, and the Delete key deletes the character at the location of the insertion point. Once you are finished editing the cell, press the Enter key to leave editing mode or to remove the insertion point from the Formula bar.

REFERENCE WINDOW   `RW`

Editing a Cell

- Double-click the cell to begin edit mode; click the cell and press the F2 key to begin edit mode; or click the cell and then click in the Formula bar.
- Use the Home, End, ←, or → keys to move the insertion point within the cell's content. Use the Delete and Backspace keys to erase characters.
- Press the Enter key when finished, or if you are working in the Formula bar, click the Enter button.

Now you'll use edit mode to change the formula in cell C16.

To edit the formula in cell C16:

1. Double-click cell **C16**.

An insertion point appears in the cell, indicating where new text will be inserted into the current cell expression. Note that the formula appears fine except for the *+#REF!* at the end of the expression. See Figure 1-27. This notation indicates that the cell reference used in the formula no longer points to a valid cell reference. In this case, the cell referenced was deleted. You can fix the error by deleting the *+#REF!* from the formula.

Figure 1-27   **EDITING THE FORMULA IN CELL C16**

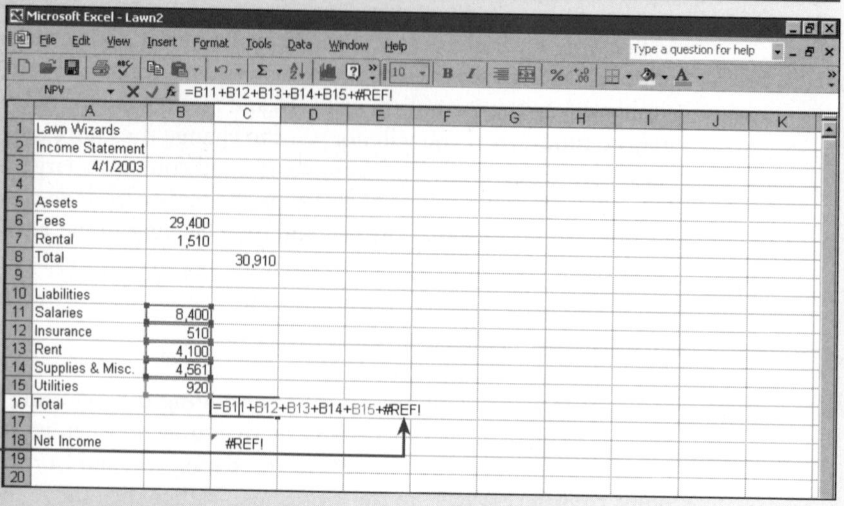

#REF! indicates a cell reference that no longer exists

2. Press the **End** key to move the blinking insertion point to the end of the cell.

3. Press the **Backspace** key six times to delete +#REF! from the formula.

4. Press the **Enter** key. The value 18,491 appears in cell C16, and the net income for the company is 12,419.

If you make a mistake as you type, you can press the Esc key or click the Cancel button on the Formula bar to cancel all changes you made while in edit mode.

Undoing an Action

Another way of fixing a mistake is to undo the action. Undoing an action cancels it, returning the workbook to its previous state. To undo an action, click the Undo button located on the Standard toolbar. As you work, Excel maintains a list of your actions, so you can undo most of the actions you perform on your workbook during your current session. To reverse more than one action, click the list arrow next to the Undo button and click the action you want to undo from the list. To see how this works, use the Undo button to remove the edit you just made to cell C16.

To undo your last action:

1. Click the **Undo** button on the Standard toolbar. The value #REF! appears again in cells C16 and C18 indicating that your last action, editing the formula in cell C16, has been undone.

If you find that you have gone too far in undoing your previous actions, you can go forward in the action list and redo those actions. To redo an action, you click the Redo button on the Standard toolbar. Use the Redo button now to return the formula in cell C16 to its edited state.

To redo your last action:

1. Click the **Redo** button ⟳ on the Standard toolbar. The edited formula has been reinserted into cell C16 and the value 18,491 again appears in the cell.

   TROUBLE? If you don't see the Redo button, click the Toolbar Options button ⟩⟩ located on the right edge of the Standard toolbar, and then click ⟳ to repeat the delete (the Redo button will now appear on the toolbar). You can also click the Repeat Delete command on the Edit menu (you might have to wait a few seconds for Excel to display the full Edit menu). After you undo an action, the Repeat command changes to reflect the action that has been undone so you can choose to repeat the action if undoing the action does not give you the result you want.

Through the use of edit mode and the Undo and Redo buttons, you should be able to correct almost any mistake you make in your Excel session.

Working with Worksheets

By default, Excel workbooks contain three worksheets labeled Sheet1, Sheet2, and Sheet3. You can add new worksheets or remove old ones. You can also give your worksheets more descriptive names. In the Lawn2 workbook, there is no data entered in the Sheet2 or Sheet3 worksheets. Mike suggests that you remove these sheets from the workbook.

Adding and Removing Worksheets

To delete a worksheet, you first select its sheet tab to make the worksheet the active sheet; then right-click the sheet tab and choose Delete from the shortcut menu. Try this now by deleting the Sheet2 and Sheet3 worksheets.

To delete the Sheet2 and Sheet3 worksheets:

1. Click the **Sheet2** tab to make Sheet2 the active sheet.

2. Right-click the sheet tab, and then click **Delete** on the shortcut menu. Sheet2 is deleted and Sheet3 becomes the active sheet.

3. Right-click the **Sheet3** tab, and then click **Delete**.

   There is now only one worksheet in the workbook.

After you have deleted the two unused sheets, Mike informs you that he wants to include a description of the workbook content and purpose. In other words, Mike wants to include a **documentation sheet**, a worksheet that provides information about the content and purpose of the workbook. A documentation sheet can be any information that you feel is important, for example, the name of the person who created the workbook or instructions on how to use the workbook. A documentation sheet is a valuable element if you intend to share the workbook with others. The documentation sheet is often the first worksheet in the workbook, though in this case Mike wants to place it at the end of the workbook.

To insert a new worksheet, you can either use the Insert Worksheet command or the right-click method. Using either method will insert a new worksheet before the active sheet.

To insert a new worksheet in the workbook:

1. Click **Insert** on the menu bar.

2. Click **Worksheet**. A new worksheet with the name "Sheet2" is placed at the beginning of your workbook.

Mike wants the documentation sheet to include the following information:

- The company name
- The date the workbook was originally created
- The person who created it
- The purpose of the workbook

You'll add this information to the new sheet in the Lawn2 workbook.

To insert the documentation information in the new worksheet:

1. Click cell **A1** if necessary, and then type **Lawn Wizards**.

2. Click cell **A3**, type **Date:** and then press the **Tab** key.

3. Enter the current date using the date format, mm/dd/yyyy. For example, if the date is April 5, 2003, enter the text string "4/5/2003." Press the **Enter** key.

4. In cell A4, type **Created By:** and then press the **Tab** key.

5. Enter your name in cell B4, and then press the **Enter** key.

6. Type **Purpose:** in cell A5, and then press the **Tab** key.

7. In cell B5, type **To record monthly income statements for the Lawn Wizards,** and then press the **Enter** key.

8. Increase the width of column A to **15** characters. Figure 1-28 shows the completed documentation sheet (your sheet will display a different name and date).

| Figure 1-28 | CREATING A DOCUMENTATION SHEET |

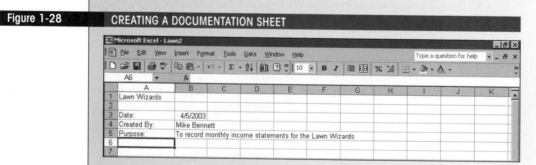

Renaming a Worksheet

The current sheet names "Sheet2" and "Sheet1" are not very descriptive. Mike suggests that you rename Sheet2 "Documentation" and Sheet1 "April Income". To rename a worksheet, you double-click the sheet tab to select the sheet name, and then you type a new name for the sheet.

Rename the sheet tabs using more meaningful names.

To rename the worksheets:

1. Double-click the **Sheet2** tab. Note that the name of the sheet is selected.

2. Type **Documentation** and then press the **Enter** key. The width of the sheet tab adjusts to the length of the name you type.

3. Double-click the **Sheet1** tab.

4. Type **April Income** and then press the **Enter** key.

Moving a Worksheet

Finally, Mike wants the Documentation sheet to appear last in the workbook. He feels that the actual data should be displayed first. To move the position of a worksheet in the workbook, you click the worksheet's sheet tab, and drag and drop it to a new location relative to the other worksheets.

You can create a copy of the entire worksheet by holding down the Ctrl key as you drag and drop the sheet tab. When you release the mouse button, a copy of the original worksheet will be placed at the new location, while the original sheet will stay at its initial position in the workbook.

REFERENCE WINDOW   **RW**

Moving or Copying a Worksheet
- Click the sheet tab of the worksheet you want to move (or copy).
- Drag the sheet tab along the row of sheet tabs until the small arrow appears in the desired location. To create a copy of the worksheet, press and hold down the Ctrl key as you drag the sheet tab to the desired location.
- Release the mouse button. Release the Ctrl key if necessary.

You'll move the Documentation sheet now.

To move the Documentation worksheet:

1. Click the **Documentation** tab to make it the active worksheet.

2. Click the **Documentation** tab again, and then press and hold down the left mouse button so the pointer changes to ▢. A small arrow appears in the upper-left corner of the sheet tab.

3. Drag the pointer to the right of the April Income tab, and then release the mouse button. The Documentation sheet is now the second sheet in the workbook.

Printing a Worksheet

Now that you are finished editing the Lawn2 workbook, you can create a hard copy of its contents for your records. You can print the contents of your workbook using either the Print command on the File menu or by clicking the Print button on the Standard toolbar. If you use the Print command, Excel displays a dialog box in which you can specify which worksheets you want to print, the number of copies, and the print quality (or resolution). If you click the Print button, you will not have a chance to set these options, but if you do not need to do so, clicking the Print button is a faster way of generating your output. Finally, you can also choose the Print Preview command on the File menu or click the Print Preview button on the Standard toolbar to see what your page will look like before it is sent to the printer. You can print directly from Print Preview.

If you are printing to a shared printer on a network, many other people might be sending print jobs at the same time you do. To avoid confusion, you will print the contents of both the Documentation sheet and the April Income sheet. You will use the Print command on the File menu since you need to print the entire workbook and not just the active worksheet (which is the default print setting). You will learn more about the Print Preview command in the next tutorial.

To print the contents of the Lawn2 workbook:

1. Click **File** on the menu bar, and then click **Print** to open the Print dialog box. See Figure 1-29.

| Figure 1-29 | PRINT DIALOG BOX |

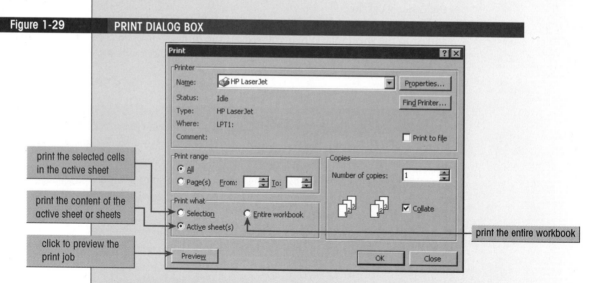

print the selected cells in the active sheet

print the content of the active sheet or sheets

click to preview the print job

print the entire workbook

2. Click the **Name** list box, and then select the printer to which you want to print.

Now you need to select what to print. To print the complete workbook, select the Entire workbook option button. To print the active worksheet, select the Active sheet(s) option button. To print the selected cells on the active sheet, click the Selection option button.

3. Click the **Entire workbook** option button.

4. Make sure "1" appears in the Number of copies list box, since you only need to print one copy of the workbook.

5. Click the **OK** button to send the workbook to the printer.

TROUBLE? If the workbook does not print, see your instructor or technical resource person for help.

You have completed your work on the Lawn2 workbook, so you can save your changes and exit Excel.

6. Click the **Save** button 🖫 on the Standard toolbar, and then click the **Close** button ✕ on the title bar.

You give Mike the hard copy of the Lawn2 workbook. He will file the report for later reference. If he needs to add new information to the workbook or if he needs you to make further changes to the structure of the workbook, he will contact you.

Session 1.2 QUICK CHECK

1. Indicate whether Excel treats the following cell entries as a value, text, or a formula:
   a. 11/09/2003
   b. Net Income
   c. 321
   d. =C11*225
   e. 201-19-1121
   f. =D1-D9
   g. 44 Evans Avenue

2. What formula would you enter to divide the value in cell E5 by the value in cell E6?

3. What formula would you enter to raise the value in cell E5 to the power of the value in cell E6?

4. When you insert a new row into a worksheet, the selected cells are moved _____.

5. When you insert a new column into a worksheet, the selected cells are moved _____.

6. To change the name of a worksheet, double-click the _____.

7. Which key do you press to clear the contents of the active cell?

8. How does clearing a cell differ from deleting a cell?

REVIEW ASSIGNMENTS

Mike has another workbook in which he wants you to make some changes. This workbook contains the income and expense figures for May. Mike has already done some work on the file, but wants you to make some modifications and additions. To complete this task:

1. Start Excel and open the workbook **Income1** located in the Tutorial.01/Review folder on your Data Disk.

2. Save the workbook as **Income2** in the same folder.

3. Change the date in cell A3 to 5/1/2003.

4. Insert new cells in the range A12:C12, shifting the other cells down. In cell A12, enter the text "Rent". In cell B12, enter the value "4,100".

Explore

5. Edit the formula in cell C16 so that the formula includes the cost of rent in the liabilities total.

Explore

6. There is a mistake in the formula for the net income. Fix the formula so that it displays the difference between the assets and the liabilities in the month of May.

7. Move the income statement values in the range A5:C18 to the range C1:E14.

8. Resize the width of column C to 15 characters.

9. Insert a sheet named "Documentation" at the beginning of the workbook.

10. In the Documentation sheet, enter the following text:

   - Cell A1: Lawn Wizards
   - Cell A3: Date:
   - Cell B3: *Enter the current date*
   - Cell A4: Created By:
   - Cell B4: *Enter your name*
   - Cell A5: Purpose:
   - Cell B5: To record income and expenses for the month of May

11. Increase the width of column A in the Documentation worksheet to 20 characters.

12. Rename Sheet1 as **May Income**.

13. Delete Sheet2 and Sheet3.

14. Print the entire contents of the Income2 workbook.

15. Save and close the workbook, and then exit Excel.

CASE PROBLEMS

Case 1. Cash Flow Analysis at Madison Federal   Lisa Wu is a financial consultant at Madison Federal. She is working on a financial plan for Tom and Carolyn Watkins. Lisa has a cash flow analysis for the couple, and she wants you to record this information for her. Here are the relevant financial figures:

Receipts
- Employment Income: 95,000
- Other Income: 5,000

Disbursements
- Insurance: 940
- Savings/Retirement: 8,400
- Living Expenses: 63,000
- Taxes: 16,300

Lisa wants you to calculate the total receipts and total disbursements and then to calculate the income surplus (receipts minus disbursements) in an Excel workbook that she has already started. To complete this task:

1. Open the **CFlow1** workbook located in the Tutorial.01/Cases folder on your Data Disk, and then save the workbook as **CFlow2** in the same folder.

2. Move the contents of the range A1:C12 to the range A3:C14.

3. Insert the text "Cash Flow Analysis" in cell A1.

4. Increase the width of column A to 130 pixels, the width of column B to 160 pixels, and the width of column C to 130 pixels.

5. Insert the financial numbers listed earlier into the appropriate cells in column C.

6. In cell C6, insert a formula to calculate the total receipts.

7. In cell C12, insert a formula to calculate the total disbursements.

8. Insert a formula to calculate the surplus in cell C14.

9. Rename Sheet1 as **Cash Flow**.

10. Insert a worksheet at the beginning of the workbook named "Documentation".

11. In the Documentation sheet, enter the following text:

   - Cell A1: Cash Flow Report
   - Cell A3: Date:
   - Cell B3: *Enter the current date*
   - Cell A4: Created By:
   - Cell B4: *Enter your name*
   - Cell A5: Purpose:
   - Cell B5: Cash flow analysis for Tom and Carolyn Watkins

12. Increase the width of column A in the Documentation worksheet to 20 characters.

13. Delete Sheet2 and Sheet3.

14. Print the contents of the entire workbook.

Explore 15. What would the surplus be if the couple's taxes increased to 18,500? Enter this value into the Cash Flow worksheet, and then print just the Cash Flow worksheet.

16. Save and close the workbook, and then exit Excel.

Case 2. Financial Report for EMS Industries   Lee Evans is an agent at New Haven Financial Services. His job is to maintain financial information on stocks for client companies. He has the annual balance sheet for a company named EMS Industries in an Excel workbook and needs your help in finishing the workbook layout and contents. To complete this task:

1. Open the **Balance1** workbook located in the Tutorial.01/Cases folder on your Data Disk, and then save the workbook as **Balance2** in the same folder.

2. Select the cells A1:C2 and insert two new rows into the worksheet.

3. Insert the text "Annual Balance Sheet for EMS Industries" in cell A1.

4. Move the contents of the range A19:C33 to the range E3:G17.

5. Move the contents of the range B36:C38 to the range B19:C21.

6. Change the width of column B to 150 pixels, the width of column D to 20 pixels, and the width of column F to 150 pixels.

7. Insert a formula in cell C10 to calculate the total current assets, in cell C17 to calculate the total noncurrent assets, in cell G10 to calculate the total current liabilities, and in cell G17 to calculate the total noncurrent liabilities.

8. In cell C19, insert a formula to calculate the total of the current and noncurrent assets.

9. In cell C20, insert a formula to calculate the total of the current and noncurrent liabilities.

10. In cell C21, insert a formula to calculate the annual balance (the total assets minus the total liabilities).

11. Rename Sheet1 as **Annual Balance Sheet**.

12. Delete Sheet2 and Sheet3.

13. Insert a worksheet named "Documentation" at the front of the workbook.

14. Enter the following text into the Documentation sheet:

   - Cell A1: Annual Balance Report
   - Cell A3: Company:
   - Cell B3: EMS Industries
   - Cell A4: Date:
   - Cell B4: *Enter the current date*
   - Cell A5: Recorded By:
   - Cell B5: *Enter your name*
   - Cell A6: Summary:
   - Cell B6: Annual Balance Sheet

15. Increase the width of column A in the Documentation worksheet to 20 characters.

16. Print the entire contents of the workbook.

17. Save and close the workbook, and then exit Excel.

Case 3. Analyzing Sites for a New Factory for Kips Shoes   Kips Shoes is planning to build a new factory. The company has narrowed the site down to four possible cities. Each city has been graded on a 1-to-10 scale for four categories: the size of the local market, the quality of the labor pool, the local tax base, and the local operating expenses. Each of these four factors is given a weight with the most important factor given the highest weight. After the sites are analyzed, the scores for each factor will be multiplied by their weights, and then a total weighted score will be calculated.

Gwen Sanchez has entered the weights and the scores for each city into an Excel workbook. She needs you to finish the workbook by inserting the formulas to calculate the weighted scores and the total overall score for each city. To complete this task:

1. Open the **Site1** workbook located in the Tutorial.01/Cases folder on your Data Disk, and then save the workbook as **Site2** in the same folder.

2. Switch to the Site Analysis sheet.

3. In cell B12, calculate the weighted Market Size score for Waukegan by inserting a formula that multiplies the value in cell B5 by the value in cell C5.

4. Insert formulas to calculate the weighted scores for the rest of the cells in the range B12:E15.

5. Insert formulas in the range B17:E17 that calculate the totals of the weighted scores for each of the four cities. Which city has the highest weighted score?

6. Switch to the Documentation sheet, and enter your name and the date in the appropriate location on the sheet.

7. Print the entire workbook.

Explore

8. Gwen reports that Brockton's score for market size should be 6 and not 5. Modify this entry in the table, and then print just the Site Analysis worksheet with the new total scores. Does this change your conclusions about which city is most preferable for the new factory?

9. Save and close the workbook, and then exit Excel.

Case 4. Cash Counting Calculator Rob Stuben works at a local town beach in Narragansett where a fee is collected for parking. At the end of each day, the parking attendants turn in the cash they have collected with a statement of the daily total. Rob is responsible for receiving the daily cash from each attendant, checking the accuracy of the daily total, and taking the cash deposit to the bank.

Rob wants to set up a simple cash counter using Excel, so that he can insert the number of bills of each denomination into a worksheet so the total cash is automatically computed. By a simple cash counter method, he only has to count and enter the number of one-dollar bills, the number of fives, and so on. To complete this task:

1. Save a new workbook with the name **CashCounter** in the Tutorial.01/Cases folder on your Data Disk.

Explore

2. In the workbook, create a worksheet named **Counter** with the following properties:

   - All currency denominations (1, 5, 10, 20, 50, 100) should be listed in the first column of the worksheet.

   - In the second column, you will enter the number of bills of each denomination, but this column should be left blank initially.

   - In the third column, insert the formulas to calculate totals for each denomination, (that is, the number of bills multiplied by the denomination of each bill).

   - In a blank cell at the bottom of the third column, which contains the formulas for calculating the totals of each denomination, a formula that calculates the grand total of the cash received should be entered.

3. Create a Documentation sheet. The sheet should include the title of the workbook, the date the workbook was created, your name, and the purpose of the workbook. Make this worksheet the first worksheet in the workbook.

4. Adjust the widths of the columns, if necessary. Delete any blank worksheets from the workbook.

Explore

5. On Rob's first day using the worksheet, the cash reported by an attendant was $1,565. Rob counted the bills and separated them by denomination. Enter the following values into the worksheet:

   - 5 fifties
   - 23 twenties
   - 41 tens
   - 65 fives
   - 120 ones

6. Print the entire contents of your workbook.

Explore

7. On Rob's second day, the cash reported by an attendant was $1,395. Again, Rob counted the money and separated the bills by denomination. Clear the previous values, and then enter the new values for the distribution of the bills into the worksheet:

- 2 hundreds
- 4 fifties
- 17 twenties
- 34 tens
- 45 fives
- 90 ones

8. Print just the Counter worksheet.

9. Save and close the workbook, and then exit Excel.

LAB ASSIGNMENTS

Spreadsheets

The New Perspectives Labs are designed to help you master some of the key computer concepts and skills presented in each chapter of the text. If you are using your school's lab computers, your instructor or technical support person should have installed the Labs software for you. If you want to use the Labs on your home computer, ask your instructor for the appropriate software. See the Read This Before You Begin page for more information on installing and starting the Lab.

Each Lab has two parts: Steps and Explore. Use Steps first to learn and review concepts. Read the information on each page and do the numbered steps. As you work through the Lab, you will be asked to answer Quick Check questions about what you have learned. At the end of the Lab, you will see a Summary Report of your answers to the Quick Checks. If your instructor wants you to turn in this Summary Report, click the Print button on the Summary Report screen.

When you have completed Steps, you can click the Explore button to complete the Lab Assignments. You can also use Explore to practice the skills you learned and to explore concepts on your own.

SPREADSHEETS Spreadsheet software is used extensively in business, education, science, and humanities to simplify tasks that involve calculations. In this Lab you will learn how spreadsheet software works. You will use spreadsheet software to examine and modify worksheets, as well as to create your own worksheets.

1. Click the Steps button to learn how spreadsheet software works. As you proceed through the Steps, answer all of the Quick Check questions that appear. After you complete the Steps, you will see a Quick Check Summary Report. Follow the instructions on the screen to print this report.

2. Click the Explore button to begin this assignment. Click OK to display a new worksheet. Click File on the menu bar, and then click Open to display the Open dialog box. Click the file **Income.xls** and then press the Enter key to open the **Income and Expense Summary** workbook. Notice that the worksheet contains labels and values for income from consulting and training. It also contains labels and values for expenses

such as rent and salaries. The worksheet does not, however, contain formulas to calculate Total Income, Total Expenses, or Profit. Do the following:

a. Calculate the Total Income by entering the formula =SUM(C4:C5) in cell C6.
b. Calculate the Total Expenses by entering the formula =SUM(C9:C12) in C13.
c. Calculate Profit by entering the formula =C6-C13 in cell C15.
d. Manually check the results to make sure you entered the formulas correctly.
e. Print your completed worksheet showing your results.

3. You can use a spreadsheet to keep track of your grades in a class and to calculate your grade average. In Explore, click File on the menu bar, and then click Open to display the Open dialog box. Click the file **Grades.xls** to open the workbook. The worksheet contains the labels and formulas necessary to calculate your grade average based on four test scores. You receive a score of 88 out of 100 on the first test. On the second test, you score 42 out of 48. On the third test, you score 92 out of 100. You have not taken the fourth test yet. Enter the appropriate data in the **Grades.xls** worksheet to determine your grade average after taking three tests. Print out your worksheet.

4. Worksheets are handy for answering "what if" questions. Suppose you decide to open a lemonade stand. You're interested in how much profit you can make each day. What if you sell 20 cups of lemonade? What if you sell 100? What if the cost of lemons increases?

   In Explore, open the file **Lemons.xls** and use the worksheet to answer questions a through d. Then print the worksheet for question e:

   a. What is your profit if you sell 20 cups a day?
   b. What is your profit if you sell 100 cups a day?
   c. What is your profit if the price of lemons increases to $.07 and you sell 100 cups?
   d. What is your profit if you raise the price of a cup of lemonade to $.30? (Lemons still cost $.07 and assume you sell 100 cups.)
   e. Suppose your competitor boasts that she sold 50 cups of lemonade in one day and made exactly $12.00. On your worksheet adjust the cost of cups, water, lemons, and sugar, and the price per cup to show a profit of exactly $12.00 for 50 cups sold. Print this worksheet.

5. It is important to make sure the formulas in your worksheet are accurate. An easy way to test this is to enter 1's for all the values on your worksheet, then check the calculations manually. In Explore, open the file **Receipt.xls**, which contains a formula that calculates sales receipts. Enter "1" as the value for Item 1, Item 2, Item 3, and Sales Tax %. Now manually calculate what you would pay for three items that each cost $1.00 in a state where sales tax is 1% (.01). Do your manual calculations match those of the worksheet? If not, correct the formulas in the worksheet, and then print out a *formula report* of your revised worksheet.

6. In Explore, create your own worksheet showing your household budget for one month. Make up the numbers for the budget. Put a title at the top of the worksheet. Use formulas to calculate your total income and expenses for the month. Add another formula to calculate how much money you were able to save. Print a formula report of your worksheet. Also, print your worksheet showing realistic values for one month.

INTERNET ASSIGNMENTS

Student Union

The purpose of the Internet Assignments is to challenge you to find information on the Internet that you can use to create effective spreadsheets. The actual assignments are updated and maintained on the Course Technology Web site. Log on to the Internet and use your Web browser to go to the Student Union on the New Perspectives Series site at **www.course.com/NewPerspectives/studentunion**. Click the Online Companions link, and then click the link for this text.

QUICK CHECK ANSWERS

Session 1.1

1. cell
2. D2
3. Ctrl + Home
4. Click the Sheet2 tab.
5. Adjacent and nonadjacent. An adjacent range is a rectangular block of cells. A nonadjacent range consists of two or more separate adjacent ranges.
6. A5:F8
7. Select the cells you want to move, and then press and hold down the Alt key and drag the selection over the Sheet2 tab. When Sheet2 becomes the active sheet, continue to drag the selection to position it in its new location in the worksheet, and then release the left mouse button and the Alt key.

Session 1.2

1. a. value
   b. text
   c. value
   d. formula
   e. text
   f. formula
   g. text
2. =E5/E6
3. =E5^E6
4. down
5. to the right
6. sheet tab and then type the new name to replace the highlighted sheet tab name
7. Delete key
8. Clearing a cell deletes the cell's contents but does not affect the position of other cells in the workbook. Deleting a cell removes the cell from the worksheet, and other cells are shifted into the deleted cell's position.

In this tutorial you will:

- Work with the Insert Function button

- Learn about Excel's financial functions

- Copy and paste formulas and functions

- Work with absolute and relative references

- Learn to use Excel's Auto Fill features

- Create logical functions

- Work with Excel's date functions

WORKING WITH FORMULAS AND FUNCTIONS

Analyzing a Mortgage

Prime Realty

You work as an assistant at Prime Realty (PR) selling real estate. One of the agents at PR, Carol Malloy, has asked you to help her develop an Excel workbook that calculates mortgages. The workbook needs to include three values: the size of the loan, the number of payments, and the annual interest rate. Using this information in the workbook, you will be able to determine the monthly payment needed to pay off the loan and the total cost of the mortgage over the loan's history. Carol wants the workbook to display a table showing the monthly payments with information describing how much of the payment is for interest and how much is applied toward the principal. Carol also wants the workbook to be flexible enough so that if a client intends on making additional payments, beyond the required monthly payment, the workbook will show how the cost of the loan and subsequent payments are affected.

In this tutorial, you will use Excel's financial functions to create the workbook for the mortgage calculations.

SESSION 2.1

In this session, you will learn about Excel's functions. You will insert functions and function arguments. You will copy and paste formulas and functions into your workbook. Finally, you will learn about absolute and relative references and how to insert them into your formulas.

Working with Excel Functions

Carol has already started the loan workbook. She has not entered any values yet, but she has entered some text and a documentation sheet. Open her workbook now.

To open Carol's workbook:

1. Start Excel and then open the **Loan1** workbook located in the Tutorial.02/Tutorial folder on your Data Disk.

2. On the Documentation sheet, enter your name in cell B3.

3. Click the **Mortgage** tab to make the sheet the active worksheet. See Figure 2-1.

| Figure 2-1 | THE LOAN WORKBOOK |

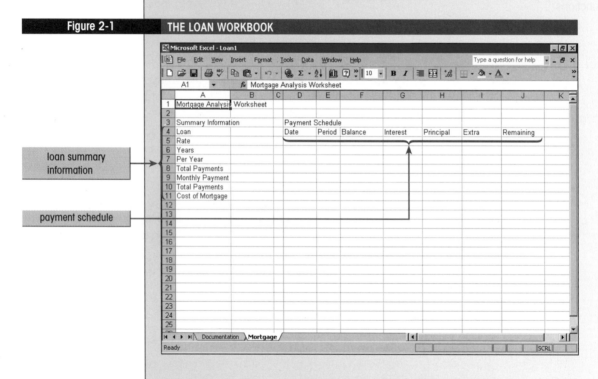

4. Save the workbook as **Loan2** in the Tutorial.02/Tutorial folder on your Data Disk.

The Mortgage worksheet is divided into two sections. The Summary Information section is the area in which you will enter the basic information about the loan, including the amount of the loan, the current interest rate, and the length of the mortgage. Figure 2-2 provides a description of the information that you will enter in the cells in that section.

Figure 2-2 **CELLS IN THE SUMMARY INFORMATION SECTION**

CELL	DESCRIPTION
B4	Enter the amount of the loan
B5	Enter the interest rate
B6	Enter the length of the mortgage in years
B7	Enter the number of periods (months) that the interest will be compounded each year
B8	Calculate the total number of periods in the loan
B9	Calculate the monthly payment
B10	Calculate the total payments on the loan
B11	Calculate the cost of the loan (total payments minus the amount of the loan)

The other section of the worksheet contains the payment schedule; it indicates how much is paid toward the principal and how much is paid in interest each month. The schedule also indicates the balance remaining on the loan each month. Figure 2-3 describes the values to be placed in each column.

Figure 2-3 **COLUMNS IN THE PAYMENT SCHEDULE**

COLUMN	DESCRIPTION
Date	Date that loan payment is due
Period	Loan payment period
Balance	Balance of loan remaining to be paid
Interest	Interest due
Principal	Portion of the monthly payment used to reduce the principal
Extra	Extra payments beyond the scheduled monthly payment
Remaining	Balance of loan remaining after the monthly payment

To make this worksheet operational, you need to use financial functions that are provided in Excel.

Function Syntax

In the previous tutorial you used formulas to calculate values. For example, the formula =$A1+A2+A3+A4$ totals the values in the range A1:A4 and places the sum in the active cell. Although calculating sums this way for small ranges works fine, a formula that calculates the sum of 100 cells would be so large that it would become unmanageable. In Excel you can easily calculate the sum of a large number of cells by using a function. A **function** is a predefined, or built-in, formula for a commonly used calculation.

Each Excel function has a name and syntax. The **syntax** specifies the order in which you must enter the different parts of the function and the location in which you must insert commas, parentheses, and other punctuation. The general syntax for an Excel function is =FUNCTION(*argument1, argument2, ...*), where FUNCTION is the name of the Excel function, and *argument1, argument2,* and so on are **arguments**—the numbers, text, or cell references used by the function to calculate a value. Some arguments are **optional arguments** because they are not necessary for the function to return a value. If you omit an optional argument, Excel assumes a default value for it. By convention, optional arguments will appear in this text within square brackets along with the default value. For example, in the function =FUNCTION(*argument1*,[*argument2=value*]), the second argument is optional, and *value* is the default value assigned to *argument2* if a value is omitted from the argument list. A convention that you will follow in this text is to display function names in uppercase letters; however, when you enter formulas into your own Excel worksheets, you can use either uppercase or lowercase letters.

Excel supplies over 350 different functions organized into 10 categories:

- Database functions
- Date and Time functions
- Engineering functions
- Financial functions
- Information functions
- Logical functions
- Lookup functions
- Math functions
- Statistical functions
- Text and Data functions

You can learn about each function using Excel's online Help. Figure 2-4 describes some of the more important math and statistical functions that you may often use in your workbooks.

Figure 2-4	MATH AND STATISTICAL FUNCTIONS
FUNCTION	**DESCRIPTION**
AVERAGE(*values*)	Calculates the average value in a set of numbers, where *values* is either a cell reference or a collection of cell references separated by commas
COUNT(*values*)	Counts the number of cells containing numbers, where *values* is either a cell reference or a range of cell references separated by commas
MAX(*values*)	Calculates the largest value in a set of numbers, where *values* is either a cell reference or a range of cell references separated by commas
MIN(*values*)	Calculates the smallest value in a set of numbers, where *values* is either a cell reference or a range of cell references separated by commas
ROUND(*number, num_digits*)	Rounds a *number* to a specified number of digits, indicated by the *num_digits* arguments
SUM(*numbers*)	Calculates the sum of a collection of numbers, where *numbers* is either a cell or a range reference or a series of numbers separated by commas

For example, the SUM function calculates the total for the values in a range of cells. The SUM function has only one argument, the cell reference containing the values to be totaled. To calculate the total of the cells in the range A1:A100, you would insert the expression =SUM(A1:A100) into the active cell.

Functions can also be combined with formulas. For example, the expression =MAX(A1:A100)/100 returns the maximum value in the range A1:A100 and then divides the value by 100. One function can also be nested inside the other. The expression =ROUND(AVERAGE(A1:A100),1) uses the AVERAGE function to calculate the average of the values in the range A1:A100 and then uses the ROUND function to round the average value off to the first decimal place.

By combining functions and formulas, you can create very sophisticated expressions to handle almost any situation.

Financial Functions

In Carol's workbook, you will use one of Excel's financial functions to calculate information about the loan. Figure 2-5 describes a few of Excel's financial functions in more detail.

Figure 2-5	FINANCIAL FUNCTIONS
FUNCTION	**DESCRIPTION**
FV(*rate,nper,pmt,*[*pv*=0],[*type*=0])	Calculates the future value of an investment based on periodic, constant payments, and a constant interest rate, where *rate* is the interest rate per period, *nper* is the number of periods, *pmt* is the payment per period, *pv* is the present value of the investment, and *type* indicates when payments are due (*type*=0 for payments at the end of each period, *type*=1 for payments at the beginning of each period)
IPMT(*rate,per,nper pv,*[*fv*=0],[*type*=0])	Calculates the interest payment for a given period for an investment based on period cash payments and a constant interest rate, where *fv* is the future value of the investment
PMT(*rate,nper,pv,*[*fv*=0],[*type*=0]	Calculates the payment for a loan based on constant payments and a constant interest rate
PPMT(*rate,per,nper,pv,*[*fv*=0],[*type*=0])	Calculates the payment on the principal for a given period for an investment based on period cash payments and a constant interest rate
PV(*rate,nper,pmt,*[*fv*=0],[*type*=0])	Calculates the present value of an investment

You need a function to calculate the monthly payment that will pay off a loan at a fixed interest rate. You can use Excel's PMT function to do just that. The syntax of the PMT function is PMT(*rate,nper,pv,*[*fv*=0],[*type*=0]) where *rate* is the interest rate per period of the loan, *nper* is the total number of periods, *pv* is the present value of the loan, *fv* is the future value, and *type* specifies whether the payment is made at the beginning of each period (*type*=1) or at the end of each period (*type*=0). Note that both the *fv* and *type* arguments are optional arguments. If you omit the *fv* argument, Excel assumes that the future value will be 0, in other words that the loan will be completely paid off. If you omit the *type* argument, Excel assumes a type value of 0 so that the loan is paid off at the end of each period.

For example, if Carol wanted to know the monthly payment for a $50,000 loan at 9% annual interest compounded monthly over 10 years, the arguments for the PMT function would be *PMT(0.09/12,10*12,50000)*. Note that the yearly interest rate is divided by the number of periods (months) for the interest rate per period. Similarly, the number of periods (months) is multiplied by the number of years in order to arrive at the total number of periods.

The value returned by the PMT function is –633.38, indicating that a client would have to spend $633.38 per month to pay off the loan in 10 years. Excel uses a negative value to indicate that the value is an expense rather than income.

You can also use the PMT function for annuities other than loans. For example, if you want to determine how much money to save at a 6% annual interest rate compounded monthly so that you will have $5000 at the end of five years, you use the following PMT function: =*PMT(0.06/12,5*12,0,5000)*. Note that the present value is 0 (since you are starting out with no money in the account) and the future value is 5000 (since that is the amount you want to have after 5 years). In this case, Excel will return a value of –71.66, indicating that you would have to invest $71.66 per month to achieve $5000 in your savings account after 5 years.

Inserting a Function

Carol wants to calculate the monthly payment for a 20-year loan of $150,000 at 7.5% annual interest compounded monthly. First you need to enter this information into the workbook. You also need to enter a formula that will calculate the total number of monthly payments.

To add the loan information:

1. Click cell **B4**, type **$150,000** and then press the **Enter** key. Even though you have added a dollar symbol in writing the loan amount, Excel still interprets cell B4 as a numeric value and not a text string.

2. In cell B5, type **7.5%** and then press the **Enter** key. Note that when you type a percentage into a worksheet cell, Excel interprets the percentage as a value. The actual value in cell B5 is 0.075; the value is just *formatted* to appear with the percent sign. You will learn more about how Excel formats numbers in the next tutorial.

3. In cell B6, type **20** and then press the **Enter** key.

4. In cell B7, type **12** since there are 12 payment periods in each year, and then press the **Enter** key.

   Note that in this text you can *enter* a cell reference in a formula or function by clicking the cell or by typing the cell reference.

5. In cell B8, enter the formula **=B6*B7** for the total number of payments in the mortgage, and then press the **Enter** key. The value 240 appears in cell B8, and cell B9 is now the active cell.

Now you will use the PMT function to calculate the required monthly payment to pay off the loan under the terms of the mortgage. You could simply type the function and its arguments into the cell, but you will often find that you have forgotten which arguments are required by the function and the correct order in which the arguments need to be entered. To assist you, Excel provides the Insert Function button on the Formula bar. Clicking this button displays a dialog box from which you can choose the function you want to enter. Once you choose a function, another dialog box opens in which you specify values for all of the function's arguments.

REFERENCE WINDOW   **RW**

Inserting a Function

- Click the cell in which you will insert the function.
- Click the Insert Function button on the Formula bar.
- Select the type of function you want from the select a category list box, and then select the function category; or type information about the function in the Search for a function text box, and then click the Go button.
- Select the function in the Select a function list box.
- Click the OK button to view the arguments for the selected function.
- Enter values for each required argument in the Function Arguments dialog box.
- Click the OK button.

You will insert the PMT function in the Summary Information section of the Mortgage worksheet to determine the monthly payment required to pay off a mortgage. You will use the Insert Function button on the Formula bar to insert the PMT function.

To insert the PMT function:

1. With cell B9 as the active cell, click the **Insert Function** button ▣ on the Formula bar. The Insert Function dialog box opens. See Figure 2-6.

Figure 2-6   INSERT FUNCTION DIALOG BOX

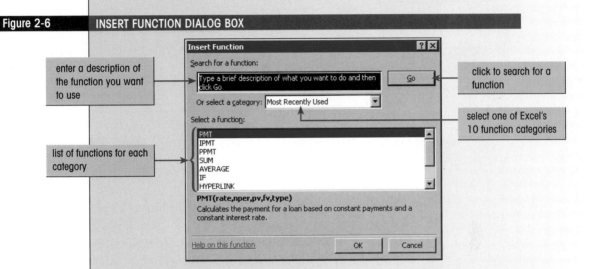

There are two ways to select a function using this dialog box. If you know something about the function but are not sure in which category the function belongs, enter a text description in the Search for a function text box and click the Go button. Excel will search for the functions that match your description. If you know the general category, select the category from the select a category list box; then Excel will list all of the functions in that category. Browse through the function list to find the function you need.

2. Type **calculate mortgage payments** in the Search for a function text box, and then click the **Go** button. Excel returns the PMT, IPMT, and NPER functions in the Select a function list box. Note that a description of the selected function and its arguments appears at the bottom of the dialog box. See Figure 2-7.

Figure 2-7   SEARCHING FOR A FUNCTION

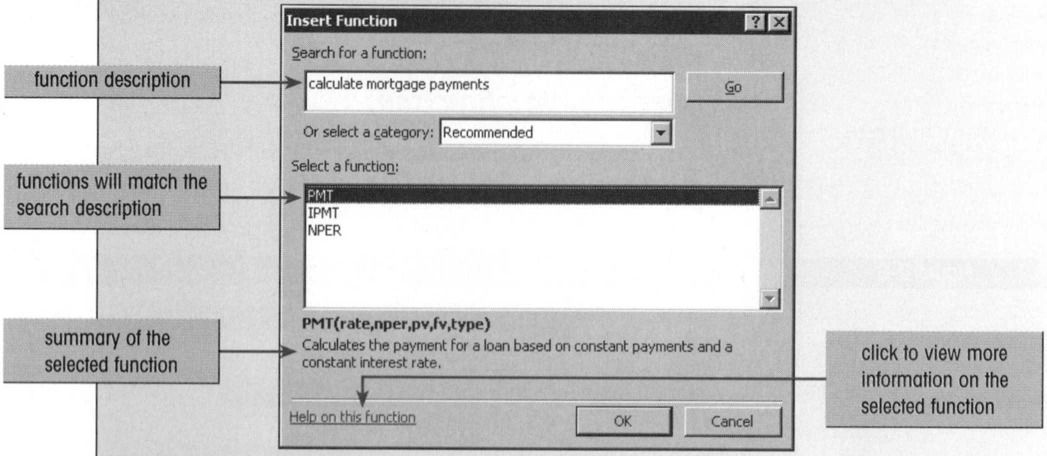

function description

functions will match the
search description

summary of the
selected function

click to view more
information on the
selected function

Insert Function

Search for a function:

calculate mortgage payments   Go

Or select a category: Recommended

Select a function:

PMT
IPMT
NPER

PMT(rate,nper,pv,fv,type)
Calculates the payment for a loan based on constant payments and a
constant interest rate.

Help on this function   OK   Cancel

3. Verify that the PMT function is selected in the Select a function list box, and
then click the **OK** button.

Excel next displays the Function Arguments dialog box, which provides all of the arguments in
the selected function and the description of each argument. From this dialog box, you can select
the cells in the workbook that contain the values required for each argument. Note that the
expression *=PMT()* appears in both the Formula bar and cell B9. This display indicates that Excel
is starting to insert the PMT function for you. You have to use the Function Arguments dialog
box to complete the process.

You will start by entering the value for the Rate argument. Remember that rate refers to the
interest rate per period. In this case, that value is 7.5% divided by 12, or if you use the cells in the
worksheet, the value in cell B5 is divided by the value in cell B7. You can enter the cell references
either by typing them into the appropriate argument boxes or by pointing to a cell with the mouse
pointer, in which case Excel will automatically insert the cell reference into the appropriate box.

To insert values into the PMT function:

1. With the blinking insertion point in the Rate argument box, click cell **B5**, type **/**,
and then click cell **B7**. The expression *B5/B7* appears in the box and the value
0.00625 appears to the right of the box.

   TROUBLE? If necessary, move the dialog box to view column B before clicking cell B5.

2. Press the **Tab** key to move to the Nper argument box.

3. Click cell **B8** for the 240 total payments needed for this loan, and then press the
Tab key.

   The present value of the loan is $150,000, which is found in cell B4.

4. Click cell **B4** to enter the value of the loan in the Pv argument box. Figure 2-8
shows the completed Function Arguments dialog box.

Figure 2-8   **ENTERING ARGUMENT VALUES**

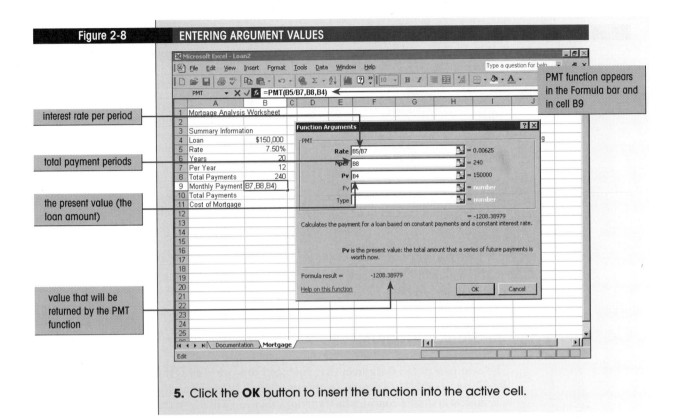

5. Click the **OK** button to insert the function into the active cell.

Excel displays the value ($1,208.39) with a red colored font in cell B9. This is a general format that Excel uses to display negative currency values. Carol would rather have the monthly payment appear as a positive value, so you will have to insert a negative sign in front of the PMT function to switch the monthly payment to a positive value. You will also complete the rest of the Summary Information section.

To complete the Summary Information section:

1. Double-click cell **B9** to enter edit mode.

2. Click directly to the right of the = (equal sign), type – so that the expression changes to =–PMT(B5/B7,B8,B4), and then press the **Enter** key.

3. In cell B10, enter **=B9*B8** and then press the **Enter** key.

4. In cell B11, enter **=B10-B4** and then press the **Enter** key. Figure 2-9 shows the complete summary information for this loan.

Figure 2-9 | **MORTGAGE SUMMARY**

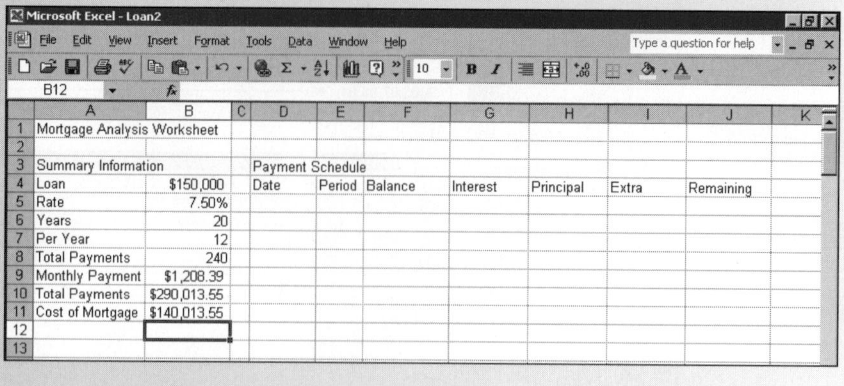

The required monthly payment for this loan will be $1,208.39. The total interest payments will be $140,013.55.

Copying and Pasting Formulas

The next part of the worksheet that you need to work with is the payment schedule, which details the monthly payments on the mortgage. Before entering values into the payment schedule, you should consider the functions that you will use in the schedule. Each row of the payment schedule represents the condition of the loan for a single month of the mortgage.

The Date column (column D in the worksheet) will contain the date on which a payment is due. At this point you will not enter any date information (you will do that later in the tutorial). The Period column specifies the number of periods in the mortgage. The first month is period 1, the second month is period 2, and so forth. Since there are 240 payment periods, this payment schedule will extend from row 5 down to row 244 in the worksheet. The Balance column displays the balance left on the loan at the beginning of each period. The initial balance value is the amount of the loan, which is found in cell B4. After the initial period, the balance will be equal to the remaining balance from the previous period.

The Interest column is the amount of interest due on the balance, which is equal to: Balance * Interest rate per period. In this example, the interest rate per period is the annual interest rate (in cell B5) divided by the number of periods in a year (in cell B7).

Subtracting the interest due from the monthly payment (cell B9) tells you how much is paid toward reducing the principal. This value is placed in column H of the worksheet. Carol knows that sometimes clients will want to make extra payments each month in order to pay off the loan quicker (and thereby reduce the overall cost of the mortgage). The Extra column (column I in the worksheet) is used for recording these values. Finally, the remaining balance will be equal to the balance at the beginning of the month minus the payment toward the principal and any extra payments.

Now that you have reviewed what values and functions will go into each column of the payment schedule, you are ready to insert the first row of the schedule.

To insert the first row of values in the payment schedule:

1. Click cell **E5**, type **1** and then press the **Tab** key.

   Now you will enter the initial balance, which is equal to the amount of the loan found in cell B4. Rather than typing in the value itself, you will enter a reference to the cell. If you change the amount of the loan, this change will be automatically reflected in the payment schedule.

2. In cell F5, enter **=B4** and then press the **Tab** key.

   Next you will enter the interest due in this period, which is equal to the balance multiplied by the interest rate per period (cell B5 divided by cell B7).

3. In cell G5, enter **=F5*B5/B7** and then press the **Tab** key.

   TROUBLE? Note that if the values in cells F5 and G5 are displayed with a different number of decimal places, do not worry. You will learn more about formatting cells in Tutorial 3.

   The payment toward the principal is equal to the monthly payment (cell B9) minus the interest payment (cell G5).

4. In cell H5, enter **=B9-G5** and then press the **Tab** key.

   At this point there are no extra payments toward the mortgage so you will enter $0 in the Extra column. The balance remaining is equal to the present balance minus the payment towards the principal and any extra payments.

5. In cell I5, type **$0** and then press the **Tab** key.

6. In cell J5, enter **=F5-(H5+I5)** and then press the **Enter** key. Figure 2-10 shows the first period values in the payment schedule.

Figure 2-10	FIRST PERIOD VALUES IN THE PAYMENT SCHEDULE

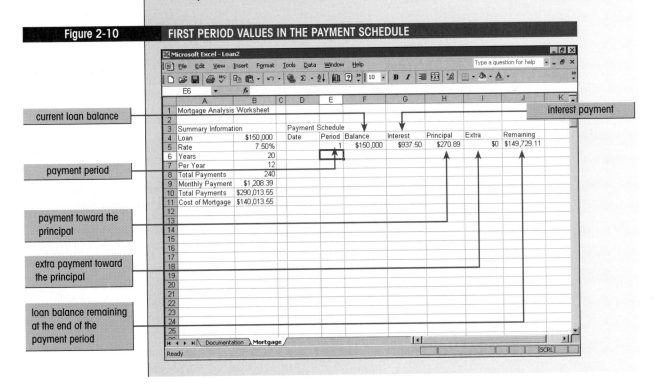

current loan balance

payment period

payment toward the principal

extra payment toward the principal

loan balance remaining at the end of the payment period

interest payment

You could have also calculated the monthly interest payment using Excel's IPMT function and the monthly payment toward the principal using the PPMT function. However, both of these functions assume that there will be no extra payments toward the principal. This assumption is something that Carol does not want to omit in her payment schedule.

The second row of the payment schedule is similar to the first. The only difference is that the balance (to be displayed in cell F6) will be carried over from the remaining balance (displayed in cell J5) in the previous row. At this point, you could retype the formulas that you used in the first row of the payment schedule. However, it is much easier and more efficient to copy and paste the formulas. When you **copy** the contents of a range, Excel places the formulas and values in those cells in a memory location called the **Clipboard**. The contents remain on the Clipboard until you **paste** them. You can paste the contents of the selected cells into another location on your worksheet, into a different worksheet or workbook, or even into another Windows application.

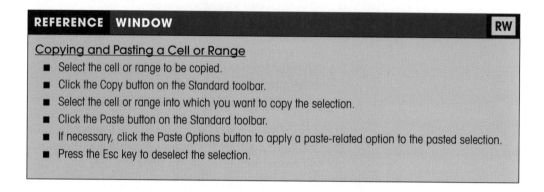

REFERENCE WINDOW   **RW**

Copying and Pasting a Cell or Range
- Select the cell or range to be copied.
- Click the Copy button on the Standard toolbar.
- Select the cell or range into which you want to copy the selection.
- Click the Paste button on the Standard toolbar.
- If necessary, click the Paste Options button to apply a paste-related option to the pasted selection.
- Press the Esc key to deselect the selection.

Next you will copy and paste a range of values in the worksheet.

To insert the second row of values in the payment schedule:

1. Click cell **E6**, type **2** and then press the **Tab** key.

2. In cell F6, enter **=J5** (since the remaining balance needs to be carried over into the second payment period), and then press the **Enter** key.

   Now you will copy the formulas from the range G5:J5 to the range G6:J6.

3. Select the range **G5:J5** and then click the **Copy** button 📋 on the Standard toolbar.

   TROUBLE? If you do not see the Copy button on the Standard toolbar, click the Toolbar Options button 》 on the Standard toolbar, and then click 📋.

   Note that the range that you copied has a moving border surrounding it. This moving border is a visual reminder of what range values are currently in the paste buffer.

4. Click cell **G6** to make it the active cell, and then click the **Paste** button 📋 on the Standard toolbar. Note that you did not have to select a range of cells equal to the range you were copying because the cells adjacent to cell G6 were empty and could accommodate the pasted range.

The formulas from the G5:J5 range are pasted into the G6:J6 range. See Figure 2-11.

| Figure 2-11 | COPYING AND PASTING FORMULAS |

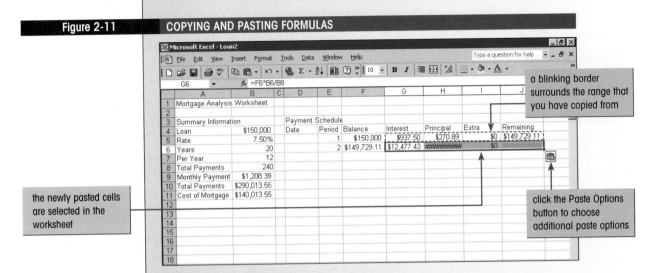

the newly pasted cells are selected in the worksheet

a blinking border surrounds the range that you have copied from

click the Paste Options button to choose additional paste options

Note that next to the pasted range is the Paste Options button. You can click this button to apply one of the available options for pasting cell values into the new range. By default, Excel pastes the values and formulas along with the format used to display those values and formulas. You will learn more about the Paste Options button in the next session.

5. Press the **Esc** key to remove the moving border.

Apparently something is wrong. Note that the interest payment in cell G6 has jumped to $12,477.43, and the principal payment in cell H6 and the remaining balance are represented with ########. Excel uses this string of symbols to represent a value that is so large that it cannot be displayed within the width of the cell. To view the value in the cell, you must either increase the width of the column or hover your mouse pointer over the cell.

To view the value in cell H6:

1. Hover your mouse pointer over cell H6. After a brief interval, the value $277,536.12 appears in a ScreenTip.

2. Click cell **G6** to make it the active cell. The Formula bar displays the formula =F6*B6/B8.

The interest payment value jumped to $12,477.43 and the payment on the principal became $277,536.12. The absurdity of these values results from the way in which Excel copies formulas. When Excel copies formulas to a new location, Excel automatically adjusts the cell references in those formulas. For example, to calculate the remaining balance for the first payment period in cell J5, the formula is =F5-(H5+I5). For the second payment period, the remaining balance in cell J6 uses the formula =F6-(H6+I6). The cell references are shifted down one row.

This automatic update of the cell references works fine for this formula, but the updating does not work for the calculation of the interest payment. The interest payment should be the balance multiplied by the interest rate per period; therefore, for the first three rows of the payment schedule, the formulas should be =F5*B5/B7, =F6*B5/B7, and =F7*B5/B7.

However, when you copied the first formula to the second row, *all* of the cell references shifted down one row and the formula automatically became *=F6*B6/B8*. You have a different formula; therefore, the result is a nonsensical value. Note that this is an issue only when copying a cell, not moving a cell. When you move a cell, Excel does *not* modify the cell references.

You need to be able to control how Excel adjusts cell references, so that Excel adjusts some of the cell references in the interest due formula, but not others. You can control this automatic adjusting of cell references through the use of relative and absolute references.

Relative and Absolute References

A **relative reference** is a cell reference that shifts when you copy it to a new location on the worksheet. As you saw in the preceding set of steps, a relative reference changes in relation to the change of location. If you copy a formula to a cell three rows down and five columns to the right, the relative cell reference shifts three rows down and five columns to the right. For example, the relative reference B5 becomes G8.

An **absolute reference** is a cell reference that does not change when you copy the formula to a new location on the workbook. To create an absolute reference, you preface the column and row designations with a dollar sign ($). For example, the absolute reference for B5 would be $B$5. No matter where you copy the formula, this cell reference would stay the same. (Relative references do not include dollars signs.)

A **mixed reference** combines both relative and absolute cell references. A mixed reference for B5 would be either $B5 or B$5. In the case of $B5, the row reference would shift, but the column reference would not. In the case of B$5, only the column reference shifts.

You can switch between absolute, relative, and mixed references by selecting the cell reference in the formula (either using edit mode or the Formula bar) and then pressing the F4 key on your keyboard repeatedly.

The problem you have encountered with the payment schedule formulas is that you need a relative reference for the remaining balance but an absolute reference for the interest rate divided by the payment periods per year (since those values are always located in the same place in the worksheet). So instead of the formula *=F5*B5/B7*, you need to use the formula *=F5*$B$5/$B$7*.

Next you will revise the formulas in the payment schedule to use relative and absolute references, and then copy the revised formulas.

To use relative and absolute references in the payment schedule:

1. Double-click cell **G5** to enter edit mode, use an arrow key to position the insertion point to the left of the column heading B if necessary, and then type **$**. Continue to use the arrow keys to position the insertion point in the formula before typing three more $ to change the formula to *=F5*$B$5/$B$7*. Press the **Enter** key.

   You also have to change the formula in cell H5, so that the formula subtracts the interest payment from the required monthly payment to calculate the payment toward the principal. Instead of typing the dollar signs to change a relative reference to an absolute reference, you will use the F4 key.

2. Double-click cell **H5**, make sure the insertion point is positioned in the B9 cell reference, and then press the **F4** key to change the formula to *=$B$9–G5*. Press the **Enter** key.

   Now copy these new formulas into the second row of the payment schedule. Note that you do not have to delete the contents of the range into which you are copying the updated formulas.

3. Select the range **G5:H5**, and then click the **Copy** button 🖻 on the Standard toolbar.

4. Click cell **G6** and then click the **Paste** button 🖻 on the Standard toolbar.

The new values are much more reasonable. The interest payment has decreased to $935.81, and the payment toward the principal has increased to $272.58. You will now add one more row to the payment schedule and copy the formulas.

To add a third row to the payment schedule:

1. Click cell **E7**, type **3** and then press the **Tab** key.

2. Select the range **F6:J6**, and then click the **Copy** button 🖻 on the Standard toolbar.

3. Click cell **F7** and then click the **Paste** button 🖻 on the Standard toolbar.

Figure 2-12 shows the first three rows of the payment schedule.

Figure 2-12	PASTING THE THIRD ROW OF THE PAYMENT SCHEDULE

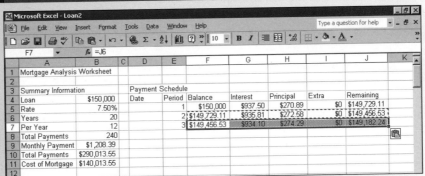

4. Examine the formulas in cells G5, G6, and G7. Note that the relative reference to the balance remaining on the loan changes from F5 to F6 to F7 as you proceed down the schedule, but the interest rate per period keeps the same absolute reference, $B$5/$B$7.

As you would expect, the interest payment schedule decreases as the remaining balance decreases, and the monthly payment that goes to the principal steadily increases. Carol would like you to complete the rest of the payment schedule for all 240 payment periods. You will explore how to complete the rest of the payment schedule in a quick and efficient way in the next session.

To close the Loan2 workbook:

1. Click **File** on the menu bar, and then click **Exit**.

2. When prompted to save your changes to Loan2.xls, click the **Yes** button.

Session 2.1 QUICK CHECK

1. Which function would you enter to calculate the minimum value in the range B1:B50?

2. What function would you enter to calculate the ratio between the maximum value in the range B1:B50 and the minimum value?

3. A 5-year loan for $10,000 has been taken out at 7% interest compounded quarterly. What function would you enter to calculate the quarterly payment on the loan?

4. Which function would you use to determine the amount of interest due in the second quarter of the first year of the loan discussed in question 3?

5. In the formula *A8+$C$1*, *$C$1* is an example of a(n) _____ reference.

6. Cell A10 contains the formula *=A1+B1*. If the contents of this cell were copied to cell B11, what formula would be inserted into that cell?

7. Cell A10 contains the formula *=$A1+B$1*. If this cell were copied to cell B11, what formula would be inserted into that cell? What would the formula be if you moved cell A10 to B11?

SESSION 2.2

In this session you will use Excel's Auto Fill feature to automatically fill in formulas, series, and dates. You will use Excel's logical functions to create functions that return different values based on different conditions. Finally, you will learn how Excel stores dates, and then you will work with dates using Excel's library of date and time functions.

Filling in Formulas and Values

So far you have entered only three periods of the 240 total payment periods into the payment schedule. You used the copy and paste technique to enter the values for the second and third rows. You could continue to copy and paste the remaining rows of the payment schedule, but you can use a more efficient technique—the fill handle. The **fill handle** is a small black square located in the lower-right corner of a selected cell or range. When you drag the fill handle, Excel automatically fills in the formulas or formats used in the selected cells. This technique is also referred to as **Auto Fill**.

REFERENCE WINDOW	RW

Copying Formulas Using Auto Fill
- Select the range that contains the formulas you want to copy.
- Click and drag the fill handle in the direction you want to copy the formulas.
- Release the mouse button.
- If necessary, click the Auto Fill Options button, and then select the Auto Fill option you want to apply to the selected range.

Copying Formulas

Carol wants you to copy the formulas from the range F6:J7 into the larger range F7:J244. Copying the formulas into the larger range will, in effect, calculate the monthly payments for all 240 periods of the loan—all 20 years of the mortgage.

To copy the formulas using the fill handle:

1. If you took a break after the previous session, make sure Excel is running and the Loan2 workbook is open.

2. Verify that the Mortgage sheet is the active worksheet.

3. Select the range **F6:J7**.

4. Position the pointer over the fill handle (the square box in the lower-right corner of cell J7) until the pointer changes to ↓.

5. Click and drag the fill handle down the worksheet to cell **J244**. As you drag the fill handle, an outline appears displaying the selected cells, and the worksheet automatically scrolls down.

6. Release the mouse button. By default, Excel copies the values and formulas found in the original range F6:J7 into the new range F7:J244. See Figure 2-13.

| Figure 2-13 | FILLING IN THE REST OF THE PAYMENT SCHEDULE VALUES |

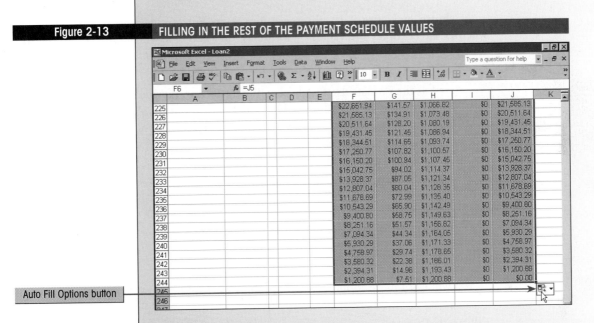

TROUBLE? It is very easy to "overshoot the mark" when dragging the fill handle down. If this happens, you can either click the Undo button [↺] on the Standard toolbar and try again, or simply select the extras formulas you created and delete them.

Excel has copied the formulas from the first few rows of the payment schedule into the rest of the rows and has also automatically adjusted any relative references in the formulas. For example, the formula in cell G244 is *=F244*$B$5/$B$7*, which is the interest due on the last loan payment, an amount of $7.51. The last row in the payment schedule shows a remaining balance of $0.00 in cell J244. The loan is paid off.

Note that to the right of the filled values is the Auto Fill Options button. Clicking this button displays the available options that you can choose from to specify how Excel should perform the Auto Fill. Click this button now to view the options.

To view the Auto Fill options:

1. Click the **Auto Fill Options** button 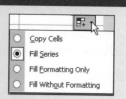 to the right of cell J244. Excel displays the Auto Fill Options menu, as shown in Figure 2-14.

Figure 2-14   **AUTO FILL OPTIONS**

- ○ Copy Cells
- ◉ Fill Series
- ○ Fill Formatting Only
- ○ Fill Without Formatting

2. Click anywhere outside of the menu to hide it.

As shown in Figure 2-14, there are four Auto Fill options. These options determine whether Excel copies the values or formulas, or whether Excel simply copies the formats used to display those values and formulas. The four options and their descriptions are:

- **Copy Cells**: Copies the values and formulas into the selected range, as well as the formats used to display those values and formulas. Relative references are adjusted accordingly. This is the default option.

- **Fill Series**: Copies the values and formulas into the selected range, and completes any arithmetic or geometric series. Relative references are adjusted accordingly.

- **Fill Formatting Only**: Copies only the formats used to display the values or formulas in the cells. Values and formulas are not copied into the selected range.

- **Fill Without Formatting**: Copies the values and formulas into the selected range. The formats used to display those values and formulas are not copied. Relative references are adjusted accordingly.

You will learn more about formatting values and formulas in the next tutorial.

Filling a Series

Missing from the payment schedule are the numbers in column E. There should be a sequence of numbers starting with the value 1 in cell E5 and ending with the value 240 in cell E244. Since these numbers are all different, you cannot simply copy and paste the values. You can, however, use the fill handle to complete a series of numbers, as long as you include the first few numbers of the series. If the numbers increase by a constant value in an arithmetic series, dragging the fill handle will continue that same increase over the length of the newly selected cells.

Use the fill handle to enter the numbers for the Period column in the payment schedule.

To fill in the payment period values:

1. Press **Ctrl + Home** to return to the top of the worksheet.

2. Select the range **E5:E7**.

3. Click and drag the fill handle down to cell **E244**. Note that as you drag the fill handle a label appears indicating the current value in the series. When you reach cell E244, the label displays the value *240*.

4. Release the mouse button. Figure 2-15 shows the values in the payment schedule through the 240th payment.

Figure 2-15	FILLING IN THE PAYMENT PERIOD NUMBERS

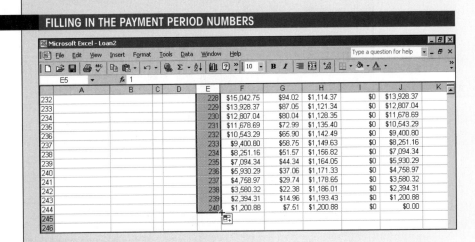

Filling In Dates

You can also use the fill handle to fill in dates—the one part of the payment schedule you have not entered yet. As with filling in a series, if you specify the initial date or dates, Excel will automatically insert the rest of the dates. The series of dates that Excel fills in depends on the dates you start with. If you start with dates that are separated by a single day, Excel will fill in a series of days. If you start with dates separated by a single month, Excel will fill in a series of months and so forth. You can also specify how to fill in the date values using the Auto Fill Options button.

Next you will insert an initial date for the loan as August 1, 2003, and then specify that each payment period is due at the beginning of the next month.

To insert the payment dates:

1. Type **8/1/2003** in cell D5, and then click the **Enter** button ☑ on the Formula bar. Note that clicking the Enter button on the Formula bar inserts the value in the cell and keeps it the active cell.

2. Drag the fill handle down to cell **D244**, and then release the mouse button. Note that as you drag the fill handle down, the date appears in the pop-up label; the date *3/27/2004* appears when you reach cell D244.

   TROUBLE? Don't worry if your computer is set up to display dates in a different format. The format doesn't affect the date value.

   By default, Excel created a series of consecutive days. You need to change the consecutive days to consecutive months.

3. Click the **Auto Fill Options** button located to the lower-right corner of cell D244.

4. Click the **Fill Months** option button. Excel fills in consecutive months in the payment schedule. The last payment date is 7/1/2023. See Figure 2-16.

Figure 2-16   ADDING DATES TO THE PAYMENT SCHEDULE

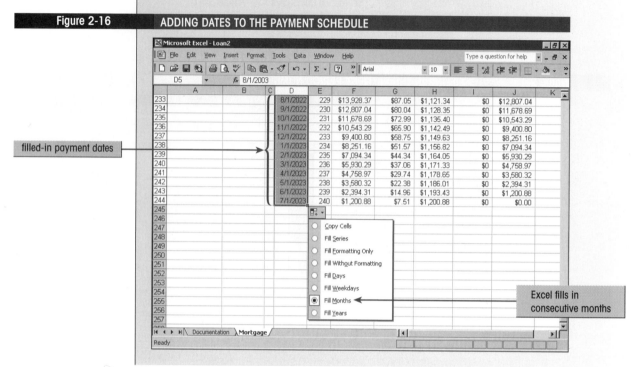

filled-in payment dates

Excel fills in consecutive months

Excel provides other techniques for automatically inserting series of numbers into your worksheets. You can even create your own customized fill series. You can use the online Help to learn how to use the other Auto Fill options. For now though, you have completed the payment schedule.

Carol wants to verify that the numbers you have inserted into the payment schedule are correct. She suggests that, as a check, you add up the interest payments in column G. The total should match the cost of the mortgage that you calculated in cell B11.

To calculate the total interest payments:

1. Click cell **A13**, and type **Observed Payments**, and then press the **Enter** key.

2. In cell A14, type **Cost of Mortgage**, and then press the **Tab** key. The observed cost of the mortgage is the sum of interest payments in the range G5:G244.

3. In cell B14, type **=SUM(G5:G244)**, and then press the **Enter** key. As shown in Figure 2-17, the total cost of the interest payments in the payment schedule, $140,013.55, matches what was calculated in cell B11.

Figure 2-17   **TOTAL INTEREST PAYMENTS FROM THE PAYMENT SCHEDULE**

	A	B	C	D	E	F	G	H	I	J	K
1	Mortgage Analysis Worksheet										
2											
3	Summary Information			Payment Schedule							
4	Loan	$150,000		Date	Period	Balance	Interest	Principal	Extra	Remaining	
5	Rate	7.50%		8/1/2003	1	$150,000	$937.50	$270.89	$0	$149,729.11	
6	Years	20		9/1/2003	2	$149,729.11	$935.81	$272.58	$0	$149,456.53	
7	Per Year	12		10/1/2003	3	$149,456.53	$934.10	$274.29	$0	$149,182.24	
8	Total Payments	240		11/1/2003	4	$149,182.24	$932.39	$276.00	$0	$148,906.24	
9	Monthly Payment	$1,208.39		12/1/2003	5	$148,906.24	$930.66	$277.73	$0	$148,628.51	
10	Total Payments	$290,013.55		1/1/2004	6	$148,628.51	$928.93	$279.46	$0	$148,349.05	
11	Cost of Mortgage	$140,013.55		2/1/2004	7	$148,349.05	$927.18	$281.21	$0	$148,067.84	
12				3/1/2004	8	$148,067.84	$925.42	$282.97	$0	$147,784.88	
13	Observed Payments			4/1/2004	9	$147,784.88	$923.66	$284.73	$0	$147,500.14	
14	Cost of Mortgage	$140,013.55		5/1/2004	10	$147,500.14	$921.88	$286.51	$0	$147,213.63	
15				6/1/2004	11	$147,213.63	$920.09	$288.30	$0	$146,925.33	
16				7/1/2004	12	$146,925.33	$918.28	$290.11	$0	$146,635.22	

Using **Excel's Logical Functions**

So far you have assumed that there are no extra payments toward the principal. In fact, the PMT function assumes constant periodic deposits with no additional payments. If extra payments were made, they would reduce the cost of the mortgage and speed up the payment of the loan. Carol would like to see what the effect would be on the payment schedule and the cost of the mortgage if an extra payment were made.

To add an extra payment to the schedule:

1. Click cell **I22**, which corresponds to the payment period for 1/1/2005.

   Now assume that a client makes an extra payment of $20,000 toward the principal on this date.

2. Type **$20,000** in cell I22, and then press the **Enter** key. The observed cost of the mortgage shown in cell B14 drops to $80,262.15.

3. Scroll down the worksheet until row **190** comes into view (corresponding to the date of 1/1/2019). See Figure 2-18.

Figure 2-18   **NEGATIVE INTEREST PAYMENTS**

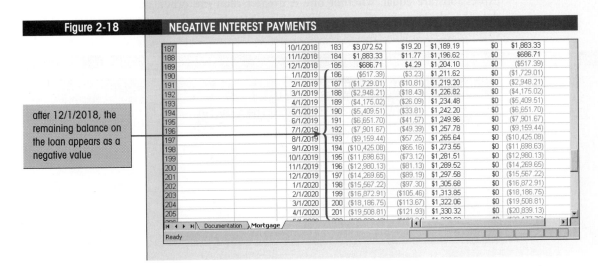

187			10/1/2018	183	$3,072.52	$19.20	$1,189.19	$0	$1,883.33
188			11/1/2018	184	$1,883.33	$11.77	$1,196.62	$0	$686.71
189			12/1/2018	185	$686.71	$4.29	$1,204.10	$0	($517.39)
190			1/1/2019	186	($517.39)	($3.23)	$1,211.62	$0	($1,729.01)
191			2/1/2019	187	($1,729.01)	($10.81)	$1,219.20	$0	($2,948.21)
192			3/1/2019	188	($2,948.21)	($18.43)	$1,226.82	$0	($4,175.02)
193			4/1/2019	189	($4,175.02)	($26.09)	$1,234.48	$0	($5,409.51)
194			5/1/2019	190	($5,409.51)	($33.81)	$1,242.20	$0	($6,651.70)
195			6/1/2019	191	($6,651.70)	($41.57)	$1,249.96	$0	($7,901.67)
196			7/1/2019	192	($7,901.67)	($49.39)	$1,257.78	$0	($9,159.44)
197			8/1/2019	193	($9,159.44)	($57.25)	$1,265.64	$0	($10,425.08)
198			9/1/2019	194	($10,425.08)	($65.16)	$1,273.55	$0	($11,698.63)
199			10/1/2019	195	($11,698.63)	($73.12)	$1,281.51	$0	($12,980.13)
200			11/1/2019	196	($12,980.13)	($81.13)	$1,289.52	$0	($14,269.65)
201			12/1/2019	197	($14,269.65)	($89.19)	$1,297.58	$0	($15,567.22)
202			1/1/2020	198	($15,567.22)	($97.30)	$1,305.68	$0	($16,872.91)
203			2/1/2020	199	($16,872.91)	($105.46)	$1,313.85	$0	($18,186.75)
204			3/1/2020	200	($18,186.75)	($113.67)	$1,322.06	$0	($19,508.81)
205			4/1/2020	201	($19,508.81)	($121.93)	$1,330.32	$0	($20,839.13)

after 12/1/2018, the remaining balance on the loan appears as a negative value

Something is wrong. With the extra payment, the loan is paid off early, at the end of the 185th payment period; but starting with 12/1/2018, the payment schedule no longer makes sense. It appears that the client is still making payments on a loan that is already paid off.

The effect of this error is that the remaining balance and the interest payments appear as negative values after the loan is paid off. But remember, in cell B14, you calculated the sum of the interest payments to determine the observed cost of the mortgage. With those negative interest payment values included, that total will be wrong.

To correct this problem, you need to revise the PMT function that determines the monthly payment directed toward the principal. Currently, this function subtracts the interest due from the monthly mortgage payment to arrive at the amount of the principal payment. You need to use a function that decides which of the two following situations is true:

- The remaining balance is greater than the payment toward the principal.
- The remaining balance is less than the payment toward the principal.

A function that determines whether a condition is true or false is called a **logical function**. Excel supports several logical functions, which are described in Figure 2-19.

Figure 2-19	EXCEL'S LOGICAL FUNCTIONS
FUNCTION	**DESCRIPTION**
AND(*logical1*,[*logical2*], …)	Returns the value TRUE if all arguments are true; returns FALSE if one or more arguments is false
FALSE()	Returns the value FALSE
IF(*logical_test*,*value_if_true*,*value_if_false*)	Returns *value_if_true* if the *logical_test* argument is true; returns the *value_if_false* if the *logical_test* argument is false
NOT(*logical*)	Returns the value TRUE if *logical* is false; returns the value FALSE if *logical* is true
OR(*logical1*,[*logical2*], …)	Returns the value TRUE if at least one argument is true; returns FALSE if all arguments are false
TRUE()	Returns the value TRUE

In this loan workbook, you will be using an IF function. The syntax of the IF function is =IF(*logical_test*,*value_if_true*,*value_if_false*) where *logical_test* is an expression that is either true or false, *value_if_true* is an expression that Excel will run if the *logical_test* is true, and *value_if_false* is an expression that runs when the *logical_test* is false. The logical test is constructed using a comparison operator. A **comparison operator** checks whether two expressions are equal, whether one is greater than the other, and so forth. Figure 2-20 describes the six comparison operators supported by Excel.

Figure 2-20	COMPARISON OPERATORS	
OPERATOR	**EXAMPLE**	**DESCRIPTION**
=	A1=B1	Checks if the value in cell A1 equals the value in cell B1
>	A1>B1	Checks if the value in cell A1 is greater than B1
<	A1<B1	Checks if the value in cell A1 is less than B1
>=	A1>=B1	Checks if the value in cell A1 is greater than or equal to B1
<=	A1<=B1	Checks if the value in cell A1 is less than or equal to B1
<>	A1<>B1	Checks if the value in cell A1 is not equal to the value in cell B1

For example, the function =*IF(A1=10,20,30)* tests whether the value in cell A1 is equal to 10. If so, the function returns the value 20, otherwise the function returns the value 30. You can also use cell references in place of values.

The function =*IF(A1=10,B1,B2)* returns the value from cell B1 if A1 equals 10, otherwise the function returns the value stored in cell B2.

You can also make comparisons with text strings. When you do, the text strings must be enclosed in quotation marks. For example, the function =*IF(A1="RETAIL",B1,B2)* tests whether the text RETAIL has been entered into cell A1. If so, the function returns the value from cell B1, otherwise it returns the value from cell B2.

Because some functions are very complex, you might find it easier to enter a logical function, such as the IF function, using Excel's Insert Function option. You will use the Insert Function option to enter an IF function in the first row of the payment schedule.

To enter the IF function in the first row of the payment schedule:

1. Click cell **H5** in the payment schedule, and then press the **Delete** key to clear the cell contents.

2. Click the **Insert Function** button f_x on the Formula bar.

3. Click the **Or select a category** list arrow, and then click **Logical** in the list of categories displayed.

4. Click **IF** in the Select a Function list box, and then click the **OK** button to open the Function Arguments dialog box.

   First, you need to enter the logical test. The test is whether the remaining balance in cell F5 is greater than the usual amount of payment toward the principal, which is equal to the monthly loan payment ($B$9) minus the interest payment (G5). The logical test is therefore *F5>($B$9–G5)*.

5. In the Logical_test argument box, enter **F5>($B$9–G5)**, and then press the **Tab** key.

   If the logical test is true (in other words, if the remaining balance is greater than the principal payment), Excel should return the usual principal payment. In this case, that value is the expression *$B$9–G5*.

6. In the Value_if_true argument box, enter **$B$9–G5**, and then press the **Tab** key.

   If the logical test is false (which means that the balance remaining is *less* than the usual principal payment), the payment should be set equal to the remaining balance—which has the effect of paying off the loan. In this case, Excel should return the value in cell F5.

7. In the Value_if_false argument box, enter **F5**. Figure 2-21 shows the completed dialog box.

Figure 2-21	INSERTING THE IF FUNCTION

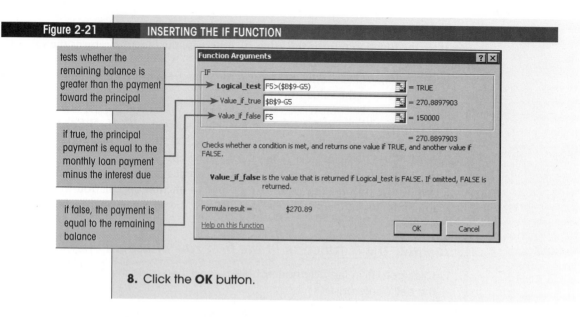

tests whether the remaining balance is greater than the payment toward the principal

if true, the principal payment is equal to the monthly loan payment minus the interest due

if false, the payment is equal to the remaining balance

8. Click the **OK** button.

Now copy this new formula into the rest of the payment schedule.

To fill in the rest of the payment schedule:

1. With cell H5 the active cell, click the fill handle and drag it down to cell **H244**.

2. Scroll up to row **190**. As shown in Figure 2-22, the payment schedule now accurately shows that once the remaining balance reaches $0, the interest payments and the payments toward the principal also become $0.

Figure 2-22	NEW PAYMENT VALUES

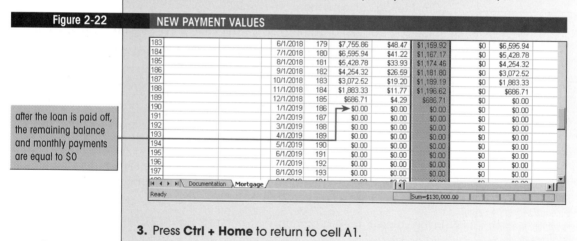

after the loan is paid off, the remaining balance and monthly payments are equal to $0

3. Press **Ctrl + Home** to return to cell A1.

Note that with the extra payment, the observed cost of the mortgage is $93,034.73. Thus, if a client were to make an extra payment of $20,000 on 1/1/2005, Carol could tell the client that there would be a savings of almost $47,000 over the history of the loan.

Making an extra payment or payments will greatly affect the number of payment periods. From the payment schedule, you can tell that the number of payment periods would be 185. The question is how can you include this information in the summary section at the top of the worksheet. To include the information, you will have to make the following change to the payment period values in column E of the payment schedule:

■ If the balance is greater than 0, the period number should be one higher than the previous period number.

■ If the balance is 0, set the period number to 0.

You'll make this change to the payment schedule now.

To add an IF function that adjusts the period numbers in case of extra payments:

1. Click cell **E6** to make it the active cell, and then press the **Delete** key.

2. Click the **Insert Function** button *fx* on the Formula toolbar.

3. Click **IF** in the Select a function list box, and then click the **OK** button.

   The logical test is whether the balance (in cell F6) is greater than $0 or not.

4. In the Logical_test argument box, enter **F6>0**, and then press the **Tab** key.

   If the logical test is true, the period number should be equal to the previous period number (E5) plus 1.

5. In the Value_if_true argument box, enter **E5+1**, and then press the **Tab** key.

   If the logical test is false, the balance is 0. Set the period number to 0.

6. In the Value_if_false argument box, type **0**, and then click the **OK** button.

7. Verify that E6 is still the active cell, and then click and drag the fill handle down to cell **E244**.

8. Scroll up the worksheet to row **190**. Note that once the loan is paid off, the period number is equal to 0. See Figure 2-23.

Figure 2-23	NEW PAYMENT PERIOD NUMBERS

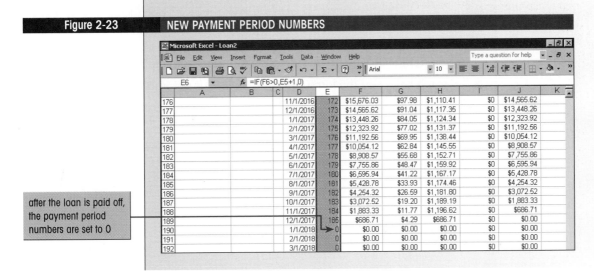

after the loan is paid off, the payment period numbers are set to 0

Using the AutoSum Button

Since the period numbers are all equal to zero after the loan is paid off, the last period number in the payment schedule will also be the largest. You can, therefore, use the MAX function to calculate the maximum, or last, payment period in the schedule. You can enter the MAX function either by typing the function directly into the active cell or by using the

Insert Function button on the Formula bar. However, Excel also provides the AutoSum button on the Standard toolbar to give you quick access to the SUM, AVERAGE, COUNT, MIN, and MAX functions. The AutoSum button can be a real timesaver, so you will use it in this situation.

To use the AutoSum button to calculate the maximum payment period:

1. Scroll to the top of the worksheet.

2. Click cell **A15**, type **Total Payments** and then press the **Tab** key.

3. Click the **list arrow** for the AutoSum button $\Sigma \ \cdot$ on the Standard toolbar to display a list of summary functions. See Figure 2-24.

Figure 2-24   **USING THE AUTOSUM BUTTON**

AutoSum button

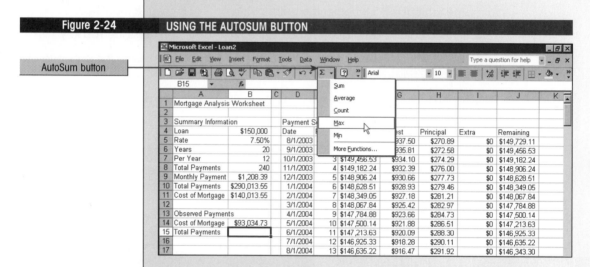

---

4. Click **Max** in the list, and then drag the pointer over the range **E5:E244** (the range containing the payment period numbers from the payment schedule).

5. Press the **Enter** key. The formula *=MAX(E5:E244)* is automatically entered into cell B15, and the value 185 appears in the cell.

Carol suggests you test the new payment schedule one more time. She asks what the effect would be if the extra payment on 1/1/2005 was increased from $20,000 to $25,000.

To test the new payment figures:

1. Click cell **I22**.

2. Type **$25,000** and then press the **Enter** key.

The cost of the mortgage decreases to $84,368.07 and the number of payments decreases to 174.

Using Excel's Date Functions

Excel stores dates as integers, where the integer values represent the number of days since January 1, 1900. For example, the integer value for the date January 1, 2008 is 39448 because that date is 39,448 days after January 1, 1900. Most of the time you do not see these values because Excel automatically formats the integers to appear as dates, such as 1/1/2008. This method of storing the dates allows you to work with dates in the same way you work with numbers. For example, if you subtract one date from another, the answer will be the number of days separating the two dates.

In addition to creating simple formulas with date values, you can use Excel's date functions to create dates or to extract information about date values. To insert the current date into your workbook, you could use the TODAY function, for example. To determine which day of the week a particular date falls on, you could use the WEEKDAY function. Note that the date functions use your computer's system clock to return a value. Figure 2-25 describes some of Excel's more commonly used date functions.

Figure 2-25	EXCEL'S DATE FUNCTIONS
FUNCTION	**DESCRIPTION**
DATE(*year, month, day*)	Returns the integer for the date represented by the *year, month,* and *day* arguments
DAY(*date*)	Extracts the day of the month from the *date* value
MONTH(*date*)	Extracts the month number from the *date* value, where January=1, February=2, and so forth
NOW(), TODAY()	Returns the integer for the current date and time
WEEKDAY(*date*)	Calculates the day of the week using the *date* value, where Sunday=1, Monday=2, and so forth
YEAR(*date*)	Extracts the year number from the *date* value

On the Documentation sheet, there is a cell for entering the current date. Rather than typing the date in manually, you will enter it using the TODAY function.

To use the TODAY function:

1. Click the **Documentation** tab to make it the active worksheet, and then click cell **B4**.

2. Click the **Insert Function** button f_x on the Formula bar.

3. Select **Date & Time** from the function category list.

4. Scroll down the list, click **TODAY**, and then click the **OK** button twice. Note that the second dialog box indicated that there are no arguments for the TODAY function. The current date is entered into cell B4 (your date will most likely be different). See Figure 2-26.

Figure 2-26	INSERTING THE CURRENT DATE

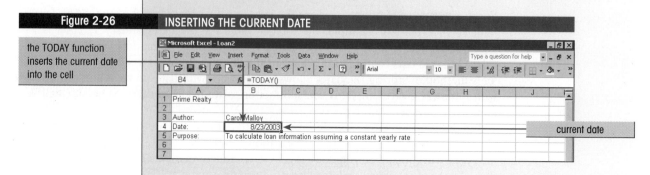

the TODAY function inserts the current date into the cell

current date

The TODAY and NOW functions will always display the current date and time. Thus, if you reopen this workbook on a different date, the date in cell B4 will be updated to reflect that change. If you want a permanent date (that might reflect when the workbook was initially developed), you enter the date directly into the cell without using a function.

You have completed your work on the Loan workbook. Carol will examine the workbook and get back to you with more assignments. For now, you can close Excel and save your work.

To save your work:

1. Click **File** on the menu bar, and then click **Exit**.

2. Click the **Yes** button when prompted to save your changes.

Session 2.2 QUICK | CHECK

1. Describe how you would create a series of odd numbers from 1 to 99 in column A of your worksheet.

2. Describe how you would create a series of yearly dates, ranging from 1/1/2003 to 1/1/2030, in column A of your worksheet.

3. What function would you enter to return the text string "Yes" if cell A1 is greater than cell B1 and "No" if cell A1 is not greater than cell B1?

4. Describe three ways of entering the SUM function into a worksheet cell.

5. Which function would you enter to extract the year value from the date entered into cell A1?

6. Which function would you enter to display the current date in the worksheet?

7. Which function would you enter to determine which day of the week a date entered into cell A1 falls on?

REVIEW ASSIGNMENTS

Carol has another workbook for you to examine. Although the loan workbook was helpful, Carol realizes that most of the time she will be working with clients who can make only a specified monthly payment. She wants to have a workbook in which she enters a specific monthly payment and from that amount determine how large a mortgage her client can afford.

To determine this information, you will use the PV function: PV(*rate*,*nper*,*pmt*,[*fv*=0],[*type*=0]) where *rate* is the interest per period, *nper* is the number of payment periods, *pmt* is the monthly payment, *fv* is the future value of the loan (assumed to be 0), and *type* specifies when the loan will be paid (assumed to be 0 at the beginning of each payment period). For a loan, the *pmt* argument must be a negative number since it represents an expense and not income. The PV function then returns the present value of the loan or annuity. In Carol's workbook, the return would be the largest mortgage her clients can afford for a given monthly payment.

As with the previous workbook, Carol wants this new workbook to contain a payment schedule. The current annual interest rate is 7.5% compounded monthly. Carol wants the payment schedule to assume a 20-year mortgage with a monthly payment of $950. What is the largest mortgage her clients could get under those conditions, and how much would the interest payments total?

To complete this task:

1. Start Excel and open the **Mort1** workbook located in the Tutorial.02/Review folder on your Data Disk.

2. Save the workbook as **Mort2** in the same folder.

3. Enter your name and the current date in the Documentation sheet (use a function to automatically insert the date). Switch to the Mortgage worksheet.

4. Enter "$950" for the monthly payment in cell B4, "7.5%" as the interest rate in cell B5, "20" as the number of years, and "12" as the number of periods per year.

5. Enter a formula in cell B8 to calculate the total number of payments over the history of the loan.

Explore 6. In cell B10, use the PV function to calculate the largest mortgage a client could receive under those conditions. Remember that you need to make the monthly payment, which appears in cell B4, a negative, so the return is a positive number.

7. Complete the first row of the payment schedule, with the following formulas:

   ■ The initial value of the payment period should be equal to 1.

   ■ The initial balance should be equal to the amount of the mortgage.

   ■ The interest due should be equal to the balance multiplied by the interest rate per period.

   ■ Use the IF function to test whether the balance is greater than the monthly payment minus the interest due. If so, the principal payment should be equal to the monthly payment minus the interest due. If not, the principal payment should be equal to the balance.

   ■ Set the extra payment value to $0.

   ■ The remaining balance should be equal to the initial balance minus the principal payment and any extra payment.

8. Complete the second row of the payment schedule with the following formulas:

   ■ Carry the remaining balance from cell J3 into the current balance in cell F4.

   ■ If the current balance is equal to 0, set the period number to 0, otherwise set the period number equal to cell E3 plus 1.

   ■ Copy the formulas in the range G3:J3 to the range G4:J4.

9. Select the range E4:J4 and then drag the fill handle down to fill range E242:J242. What happens to the values in the Extra column when you release the mouse button?

Explore 10. Click the Auto Fill Options button next to the filled in values. Which option button is selected? Does this help you understand what happened in the previous step? Click the Copy Cells option button to fix the problem.

11. In cell D3, enter the initial date of the loan as "4/1/2003".

12. Payments are due at the beginning of each month. Fill in the rest of the payment dates in the range D3:D242 using the appropriate Auto Fill option.

13. In cell B11, enter the cost of the mortgage, which is equal to the sum of the interest payments in the payment schedule.

14. In cell B12, enter the number of observed payments, which is equal to the maximum payment period number in the payment schedule.

Explore   15. If a client pays an extra $100 for each period of the first five years of the loan, what is the cost of the mortgage and how many months will it take to pay off the loan? On what date will the loan be paid?

16. Print the entire Mort2 workbook.

17. Save and close the workbook, and then exit Excel.

CASE PROBLEMS

Case 1. Setting Up a College Fund   Lynn and Peter Chao have recently celebrated the birth of their first daughter. The couple is acutely aware of how expensive a college education is. Although the couple does not have much money, they realize that if they start saving now, they can hopefully save a nice sum for their daughter's education. They have asked you for help in setting up a college fund for their daughter.

The couple has set a goal of saving $75,000 that they will use in 18 years for college. Current annual interest rates for such funds are 6.5% compounded monthly. Lynn and Peter want you to determine how much money they would have to set aside each month to reach their goal. They would also like you to create a schedule so they can see how fast their savings will grow over the next few years.

You can calculate how fast monthly contributions to a savings account will grow using the same financial functions used to determine how fast monthly payments can pay back a loan. In this case, the present value is equal to 0 (since the couple is starting out with no savings in the college fund) and the future value is $75,000 (the amount that the couple wants to have saved after 18 years.)

To complete this task:

1. Open the **School1** workbook located in the Tutorial.02/Cases folder on your Data Disk, and then save the workbook as **School2** in the same folder.

2. Enter your name and the current date in the Documentation sheet. Switch to the College Fund worksheet.

3. Enter the Chaos' saving goal in cell B3 and the assumed annual interest rate in cell B4. Enter the number of years they plan to save in cell B5 and the number of payments per year in cell B6.

4. Enter a formula to calculate the total number of payments in cell B7.

Explore   5. In cell B9, use the PMT function to calculate the monthly payment required for the Chaos to meet their savings goal. Express your answer as a positive value rather than a negative value.

6. Begin filling out the savings schedule. In the first row, enter the following information:
   - The initial date is 1/1/2003.
   - The payment period is 1.
   - The starting balance is equal to the first monthly payment.

   Explore
   - Calculate the accrued interest using the IPMT function, assuming that payments are made at the beginning of each month. (*Hint*: Scroll the IPMT arguments list to display all the necessary arguments.)
   - Calculate the ending balance, which is equal to the starting balance plus the interest accrued in the current month.

7. Enter the second row of the table, using the following guidelines:
   - The date is one month later than the previous date.
   - The payment period is 2.
   - The starting balance is equal to the previous month's ending balance plus the monthly payment.
   - Use the IPMT function to calculate the interest for the second payment period.
   - The ending balance is once again equal to the starting balance plus the accrued interest.

8. Use the fill handle to fill in the remaining 214 months of the savings schedule. Choose the appropriate fill options to ensure that the values in the dates and the period and interest values fill in correctly.

9. Save your changes.

10. Print a copy of the College Fund worksheet, and then indicate on the printout how much the couple will have to save each month to reach their savings goal.

11. Save and close the workbook, and then exit Excel.

Case 2. Payroll Information at Sonic Sounds Jeff Gwydion manages the payroll at Sonic Sounds. He has asked you for help in setting up a worksheet to store payroll values. The payroll contains three elements: the employee's salary, the 401(k) contribution, and the employee's health insurance cost. The company's 401(k) contribution is 3% of the employee's salary for employees who have worked for the company at least one year; otherwise the company's contribution is zero. Sonic Sounds also supports two health insurance plans: Premier and Standard. The cost of the Premier plan is $6,500, and the cost of the Standard plan is $5,500.

The workbook has already been set up for you. Your job is to enter the functions and formulas to calculate the 401(k) contributions and health insurance costs for each employee.

To complete this task:

1. Open the **Sonic1** workbook located in the Tutorial.02/Cases folder on your Data Disk, and save the workbook as **Sonic2** in the same folder.

2. Enter your name and the current date (calculated using a function) in the Documentation sheet. Switch to the Payroll worksheet.

3. In cell C13, determine the number of years the employee Abbot has been employed by subtracting the date Abbot was hired from the current date and then dividing the difference by 365.

4. Use the fill handle to compute the years employed for the rest of the employees.

Explore

5. Use an IF function to compute the 401(k) contribution for each employee (*Note*: Remember that an employee must have worked at Sonic for at least one year to be eligible for the 401(k) contribution.)

Explore

6. Use an IF function to calculate the health insurance cost for each employee at the company. (*Hint*: Test whether the employee's health plan listed in column E is equal to the value in cell B4. If so, the employee is using the Premier plan, and the health cost is equal to the value in cell C4. If not, the employee is using the Standard plan, and the health cost is equal to the value in cell C5.)

7. Calculate the total salaries, total 401(k) contributions, and total health insurance expenses for all of the employees at Sonic Sounds. Place the functions in the range B7:B9.

8. Print the contents of the **Sonic2** workbook.

9. Redo the analysis, assuming that the cost of the Premier plan has risen to $7,000 and the cost of the Standard plan has risen to $6,100. What is the total health insurance cost to the company's employees?

10. Print just the Payroll sheet.

11. Save and close the workbook, and then exit Excel.

Case 3. Depreciation at Leland Hospital Leland Hospital in Leland, Ohio, has purchased a new x-ray machine for its operating room. Debra Sanchez in purchasing wants your assistance in calculating the yearly depreciation of the machine. **Depreciation** is the declining value of an asset over its lifetime. To calculate the depreciation, you need the initial cost of the asset, the number of years or periods that the asset will be used, and the final or salvage value of the asset. The new x-ray machine costs $450,000. The hospital expects that the x-ray machine will be used for 10 years and that at the end of the 10-year period the salvage value will be $50,000. Debra wants you to calculate the depreciation of the machine for each year in that 10-year period.

Accountants use several different methods to calculate depreciation. The difference between each method lies in how fast the asset declines in value. Figure 2-27 describes four Excel functions that you can use to calculate depreciation.

Figure 2-27	EXCEL'S DEPRECIATION FUNCTIONS	
METHOD	**FUNCTION**	**DESCRIPTION**
Straight-line	SLN(*cost, salvage, life*)	The straight-line method distributes the depreciation evenly over the life of the asset, so that the depreciation is the same in each period. The argument *cost* is the cost of the asset, *salvage* is the salvage value at the end of the life of the asset, and *life* is the number of periods that the asset is being depreciated.
Sum-of-years	SYD(*cost, salvage, life, per*)	The sum-of-years method concentrates the most depreciation in the earliest periods of the lifetime of the asset. The argument *per* is the period that you want to calculate the depreciation for.
Fixed-declining balance	DB(*cost, salvage, life, period,* [*month=12*])	The fixed-declining balance method is an accelerated depreciation method in which the highest depreciation occurs in the earliest periods. The argument *month* is an optional argument that specifies the number of months in the first year (assumed to be 12).
Double-declining balance	DDB(*cost, salvage, life, period,* [*factor=2*])	The double-declining balance method is an accelerated method in which the highest depreciation occurs in the earliest periods. The optional *factor* argument controls that rate at which the balance declines.

Debra wants you to calculate the depreciation using all four methods so that she can see the impact on each method on the asset's value. She has already created the workbook containing the basic figures; she needs you to add the formulas.

To complete this task:

1. Open the **Leland1** workbook located in the Tutorial.02/Cases folder on your Data Disk and save the workbook as **Leland2** in the same folder.

2. Enter your name and the current date (calculated using a function) in the Documentation sheet. Switch to the Depreciation worksheet.

3. Enter the cost of the x-ray machine in cell B3, the lifetime of the machine in cell B4, and the salvage value in B5.

Explore ▷ 4. In the range B9:B18, enter the depreciation of the x-ray machine using the straight-line method.

5. In the range C9:C18, enter the yearly value of the machine after the depreciation is applied (*Hint*: After the first year, you must subtract the yearly depreciation from the previous year's value).

Explore ▷ 6. In the range F9:F18, enter the depreciation using the sum-of-years method.

7. In the range G9:G18, calculate the yearly value of the machine after the sum-of-years depreciation.

Explore ▷ 8. In the range B22:B31, calculate the fixed-declining depreciation for each year.

9. In the range C22:C31, calculate the value of the x-ray machine after applying the fixed-declining depreciation.

Explore   10. In the range F22:F31, calculate the double-declining depreciation for each year.

11. In the range G22:G31, calculate the yearly value of the x-ray machine after applying the double-declining depreciation.

12. Print the entire workbook.

13. Save and close the workbook, and then exit Excel.

Case 4. Analyzing Faculty Salaries at Glenmore Junior College A complaint has been raised at Glenmore Junior College, a liberal arts college in upstate New York, that female faculty members are being paid less than their male counterparts. Professor Lawton, a member of the faculty senate, has asked you to compile basic statistics on faculty salaries, broken down by gender. The current salary figures are shown in Figure 2-28.

Figure 2-28	FACULTY SALARIES

MALE FACULTY	MALE FACULTY	MALE FACULTY	FEMALE FACULTY	FEMALE FACULTY
$40,000	$55,000	$75,000	$25,000	$60,000
$45,000	$55,000	$75,000	$30,000	$60,000
$45,000	$60,000	$75,000	$35,000	$60,000
$45,000	$60,000	$75,000	$40,000	$60,000
$45,000	$60,000	$80,000	$42,000	$62,000
$45,000	$62,000	$85,000	$45,000	$62,000
$45,000	$62,000	$95,000	$47,000	$65,000
$50,000	$65,000	$115,000	$50,000	$65,000
$50,000	$65,000		$55,000	$67,000
$52,000	$65,000		$55,000	$70,000
$55,000	$70,000		$57,000	$75,000

To complete this task:

1. Create a new workbook named **JrCol** and store it in the Tutorial.02/Cases folder on your Data Disk.

2. Insert a Documentation sheet into the workbook containing your name, the current date (calculated using a function), and the purpose of the workbook.

3. Rename Sheet1 as "Statistical Analysis" and delete any unused worksheets.

4. In the Statistical Analysis worksheet, enter the male and female faculty salaries in two separate columns labeled "Male Faculty" and "Female Faculty."

Explore

5. Use Excel's statistical functions to create a table of the following statistics for all faculty members, male faculty members, and female faculty members:

  ■ the count

  ■ the sum of the salaries

  ■ the average salary

  ■ the median salary

  ■ the minimum salary

  ■ the maximum salary

  ■ the range of salary values (maximum minus minimum)

  ■ the standard deviation of the salary values

  ■ the standard error of the salary values (the standard deviation divided by the square root of the number of salaries)

6. Compare the average male salary to the average female salary. Is there evidence that the female faculty members are paid significantly less?

7. Average values can sometimes be skewed by high values. Compare the median male salary to the median female salary. Is the evidence supporting the complaint stronger or weaker using the median salary figures?

Explore

8. Select the cell range containing the statistics you calculated, and then print only that selected range.

9. Save and close the workbook, and then exit Excel.

INTERNET ASSIGNMENTS

Student Union

The purpose of the Internet Assignments is to challenge you to find information on the Internet that you can use to create effective spreadsheets. The actual assignments are updated and maintained on the Course Technology Web site. Log on to the Internet and use your Web browser to go to the Student Union on the New Perspectives Series site at **www.course.com/NewPerspectives/studentunion**. Click the Online Companions link, and then click the link for this text.

QUICK CHECK ANSWERS

Session 2.1

  1. =MIN(B1:B50)

  2. =MAX(B1:50)/MIN(B1:B50)

  3. =PMT(0.07/4,20,10000)

  4. =IPMT(0.07/4,2,20,10000)

  5. absolute reference

  6. =B2+C2

  7. =$A2+C$1; if moved, the formula would stay the same, =$A1+B$1

Session 2.2

1. Enter the values *1* and *3* in the first two rows of column A. Select the two cells and then drag the fill handle down to complete the rest of the series.

2. Enter *1/1/2003* in the first cell. Select the first cell and then drag the fill handle down 27 rows. Click the Auto Fill Options button, and then click the Fill Years option button.

3. =IF(A1>B1,"Yes","No")

4. Type the SUM function directly into the cell while in edit mode, using the Insert Function button on the Formula bar or using the AutoSum button on the Standard toolbar.

5. =YEAR(A1)

6. =TODAY()

7. =WEEKDAY(A1)

In this tutorial you will:

- Format data using different fonts, sizes, and font styles

- Align cell contents

- Add cell borders and backgrounds

- Merge cells and hide rows and columns

- Format the worksheet background and sheet tabs

- Find and replace formats within a worksheet

- Create and apply styles

- Apply an AutoFormat to a table

- Format a printout using Print Preview

- Create a header and footer for a printed worksheet

- Define a print area and add a page break to a printed worksheet

DEVELOPING A PROFESSIONAL-LOOKING WORKSHEET

Formatting a Sales Report

CASE

NewGeneration Monitors

NewGeneration Monitors is a computer equipment company that specializes in computer monitors. Joan Sanchez has been entering sales data on three of the company's monitors into an Excel workbook. She plans on including the sales data in a report to be presented later in the week. Joan has made no attempt to make this data presentable to her coworkers. She has simply entered the numbers. She needs you to transform her raw figures into a presentable report.

To create a professional-looking document, you will learn how to work with Excel's formatting tools to modify the appearance of the data in each cell, the cell itself, and the entire worksheet. You will also learn how to format printouts that Joan wants to generate based on her workbook. You will learn how to create headers and footers, and control which parts of the worksheet are printed on which pages.

SESSION 3.1

In this session, you will format the contents of individual cells in your worksheet by modifying the font used in the cell or by changing the font size or style. You will also use color in your worksheet, modifying the background color of worksheet cells as well as the color of the text in a cell. You will also have an opportunity to examine various Excel commands that you can use to control text alignment and to wrap a line of text within a single cell. Finally, you will create borders around individual cells and cell ranges.

Formatting Worksheet Data

The data for Joan's sales report has already been stored in an Excel workbook. Before going further, open the workbook and save it with a new filename.

To open the Sales report workbook:

1. Start Excel, and open the **Sales1** workbook located in the Tutorial.03/Tutorial folder on your Data Disk.

2. On the Documentation worksheet, enter your name in cell B3, and enter the current date in cell B4.

3. Save the workbook as **Sales2** in the Tutorial.03/Tutorial folder on your Data Disk.

4. Click the **Sales** tab. Figure 3-1 shows the current appearance of the sales report, which is unformatted.

Figure 3-1   **THE UNFORMATTED SALES WORKSHEET**

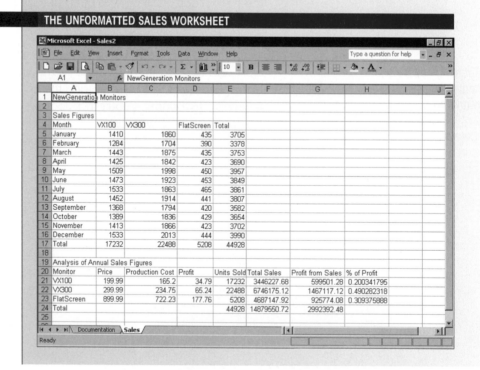

The Sales worksheet contains two tables. The first table displays the monthly sales for three of NewGeneration's monitors: the VX100, VX300, and the FlatScreen. The second table presents an analysis of these sales figures, showing the profit from the monitor sales and the percentage that each monitor contributes to the overall profit. In its current state, the worksheet is difficult to read and interpret. This is a problem that Joan wants you to solve by using Excel's formatting tools.

Formatting is the process of changing the appearance of your workbook. A properly formatted workbook can be easier to read, appear more professional, and help draw attention to important points you want to make. Formatting changes only the appearance of the data; formatting does not affect the data itself. For example, if a cell contains the value 0.124168, and you format the cell to display only up to the thousandths place (for example, 0.124), the cell still contains the precise value, even though you cannot see it displayed in the worksheet.

Up to now, Excel has been automatically formatting your cell entries using a formatting style called the General format. The **General format** aligns numbers with the right edge of the cell without dollar signs or commas, uses the minus sign for negative values, and truncates any trailing zeros to the right of the decimal point. For more control over your data's appearance, you can choose from a wide variety of other number formats. Formats can be applied using either the Formatting toolbar or the Format menu from Excel's menu bar. Formats can also be copied from one cell to another, giving you the ability to apply a common format to different cells in your worksheet.

Using the Formatting Toolbar

The Formatting toolbar is the fastest way to format your worksheet. By clicking a single button on the Formatting toolbar you can increase or decrease the number of decimal places displayed in a selected range of cells, display a value as a currency or percentage, or change the color or size of the font used in a cell.

When Joan typed in the monthly sales figures for the three monitors, she neglected to include a comma to separate the thousands from the hundreds and so forth. Rather than retype these values, you can use the Comma Style button on the Formatting toolbar to format the values with a comma. You can use the Increase Decimal or Decrease Decimal button on the Formatting toolbar to change the number of decimal places displayed in a number.

To apply the Comma format and adjust the number of decimal places displayed:

1. Select the range **B5:E17** in the Sales worksheet.

2. Click the **Comma Style** button on the Formatting toolbar. Excel adds the comma separator to each of the values in the table and displays the values with two digits to the right of the decimal point.

   TROUBLE? If you do not see the Comma Style button on the Formatting toolbar, click the Toolbar Options button on the Formatting toolbar, and then click .

   TROUBLE? If the Standard and Formatting toolbars appear on separate rows on your computer, then the Toolbar Options button might look slightly different from the Toolbar Options button used throughout this text. If you are unsure about the function of a toolbar button, hover the pointer over the button to display its name.

   Because all of the sales figures are whole numbers, you will remove the zeros.

3. Click the **Decrease Decimal** button on the Formatting toolbar twice to remove the zeros. See Figure 3-2.

Figure 3-2	APPLYING THE COMMA STYLE TO THE SALES FIGURES

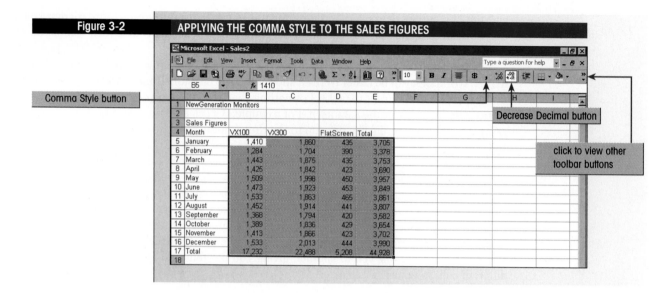

Joan's worksheet also displays the price and production cost of each monitor as well as last year's total sales and profit. She wants this information displayed using dollar signs, commas, and two decimal places. To format the values with these attributes, you can apply the Currency style.

To apply the Currency format:

1. Select the nonadjacent range **B21:D23;F21:G24**.

   TROUBLE? To select a nonadjacent range, select the first range, press and hold the Ctrl key, and then select the next range.

2. Click the **Currency Style** button $ on the Formatting toolbar. Excel adds the dollar signs and commas to the currency values and displays each value (price) to two decimal places. See Figure 3-3.

Figure 3-3	APPLYING THE CURRENCY STYLE

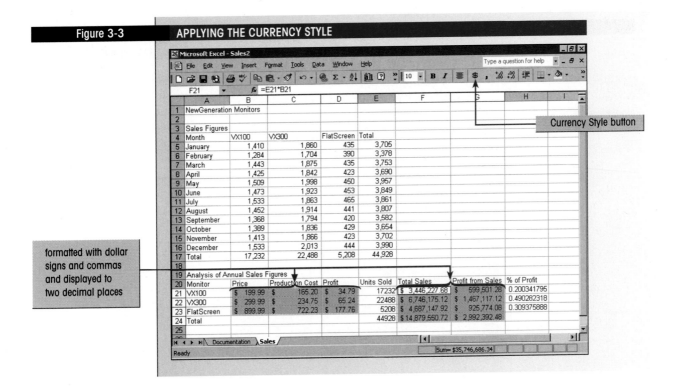

formatted with dollar signs and commas and displayed to two decimal places

Finally, the range H21:H23 displays the percentage that each monitor contributes to the overall profit from sales. Joan wants these values displayed with a percent sign and to two decimal places. You will apply the Percent format; however, Excel, by default, does not display any decimal places with the Percent format. You need to increase the number of decimal places displayed.

To apply the Percent format and increase the number of decimal places:

1. Select the range **H21:H23**.

2. Click the **Percent Style** button 🔲 on the Formatting toolbar.

3. Click the **Increase Decimal** button 🔲 on the Formatting toolbar twice to display the percentages to two decimal places. See Figure 3-4.

Figure 3-4   **APPLYING THE PERCENT STYLE**

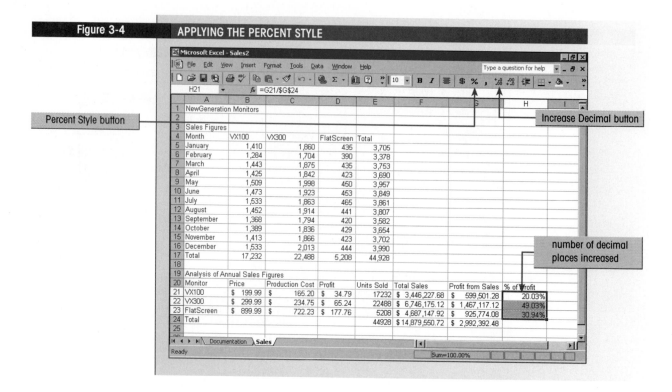

By displaying the percent values using the Percent format, you can quickly see that one monitor, the VX300, accounts for almost half of the profit from monitor sales.

Copying Formats

As you look over the sales figures, you see that one area of the worksheet still needs to be formatted. The Units Sold column in the range E21:E24 still does not display the comma separator you used in the sales figures table. To fix a formatting problem like this one, you can use one of the methods that Excel provides for copying a format from one location to another.

One of these methods is the Format Painter button located on the Standard toolbar. When you use the Format Painter option, you "paint" a format from one cell to another cell or to a range of cells. You can also use the fill handle and its Auto Fill options to copy a format from one cell to another. Another method for copying a format is using the Copy and Paste commands, which are available on both the Standard toolbar and the Edit menu. The Copy and Paste method requires you to click the Formatting Only option button that appears when you paste the selected cell, so that only the formatting of the pasted cell, not its content, is applied. Using the Format Painter button does all of this in fewer steps.

You will use the Format Painter button to copy the format used in the sales figures table and to paste that format into the range E21:E24.

To copy the format using the Format Painter button:

1. Select cell **B5**, which contains the formatting that you want to copy. You do not have to copy the entire range, because the range is formatted in the same way.

2. Click the **Format Painter** button 🖌 on the Standard toolbar.

As you move the pointer over the worksheet area, the pointer changes to 🔂🖌.

> **TROUBLE?** If you do not see the Format Painter button, click the Toolbar Options button ⁝ on the Standard toolbar, and then click ◊.
>
> 3. Select the range **E21:E23**. The format that you used in the sales figures table is applied to the cells in the range E21:E23.

You have not applied the format to cell E24 yet. Rather than using the Format Painter button again, you can drag the fill handle down over the cell. Recall that you can use the fill handle to copy formulas and values from one range into another. You can also use the fill handle to copy formats.

> ### To copy the format using the fill handle:
>
> 1. Click and drag the fill handle down to the range **E21:E24**.
>
>   When you release the mouse button, the word "Price" appears. This occurs because the default action of the fill handle in this case is to fill the values in the range E21:E23 into cell E24. You'll override this default behavior by choosing a different option from the list of Auto Fill options.
>
> 2. Click the **Auto Fill Options** button located at the lower-right corner of the selected range.
>
> 3. Click the **Fill Formatting Only** option button. Excel extends the format from the range E21:E23 into cell E24.

The Formatting toolbar is a fast and easy way to copy and apply cell formats, but there are other ways of formatting your data.

Using the Format Cells Dialog Box

Joan stops by to view your progress. She agrees that formatting the values has made the worksheet easier to read, but she has a few suggestions. She does not like the way the currency values are displayed with the dollar signs ($) placed at the left edge of the cell, leaving a large blank space between the dollar sign and the numbers. She would like to have the dollar sign placed directly to the left of the dollar amounts, leaving no blank spaces.

The convenience of the Formatting toolbar's one-click access to many of the formatting tasks you will want to perform does have its limits. As you can see in the worksheet, when you use the Formatting toolbar, you cannot specify how the format is applied. To make the change that Joan suggests, you need to open the Format Cells dialog box, which gives you more control over the formatting.

> ### To open the Format Cells dialog box:
>
> 1. Select the nonadjacent range **B21:D23;F21:G24**.
>
> 2. Click **Format** on the menu bar, and then click **Cells**. The Format Cells dialog box opens. See Figure 3-5.

Figure 3-5 FORMAT CELLS DIALOG BOX

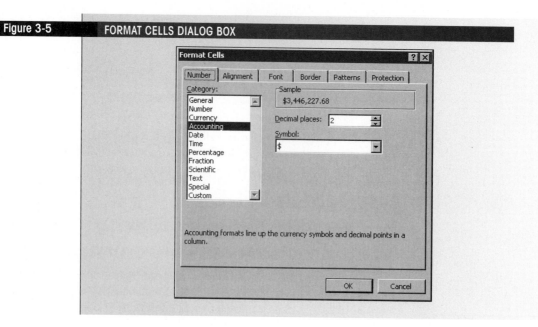

The Format Cells dialog box contains the following six tabs, each dedicated to a different set of format properties:

- **Number**—used to format the appearance of text and values within selected cells
- **Alignment**—used to control how text and values are aligned within a cell
- **Font**—used to choose the font type, size, and style
- **Border**—used to create borders around selected cells
- **Patterns**—used to create and apply background colors and patterns for selected cells
- **Protection**—used to lock or hide selected cells, preventing other users from modifying the cells' contents

So far, you have worked with number formats only. Excel supports several categories of number formats, ranging from Accounting and Currency formats to Scientific formats that might be used for recording engineering data. Figure 3-6 describes some of the number format categories.

Figure 3-6 NUMBER FORMAT CATEGORIES

CATEGORY	DESCRIPTION
General	Default format; numbers are displayed without dollar signs, commas, or trailing decimal places
Number	Used for a general display of numbers
Currency, Accounting	Used for displaying monetary values; use Accounting formats to align decimal points within a column
Date, Time	Used for displaying date and time values
Percentage	Used for displaying decimal values as percentages
Fraction, Scientific	Used for displaying values as fractions or in scientific notation
Text	Used for displaying values as text strings
Special	Used for displaying zip codes, phone numbers, and social security numbers

As shown in Figure 3-5, Excel applied an Accounting format, displaying the dollar sign and two decimal places, to the sales figures. The Accounting format differs from the Currency format; the Accounting format lines up the decimal points and the dollar signs for values within a column so that all the dollar signs appear at the left edge of the cell border. To align the dollar signs closer to the numbers, you can change the format to the Currency format.

To apply the Currency format:

1. On the Number tab, click **Currency** in the Category list box.

   As shown in the Negative numbers list box, Excel displays negative currency values either with a minus sign (-) or with a combination of a red font and parentheses. Joan wants any negative currency values to be displayed with a minus sign.

2. Click the first entry in the Negative numbers list box.

3. Click the **OK** button. Excel changes the format of the currency values, removing the blank spaces between the dollar signs and the currency values, rather than having the dollar signs lined up within each column.

By using the Format Cells dialog box, you can control the formatting to ensure that text and values are displayed the way you want them to be.

Working **with Fonts and Colors**

A **font** is the design applied to characters, letters, and punctuation marks. Each font is identified by a **font name** (or **typeface**). Some of the more commonly used fonts are Arial, Times Roman, and Courier. Each font can be displayed using one of the following styles: regular, italic, bold, or bold italic. Fonts can also be displayed with special effects, such as strikeout, underline, and color.

Fonts can also be rendered in different sizes. Sizes are measured using "points." By default, Excel displays characters using a 10-point Arial font in a regular style. To change the font used in a selected cell, you either click the appropriate buttons on the Formatting toolbar or select options in the Format Cells dialog box.

In the logo that the company uses on all its correspondence and advertising materials, the name "NewGeneration Monitors" appears in a large Times New Roman font. Joan wants you to modify the title in cell A1 to reflect this company-wide format.

To change the font and font size of the title:

1. Click cell **A1** to make it the active cell.

2. Click the **list arrow** for the Font button ⎡Arial   ▾⎤ on the Formatting toolbar, scroll down the list of available fonts, and then click **Times New Roman**.

   TROUBLE? If you do not have the Times New Roman font installed on your computer, choose a different Times Roman font or choose MS Serif in the list.

3. Click the **list arrow** for the Font Size button ⎡10 ▾⎤ on the Formatting toolbar, and then click **18**. Figure 3-7 shows the revised format for the title in cell A1.

Figure 3-7	CHANGING THE FONT AND FONT SIZE

Times New Roman font, 18 point

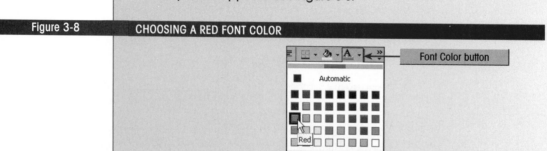

Joan wants the column titles of both tables displayed in bold font and the word "Total" in both tables displayed in italics. To make these modifications, you will again use the Formatting toolbar.

To apply the bold and italic styles:

1. Select the nonadjacent range **A4:E4;A20:H20**.

2. Click the **Bold** button **B** on the Formatting toolbar. The titles in the two tables now appear in a boldface font.

3. Select cell **A17**, press and hold the **Ctrl** key, and then click cell **A24**.

4. Click the **Italic** button **I** on the Formatting toolbar. The word "Total" in cells A17 and A24 is now italicized.

Joan points out that NewGeneration's logo usually appears in a red font. Color is another one of Excel's formatting tools. Excel allows you to choose a text color from a palette of 40 different colors. If the color you want is not listed, you can modify Excel's color configuration to create a different color palette. Excel's default color settings will work for most situations, so in this case you will not modify Excel's color settings.

To change the font color of the title to red:

1. Click cell **A1** to make it the active cell.

2. Click the **list arrow** for the Font Color button **A** on the Formatting toolbar. A color palette appears. See Figure 3-8.

Figure 3-8	CHOOSING A RED FONT COLOR

Font Color button

Automatic

Red

3. In the color palette, click the **Red** square (third row, first column). Excel changes the color of the font in cell A1 to red. See Figure 3-9.

Figure 3-9 **CHANGING FONT COLOR**

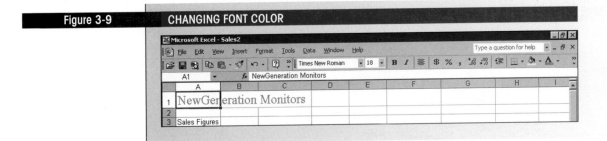

Aligning Cell Contents

When you enter numbers and formulas into a cell, Excel automatically aligns them with the cell's right edge and bottom border. Text entries are aligned with the left edge and bottom border. The default Excel alignment does not always create the most readable worksheets. As a general rule, you should center column titles, format columns of numbers so that the decimal places are lined up within a column, and align text with the left edge of the cell. You can change alignment using the alignment tools on the Formatting toolbar or the options on the Alignment tab in the Format Cells dialog box.

Joan wants the column titles centered above the values in each column.

To center the column titles using the Formatting toolbar:

1. Select the nonadjacent range **B4:E4;B20:H20**.

2. Click the **Center** button ▤ on the Formatting toolbar. Excel centers the text in the selected cells in each column.

The Formatting toolbar also provides the Align Left button and the Align Right button so that you can left- and right-align cell contents. If you want to align the cell's contents vertically, you have to open the Format Cells dialog box and choose the vertical alignment options on the Alignment tab.

Another alignment option available in the Format Cells dialog box is the Merge and Center option, which centers the text in one cell across a range of cells. Joan wants the company logo to be centered at the top of the worksheet. In other words, she wants the contents of cell A1 to be centered across the range A1:H1.

To center the text across the range A1:H1:

1. Select the range **A1:H1**.

2. Click **Format** on the menu bar, and then click **Cells**.

3. Click the **Alignment** tab.

4. Click the **Horizontal** list arrow in the Text alignment pane, and then click **Center Across Selection**. See Figure 3-10.

Figure 3-10 | **ALIGNMENT TAB**

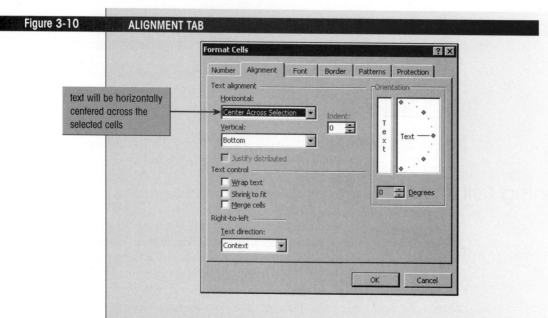

5. Click the **OK** button. See Figure 3-11.

Figure 3-11 | **CENTERING TEXT WITHIN CELLS AND ACROSS COLUMNS**

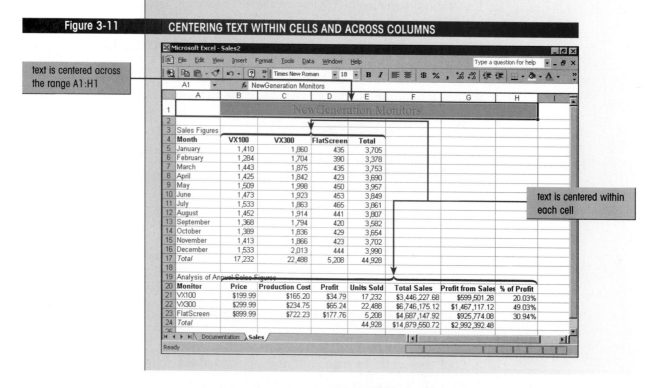

Indenting and Wrapping Text

Sometimes you will want a cell's contents offset, or indented, a few spaces from the cell's edge. This is particularly true for text entries that are aligned with the left edge of the cell. Indenting is often used for cell entries that are considered "subsections" of your worksheet. In the sales figures table, Joan wants you to indent the names of the months in the range A5:A16 and the monitor titles in the range A21:A23.

To indent the months and monitor titles:

1. Select the nonadjacent range **A5:A16;A21:A23**.

2. Click the **Increase Indent** button ![button] on the Formatting toolbar. Excel shifts the contents of the selected cells to the right.

   TROUBLE? You may have to click the Toolbar Options button ![button], and then choose the Add or Remove Buttons option before you can click the Increase Indent button. As you use more buttons on the Formatting toolbar, they are added to the toolbar. If your Standard and Formatting toolbars now appear on separate rows, that is okay. The rest of the figures in this book might not look exactly like your screen, but this will not affect your work.

Clicking the Increase Indent button increases the amount of indentation by roughly one character. To decrease or remove an indentation, click the Decrease Indent button or modify the indent value using the Format Cells dialog box.

If you enter text that is too wide for a cell, Excel either extends the text into the adjoining cells (if the cells are empty) or truncates the display of the text. You can also have Excel wrap the text within the cell so that the excess text is displayed on additional lines within the cell. To wrap text, you use the Format Cells dialog box.

Joan notes that some of the column titles in the second table are long. For example, the "Production Cost" label in cell C20 is much longer than the values below it. This formatting has caused some of the columns to be wider than they need to be. Joan suggests that you wrap the text within the column titles and then reduce the width of the columns.

To wrap the title text within a cell and reduce the column widths:

1. Select the cell range **A20:H20**.

2. Click **Format** on the menu bar, and then click **Cells**.

3. Click the **Wrap text** check box in the Text control pane.

4. Click the **OK** button. The text in cells C20 and G20 now appears on two rows within the cells.

5. Reduce the width of column **C** to about **10** characters.

6. Reduce the width of column **G** to about **12** characters.

7. Reduce the width of column **H** to about **8** characters. See Figure 3-12.

| Figure 3-12 | | WRAPPING TEXT WITHIN A CELL |

long column titles wrap to a new line and the widths of the columns are reduced

		Price	Production Cost	Profit	Units Sold	Total Sales	Profit from Sales	% of Profit
13	September	1,368	1,794	420	3,582			
14	October	1,389	1,836	429	3,654			
15	November	1,413	1,866	423	3,702			
16	December	1,533	2,013	444	3,990			
17	Total	17,232	22,488	5,208	44,928			
18								
19	Analysis of Annual Sales Figures							
20	Monitor	Price	Production Cost	Profit	Units Sold	Total Sales	Profit from Sales	% of Profit
21	VX100	$199.99	$165.20	$34.79	17,232	$3,446,227.68	$599,501.28	20.03%
22	VX300	$299.99	$234.75	$65.24	22,488	$6,746,175.12	$1,467,117.12	49.03%
23	FlatScreen	$899.99	$722.23	$177.76	5,208	$4,687,147.92	$925,774.08	30.94%
24	Total				44,928	$14,879,550.72	$2,992,392.48	

TROUBLE? Different monitors have different screen resolutions and column widths. If your screen does not match Figure 3-12, resize the columns accordingly.

Other Formatting Options

Excel supports even more formatting options than have been discussed so far. For example, instead of wrapping the text, you can have Excel shrink it to fit the size of the cell. If you reduce the cell later on, Excel will automatically resize the text to match. You can also rotate the contents of the cell, displaying the cell entry at almost any angle (see Figure 3-13). Joan does not need to use either of these options in her workbook, but they might be useful later on another project.

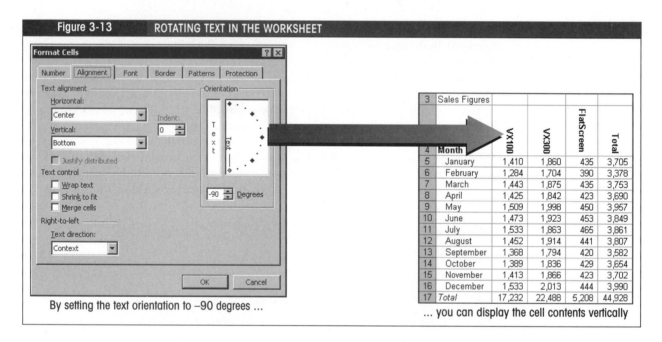

Figure 3-13   ROTATING TEXT IN THE WORKSHEET

By setting the text orientation to –90 degrees …

… you can display the cell contents vertically

Working with Cell Borders and Backgrounds

Up to now, all the formatting you have done has been applied to the contents of a cell. Excel also provides a range of tools to format the cells themselves. Specifically, you can add borders to the cells and color the cell backgrounds.

Adding a Cell Border

As you may have noticed from the printouts of other worksheets, the gridlines that appear in the worksheet window are not displayed on the printed page. In some cases, however, you might want to display borders around individual cells in a worksheet. This would be particularly true when you have different sections or tables in a worksheet, as in Joan's Sales worksheet.

You can add a border to a cell using either the Borders button on the Formatting toolbar or the options on the Border tab in the Format Cells dialog box. The Borders button allows you to create borders quickly, whereas the Format Cells dialog box lets you further refine your choices.

Joan wants you to place a border around each cell in the two tables in the worksheet. You'll select the appropriate border style from the list of available options on the Borders palette.

To create a grid of cell borders in the two tables:

1. Select the nonadjacent range **A4:E17;A20:H24**.

2. Click the **list arrow** for the Borders button on the Formatting toolbar. See Figure 3-14.

Figure 3-14	BORDER OPTIONS

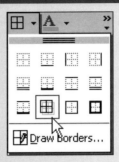

3. Click the **All Borders** option (third row, second column) in the gallery of border options. A thin border appears around each cell in the selected range.

4. Click cell **A1** to deselect the range.

You can also place a border around the entire range itself (and not the individual cells) by selecting a different border style. Try this by creating a thick border around the cell range.

To create a thick border around the selected range:

1. Select the range **A4:E17;A20:H24** again.

2. Click the **list arrow** for the Borders button on the Formatting toolbar, and then click the **Thick Box Border** option (third row, fourth column) in the border gallery.

3. Click cell **A2**. Figure 3-15 shows the two tables with their borders.

| Figure 3-15 | BORDERS WITHIN AND AROUND THE TWO SALES TABLES |

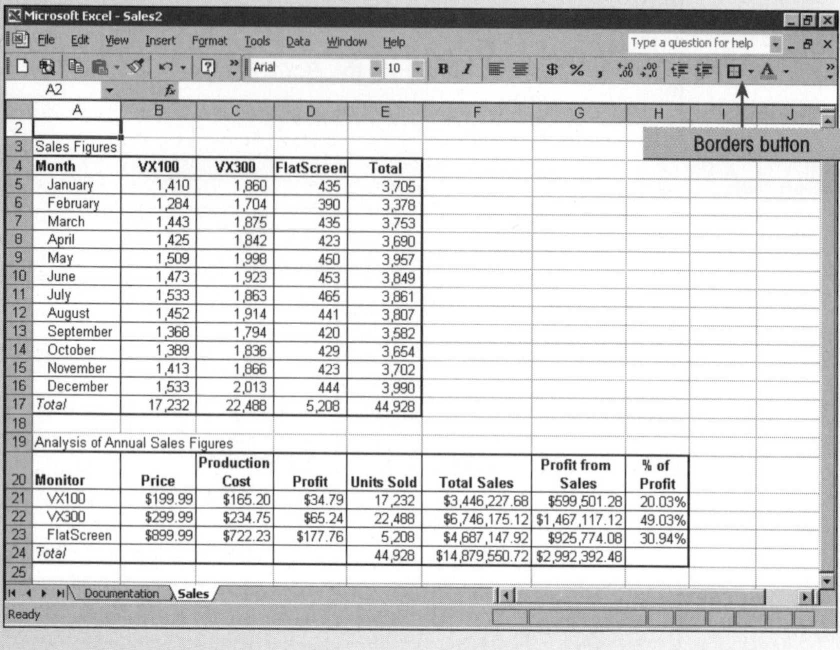

If you want a more interactive way of drawing borders on your worksheet, you can use the Draw Border button, which is also one of the options on the Borders palette. To see how this option works, you will add a thick black line under the column titles in both of the tables.

To draw borders using the Draw Border tool:

1. Click the **list arrow** for the Borders button ▣▾ on the Formatting toolbar, and then click the **Draw Border** button 🔲 at the bottom of the border gallery.

   The pointer changes to ✏, and a floating Borders toolbar opens with four tools. The Draw Border button ✏▾ (currently selected) draws a border line on the worksheet; the Erase Border button 🔲 erases border lines; the Line Style button ▭▾ specifies the style of the border line; and the Line Color button 🔲 specifies the line color.

2. Click the **list arrow** for the Line Style button ▭▾, and then click the **thick line** option (the eighth from the top) in the list.

3. Click and drag the pointer over the lower border of the range **A4:E4**.

4. Click and drag the pointer over the lower border of the range **A20:H20**.

5. Click the **Close** button ✕ on the floating Borders toolbar to close it.

Finally, you will add a double line above the Total row in each table. You will add the line using the options in the Format Cells dialog box.

To create the double border lines:

1. Select the nonadjacent range **A16:E16;A23:H23**.

2. Click **Format** on the menu bar, and then click **Cells**.

3. Click the **Border** tab. The Border tab displays a diagram showing what borders, if any, are currently surrounding the selected cells.

   The bottom border is currently a single thin line. You want to change this to a double line.

4. Click the **double line** style in the Line Style list box located on the right side of the tab.

5. Click the **bottom border** in the border diagram. The bottom border changes to a double line. See Figure 3-16.

Figure 3-16   **BORDER TAB**

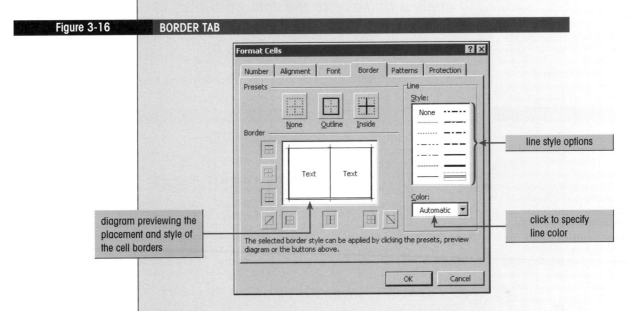

diagram previewing the placement and style of the cell borders

line style options

click to specify line color

---

6. Click the **OK** button.

7. Click cell **A2** to deselect the ranges. See Figure 3-17.

Figure 3-17   **TOTAL ROWS SEPARATED WITH DOUBLE LINES**

double lines

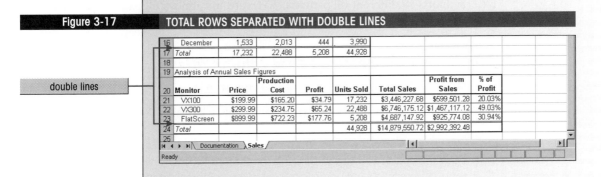

						Profit from	% of
16	December	1,533	2,013	444	3,990		
17	Total	17,232	22,488	5,208	44,928		
18							
19	Analysis of Annual Sales Figures						
20	Monitor	Price	Production Cost	Profit	Units Sold	Total Sales	Profit from Sales	% of Profit
21	VX100	$199.99	$165.20	$34.79	17,232	$3,446,227.68	$599,501.28	20.03%
22	VX300	$299.99	$234.75	$65.24	22,488	$6,746,175.12	$1,467,117.12	49.03%
23	FlatScreen	$899.99	$722.23	$177.76	5,208	$4,687,147.92	$925,774.08	30.94%
24	Total				44,928	$14,879,550.72	$2,992,392.48	
25								

Documentation \ Sales /
Ready

You can also specify a color for the cell borders by using the Color list box located on the Border tab (see Figure 3-16). Joan does not need to change the border colors, but she would like you to change the background color for the column title cells.

Setting the Background Color and Pattern

Patterns and color can be used to enliven a dull worksheet or provide visual emphasis to the sections of the worksheet that you want to stress. If you have a color printer or a color projection device, you might want to take advantage of Excel's color tools. By default, worksheet cells are not filled with any color (the white you see in your worksheet is not a fill color for the cells). To change the background color in a worksheet, you can use the Fill Color button on the Formatting toolbar, or you can use the Format Cells dialog box, which also provides patterns that you can apply to the background.

Joan wants to change the background color of the worksheet. When she makes her report later in the week, she will be using the company's color laser printer. So she would like you to explore using background color in the column titles for the two sales tables. She suggests that you try formatting the column titles with a light yellow background.

To apply a fill color to the column titles:

1. Select the nonadjacent range **A4:E4;A20:H20**.

2. Click the **list arrow** for the Fill Color button 🖌️ on the Formatting toolbar.

3. Click the **Light Yellow** square (fifth row, third column). See Figure 3-18.

Figure 3-18   SELECTING A FILL COLOR

4. Click cell **A2** to deselect the column titles. The column titles now have light yellow backgrounds.

Joan would also like to investigate whether you can apply a pattern to the fill background. Excel supports 18 different fill patterns. To create and apply a fill pattern, you have to open the Format Cells dialog box.

To apply a fill pattern to the column titles:

1. Select the nonadjacent range **A4:E4;A20:H20**.

2. Click **Format** on the menu bar, and then click **Cells**.

3. Click the **Patterns** tab.

4. Click the **Pattern** list arrow. Clicking the Pattern list arrow displays a gallery of patterns and a palette of colors applied to the selected pattern. The default pattern color is black. You will choose just a pattern now.

5. Click the **50% Gray** pattern (first row, third column) in the pattern gallery. See Figure 3-19.

Figure 3-19	SELECTING A FILL PATTERN

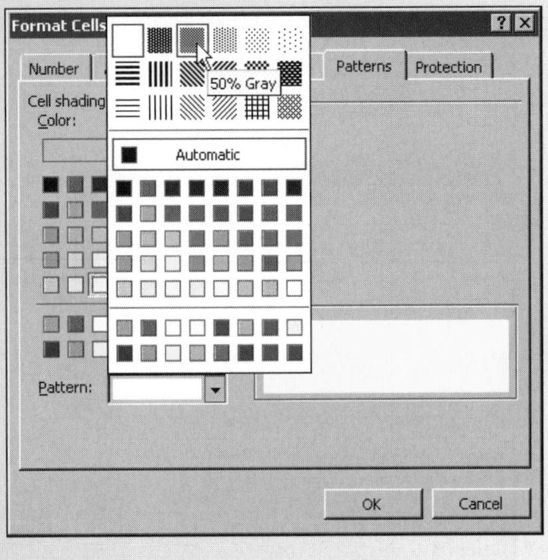

6. Click the **OK** button.

7. Click cell **A2** to deselect the ranges and to see the pattern.

The background pattern you have chosen overwhelms the text in these column titles. You can improve the appearance by changing the color of the pattern itself from black to a light orange.

To change the pattern color:

1. Select the range **A4:E4;A20:H20** again.

2. Click **Format** on the menu bar, and then click **Cells**.

3. Click the **Pattern** list arrow. The default (or automatic) color of a selected pattern is black. You can choose a different color for the pattern using the color palette below the patterns.

4. Click the **Light Orange** square (third row, second column) in the color palette.

5. Click the **OK** button.

6. Click cell **A2** to deselect the ranges. Figure 3-20 shows the patterned background applied to the column titles. Note that the light orange pattern does not overwhelm the column titles.

Figure 3-20   COLUMN TITLES WITH FORMATTED BACKGROUND

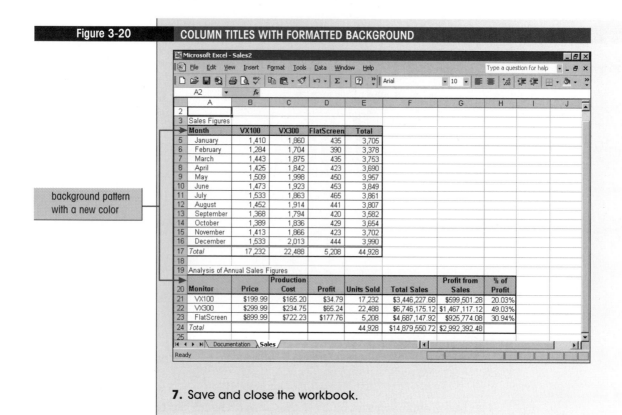

background pattern
with a new color

7. Save and close the workbook.

Joan is pleased with the progress you have made. In the next session, you will explore other formatting features.

Session 3.1 QUICK CHECK

1. Describe two ways of applying a Currency format to cells in your worksheet.

2. If the number 0.05765 has been entered into a cell, what will Excel display if you:

   a. format the number using the Percent format with one decimal place?

   b. format the number using the Currency format with two decimal places and a dollar sign?

3. Which two buttons can you use to copy a format from one cell range to another?

4. A long text string in one of your worksheet cells has been truncated. List three ways to correct this problem.

5. How do you center the contents of a single cell across a range of cells?

6. Describe three ways of creating a cell border.

7. How would you apply a background pattern to a selected cell range?

SESSION 3.2

In this session, you will format a worksheet by merging cells, hiding rows and columns, inserting a background image, and finding and replacing formats. You will also be introduced to styles. You will see how to create and apply styles, and you will learn how styles can be used to make formatting more efficient. You will also learn about Excel's gallery of AutoFormats. Finally, you will work with the Print Preview window to control the formatting applied to your printed worksheets.

Formatting the Worksheet

In the previous session you formatted individual cells within the worksheet. Excel also provides tools for formatting the entire worksheet or the entire workbook. You will explore some of these tools as you continue to work on Joan's Sales report.

Merging Cells into One Cell

Joan has reviewed the Sales worksheet and has a few suggestions. She would like you to format the titles for the two tables in her report so that they are centered in a bold font above the tables. You could do this by centering the cell title across a cell range, as you did for the title in the last session. Another way is to merge several cells into one cell and then center the contents of that single cell. Merging a range of cells into a single cell removes all of the cells from the worksheet, except the cell in the upper-left corner of the range. Any content in the other cells of the range is deleted. To merge a range of cells into a single cell, you can use the Merge option on the Alignment tab in the Format Cells dialog box or click the Merge and Center button on the Formatting toolbar.

To merge and center the cell ranges containing the table titles:

1. If you took a break after the previous session, start Excel and open the Sales2 workbook.

2. In the Sales worksheet, select the range **A3:E3**.

3. Click the **Merge and Center** button ▦ on the Formatting toolbar. The cells in the range A3:E3 are merged into one cell at the cell location, A3. The text in the merged cell is centered as well.

4. Click the **Bold** button **B** on the Formatting toolbar.

5. Select the range **A19:H19**, click ▦, and then click **B**.

6. Click cell **A2** to deselect the range. Figure 3-21 shows the merged and centered table titles.

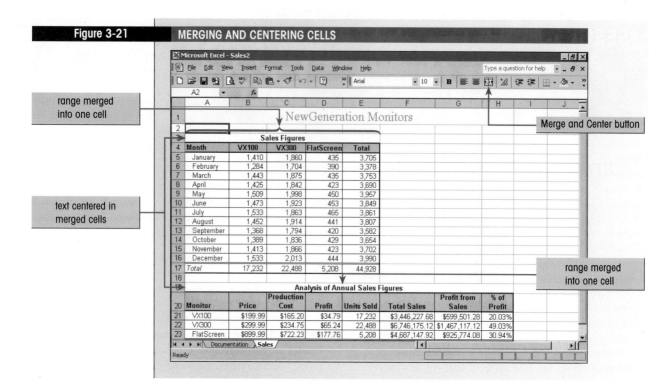

Figure 3-21 MERGING AND CENTERING CELLS

To split a merged cell back into individual cells, regardless of the method you used to merge the cells, you select the merged cell and then click the Merge and Center button again. You can also merge and unmerge cells using the Alignment tab in the Format Cells dialog box.

Hiding Rows and Columns

Sometimes Joan does not need to view the monthly sales for the three monitors. She does not want to remove this information from the worksheet, but she would like the option of temporarily hiding that information. Excel provides this capability. Hiding a row or column does not affect the data stored there, nor does it affect any other cell that might have a formula referencing a cell in the hidden row or column. Hiding part of your worksheet is a good way of removing extraneous information, allowing you to concentrate on the more important data contained in your worksheet. To hide a row or column, first you must select the row(s) or column(s) you want to hide. You can then use the Row or Column option on the Format menu or right-click the selection to open its shortcut menu.

You will hide the monthly sales figures in the first table in the worksheet.

To hide the monthly sales figures:

1. Select the headings for rows **5** through **16**.

2. Right-click the selection, and then click **Hide** on the shortcut menu. Excel hides rows 5 through 16. Note that the total sales figures in the range B17:E17 are not affected by hiding the monthly sales figures. See Figure 3-22.

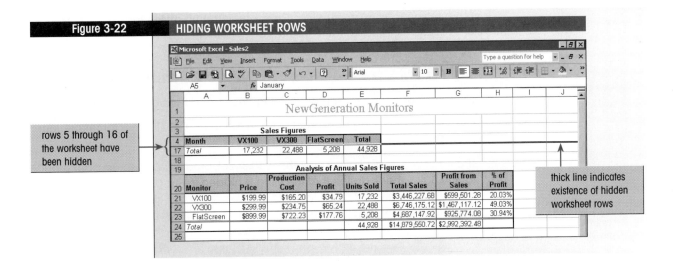

Figure 3-22   **HIDING WORKSHEET ROWS**

rows 5 through 16 of the worksheet have been hidden

thick line indicates existence of hidden worksheet rows

To unhide a hidden row or column, you must select the headings of the rows or columns that border the hidden area; then you can use the right-click method or the Row or Column command on the Format menu. You will let Joan know that it is easy to hide any row or column that she does not want to view. But for now you will redisplay the hidden sales figures.

To unhide the monthly sales figures:

1. Select the row headings for rows **4** and **17**.

2. Right-click the selection, and then click **Unhide** on the shortcut menu. Excel redisplays rows 5 through 16.

3. Click cell **A2** to deselect the rows.

Hiding and unhiding a column follows the same process, except that you select the worksheet column headings rather than the row headings.

Formatting the Sheet Background

In the previous session you learned how to create a background color for individual cells within the worksheet. Excel also allows you to use an image file as a background. The image from the file is tiled repeatedly until the images fill up the entire worksheet. Images can be used to give the background a textured appearance, like that of granite, wood, or fibered paper. The background image does not affect the format or content of any cell in the worksheet, and if you have already defined a background color for a cell, Excel displays the color on top, hiding that portion of the image.

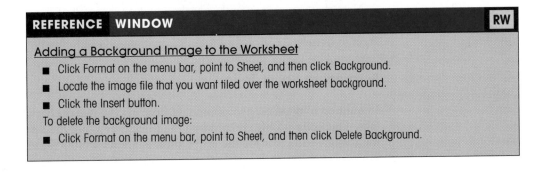

REFERENCE   WINDOW   **RW**

Adding a Background Image to the Worksheet
- Click Format on the menu bar, point to Sheet, and then click Background.
- Locate the image file that you want tiled over the worksheet background.
- Click the Insert button.

To delete the background image:
- Click Format on the menu bar, point to Sheet, and then click Delete Background.

Joan wants you to experiment with using a background image for the Sales worksheet. She has an image file that she wants you to try.

To add a background image to the worksheet:

1. Click **Format** on the menu bar, point to **Sheet**, and then click **Background**.

2. Locate and select the **Back** image file in the Tutorial.03/Tutorial folder on your Data Disk, and then click the **Insert** button.

   The Back image file is tiled over the worksheet, creating a textured background for the Sales sheet. Notice that the tiling is hidden in the cells that already contained a background color. In order to make the sales figures easier to read, you'll change the background color of those cells to white.

3. Select the nonadjacent range **A5:E17;A21:H24**.

4. Click the **list arrow** for the Fill Color button ![Fill Color] on the Formatting toolbar, and then click the **White** square (last row, last column) in the color palette.

5. Click cell **A2**. Figure 3-23 shows the Sales worksheet with the formatted background.

Figure 3-23   **ADDING A BACKGROUND IMAGE**

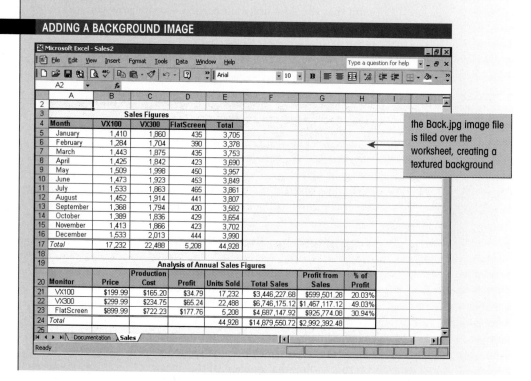

the Back.jpg image file is tiled over the worksheet, creating a textured background

Note that you cannot apply a background image to all of the sheets in a workbook at the same time. If you want to apply the same background to several sheets, you must format each sheet separately.

Formatting Sheet Tabs

In addition to the sheet background, you can also format the background color of worksheet tabs. This color is only visible when the worksheet is not the active sheet in the workbook; the background color for the active sheet is always white. You can use tab colors to better organize the various sheets in your workbook. For example, worksheets that contain sales information could be formatted with blue tabs, and sheets that describe the company's cash flow or budget could be formatted with green tabs.

If Joan's workbook contained many sheets, it would be easier to locate information if the sheet tabs were different colors. To explore how to color sheet tabs, you will change the tab color of the Sales worksheet to light orange.

To change the tab color:

1. Right-click the **Sales** tab, and then click **Tab Color** on the shortcut menu.

2. Click the **Light Orange** square (third row, second column) in the color palette.

3. Click the **OK** button. A light orange horizontal stripe appears at the bottom of the tab, but because Sales is the active worksheet, the background color is still white.

4. Click the **Documentation** tab. Now that Documentation is the active sheet, you can see the light orange color of the Sales sheet tab.

5. Click the **Sales** tab to make it the active sheet again.

Clearing **and Replacing Formats**

Sometimes you might want to change or remove some of the formatting from your workbooks. As you experiment with different formats, you will find a lot of use for the Undo button on the Standard toolbar as you remove formatting choices that did not work out as well as you expected. Another choice is to clear the formatting from the selected cells, returning the cells to their initial, unformatted appearance. To see how this option works, you will remove the formatting from the company name in cell A1 on the Sales worksheet.

To clear the format from cell A1:

1. Click cell **A1** to select it.

2. Click **Edit** on the menu bar, point to **Clear**, and then click **Formats**. Excel removes the formatting that was applied to the cell text and removes the formatting that centered the text across the range A1:H1.

3. Click the **Undo** button 🔄 on the Standard toolbar to undo your action, restoring the formats you cleared.

Sometimes you will want to make a formatting change that applies to several different cells. If those cells are scattered throughout the workbook, you may find it time-consuming to search and replace the formats for each individual cell. If the cells share a common format that you want to change, you can use the Find and Replace command to locate the formats and modify them.

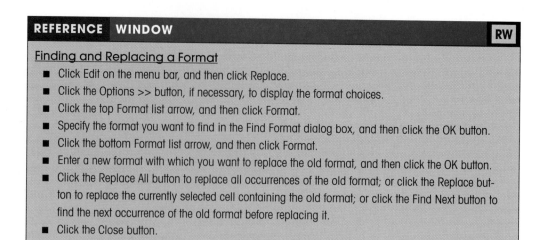

<u>Finding and Replacing a Format</u>

- Click Edit on the menu bar, and then click Replace.
- Click the Options >> button, if necessary, to display the format choices.
- Click the top Format list arrow, and then click Format.
- Specify the format you want to find in the Find Format dialog box, and then click the OK button.
- Click the bottom Format list arrow, and then click Format.
- Enter a new format with which you want to replace the old format, and then click the OK button.
- Click the Replace All button to replace all occurrences of the old format; or click the Replace button to replace the currently selected cell containing the old format; or click the Find Next button to find the next occurrence of the old format before replacing it.
- Click the Close button.

For example, in the Sales worksheet, the table titles and column titles are displayed in a bold font. After seeing how the use of color has made the worksheet come alive, Joan wants you to change the titles to a boldface blue. Rather than selecting the cells that contain the table and column titles and formatting them, you can replace all occurrences of the boldface text with blue boldface text.

To find and replace formats:

1. Click **Edit** on the menu bar, and then click **Replace**. The Find and Replace dialog box opens. You can use this dialog box to find and replace the contents of the cells. In this case, you will use it only for finding and replacing formats, leaving the contents of the cells unchanged.

2. Click the **Options >>** button to display additional find and replace options. See Figure 3-24.

   TROUBLE? If the button on your workbook appears as Options <<, the additional options are already displayed, and you do not need to click any buttons.

Figure 3-24   **FIND AND REPLACE DIALOG BOX**

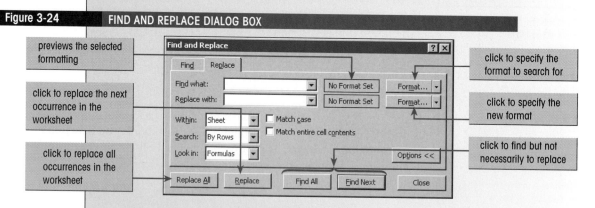

The dialog box expands to display options that allow you to find and replace cell formats. It also includes options to determine whether to search within the active sheet or the entire workbook. Currently no format options have been set.

3. Click the top **Format** list arrow, and then click **Format**.

The Find Format dialog box opens. Here is where you specify the format you want to search for. In this case, you are searching for cells that contain boldface text.

4. Click the **Font** tab, and then click **Bold** in the Font style list box. See Figure 3-25.

| Figure 3-25 | FIND FORMAT DIALOG BOX |

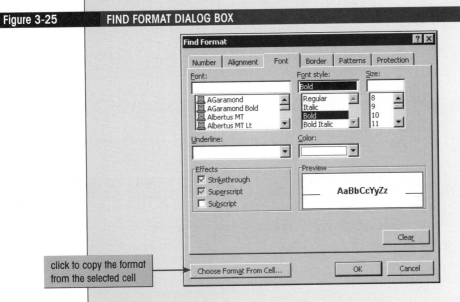

click to copy the format from the selected cell

5. Click the **OK** button.

Next, you have to specify the new format that you want to use to replace the boldface text. In this case, you need to specify a blue boldface text.

6. Click the bottom **Format** list arrow, and then click **Format**.

7. Click **Bold** in the Font style list box.

8. Click the **Color** list box, and then click the **Blue** square (second row, sixth column) in the color palette.

9. Click the **OK** button.

10. Click the **Replace All** button to replace all boldface text in the worksheet with boldface blue text. Excel indicates that it has completed its search and made 15 replacements.

11. Click the **OK** button, and then click the **Close** button. See Figure 3-26.

Figure 3-26 | SALES WORKSHEET WITH BOLDFACE BLUE TEXT

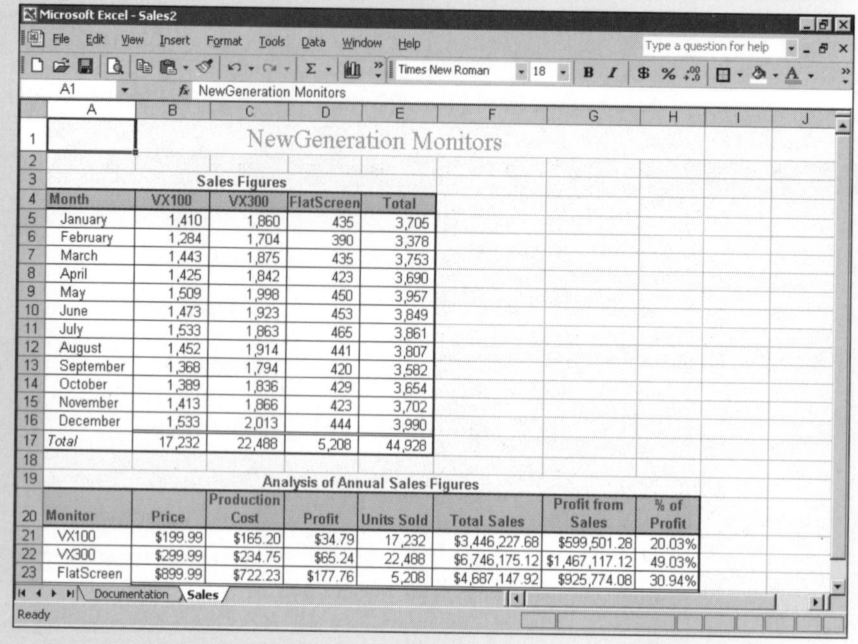

Using Styles

If you have several cells that employ the same format, you can create a style for those cells. A **style** is a saved collection of formatting options—number formats; text alignment; font sizes and colors; borders; and background fills—that can be applied to cells in the worksheet. When you apply a style, Excel remembers which styles are associated with which cells in the workbook. If you want to change the appearance of a particular type of cell, you need only modify the specifications for the style, and the appearance of any cell associated with that style would be automatically changed to reflect the new style.

You can create a style in one of two ways: by selecting a cell from the worksheet and basing the style definition on the formatting choices already defined for that cell or by manually entering the style definitions into a dialog box. Once you create and name a style, you can apply it to cells in the workbook.

Excel has eight built-in styles named Comma, Comma [0], Currency, Currency [0], Followed Hyperlink, Hyperlink, Normal, and Percent. You have been using styles all of this time without knowing it. Most cells are formatted with the Normal style, but when you enter a percentage, Excel formats it using the Percent style. Similarly, currency values are automatically formatted using the Currency style, and so forth.

Creating a Style

Joan wants you to further modify the appearance of the worksheet by changing the background color of the months in the first table and the monitor names in the second table to yellow. Rather than applying new formatting to the cells, you decide to create a new style called "Category" that you will apply to the category columns of the tables in your workbook. You will create the style using the format already applied to cell A5 of the worksheet as a basis.

To create a style using a formatted cell:

1. Click cell **A5** to select it. The format applied to this cell becomes the basis of the new style that you want to create.

2. Click **Format** on the menu bar, and then click **Style**. The Style dialog box opens. All of the formatting options associated with the style of the active cell are listed. For example, the font is 10-point Arial.

   To create a new style for this cell, you simply type a different name into the list box.

3. Verify that Normal is highlighted in the Style name list box, and then type **Category**. See Figure 3-27.

Figure 3-27   **STYLE DIALOG BOX**

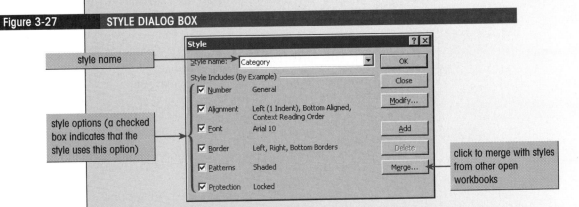

If you do not want all of these formatting options to be part of the Category style, you can deselect the options you no longer want included. You can also modify a current format option or add a new format option. You'll change the background color in the Category style to yellow.

4. Click the **Modify** button. The Format Cells dialog box opens.

5. Click the **Patterns** tab, and then click the **Yellow** square (fourth row, second column) in the color palette.

6. Click the **OK** button to close the Format Cells dialog box.

   If you click the OK button in the Style dialog box, the style definition changes and the updated style is applied to the active cell. If you click the Add button in the dialog box, the change is added, or saved, to the style definition but the updated style is not applied to the active cell.

7. Click the **OK** button. The background color of cell A5 changes to yellow.

Now you need to apply this style to other cells in the workbook.

Applying a Style

To apply a style to cells in a worksheet, you first select the cells you want associated with the style and then open the Styles dialog box.

To apply the Category style:

1. Select the nonadjacent range **A6:A16;A21:A23**.

2. Click **Format** on the menu bar, and then click **Style**.

3. Click the **Style name** list arrow, and then click **Category**.

4. Click the **OK** button, and then click cell **A2** to deselect the cells. A yellow background color is applied to all of the category cells in the two tables.

The yellow background appears a bit too strong. You decide to change it to a light yellow background. Since all the category cells are now associated with the Category style, you need only modify the definition of the Category style to make this change.

To modify the Category style:

1. Click **Format** on the menu bar, and then click **Style**.

2. Click the **Style name** list arrow, and then click **Category**.

3. Click the **Modify** button, and then click the **Patterns** tab, if necessary.

4. Click the **Light Yellow** square (fifth row, second column) in the color palette, and then click the **OK** button.

5. Click the **Add** button. Excel changes the background color of all the cells associated with the Category style.

   TROUBLE? Do not click the OK button. Clicking the OK button will apply the Category style only to the active cell.

6. Click the **Close** button. See Figure 3-28.

Figure 3-28   **CATEGORY STYLE IN THE SALES WORKSHEET**

formatted with the
Category style

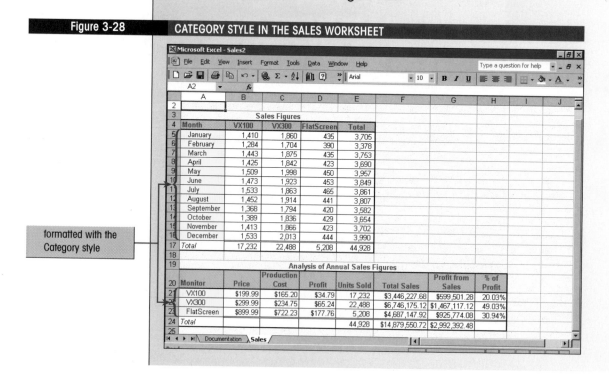

You can also copy styles from one workbook to another. Copying styles allows you to create a collection of workbooks that share a common look and feel.

Using AutoFormat

Excel's **AutoFormat** feature lets you choose an appearance for your worksheet cells from a gallery of 17 predefined formats. Rather than spending time testing different combinations of fonts, colors, and borders, you can apply a professionally designed format to your worksheet by choosing one from the AutoFormat Gallery. You have done a lot of work already formatting the data in the Sales workbook to give it a more professional and polished look, but you decide to see how the formatting you have done compares to one of Excel's AutoFormat designs.

Apply an AutoFormat to the Sales Figures table so that you can compare the professionally designed format to the format you have worked on.

To apply an AutoFormat to the table:

1. Select the range **A3:E17**.

2. Click **Format** on the menu bar, and then click **AutoFormat**. The AutoFormat dialog box opens. See Figure 3-29.

Figure 3-29	AUTOFORMAT GALLERY

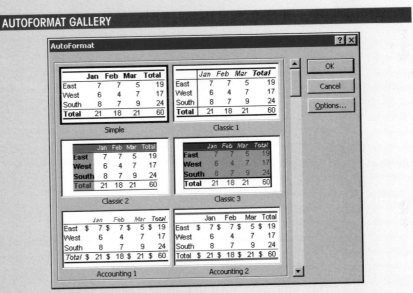

The dialog box displays a preview of how each format will appear when applied to cells in a worksheet.

3. Click **Classic 3** in the list of available designs, and then click the **OK** button.

4. Click cell **A2** to remove the highlighting from the first table. Figure 3-30 shows the appearance of the Classic 3 design in your workbook.

Figure 3-30 | **APPLYING AN AUTOFORMAT**

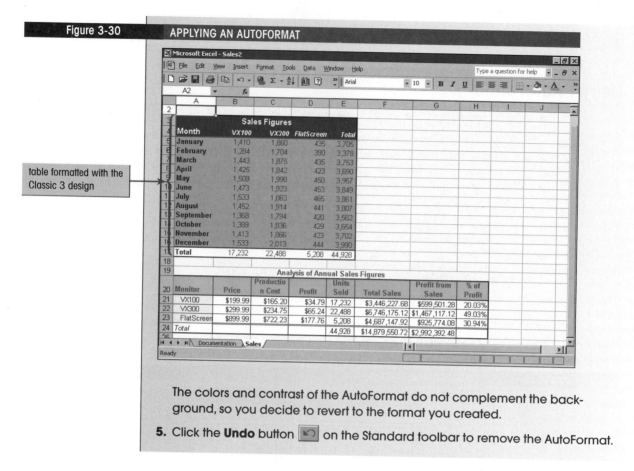

table formatted with the Classic 3 design

The colors and contrast of the AutoFormat do not complement the background, so you decide to revert to the format you created.

5. Click the **Undo** button on the Standard toolbar to remove the AutoFormat.

Although you will not use an AutoFormat in this case, you can see how an AutoFormat can be used as a starting point. You could start with Excel's professional design and then make modifications to the worksheet to fit your own needs.

Formatting **the Printed Worksheet**

You have settled on an appearance for the Sales worksheet—at least the appearance that is displayed on your screen. But that is only half of your job. Joan also wants you to format the appearance of this worksheet when it is printed out. You have to decide how to arrange the report on the page, the size of the page margins, the orientation of the page, and whether the page will have any headers or footers. You can make many of these choices through Excel's Print Preview.

Opening the Print Preview Window

As the name implies, the **Print Preview window** shows you how each page of your worksheet will look when it is printed. From the Print Preview window, you can make changes to the page layout before you print your worksheet.

To preview the Sales worksheet printout:

1. Click the **Print Preview** button on the Standard toolbar. The Print Preview window opens, displaying the worksheet as it will appear on the printed page. See Figure 3-31.

Figure 3-31 | PRINT PREVIEW

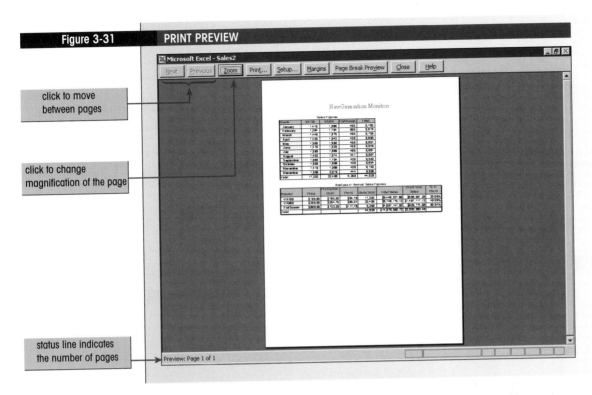

click to move
between pages

click to change
magnification of the page

status line indicates
the number of pages

Excel displays the full page in the Print Preview window. You might have difficulty reading the text because it is so small. Do not worry if the preview is not completely readable. One purpose of Print Preview is to see the overall layout of the worksheet. If you want a better view of the text, you can increase the magnification by either using the Zoom button on the Print Preview toolbar or by clicking the page with the 🔍 pointer. Clicking the Zoom button again, or clicking the page a second time with the pointer, reduces the magnification, bringing the whole page back into view.

To enlarge the preview:

1. Click the **Zoom** button on the Print Preview toolbar.

2. Use the horizontal and vertical scroll bars to move around the worksheet.

3. Click anywhere within the page with the pointer to reduce the magnification.

You can also make changes to the layout of a worksheet page using the Setup and Margins buttons on the Print Preview toolbar.

Defining the Page Setup

You can use the Page Setup dialog box to control how a worksheet is placed on a page. You can adjust the size of the **margins**, which are the spaces between the page content and the edges of the page. You can center the worksheet text between the top and bottom margins (horizontally) or between the right and left margins (vertically). You can change the **page orientation**, which determines if the page is wider than it is tall or taller than it is wide. You can also use the Page Setup dialog box to display text that will appear at the top (a header) or bottom (a footer) of each page of a worksheet. You can open the Page Setup dialog box using the File menu or using the Print Preview toolbar.

By default, Excel places a 1-inch margin above and below the report and a ¼-inch margin to the left and right. Excel also aligns column A in a worksheet at the left margin and row 1 at the top margin. Depending on how many columns and rows there are in the worksheet, you might want to increase or decrease the page margins or center the worksheet between the left and right margins or between the top and bottom margins.

You want to increase the margin size for the Sales worksheet to 1 inch all around. You also want the worksheet to be centered between the right and left margins.

To change the margins and center the worksheet horizontally on the page:

1. Click the **Setup** button on the Print Preview toolbar.

2. Click the **Margins** tab. See Figure 3-32.

| Figure 3-32 | MARGINS TAB |

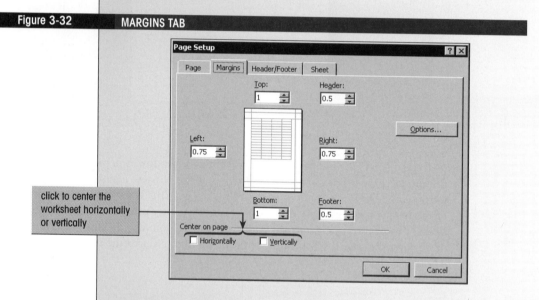

click to center the worksheet horizontally or vertically

The Margins tab provides a diagram showing the placement of the worksheet on the page. In addition to adjusting the sizes of the margins, you can also adjust the space allotted to the header and footer.

3. Click the **Left** up arrow to set the size of the left margin to **1** inch.

4. Click the **Right** up arrow to increase the size of the right margin to **1** inch.

5. Click the **Horizontally** check box, and then click the **OK** button.

The left and right margins change, but there is now less room for the worksheet. As indicated in the status line located in the lower-left corner of the Print Preview window, the worksheet now covers two pages instead of one; the last column in the Sales Analysis table has been moved to the second page. You can restore the margins to their default sizes, and the worksheet will once again fit on a single page. Another option is to change the orientation of the page from portrait to landscape. **Portrait orientation** (which is the default) displays the page taller than it is wide. **Landscape orientation** displays the page wider than it is tall.

You want to change the page orientation to landscape so the last column of the Sales Analysis table will fit on the same page as the rest of the columns in the table.

To change the page orientation:

1. Click the **Setup** button, and then click the **Page** tab.

2. Click the **Landscape** option button. See Figure 3-33.

Figure 3-33   PAGE SETUP DIALOG BOX

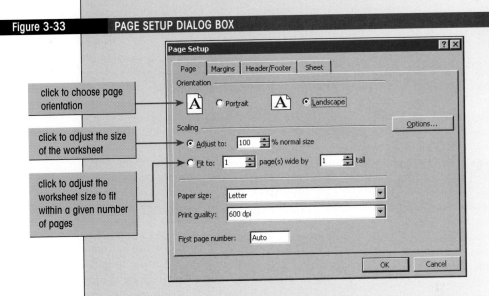

click to choose page orientation

click to adjust the size of the worksheet

click to adjust the worksheet size to fit within a given number of pages

3. Click the **OK** button. Excel changes the orientation to landscape. Note that the entire report now fits on a single page.

The Page tab in the Page Setup dialog box contains other useful formatting features. You can reduce or increase the size of the worksheet on the printed page. The default size is 100%. You can also have Excel automatically reduce the size of the report to fit within a specified number of pages.

Working with Headers and Footers

Joan wants you to add a header and footer to the report. A **header** is text printed in the top margin of every worksheet page. A **footer** is text printed at the bottom of every page. Headers and footers can add important information to your printouts. For example, you can create a header that displays your name and the date the report was created. If the report covers multiple pages, you can use a footer to display the page number and the total number of pages. You use the Page Setup dialog box to add headers and footers to a worksheet.

Excel tries to anticipate headers and footers that you might want to include in your worksheet. Clicking the Header or Footer list arrow displays a list of possible headers or footers (the list is the same for both). For example, the "Page 1" entry inserts the page number of the worksheet prefaced by the word "Page" in the header; the "Page 1 of ?" displays the page number and the total number of pages. Other entries in the list include the name or the worksheet or workbook.

If you want to use a header or footer not available in the lists, you click the Custom Header or Custom Footer button and create your own header and footer. The Header dialog box and the Footer dialog box are similar. Each dialog box is divided into three sections, left, center, and right. If you want to enter information such as the filename or the day's date into the header or footer, you can either type the text or click one of the format buttons located above the three section boxes. Figure 3-34 describes the format buttons and the corresponding format codes.

Figure 3-34 HEADER/FOOTER FORMATTING BUTTONS

BUTTON	NAME	FORMATTING CODE	ACTION
A	Font	None	Sets font, text style, and font size
[#]	Page number	&[Page]	Inserts page number
	Total pages	&[Pages]	Inserts total number of pages
	Date	&[Date]	Inserts current date
	Time	&[Time]	Insert current time
	Path	&[Path]&[File]	Inserts path and filename
	Filename	&[File]	Insert filename
	Sheet name	&[Tab]	Inserts name of active worksheet
	Picture	&[Picture]	Inserts an image file
	Format picture	None	Formats the picture inserted into the header/footer

Joan wants a header that displays the filename at the left margin and today's date at the right margin. She wants a footer that displays the name of the workbook author, with the text aligned at the right margin of the footer. You'll create the header and footer now.

To add a custom header to the workbook:

1. Click the **Setup** button on the Print Preview toolbar, and then click the **Header/Footer** tab.

2. Click the **Custom Header** button. The Header dialog box opens. See Figure 3-35.

Figure 3-35 HEADER DIALOG BOX

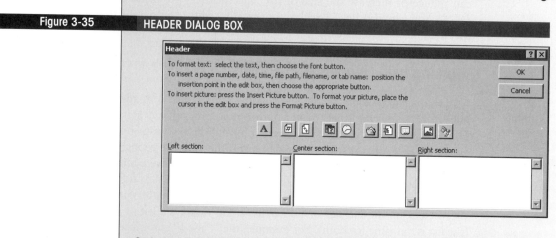

3. In the Left section box, type **Filename:** and then press the **spacebar**.

4. Click the **Filename** button to insert the format code. The formatting code for the name of the file, &(File), appears after the text string that you entered in the Left section box.

5. Click the **Right section** box, and then click the **Date** button . Excel inserts the &(DATE) format code into the section box.

6. Click the **OK** button to close the Header dialog box.

7. Click the **Custom Footer** button. The Footer dialog box opens.

8. Click the **Right section** box, type **Prepared by:** and then type your name.

9. Click the **OK** button. The Page Setup dialog box displays the custom header and footer that you created.

10. Click the **OK** button. The Print Preview window displays the worksheet with the new header and footer.

11. Click the **Close** button on the Print Preview toolbar.

Working with the Print Area and Page Breaks

When you displayed the worksheet in the Print Preview window, how did Excel know which parts of the active worksheet you were going to print? The default action is to print all parts of the active worksheet that contain text, formulas, or values, which will not always be what you want. If you want to print only a part of the worksheet , you can define a **print area** that contains the content you want to print. To define a print area, you must first select the cells you want to print, and then select the Print Area option on the File menu.

A print area can include an adjacent range or nonadjacent ranges. You can also hide rows or columns in the worksheet in order to print nonadjacent ranges. For her report, Joan might decide against printing the sales analysis information. To remove those cells from the printout, you need to define a print area that excludes the cells for the second table.

To define the print area:

1. Select the range **A1:H17**.

2. Click **File** on the menu bar, point to **Print Area**, and then click **Set Print Area**.

3. Click cell **A2**. Excel places a dotted black line around the selected cells of the print area. This is a visual indicator of what parts of the worksheet will be printed.

4. Click the **Print Preview** button on the Standard toolbar. The Print Preview window displays only the first table. The second table has been removed from the printout because it is not in the defined print area.

5. Click the **Close** button on the Print Preview toolbar.

Another approach that Joan might take is to place the two tables on separate pages. You can do this for her by creating a **page break**, which forces Excel to place a portion of a worksheet on a new page.

Before inserting a page break, you must first redefine the print area to include the second table.

To redefine the print area, and then insert a page break:

1. Select the range **A1:H24**.

2. Click **File** on the menu bar, point to **Print Area**, and then click **Set Print Area**.

   Before you insert the page break, you need to indicate where in the worksheet you want the break to occur. Because you want to print the second table on a separate page, you will set the page break at cell A18, which will force rows 18 through 24 to a new page.

3. Click cell **A18**, click **Insert** on the menu bar, and then click **Page Break**. Another blank dotted line appears—this time above cell A18, indicating there is a page break at this point in the print area. See Figure 3-36.

Figure 3-36   ADDING A PAGE BREAK TO THE PRINT AREA

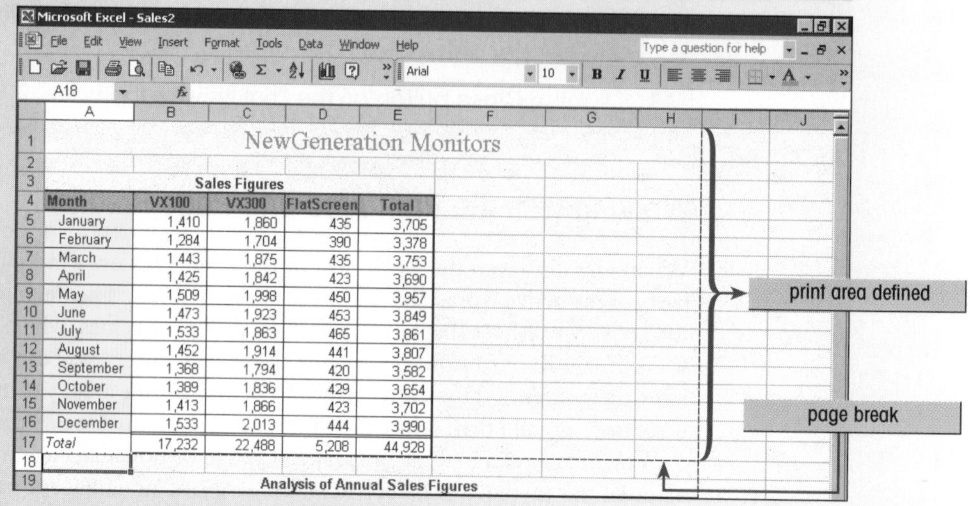

4. Click the **Print Preview** button on the Standard toolbar. Excel displays the first table on page 1 in the Print Preview window.

5. Click the **Next** button to display page 2.

6. Click the **Close** button on the Print Preview toolbar.

You show the print preview to Joan and she notices that the name of the company, "NewGeneration Monitors," appears on the first page, but not on the second. That is not surprising because the range that includes the company name is limited to the first page of the printout. However, Joan would like to have this information repeated on the second page.

You can repeat information, such as the company name, by specifying which cells in the print area should be repeated on each page. This is particularly useful in long tables which extend over many pages. In such cases, you can have the column titles repeated for each page in the printout.

To set rows or columns to repeat on each page, you have to open the Page Setup dialog box from the worksheet window.

To repeat the first row on each page:

1. Click **File** on the menu bar, and then click **Page Setup**.

2. Click the **Sheet** tab. See Figure 3-37.

| Figure 3-37 | ADDING A PAGE BREAK TO THE PRINT AREA |

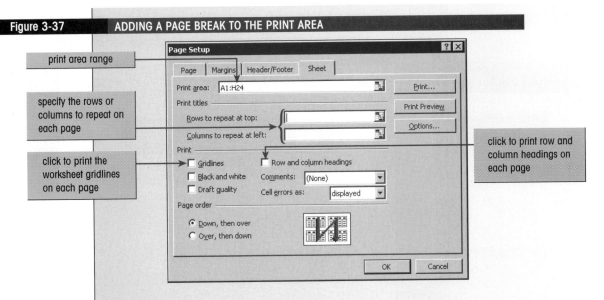

The Sheet tab displays options you can use to control how the worksheet is printed. As shown in Figure 3-37, the print area you have defined is already entered into the Print area box. Joan wants the company name to appear above the second table, so you need to have Excel repeat the first row on the second page.

3. Click the **Rows to repeat at top** box.

4. Click cell **A1**. A flashing border appears around the first row in the worksheet. This is a visual indicator that the contents of the first row will be repeated on all pages of the printout. In the Rows to repeat at top box, the format code *$1:$1* appears.

5. Click the **OK** button.

The Sheet tab also provides other options, such as the ability to print the worksheet's gridlines or row and column headings. You can also have Excel print the worksheet in black and white or draft quality. If there are multiple pages in the printout, you can indicate whether the pages should be ordered going down the worksheet first and then across, or across first and then down.

Next, you'll preview the worksheet to see how the pages look with the company name above each table, and then you'll print the worksheet.

To preview and print the worksheet:

1. Click the **Print Preview** button on the Standard toolbar. The first page of the printout appears in the Print Preview window.

2. Click the **Next** button to display the second page of the printout. Note that the title "NewGeneration Monitors" appears on the page. See Figure 3-38.

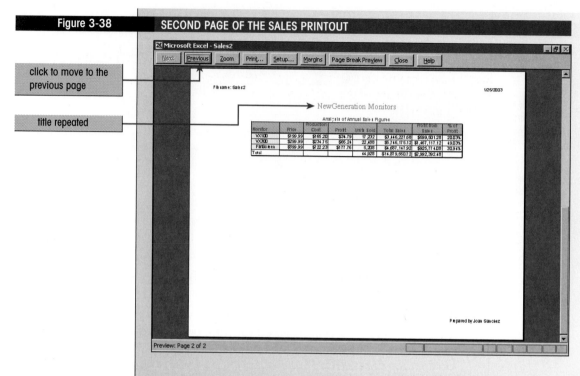

| Figure 3-38 | SECOND PAGE OF THE SALES PRINTOUT |

click to move to the previous page

title repeated

3. Click the **Print** button, select your printer from the Name list box, and then click the **OK** button.

For now your work is done. When you save the workbook, your printing options are saved along with the file, so you will not have to re-create the print format in the future.

4. Save and close the workbook, and then exit Excel.

You show the final version of the workbook and the printout to Joan. She is very happy with the way in which you have formatted her report. She will spend some time going over the printout and will get back to you with any further changes she wants you to make.

Session 3.2 QUICK CHECK

1. Describe two ways of merging a range of cells into one.

2. How do you clear a format from a cell without affecting the underlying data?

3. How do you add a background image to the active worksheet?

4. To control the amount of space between the content on a page and its edges, you can adjust the page's _____.

5. By default, Excel prints what part of the active worksheet?

6. How do you define a print area? How do you remove a print area?

7. How do you insert a page break into your worksheet?

REVIEW ASSIGNMENTS

Joan Sanchez has another report that she wants to format. The report displays regional sales for the three monitor brands you worked on earlier. As before, Joan wants to work on the overall appearance of the worksheet so the printout of the report is polished and professional looking.

To format the report:

1. Start Excel and open the **Region1** workbook located in the Tutorial.03/Review folder on your Data Disk.

2. Save the workbook as **Region2** in the same folder.

Explore

3. Enter your name and the current date in the Documentation sheet. Format the date to display the day of the week and the name of the month as well as the day and year. Switch to the Regional Sales worksheet.

4. Format the text in cell A1 with a 20-point, boldfaced, italicized, red Times New Roman font. Select the cell range A1:F1, and then center the text in cell A1 across the selection (do not merge the cells).

5. Select the range A3:E14, and then apply the List 2 format from the AutoFormat Gallery.

6. Change the format of all the values in the Sales by Region table to display a comma separator, but no decimal places.

7. Change the format of the units sold values in the second table to display a comma separator, but no decimal places.

8. Indent the region names in the range A5:A13 by one character.

9. Display the text in cell A16 in bold.

10. Change the format of the values in the Total Sales and Profit from Sales columns to display a dollar sign directly to the left of the values and no decimal places.

11. Change the format of the % of Profit column as percentages with two decimal places.

12. Allow the text in the range A17:F17 to wrap to a second line of text. Change the font of the text to bold.

Explore

13. Merge the cells in the range A18:A20, and then vertically align the text with the top of the cell. Apply this format to the cells in the following ranges: A21:A23, A24:A26, and A27:A29.

14. Change the background color of the cells in the range A17:F17;A18:A29 to Sea Green (third row, fourth column of the color palette). Change the font color to white.

15. Change the background color of the cells in the range B18:F29 to white. Change the background color of the cells in the range B20:F20;B23:F23;B26:F26;B29:F29 to Light Green (fifth row, fourth column of the color palette).

16. Surround the borders of all cells in the range A17:F29 with a black line.

Explore

17. Place a double red line on the bottom border of the cells in the range B20:F20;B23:F23;B26:F26.

18. Set the print area as the range A1:F29. Insert a page break above row 16. Repeat the first row of the worksheet on every page of any printouts you produce from this worksheet.

19. Set up the page to print in portrait orientation with 1-inch margins on all sides. Center the contents of the worksheet horizontally on the page.

20. Add a footer with the following text in the Left section box of the footer (with the date on a separate line): "Filename: *the name of the file*" and "Date: *current date*," and then the following text in the Right section box of the footer: "Prepared by: *your name*."

Explore 21. Add a header with the text "Regional Sales Report" displayed in the Center section using a 14-point Times New Roman font with a double underline. (*Hint*: Select the text in the Center section, and then use the Formatting toolbar to change the appearance of the text.)

22. Print the Regional Sales worksheet.

23. Save and close the workbook, and then exit Excel.

CASE PROBLEMS

Case 1. Jenson Sports Wear Quarterly Sales Carol Roberts is the national sales manager for Jenson Sports Wear, a company that sells sportswear to major department stores. She has been using an Excel worksheet to track the results of her staff's sales incentive program. She has asked you to format the worksheet so that it looks professional. She also wants a printout before she presents the worksheet at the next sales meeting.

Complete these steps to format and print the worksheet:

1. Open the **Running1** workbook located in the Tutorial.03/Cases folder on your Data Disk, and then save the file as **Running2** in the same folder.

2. Enter your name and the current date in the Documentation sheet. Switch to the Sales worksheet.

3. Complete the following calculations:
   a. Calculate the totals for each product.
   b. Calculate the quarterly subtotals for the Shoes and Shirts departments.
   c. Calculate the totals for each quarter and an overall total.

Explore 4. Format the data in the range A1:F14 so that it resembles the table shown in Figure 3-39.

Figure 3-39

Jenson Sports Wear					
Quarterly Sales by Product					
Shoes	**Qtr1**	**Qtr2**	**Qtr3**	**Qtr4**	**Total**
Running	2,250	2,550	2,650	2,800	10,250
Tennis	2,800	1,500	2,300	2,450	9,050
Basketball	1,250	1,400	1,550	1,550	5,750
Subtotal	6,300	5,450	6,500	6,800	25,050
Shirts	**Qtr1**	**Qtr2**	**Qtr3**	**Qtr4**	**Total**
Tee	1,000	1,150	1,250	1,150	4,550
Polo	2,100	2,200	2,300	2,400	9,000
Sweat	250	250	275	300	1,075
Subtotal	3,350	3,600	3,825	3,850	14,625
Grand Total	**9,650**	**9,050**	**10,325**	**10,650**	**39,675**

Explore 5. Create a style named "Subtotal" that is based on the font, border, and pattern formats found in the cell ranges A7:F7 and A13:F13.

6. Use the Page Setup dialog box to center the table both horizontally and vertically on the printed page and to change the page orientation to landscape.

7. Add the filename, your name, and the date on separate lines in the Right section box of the footer.

8. Print the sales report.

9. Save and close the workbook, and then exit Excel.

Case 2. *Wisconsin Department of Revenue* Ted Crawford works for the Wisconsin Department of Revenue. Recently he compiled a list of the top 50 women-owned businesses in the state. He would like your help in formatting the report, in regard to both how it appears in the worksheet window and how it appears on the printed page.

Complete the following:

1. Open the **WBus1** workbook located in the Tutorial.03/Cases folder on your Data Disk, and then save the file as **WBus2** in the same folder.

2. Enter your name and the current date in the Documentation sheet. Switch to the Business Data worksheet.

3. Change the font in cell A1 to a boldface font that is 14 points in size. Merge and center the title across the range A1:F1.

4. Display the text in the range A2:F2 in bold, and then center the text in the range C2:F2. Place a double line on the bottom border of the range A2:F2.

5. Display the sales information in the Accounting format with no decimal places; enlarge the width of the column, if necessary.

6. Display the employees' data using a comma separator with no decimal places.

7. Change the background color of the cells in the range A3:F3 to light green. Change the background color of the cells in A4:F4 to white.

Explore 8. Select the range A3:F4 and use the Format Painter to apply the format to the cells in the range A5:F52. How is the format applied to the cells?

9. Change the page orientation of the worksheet to landscape. Set the bottom margin to 1.5 inches. Center the contents of the worksheet horizontally on the page.

10. Set the print area as the cell range A1:F52. Repeat the first two rows of the worksheet in any printouts.

11. Remove any header from the printed page. Display the following text on separate lines in the Right section box of the footer: "Compiled by *your name*," "*the current date*," "Page *the current page* of *total number of pages*."

Explore 12. Fit the worksheet on output that is 1 page wide by 2 pages tall.

13. Preview the worksheet, and then print it.

14. Save and close the workbook, and then exit Excel.

Case 3. *Sales Report at Davis Blades* Andrew Malki is a financial officer at Davis Blades, a leading manufacturer of roller blades. He has recently finished entering data for the yearly sales report. Andrew has asked you to help him with the design of the main table in the report. A preview of the format you will apply is shown in Figure 3-40.

Figure 3-40

Davis Blades Yearly Sales Report
Units Sold

		Northeast	East	Southeast	Midwest	Southwest	West	All Regions
Black Hawk	Qtr 1	641	748	733	676	691	783	4,272
	Qtr 2	708	826	811	748	763	866	4,722
	Qtr 3	681	795	780	719	734	833	4,542
	Qtr 4	668	779	764	705	720	816	4,452
	Total	2,698	3,148	3,088	2,848	2,908	3,298	17,988
Blademaster	Qtr 1	513	598	587	541	552	627	3,418
	Qtr 2	567	661	648	598	611	693	3,778
	Qtr 3	545	636	624	575	587	666	3,633
	Qtr 4	534	623	611	564	576	653	3,561
	Total	2,159	2,518	2,470	2,278	2,326	2,639	14,390
The Professional	Qtr 1	342	399	391	361	368	418	2,279
	Qtr 2	378	441	432	399	407	462	2,519
	Qtr 3	363	424	416	383	391	444	2,421
	Qtr 4	356	415	407	376	384	435	2,373
	Total	1,439	1,679	1,646	1,519	1,550	1,759	9,592
All Models	Qtr 1	1,496	1,745	1,711	1,578	1,611	1,828	9,969
	Qtr 2	1,653	1,928	1,891	1,745	1,781	2,021	11,019
	Qtr 3	1,589	1,855	1,820	1,677	1,712	1,943	10,596
	Qtr 4	1,558	1,817	1,782	1,645	1,680	1,904	10,386
	Total	6,296	7,345	7,204	6,645	6,784	7,696	41,970

Complete the following:

1. Open the **Blades1** workbook located in the Tutorial.03/Cases folder on your Data Disk, and then save the file as **Blades2** in the same folder.

2. Enter your name and the current date in the Documentation sheet. Switch to the Sales worksheet.

3. Change the font of the title in cell A1 to a 14–point, dark blue, boldface Arial font. Change the subtitle in cell A2 to a 12-point, dark blue, boldface Arial font.

Explore ▷ 4. Merge the cells in the range A4:A8, and align the contents of the cell with the upper-left corner of the cell. Repeat this for the following ranges: A9:A13, A14:A18, and A19:A23.

5. Change the background color of the cell range A4:I8 to light yellow. Change the background color of the range A9:I13 to light green. Change the background color of the range A14:I18 to light turquoise. Change the background color of the range A19:I23 to pale blue.

6. Reverse the color scheme for the subtotal values in the range B8:I8, so that instead of black on light yellow, the font color is light yellow on a black background. Reverse the subtotal values for the other products in the table.

7. Apply the gridlines as displayed in Figure 3-40 to the cells in the range A4:I23.

Explore ▷ 8. Rotate the column titles in the range C3:I3 by 45 degrees. Align the contents of each cell with the cell's bottom right border. Change the background color of these cells to white and add a border to each cell.

9. Set the print area as the range A1:K23.

10. Leave the page orientation as portrait, but center the worksheet horizontally on the page.

11. Remove any headers from the page. Create a custom footer with the the text "Filename: *name of the file*" left-aligned, and "Prepared by: *your name*" and "*the current date*" right-aligned, with your name and date on separate lines.

12. Print the worksheet.

13. Save and close the workbook, and then exit Excel.

Case 4. Oritz Marine Services Vince DiOrio is an information systems major at a local college. He works three days a week at a nearby marina, Oritz Marine Services, to help pay for his tuition. Vince works in the business office, and his responsibilities range from making coffee to keeping the company's books.

Recently, Jim Oritz, the owner of the marina, asked Vince if he could help computerize the payroll for the employees. He explained that the employees work a different number of hours each week at different rates of pay. Jim does the payroll manually now and finds it time-consuming. Moreover, whenever he makes an error, he is annoyed at having to take the additional time to correct it. Jim is hoping that Vince can help him.

Vince immediately agrees to help. He tells Jim that he knows how to use Excel and that he can build a worksheet that will save him time and reduce errors. Jim and Vince meet to review the present payroll process and discuss the desired outcome of the payroll spreadsheet. Figure 3-41 displays the type of information that Jim records in the spreadsheet.

Figure 3-41

Oritz Marine Service Payroll
Week Ending

Employee	Hours	Pay Rate	Gross Pay	Federal Withholding	State Withholding	Total Deductions	Net Pay
Bramble	16	9.50					
Juarez	25	12.00					
Smith	30	13.50					
DiOrio	25	12.50					
Smiken	10	9.00					
Cortez	30	10.50					
Fulton	20	9.50					
Total							

Complete the following:

1. Create a new workbook named **Payroll** and save it in the Tutorial.03/Cases folder on your Data Disk.

2. Name two worksheets Documentation and Payroll.

3. On the Documentation sheet, include the name of the company, your name, the date, and a brief description of the purpose of the workbook.

4. On the Payroll worksheet, enter the payroll table shown in Figure 3-41.

5. Use the following formulas in the table to calculate total hours, gross pay, federal withholding, state withholding, total deductions, and net pay:
   a. Gross pay is hours times pay rate
   b. Federal withholding is 15% of gross pay
   c. State withholding is 4% of gross pay
   d. Total deductions are the sum of federal and state withholdings
   e. Net pay is the difference between gross pay and total deductions

Explore   6. Format the appearance of the payroll table using the techniques you learned in this tutorial. The appearance of the payroll table is up to you; however, do not use an AutoFormat to format the table.

Explore   7. Format the printed page, setting the print area and inserting an appropriate header and footer. Only a few employees are entered into the table at present. However, after Jim Oritz approves your layout, many additional employees will be added, which will cause the report to cover multiple pages. Format your printout so that the page title and column titles will appear on every page.

8. Remove the hours for the seven employees, and enter the following new values: 18 for Bramble, 25 for Juarez, 35 for Smith, 20 for DiOrio, 15 for Smiken, 35 for Cortez, and 22 for Fulton.

9. Print the worksheet.

10. Save and close the workbook, and then exit Excel.

INTERNET ASSIGNMENTS

Student Union

The purpose of the Internet Assignments is to challenge you to find information on the Internet that you can use to create effective spreadsheets. The actual assignments are updated and maintained on the Course Technology Web site. Log on to the Internet and use your Web browser to go to the Student Union on the New Perspectives Series site at **www.course.com/NewPerspectives/studentunion**. Click the Online Companions link, and then click the link for this text.

QUICK CHECK ANSWERS

Session 3.1

1. Click the Currency Style button on the Formatting toolbar; or click Cells on the Format menu, click the Number tab, and then select Currency from the Category list box.

2. Excel will display the following:
   a. 5.8%
   b. $0.06

3. the Format Painter button and the Copy button

4. Increase the width of the column; decrease the font size of the text; or select the Shrink to fit check box or the Wrap text check box on the Alignment tab in the Format cells dialog box.

5. Select the range, click Cells on the Format menu, click the Alignment tab, and then choose Center Across Selection from the Horizontal list box.

6. Use the Borders button on the Formatting toolbar; use the Draw Borders tool in the Border gallery; or click Cells on the Format menu, click the Border tab, and then choose the border options in the dialog box.

7. Click Cells on the Format menu, click the Patterns tab, and then click the Pattern list arrow to choose the pattern type and color.

Session 3.2

1. Select the cells and either click the Merge and Center button on the Formatting toolbar; or click Cells on the Format menu, click the Alignment tab, and then click the Merge cells check box.

2. Select the cell, point to Clear on the Edit menu, and then click Formats.

3. Point to Sheet on the Format menu, and then click Background. Locate and select an image file to use for the background.

4. margins

5. Excel prints all parts of the active worksheet that contain text, formulas, or values.

6. To define a print area, select a range in the worksheet, point to Print Area on the File menu, and then click Set Print Area. To remove a print area, point to Print Area on the File menu, and then click Clear Print Area.

7. Select the first cell below the intended place for the page break, and then click Page Break on the Insert menu.

OBJECTIVES

In this tutorial you will:

- Create column and pie charts using the Chart Wizard

- Resize and move an embedded chart

- Create a chart sheet

- Modify the properties of your charts

- Format chart elements

- Create 3-D charts

- Insert drawing objects into your workbook

- Print a chart sheet

WORKING
WITH CHARTS
AND GRAPHICS

Charting Sales Data for
Vega Telescopes

CASE

Vega Telescopes

Alicia Kendall is a sales manager at Vega Telescopes, one of the leading manufacturers of telescopes and optics. She has been asked to present information on last year's sales for four of Vega's top telescope models: the 6- and 8-inch BrightStars, and the 12- and 16-inch NightVisions. Her report should include the sales figures on each model organized by the United States, European, and Asian sales. Her presentation will be part of the sales conference that will be held next week in Charlotte, North Carolina.

Alicia has the basic sales information and knows that this kind of sales information is often best understood when presented visually, that is, in a graphical or pictorial form. Therefore, she wants you to help her create charts that will clearly and easily present the sales data. She would like to show the sales data in a column chart, but she would also like to use a pie chart that shows how each model contributes to Vega's overall sales of these top telescope models.

Alicia wants to format the charts so they are visually appealing. She wants to draw attention to the product that is the top-selling model. She also will need printouts of the charts.

In this tutorial you will create two charts: a column chart and a pie chart. You will format the charts and individual chart components. You will also add a drawing object that points out the top-selling telescope and then print the completed charts.

SESSION 4.1

In this session, you will create a chart using Excel's Chart Wizard. You will learn about embedded charts and chart sheets. You will resize and move an embedded chart. You will work with pie charts by rotating them and exploding a pie slice.

Excel **Charts**

Alicia's sales data has already been entered into a workbook for you. Open the workbook and examine the data.

To open Alicia's workbook:

1. Start Excel, if necessary, and open the **Vega1** workbook located in the Tutorial.04/Tutorial folder on your Data Disk.

2. Enter your name and the current date in the Documentation sheet.

3. Save the workbook as **Vega2** in the same folder.

4. Switch to the Sales worksheet. See Figure 4-1.

Figure 4-1   THE SALES WORKSHEET FOR VEGA TELESCOPES

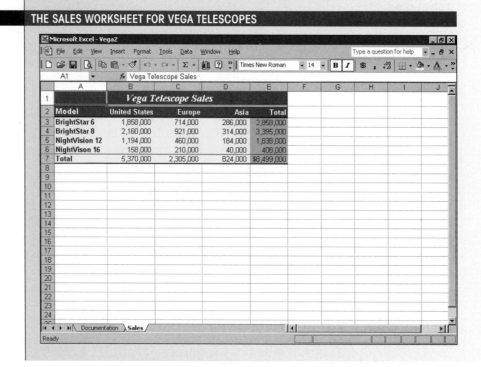

The Sales worksheet shows the annual sales, in dollars, for each of the four Vega telescope models. The sales data are broken down by world region. As Alicia has explained, she wants two charts. The first chart should show the sales for each telescope in each region represented by columns, in which the height of the column represents the sales volume for each model. The second should be a pie chart, in which the size of each slice is proportional to the total sales for each telescope model. The sketches of the charts Alicia wants to create are shown in Figure 4-2.

Figure 4-2	SKETCH OF COLUMN AND PIE CHARTS

Sales by Region and Model

United States   Europe   Asia

Legend

NightVision 12

BrightStar 6

NightVision 16

BrightStar 8

Charts, also referred to in Excel as graphs, provide visual representations of the workbook data. Excel makes it easy to create charts through the use of the **Chart Wizard**, a series of dialog boxes that prompt you for information about the chart you want to generate. You will use the Chart Wizard to create the first graph that Alicia sketched for you—the column chart of the sales figures broken down by region and telescope model.

Creating a Chart with the Chart Wizard

Before starting the Chart Wizard, you should (although it is not necessary) select the data that will be used in the chart. In this case, you will select the data in the range A2:D6. Note that you will not include any of the subtotals in the selection. The column chart that you need to create will only display the sales figures broken down by model type and region; it will not display any overall totals.

Once you start the Chart Wizard, you go through a series of four dialog boxes that prompt you for different information about the chart you are creating. Figure 4-3 describes each of the four dialog boxes.

Figure 4-3	TASKS PERFORMED IN EACH STEP OF THE CHART WIZARD

DIALOG BOX	TASK OPTIONS
Chart Type	Select from list of available chart types and corresponding type sub-type, or choose to customize a chart type
Chart Source Data	Specify the worksheet cells that contain the data on which the chart will be based and the worksheet cells that contain the labels that will appear in the chart
Chart Options	Change the appearance of the chart by selecting the options that affect titles, axes, gridlines, legends, data labels, and data tables
Chart Location	Specify where the chart will be placed: embedded as an object in the worksheet containing the data or on a separate worksheet, also called a chart sheet

Note that you can quit the Chart Wizard at any time in the process, and Excel will complete the remaining dialog boxes for you, using the default configuration for the chart you have chosen.

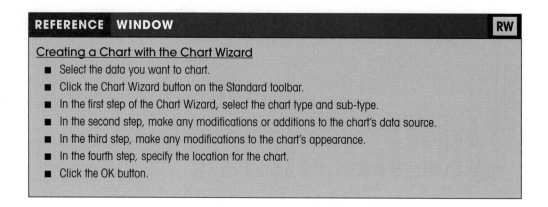

Start the Chart Wizard.

To start the Chart Wizard:

1. Select the range **A2:D6**.

2. Click the **Chart Wizard** button ▦ on the Standard toolbar. The first step of the Chart Wizard is shown in Figure 4-4.

> **TROUBLE?** If the Chart Wizard button is not displayed on the toolbar, click the Toolbar Options button ⏷ on the Standard toolbar, and then click ▦.

Figure 4-4 **STEP 1 OF THE CHART WIZARD**

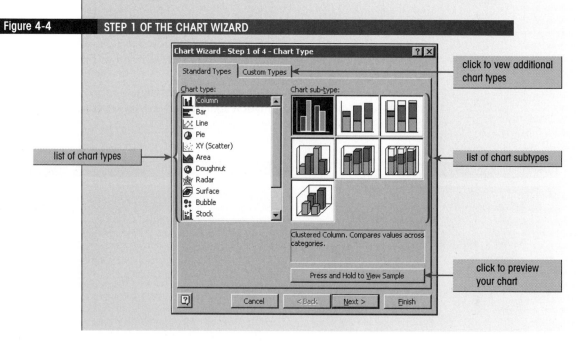

Choosing a Chart Type

The first step of the Chart Wizard provides the chart types from which you choose the one you think will best represent the data you want to present visually. Excel supports 14 types of charts ranging from the column chart, similar to the one shown in Alicia's first sketch, to stock market charts used to record the daily behavior of stocks. Figure 4-5 provides information about some of the chart types.

Figure 4-5	EXCEL CHART TYPES	

ICON(S)	CHART TYPE(S)	DESCRIPTION
	Column	Compares values within different categories based on the height of the columns
	Bar	Compares values within different categories based on the width of the bars
	Line	Compares values using different lines for different categories
	Pie	Compares values within different categories based on the size of the pie slice
	XY (Scatter)	Shows the pattern or relationship between sets of (x, y) data points
	Area	Similar to the Line chart, except that the areas under the lines are filled in with color
	Stock	Displays stock market data, including the high, low, open, and close prices of a stock
	Cylinder, Cone, Pyramid	Similar to the Column chart, except that cylinders, cones, and pyramids are substituted for the columns

Each chart type has its own collection of sub-types that provide alternative formats for the chart. For example, the column chart type has seven different sub-types, including the clustered column and the stacked column. There are also 3-D, or three-dimensional, sub-types.

Excel also supports 20 additional "custom" chart types that either combine two of the 14 main chart types or that provide additional formatting of the chart's appearance. You can also create your own customized chart designs and add them to the custom chart list.

Alicia wants you to create a column chart for the sales data, in which values are arranged into separate columns. To see whether the chart you are creating is the right one, you can click a button to preview the chart before continuing in the Chart Wizard.

To select the chart type and preview it:

1. Verify that the Column chart type is selected in the Chart type list box and that the first sub-type, Clustered Column, is also selected.

2. Press the **Press and Hold to view Sample** button, but do not release the mouse button. Figure 4-6 shows the contents of the preview window.

Figure 4-6	PREVIEW OF THE CLUSTERED COLUMN CHART

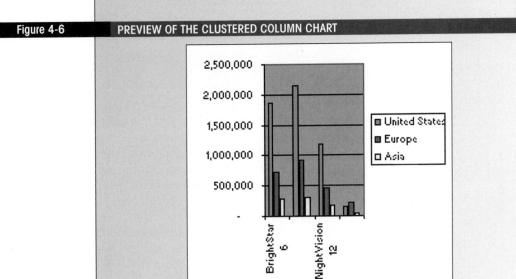

A different colored column represents each region in this chart. The blue columns represent the United States sales, the maroon columns the European sales, and the yellow columns the Asian sales. Though the size of the Preview pane prevents you from viewing much of the chart detail, you can see that the columns are clustered into groups, where each group represents a different model. The first cluster represents sales for the BrightStar 6 telescope. The second cluster represents sales for the BrightStar 8 and so forth. Since this is the chart type that Alicia wants you to create, you can continue to the next step of the Chart Wizard.

3. Release the mouse button, and then click the **Next** button to go to step 2 of the Chart Wizard.

Choosing a Data Source

In the second step of the Chart Wizard, shown in Figure 4-7, you specify the data to be displayed in the chart, also known as the chart's **data source**. Excel organizes the data source into a collection of **data series**, where each data series is a range of data values that are plotted on the chart. A data series consists of data values, which are plotted on the chart's vertical axis, or y-axis. On the horizontal axis, or x-axis, are the data series' **category values**, or **x values**. A chart can have several data series, which are plotted against a common set of category values. For example, the column chart preview shown in Figure 4-7 illustrates the three data series that present the sales for the United States, Europe, and Asia. Those sales values are matched against the category values that indicate the telescope model.

Figure 4-7	SPECIFYING THE DATA SOURCE

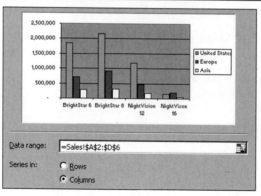

In Alicia's sketch, she has illustrated that she wants the category values to be the three regions, and not the four telescope models. Currently Excel has drawn the data from the range A2:D6, which is the range of data you selected before starting the Chart Wizard. By default, Excel organized these values by columns, so that the leftmost column contains the category values and the subsequent columns each contain a data series. The first row of the data used in the chart contains the labels that identify each data series. In general, if the data spans more rows than columns, then the Chart Wizard organizes the data series by columns, otherwise the Chart Wizard organizes the data series by rows. However, you can override this behavior and have Excel organize the data by rows. Therefore, the first row will contain the category values, and each subsequent row will contain a data series. The first column will then contain the label of each series.

To organize the data source by rows:

1. Click the **Rows** option button. Excel changes the orientation of the data source. The category values now represent the three regions rather than the four telescope models. See Figure 4-8.

| Figure 4-8 | CHANGING THE ORIENTATION OF THE DATA SOURCE |

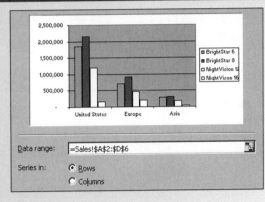

You can further define the data series used by the Chart Wizard using the Series tab. From this tab, you can add or remove data series from the chart or change the category values. Although it is recommended that you select the data series before starting the Chart Wizard, you do not have to since you can define all of the data series and chart values using the Series tab. However, selecting the data series first does save time.

To view the Series tab:

1. Click the **Series** tab. The Series tab lists all of the data series used in the chart and the cell references for the category labels. Note that the cell references include the name of the sheet from which the values are selected. See Figure 4-9.

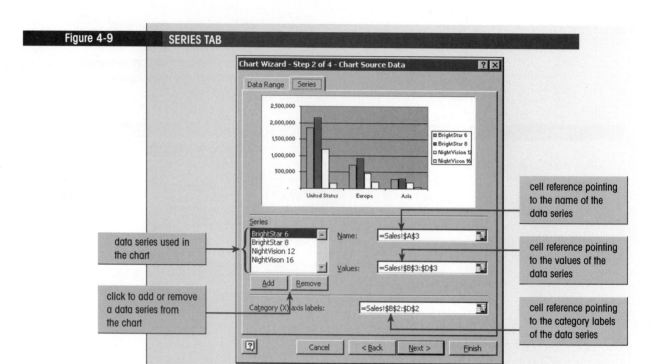

Figure 4-9   SERIES TAB

data series used in
the chart

click to add or remove
a data series from
the chart

cell reference pointing
to the name of the
data series

cell reference pointing
to the values of the
data series

cell reference pointing
to the category labels
of the data series

You do not have to make any changes in the data series at this point, so you
will continue in the Chart Wizard.

2. Click the **Next** button to go to step 3 of the Chart Wizard.

Choosing Chart Options

The third step of the Chart Wizard provides the options that you can use to control the
appearance of the chart. To better understand the options available to you, first explore
the terminology that Excel uses with respect to charts. Figure 4-10 shows the elements of
a typical Excel chart.

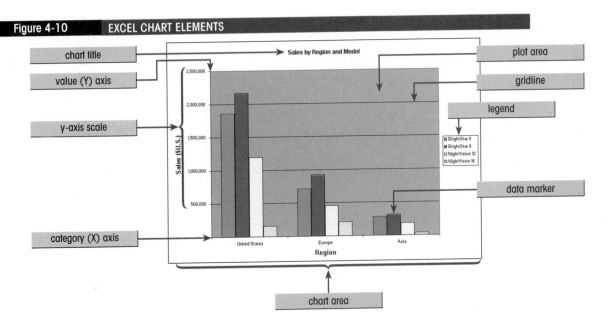

Figure 4-10   **EXCEL CHART ELEMENTS**

The basic element of the chart is the **plot area**, a rectangular area that contains a graphical representation of the values in the data series. These graphical representations are called **data markers**. The columns displayed in Column charts are examples of data markers. Other examples of data markers include the pie slices used in pie charts, or the points used in the XY (scatter) charts.

Most charts have two axes that border the plot area: a vertical, or x, axis and a horizontal, or y, axis. As mentioned earlier, values from the data series are plotted along the y-axis, whereas the category labels are plotted alongside the x-axis. Each axis can have a title that describes the values or labels displayed on the axis. In Figure 4-10, the x-axis title is "Region" and the y-axis title is "Sales ($U.S.)".

An axis covers a range of values, called a **scale**. The scale is displayed with values placed alongside the axes. Next to the values are **tick marks**, which act like the division lines on a ruler. Excel automatically displays a scale that represents the range of values in the data series. In the chart shown in Figure 4-10, the scale of the y-axis ranges from 0 up to 2,500,000. To make it easier to read the data markers on the axis scale, a chart might contain **gridlines**, which extend the tick marks into the plot area.

If several data series appear on the chart, a **legend** can be placed next to the plot area to identify each data series with a unique color or pattern. Above the plot area, Excel can display a **chart title** describing the contents of the plot and the data series. The entire chart and all of the elements discussed so far are contained in the **chart area**.

You can format these various elements of a chart in the Chart Wizard's third dialog box. You can also format these features later on, after the chart has been created. Figure 4-11 shows step 3 of the Chart Wizard. Excel divides the Step 3 dialog box into six tabs: Titles, Axes, Gridlines, Legend, Data Labels, and Data Table. Each tab provides tools for formatting different elements of your chart.

Figure 4-11   **STEP 3 OF THE CHART WIZARD**

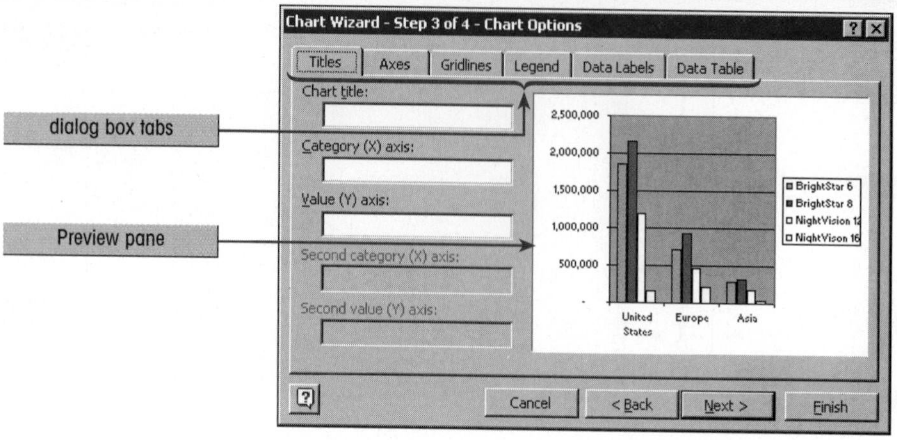

Alicia wants you to add descriptive titles to the chart and to each of the axes. She also wants you to remove the gridlines.

To insert titles into the chart:

1. Verify that the Titles tab is active.

2. Click the **Chart title** text box, type **Telescope Sales by Region**, and then press the **Tab** key. The Preview pane updates automatically to reflect the addition of the chart title to the chart area.

3. Type **Region** in the Category (X) axis box, and then press the **Tab** key.

4. Type **Sales ($U.S.)** in the Value (Y) axis box, and then press the **Tab** key. The Preview pane shows all of the new titles you entered into the chart.

5. Click the **Gridlines** tab.

6. Click the **Major gridlines** check box on the Value (Y) axes to remove the major gridlines from the chart.

7. Click the **Next** button.

Choosing the Chart Location

In the final step of the Chart Wizard, you choose a location for the chart. You have two choices: 1) you can save the chart as an embedded chart in a worksheet, or 2) you can create a sheet called a chart sheet that contains only the chart. Figure 4-12 shows both options.

Figure 4-12 **EMBEDDED CHARTS AND CHART SHEETS**

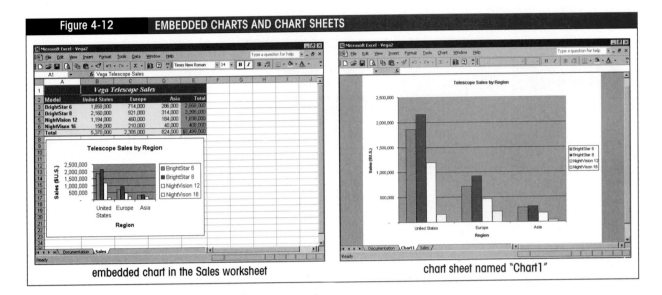

embedded chart in the Sales worksheet

chart sheet named "Chart1"

An **embedded chart** is a chart that is displayed within a worksheet. The advantage of creating an embedded chart is that you can place the chart alongside the data source, giving context to the chart. On the other hand, a **chart sheet** is a new sheet that is automatically inserted in the workbook, occupying the entire document window and thus providing more space and details for the chart. For this chart, you will save it as an embedded chart in the Sales worksheet.

To save the chart:

1. Verify that the As object in option button is selected and that "Sales" is selected in the adjacent list box. See Figure 4-13.

Figure 4-13 **STEP 4 OF THE CHART WIZARD**

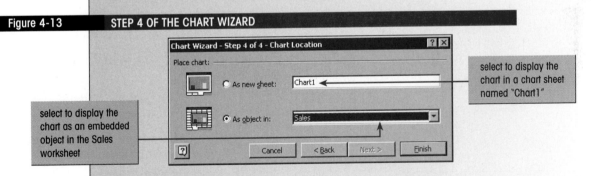

select to display the chart in a chart sheet named "Chart1"

select to display the chart as an embedded object in the Sales worksheet

2. Click the **Finish** button. Excel creates the column chart with the specifications you selected and embeds the chart in the Sales worksheet. Figure 4-14 shows the chart.

| Figure 4-14 | COMPLETED COLUMN CHART |

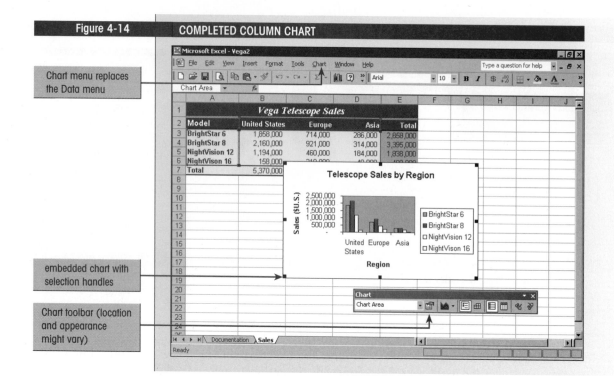

Chart menu replaces the Data menu

embedded chart with selection handles

Chart toolbar (location and appearance might vary)

When Excel creates the embedded chart, several things happen. First, note that the chart appears with selection handles around it. The selection handles indicate that the chart is an **active chart**, and it is ready for additional formatting. The Chart toolbar also appears automatically when the chart is selected (on some systems, where the Chart toolbar has been previously closed, this will not be true). Also note that the Chart menu has replaced the Data menu on Excel's menu bar. You will also find certain Excel commands are not available to you when a chart is the active object in the document window. When a chart is not active, the worksheet menus return and the Chart toolbar disappears.

To switch between the embedded chart and the worksheet:

1. Click anywhere in the worksheet outside of the chart to deselect it. The Chart toolbar disappears and the Data menu replaces the Chart menu on the menu bar. There are no selection handles around the chart.

2. Move the pointer over a blank area in the chart until the label, "Chart Area" appears, and then click the blank area. The Chart toolbar and the Chart menu reappear. Selection handles appear around the chart.

TROUBLE? If you do not see the Chart toolbar, it may have been closed during a previous Excel session. Click View on the menu bar, point to Toolbars, and then click Chart to redisplay the toolbar.

TROUBLE? If you clicked one of the chart's elements, you made that element active rather than the entire chart. Click a blank area in the chart area to select the entire embedded chart.

The new chart is obscuring some of the data from the sales table. The chart might also look better if it were bigger. You decide to make some additional changes to the chart's appearance.

Moving and Resizing an Embedded Chart

The Chart Wizard has a default size and location for embedded charts, which might not match what you want in your worksheet. The chart may be too small to accentuate relationships between the data markers, or labels might not be displayed correctly. An embedded chart is an object that you can move, resize, or copy. To work with an embedded chart, you first must make the chart active so that the selection handles appear.

Even though you are not sure where Alicia wants the chart to appear, you decide to move it so the chart appears directly under the worksheet.

To move the embedded chart:

1. Verify that the embedded chart is active and that the selection handles appear around the chart, and not around any element within the chart.

2. Move the pointer over a blank area of the chart so that the label "Chart Area" appears.

3. Drag the embedded chart so that the upper-left corner of the chart aligns with the upper-left corner of cell A8. Note that as you drag the chart with the pointer, an outline of the chart area appears. Use the outline as a guideline.

4. Release the mouse button. The chart moves to a new location in the worksheet.

To resize the chart, you drag the selection handles in the direction that you want the chart resized, that is, to increase or decrease the size of the chart. To keep the proportions of the chart the same, press and hold the Shift key as you drag one of the corner selection handles. Now that you have moved the chart, you can increase its size, which will improve its readability. Increasing the size of the chart will help to draw the audience's attention immediately to it.

To resize the embedded chart:

1. Move your mouse pointer over the lower-right corner selection handle until the pointer changes to ⬂.

2. Press and hold down the mouse button.

3. Drag the lower-right corner of the embedded chart until that corner is aligned with the lower-right corner of cell F24.

   TROUBLE? If the Chart toolbar obscures cell F24, you can still move the pointer to the approximate location of cell F24, or you can release the mouse button, and then drag the Chart toolbar by its title bar to a new location on the worksheet, out of the way.

4. Release the mouse button. Figure 4-15 shows the final resized and moved chart.

Figure 4-15 | **EMBEDDED CHART RESIZED AND MOVED TO A NEW LOCATION**

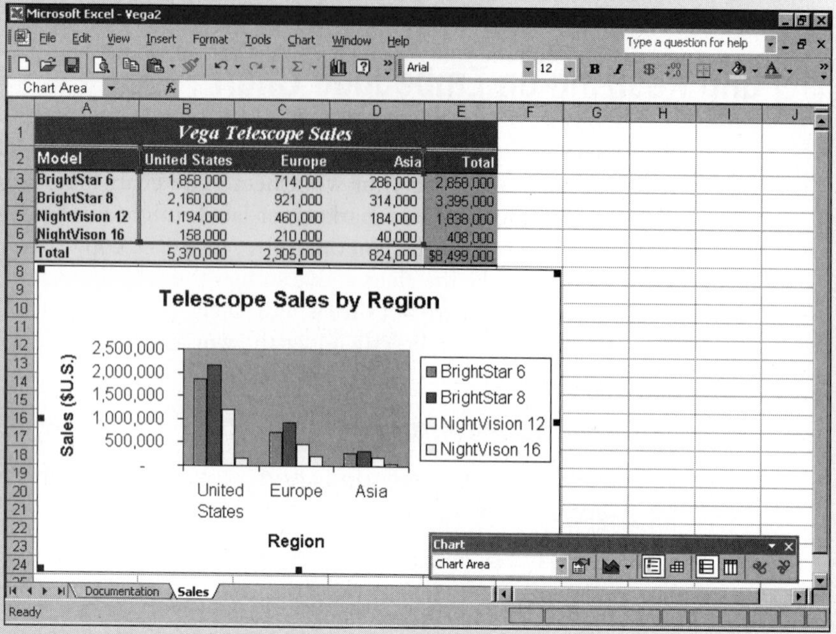

Updating a Chart

Every chart you create is linked to the data in a worksheet. As a result, if you change the data in the worksheet, Excel will automatically update the chart to reflect the change. This is true for category labels as well as for data values.

Alicia notices two mistakes in the Sales worksheet. First, the sales amount in cell C3 should be 914,000 and not 714,000. The second mistake is that the name of the telescope model in cell A6 is misspelled. The name of the telescope is "NightVision" and not "NightVison". You'll correct these mistakes and observe how the embedded chart is automatically updated.

To update the column chart:

1. Click cell **C3**, type **914000**, and then press the **Enter** key. The data marker corresponding to European sales for the BrightStar 6 changes to reflect the new sales value.

2. Click cell **A6**, type **NightVision 16**, and then press the **Enter** key. The entry in the chart's legend displays the correct spelling of the telescope.

Creating a Pie Chart

The second chart that Alicia sketched (shown in Figure 4-2) is a pie chart that shows the contribution of each telescope model to the total sales. In a pie chart, the size of each slice is determined by the value of a single data point to the sum of all values. Unlike the column chart you just created, a pie chart will have only one data series. In this case, the data series will contain the totals for each model across all regions. If you want to create a pie-like chart that contains several data series, you would choose the doughnut chart type in which the pie slices are nested inside one another.

The pie chart that you need to create will have four slices, each corresponding to one of the four telescope models. Alicia's sketch also shows percentages next to the slices, so that people viewing her report will be able to see instantly what percentage each model contributed to the total sales.

As with the column chart, you will create the pie chart using the Chart Wizard. You need to select two columns from the sales table. The first column, range A2:A6, contains the names of the different telescope models. The second column, range E2:E6, contains the totals sales for each model. Remember that a pie chart uses only one data series.

To create the pie chart:

1. Select the nonadjacent range **A2:A6;E2:E6**.

2. Click the **Chart Wizard** button 📊 on the Standard toolbar.

3. Click the **Pie** chart in the Chart type list box, and verify that the first chart sub-type is selected.

4. Click the **Next** button.

   Since you already chose the data series for the chart, you do not have to make any changes, so you can bypass the second step of the Chart Wizard.

5. Click the **Next** button.

   According to Alicia's sketch, you need to add a title to the chart.

6. Verify that the Titles tab is active, double-click the **Chart title** text box, and then type **Total Telescope Sales** (which replaces the title "Total" that displayed automatically based on the data series in range E2:E6).

   Next you will add data labels to the chart that display the percentage of sales for each model.

7. Click the **Data Labels** tab, and then click the **Percentage** check box. See Figure 4-16.

| Figure 4-16 | DISPLAYING PERCENTAGE LABELS IN A PIE CHART |

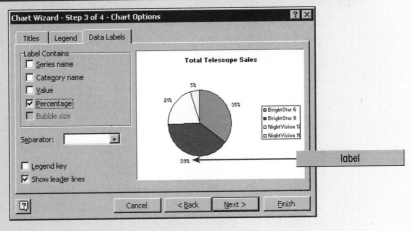

8. Click the **Next** button.

Finally, you will place the pie chart in its own chart sheet and name the sheet "Pie Chart of Sales."

9. Click the **As new sheet** option button, and then type **Pie Chart of Sales** in the adjacent list box. The text you type in the text box appears as the name of the chart sheet on the tab.

10. Click the **Finish** button. Figure 4-17 shows the completed pie chart. Note that the chart sheet is inserted before the Sales sheet.

Figure 4-17	PIE CHART OF TOTAL TELESCOPE SALES

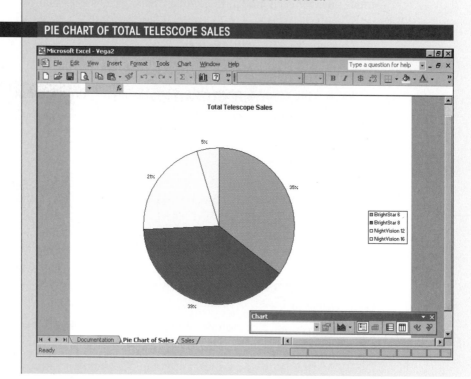

After reviewing the pie chart, Alicia has a few questions about the chart's appearance. She wonders why the slices are organized the way they are and whether the arrangement of the pie slices can be changed. The slices are arranged in a counter-clockwise direction following the order that they appeared in the table. The first entry is for the BrightStar 6 scope, the next is for the BrightStar 8, and so forth. Alicia asks whether it would be possible to move the BrightStar 6 slice away from the legend.

Rotating the Pie Chart

You cannot change the order in which the slices are arranged in the pie without changing their order in the data series, but you can rotate the chart. If you break the chart in 360 degree increments, starting from the top of the pie, the first slice starts at 0 degrees. You can specify a different starting point for the first slice.

Based on Alicia's suggestion, you decide to change the starting point to 180 degrees—the bottom of the chart.

To complete this task:

1. Create a new workbook named **BCancer** that contains a Documentation sheet displaying your name, the date, and the purpose of the workbook, and a worksheet named "Breast Cancer Data" that contains the data from Figure 4-42 entered in the range A1:C17.

2. Select the temperature and mortality data, and then start the Chart Wizard.

3. Use the Chart Wizard to create an embedded XY (Scatter) chart with no data points connected. Specify "Mortality vs. Temperature" as the chart title. Specify "Temperature" as the title of the x-axis and "Mortality Index" as the title of the y-axis. Remove the grid-lines. Do not include the legend. The scatter chart should be embedded on the Breast Cancer Data worksheet, with the chart covering the cell range D1:K23.

4. Change the scale of the x-axis to cover the temperature range 30 to 55 degrees.

5. Change the scale of the y-axis to cover the mortality index range 50 to 110.

Explore ▷ 6. Double-click one of the data points in the chart to open the Format Data Series dialog box, and make the following changes to the appearance of the data points:

   ■ Change the marker style to a circle that is 7 points in size.
   ■ Change the background color of the circle to white.
   ■ Change the foreground color of the circle to red.

Explore ▷ 7. Click Chart on the menu bar, and then click Add Trendline. On the Type tab, click the Linear trend line, and then click the OK button. The purpose of the linear trend line is to display whether a linear relationship exists between the 16 regions' mean annual temperature and their annual mortality index. Does it appear that such a relationship exists? What does a high mean annual temperature imply about the annual mortality index?

8. Change the fill color of the plot area to light yellow.

9. Set up the worksheet to print in landscape orientation. Center the worksheet horizontally and vertically on the page. Enter your name and the date in the right section of the page's header. Print the chart.

10. Save and close the workbook, and then close Excel.

INTERNET ASSIGNMENTS

Student Union

The purpose of the Internet Assignments is to challenge you to find information on the Internet that you can use to create effective spreadsheets. The actual assignments are updated and maintained on the Course Technology Web site. Log on to the Internet and use your Web browser to go to the Student Union on the New Perspectives Series site at **www.course.com/NewPerspectives/studentunion**. Click the Online Companions link, and then click the link for this text.

QUICK | CHECK ANSWERS

Session 4.1

1. A chart type is one of the 14 styles of charts supported by Excel. Each chart type has various alternate formats, called chart sub-types.

2. stock chart

3. A data series is a range of data values that is plotted on the chart.

4. The plot area contains the actual data values that are plotted in the chart, as well as any background colors or images for that plot. The chart area contains the plot area and any other element (such as titles and legend boxes) that may be included in the chart.

5. Gridlines are lines that extend out from the tick marks on either axis into the plot area.

6. embedded charts, which are placed within a worksheet, and chart sheets, which contain only the chart itself

7. pie

8. exploded pie

Session 4.2

1. Click Chart on the menu bar, click Source Data, and then click the Series tab. Select the data series in the Series list box, and click the Remove button.

2. Click Chart on the menu bar, and then click Location. Select a new location from the dialog box.

3. Label text is text that consists of category names, tick mark labels, and legend text. Attached text is text that is attached to other elements of the chart, such as the chart title or axes titles. Unattached text is additional text that is unassociated with any particular element of the chart.

4. Major tick marks are tick marks that appear on the axis alongside the axis values. Minor tick marks do not appear alongside any axis value, but instead are used to provide a finer gradation between major tick marks.

5. Click Chart on the menu bar, and then click Chart Type. Select one of the 3-D chart sub-types for the column chart.

6. An AutoShape is a predefined shape available on the Drawing toolbar. You can add an AutoShape to any worksheet or chart. You can change the size or shape of an AutoShape, and you can change its fill color.

7. a) Use full page, which resizes the chart to fit the full size of the printed page; the proportions of the chart may change in the resizing, b) Scale to fit page, in which the chart is resized to fit the page, but it retains its proportions, c) Custom, in which the dimensions of the printed chart are specified in the chart sheet

New Perspectives on

MICROSOFT®
EXCEL 2002

Read This Before You Begin

To the Student

Data Disks

To complete the Level II tutorials, Review Assignments, and Case Problems, you need six Data Disks. Your instructor will either provide you with the Data Disks or ask you to make your own.

If you are making your own Data Disks, you will need **six** blank, formatted high-density disks. You will need to copy a set of files and/or folders from a file server, standalone computer, or the Web onto your disk. Your instructor will tell you which computer, drive letter, and folders contain the files you need. You could also download the files by going to **www.course.com** and following the instructions on the screen.

The information below shows you which folders go on your disks, so that you will have enough disk space to complete all the tutorials, Review Assignments, and Case Problems:

Data Disk 1

Write this on the disk label:
Data Disk 1: Excel 2002 Tutorial 5

Put this folder on the disk: Tutorial.05

Data Disk 2

Write this on the disk label:
Data Disk 2: Excel 2002 Tutorial 6

Put this folder on the disk: Tutorial.06

Data Disk 3

Write this on the disk label:
Data Disk 3: Excel 2002 Tutorial 7 (Tutorial and Review)

Put these folders on the disk: Tutorial.07\Tutorial and Tutorial.07\Review

Data Disk 4

Write this on the disk label:
Data Disk 4: Excel 2002 Tutorial 7 (Cases)

Put this folder on the disk: Tutorial.07\Cases

Data Disk 5

Write this on the disk label:
Data Disk 5: Excel 2002 Tutorial 8

Put this folder on the disk: Tutorial.08

Data Disk 6

Write this on the disk label:
Data Disk 6: Excel 2002 Appendices 1 and 2

Put these folders on the disk: Appendix.01 and Appendix.02

When you begin each tutorial, be sure you are using the correct Data Disk. Refer to the "File Finder" chart at the back of this text for more detailed information on which files are used in which tutorials. See the inside front or inside back cover of this book for more information on Data Disk files, or ask your instructor or technical support person for assistance.

Using Your Own Computer

If you are going to work through this book using your own computer, you need:

- **Computer System** Microsoft Windows 98, NT, 2000 Professional, or higher must be installed on your computer. This book assumes a typical installation of Microsoft Excel.

- **Data Disks** You will not be able to complete the tutorials or exercises in this book using your own computer until you have your Data Disks.

Visit Our World Wide Web Site

Additional materials designed especially for you are available on the World Wide Web.
Go to **www.course.com/NewPerspectives**.

To the Instructor

The Data Disk Files are available on the Instructor's Resource Kit for this title. Follow the instructions in the Help file on the CD-ROM to install the programs to your network or standalone computer. For information on creating Data Disks, see the "To the Student" section above.

You are granted a license to copy the Data Files to any computer or computer network used by students who have purchased this book.

OBJECTIVES

In this tutorial you will:

- Identify the elements of an Excel list

- Freeze rows and columns

- Change zoom settings for displaying a worksheet

- Find and replace values in a worksheet

- Sort data in a list

- Use a data form to enter, search for, edit, and delete records

- Filter data in a list using AutoFilters

- Apply conditional formatting to a range

- Insert subtotals into a list

- Use the subtotals outline view

- Summarize a list using a PivotTable and a PivotChart

WORKING WITH EXCEL LISTS

Tracking Vehicle Data

CASE

Keeping Track of Campus Vehicles

Linda Pell was recently hired as coordinator of facilities, a new position, at a local university. One of her first assignments is to get a handle on the fleet of vehicles owned by the institution. In the past, the automotive department was responsible for keeping these records, but it was more interested in repairing the vehicles than in doing the recordkeeping. As a result, the administration really has no idea which department has been assigned what vehicles, how much each vehicle is being used, which vehicles are insured, as well as many other questions.

To track the information on the fleet of vehicles, Linda set up an Excel database. She recorded information such as the vehicle identification number, type of car, model year, purchase price, department to which a vehicle was assigned, maintenance cost, and other pieces of information. Linda has asked that you help her maintain this database of information so she can provide up-to-date and accurate information to the administration about the university's vehicles.

In this tutorial, you will use Excel to manage Linda's list of vehicle data. You will sort data in an Excel list, and then enter, edit, and delete data in the list using a data form. You will also use the data form to search for information that meets certain criteria. You will filter the information to display only data that meets certain criteria. You will also apply conditional formatting to a range of cells to highlight specific values in the range. You will insert subtotals and view the subtotals. You will summarize a list using a PivotTable and PivotChart.

SESSION 5.1

In this session, you will use Excel to manage a list of information. You will sort information using different fields. You will enter, edit, and delete information using a data form, and then use the data format to search for specific information. Finally, you will filter the information in the list to display only the data that meets certain criteria.

Introduction **to Lists**

One of the more common uses of a worksheet is to manage lists of data, such as client lists, phone lists, and transaction lists. Excel provides you with the tools to manage such tasks. Using Excel, you can store and update data, sort data, search for and retrieve data, summarize and compare data, and create reports.

In Excel a **list** is a collection of similar data stored in a structured manner, in rows and columns. Figure 5-1 shows a portion of the vehicles list. Within an Excel list, each column represents a **field** that describes some attribute or characteristic of an object, person, place, or thing. In this list, a vehicle's identification number, the department that is responsible for the vehicle, and the purchase price of the vehicle are examples of fields. When related fields are grouped together in a row, they form a **record**, a collection of fields that describes a person, place, or thing. For example, the data for each vehicle—ID number, model year, make, vehicle type, department to which the vehicle is assigned, odometer reading, purchase price, and annual maintenance cost—represents a record. A collection of related records makes up an Excel list.

Figure 5-1 PORTION OF THE VEHICLES LIST

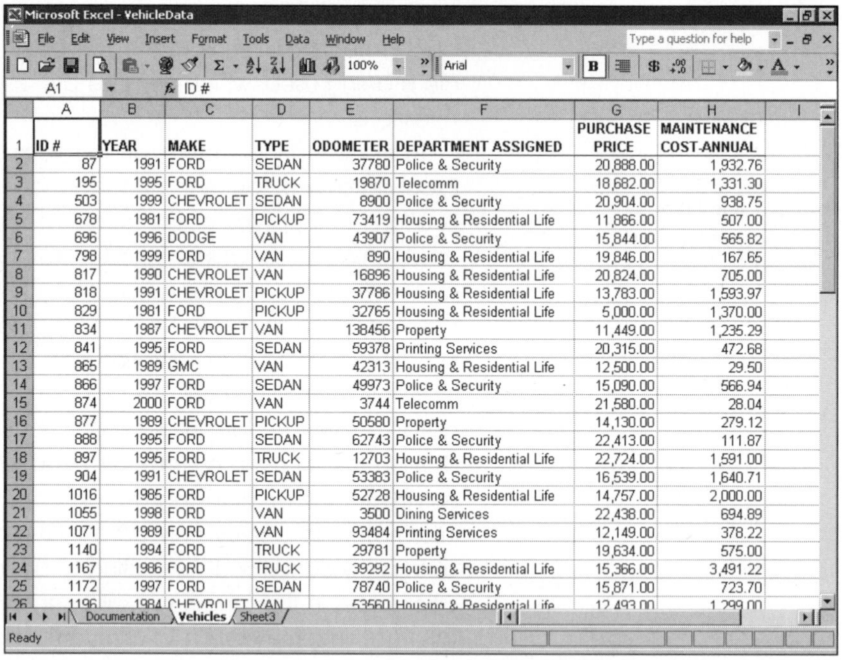

ID #	YEAR	MAKE	TYPE	ODOMETER	DEPARTMENT ASSIGNED	PURCHASE PRICE	MAINTENANCE COST-ANNUAL
87	1991	FORD	SEDAN	37780	Police & Security	20,888.00	1,932.76
195	1995	FORD	TRUCK	19870	Telecomm	18,682.00	1,331.30
503	1999	CHEVROLET	SEDAN	8900	Police & Security	20,904.00	938.75
678	1981	FORD	PICKUP	73419	Housing & Residential Life	11,866.00	507.00
696	1996	DODGE	VAN	43907	Police & Security	15,844.00	565.82
798	1999	FORD	VAN	890	Housing & Residential Life	19,846.00	167.65
817	1990	CHEVROLET	VAN	16896	Housing & Residential Life	20,824.00	705.00
818	1991	CHEVROLET	PICKUP	37786	Housing & Residential Life	13,783.00	1,593.97
829	1981	FORD	PICKUP	32765	Housing & Residential Life	5,000.00	1,370.00
834	1987	CHEVROLET	VAN	138456	Property	11,449.00	1,235.29
841	1995	FORD	SEDAN	59378	Printing Services	20,315.00	472.68
865	1989	GMC	VAN	42313	Housing & Residential Life	12,500.00	29.50
866	1997	FORD	SEDAN	49973	Police & Security	15,090.00	566.94
874	2000	FORD	VAN	3744	Telecomm	21,580.00	28.04
877	1989	CHEVROLET	PICKUP	50580	Property	14,130.00	279.12
888	1995	FORD	SEDAN	62743	Police & Security	22,413.00	111.87
897	1995	FORD	TRUCK	12703	Housing & Residential Life	22,724.00	1,591.00
904	1991	CHEVROLET	SEDAN	53383	Police & Security	16,539.00	1,640.71
1016	1985	FORD	PICKUP	52728	Housing & Residential Life	14,757.00	2,000.00
1055	1998	FORD	VAN	3500	Dining Services	22,438.00	694.89
1071	1989	FORD	VAN	93484	Printing Services	12,149.00	378.22
1140	1994	FORD	TRUCK	29781	Property	19,634.00	575.00
1167	1986	FORD	TRUCK	39292	Housing & Residential Life	15,366.00	3,491.22
1172	1997	FORD	SEDAN	78740	Police & Security	15,871.00	723.70
1196	1984	CHEVROLET	VAN	53560	Housing & Residential Life	12,493.00	1,299.00

If you have worked with spreadsheets before, you might be aware that Microsoft uses the term "list" instead of "database" for data in a worksheet that is structured in a row and column format. The term **database** refers to files created using database management software, such as Access, SQL Server, and Oracle. In this tutorial you will focus on Excel lists.

Planning **and Creating a List**

Before you create a list, you will want to do some planning. As you spend time thinking about how you will use the list, consider the types of reports, queries, and searches you might need. This process should help you determine the kind of information to include for each record and the contents of each field. As with most projects, the planning that you do before you create your list will help you avoid redesigning the list later.

To create the vehicles list, Linda first determined her information requirements. As a way of documenting the information requirements of the vehicles list, she developed a **data definition table**, which is a table that describes the fields she plans to maintain for each vehicle. Figure 5-2 shows the data definition table Linda developed to define her data requirements. She used this table as a guide in creating the vehicles list.

Figure 5-2	DATA DEFINITION TABLE FOR THE VEHICLES LIST

FIELD NAME	DESCRIPTION
ID #	Vehicle's identification number
YEAR	Model year of vehicle
MAKE	Manufacturer (CHEVROLET, DODGE, FORD, GMC)
TYPE	Category of vehicle (PICKUP, SEDAN, TRUCK, VAN)
ODOMETER	Latest reading of odometer
DEPARTMENT ASSIGNED	Department responsible for vehicle
PURCHASE PRICE	Purchase price of vehicle
MAINTENANCE COST-ANNUAL	Annual maintenance cost

Once you determine the design of your list, you can create the list in a worksheet. You can use a blank worksheet or one that already contains data. When creating a list in Excel, use the following guidelines:

- The top row of the list should contain a **field name**, a unique label describing the contents of the data in the rows below it. This row of field names is sometimes referred to as the **field header row**. Although the field header row often begins in row 1, the field header row can begin in any row.

- Field names can contain up to 255 characters. Usually a short name is easier to understand and remember. Short field names also enable you to display more fields on the screen at one time.

- You format the field names to make it easier for Excel to distinguish between the data in the list and the field names. For example, you can use a different font, font size, font style (such as bold or italic), or color.

- Each column should contain the same kind of information for each row in the list.

- The list should be separated from any other information in the same worksheet by at least one blank row and one blank column. Separating the list from the other parts of the worksheet will enable Excel to automatically determine the range of the list by identifying the blank row and column. For the same reason, you should avoid blank rows and columns within the list.

Now you will open the workbook that Linda created that contains the vehicles list.

To open the Vehicles workbook:

1. Start Excel and then open the **Vehicles** workbook located in the Tutorial.05/Tutorial folder on your Data Disk.

2. On the Documentation sheet, enter the current date and your name.

3. Save the workbook as **VehicleData** in the Tutorial.05/Tutorial folder on your Data Disk.

4. Switch to the Vehicles sheet to display the list of vehicles. This worksheet (which is the same worksheet as shown in Figure 5-1) contains the list of vehicles. Currently there are 71 vehicles. Each vehicle record is stored as a separate row (row 2 through 72). There are eight fields (columns A through H) for each record. Notice that the field names have been boldface to make it easier for Excel to distinguish the field names from the data in the list.

   To view the current information, scroll through the vehicles list.

5. Drag the **vertical scroll bar** down to move to the bottom of the list (row 72). As the list scrolls, notice that the column headings are no longer visible.

6. Press **Ctrl + Home** to return to cell A1.

You want to be able to keep the column headings on the screen as you scroll the vehicles list. Not being able to see the column headings makes it difficult to know what the data in each column represents.

Freezing **Rows and Columns**

You can select rows and columns so they "freeze" onscreen and don't scroll off the screen as you move around the worksheet. Freezing a row or column lets you keep headings on the screen as you work with the data in a large worksheet. To freeze a row or column, you select the cell below and to the right of the row(s) or column(s) you want to freeze. For example, if you want to keep just the top row of column headings displayed on the screen, you click cell A2 (first column, second row), and then you select the Freeze Panes option on the Window menu. As you scroll down the list, the first row will remain on the screen so the column headings are visible, making it easier for you to understand the data in each record. The Freeze Panes option is a toggle—once you freeze the rows or columns, the option on the Window menu changes to Unfreeze Panes.

Freeze the first row, which contains the column headings, and the ID # column so that they remain on the screen as you scroll the list.

To freeze the first row and column in the worksheet:

1. Click cell **B2** to make it the active cell.

2. Click **Window** on the menu bar, and then click **Freeze Panes** to freeze the rows above row 2 and the columns to the left of column B. Excel displays dark horizontal and vertical lines to indicate which rows and columns are frozen.

   Now scroll the list, and watch the column headings.

3. Drag the **vertical scroll box** down to move to the bottom of the list (row 72). This time as the list scrolls, notice that the column headings remain visible. See Figure 5-3.

Figure 5-3 **COLUMN HEADINGS REMAIN VISIBLE AS THE LIST SCROLLS**

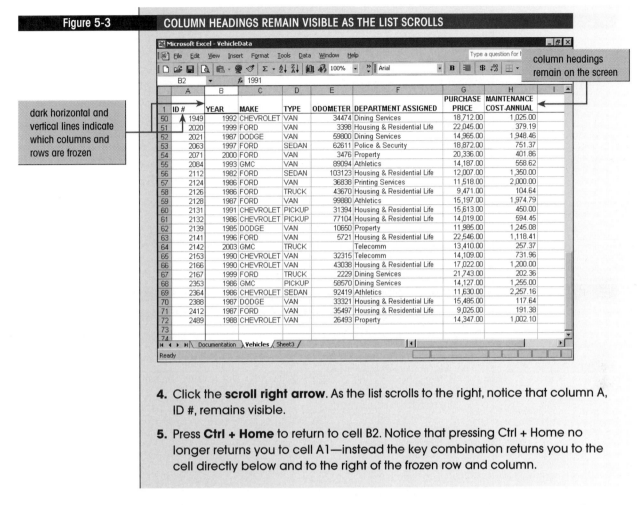

dark horizontal and vertical lines indicate which columns and rows are frozen

column headings remain on the screen

4. Click the **scroll right arrow**. As the list scrolls to the right, notice that column A, ID #, remains visible.

5. Press **Ctrl + Home** to return to cell B2. Notice that pressing Ctrl + Home no longer returns you to cell A1—instead the key combination returns you to the cell directly below and to the right of the frozen row and column.

The Freeze Panes option is a toggle—once you freeze the rows or columns, the option on the Window menu changes to Unfreeze Panes.

Changing the Zoom Setting of a Worksheet

Normally a worksheet appears at 100% magnification. The Zoom command on the View menu (or the Zoom list box on the Standard toolbar) enables you to change the zoom setting so you can see more or less of the worksheet on a screen. To see more of the worksheet, you can zoom out by decreasing the zoom percentage. To see less of the worksheet, you can zoom in, or magnify, a portion of the worksheet by increasing the zoom percentage, making it easier to read the contents of the worksheet.

Try changing the zoom setting using the Zoom command on the View menu.

To change the zoom setting of the Vehicles worksheet:

1. Click **View** on the menu bar, and then click **Zoom**. The Zoom dialog box opens. See Figure 5-4.

Figure 5-4   **ZOOM DIALOG BOX**

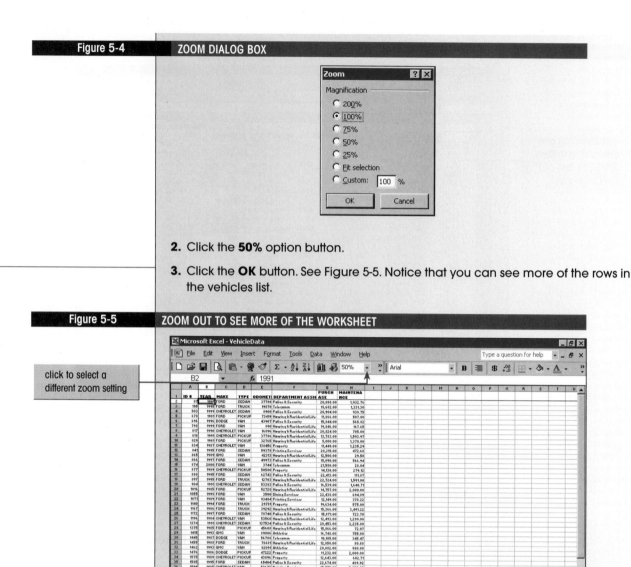

2. Click the **50%** option button.

3. Click the **OK** button. See Figure 5-5. Notice that you can see more of the rows in the vehicles list.

Figure 5-5   **ZOOM OUT TO SEE MORE OF THE WORKSHEET**

click to select a different zoom setting

Although you can see the entire list of vehicles, the values are small and too hard to read at 50% magnification, so you decide to return to the standard 100% setting. Although you can use the Zoom command to make this change, you'll use the Zoom button on the Standard toolbar instead.

To return the zoom setting to 100% using the Zoom list box:

1. Click the **list arrow** for the Zoom button 100% on the Standard toolbar to display the list of magnification options.

TROUBLE? If the Zoom button is not visible on the Standard toolbar, click the Toolbar Options button ⏬ on the toolbar, and then click the list arrow to the right of the 50% option, which is the current zoom setting.

TROUBLE? If the Standard and Formatting toolbars appear on separate rows on your screen, then the Toolbar Options button might look slightly different from the Toolbar Options button ⏬ used throughout this text. If you are unsure about the function of a toolbar button, hover the pointer over the button to display its name.

2. Click **100%**. Notice the worksheet returns to normal view.

As you review the worksheet, you notice the value "Telecomm" in the DEPARTMENT ASSIGNED column of the vehicles list reflects the abbreviated name. You want to change the name to "Telecommunications" instead of "Telecomm" before any reports are prepared.

Using **Find and Replace**

To find every occurrence of a character string or value in a large worksheet, you can use the Find and Replace commands. The Find command locates a value or character string, and the Replace command overwrites values or character strings.

Change every DEPARTMENT ASSIGNED field that contains the value "Telecomm" to "Telecommunications."

To replace the value Telecomm with Telecommunications in the DEPARTMENT ASSIGNED field:

1. Select the entire column **F** (DEPARTMENT ASSIGNED).

2. Click **Edit** on the menu bar, and then click **Replace** to open the Find and Replace Dialog box. See Figure 5-6.

Figure 5-6	FIND AND REPLACE DIALOG BOX

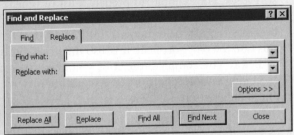

3. Type **Telecomm** in the Find what list box, and then press the **Tab** key.

4. Type **Telecommunications** in the Replace with list box.

5. Click the **Replace All** button to replace all matches. A message informs you that five replacements were changed.

6. Click the **OK** button in the message box, click the **Close** button in the Find and Replace dialog box, and then click any cell in the worksheet. See Figure 5-7. Notice the Telecomm entries have been changed to Telecommunications.

Figure 5-7 | **TELECOMMUNICATIONS REPLACES TELECOMM**

	A	B	C	D	E	F	G PURCHASE PRICE	H MAINTENANCE COST-ANNUAL	I
1	ID #	YEAR	MAKE	TYPE	ODOMETER	DEPARTMENT ASSIGNED			
2	87	1991	FORD	SEDAN	37780	Police & Security	20,888.00	1,932.76	
3	195	1995	FORD	TRUCK	19870	Telecommunications	18,682.00	1,331.30	
4	503	1999	CHEVROLET	SEDAN	8900	Police & Security	20,904.00	938.75	
5	678	1981	FORD	PICKUP	73419	Housing & Residential Life	11,866.00	507.00	
6	696	1996	DODGE	VAN	43907	Police & Security	15,844.00	5	
7	798	1999	FORD	VAN	890	Housing & Residential Life	19,846.00	1	
8	817	1990	CHEVROLET	VAN	16896	Housing & Residential Life	20,824.00	7	
9	818	1991	CHEVROLET	PICKUP	37786	Housing & Residential Life	13,783.00	1,59	
10	829	1981	FORD	PICKUP	32765	Housing & Residential Life	5,000.00	1,370.00	
11	834	1987	CHEVROLET	VAN	138456	Property	11,449.00	1,235.29	
12	841	1995	FORD	SEDAN	59378	Printing Services	20,315.00	472.68	
13	865	1989	GMC	VAN	42313	Housing & Residential Life	12,500.00	29.50	
14	866	1997	FORD	SEDAN	49973	Police & Security	15,090.00	566.94	
15	874	2000	FORD	VAN	3744	Telecommunications	21,580.00	28.04	
16	877	1989	CHEVROLET	PICKUP	50580	Property	14,130.00	279.12	
17	888	1995	FORD	SEDAN	62743	Police & Security	22,413.00	111.87	

full name of department is displayed

7. Scroll to view the other occurrences of the replacement text, and then press **Ctrl + Home**.

With the name of the Telecommunications department correct, you can now continue working with the data.

Sorting Data

In preparation for her meetings this week, Linda wants a list of vehicles sorted by the departments to which the vehicles are assigned so she can answer questions from department managers about their inventory of vehicles. She asks you to prepare a list of vehicles arranged by department.

When you enter a new record into a list, the new record is usually placed at the bottom of the list. To rearrange the records in a list, you can sort the records based on the data in one or more of the fields (columns). The fields you use to order your data are called **sort fields**, or **sort keys**. For example, to prepare a list of vehicles by department, you sort the data using the values in the DEPARTMENT ASSIGNED field. DEPARTMENT ASSIGNED becomes the sort field. Because DEPARTMENT ASSIGNED is the first sort field, and in this case the only sort field, it is also the **primary sort field**.

Before you complete the sort, you need to decide whether you want to put the list in ascending or descending order. **Ascending order** arranges labels alphabetically from A to Z and numbers from smallest to largest. **Descending order** arranges labels in reverse alphabetical order from Z to A and numbers from largest to smallest. In both ascending and descending order, any blank fields are placed at the bottom of the list.

Sorting a List Using One Sort Field

To sort data in an Excel worksheet, you can use the Sort Ascending and Sort Descending buttons on the Standard toolbar, or you can use the Sort command on the Data menu. The easiest way to sort data when there is only one sort field is to use the Sort Ascending or Sort Descending button on the Standard toolbar. If you are sorting using more than one sort field, you should use the Sort command on the Data menu to specify the columns on which you want to sort.

For the quick reference list of vehicles, Linda wants to sort the list by DEPARTMENT ASSIGNED in ascending order. Generate the alphabetized list of vehicles using the Standard toolbar.

To sort the list of vehicles using a single sort field:

1. Click any cell in the DEPARTMENT ASSIGNED column. You do not have to select the entire vehicles list, which consists of range A1:H72. Excel automatically determines the range of the list when you click any cell inside the list range, using the column that contains the active cell as the sort field.
2. Click the **Sort Ascending button** on the Standard toolbar. The data is sorted in ascending order by DEPARTMENT ASSIGNED. See Figure 5-8.

   TROUBLE? If the Sort Ascending button is not displayed on the Standard toolbar, click the Toolbar Options button on the toolbar, and then click .

   TROUBLE? If you selected the wrong column before sorting the list or if your data is sorted in the wrong order, you can undo it. To undo a sort, click the Undo button on the Standard toolbar. Then repeat Steps 1 and 2.

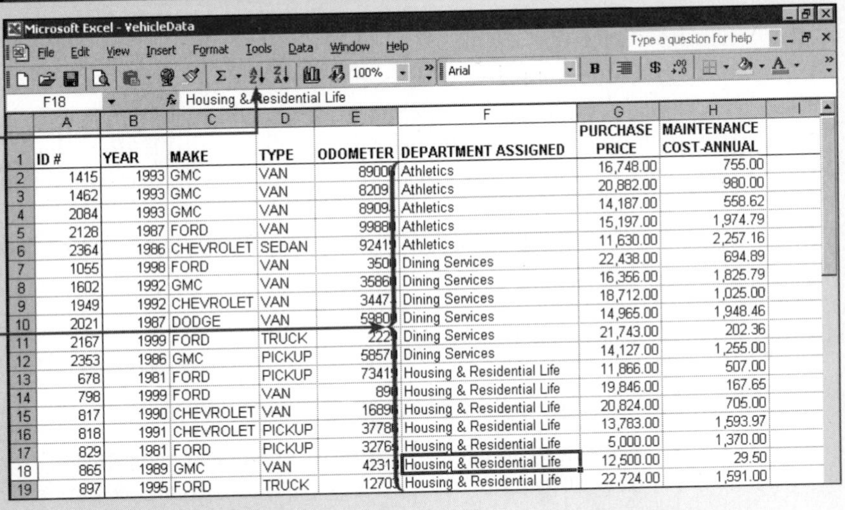

Figure 5-8 VEHICLES LIST SORTED BY DEPARTMENT ASSIGNED

Sort Ascending button

departments in alphabetical order

	A	B	C	D	E	F	G	H
1	ID #	YEAR	MAKE	TYPE	ODOMETER	DEPARTMENT ASSIGNED	PURCHASE PRICE	MAINTENANCE COST-ANNUAL
2	1415	1993	GMC	VAN	8900	Athletics	16,748.00	755.00
3	1462	1993	GMC	VAN	8209	Athletics	20,882.00	980.00
4	2084	1993	GMC	VAN	8909	Athletics	14,187.00	558.62
5	2128	1987	FORD	VAN	9988	Athletics	15,197.00	1,974.79
6	2364	1986	CHEVROLET	SEDAN	9241	Athletics	11,630.00	2,257.16
7	1055	1998	FORD	VAN	350	Dining Services	22,438.00	694.89
8	1602	1992	GMC	VAN	3586	Dining Services	16,356.00	1,825.79
9	1949	1992	CHEVROLET	VAN	3447	Dining Services	18,712.00	1,025.00
10	2021	1987	DODGE	VAN	5980	Dining Services	14,965.00	1,948.46
11	2167	1999	FORD	TRUCK	222	Dining Services	21,743.00	202.36
12	2353	1986	GMC	PICKUP	5857	Dining Services	14,127.00	1,255.00
13	678	1981	FORD	PICKUP	7341	Housing & Residential Life	11,866.00	507.00
14	798	1999	FORD	VAN	89	Housing & Residential Life	19,846.00	167.65
15	817	1990	CHEVROLET	VAN	1689	Housing & Residential Life	20,824.00	705.00
16	818	1991	CHEVROLET	PICKUP	3778	Housing & Residential Life	13,783.00	1,593.97
17	829	1981	FORD	PICKUP	3276	Housing & Residential Life	5,000.00	1,370.00
18	865	1989	GMC	VAN	4231	Housing & Residential Life	12,500.00	29.50
19	897	1995	FORD	TRUCK	1270	Housing & Residential Life	22,724.00	1,591.00

When sorting records, you do not select the entire sort field column. If you do select the column, Excel will only sort the values in the selected column rather than sort the entire list.

Linda also needs a list of vehicles sorted by vehicle type, and within each vehicle type, sorted by model year with new vehicles displayed before older ones.

Sorting a List Using More Than One Sort Field

Sometimes sorting by one sort field results in a tie—a **tie** occurs when more than one record has the same value for a field. For example, if you were to sort the vehicles list on the TYPE field, all vehicles with the same type would be grouped together. To break a tie, you can sort the list on multiple fields. For example, you can sort the vehicles list by type and then by year within each type. In this case, you specify the TYPE field as the **primary sort field** and the YEAR field as the **secondary sort field**.

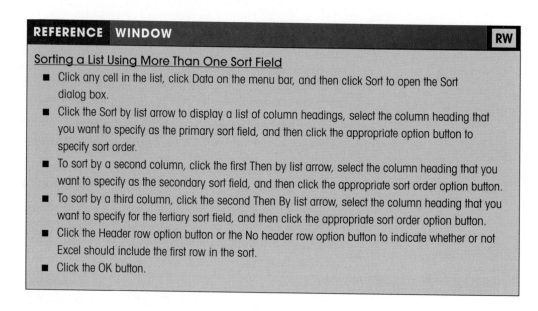

REFERENCE WINDOW   RW

Sorting a List Using More Than One Sort Field
- Click any cell in the list, click Data on the menu bar, and then click Sort to open the Sort dialog box.
- Click the Sort by list arrow to display a list of column headings, select the column heading that you want to specify as the primary sort field, and then click the appropriate option button to specify sort order.
- To sort by a second column, click the first Then by list arrow, select the column heading that you want to specify as the secondary sort field, and then click the appropriate sort order option button.
- To sort by a third column, click the second Then By list arrow, select the column heading that you want to specify for the tertiary sort field, and then click the appropriate sort order option button.
- Click the Header row option button or the No header row option button to indicate whether or not Excel should include the first row in the sort.
- Click the OK button.

Linda wants to sort by type in alphabetical order and then by year in descending order within each type. To generate this second list, you will need to sort the data using two columns: TYPE as the primary sort field and YEAR as the secondary sort field. When you have more than one sort field, you must use the Sort command on the Data menu to specify the columns you want to sort.

Now sort the vehicles list by type in ascending order, and within type by year in descending order.

To sort the records by type and within type by year:

1. Make sure the active cell is inside the list.

2. Click **Data** on the menu bar, and then click **Sort**. The Sort dialog box opens. See Figure 5-9. Notice that all the rows and columns, except for the first row (that is, the header row), are automatically selected.

Figure 5-9   SORT DIALOG BOX

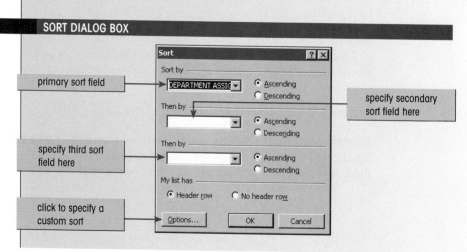

3. Click the **Sort by** list arrow to display the list of column headings, click **TYPE**, and then make sure the **Ascending** option button is selected.

Now specify the secondary sort field.

4. Click the first **Then by** list arrow, click **YEAR**, and then click the **Descending** option button.

5. Make sure the **Header row** option button is selected, and then click the **OK** button to sort the records by type and within type by year.

6. Scroll the list to view the data sorted by type and within type by year. Notice for each vehicle type that the newer vehicles are displayed before the older ones. See Figure 5-10.

Figure 5-10	VEHICLES LIST SORTED BY TYPE AND WITHIN TYPE BY YEAR

list sorted alphabetically by type of vehicles

list sorted within type by year in descending order

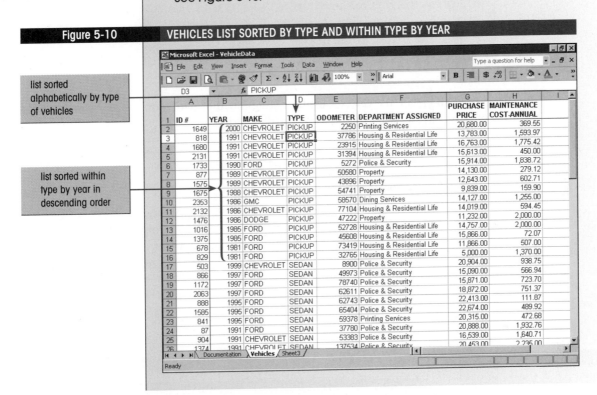

Now Linda has a list of vehicles sorted by type and within type by year. This sorted list will make finding information about the age of each type of vehicle much easier to find.

Maintaining a List Using a Data Form

Linda has several changes regarding the vehicle status that need to be reflected in the vehicles list. First, the Police & Security department has purchased a new patrol car that needs to be added to the vehicles list. Second, Linda just received the latest odometer reading for vehicle ID # 2142. This vehicle's record must be updated to reflect the new information. Finally, one of the older pickup trucks used by the Housing & Residential department is being scrapped because of its high mileage and high annual maintenance cost; the record for this vehicle, with ID # 678, needs to be deleted from the vehicles list. Linda asks you to update the vehicles list to reflect all these changes.

One way to maintain a list in Excel is to use a data form. A **data form** is a dialog box in which you can add, find, edit, and delete records in a list. A data form displays one record at a time, as opposed to the table of rows and columns you see in the worksheet. Although experienced users often use the worksheet to make changes directly to the list, using the data form can help prevent mistakes that can occur if you accidentally enter data in the wrong column or in a row above or below the correct one.

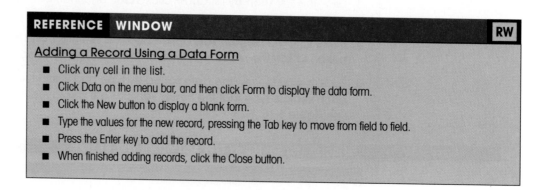

REFERENCE WINDOW   **RW**

Adding a Record Using a Data Form
■ Click any cell in the list.
■ Click Data on the menu bar, and then click Form to display the data form.
■ Click the New button to display a blank form.
■ Type the values for the new record, pressing the Tab key to move from field to field.
■ Press the Enter key to add the record.
■ When finished adding records, click the Close button.

You will update the vehicles list by adding the information on the new patrol car for the Police & Security department, using the data form.

To add the new record using the data form:

1. Make sure the active cell is within the list.

2. Click **Data** on the menu bar, and then click **Form** to display the Vehicles data form. The first record in the list appears. See Figure 5-11. Notice that Excel uses the worksheet name, Vehicles, as the title of the data form. The labels that appear on the left side of the data form are taken from the header row of the vehicles list (ignore the small boxes that appear in the last two labels—the boxes are just placeholders for the spaces in the headings). In the upper-right corner of the form, there is information on how many records there are in the list and which record is currently selected.

Figure 5-11   VEHICLES DATA FORM

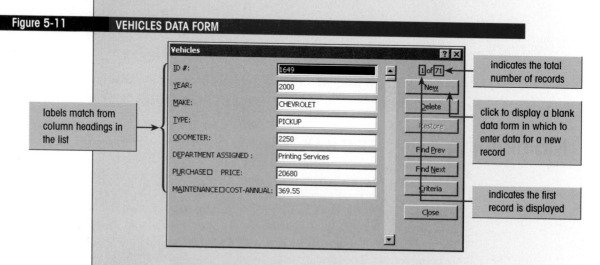

3. Click the **New** button to display a blank data form. Notice that the label "New Record" appears in the upper-right corner of the data form.

   Now you can enter the values for the new record in the text boxes next to each label.

4. Type **2525** in the ID # text box, and then press the **Tab** key to move to the YEAR text box.

   TROUBLE? If you pressed the Enter key or the ↓ key instead of the Tab key, a blank data form appears. Click the Find Prev button to return to the previous record, the record you were entering. Click in the YEAR box text and continue with Step 5.

5. Type **2003** in the YEAR text box, press the **Tab** key to move to the MAKE text box, and then type **CHEVROLET**. Note that you must enter the make of the vehicle in all caps so the data in the MAKE field will be formatted consistently.

6. Press the **Tab** key to move to the TYPE text box, and then enter the following data, pressing the Tab key after you enter each value:

   TYPE: **SEDAN**

   ODOMETER: **203**

   DEPARTMENT ASSIGNED: **Police & Security**

   PURCHASE PRICE: **22400**

   MAINTENANCE COST-ANNUAL: **0**

7. Press the **Enter** key. Pressing the Enter key after typing in the last value automatically adds a new record to the bottom of the list and displays a blank data form, ready for you to add another new record.

   You do not have any new records to add now, so you can return to the worksheet.

8. Click the **Close** button to close the data form and return to the worksheet.

   To make sure that the new record has been added to the vehicles list, display the bottom of the list.

9. Press **Ctrl + End** to move to the bottom of the list. The last record contains the data for the police sedan.

10. Press **Ctrl + Home** to return to cell B2.

Now you can make the other updates to the vehicles list. You still need to complete two tasks: update the odometer reading for vehicle ID # 2142, and delete the record for the vehicle ID # 3544. Although you can manually scroll through the list to find a specific record, with larger lists of data this method is slow and prone to error. A quicker and more accurate way to find a record is to use the data form's search capabilities. You will use this method to update the vehicle's odometer reading and to delete the pickup truck no longer in use.

Using the Data Form to Search for Records

You can use the data form to search for a specific record or group of records. When you initiate a search, you specify the search criteria, or instructions, for the search. Excel starts from the current record and moves through the list, searching for any records that match the search criteria. If Excel finds more than one record that matches the search criteria, Excel displays the first record that matches the criteria. You can use the Find Next button in the data form to display the next record that matches the search criteria.

You need to find vehicle ID # 2142 to update the odometer reading. Use the data form to find this record.

To search for the record for vehicle ID# 2141 using the data form:

1. Make sure the active cell is inside the list.

2. Click **Data** on the menu bar, and then click **Form** to display the Vehicles data form.

3. Click the **Criteria** button to display a blank data form. The label "Criteria" in the upper-right corner of the data form indicates that the form is ready to accept search criteria.

   Now enter the search criteria in the appropriate field.

4. Type **2142** in the ID # text box.

   You can enter multiple criteria if necessary. However, when you enter multiple criteria, only records that match all the criteria that you have entered will be displayed. There is only one specification that the record must match so you do not have to enter anything else.

5. Click the **Find Next** button to display the next record in the list that meets the specified criteria. The record that you are searching for is ID # 2142. See Figure 5-12.

Figure 5-12	RECORD FOR VEHICLE ID# 2142 FOUND

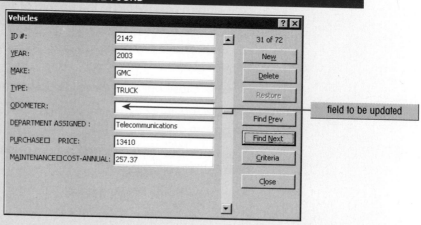

field to be updated

If there were more than one vehicle with the same ID # and the current record was not the one you were interested in, you could click the Find Next button again, and the next record meeting the search criteria would be displayed. If no records meet the search criteria, no message is displayed. Instead, the data form simply displays the current record.

Now update this record.

6. Click in the ODOMETER text box, and then type **3456**.

7. Click the **Close** button to return to the vehicles list.

8. Scroll the list to find this vehicle. Note that the odometer reading for this vehicle now displays 3456.

Now you need to complete the final update to the list by deleting the pickup truck record assigned to Housing & Residential Life.

Using the Data Form to Delete a Record

To delete a record, you first need to locate it. You can use the data form to search the list to find and then delete the record.

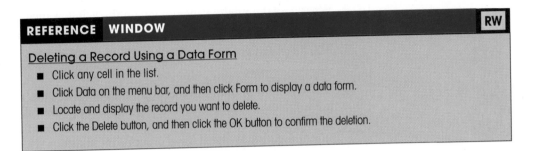

REFERENCE WINDOW | **RW**

<u>Deleting a Record Using a Data Form</u>
- Click any cell in the list.
- Click Data on the menu bar, and then click Form to display a data form.
- Locate and display the record you want to delete.
- Click the Delete button, and then click the OK button to confirm the deletion.

You need to find the correct pickup truck record and then delete it. The record ID # for the pickup truck assigned to Housing & Residential Life is 678.

To search for and delete the pickup truck record:

1. Make sure the active cell is inside the list, click **Data** on the menu bar, and then click **Form** to display the Vehicles data form.

2. Click the **Criteria** button, type **678** in the ID # text box, and then click the **Find Next** button. The record for a 1981 Ford pickup truck record assigned to Housing & Residential Life is displayed.

3. Click the **Delete** button. A message box appears, warning you that the displayed record will be permanently deleted from the list.

4. Click the **OK** button to confirm the record deletion. The vehicle with ID # 678 record has been deleted from the list, and the next record in the list is displayed in the data form. Note that the next record shows another pickup truck assigned to Housing & Residential Life, but the ID # is different.

5. Click the **Close** button to close the data form and return to the worksheet.

   You have made all the necessary changes to update the vehicles list. You can now save your changes and exit Excel.

6. Click the **Save** button 🖫 on the Standard toolbar, and then click the **Close** button ⊠ on the Excel title bar.

You can also delete a record directly from the list. First you need to select the entire row that you want to delete, click Edit on the menu bar, and then click Delete. You will not be asked to confirm the deletion, so make sure you have selected the correct row.

You have now provided Linda with a current and updated list of all vehicles, sorted by type and within type by year. Next you will use the vehicles list to retrieve specific information on only some of the vehicles. To find the information that you need, you will create a customized list, which will be limited to just the information you need, by filtering the vehicles list to show just the necessary information. You will do this in Session 5.2.

Session 5.1 QUICK CHECK

1. In Excel, a(n) _____ is a collection of similar data stored in a structured manner.

2. What does the Freeze Panes option on the Window menu do? Why is this feature helpful?

3. The fields that you use to order your data are called _____ or _____ .

4. You have a list of college students. First name, last name, major, current year (that is, freshman, sophomore, and so on), and year of matriculation are the fields used in the list. Explain how to order the list of students so that those with the same major appear together in alphabetical order by the student's last name.

5. To locate a record quickly, you can use the _____ associated with the list.

6. You have a list of 250 employees. Social Security number, first name, last name, and address are fields you track for each employee. Explain how to find Jin Shinu's record using the data form.

7. A(n) _____ sort key is a field used to arrange records in a list.

8. If you sort the vehicles list from the most recent purchase date to the oldest purchase date, you have sorted the vehicles in _____ order.

SESSION 5.2

In this session, you will filter a list to display only specific information using AutoFilters, and you will customize a filter to meet more complex criteria. You will also use conditional formatting to highlight data in the list. Finally, you insert subtotals to display summary information in the list.

Filtering a List Using AutoFilters

Linda received a letter indicating that there might be a recall of certain Ford vans manufactured between 1995 and 1999. To be prepared for any such recall and the associated upgrades, Linda needs information on these vehicles so that she can alert the Property department.

To get a list of Ford vans whose model year is between 1995 and 1999, you could scan the entire vehicles list. However, with large lists, locating specific data can be difficult and time-consuming. Sorting can help because you group the data; however, you're still working with the entire list. You could use a data form, but if you use a data form to find records that meet specified criteria, you will only display one record at a time. A better solution is to have Excel find the specific records you want and display only these records in the worksheet. This process of displaying the ones you want and therefore "hiding" the records you don't need is called **filtering** the data. All records that do not meet your criteria are temporarily hidden from view.

RW

REFERENCE WINDOW

Filtering a List with AutoFilter
- Click any cell in the list.
- Click Data on the menu bar, point to Filter, and then click AutoFilter to insert list arrows next to each column heading in the list.
- Click the list arrow in the column that contains the data you want to filter.
- Click the criteria by which you want to filter the data in the list.

You can use Excel's AutoFilter feature to create the list of Ford vans that may be recalled. Remember, by filtering the list you will be hiding some of the records.

To filter the vehicles list using AutoFilter:

1. If you took a break after the last session, make sure Excel is running and that the VehicleData workbook is open.

2. Switch to the Vehicles worksheet, and then click any cell within the vehicles list. Note that the Freeze Panes option for column A and row 1 should still be turned on.

3. Click **Data** on the menu bar, point to **Filter**, and then click **AutoFilter**. List arrows appear next to each column heading in the list. To see a list of filtering criteria for a specific column, you must click the list arrow next to the column heading.

4. Click the **MAKE** column list arrow in cell C1 to display a list of criteria you can use to filter the data. See Figure 5-13.

| Figure 5-13 | FILTERING OPTIONS FOR THE MAKE FIELD |

displays all items in the column and removes filtering for the column

specifies more complex criteria

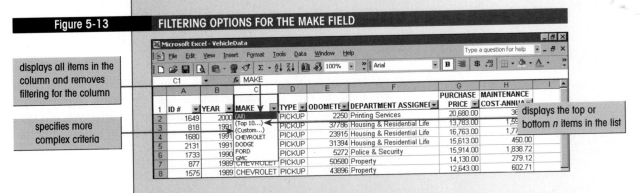

displays the top or bottom *n* items in the list

Besides the unique values—CHEVROLET, DODGE, FORD, GMC—in the list of criteria for the MAKE column, there are three other choices that appear and can be applied to every column. Now select your criterion for filtering the data.

5. Click **FORD** to display only Ford vehicles. See Figure 5-14. In the status bar, Excel displays the number of records found out of the total records in the list.

Figure 5-14	VEHICLES LIST DISPLAYING ONLY FORD VEHICLES

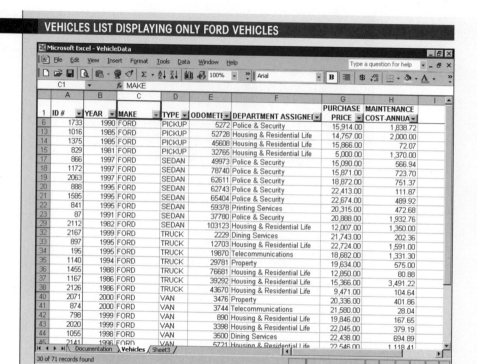

6. Review the list to verify that only records with a value equal to FORD in the MAKE column are visible. Excel hides all rows (records) that do not have the value Ford in this column.

Notice the gaps in the row numbers in the worksheet, and the blue color of the row numbers of the filtered records. The color of the list arrow next to the MAKE column changes to blue to let you know that this column has been used to filter the list.

If you need to further restrict the records that appear in the filtered list, you can select entries from the lists of criteria for the other columns. Linda wants to display only Ford vans, rather than all Ford vehicles. To add another criterion to the filter, you can click the list arrow for TYPE column that contains the value you need to use to further filter the data to display just Ford vans.

To add another criterion by which to filter the vehicles list:

1. Click the **TYPE** column list arrow in cell D1.

2. Click **VAN** to display Ford Vans. See Figure 5-15.

Figure 5-15   **VEHICLES LIST SHOWING FORD VANS**

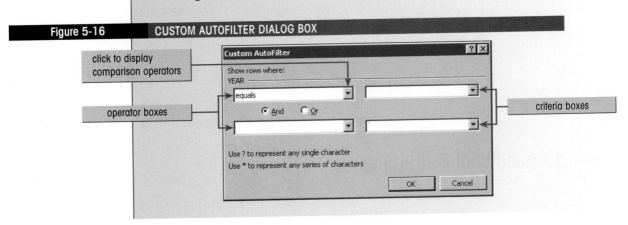

	A	B	C	D	E	F	G	H	I
1	ID #	YEAR	MAKE	TYPE	ODOMETE	DEPARTMENT ASSIGNE	PURCHASE PRICE	MAINTENANCE COST-ANNUA	
40	2071	2000	FORD	VAN	3476	Property	20,336.00	401.86	
41	874	2000	FORD	VAN	3744	Telecommunications	21,580.00	28.04	
42	798	1999	FORD	VAN	890	Housing & Residential Life	19,846.00	167.65	
43	2020	1999	FORD	VAN	3398	Housing & Residential Life	22,045.00	379.19	
44	1055	1998	FORD	VAN	3500	Dining Services	22,438.00	694.89	
45	2141	1996	FORD	VAN	5721	Housing & Residential Life	22,546.00	1,118.41	
56	1678	1989	FORD	VAN	25126	Housing & Residential Life	12,957.00	675.00	
57	1071	1989	FORD	VAN	93484	Printing Services	12,149.00	378.22	
60	2128	1987	FORD	VAN	99880	Athletics	15,197.00	1,974.79	
64	2412	1987	FORD	VAN	35497	Housing & Residential Life	9,025.00	191.38	
68	2124	1986	FORD	VAN	36838	Printing Services	11,518.00	2,000.00	
73									

If you wanted to remove the filter from the TYPE field, you would click the TYPE column list arrow again and then click All to remove the filter from this field. All Ford vehicles would be displayed in the list again.

Using Custom AutoFilters to Specify More Complex Criteria

Although you can often find the information you need by selecting a single item from a list of values in the filter list, there are times when you need to specify a custom set of criteria to find certain records. **Custom AutoFilters** allow you to specify relationships other than those that are "equal to" the criteria specified in the filter records. For example, you filtered records by type; that is, the values in the TYPE field were equal to the specified criterion, which was FORD. But the type of vehicle is only part of the information that you need. The recall specified that the vehicles were manufactured between 1995 and 1999. Therefore, you need to complete the search by filtering for vehicles manufactured between 1995 and 1999.

To complete the search, you need to develop a custom set of criteria. You can create this set of criteria to retrieve these records using the Custom AutoFilter dialog box.

To use a custom AutoFilter to filter the vehicles list:

1. Click the **YEAR** column list arrow, and then click **Custom**. The Custom AutoFilter dialog box opens. See Figure 5-16.

Figure 5-16   **CUSTOM AUTOFILTER DIALOG BOX**

You use the operator list box, which is the first list box in the dialog box, to specify a comparison operator that you need to use for the filter by selecting an operator from the list. You use the criteria list box, the list box to the right of the operator list box, to specify the field value that you want to use for the filter by typing the value or selecting an item from a list. You can select the And or Or option button if you want to display rows that meet two conditions for the field. You select And to display rows that meet both criteria. You select Or to display rows that meet either criterion.

2. Click the **first operator** list arrow, and then click **is greater than or equal to**.

3. Click in the criteria list box to right, and then type **1995** as the first value.

4. If necessary, click the **And** option button.

5. Click the **second operator** list arrow, and then click **is less than or equal to**.

6. Click in the second criteria list box, and then type **1999**.

7. Click the **OK** button to display the filtered list consisting of all Ford vans manufactured between 1995 and 1999. See Figure 5-17. The status bar indicates 4 of 71 records found.

Figure 5-17	FILTERED LIST SHOWING FORD VANS WITH MODEL YEARS BETWEEN 1995 AND 1999

You have completed your task. You can now remove all the filters and return to the original complete vehicles list.

To remove the filter arrows from the vehicles list:

1. Click **Data** on the menu bar, point to **Filter**, and then click **AutoFilter** to remove all the filters. All the records are displayed, and the list arrows no longer appear in the column headings.

If you wanted to restore the original list and then enter new filtering criteria, you would select Show All instead of clicking AutoFilter.

Linda wants to be able to quickly identify "high" use vehicles as she views the vehicles lists and asks you to apply Excel's conditional formatting feature to the ODOMETER field.

Using Conditional Formatting

Excel's **conditional formatting** is formatting that appears in a cell only when data in the cell meets conditions that you specify or is the result of a formula. You can apply conditional formatting so you can easily identify critical highs or lows in a report. For example, cells representing large amounts of overtime or sales that do not meet projections can be formatted in bold font style or with a red background. You can specify up to three conditions that apply to the value of a cell or the formula that produces the value for each condition. You specify the formatting (font, font style, font color, border, and so on) that will be applied to the cell if the condition is true.

REFERENCE WINDOW | **RW**

Applying Conditional Formatting to Cells

- Select the cells you want to format.
- Click Format on the menu bar, and then click Conditional Formatting to open the Conditional Formatting dialog box.
- Specify the condition on which to apply formatting using the Condition 1 boxes.
- Click the Format button to open the Format Cells dialog box.
- Select the font style, font color, underlining, borders, shading, or patterns that you want to apply, then click the OK button to return to the Conditional Formatting dialog box.
- To specify another condition, click the Add >> button and enter the necessary specifications for the condition and formatting.
- Click the OK button to apply the conditional format(s) to the selected cells.

Linda wants to determine the best time to trade in vehicles that have higher mileage. She wants to format high-mileage vehicles using two categories—those with over 100,000 miles and those between 80,000 and 100,000 miles—so she can easily spot the "high-mileage" vehicles. To highlight these two categories of vehicles you want to apply a red background to any cell in the ODOMETER field containing a value exceeding 100,000 and a blue background for any vehicles with an odometer reading between 80,000 and 100,000. You need to apply this conditional formatting to the ODOMETER field.

To apply conditional formatting to the ODOMETER field:

1. Select the range **E2:E72**.

2. Click **Format** on the menu bar, and then click **Conditional Formatting**. The Conditional Formatting dialog box opens. See Figure 5-18.

Figure 5-18	CONDITIONAL FORMATTING DIALOG BOX

First, you need to specify the condition that will be applied to the range of odometer readings. Because the contents of the cell in the ODOMETER field are values as opposed to formulas or text, you don't need to specify any additional criteria.

3. Make sure that **Cell Value Is** appears in the Condition 1 list box.

Next, you need to choose the comparison operator that will compare the cell value to the condition you specify.

4. Click the **list arrow** in the second box to display a list of comparison operators, and then click **greater than**. Notice that the number of boxes changes to reflect the comparison operator you selected.

Now you need to enter the value for the condition that the values in the ODOMETER field must meet.

5. Click in the third box for Condition 1, and then type **100000**. The condition is now defined.

Now you need to define the formatting to be applied to the cell or range if the condition is true.

6. Click the **Format** button to open the Format Cells dialog box.

7. Click the **Patterns** tab, and then click the **Red** color square (third row, first column) in the color palette.

8. Click the **OK** button to return to the Conditional Formatting dialog box. Notice that red shading appears in the Preview box.

Now you will develop the second condition.

9. Click the **Add>>** button to display the boxes that you can use to specify the criteria for a second condition.

10. Repeat Steps 3 to 8 to format vehicles driven *between* 80000 and 100000 miles by applying a bright blue background (fourth row, sixth column).

If you had a third condition to specify (only three can be entered), you would click the Add>> button again and return to Step 3.

11. Click the **OK** button to apply the conditional formatting to the selected cells.

12. Click any cell to deselect the range. Scroll the list so you can see where the conditional formatting has been applied. See Figure 5-19. Notice that the background color of several cells in the range is now blue, and others are red.

Figure 5-19	VEHICLES LIST WITH CONDITIONAL FORMATTING APPLIED

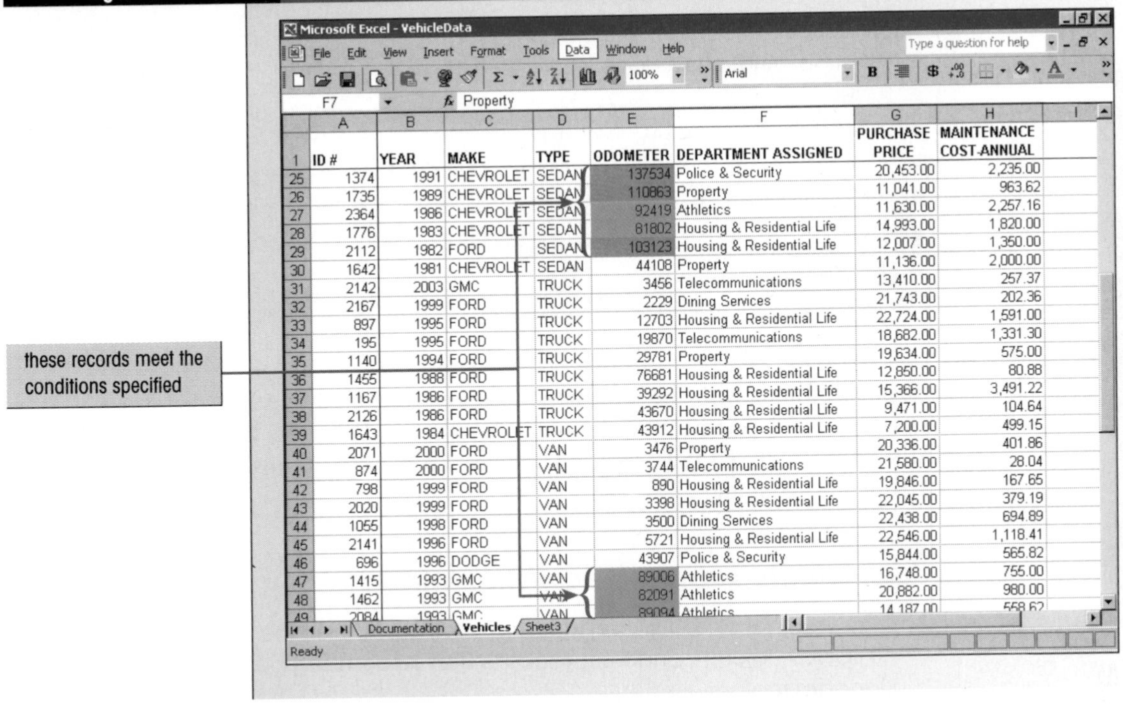

these records meet the conditions specified

Note that if the value of the cell changes and no longer meets the specified condition(s), Excel temporarily suppresses the formats associated with that cell. Likewise, if the value of the cell changes and now the specified condition is met, then Excel applies the format associated with the condition to the cell. In all cases, the conditional formats remain applied to the cells until you remove conditional formatting specifications, even when none of the conditions is met and the specified cell formats are not displayed. To remove a conditional format, you must select the range of cells to which the conditional formatting has been applied, and then open the Conditional Formatting dialog box. In the dialog box, you click the Delete button to open the Delete Condition Format dialog box in which you clear the check box of the condition(s) that you want to delete. Click the OK button twice to remove the formatting from the selected cells.

Linda has a request for information that she needs for her meeting with the budget director, and she meets with you to discuss how the vehicles list can be used in this task. The budget director has asked to see each department's total expenditures for vehicles, so Linda will need to see those numbers in a subtotal format.

Inserting **Subtotals into a List**

Excel can summarize data in a list by inserting subtotals. The Subtotals command offers many kinds of summary information, including counts, sums, averages, minimums, and maximums. The Subtotals command automatically inserts a subtotal line into the list for each group of data in the list. A grand total line is also added to the bottom of the list. Because Excel inserts subtotals whenever the value in a specified field changes, you need to sort the list so that records with the same value in a specified field are grouped together before you can use the subtotals command.

REFERENCE   WINDOW   **RW**

Calculating Subtotals In a List

- Sort the list by the column for which you want a subtotal, and then make sure the active cell is in the list.
- Click Data on the menu bar, and then click Subtotals to open the Subtotal dialog box.
- In the At each change in list box, select the column that contains the group you want to subtotal.
- In the Use function list box, select the function that you want to use to summarize the data.
- In the Add subtotal to list box, select the column that contains the values you want to summarize.
- Click the OK button.

To supply Linda with the information she requested, you need to develop a list of vehicles, sorted by department, with subtotals calculated for the PURCHASE PRICE and MAINTENANCE COST-ANNUAL fields. You need to insert a subtotal after each departmental grouping.

To calculate subtotals by department:

1. If the list is not sorted by department, click any cell in the DEPARTMENT ASSIGNED column, and then click the **Sort Ascending** button 🔼 on the Standard toolbar.

Now you need to calculate the subtotals in the list.

2. Click **Data** on the menu bar, and then click **Subtotals** to display the Subtotal dialog box. See Figure 5-20.

Figure 5-20	SUBTOTAL DIALOG BOX

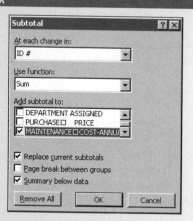

3. Click the **At each change in** list arrow, and then click **DEPARTMENT ASSIGNED** to select the column containing the field for which you want subtotals.

4. If necessary, click the **Use function** list arrow, and then click **Sum** to select the function you need to use to summarize the data. The Use function lists many other ways to summarize data, including counts, averages, minimums, and maximums.

You want departmental subtotals for the PURCHASE PRICE and MAINTENANCE COST-ANNUAL fields.

5. In the Add subtotal to list box, scroll the list and select the **PURCHASE PRICE** check box, and if necessary click the **MAINTENANCE COST-ANNUAL** check box. These are the columns that contain the fields you want to summarize. If necessary, remove any other check marks that appear in the Add subtotal to list.

   If you're preparing a new subtotal and want to replace existing subtotals in the list, select the Replace current subtotals check box; otherwise, new subtotals will be displayed on a separate row above the existing subtotal. Since there currently are no subtotals in the list, whether you select this option or not will make no difference.

6. Make sure the **Summary below data** check box is selected so that the subtotals appear below the related data; otherwise Excel places the subtotals above the first entry in each group and places the grand total at the top of the column just below the row of column headings.

7. Click the **OK** button to insert subtotals into the list. Rows that display subtotals for the MAINTENANCE COST-ANNUAL and PURCHASE PRICE columns have been inserted throughout the list, showing the totals for each department. Note that a series of Outline buttons now appears to the left of the worksheet. These buttons allow you to display or hide the detail rows within each subtotal while the Subtotals feature is active.

   TROUBLE? If necessary, increase the column width so you can view the subtotal values.

8. Scroll through the list to see all the subtotals, moving to the bottom of the list to view the grand total. See Figure 5-21.

| Figure 5-21 | **VEHICLES LIST WITH SUBTOTALS** |

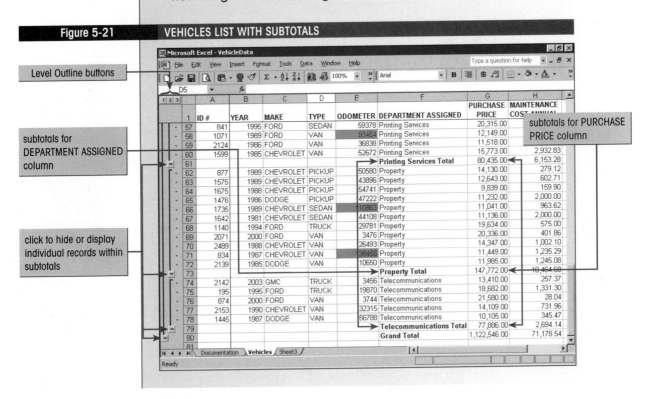

The subtotals are useful, but Linda asks if there is a way to isolate the different subtotal sections so that she can focus on them individually.

Using the Subtotals Outline View

In addition to displaying subtotals, the Subtotals feature "outlines" your worksheet so you can control the level of detail that is displayed. The three Outline buttons displayed at the top of the outline area, as shown in Figure 5-21, allow you to show or hide different levels of detail in your worksheet. By default, the highest level is active, in this case Level 3. Level 3 displays the most detail—the individual vehicle records, the subtotals, and the grand total. If you click the Level 2 Outline button, Excel displays the subtotals and the grand total, but not the individual records. If you click the Level 1 Outline button, Excel displays only the grand total.

Use the Outline buttons to prepare a report for Linda that includes only subtotals and the grand total.

To use the Outline buttons to hide the detail:

1. Click the **Level 2 Outline** button. See Figure 5-22. Notice that the worksheet hides the individual vehicle records and shows only the subtotals for each department and the grand total.

   TROUBLE? If necessary, scroll the window up to see the complete level 2 list.

Figure 5-22	SUBTOTALS AFTER LEVEL 2 OUTLINE BUTTON IS SELECTED

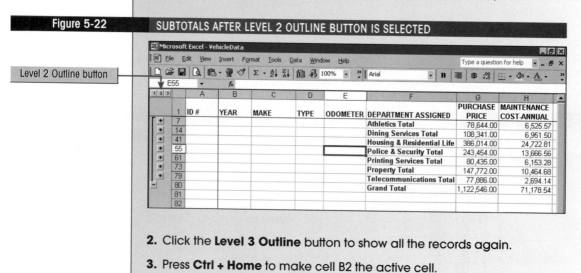

2. Click the **Level 3 Outline** button to show all the records again.

3. Press **Ctrl + Home** to make cell B2 the active cell.

Now that you have prepared the list with subtotals, you can remove the subtotals from the list so that you can perform other list-related tasks in the next section of the tutorial.

To remove the subtotals from the list:

1. Click **Data** on the menu bar, and then click **Subtotals** to open the Subtotal dialog box.

2. Click the **Remove All** button to remove the subtotals from the list.

   You have supplied Linda with the information she needs for her meeting with the budget director to review financial plans for the next fiscal cycle. You can now save your changes and exit Excel.

3. Click the **Save** button 🖫 on the Standard toolbar, and then click the **Close** button ⊠ on the Excel title bar.

Now Linda needs to generate some information for a meeting with the budget director to review financial plans for the next fiscal cycle. You will work with the vehicles list in the next session to gather the information she needs for that meeting.

QUICK CHECK Session 5.2

1. Explain the relationship between the Sort and Subtotals commands.

2. If you have a list of 300 students in the College of Business Administration and wanted to list only finance majors, you would use the _____ command on the _____ menu.

3. Explain how you can display a list of marketing majors with a GPA of 3.0 or greater from a list of 300 students.

4. Once subtotals are displayed, you can use the _____ button to control the level of detail displayed.

5. True or False: The Count function is a valid subtotal function when using the Subtotals command.

6. _____ enables formatting to appear only when the data in a cell meets a condition you specify.

7. You can specify up to _____ different conditions when using conditional formatting

SESSION 5.3

In this session, you will summarize data from an Excel list in different formats using the PivotTable and PivotChart Wizard.

Creating and Using PivotTables to Summarize a List

An Excel list can contain a wealth of information, but because of the large amounts of detailed data, it is often difficult to form a clear overall view of the information. You can use a PivotTable to help organize the data into a meaningful summary. A **PivotTable** report is an interactive table that enables you to group and summarize an Excel list into a concise, tabular format for easier reporting and analysis. A PivotTable summarizes data into different categories using functions such as COUNT, SUM, AVERAGE, MAX, and MIN. You can also summarize the list by creating a PivotChart. A **PivotChart** report contains the same elements as a regular chart but also contains fields and items that can be added to, rotated, or removed to display different views of your data. A PivotChart report must be associated with a PivotTable report in the same workbook. When you create a PivotChart report, Excel automatically creates an associated PivotTable report. If you have an existing PivotTable report, you can use it to create the PivotChart report, which will reflect the view of that table.

To generate a PivotTable report, you need to specify which fields you want to summarize. Salaries, sales, and costs are examples of fields that are often summarized for reports. In PivotTable terminology these fields are known as **data fields**. In addition to data fields, a PivotTable uses **category fields**, which are values such as department, model, year, and vehicle type. Category fields appear in PivotTables as rows, columns, or pages and are referred to as **column fields**, **row fields**, and **page fields**. Figure 5-23 shows an example of a PivotTable.

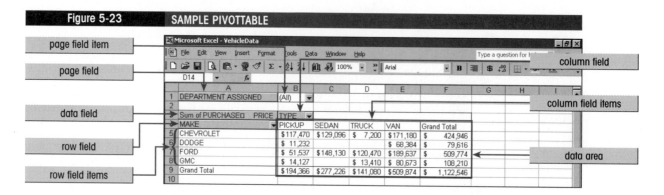

Figure 5-23	SAMPLE PIVOTTABLE

page field item
page field
data field
row field
row field items
column field
column field items
data area

One advantage of PivotTables is that you can easily rearrange, hide, and display different category fields in the PivotTable to provide alternative views of the data. The ability to "pivot" your table —for example, change column headings to row positions and vice versa— gives the PivotTable its name and makes the PivotTable a powerful analytical tool.

At budget time, Linda meets with the head of the Property department to discuss the department's budget for the upcoming fiscal year. The Property department is responsible for vehicle maintenance and has a budget for upcoming maintenance expenses for all the vehicles owned by the university. Linda needs a report showing the average annual maintenance cost by type of vehicle and by department.

The best approach to generating the information that Linda needs is to create a PivotTable. A useful first step in creating a PivotTable is to plan it and sketch its layout. Your plan and sketch, shown in Figures 5-24 and 5-25, will help you work with the PivotTable and PivotChart Wizard to produce the PivotTable you want.

Figure 5-24	PIVOTTABLE PLAN FOR CALCULATING AVERAGE ANNUAL MAINTENANCE COSTS

My Goal
Create a table that compares average maintenance costs for each department by type of vehicle

What results do I want to see?
Average departmental maintenance cost for each type of vehicle
Overall average maintenance cost for each department
Overall average maintenance cost for each type of vehicle
Overall average maintenance cost for each vehicle

What information do I need?
The table rows will show the data for each department.
The table columns will show the data for each type of vehicle.
The table will summarize annual maintenance cost.

What calculation method will I use?
The annual maintenance cost will be averaged.

Figure 5-25	SKETCH OF TABLE TO COMPARE AVERAGE ANNUAL MAINTENANCE COSTS

Average Maintenance Cost by Department and Type of Vehicle

Department	PICKUP	SEDAN	TRUCK	VAN	Total
Athletics					
Dining Services					
Housing & Residential Life					
Police & Security					
Printing Services					
Property					
Telecommunications					
Total					

Now you are ready to create a PivotTable summarizing average annual maintenance costs of the different types of vehicles by departments.

Creating a PivotTable

To create the PivotTable that will provide Linda with the information she needs, you will use Excel's PivotTable and PivotChart Wizard to guide you through a three-step process. Although the PivotTable and PivotChart Wizard will prompt you for the information necessary to create the table, the preliminary plan and sketch you created will be helpful in achieving the layout Linda wants.

Most often when creating a PivotTable, you begin with a list stored in a worksheet, although a PivotTable can also be created using data stored in an external database file, such as one in Access. In this case, you will use the vehicles list to create the PivotTable.

To create the PivotTable using the vehicles list:

1. If you took a break after the last session, make sure Excel is running and that the VehicleData workbook is open.

2. Switch to the Vehicles worksheet, and then click any cell within the vehicles list. Note that the Freeze Panes option for column A and row 1 should still be turned on.

3. Click **Data** on the menu bar, and then click **PivotTable and PivotChart Report** to display the first step in the PivotTable and PivotChart Wizard. See Figure 5-26. In this step, you specify the kind of report you want to display—either a PivotTable or a PivotChart along with a PivotTable. You also indicate where the data for the PivotTable can be found. You can select from an Excel list, an external data source (such as an Access database file), multiple consolidation ranges, or another PivotTable. To develop the average annual maintenance cost PivotTable, you will use the Excel list in the Vehicles worksheet.

Figure 5-26   STEP 1 OF THE PIVOTTABLE AND PIVOTCHART WIZARD

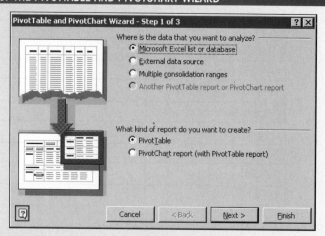

4. Make sure the **Microsoft Excel list or database** option is selected and the **PivotTable** option is selected as the kind of report. Then click the **Next** button to display the next step in the PivotTable and PivotChart Wizard. See Figure 5-27.

Figure 5-27   STEP 2 OF THE PIVOTTABLE AND PIVOTCHART WIZARD

At this point, you need to identify the location of the data you are going to summarize in the PivotTable. Because the active cell is located inside the range of the Excel list, the wizard automatically selects the range of the vehicles list $A$1:$H$72 as the source of data for the PivotTable.

TROUBLE? If the Range box in the second wizard dialog box displays "Database" instead of $A$1:$H$72 as the source of the data, click the Next button to go to the third step of the wizard. If an error message appears when you click the Next button, click the Collapse Dialog Box button , select the range A1:H72, and then click the Expand Dialog Box button . Then read but do not perform Step 5. Continue with Step 6.

5. Click the **Next** button to display the last step in the PivotTable and PivotChart Wizard. See Figure 5-28. In this step you need to decide where to place the PivotTable—either in a new worksheet or in an existing worksheet. You also have the opportunity to complete the layout of the PivotTable within the wizard by selecting the Layout button; otherwise you can complete the PivotTable directly on the worksheet.

Figure 5-28	STEP 3 OF THE PIVOTTABLE AND PIVOTCHART WIZARD

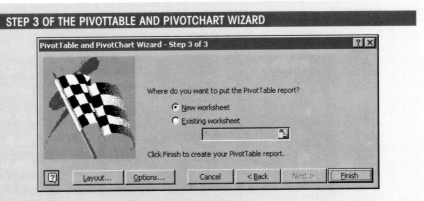

You will place the PivotTable in a new worksheet and complete the PivotTable directly in the worksheet.

6. Make sure the **New worksheet** option button is selected, and then click the **Finish** button to create the PivotTable report layout. See Figure 5-29. A new worksheet, Sheet1, appears to the left of the Vehicles sheet. Sheet1 contains a blank PivotTable report layout, a diagram containing blue outlined drop areas. You use this diagram to complete the PivotTable and the PivotTable Field List. The PivotTable Field List includes the names of each field in your Excel list.

Figure 5-29	PIVOTTABLE REPORT DIAGRAM DISPLAYING DROP AREAS

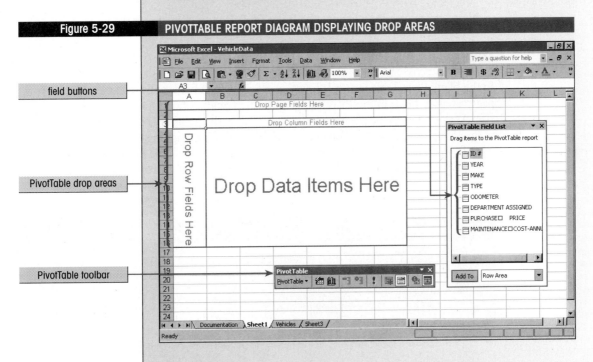

TROUBLE? The PivotTable toolbar and PivotTable Field List might not appear in the same location as shown in Figure 5-29. If necessary, move the PivotTable toolbar and PivotTable Field List so that they are visible on your screen and more accessible.

The worksheet also includes the PivotTable toolbar. Figure 5-30 describes the tools available on this toolbar.

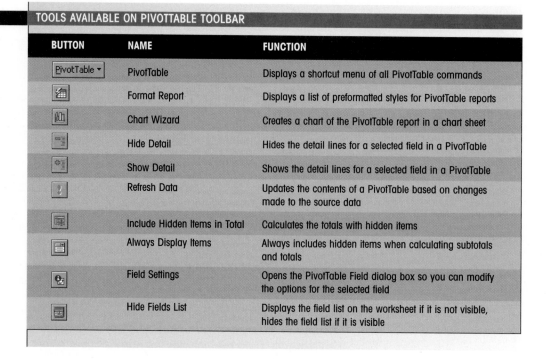

Figure 5-30   **TOOLS AVAILABLE ON PIVOTTABLE TOOLBAR**

BUTTON	NAME	FUNCTION
PivotTable ▾	PivotTable	Displays a shortcut menu of all PivotTable commands
	Format Report	Displays a list of preformatted styles for PivotTable reports
	Chart Wizard	Creates a chart of the PivotTable report in a chart sheet
	Hide Detail	Hides the detail lines for a selected field in a PivotTable
	Show Detail	Shows the detail lines for a selected field in a PivotTable
	Refresh Data	Updates the contents of a PivotTable based on changes made to the source data
	Include Hidden Items in Total	Calculates the totals with hidden items
	Always Display Items	Always includes hidden items when calculating subtotals and totals
	Field Settings	Opens the PivotTable Field dialog box so you can modify the options for the selected field
	Hide Fields List	Displays the field list on the worksheet if it is not visible, hides the field list if it is visible

Now you are ready to lay out the PivotTable Report directly on the worksheet.

Laying Out the PivotTable Directly on the Worksheet

In the blank PivotTable report layout you specify which fields will appear as column, row, and page category fields in the PivotTable, and which fields contain the data you want to summarize. At this point in the creation of the PivotTable, the fields are represented by a set of fields in the PivotTable Field list. You create the PivotTable by dragging the fields with the data you want from the Field List to any of the four areas of the PivotTable diagram: Drop Rows Fields Here, Drop Column Fields Here, Drop Page Fields Here, or Drop Data Items Here.

REFERENCE   WINDOW   **RW**

Laying Out the PivotTable on the Worksheet
- Click and drag the fields you want to display in rows to the area of the PivotTable diagram labeled Drop Row Fields Here.
- Click and drag the fields you want to display in columns to the area of the PivotTable diagram labeled Drop Column Fields Here.
- Click and drag the fields you want to display in pages to the area of the PivotTable diagram labeled Drop Page Fields Here.
- Click and drag the fields that contain the data you want to summarize to the area of the PivotTable diagram labeled Drop Data Items Here.

You need to compute average annual maintenance cost by department for each type of vehicle. In the PivotTable, you want the values in the DEPARTMENT ASSIGNED field to appear as row labels, the values in the TYPE field to appear as column headings, and the data in the MAINTENANCE COST-ANNUAL field to be summarized.

You now need to lay out the PivotTable in the worksheet.

To lay out the PivotTable on the worksheet:

1. From the list of fields in the PivotTable Field List, click and drag the **DEPARTMENT ASSIGNED** field to the area on the PivotTable diagram labeled Drop Row Fields Here. When you release the mouse button, the DEPARTMENT ASSIGNED button appears in the PivotTable report along with a row label for each unique value in the DEPARTMENT ASSIGNED field. See Figure 5-31.

| Figure 5-31 | PIVOTTABLE DIAGRAM WITH DEPARTMENT ASSIGNED FIELD ADDED |

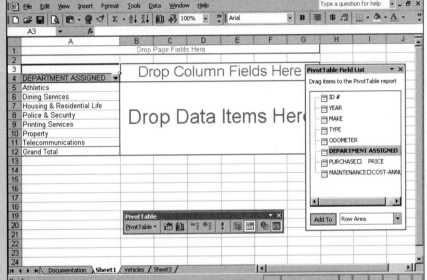

TROUBLE? If you moved the wrong field into the PivotTable diagram, you can remove the field by dragging it anywhere outside the diagram or by clicking the Undo button [icon] on the Standard toolbar. Then repeat Step 1.

2. Click and drag the **TYPE** field from the PivotTable Field List to the area of the diagram labeled Drop Column Fields Here. When you release the mouse button, the TYPE button appears in the report framework, and each unique value in the TYPE field appears as a column heading.

3. Click and drag the **MAINTENANCE COST-ANNUAL** field from the PivotTable Field List to the area of the diagram labeled Drop Data Items Here. When you release the mouse button, the Sum of MAINTENANCE COST-ANNUAL appears above the DEPARTMENT ASSIGNED button to indicate the type of summary; the report contains the total annual maintenance cost for each department for each vehicle type. See Figure 5-32.

Figure 5-32   **PIVOTTABLE SHOWING ANNUAL MAINTENANCE COST**

this button indicates the field and the type of summary function in the data area

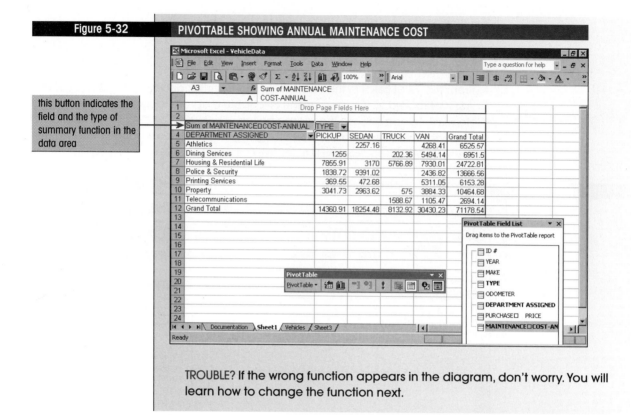

TROUBLE? If the wrong function appears in the diagram, don't worry. You will learn how to change the function next.

By default, the PivotTable report uses the SUM function for calculations involving numeric values placed in the Drop Data Items Here area and the COUNT function for nonnumeric values. If you want to use a different summary function, such as AVERAGE, MAX, or MIN, you can click the Field Settings button on the PivotTable toolbar and select the summary function from a list of available functions in the PivotTable Field dialog box.

Linda wants to compare average cost by department and vehicle type. You need to change the summary function from Sum to Average.

To change the PivotTable report to compute average cost by department and type:

1. Select a value inside the PivotTable report, and then click the **Field Settings** button ▦ on the PivotTable toolbar. The PivotTable Field dialog box opens. See Figure 5-33.

Figure 5-33   **PIVOTTABLE FIELD DIALOG BOX**

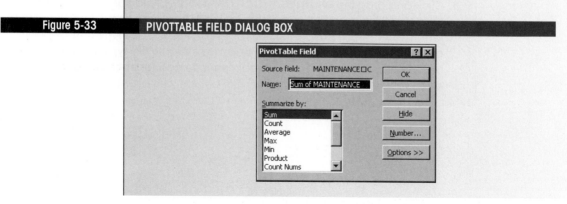

2. Click **Average** in the Summarize by list box, and then click the **OK** button to
   return to the PivotTable report. See Figure 5-34. Notice that the summary button
   displays "Average of MAINTENANCE COST-ANNUAL" and the data in the
   PivotTable report represents the averages.

| Figure 5-34 | PIVOTTABLE SHOWING AVERAGE ANNUAL MAINTENANCE COST |

button label changes
to indicate the type of
summary function in the
data area

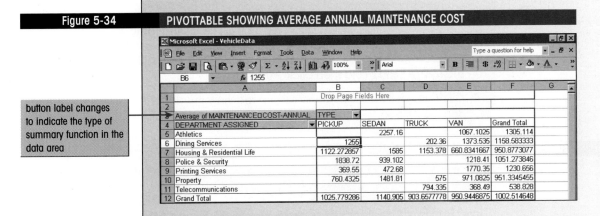

TROUBLE? If some of the values in the report are displayed with several decimal
places, don't worry about formatting at this time.

3. Rename the worksheet **AvgMaintCost**.

You can also change the type of summary information in a PivotTable by double-clicking
the field button that appears inside the PivotTable.

The PivotTable in Figure 5-34 shows the average annual maintenance cost of each vehicle by department and type. Although the data in a PivotTable might look like data in any
other worksheet, you cannot directly enter or change data in the DATA area of the
PivotTable because the PivotTable is linked to the source data. Any changes that affect the
PivotTable must first be made to the Excel list. Later in the tutorial you will change a vehicle's department and learn how to reflect that change in the PivotTable.

Changing the Layout of a PivotTable

Although you cannot change the values inside the PivotTable, there are many ways you can
change the layout, formatting, and computational options of a PivotTable. For example,
once the PivotTable is created, you have numerous ways of rearranging, adding, and removing fields.

Formatting Numbers in the PivotTable

Linda feels that the numbers in the PivotTable are too difficult to read. You can apply standard formatting to the cells in the PivotTable just as you would to any cell in a worksheet.
You can also select from a list of over 20 AutoFormats that apply predefined fonts, colors,
and borders to your PivotTable. You will first format the PivotTable using an AutoFormat.

To apply an AutoFormat to PivotTable values:

1. Click inside the PivotTable, and then click the **Format Report** button 📊 on the
   PivotTable toolbar to open the AutoFormat dialog box.

2. Scroll down the list of AutoFormats until Table 2 is displayed, click the **Table 2** AutoFormat, and then click the **OK** button. The AutoFormat is applied to the PivotTable.

To make the appearance of the numbers more consistent, you will apply the Currency number format to the numbers in the PivotTable.

3. Click the **Currency Style** button 💲 on the Formatting toolbar.

TROUBLE? If you deselected the PivotTable after applying the AutoFormat, select the range B5:F12 and then click 💲.

4. Click any cell to deselect the range and view the newly formatted PivotTable. See Figure 5-35.

Figure 5-35   PIVOTTABLE WITH AN AUTOFORMAT APPLIED

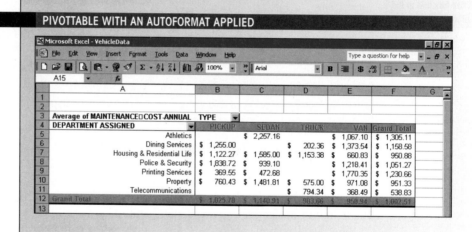

With the AutoFormat applied and the numbers formatted as currency, the data in the PivotTable is much easier to interpret.

Changing the Layout of the PivotTable

Recall that the benefit of a PivotTable is that it summarizes large amounts of data into a readable format. Once you have created the table, you can also choose to view the same data in different ways. At the top of the PivotTable's Row and Column areas are field buttons that enable you to change, or pivot, the view of the data by dragging these buttons to different locations in the PivotTable.

Linda reviews the tabular format of the PivotTable you have created and decides it might be more useful if the information in the PivotTable displayed the vehicle type as the row classifications under the departments. To change the presentation of the data, you can reposition the column headings for the TYPE field as row labels.

To move the TYPE column field to a row field in the PivotTable:

1. Click and drag the **TYPE** field button down and position it immediately below the list arrow for the DEPARTMENT ASSIGNED field button. As you drag the TYPE field button to reposition it, the pointer changes to 🔲.

2. Release the mouse button. See Figure 5-36. The PivotTable is reordered so that the TYPE field is treated as a row field instead of a column field.

TROUBLE? If the TYPE field appears to the left of the DEPARTMENT ASSIGNED field, click the Undo button 🔄 on the Standard toolbar, and then repeat Step 1. When you drag the TYPE field button, drag the button into the blank area directly under the list arrow for the DEPARTMENT ASSIGNED field button. If you drag the button much further to the left, you will change the order of the fields.

| Figure 5-36 | PIVOTTABLE REARRANGED WITH TYPE AS ROW FIELD ITEMS |

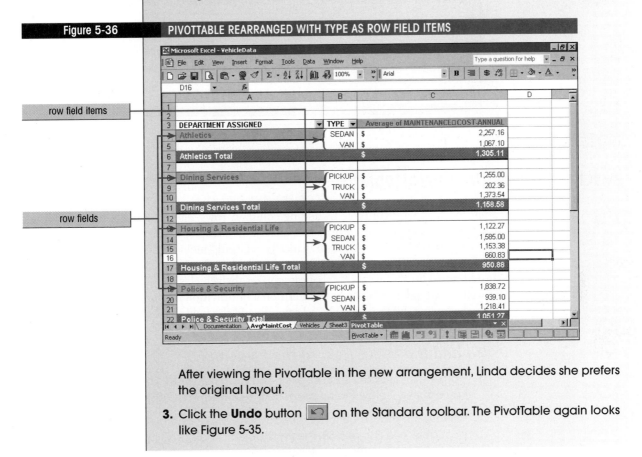

After viewing the PivotTable in the new arrangement, Linda decides she prefers the original layout.

3. Click the **Undo** button 🔄 on the Standard toolbar. The PivotTable again looks like Figure 5-35.

Sorting Items Within the PivotTable

Linda wants you to rearrange the PivotTable so that it displays the vehicle type with the highest average annual maintenance cost first. To complete this task, you can sort the data that is already laid out in the PivotTable.

To sort the PivotTable to display the highest average maintenance cost first:

1. Click cell **F5** to select the cell that contains the field you want to sort.

2. Click the **Sort Descending** button 🔽 on the Standard toolbar. See Figure 5-37. The average annual departmental maintenance costs are now sorted from most costly to least costly.

Figure 5-37	PIVOTTABLE WITH VALUES SORTED

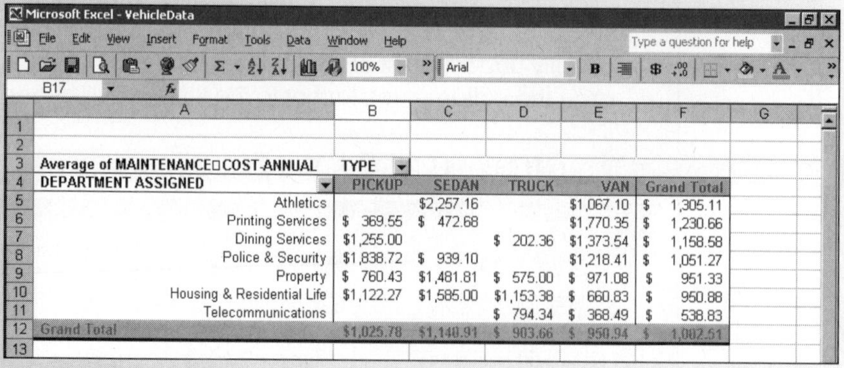

Microsoft Excel - VehicleData

	A	B	C	D	E	F	G
1							
2							
3	Average of MAINTENANCE☐COST-ANNUAL	TYPE ▾					
4	DEPARTMENT ASSIGNED ▾	PICKUP	SEDAN	TRUCK	VAN	Grand Total	
5	Athletics		$2,257.16		$1,067.10	$ 1,305.11	
6	Printing Services	$ 369.55	$ 472.68		$1,770.35	$ 1,230.66	
7	Dining Services	$1,255.00		$ 202.36	$1,373.54	$ 1,158.58	
8	Police & Security	$1,838.72	$ 939.10		$1,218.41	$ 1,051.27	
9	Property	$ 760.43	$1,481.81	$ 575.00	$ 971.08	$ 951.33	
10	Housing & Residential Life	$1,122.27	$1,585.00	$1,153.38	$ 660.83	$ 950.88	
11	Telecommunications			$ 794.34	$ 368.49	$ 538.83	
12	Grand Total	$1,025.78	$1,148.91	$ 903.66	$ 950.94	$ 1,002.51	
13							

Adding a Field to a PivotTable

You can expand a PivotTable by adding columns, rows, and page fields and by adding data fields; this creates a more informative table. For example, Linda believes that a more accurate comparison of average maintenance costs would include the MAKE field. Adding this field to the PivotTable would enable you to calculate the average maintenance cost based on an additional breakdown—one that categorizes the vehicles in each department by the make as well as by type. Linda thinks the additional information might be useful in her discussion with the budget director, and she asks you to add the field to the PivotTable.

To add the MAKE field to the PivotTable:

1. From the PivotTable Field List, click and drag the **MAKE** field up and position it immediately below the list arrow for the DEPARTMENT ASSIGNED field button.

2. Release the mouse button. Excel adds the MAKE field button and redisplays the PivotTable. See Figure 5-38. The PivotTable now displays the MAKE subcategories for each department.

   TROUBLE? If the MAKE field button appears to the left of the DEPARTMENT ASSIGNED field button, click and drag the DEPARTMENT ASSIGNED button over the MAKE button, and then release the mouse button.

   TROUBLE? If the PivotTable toolbar and PivotTable Field List are in the way, drag them to a different location on your screen.

Figure 5-38 | PIVOTTABLE WITH MAKE FIELD ADDED

field added

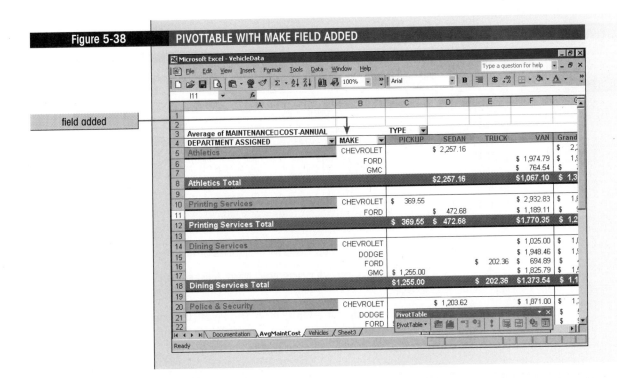

Linda doesn't like the look of the report with the MAKE field added; the report looks too busy and is difficult to read. She asks you if there is another way to use the MAKE field information in the report, but in a way that adds value to the report and doesn't distract from it.

Adding a Page View of a PivotTable

You can drag a field to the Drop Page Field area to create a page view of the PivotTable report. A **page view** allows you to filter the PivotTable so it displays summarized data for either a single field item or all field items. For example, creating a page view for the MAKE field allows you to display average annual maintenance costs for Fords, Chevrolets, or any other make.

Try adding a page view for the MAKE field to see if using this information adds value to the report.

To display a page view of the average annual maintenance costs:

1. Click and drag the **MAKE** field button to the area labeled Drop Page Fields Here. See Figure 5-39. Notice that the item All appears as the page field item. This item indicates that the PivotTable report displays all the summarized data associated with the MAKE field.

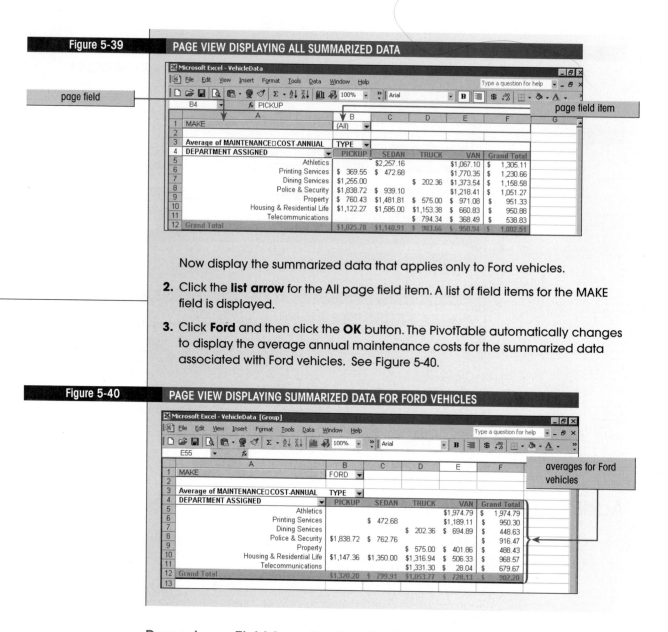

Figure 5-39   PAGE VIEW DISPLAYING ALL SUMMARIZED DATA

Now display the summarized data that applies only to Ford vehicles.

2. Click the **list arrow** for the All page field item. A list of field items for the MAKE field is displayed.

3. Click **Ford** and then click the **OK** button. The PivotTable automatically changes to display the average annual maintenance costs for the summarized data associated with Ford vehicles. See Figure 5-40.

Figure 5-40   PAGE VIEW DISPLAYING SUMMARIZED DATA FOR FORD VEHICLES

Removing a Field from the PivotTable

If you decide you want to remove a field from the PivotTable, just drag the field button outside the PivotTable. Linda reviews the PivotTable showing the data arranged by vehicle type, department, and make. Although Linda thinks this is important information, she feels the additional breakdown is not needed to show the difference in average annual maintenance costs between departments and vehicles. She asks you to remove the MAKE field from the PivotTable.

To remove a field from the PivotTable:

1. Click and drag the **MAKE** field button outside the PivotTable range to column G.

2. Release the mouse button. The MAKE field is removed from the PivotTable, and the PivotTable reverts to its previous layout. Removing a field from the PivotTable has no effect on the underlying list; the MAKE field is still in the vehicles list.

Linda wants to focus the analysis on sedans, vans, and pickups. She asks you to remove trucks from the PivotTable report.

Hiding Field Items on a PivotTable

You can hide row or column field items in the PivotTable by clicking the list arrow for the field button that represents the data you want to hide and then by clearing the check box for each item you want to hide. To show hidden items, you click the list arrow for the field button and select the check box for the item you want to show. Now hide the truck item from the PivotTable.

To hide the TRUCK item on the PivotTable:

1. Click the **list arrow** for the TYPE field button to display a list of each item in the TYPE field. See Figure 5-41.

| Figure 5-41 | LIST OF FIELD ITEMS FOR TYPE FIELD |

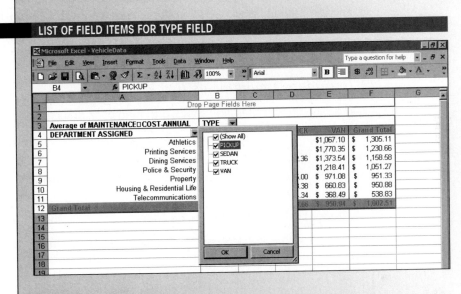

2. Click the **TRUCK** check box next to deselect the item.

3. Click the **OK** button. See Figure 5-42.

| Figure 5-42 | PIVOTTABLE WITH TRUCK ITEM HIDDEN |

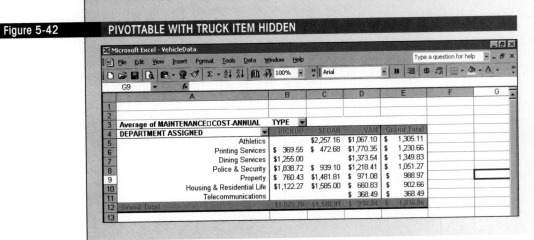

Now the report contains the vehicle data Linda wants to review. Although the item is hidden, you can show the item again by clicking the field button and checking the check box for the hidden item.

You receive a memo from Linda informing you that vehicle ID # 818, a vehicle in the Housing department, will be reassigned to Dining Services. You want to update the PivotTable before you print a copy of it for Linda.

Refreshing a PivotTable

Recall that you cannot directly change the data in the PivotTable. In order to change the data in the PivotTable, you must make the changes to the original Excel list first, and then you need to update the PivotTable. To update a PivotTable so that it reflects the current state of the vehicles list, you update, or "refresh," the PivotTable by using the Refresh command.

You need to update the record for vehicle ID # 818 in the vehicles list. Making this change will affect the PivotTable because the average annual maintenance cost for vehicles assigned to Dining Services (which is currently $1349.83) and to Housing & Residential Life (which is currently $902.66) will change. After you update the vehicle information in the Excel list, check to see if there is any change in the PivotTable.

To update the vehicles list:

1. Switch the Vehicles worksheet, and then click any cell in the list.

2. Click **Data** on the menu bar, and then click **Form** to display the Vehicles data form.

3. Click the **Criteria** button to display a blank data form.

4. Type **818** in the ID # text box, and click the **Find Next** button to display the next record in the list that meets the specified criteria—the ID # must equal 818.

5. Change the vehicle's assigned department to **Dining Services**, and then click the **Close** button. The department for this vehicle has been updated in the vehicles list.

Now return to the PivotTable to see whether there is any change in the average annual maintenance cost.

6. Switch to the AvgMaintCost worksheet. Notice that the average annual maintenance costs for Dining Services and Housing & Residential Life remain at $1349.83 and $902.66, respectively.

Because the PivotTable is not automatically updated when data in the source list is updated, you must "refresh" the PivotTable yourself.

To refresh the PivotTable to reflect the changes in the vehicles list:

1. Select any cell inside the PivotTable.

2. Click the **Refresh Data** button on the PivotTable toolbar to update the PivotTable. See Figure 5-43. The new average annual maintenance cost for Dining Services increases to $1,390.52 and Housing & Residential Life decreases to $868.10.

Figure 5-43	PIVOTTABLE AFTER BEING REFRESHED

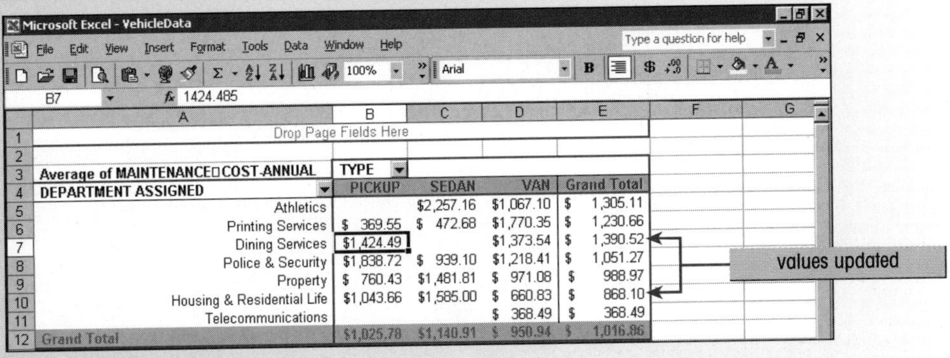

	A	B	C	D	E	F	G
1		Drop Page Fields Here					
2							
3	Average of MAINTENANCE□COST-ANNUAL	TYPE					
4	DEPARTMENT ASSIGNED	PICKUP	SEDAN	VAN	Grand Total		
5	Athletics		$2,257.16	$1,067.10	$ 1,305.11		
6	Printing Services	$ 369.55	$ 472.68	$1,770.35	$ 1,230.66		
7	Dining Services	$1,424.49		$1,373.54	$ 1,390.52		
8	Police & Security	$1,838.72	$ 939.10	$1,218.41	$ 1,051.27		
9	Property	$ 760.43	$1,481.81	$ 971.08	$ 988.97		
10	Housing & Residential Life	$1,043.66	$1,585.00	$ 660.83	$ 868.10		
11	Telecommunications			$ 368.49	$ 368.49		
12	Grand Total	$1,025.78	$1,140.91	$ 950.94	$ 1,016.86		

values updated

3. Click any cell outside the PivotTable area to remove the blue outline from the PivotTable report.

The PivotTable shows that the average annual maintenance cost by vehicle type and department.

Creating a PivotChart

Linda thinks a chart can more effectively convey the summary information of the PivotTable. She asks you to create a clustered column chart. You can create a PivotChart using the PivotTable and PivotChart Wizard, or you can first create a PivotTable and then click Chart Wizard button on the PivotTable toolbar to create a PivotChart. The second approach takes a single mouse click. Since you already have created a PivotTable, you decide on the single mouse click approach.

To create the PivotChart based on the PivotTable:

1. Click any cell inside the PivotTable, and then click the **Chart Wizard** button 📊 on the PivotTable toolbar. A stacked column chart and Chart toolbar appear in a new chart sheet. See Figure 5-44.

Figure 5-44 | **STACKED COLUMN PIVOTCHART LINKED TO PIVOTTABLE**

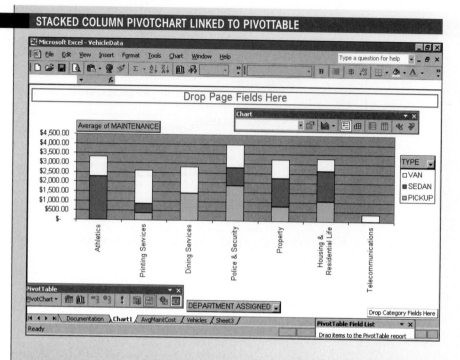

Next you will change the chart type to a clustered column chart.

2. Click the **list arrow** for the Chart Type button 🔽 on the Chart toolbar, and then click the **Column Chart** icon (third row, first column). A clustered column chart appears. See Figure 5-45.

Figure 5-45 | **CLUSTERED COLUMN PIVOTCHART**

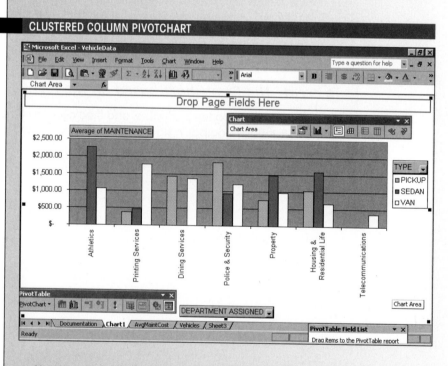

You have completed your work on the VehicleData workbook. Save your changes and exit Excel.

3. Click the **Save** button 🔲 on the Standard toolbar, and then click the **Close** button 🗙 on the Excel title bar.

Linda is pleased with the PivotTable and PivotChart. Both show the average annual maintenance cost by department and vehicle type, which will be important information for her upcoming budget meeting.

QUICK CHECK Session 5.3

1. What is the default calculation method for numeric data in a PivotTable?

2. When creating a PivotTable, you use the _____ to layout a PivotTable report.

3. After the data in a list has been updated, you would have to _____ the PivotTable in order to see an updated version of it.

4. Fields such as region, state, country, and zip code are most likely to appear as _____ in a PivotTable.

5. Fields such as revenue, costs, and profits are most likely to appears as _____ in a PivotTable.

6. Assume that you have a list of college students, and in the list there is a code for males and females, and there is a field identifying the student's major. Which tool, AutoFilter or PivotTable, would you use in each of the following situations:

   a. You want a list of all females majoring in history.

   b. You want a count of the number of males and females in each major at your institution.

REVIEW ASSIGNMENTS

Linda has another vehicle that needs to be entered in the VehicleData workbook. To further understand the information in the workbook, she wants to know which type of vehicle has been purchased the most often and which types of vehicle each department uses the most often. She also wants to analyze the age of the vehicles in the fleet. She also wants several PivotTables that will show the minimum annual maintenance cost by make and type and then by department assigned and average annual maintenance cost by year. She wants the last PivotTable converted to a PivotChart. To gather the information she needs for further analysis of the university's fleet, Linda has asked to you to complete the following:

1. Start Excel and make sure your Data Disk is in the disk drive. Open the workbook **VehicleData1** in the Tutorial.05/Review folder on your Data Disk.

2. On the Documentation sheet, enter the date and your name, and then switch to the Vehicles sheet.

3. Save the workbook as **VehicleData2** in the Tutorial.05/Review folder on your Data Disk.

4. Add the following information for the latest vehicle assigned to the Athletics department:

   ID #: **12345**   ODOMETER: **789**
   YEAR: **2003**   DEPARTMENT: **Athletics**
   MAKE: **GMC**   PURCHASE PRICE: **25000**
   TYPE: **VAN**   MAINTENANCE COST-ANNUAL: **0**

5. Use the Vehicles data form to determine how many Ford vehicles there are in the list. Explain the steps you followed to get your answer.

6. Sort the vehicles list by TYPE, within TYPE by MAKE, and within MAKE by MAINTENANCE COST-ANNUAL. Arrange MAINTENANCE COST-ANNUAL in descending order.

7. Use the Subtotals command to count how many vehicles there are for each type of vehicle. Display the count in the ID # column. Print the vehicles list with the subtotals. Remove all subtotals after printing the list.

8. Use the AVERAGE function to compute the average annual maintenance cost for all the vehicles, and then use the AutoFilter feature to print a list of all vehicles with above average annual maintenance costs.

9. Use conditional formatting to boldface the YEAR field for vehicles with a model year between 1990 and 2000. Format the YEAR field with a yellow background color. Print the vehicles list.

Explore 10. Use the Excel AutoFilter to produce a list of the vehicles with the top five odometer readings in descending order. (*Hint*: Check out the Top 10 option in the list of available AutoFilters.) Print the list.

11. Create a PivotTable to show the maximum annual maintenance cost by MAKE and TYPE. Place your PivotTable in a new worksheet. Format your PivotTable to produce an attractive report. Rename the PivotTable sheet using an appropriate name. Include your name in the custom footer, and then print the PivotTable.

12. Modify the PivotTable in Question 11 to also display the minimum annual maintenance cost by MAKE and TYPE. Print the modified PivotTable.

13. Modify the PivotTable in Question 12 to include the DEPARTMENT ASSIGNED as a page field. Print the modified PivotTable. Explain how the page field can be used.

Explore 14. Create a second PivotTable that displays the average annual maintenance cost by YEAR. Display the costs in five-year periods: 1981-1985, 1986-1990, and so on. (*Hint*: Check out the Group and Outline option on the shortcut menu.) Prepare a PivotChart based on the PivotTable. Print the PivotTable and PivotChart.

15. Save and close the workbook, and then exit Excel.

CASE PROBLEMS

Case 1. Revenue at the Tea House Arnold Taymore, sales manager for Tea House Distributors, is getting ready for a semiannual meeting at the company headquarters. At this meeting, Arnold plans to present summary data on the product line. The data that he has accumulated consists of revenues by product, by month, and by region for the last six months. Help him summarize and analyze the data.

To complete this task:

1. Open the workbook **Teahouse1** located in the Tutorial.05/Cases folder on your Data Disk. Enter the date and your name in the Documentation sheet. Save the workbook as **Teahouse2** in the same folder.

2. Improve the formatting of the revenue field so it is clear that this field deals with dollars.

3. Freeze the column headings so they remain on the screen as you scroll the worksheet.

4. Revenue for Duke Gray Tea for June in the West region was $48,420. Use the data form to enter the following data: Duke Gray Tea, June, West, 48420.

5. Sort the tea list by month and within month by region. Insert subtotals by month. Include your name in a custom footer, and then print the information for each month on a separate page.

6. Use conditional formatting to display revenue below $25,000 using a formatting that you feel will best highlight the results. Print the list.

Explore ▷ 7. Sort the data by month and within month by region. The months should appear in January through December sequence. (*Hint*: Click the Options button in the Sort dialog box to customize your sort options.) Print the list.

8. Which product was the company's bestseller in the West region during May and June? Identify the product, month, and revenue in that month. Print the analysis that enabled you to answer the question.

9. Which product had the highest revenue in each month? Create a PivotTable that provides you with the answer to the question. Place your PivotTable in a new worksheet. Format the PivotTable to emphasize the highest revenue in each month. Rename the PivotTable sheet "HighSales." Print the PivotTable.

10. Create a PivotChart of total revenue by product. Choose an appropriate chart type. Assign descriptive names to all new sheets. Print the PivotTable and PivotChart.

Explore ▷ 11. Create a PivotTable that displays total revenue and average revenue by Region (row field) and Month (column field). Format the PivotTable, and then print it.

12. Save and close the workbook, and then exit Excel.

Case 2. Eastern State College Michelle Long is the dean of the College of Business Administration at Eastern State College. The College of Business Administration has three academic departments: Management, Marketing, and Accounting. Each faculty member holds an academic rank, such as professor or associate professor. Most faculty members are hired as instructors or assistant professors. After a period of time, the faculty member might be promoted to associate professor and then to full professor. Faculty salaries usually reflect the faculty member's rank and length of service in the department.

The dean frequently asks you to locate and summarize information about the College of Business Administration faculty. This week she has several important budget and staffing meetings to attend for which she will need to produce detailed and specific information on her faculty. She asks for your help to compile the necessary data. She has created an Excel workbook that contains a worksheet with the name, academic rank, department, hire date, salary, and sex of each faculty member in the College of Business Administration. She asks you to use the worksheet to create several reports that will organize the information to produce the specific output she requires for each meeting.
To complete this task:

1. Open the **Faculty1** workbook located in Tutorial.05/Cases folder of your Data Disk, and then save the workbook as **Faculty2** in the same folder.

2. Enter the date and your name in the Documentation sheet. Switch to the Faculty Data worksheet.

3. Complete the worksheet by calculating the matching retirement dollar amount for each faculty member (column I). Note that not all of the faculty members participate in the

plan (column H). For any faculty member who is participating in the retirement plan, the institution will contribute (match) 3% (cell I1) of the faculty member's salary, placing the contribution in the retirement fund. If the faculty member is not participating, enter a zero in the appropriate cell. Create a formula using the IF function to compute the contribution to the retirement fund (column I).

4. Freeze the panes so the column headings and the first and last name row labels remain on the screen as you scroll the faculty list.

5. Use the Find and Replace command to change all faculty members with the rank Full Prof to Full.

6. Display only the faculty with the rank Full, and then sort by salary from the highest salary to the lowest. Print the list of full professors beginning with the professor with the highest salary.

Explore

7. Sort the data so the faculty is sorted by rank in the following order: Full, Associate, Assistant, and Instructor. Print the sorted worksheet. (*Hint*: Use the Custom Lists tab found in the Options dialog box, which you can access from the Options command on the Tools menu.)

8. The institution is studying an early retirement program. To make it easier to identify eligible faculty, apply conditional formatting to all faculty hired before 1980. Apply a format of your choice to the YearHired column.

9. Use the Subtotals command to compute the total number of faculty in each department. Print the faculty list with subtotals.

Explore

10. Use the SUM function to compute the total salary for all faculty (display the total salary in cell G48). Use the subtotal function (*not* the Subtotals command on the Data menu) to compute the total salary (display the total in cell G49). Filter the list so only full professors are displayed. Observe the two totals. Filter the list again, but this time display only assistant professors. Observe the totals. Comment on the two functions used to compute total salaries after filtering has been applied.

11. Create a PivotTable to compute the average salary by gender and department. Place the PivotTable in a new worksheet. Give a descriptive name to the new worksheet. Print the PivotTable.

12. Use the PivotTable in Question 11 to develop a PivotChart. Choose an appropriate type of chart. Print the PivotChart.

13. Save and close the workbook, and then exit Excel.

Case 3. Outstanding Accounts Marcus Choy is an accounts receivable specialist for a company that provides research services to various government agencies and private corporations. Marcus is assigned to manage the government contracts. Each month Marcus provides his supervisor with an analysis of the accounts for which his supervisor is responsible. Marcus uses Excel to help him with the analysis.

The Excel list consists of the following fields:

Field	Description
Customer #	A number assigned to each customer
Invoice #	Each month a bill is sent for expenses on a contract. For each bill on a contract, the voucher is increased by 1.
Date Billed	Date bill mailed
Balance	Amount owed
Agency Name	Government agency funding the research

PI	Principal investigator who has major responsibility for the research
Days Outstanding	Number of days since Date Billed
Over 120 Days Old	Contains "Follow Up" if the invoice is over 120 days old; otherwise cell is blank

Marcus needs to analyze the government receivables so that he can compare them to the payments. He believes that some of the receivables are running well past the due dates. The company will need to notify the government agencies involved so that payments can be obtained in a more timely manner.

To complete this task:

1. Open the **Receivables1** workbook located in Tutorial.05/Cases folder on your Data Disk, and then save the workbook as **Receivables2** in the same folder.

2. Enter the date and your name in the Documentation sheet. Switch to the Amount Owed worksheet.

3. Complete the worksheet by calculating the number of Days Outstanding (column G) by subtracting the Date Billed (column C) of each invoice from the Age As of date in cell B1. Format the number of Days Outstanding column using the Number format. In column H use an IF function to place the words "Follow Up" in the cell for any invoice that is overdue by over 120 days; otherwise leave the cell blank.

4. Freeze the panes so that the Customer # and Invoice # column headings remain on the screen as you scroll the amount owed list.

5. Sort the list by PI (principal investigator), Agency Name, and Balance. Print the results.

6. Display only the invoices to NASA that have an amount due (Balance) over $25,000. Print the results, and then remove the filter arrows.

7. Apply conditional formatting to all invoices that have been due for more than 120 days. Apply a format of your choice to the Days Outstanding column. (*Hint*: You should select only the range to be formatted when applying conditional formatting.) Print the results.

8. Use the Subtotals command to compute the total owed by each customer (Customer #). Print the results. Remove the subtotals after printing.

Explore ▶ 9. Use the Subtotals command from the Data menu to compute the average balance owed by Agency. Place each subtotal immediately *before* the data for the associated agency. Print the report with subtotals.

10. Create a PivotTable that summarizes the total owed (Balance) by each agency. Place the PivotTable in a new worksheet. Give a descriptive name to the new worksheet. Print the PivotTable.

Explore ▶ 11. Modify the PivotTable in Question 10 to summarize by agency and month (*Hint*: Check out the Group and Outline option on the shortcut menu.)

12. Save and close the workbook, and then exit Excel.

Case 4. E-Gourmet Express Jerry Mayer is operations manager at E-Gourmet Express, an Internet startup company. The company sells gourmet food products to specialty food stores around the world. E-Gourmet sells a wide range of premium beverages, bakery goods, spices, desserts, and gourmet meat items through the use of a Web storefront. E-Gourmet Express guarantees shipments within 48 hours.

The company has been in operation a little over a year, and Jerry wants to analyze where it stands. Jerry downloaded a portion of the company's sales data and stored it in an Excel file. He wants to summarize sales by country, product categories, products, months, and the like. He asks for your help with the analysis.

To complete this task:

1. Open the **GourmetSales1** workbook located in Tutorial.05/Cases folder on your Data Disk, and then save the workbook as **GourmetSales2** in the same folder.

2. Insert a new worksheet and rename the sheet Documentation. Enter your name, the date, and a purpose statement in the Documentation sheet. Switch to the CustSales worksheet.

3. Freeze the panes so that the column headings and the CompanyName, Country, and OrderDate row values remain on the screen as you scroll the customer sales list.

4. Compute the total sales for each item sold, and include the amount in column L (column labeled "Total"). Use the following formula: Quantity multiplied by the UnitPrice multiplied by the Adjustment plus Freight. The Adjustment is computed using the formula 1 –Discount % (1 minus the value in the Discount % field).

5. Display all the beverages sold in Brazil between January 1 and March 15. Sort by the company name and within company name by order date (with the most recent order date displayed first). Print these records. If a second page is needed to print all the fields for each record, make sure the company name appears on the second page. After printing the results, remove the filter arrows.

Explore
6. Sort the worksheet by Country; within country by category; within category by Product; and within product by Order date. Print *only the first* page of the sorted worksheet. (*Hint*: You must make two passes for the data to be sorted correctly.)

7. Apply conditional formatting to two products: Tofu and Chai. Choose different formatting in the Product Name column for each product.

8. Create a PivotTable that summarizes the total sales by country, by category, and then by sales rep. Place the PivotTable in a new worksheet. Give a descriptive name to the new worksheet. You decide the formatting and layout of the PivotTable. Print the PivotTable.

9. For each country, who is E-Gourmet's largest customer based on total sales? Format the PivotTable so the largest customer in each country can be easily identified. What are the total sales for this company? Print the analysis that supports your answer.

Explore
10. How many unique products are sold by E-Gourmet? Explain how you determined your answer. Print a list of the unique products sold by E-Gourmet. (*Hint*: Use the Advanced Filter dialog box, which you can open from the Filter submenu on the Data menu.)

11. Create a PivotTable that displays the number of orders made (treat each row as an order), the total number of units shipped, and the total freight charges by shipper and country. Place the PivotTable in a new worksheet. Give a descriptive name to the new worksheet. You decide the formatting and layout of the PivotTable.

12. Use the page field feature of the PivotTable to expand the analysis in Question 11. Print the modified PivotTable. Comment on how the page field can be used.

13. Create a PivotChart that shows the total sales by country and category. Choose an appropriate chart type. Print the PivotChart

14. Save and close the workbook, and then exit Excel.

INTERNET ASSIGNMENTS

Student Union

The purpose of the Internet Assignments is to challenge you to find information on the Internet that you can use to create effective spreadsheets. The actual assignments are updated and maintained on the Course Technology Web site. Log on to the Internet and use your Web browser to go to the Student Union on the New Perspectives Series site at **www.course.com/NewPerspectives/studentunion**. Click the Online Companions link, and then click the link for this text.

QUICK CHECK ANSWERS

Session 5.1

1. list
2. The Freeze Panes option allows you to keep, or freeze, rows and columns that will not scroll off the screen as you move around the worksheet. Freezing the rows and columns, which often contain headings, on the screen makes understanding the data in each record easier.
3. sort fields, sort keys
4. sort by major and then within major sort by last name
5. data form
6. Assuming that you have the fields FirstName and LastName as part of the employee list, you would click the Criteria button in the Data Form dialog box. In the FirstName field text box, type "Jin"; in the LastName field text box, type "Shinu". Click the Find Next button to display the record in the data form.
7. primary (sort field or sort key)
8. descending

Session 5.2

1. In order to have Excel calculate subtotals correctly, you must first sort the data because the subtotals are inserted whenever the value in the specified field changes.
2. AutoFilter, Data
3. Use the AutoFilter feature. Click the Major column list arrow, and then click Marketing. For the GPA field, click Custom in the list of filtering options. Enter the comparison operator > (greater than) and the constant 3.0 to form the condition for a GPA greater than 3.0.
4. Outline
5. True
6. Conditional formatting
7. three

Session 5.3

1. sum, or add, the field
2. PivotTable Field List
3. refresh
4. row, columns, or pages fields, or category fields
5. data items
6. a. AutoFilter
   b. PivotTable

In this tutorial you will:

- Create and print a worksheet group

- Edit multiple work-sheets at the same time

- Create 3-D cell refer-ences and workbook references

- Consolidate information from multiple work-sheets and workbooks

- Create a workbook template

- Learn how to store and access templates

- Create a lookup table and use Excel's lookup functions

- Create and use an Excel workspace

WORKING
WITH MULTIPLE WORKSHEETS AND WORKBOOKS

Tracking Cash Flow for the Lakeland Boychoir

CASE

Lakeland Boychoir

The Lakeland Boychoir is a nonprofit performing choir for boys aged 8 through 14, who live in and around the city of Lakeland, Nebraska. The choir of almost 60 boys performs several concerts throughout the year for the people of central and western Nebraska. The choir also tours the Midwest and participates in several regional and national com-petitions.

Because of its nonprofit status, the choir relies heavily on volunteer support, particularly from the parents. Joy Ling is one such parent. She has two children in choir, and she also acts as the choir's treasurer. The executive director has asked Joy to place the choir's budget informa-tion in an Excel workbook so information can then be printed in the choir's annual financial report given to its members and supporters.

Joy has asked you to help her with a cash flow report that will show the monthly expenses and inflows for the past year. She has already entered each month's values on separate worksheets, but she needs your assistance in making all the sheets work together. She wants to be able to summarize all of the information in the 12 sheets into a single sheet. Joy realizes that this will be a yearly task, so she also wants to be able to access the financial information of a previ-ous year's workbook and use that information as the basis of the cur-rent year's workbook.

SESSION 6.1

In this session, you'll work with multiple worksheets by creating and formatting worksheet groups. You'll also insert cell references to cells on other worksheets using 3-D cell references. Finally, you'll consolidate data from several worksheets into a single cell.

Using **Multiple Worksheets**

One of the most useful ways to organize your workbook data is to place that data in several different worksheets. Using multiple worksheets makes it easier for you to group your data. For example, a company with branches located in different geographic regions could place sales information for each region on a separate worksheet. Employees could then view regional sales information by clicking a sheet in the workbook, rather than having to scroll through a single large and complicated worksheet.

You can also use multiple worksheets to place the most important information first. If your supervisor were only interested in the bottom line, the first worksheet could contain your conclusions and summary data, whereas more detailed information would be available on separate worksheets placed later in the workbook.

In the case of the Lakeland Boychoir, Joy Ling has created separate worksheets that display the cash flow for each month of the 2003 season. She has already entered the data in an Excel workbook. Open the workbook and review the current information.

To open the Lakeland Boychoir workbook:

1. Start Excel and open the **LBC1** workbook located in the Tutorial.06/Tutorial folder on your Data Disk.

2. On the Documentation sheet, enter today's date and your name.

3. Save the workbook as **LBC2003** in the Tutorial.06/Tutorial folder on your Data Disk.

4. Switch to the January worksheet to view the cash flow figures for the first month of the year. See Figure 6-1.

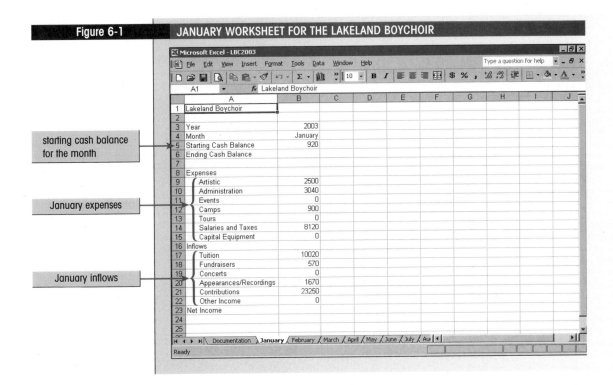

Figure 6-1   JANUARY WORKSHEET FOR THE LAKELAND BOYCHOIR

Joy hasn't entered any formulas in the workbook yet. For each month, she needs to calculate the total of the expenses entered in the range B9:B15, the total inflows entered in the range B17:B22, and the net income (the total inflows minus the total expenses) which will appear in cell B23. Finally, Joy needs to calculate the ending cash balance for the month, which is equal to the starting cash balance plus the net income.

Joy needs to add these formulas to all 12 worksheets, but rather than laboriously retyping the commands in each sheet, she can enter them all at once by creating a worksheet group.

Grouping Worksheets

A **worksheet group** is a collection of several worksheets. Once you group a collection of worksheets, any changes you make to one worksheet are applied to all sheets in the group. Like cell ranges, the collection can contain adjacent or nonadjacent sheets. To select adjacent worksheets, you click the sheet tab of the first sheet in the group, press and hold down the Shift key, and then click the sheet tab of the last sheet in the group. To select nonadjacent worksheets, you click a sheet tab of one of the worksheets, and then press and hold down the Ctrl key as you click the sheet tabs of other worksheets you want included in the group.

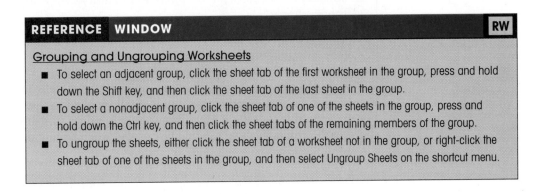

REFERENCE WINDOW   **RW**

Grouping and Ungrouping Worksheets
- To select an adjacent group, click the sheet tab of the first worksheet in the group, press and hold down the Shift key, and then click the sheet tab of the last sheet in the group.
- To select a nonadjacent group, click the sheet tab of one of the sheets in the group, press and hold down the Ctrl key, and then click the sheet tabs of the remaining members of the group.
- To ungroup the sheets, either click the sheet tab of a worksheet not in the group, or right-click the sheet tab of one of the sheets in the group, and then select Ungroup Sheets on the shortcut menu.

Entering Formulas in a Worksheet Group

In the choir workbook, you'll select an adjacent range of worksheets from the January worksheet through the December sheet.

To group the choir worksheets:

1. Verify that the January worksheet is still selected.

2. Click the **Last Sheet** button ▶| to display the last tab in the workbook (December).

3. Press and hold down the **Shift** key, and click the **December** tab. Release the Shift key. The worksheet tabs for January through December are highlighted, indicating that they are all selected. Note that the Excel title bar includes the caption "(Group)", which indicates that a worksheet group has been selected.

4. Click the **First Sheet** button |◀ to return to the first sheet in the worksheet group, which is January.

With the monthly sheets grouped together, you can now enter the formulas for total expenses, total inflows, net income, and ending cash balance.

To enter the worksheet formulas:

1. Click cell **B8** and enter the formula **=SUM(B9:B15)**. Note that you can enter the cell reference in a function or formula by typing the cell reference or by pointing to the cell. To enter the SUM function, you can use the AutoSum button Σ on the Standard toolbar. If you select the AutoSum button, drag the pointer down over the cell range.

2. Click cell **B16** and enter the formula **=SUM(B17:B22)**.

3. Click cell **B23** and enter the formula **=B16-B8**.

4. Click cell **B6** and enter the formula **=B5+B23**. The ending cash balance (cell B6) for January should be 21870.

   As you entered formulas into the January worksheet, the same formulas were added to the rest of the sheets in the group.

5. Click the **February** tab. The ending cash balance for February is –2690.

   Note that the starting cash balance in cell B5 has been set to zero. This starting cash balance doesn't take into account the cash that will carry over from January into February. You'll learn how to carry over values from the previous month shortly.

6. Click the **January** tab to return to the January cash figures.

You should remember that when entering or editing cells in a worksheet group, any changes you make to one sheet are automatically applied to the other sheets in the group. For example, if you delete a value from one cell, values in that cell will be deleted in all sheets in the group. Thus you should be cautious when editing the contents of the group.

Formatting a Worksheet Group

As with inserting formulas and text, any formatting changes you make to a single sheet in a group are applied to all sheets. You decide to use one of Excel's AutoFormats to change the appearance of the cash flow data. You will also make some individual formatting changes using the Format Cells dialog box and Formatting toolbar.

To format the worksheet group:

1. Select the range **A3:B23**.

2. Click **Format** on the menu bar, and then click **AutoFormat**. The AutoFormat dialog box opens.

3. Click the **Classic 3** AutoFormat in the list of available formats, and then click the **Options** button.

   When you apply the Classic 3 format to a selected range, the text in the range will be right-aligned. You do not want the current alignment of text in the worksheets to change, so you will deselect the Alignment option.

4. Deselect the **Alignment** check box, click the **OK** button, and then click outside the selected range to view the AutoFormat applied to the cells.

   The formatting applied to the Net Income cells includes a white background and a solid black border. You can apply this portion of the Classic 3 AutoFormat to the Expenses cells and the Inflows cells.

5. Select the range **A23:B23**, and then double-click the **Format Painter** button ⬚ on the Formatting toolbar. Double-clicking the Format Painter button allows you to apply the format in the range A23:B23 to multiple cell ranges.

6. Click cell **A8**, and then click cell **A16**. Excel displays the contents of the ranges A8:B8 and A16:B16 with a white background and a solid black border.

   TROUBLE? If Excel does not apply the format to both cell ranges, you might not have double-clicked the Format Painter button. Select the range A23:B23 again, and then double-click ⬚. Repeat Step 6 to apply the format to both ranges.

7. Click ⬚ again to turn Format Painter off.

   You want the numbers to appear with commas only.

8. Select the range **B5:B23**, click **Format** on the menu bar, and then click **Cells**. The Format Cells dialog box opens.

9. Click the **Number** tab if necessary, click **Number** in the Category list, reduce the number of decimal places to **0**, click to select the **Use 1000 Separator (,)** check box, and then click the **OK** button. The numbers now appear with commas.

   Next you will format the title of the worksheet.

10. Click cell **A1**, click the **Bold** button **B** on the Formatting toolbar, and then increase the font size to **14** points.

    Finally, you will change the width of column B to better accommodate the numbers.

11. Increase the width of column B to **10** characters. See Figure 6-2.

Figure 6-2   FORMATTED JANUARY WORKSHEET

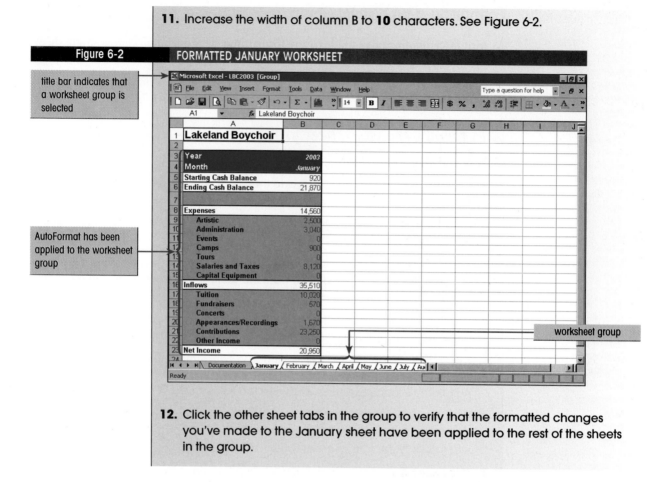

title bar indicates that a worksheet group is selected

AutoFormat has been applied to the worksheet group

worksheet group

12. Click the other sheet tabs in the group to verify that the formatted changes you've made to the January sheet have been applied to the rest of the sheets in the group.

Now that you've applied a common set of formulas and formats to the monthly worksheets, you can ungroup the selected sheets. To remove a worksheet group, you can click a sheet tab of a sheet not in the group, or you can right-click the sheet tab of a selected sheet and then click Ungroup Sheets on the shortcut menu that appears.

To ungroup the monthly worksheets:

1. Right-click the **January** tab. A shortcut menu appears.

2. Click **Ungroup Sheets** on the shortcut menu. Only the January tab should be highlighted now, and the word "(Group)" disappears from the title bar.

The formulas in the worksheets are all correct, but you still need a way of carrying the cash balance over from one month to another. You'll do this next using a 3-D reference.

Working with 3-D Cell References

In a worksheet, you can consider the rows and columns as representing two dimensions. As shown in Figure 6-3, the collection of worksheets in the workbook constitutes a third dimension.

Figure 6-3   **THE THREE DIMENSIONS OF A WORKBOOK**

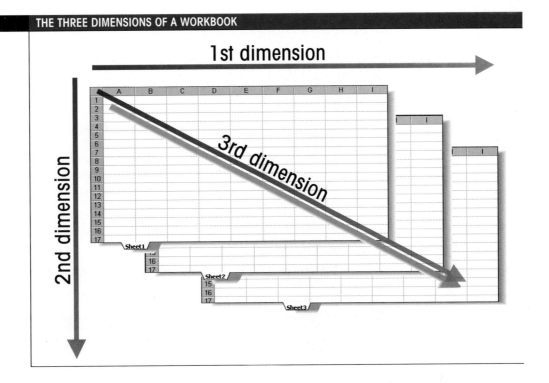

A **3-D cell reference** is a reference that specifies not only the rows and columns of a cell range, but also the sheet (or sheets) that the cells appear on. The general format of a 3-D cell reference is *'Sheet Range'!Cell Range*, where *Sheet Range* is the range of sheets, and *Cell Range* is the cell range within those sheets. The sheet range can be either a single sheet or a range of adjacent sheets. If the sheet range includes more than one sheet, you specify the first and last sheet in the range separated by a colon. For example, to reference the range B2:B21 on the "Sheet1" worksheet, you would use the cell reference: *'Sheet1'!B2:B21*. To reference the range B2:B21 on three adjacent sheets named "Sheet1," "Sheet2," and "Sheet3," you would use the reference *'Sheet1:Sheet3'!B2:B21*.

Although the "Sheet2" worksheet isn't mentioned in this 3-D reference, the worksheet is included since it is part of the adjacent range of worksheets. Note that the quotation marks that enclose the sheet range are only necessary if the worksheet names include spaces in the name. For example, the 3-D reference *Sheet1!B2:B21* does not need quotation marks because there is no space in the sheet name.

A note of caution: 3-D cell references based on a worksheet group may become inaccurate if you change the positions of the worksheets or remove one of the worksheets from the workbook. On the other hand, you *can* rename worksheets, and the 3-D reference will be automatically updated to reflect the change.

You enter a 3-D reference either by typing the reference directly into the formula or by using your mouse to select the appropriate worksheet cells in the workbook. If you use the mouse, you must first select the sheet range, followed by the cell range.

In the choir workbook, the starting cash balance for each month after January is based on the ending cash balance of the previous month. For February this amount would be equal to the value of cell B6 in the January worksheet. Enter a reference to this cell now in the February worksheet.

To insert the 3-D cell reference:

1. Click the **February** tab, and then click cell **B5**.

2. Type **=** but do *not* press the Enter key.

3. Click the **January** tab.

4. Click cell **B6**, and then click the **Enter** button ☑ on the Formula bar in the January worksheet window. The February sheet is redisplayed. As indicated in the Formula bar for the February worksheet, Excel automatically inserted the formula *"=January!B6"* in cell B5. The starting cash balance for February changes to 21,870, and the ending cash balance changes to 19,180.

5. Repeat Steps 1 through 4 for the remaining 10 months of the year to calculate each month's starting cash balance based on the previous month's ending cash balance.

At the end of 2003, the ending cash balance for the entire year is 2,170. See Figure 6-4.

Figure 6-4	DECEMBER WORKSHEET

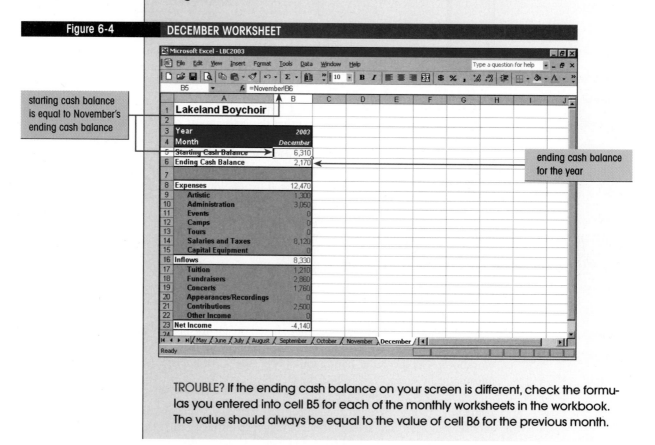

TROUBLE? If the ending cash balance on your screen is different, check the formulas you entered into cell B5 for each of the monthly worksheets in the workbook. The value should always be equal to the value of cell B6 for the previous month.

You show Joy the progress you've made on the workbook. She's pleased with your results and would like you to add a new worksheet that contains a summary of the expenses and inflows for the entire year.

Consolidating Data from Several Worksheets

When you consolidate data, you use formulas that summarize the results contained in several worksheets (or workbooks) in a single cell. For example, consolidation formulas can combine sales figures from several regional sales worksheets. In the choir workbook, you'll do something similar by creating a single worksheet named "Annual" that will display the total cash flow values for the entire fiscal year.

To insert the Annual worksheet:

1. Click the **First Sheet** button [◄], right-click the **January** tab, and then click **Insert** on the shortcut menu. The Insert dialog box opens.

2. On the General tab, click the **Worksheet** icon if necessary, and then click the **OK** button. Excel inserts a new worksheet to the left of the January sheet.

3. Double-click the new sheet tab, type **Annual** as the new sheet name, and then press the **Enter** key.

The Annual worksheet needs to have the same format and structure as the monthly worksheets that you've been working on. To ensure consistency among the worksheets, you can copy the format from the January worksheet to the Annual worksheet.

Copying Information Across Worksheets

To copy information from one worksheet into another sheet (or worksheet group), you can use the same fill command that you used to copy formulas, values, and formats from one cell into a range of cells. Try this now with the January and Annual worksheets.

To copy the values and formats from one worksheet into another:

1. Click the **January** tab to make it the active sheet.

2. Press and hold down the **Shift** key, click the **Annual** tab, and then release the Shift key. The Annual tab is highlighted, and the word "(Group)" appears in the title bar. Note also that the January worksheet is still the active sheet.

3. Select the range **A1:B23** on the January worksheet.

4. Click **Edit** on the menu, point to **Fill**, and then click **Across Worksheets**. The Fill Across Worksheets dialog box opens. You can choose to copy only the contents of the selected cells, the formats, or both.

5. Verify that the **All** option button is selected. See Figure 6-5.

| **Figure 6-5** | **FILL ACROSS WORKSHEETS DIALOG BOX** |

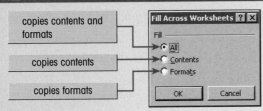

6. Click the **OK** button.

7. Right-click the **January** tab, and click **Ungroup Sheets** on the shortcut menu.

8. Click the **Annual** tab. The contents and formats have been copied to the worksheet.

   You need to adjust the width of the columns so all of the cell entries are visible.

9. Increase the width of column A to **27** characters and the width of column B to **10** characters, and then click any cell to view the formatted table.

You next need to revise the contents of the Annual worksheet so that it displays the total expenses and inflows for the entire year.

Summing Values Across Worksheets

To calculate the total expenses and inflows, you'll insert a formula that references a worksheet group which includes the January sheet through the December sheet.

To insert the total expenses and inflows:

1. In the Annual sheet, click cell **B9**, and then type **=SUM(**. Do *not* press the Enter key). Note that a ScreenTip with the SUM function and its arguments appears.

2. Click the **January** tab.

3. Click the **Last Sheet** button ⏭, press and hold down the **Shift** key, and then click the **December** tab. Release the Shift key.

4. In the December worksheet, click cell **B9**, type **)**, and then click the **Enter** button ✓ on the Formula bar. The Annual worksheet is redisplayed, and the formula *=SUM(January:December!B9)* appears in cell B9. The total artistic expenses for the year is 7,500.

   You need to copy the SUM formula to the other Expenses cells.

5. If necessary click cell **B9**, and then drag the fill handle down over the range **B9:B15**. Excel fills in the rest of the expense values for the entire year. The Expenses total for the choir is 163,700.

6. Click cell **B17**, and then using the same method described above, enter the formula **=SUM(January:December!B17)** in the cell.

   You need to copy the formula to the other Inflows cells.

7. If necessary click cell **B17**, and then drag the fill handle down over the range **B17:B22**. Excel fills in the total inflows for the year. The choir received a total of 164,950 from contributions, concerts, and other sources of income.

   Note that the ending cash balance for the entire year in cell B6 is equal to the ending cash balance in the month of December, as it should be.

8. Click cell **B4**, and then change the cell content to **All Months**. See Figure 6-6.

| Figure 6-6 | COMPLETED ANNUAL WORKSHEET |

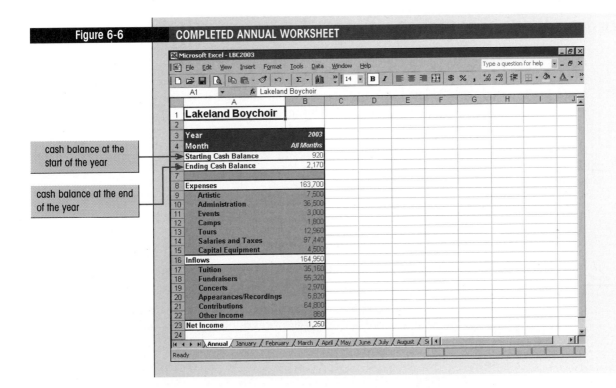

cash balance at the start of the year

cash balance at the end of the year

Joy reports that there's an error in the information she gave you. It turns out that there was a $500-Events expense in January that she was not aware of. One of the advantages of consolidating data using formulas across the worksheets is that if you change the value in one worksheet, the consolidation formula will automatically show the result of the change.

To change the events expense from January:

1. Click the **January** tab.

2. Click cell **B11**, and then change the value to **500**.

   Now examine the impact this change has had on the annual cash flow.

3. Switch to the Annual worksheet. The ending cash balance has dropped to 1,670, whereas the total expense has increased to 164,200.

   To verify that the worksheet is operating properly, compare the ending cash balance for the year with the ending cash balance for December.

4. Switch to the December sheet to view the ending cash balance for December, which should be 1,670 as well.

5. Switch to the Annual worksheet.

Now that you've completed filling in the values for the Annual worksheet, you can print the entire contents of the workbook for Joy to include in her report.

Printing **Worksheet Groups**

You can set up the page layout and print area for all of the worksheets in the choir workbook by selecting a worksheet group and then accessing the Page Setup dialog box. You want the worksheets printed in portrait orientation, and you want the name of the worksheet to appear as part of the header on each page.

To print the cash flow sheets with a customized header and footer:

1. Select the worksheets from the **Annual** sheet through the **December** sheet.

2. Click **File** on the menu bar, and then click **Page Setup**.

3. On the Page tab, verify that the **Portrait** option button is selected.

4. Click the **Margins** tab, and then click the **Horizontally** check box to center the output horizontally on the page.

5. Click the **Header/Footer** tab, click the **Header** list arrow, and then click **Annual** in the list. The worksheet name appears centered in the Header box at the top of the dialog box.

6. Click the **Custom Footer** button, type your name and insert the date on separate lines in the Right section box, and then click the **OK** button.

7. Click the **Print Preview** button.

8. Click the **Next** and **Previous** buttons to view all 13 pages of the printout and to verify that Excel has applied the same page layout to each sheet. See Figure 6-7.

Figure 6-7	PRINT PREVIEW OF THE WORKSHEET GROUP

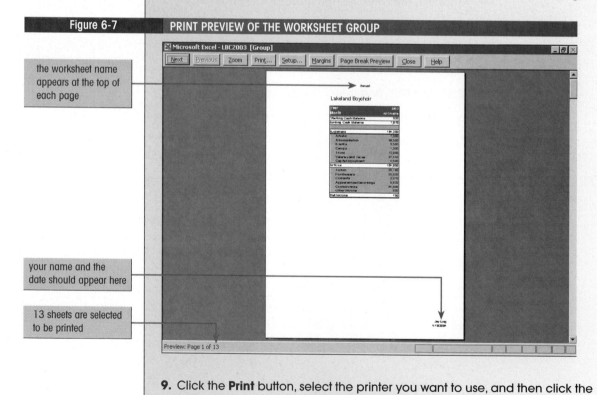

the worksheet name appears at the top of each page

your name and the date should appear here

13 sheets are selected to be printed

9. Click the **Print** button, select the printer you want to use, and then click the **OK** button.

> **10.** Click the **Documentation** tab so that the next time this workbook is opened the user sees the Documentation sheet first.
>
> **11.** Save and close the workbook, and then exit Excel.

You show the printouts to Joy, and she is so pleased that she would like to apply the same format to financial data from previous years. In the next session, you'll learn how to create workbooks that follow a customized format.

Session 6.1 QUICK CHECK

1. What is a worksheet group?

2. How do you select and deselect a worksheet group?

3. What is the 3-D cell reference to cell A10 on the "Summary Data" worksheet?

4. What is the 3-D cell reference to cell A10 on the worksheets "Summary 1," "Summary 2," and "Summary 3" (assuming that these sheets occupy an adjacent range in the workbook)?

5. How do you copy the contents and format from a range in one worksheet to the rest of the worksheets in a worksheet group?

6. How do you apply the same page layout to all sheets in your workbook?

SESSION 6.2

In this session, you'll create an Excel template. You'll learn how Excel organizes templates on your computer. You will use some of the built-in templates that Excel provides. Finally, you'll open a workbook based on another workbook.

Using Templates

In the last session you created a workbook for the 2003 budget of the Lakeland Boychoir. Joy wants to use the same workbook format for the financial data from previous years, but how should she go about it? One possibility is to reopen the workbook, save it under a new name, and then replace the 2003 values with new figures. Joy is reluctant to use that approach. She's concerned that she might make a mistake and forget to save the workbook under a new name. If that happens, she risks overwriting the 2003 figures. What Joy would like to have is a blank workbook that she can open with the formats and formulas already built into it.

Such a document is called a **template**. When you open a template, Excel opens a blank workbook with all the contents and formatting you applied to the template file. You can make any changes or additions you want to the workbook without affecting the template file. The original template retains its formatting and content, and the next time you open a blank workbook based on the template, those original settings will still be present. From Joy's point of view, the best thing about a template is that she runs no risk of affecting the data she entered into the 2003 workbook because she never opens that workbook file.

Excel has several templates that are automatically installed on your hard disk. In fact, when you start Excel and see the blank workbook called Book1, you are actually using a workbook based on a template known as the **default template**. Excel also includes the following specialized templates:

- **Balance Sheet**—used for tracking account balances over time
- **Expense Statement**—used for creating an expense report
- **Loan Amortization**—used for tracking the costs of loans and mortgages
- **Sales Invoice**—used for creating a sales invoice
- **Time Card**—used for creating an online time card to track employees' work hours

By using these templates, you can save yourself the trouble of "reinventing the wheel." You can also download additional templates from the Microsoft Web site or from third-party vendors.

Opening a Workbook Based on a Template

To see how templates work, you'll create a new workbook based on one of the built-in Excel templates.

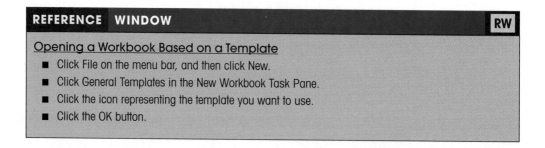

REFERENCE WINDOW   **RW**

Opening a Workbook Based on a Template
- Click File on the menu bar, and then click New.
- Click General Templates in the New Workbook Task Pane.
- Click the icon representing the template you want to use.
- Click the OK button.

You'll open the Excel Balance Sheet template.

To open a Workbook based on a Template:

1. If you took a break at the end of the last session, make sure Excel is running.

   TROUBLE? If you did not exit Excel at the end of the last session, click **File** on the menu bar, and then click **New** to open a blank workbook and the New Workbook Task Pane.

2. Click **General Templates** in the New from template section of the New Workbook Task Pane. The Templates dialog box opens.

3. Click the **Spreadsheet Solutions** tab, and then if necessary click the **Balance Sheet** icon. See Figure 6-8.

   TROUBLE? Depending on how Excel has been installed on your system, you might not see the Balance Sheet template; you can open any other template in the list.

   TROUBLE? You might be asked to insert the installation CD to access this template file. If so, insert the CD if you have it, and follow the installation instructions. If the CD is not available or if you have other problems, contact your instructor or technical support person.

| Figure 6-8 | BUILT-IN TEMPLATES |

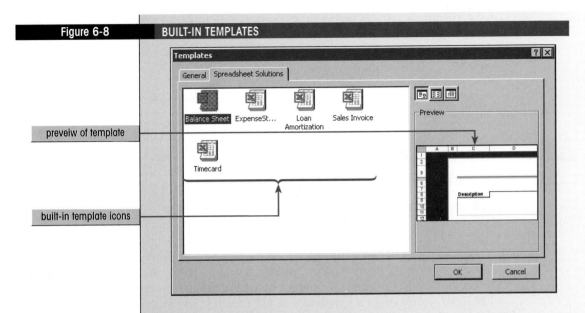

preveiw of template

built-in template icons

4. Click the **OK** button. Excel opens a workbook based on the Balance Sheet template, as shown in Figure 6-9.

| Figure 6-9 | BALANCE SHEET TEMPLATE |

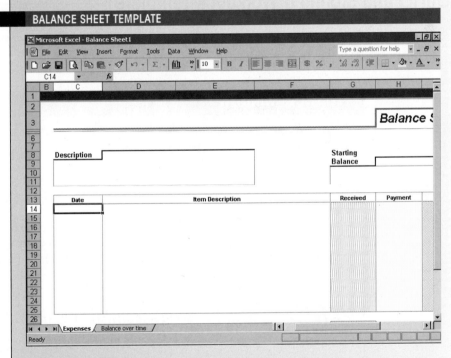

TROUBLE? Don't worry if your screen doesn't look exactly like the one in the figure. You can click the right scroll arrow on the horizontal scroll bar to see more of the layout of the worksheet.

Figure 6-9 displays a workbook based on the Balance Sheet template. Notice that the name in the title bar is not Balance Sheet, but Balance Sheet1. Just as a blank workbook that you open is named sequentially, Book1, Book2, and so forth, a workbook based on a specific template always displays the name of the template followed by a sequential number. Any changes or additions that you make to this workbook only affect the new document you are creating and do not affect the template, in this case the Balance Sheet template, itself. If you want to save your changes, you save the workbook in the same way as you would save any new workbook based on the default template.

Having seen how to create a workbook based on a template, you can close the Balance Sheet1 workbook.

To close the Balance Sheet1 workbook:

1. Click the **Close Window** button ☒ to close the workbook.

2. If prompted to save your changes, click the **No** button.

Now that you've had some experience in opening a template, you can see how useful a template that would provide the formatting and formulas for the workbooks that Joy wants to create would be. Instead of using one of Excel's built-in templates, you can save the LBC2003 workbook as a template file, and then Joy can create new workbooks based on that template.

Creating and Storing a Workbook Template

To create a template, you simply save an Excel workbook in template format using the Save As dialog box.

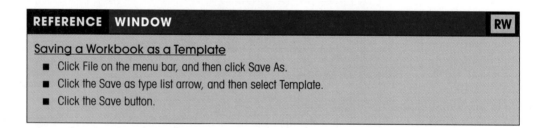

REFERENCE WINDOW   **RW**

Saving a Workbook as a Template
- Click File on the menu bar, and then click Save As.
- Click the Save as type list arrow, and then select Template.
- Click the Save button.

To save the LBC2003 workbook as a template, you'll reopen the workbook, remove the data values from the worksheets (but keep all of the formulas), and then save the workbook in template format.

To remove the data values from the choir workbook:

1. Open the **LBC2003** workbook from the Tutorial.06/Tutorial folder on your Data Disk.

2. Select the sheets from **January** through **December** (do *not* select the Annual worksheet).

3. Click cell **B5**, type **0**, and then press the **Enter** key.

4. Click cell **B9**, type **0**, and then press the **Enter** key.

5. Click cell **B9**, and then drag the fill handle down over the range **B9:B15**, filling in zeroes for all of the expense categories.

6. Click cell **B17**, type **0**, and then press the **Enter** key.

7. Click cell **B17**, and then drag the fill handle down over the range **B17:B22**, filling in zeroes for all of the inflow categories.

8. Click cell **A1**, and then click the **Annual** tab.

9. Change the value in cell B5 to **0**, and then change the value in cell B3 to **0**.

10. Click cell **A1**, and then click the **Documentation** tab.

Now you'll save the workbook in template format.

To save the workbook as a template:

1. Click **File** on the menu bar, and then click **Save As**.

2. Click the **Save as type** list arrow, and then click **Template** in the list.

   TROUBLE? When you select the Template file type, Excel automatically opens a folder named "Templates" in which all template files are stored. Excel automatically looks for template files in this particular folder, but you might not have access to your computer network's Templates folder; therefore you should save the template file to your Data Disk.

3. In the Save in list box, locate and select the **Tutorial.06/Tutorial** folder on your Data Disk.

4. Type **LBC Cash Flow** in the File name list box, and then click the **Save** button.

5. Close the LBC Cash Flow workbook template.

All template files have an .xlt extension. This extension differentiates template files from workbook files that have the .xls file extension. Once you've saved a workbook in template format, you have to make the template accessible to other users. To do this, you have to understand a bit more about how Excel stores template files.

Using the Templates Folder

To use a template like the one you just created, the template file must be placed in the Templates folder. The location of this folder will vary from user to user, but the general path is often C:\Documents and Settings*user_name*\Application Data\Microsoft\Templates where *user_name* is the name of user account. In some cases, such as on a computer network, you will have to check with the network administrator to discover the location of the Templates folder. Figure 6-10 shows a typical Templates folder location as viewed in Windows Explorer. Note that this folder is usually hidden, so to view it you would have to change your Windows Explorer settings to view hidden files by clicking the Folder Options command on the View menu and then selecting the appropriate Hidden files option on the View tab.

Figure 6-10   CONTENTS OF THE TEMPLATES FOLDER

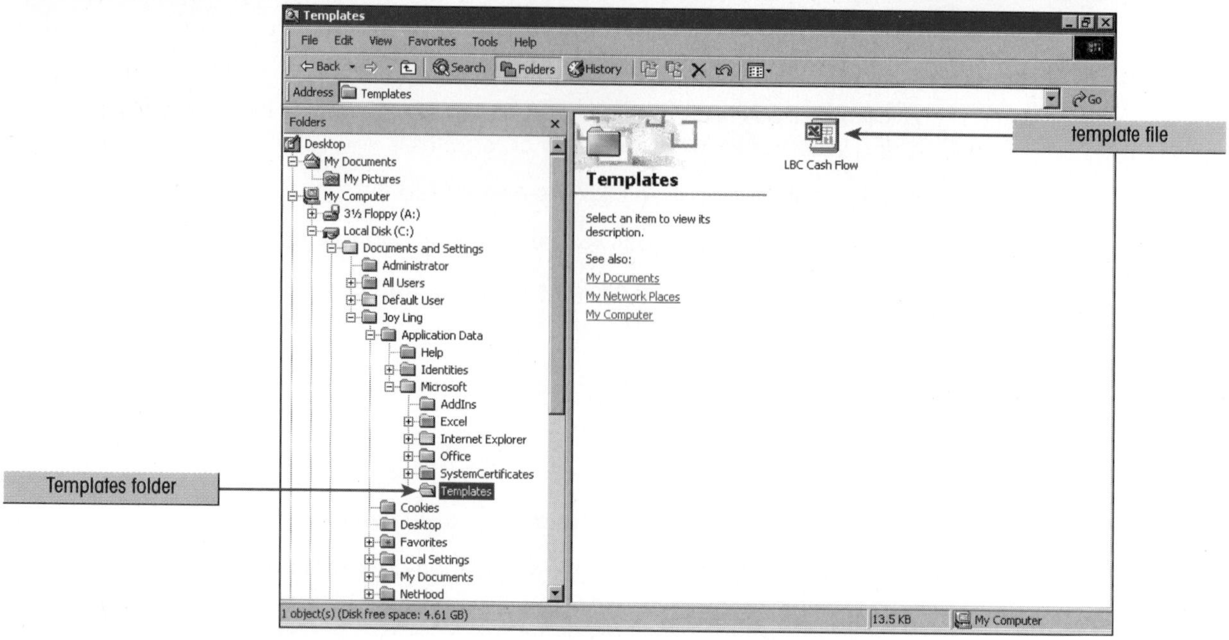

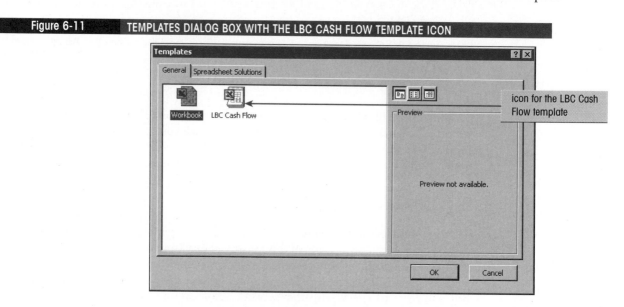

Once a file has been stored in the Templates folder (either by saving it to that folder directly via the Save As dialog box or by moving the file to the folder using Windows Explorer), the template file becomes an icon on the General tab in Templates dialog box. Figure 6-11 shows the General tab with an icon for the LBC Cash Flow template.

Figure 6-11   TEMPLATES DIALOG BOX WITH THE LBC CASH FLOW TEMPLATE ICON

The Templates folder can include subfolders used to organize your templates. The Templates folder shown in Figure 6-12 contains a single subfolder named LBC Templates, which contains the LBC Cash Flow template file.

Figure 6-12	LBC TEMPLATES SUBFOLDER

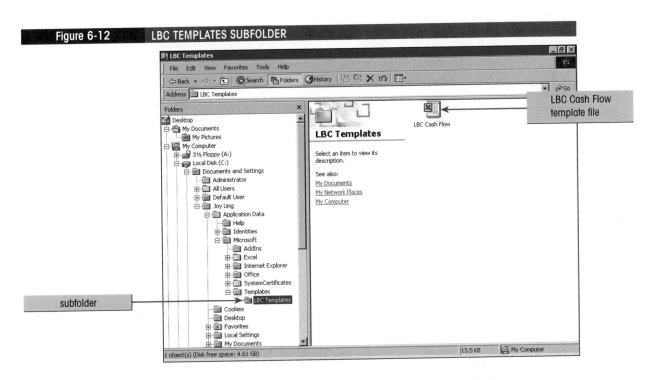

Subfolders of the Templates folder appear as tabs in the Templates dialog box. For example, the LBC Templates subfolder appears as the LBC Templates tab in Figure 6-13.

Figure 6-13	LBC TEMPLATES TAB IN THE TEMPLATES DIALOG BOX

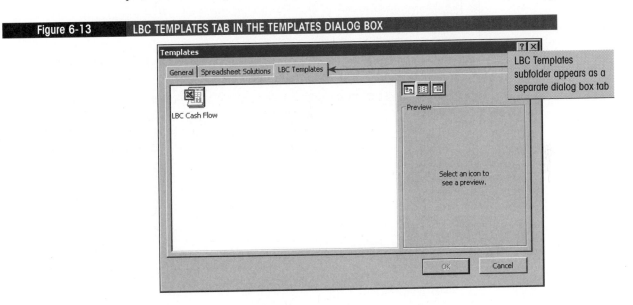

You discuss the issue of creating templates and using the Templates folder with Joy. She agrees that using templates would be very useful to her work.

Creating a New Workbook Based on an Existing File

If you don't want to create a template file or use one of Excel's templates, you can also create a new workbook based on an existing workbook. This option is available on the Task Pane. You decide to try this method with the LBC2003 workbook.

To create a workbook based on an existing workbook:

1. Click **File** on the menu bar, and then click **New**. The New Workbook Task Pane opens. See Figure 6-14.

BASING A NEW WORKBOOK ON AN EXISTING FILE

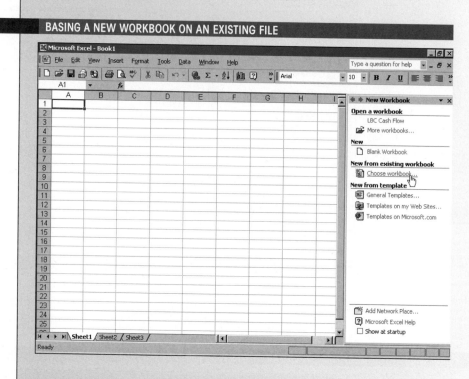

2. Click **Choose workbook** in the New from existing workbook section of the Task Pane.

3. Select the **LBC2003** workbook located in the Tutorial.06/Tutorial folder on your Data Disk, and then click the **Create New** button. Excel opens a copy of the LBC2003 workbook. See Figure 6-15. Note that the filename in the title bar is LBC20031, indicating that it is the first copy of the LBC2003 workbook created in this Excel session.

Figure 6-15 | NEW WORKBOOK BASED ON LBC2003

title bar indicates that this is copy 1 of the LBC2003 workbook

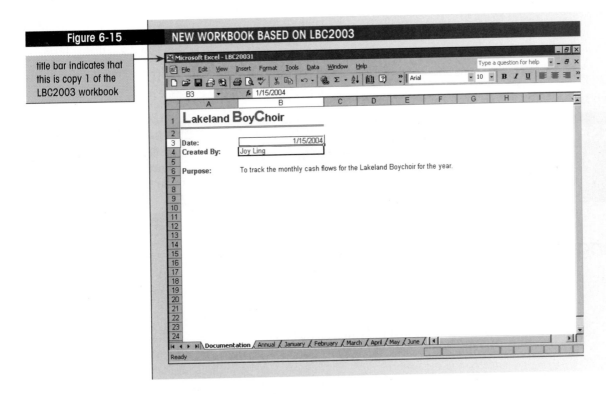

The Task Pane option of creating a new workbook works much like creating a workbook based on a template. The advantage of this option is that you are not limited to storing a workbook file in the Templates folder. This option also protects the original workbook from being inadvertently altered. However, some users may feel more comfortable using a template because it doesn't involve the original workbook at all. Which method you decide to use is a matter of personal preference.

You can close the LBC20031 workbook now without saving your changes.

To close the workbook:

1. Click the **Close Window** button [×], and then click **No** button when prompted to save your changes.

2. Exit Excel.

Joy has received a copy of the template file you created and stored it in the Templates folder on her computer. Using that template, she'll create cash flow reports for the previous years of the choir. In the next session, you'll learn how to make those files work together.

Session 6.2 QUICK CHECK

1. What is a template?

2. What is an advantage of using a template over simply using the original workbook file?

3. What is the default workbook template?

4. How do you save a file as a template?

5. Where must a template file be stored?

6. How do you place a template into a separate tab in the Templates dialog box?

7. How do you create a workbook based on another file without creating a template?

SESSION 6.3

In this session, you'll create workbook references to access data on other workbooks. You'll create links between workbooks, and learn how to manage those links. You'll also work with a lookup table and learn how to retrieve information from a lookup table using the VLOOKUP function. Finally, you will create an Excel workspace file to access several workbooks at the same time.

Using Data from Multiple Workbooks

Joy has completed the process of entering data from other years into Excel. She has created three additional workbooks, named LBC2000, LBC2001, and LBC2002, which contain monthly cash flow statements for the years 2000 through 2002.

When you created the LBC2003 workbook in the first session, you had to insert a formula that would carry the ending cash balance from one month into the starting cash balance of the next month. Joy wants you to do something similar with her other cash flow workbooks. She would like each year's starting cash balance to be based on the ending cash balance for the previous year. The previous year's cash flow statements for 2003 are located in the LBC2002 workbook (the previous year's workbook). Open that workbook and the LBC2003 workbook now.

To open the two workbooks:

1. If you took a break at the end of the last session, make sure Excel is running.

2. Open the **LBC2003** workbook located in the Tutorial.06/Tutorial folder on your Data disk, and then open the **LBC2002** workbook located in the same folder. Both workbook files are opened.

3. Switch to the LBC2003 workbook.

Because you need to use data located in one workbook in the other workbook, you have to create a link between the two workbooks. A **link** is a connection between two files allowing information to be transferred from one file to the other. When two files are linked together, one workbook is called the **source file** because it contains the information, and the other workbook is called the **destination file** because it receives the information. In this case, LBC2002 is the source file because this workbook contains the ending cash balance data for the year 2002, and LBC2003 is the destination file because this workbook will receive that ending cash balance data to determine the starting cash balance for 2003. See Figure 6-16.

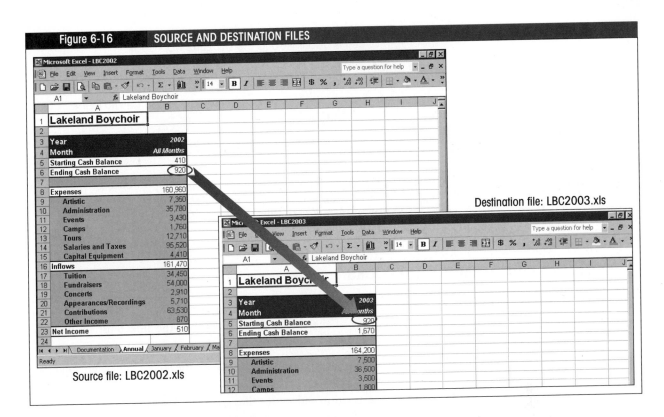

Figure 6-16   SOURCE AND DESTINATION FILES

Destination file: LBC2003.xls

Source file: LBC2002.xls

To create this link, you have to insert a formula in the LBC2003 workbook that points to a specific cell range in the LBC2002 workbook. The general form of a workbook reference is: '*Path*[*Workbook Name*]*Sheet Range*'!*Cell Range* where *Path* is the path of the workbook file on the computer or network, *Workbook Name* is the filename of the workbook (including the file extension), and *Sheet Range* and *Cell Range* are worksheets and cells in the workbook, respectively. For example, if you want to create a cell reference to the range B5:E5 on the Summary Info worksheet of the Sales.xls workbook, and the workbook file is located in the Business folder on drive E of your network, you would use the following workbook reference: '*E:\Business\[Sales.xls]Summary Info*'!*B5:E5*.

If the two workbooks are located in the same folder, you do not need to include the location information in the workbook reference. However, if you move one of the workbooks into a different folder, then you will have to modify the workbook reference to reflect the new location.

Now that you've seen the form of the workbook reference, replace the starting cash balance value in the LBC2003 workbook with a reference to the ending cash balance in the LBC2002 workbook. To create this reference you can use the same point-and-click method you used in creating the 3-D cell references in the first session.

To create the workbook reference:

1. Click the **Annual** tab in the LBC2003 workbook, click cell **B5**, and then type **=** (do *not* press the Enter key).

2. Switch to the LBC2002 workbook, and then click the **Annual** tab.

3. Click cell **B6**, and then click the **Enter** button on the Formula bar. The LBC2003 workbook redisplays, and the formula =(LBC2002.xls)Annual!$B$6 appears in cell B5 and in the Formula bar of the workbook.

You also have to change the starting cash balance formula in the January worksheet so that cell is also linked to the LBC2002 workbook.

4. Click the **January** tab in the LBC2003 workbook, click cell **B5**, and then create a link to cell **B6** in the **Annual** worksheet of the **LBC2002** workbook using the method you just used to create the first link. The formula in cell B5 in the January worksheet in the LBC2003 workbook should be =(LBC2002.xls)Annual!$B$6.

Joy likes what you've done in creating the link between the two workbooks, but wonders what will happen if she changes a value in the LBC2002 workbook. How soon will that change be reflected in the starting cash flow value in 2003? To answer Joy's question, you need to look further at the concept of linking.

Working with Linked Workbooks

When two workbooks are linked, it's important that the data in the destination file accurately reflects the contents of the source file. To do this, the link must be periodically updated. Excel updates a link in the following circumstances:

■ Excel will prompt you to update the link with the source file when you initially open the destination file.

■ If both the destination and source files are open, Excel will update the link automatically whenever a value in the source file is changed.

■ If only the destination file is open, you can manually update the link at any time during your Excel session without opening the source file.

You currently have both the source and destination files open. You decide to show Joy what would happen if you modify a value in the LBC2002 workbook.

To change a value in the 2002 cash flow:

1. Switch to the LBC2002 workbook, and then click the **January** tab.

To illustrate the effect of changing a value in a linked workbook, you will increase the value of the January fundraiser by 1,000 to 1,360. This change should increase the starting 2003 cash balance as well, from 920 to 1,920.

2. Click cell **B18**, type **1360**, press the **Enter** key, and then switch to the Annual sheet. The ending cash balance has changed to 1,920.

Now check the starting cash balance for 2003, which should match the ending cash balance for 2002.

3. Switch to the LBC2003 workbook, and then click the **Annual** tab. The value in cell B5 has changed to 1,920, reflecting the new value you entered into the LBC2002 workbook.

Since this was just a test of the link feature, you can close the LBC2002 workbook now, but do not save your changes.

To close the LBC2002 workbook:

1. Switch to the LBC2002 workbook.

2. Click the **Close Window** button ⊠, and then click the **No** button when prompted to save your changes to the file. The workbook closes, and the original values are restored.

Being able to change values in linked workbooks will save time and ensure accuracy across the workbooks.

Editing Workbook References

Joy is impressed with the concept of linking workbooks. She asks you to create a summary workbook that will contain a table showing the annual expenses and inflows over the past four years. A formatted workbook has already been created for you. Your job will be to add the appropriate formulas to the workbook.

To create the summary workbook:

1. Click **File** on the menu bar, click **Open**, and then open the **LBCSum1** workbook located in the Tutorial.06/Tutorial folder on your Data Disk.

2. Enter the date and your name on the Documentation sheet.

3. Save the workbook as **LBCSum2** in the Tutorial.06/Tutorial folder on your Data Disk.

4. Click the **Summary** tab. Figure 6-17 shows the contents of the Summary worksheet.

Figure 6-17	SUMMARY WORKSHEET

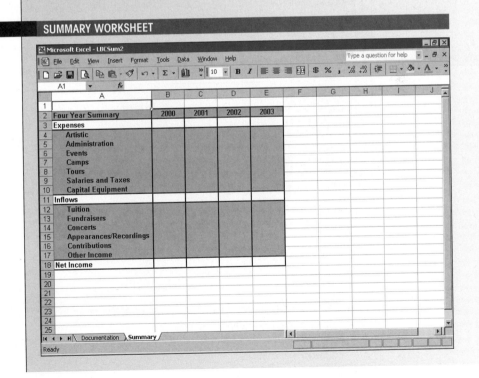

There are four columns in the table, which cover the annual expenses and inflows for the past four years. Your job will be to link the contents of this table to the four different annual workbooks. You'll start by linking the last column of the table to the annual values in the LBC2003 workbook.

To link the LBCSum2 workbook to the 2003 values:

1. Click cell **E3**, and then type **=** (do *not* press the Enter key).

2. Switch to the LBC2003 workbook.

3. Click cell **B8** in the Annual worksheet of the LBC2003 workbook.

4. Click in the Formula bar, and change the cell reference from "$B$8" to the mixed reference **$B8**, and then click the **Enter** button ☑ on the Formula bar. The formula *=(LBC2003.xls)Annual!$B8* appears in cell E3 in the LBCSum2 workbook.

   By default, Excel uses an absolute cell reference when linking to a different workbook. You had to change the absolute reference to a mixed reference because you are going to fill in the rest of the values in the table using the fill handle. You want the column reference to stay the same, but the row reference to adjust.

   TROUBLE? To change a cell reference, you can press the F4 key.

5. If necessary, click cell **E3**, and then drag the fill handle down over the range **E3:E18**. Figure 6-18 shows the revised 2003 column.

Figure 6-18 INSERTING WORKBOOK REFERENCES TO THE LBC2003 WORKBOOK

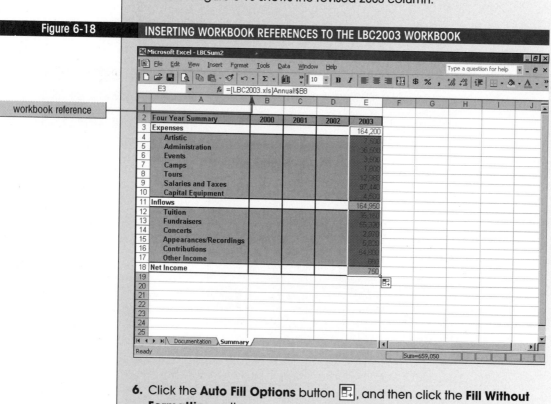

6. Click the **Auto Fill Options** button 🔽, and then click the **Fill Without Formatting** option.

Now that you have linked the column values for 2003, you can link the remaining column values. You can't use the fill handle or Auto Fill options to fill across different workbooks. Instead, you'll copy the formulas from column E into the remaining columns, and then replace the workbook references with new references by pointing to the other workbooks.

To enter the remaining values:

1. With the range E3:E18 still selected, click the **Copy** button on the Standard toolbar.

2. Select the range **B3:D18**, and then click the **Paste** button on the Standard toolbar. The formulas with the correct formatting are now copied to the other columns.

   Now you can use Excel's Find and Replace feature to change the workbook references in each column.

3. Select the range **D3:D18**.

4. Click **Edit** on the menu bar, and then click **Replace**. The Find and Replace dialog box opens.

5. Type **(LBC2003.xls)** in the Find what list box, and press the **Tab** key.

6. Type **(LBC2002.xls)** in the Replace with list box. See Figure 6-19.

Figure 6-19 | FIND AND REPLACE DIALOG BOX

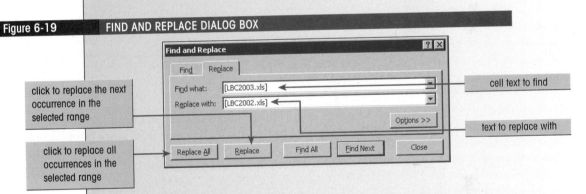

7. Click the **Replace All** button to replace all LBC2003 workbook references with LBC2002 workbook references in the selected range. Excel replaces 16 occurrences.

8. Click the **OK** button.

   You don't have to close the Find and Replace dialog box yet. You can select the next column, and then change the workbook references in that column from (LBC2003.xls) to (LBC2001.xls).

9. With the Find and Replace dialog box still open, select the range **C3:C18**, change the text in the Replace with list box to **(LBC2001.xls)**, and then click the **Replace All** button. Excel replaces another 16 occurrences.

10. Click the **OK** button.

11. Select the range **B3:B18**, change the text in the Replace with list box to **(LBC2000.xls)**, and then click the **Replace All** button. Excel replaces another 16 occurrences.

12. Click the **OK** button, click the **Close** button to close the Find and Replace dialog box, and then press the **Esc** key to remove the blinking selection border around the range E3:E18.

13. Click cell **A1**. Figure 6-20 shows the revised summary table.

Figure 6-20   ANNUAL BUDGET FIGURES FOR 2000 – 2003

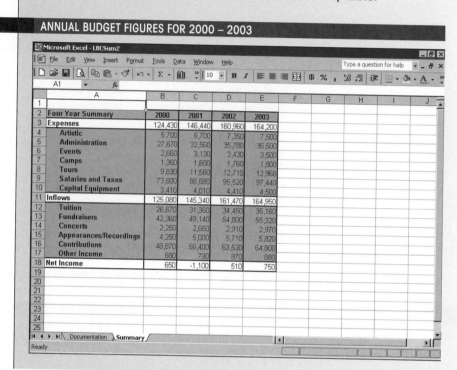

Each of the values in the table is linked to a cell in one of the cash flow workbooks. For example, the total artistic expenses in cell B4 come from a cell in the Annual worksheet of the LBC2000 workbook. By examining the table, Joy can quickly see that expenses and inflows for the choir have both increased by about $40,000 over the past four years.

Working with the List of Links

Joy wonders how one would know what links are present in a workbook without viewing the contents of each cell. One way would be to use Excel's Find feature and search through the workbook for cell references containing the text string *.xls]* because this text string implies a workbook reference.

Another way is to view a list of links in the Edit Links dialog box. You decide to show Joy how this works with the current workbook.

To view the list of linked workbooks:

1. Click **Edit** on the menu bar, and then click **Links**. The Edit Links dialog box opens, as shown in Figure 6-21.

Figure 6-21   **EDIT LINKS DIALOG BOX**

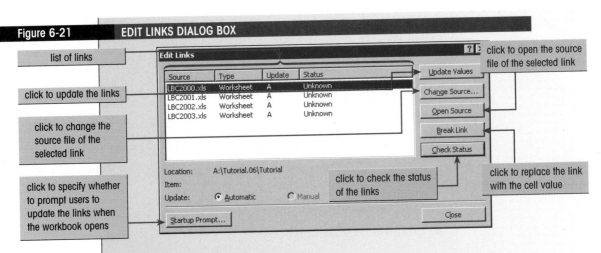

TROUBLE? It is okay if your list of links are sorted in a different order from that shown in Figure 6-21.

The Edit Links dialog box lists all of the links in the current workbook. Currently there are four links pointing to the four cash flow workbooks: LBC2000.xls, LBC2001.xls, LBC2002.xls, and LBC2003.xls. The list also indicates the type of each source file. In this case, the type is an Excel worksheet. The third column indicates how values are updated from the source file. The letter "A" indicates that these links are updated automatically either when you initially open the workbook or when you have both the source and the destination file open at the same time. A letter "M" would indicate that the link has to be updated manually by the user. The final column gives the status of the link, indicating whether Excel has been able to successfully access the link and update the values from the source document. Currently the status of all four links is unknown because Excel has not attempted to update the links in this session.

Joy wants to know how to update all of the links in the workbook. You can do that by selecting the links in the list and then clicking the Update Values button. Try this now.

To update the links in the summary workbook:

1. Click **LBC2000.xls** in the list of links, press and hold the **Shift** key, and then click **LBC2003.xls**. Release the Shift Key. Excel selects all of the links in the list.

   TROUBLE? If the list of links is not selected, the workbooks might not be listed in the same order as shown in the Figure 6-21. To select all the workbook links, click the first workbook in the list, press and hold the Shift key, and then click the last workbook in the list. All the links should be selected.

2. Click the **Update Values** button. The status column changes to indicate the current status of each linked workbook. Excel displays the text "OK" for the first three links, indicating that those links are acting correctly and have been updated in this session. The LBC20003 link displays the text "Source is open," indicating that the source file is currently open. Any changes you make in the LBC2003 file will be automatically reflected in the summary workbook.

Joy wants to view the January 2002 cash flow figures. She wants to examine how much the choir received in contributions for that month. Rather than searching for the workbook, she can open the file directly from the Edit Links dialog box.

To open the LBC2002 workbook:

1. Click **LBC2002.xls** in the list of links.

2. Click the **Open Source** button. Excel opens the LBC2002 workbook.

   You can now examine in more detail the year 2002 figures for the Lakeland Boychoir.

3. Click the **January** tab, which shows that the January contributions were 22,790.

4. Close the LBC2002 workbook.

The Edit Links dialog box provides other options. Sometimes Joy will want to provide the cash flow figures to other members of the choir board. Joy tells you that the board members are usually only interested in the summary figures—not the monthly totals. Rather than handing those board members a workbook that contains links to several different workbooks (which the board members might not have), Joy can use the Edit Links dialog box to break those links, replacing the workbook references with the most recent values obtained from the source file. Note that if you do break a link, you cannot undo that action. To restore the link, you would have to retype the workbook references.

Using Lookup Tables

Joy likes using the summary table to review budget figures from previous years, but she wonders if there is a quicker way of retrieving that information without having to open the LBSum2 workbook. Joy would like to have the ability within the LBC2003 workbook to type in the budget category and the year and to have Excel report the value without opening up any additional workbooks.

To do this Excel, you need a lookup table. A **lookup table** is a table that organizes values that you want to retrieve into different categories. The categories for the lookup table, called **compare values**, are usually located in the table's first row or column. To retrieve a particular value from the table, you need a **lookup value** that is matched against the compare values. When the lookup value matches a particular compare value, a value from an appropriate column (or row) in the table is returned.

The table you just created can function as a lookup table. For example, Joy wants to know the administration expenses for 2001. The lookup value is "Administration" and the compare values come from the first column of the summary table. To retrieve the administration expense for 2001, she moves down the first column until she finds the Administration category and then moves to the third column to view the answer, which is 32,560, as shown in Figure 6-22.

Figure 6-22   USING THE SUMMARY DATA AS A LOOKUP TABLE

	A	B	C	D	E	F
1						
2	Four Year Summary	2000	2001	2002	2003	
3	Expenses	124,430	146,440	160,960	164,200	
4	Artistic	5,790	6,700	7,350	7,500	
5	Administrat		32,560	35,780	36,500	
6	Events	2,060	3,130	3,430	3,500	
7	Camps	1,360	1,600	1,760	1,800	
8	Tours	9,830	11,560	12,710	12,960	
9	Salaries and Taxes	73,800	86,880	95,520	97,440	
10	Capital Equipment	3,410	4,010	4,410	4,500	
11	Inflows	125,080	145,340	161,470	164,950	
12	Tuition	26,670	31,360	34,450	35,160	
13	Fundraisers	42,360	49,140	54,000	55,320	
14	Concerts	2,250	2,650	2,910	2,970	
15	Appearances/Recordings	4,250	5,000	5,710	5,820	
16	Contributions	48,870	56,400	63,530	64,800	
17	Other Income	680	790	870	880	
18	Net Income	650	-1,100	510	750	
19						

compare values

The categories in the first row or column of a lookup table can also represent a range of values. Figure 6-23 shows a sample table of tax rates for different income categories.

Figure 6-23   TAX RATES FOR DIFFERENT INCOME RANGES

INCOME RANGE	TAX RATE
$0–$26250	15.0%
$26,251–$63,550	28.0%
$63,551–$132,600	31.9%
$132,601–$288,350	36.0%
$288,351 and above	39.6%

In the tax rate table, you would not be looking for an exact match for the lookup value. Instead you would want to test whether the lookup value falls within a range of values. To do this, the compare values represent the upper end of the range for each category. You go through the compare values until you locate the largest compare value that is still less than the lookup value. At that point, you would move across the table to retrieve the appropriate value. In the example in Figure 6-24, a person with an income of $45,000 would fall into the 28% tax bracket.

Figure 6-24 **A LOOKUP TABLE FOR A RANGE OF VALUES**

the tax rate for $45,000 is 28.0%

lookup value = $45,000

$26,251 is the largest compare value that is less than the lookup value

	A	B	C	D
1				
2		**Income Range**	**Tax Rate**	
3		$0	15.0%	
4		$26,251	28.0%	
5		$63,551	31.0%	
6		$132,601	36.0%	
7		$288,351	39.6%	
8				

Note that when the lookup table is used with a range of values, the compare values *must* be sorted in ascending order, or Excel will not be able to correctly retrieve the results.

You've seen that the summary table you created will work as a lookup table, but how do you use Excel to retrieve the correct value from the table? To retrieve correct values from a table, you use one of Excel's lookup functions.

Using Lookup Functions

Excel has two lookup functions: VLOOKUP and HLOOKUP. The VLOOKUP (or vertical lookup) function is used for lookup tables in which the compare values are placed in the table's first column. The HLOOKUP (or horizontal lookup) function is used when the compare values are placed in the table's first row. The summary table you created places the compare values in the first column, so you would use the VLOOKUP function. The general form of the VLOOKUP function is VLOOKUP(*lookup_value*, *table_array*, *col_index_num*, [*range_lookup*]) where *lookup_value* is the lookup value you want to send to the table, *table_array* is the cell reference of the table, *col_index_num* is the number of the column in the lookup table containing the value you want to retrieve, and *range_lookup* indicates whether the compare values constitute a range or not. If you're using range values (as you would in the tax rate table), set the *range_lookup* value to TRUE; otherwise the *range_lookup* value should be set to FALSE. If you omit a *range_lookup* value, Excel will assume that the value is TRUE.

For example, in the tax rate table shown earlier in Figure 6-24, the following function VLOOKUP(45000, B2:C7, 2, TRUE) returns the value "28%." Note that the value of the *col_index_num* parameter is 2 because the tax rate values appear in the second column of the lookup table.

Similarly, to determine the administration expenses for 2001 from the summary table shown earlier in Figure 6-22, you could use the function VLOOKUP(*"Administration"*, *A2:E18,3,FALSE*).

Now that you've seen how the VLOOKUP function works, you can add lookup capability to the LBC2003 workbook. First you need to insert the cells containing the necessary information.

To set up the lookup section:

1. Switch to the LBC2003 workbook.

2. Click the **Annual** tab, if necessary.

3. Click cell **D3**, type **Lookup Previous Year's Values**, and then press the **Enter** key.

4. Type **Category** in cell D4, and then press the **Enter** key.

5. Type **Year** in cell D5, and then press the **Enter** key.

6. Type **Value** in cell D6, and then press the **Enter** key.

   Next you will add a sample lookup value and category. You'll start with the Administration category for year 2001, which you've already seen is equal to $32,560.

7. Click cell **E4**, type **Administration**, and then press the **Enter** key.

8. Type **2001** in cell E5, and then press the **Enter** key. See Figure 6-25.

Figure 6-25	SETTING UP THE LOOKUP SECTION

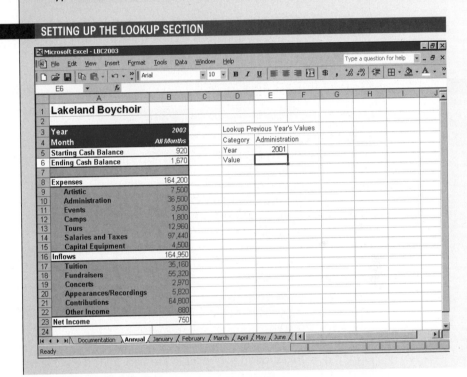

In cell E6, you'll insert the VLOOKUP function to lookup the values from the summary table.

To insert the VLOOKUP function:

1. Click **Insert** on the menu bar, and then click **Function**.

2. Click **Lookup & Reference** in the Or select a category list box.

3. Scroll to the bottom of the list of functions, and then double-click **VLOOKUP**. The Function Arguments dialog box opens.

   The Lookup_value parameter is equal to the value you entered into cell E4 of the current worksheet.

4. Click cell **E4**, and then press the **Tab** key.

The Table_array parameter is equal to the range containing the summary table located in the LBCSum2 workbook.

5. Switch to the LBCSum2 workbook, select the range **A3:E18**, and then press the **Tab** key.

The next parameter you must enter is the Col_index_num. This parameter indicates the column number in the lookup table. For the year 2000, the value would be column 2. For the year 2001, the value would be column 3, and so forth. However, Joy doesn't want to have a column index number for every year; she simply wants to enter the year number. Entering the year number is an easier value to calculate. The column index number is equal to the year number minus 1998. For example, 2001 minus 1998 equals 3, which is the correct column index number in the summary table. You can enter this formula into the VLOOKUP function. Because the year is found in cell E5, the formula will be *E5–1998*.

6. Click cell **E5**, type **–1998**, and then press the **Tab** key.

7. Type **FALSE** in the Range_lookup parameter box because you are not using range values as compare values in the lookup table. See Figure 6-26 for the completed Function Arguments dialog box.

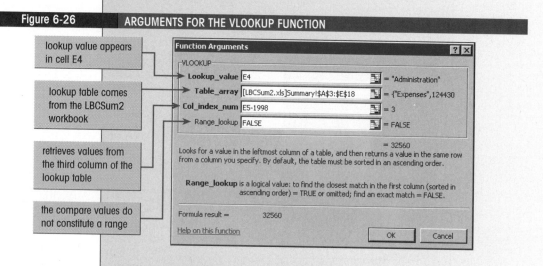

Figure 6-26   ARGUMENTS FOR THE VLOOKUP FUNCTION

lookup value appears in cell E4

lookup table comes from the LBCSum2 workbook

retrieves values from the third column of the lookup table

the compare values do not constitute a range

8. Click the **OK** button. The value 32,560 appears in cell E6, indicating to Joy that the Administration expenses in the year 2001 were $32,560.

You decide to test this lookup feature with other values. For example, what were the total inflows and expenses for the year 2002?

To view other values:

1. Click cell **E4**, type **Expenses**, and then press the **Enter** key.

2. Type **2002** in cell E5, and then press the **Enter** key. Excel displays the value 160,960 in cell E6, indicating that the total expenses for the year 2002 were $160,960.

3. Click cell **E4**, type **Inflows**, and then press the **Enter** key. The value 161470 appears in cell E6, indicating that the total inflows for 2002 were $161,470.

Before going further you decide to format the values in the lookup section of the Annual worksheet to complement the look of all the tables in the cash flow workbooks.

To format the lookup section:

1. Select the range **D3:E6**, click **Format** on the menu bar, and then click **AutoFormat**. The AutoFormat dialog box opens.

2. Click the **Classic 2** AutoFormat, and then click the **OK** button.

3. Click cell **E6**, click **Format**, and then click **Cells**. The Format Cells dialog box opens.

4. If necessary, click the **Number** tab, click **Number** in the Category list, reduce the number of decimal places to **0**, click to select the **Use 1000 Separator (,)** check box, and then click the **OK** button.

5. Increase the width of column E to **10** characters. See Figure 6-27.

| Figure 6-27 | FORMATTED LOOKUP SECTION |

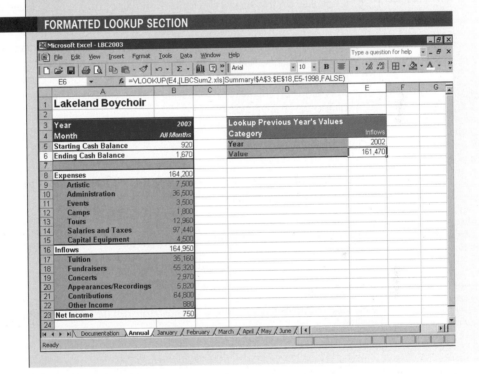

The lookup feature will provide an easy method for viewing information from previous years.

Creating an Excel Workspace

Joy now has five different workbooks containing budget data for the choir. Most of the time she'll only need to access one workbook at a time, but there will be those occasions when she'll want to be able access all of the workbooks. It would be great help if Joy could open all those workbooks at once. Being able to open all the workbooks would save time, but more importantly, it would save Joy the trouble of remembering all those filenames and folder locations.

To have the ability to open multiple workbooks at one time, you can create a workspace. A **workspace** is an Excel file that saves information about all of the currently opened workbooks, such as their locations, their window sizes, and screen positions. The workspace does not contain the workbooks themselves—only information about them. To open that set of workbooks again, Joy will only have to open the workspace file, and Excel will open the workbooks.

To create the choir workspace file:

1. Open the **LBC2000**, **LBC2001**, and **LBC2002** workbooks from the Tutorial/Tutorial.06 folder on your Data Disk.

   TROUBLE? If you closed the LBC2002 or the LBCSum2 workbook, make sure you open them as well. All five workbooks should be open.

2. Switch to the LBCSum2 workbook.

3. Click **File** on the menu bar, and then click **Save Workspace**. The Save Workspace dialog box opens.

4. Type **Choir Files** in the File name list box, verify that "Workspaces" is selected in the Save as type list box and that the Tutorial subfolder for Tutorial.06 appears in the Save in list box, and then click the **Save** button. Excel prompts you to save your changes to the various open workbook files. You will save change to all the open workbooks.

5. Click the **Yes To All** button. The Choir Files workspace is created on your Data Disk.

Now that you've created the workspace file, your next step is to open it to confirm that it opens all five choir workbooks.

To test the Choir Files workspace:

1. Close all five of the choir workbooks.

2. Click **File** on the menu bar, and then click **Open**.

3. Select **Choir Files** from the Tutorial/Tutorial.06 folder on your Data Disk. See Figure 6-28.

Figure 6-28	OPENING THE CHOIR FILES WORKSPACE FILE

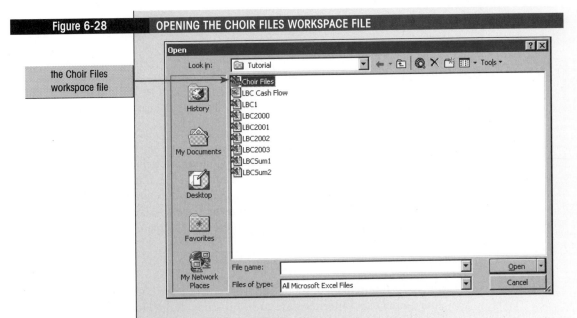

the Choir Files workspace file

4. Click the **Open** button, and then click the **Update** button when you are prompted to update any links contained in these files. The five choir workbooks are all opened.

5. Close all of the choir workbooks without saving any changes, and then exit Excel.

In this tutorial, you have worked with multiple worksheets and workbooks. You've learned about templates, the Excel LOOKUP function, and Excel workspaces. Joy will study the workbooks you created further and get back to you with any additional projects.

Session 6.3 QUICK CHECK

1. What is the workbook reference for the A1:A10 cell range on the Sales Info worksheet in the Product Report workbook located in the Reports folder on drive D?

2. What is a source file? What is a destination file?

3. Name three ways of updating a link in a workbook.

4. How would you view a list of links to other workbooks in your current workbook?

5. Define lookup table, lookup value, and compare value.

6. What are two of the functions that Excel uses to retrieve values from a lookup table?

7. What is the Range_lookup parameter? What does a value of TRUE mean for the Range_lookup parameter?

8. What is a workspace file? Explain how workspace files can help you organize your work.

REVIEW ASSIGNMENTS

Joy Ling has approached you with another workbook problem. She wants to create a workbook that displays monthly contributions for the year. The workbook should contain a separate worksheet for each month of the year, showing the total contributions for that month, and for the year up through that month.

Each contributor has been assigned an ID number. Joy has a separate workbook that contains the contributor's name, address, and phone number, as well as whether the contribution came from a personal, business, or governmental source. Rather than repeating this information in the new workbook, Joy has only included the contributor's ID number. She wants you to insert the remaining information using Excel's lookup feature. When you're finished working with the file, she wants you to create a template so that she could use the workbook in future years.

To complete this task:

1. Open the **Contrib1** workbook located in the Tutorial.06/Review folder on your Data Disk. Enter the date and your name in the Documentation sheet. Save the workbook as **Contrib2003** in the same folder.

2. Create a worksheet group that contains the January through December worksheets.

3. In the worksheet group, insert a formula in cell B5 to display the sum of the contributions in column E.

4. Ungroup the worksheets, and then insert a formula in cell B6 that displays the total contributions for the current month plus the total of all previous months for the year. (*Hint*: Enter the formula using a 3-D cell reference in cell B6 in each of the monthly worksheets.)

5. Open the **CList** workbook located in the Tutorial.06/Review folder on your Data Disk. This workbook contains the list of choir contributors in the range A1:E44 of the Contributors worksheet.

Explore

6. Switch to the Contrib2003 workbook. Regroup the monthly worksheets. In cell F3, insert the VLOOKUP function where the lookup value is the contributor ID found in cell D3, the lookup table is located in the range A1:E44 in the Contributors worksheet of the CList workbook, the column index number is 2, and the range lookup value is FALSE. Insert the VLOOKUP function for the rest of the values in row 3, making sure that you use the correct column index number: for column G the column index number is 3; for column H the column index number is 4; for column I the column index number is 5. (*Hint*: Use the mixed reference $D3 to refer to the lookup value so that you can copy the VLOOKUP formula to the right.) Use the fill handle to fill in the VLOOKUP formulas from the third row into the range F3:I25. (*Note*: You will see the result *#N/A* for those rows in which no contribution ID has been entered. This is not an error—the *#N/A* results indicates that there is no value in the lookup table corresponding to a missing ID.)

7. Format the range D2:I25 using the List 1 AutoFormat. Format the entries in the range H3:H25 so that the text is wrapped within the cell. Reduce the width of column H to 22 characters. Format the values in the nonadjacent range B5:B6;E3:E25 with the Number format applying the 1000 Separator (,) option, but no decimal places. Increase the width of column E to 9 characters.

8. Format each page in the workbook so that each worksheet is displayed in landscape orientation with the sheet fitted to a single page. Display the name of the workbook and the name of the worksheet on separate lines in the upper-right corner of the header. Display your name and the date on separate lines in the lower-right corner of the footer. Preview the worksheets, and then print the contents of the January through December worksheets.

9. Ungroup the worksheets, switch to the Documentation sheet, and then save your changes.

10. Regroup the monthly worksheets. Clear all contributor ID values and contribution values in the range D3:E25. Delete the year value in cell B3. Click cell A1 and then ungroup the worksheets. Return to the Documentation sheet, and make cell A1 the active cell.

11. Save the workbook as an Excel template named **Contribution Record** to the Tutorial.06/Review folder on your Data Disk.

12. Close all workbooks and the template file, and then exit Excel.

CASE PROBLEMS

Case 1. **Creating a Grading Workbook at MidWest University** You're an assistant to Professor David Templeton, who teaches Math 220 at MidWest University. He's asked you to help him develop a grading workbook. There are three sections for his course, and he wants to enter the grades for each section in a separate worksheet. The workbook should track three sets of grades: the first and second exams and the final exam. The workbook should also calculate an overall final score, which is equal to 25% of the first exam score, plus 25% of the second exam, plus 50% of the final exam. Finally, the workbook should display a final grade based on the overall score. Professor Templeton plans to assign grades according to the following range of points:

- 0 to 49 = F
- 50 to 59 = D
- 60 to 74 = C
- 75 to 89 = B
- 90 to 100 = A

A set of exam scores has already been entered for you. Your job will be to calculate an overall score and grade for each student in each session. You should also format the worksheets and the output. Finally, Professor Templeton will want to use this workbook again, so he will want you to create a template based on your work.

To complete this task:

1. Open the **Grade1** workbook located in the Tutorial.06/Cases folder on your Data Disk. Enter the date and your name in the Documentation sheet. Save the workbook as **Grade2** in the same folder.

2. Group the Section 1 through Section 3 worksheets. Insert a formula in column E to calculate the overall score for each student based on the results of the three exams.

3. Open the **GRange1** workbook in the Tutorial.06/Cases folder on your Data Disk. Enter the date and your name in the Documentation sheet. Save the workbook as **GRange2** in the same folder.

Explore   4. Insert a worksheet named "Grades" after the Documentation sheet. Enter the text "Exam Average" in cell A1 and the text "Grade" in cell B1. In the range A2:B6, create a lookup table for the range of grades specified by Professor Templeton. (*Hint*: Each letter grade should be matched up with the lowest score possible for that grade.)

Explore   5. Switch to the Grade2 workbook. In column F, insert a lookup function to calculate the final letter grade for each student based on the lookup table you created in the GRange2 workbook. (*Hint*: Be sure that the lookup function assumes that the compare values constitute a range of values, not an exact match.)

6. Format the grade data in the range A1:F16 using the Classic 1 AutoFormat.

7. Define the page setup for the three section worksheets so that each worksheet is centered horizontally on the page, with the name of the section centered in the header, and your name and the date on the separate lines in the right section of the footer. Print the grades for the three sections.

8. Ungroup the section worksheets, and switch to the Documentation sheet in the Grade2 and GRange2 workbooks. Save your changes to both workbooks.

9. Regroup the section worksheets. Clear the data values from the range A2:D16 in all three worksheets. Ungroup the worksheets again. Switch to the Documentation sheet.

10. Save the workbook as an Excel template named **Grading Template** to the Tutorial.06/Cases folder on your Data Disk.

11. Close the workbook and the template file, and then exit Excel.

Case 2. Consolidating Refrigerator Sales Freezing Point makes six brands of refrigerators. They track sales information from four sales regions—North, South, East and West—in a sales workbook. Your supervisor, Jayne Mitchell, has asked you to format the workbook and to create a summary worksheet that will total up the sales information from all four regions.

To complete this task:

1. Open the **Refrig1** workbook located in the Tutorial.06/Cases folder on your Data Disk. Enter the date and your name in the Documentation sheet. Save the workbook as **Refrig2** in the same folder.

2. Insert a new blank worksheet named "Total Sales" at the end of the workbook.

Explore   3. Using the Fill Across Sheets command on the Edit menu, copy the row titles and column titles from the East worksheet into the Total Sales worksheet.

4. In the range B3:F9 of the Total Sales worksheet, insert the formula that sums the sales in the corresponding cells of the North through East worksheets.

5. Format the numbers in the five sales worksheets with the Number format, reducing the number of decimal places to zero and adding the 1000 (,) separator. Apply the Classic 2 AutoFormat to the sales data.

6. Print the five sales worksheets centered horizontally in landscape orientation with the name of the sheet centered in the header, and your name and the date placed on separate lines in the right section of the footer.

7. Save your changes to the Refrig2 workbook.

8. Remove the sales data, but not the formulas from the workbook. Return to cell A1 of the Documentation sheet.

9. Save the workbook as an Excel template named **Refrigerator Sales Form** to the Tutorial.06/Cases folder on your Data Disk.

10. Close the workbook template, and then exit Excel.

Case 3. *Examining Sales Information at the Kitchen WareHouse* Jaya Torres tracks the sales of kitchen appliances at Kitchen WareHouse. Kitchen WareHouse has stores in five regions. Jaya has recorded the monthly sales of refrigerators, microwaves, ovens, and dishwashers for each region. Jaya would like to include a worksheet that consolidates the sales information from the five regions. She would also like to take advantage of the Excel lookup feature to allow users to quickly retrieve the total sales of a particular product in a specific month.

To complete this task:

1. Open the **Kitchen1** workbook in the Tutorial.06/Cases folder on your Data Disk. Enter your name and the date in the Documentation sheet. Save the workbook as **Kitchen2** in the same folder.

2. In the range B4:N8 of the Summary worksheet, enter a formula that sums the values in the corresponding cells from Region 1 to Region 5 worksheets.

3. Print the Summary worksheet center horizontally on the page in landscape mode, with your name and the date on separate lines in the right section of the footer.

Explore ▶ 4. In cell B5 of the Sales Results worksheet, create a lookup formula that will display annual sales figures based on the Month Number entered into cell B3 and the Product Number entered into cell B4. (*Hint:* Use the Product Number as your lookup value. Retrieve sales figures from the column in the lookup table corresponding to the month number plus one.)

5. Test the lookup function by using it to answer the following questions:
   a. How many refrigerators were sold in all regions in January?
   b. How many dishwashers were sold in all regions over the entire year?
   c. How many appliances were sold in all regions in March?
   d. How many ovens were sold in all regions in June?

6. Save and close the workbook, and then exit Excel

Case 4. *Projected Income Statement for Tour Bikes* You work at Tour Bikes, an up-and-coming manufacturer of touring bikes. Your supervisor, Ken Delaney, has asked you to prepare the annual projected income statement for the company. You've been given workbooks from three regions in the country. Each workbook has quarterly projected income statements for three of the company's bikes: Tour, Tour XL, and Cross Country. Ken wants you to summarize each workbook for him, reporting the annual totals for Earnings Before Tax in a new worksheet. Once you have added this information to each workbook, he wants you to consolidate the information from the three regional workbooks, reporting in a single workbook the same information for each company.

To complete this task:

1. Open each of the regional sales workbooks **Bike1, Bike2, and Bike3** located in the Tutorial.06/Cases folder on your Data Disk. Save Bike1 as **North**, Bike2 as **South**, and Bike3 as **Southwest**.

2. On the Documentation sheet in each regional sales workbook, enter the name of the workbook, your name, and the date.

3. In each regional sales workbook, insert a worksheet named "Summary" after the Documentation sheet. Use the Summary sheet to display the total all the Earnings Before Tax figures for each of the bike models for each of the four quarters. Also include the summary figures for the Earning Before Tax values across all four quarters and for all models.

4. Format the Summary sheet using any format you choose.

5. Create a new workbook named **Tour Bikes Report** in the Tutorial.06/Cases folder on your Data Disk.

6. Insert a Documentation sheet in the beginning of the workbook, and enter your name and the date in the sheet.

Explore

7. Create a Summary worksheet in the Tour Bikes Report workbook that displays the Earnings Before Tax value summarized over region, bike model, and quarter. Include summary totals over these categories.

8. Format the workbook in any format you choose.

9. Print the summary worksheets from the four workbooks you created. Include your name and the date on separate lines in the right section of the footer.

10. Create a workspace named **Tour Bike Files** for the four workbooks you created. Save the workspace file in the Tutorial.06/Cases folder on your Data Disk.

11. Save and close the workbook, and then exit Excel.

INTERNET ASSIGNMENTS

Student Union

The purpose of the Internet Assignments is to challenge you to find information on the Internet that you can use to create effective spreadsheets. The actual assignments are updated and maintained on the Course Technology Web site. Log on to the Internet and use your Web browser to go to the Student Union on the New Perspectives Series site at **www.course.com/NewPerspectives/studentunion**. Click the Online Companions link, and then click the link for this text.

QUICK CHECK

Session 6.1

1. A worksheet group is a collection of worksheets that have all been selected for editing and formatting.

2. Select the worksheet group either by pressing and holding down the Ctrl key and clicking the sheet tab of each worksheet in the group, or if the worksheets occupy an adjacent range in the workbook, by clicking the first sheet tab in the range, pressing and holding down the Shift key, and clicking the sheet tab of the last sheet in the range. Deselect a worksheet group by either clicking the sheet tab of a worksheet not in the group or right-clicking one of the sheet tabs in the group and clicking Ungroup Sheets on the shortcut menu.

3. 'Summary Data'!A10

4. 'Summary 1:Summary 3'!A10

5. Create a worksheet group consisting of the range of worksheets. In the first worksheet in the group, select the text and formulas you want to copy, click Edit on the menu bar, point to Fill, and then click Across Worksheets. Next select whether you want to copy the contents, formulas, or both, and then click the OK button.

6. Select a worksheet group consisting of all sheets in the workbook, click File on the menu bar, and then click Page Layout.

Session 6.2

1. A template is a workbook that contains specific content and formatting that you can use as a model for other similar workbooks.

2. A user can modify the contents of a workbook based on a template without changing the template file itself. The next time a new workbook is created based on a template the workbook opens with all the original properties intact.

3. the template used in creating the blank workbook that you first see when starting a new Excel session

4. Click File on the menu bar, click Save As, click the Save as type list arrow, click Template, type a filename for the template, and then click the Save button.

5. in the Templates folder (usually located in C:\Document and Settings*user_name*\Application Data\Microsoft\Templates)

6. Create a subfolder in the Templates folder, and then move the template file into the subfolder.

7. Click the Choose workbook in the New from existing workbook section in the New Workbook Task Pane.

Session 6.3

1. 'D:\Reports\[Product Report]Sales Info'!A1:A10

2. The source file is the file that contains the values to be linked. The destination file displays the value placed in the source file.

3. a) When you initially open the workbook, Excel will prompt you to update the link; b) if both the destination and source files are open, Excel will update the link automatically; and 3) if only the destination file is open, click Edit on the menu bar, click Links, and then click the Update Link button to manually update the link.

4. Click Edit on the menu bar, and then click Links.

5. A lookup table is a table in which rows and columns of information are organized into separate categories. The lookup value is the value that indicates the category in which you are looking. The categories for the lookup table are usually located in the table's first row or column and are called compare values.

6. VLOOKUP and HLOOKUP

7. The range_lookup value is a parameter in the VLOOKUP and HLOOKUP functions that tell Excel where to look for an exact match in a lookup table. A value of TRUE means that Excel does not have to find an exact match.

8. A workspace file is a file containing information about all of the currently opened workbooks, including their locations, window sizes, and screen positions. By opening a workspace file, you open all workbooks defined in the workspace. Using a workspace helps you organize projects that might involve several workbooks.

OBJECTIVES

In this tutorial you will:

- Check the spelling in a workbook

- Audit formulas

- Trace and fix formula errors

- Insert and edit cell comments

- Track, highlight, and review changes to the workbook

- Mail and merge workbooks

- Save the workbook as a Web page

- Create and edit hyperlinks

WORKING
WITH EXCEL'S EDITING AND WEB TOOLS

Collaborating on a Workbook and Web Page

Digital Products

Digital Products is a company specializing in digital video editing software and hardware. Each year the company publishes a financial report for its stockholders. The company also publishes the report on the World Wide Web for the general public. You work with Kevin Whyte in the group that will create and publish this year's report.

In the process of creating the report, there will be several drafts of the workbook as different employees review and edit the workbook's content. Kevin has asked your help in managing the development of this workbook from its initial draft to its final form. Because stockholders will see this report, Kevin is acutely interested in making sure that there are no errors in the workbook.

Once the report becomes finalized, the workbook will be printed in a booklet. Kevin also wants to have a summary of the report converted into a form that can be published on the company's Web site, to be shared with a larger community. Kevin has asked for your assistance in creating that file as well.

In this tutorial, you will use Excel's spelling checker and auditing tools to make sure the workbook contains no errors. You will also review the comments and edits made by other users on the workbook and incorporate their suggestions into the final document. Finally, you will convert the workbook into a format for publishing on the Web.

SESSION 7.1

In this session, you'll check a workbook for spelling errors and mistakes in formulas. To evaluate a formula, you'll create tracer arrows that graphically display a formula's dependent and precedent cells. If a formula contains an error, you'll learn how to trace the error back to its source so you can correct the error. Finally, you'll learn how to display formulas in your workbook rather than their resulting values.

Checking Spelling in a Workbook

You're ready to start working on the financial report workbook for the company. Andrew Thomason, a summer intern working at Digital Products, has created a rough draft of the report containing the initial figures, formulas, and text. Open the financial report workbook now.

To open the workbook:

1. Start Excel and open the **DPReport1** workbook located in the Tutorial.07\Tutorial folder on your Data Disk.

2. Enter the date and your name on the Documentation sheet.

3. Save the workbook as **DPReport2** in the Tutorial.07\Tutorial folder on your Data Disk.

The DPReport2 workbook contains four other worksheets besides the Documentation sheet. These are labeled:

- **Balance Sheet**: Contains the company's balance sheet for the past three years
- **Financial Data**: Contains an overview of selected financial figures
- **Income Statement**: Contains the company's income statement for the past three years
- **Cash Flows**: Contains the company's cash flow over the past three years

Your first task is to check for spelling errors. All Microsoft Office XP products use a common spelling checker tool. Excel checks the words in the selected worksheets against its internal dictionary. If Excel finds a word that is not in its dictionary, Excel displays the word in a dialog box along with a list of suggested replacements. You can replace the word with one from the list, or you can have Excel ignore the word and go to the next word that might be misspelled. You can also add the word to the dictionary so that the word is not flagged in future. Note that there are words that not are included in the online dictionary (for example, a person's name or product name); Excel will stop at these words, and you can then choose to ignore the word or all occurrences of the word, change the word, or add the word to the dictionary.

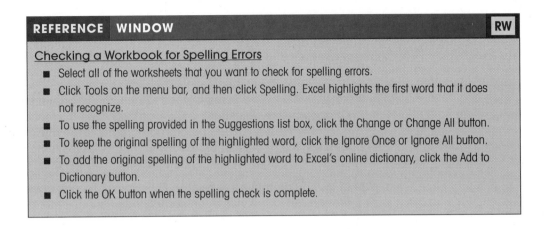

REFERENCE   WINDOW   **RW**

Checking a Workbook for Spelling Errors
- Select all of the worksheets that you want to check for spelling errors.
- Click Tools on the menu bar, and then click Spelling. Excel highlights the first word that it does not recognize.
- To use the spelling provided in the Suggestions list box, click the Change or Change All button.
- To keep the original spelling of the highlighted word, click the Ignore Once or Ignore All button.
- To add the original spelling of the highlighted word to Excel's online dictionary, click the Add to Dictionary button.
- Click the OK button when the spelling check is complete.

You need to check the spelling in all the worksheets, so you need to group the worksheets first before using the spelling checker.

To check the spelling in the workbook:

1. Select the **Balance Sheet** through **Cash Flows** worksheets as a group. The sheet tabs are highlighted, and the word "(Group)" appears in the title bar after the name of the workbook.

   TROUBLE? To select a group of worksheets in a workbook, click the first sheet tab, press and hold the Shift key, and then click the last sheet tab.

2. Click the **Spelling** button [icon] on the Standard toolbar. Excel locates the first potential spelling error in the selected worksheets, "contigencies." Excel suggests replacing it with the correct spelling, "contingencies." See Figure 7-1.

Figure 7-1   SPELLING DIALOG BOX

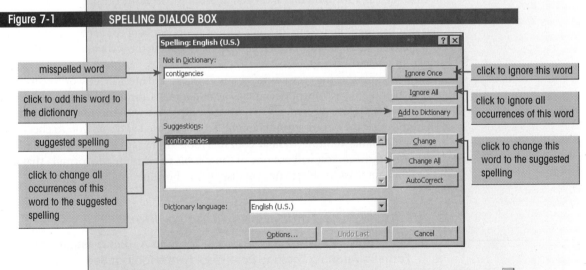

TROUBLE? If you don't see the Spelling button, click the Toolbar Options [icon] on the Standard toolbar, and then click [icon]. If the toolbars on your screen appear on separate rows, the Toolbar Options button might look different.

3. Click the **Change All** button to replace this misspelling and all other occurrences of this word in the selected worksheets with the correct spelling. Excel replaces the occurrences and moves to the next misspelled word "Incone." Excel suggests several possible corrections. The first word listed is "Income."

4. Verify that "Income" is highlighted in the Suggestions list box, and then click the **Change** button. Clicking the Change button will correct the misspelling of the current word, but you will be prompted again if the misspelling occurs elsewhere in the selected worksheets. Next Excel displays the misspelling "tousands." The correct spelling is "thousands."

5. Click the **Change All** button. An Excel message box appears, indicating that the spelling check has been completed.

   TROUBLE? If Excel locates other misspellings, click the Ignore button.

6. Click the **OK** button.

7. Right-click the **Balance Sheet** tab, and then click **Ungroup Sheets** on the shortcut menu.

Note that you had to group the worksheets in the workbook before running the spelling checker. If you had not grouped the worksheets, Excel would have checked for spelling errors only in the active sheet.

Auditing Formulas

Now that you've checked the spelling in the workbook, you next have to check the values and the formulas in the workbook for mistakes. Mistakes can occur in several different forms, such as a formula that has been entered incorrectly, causing Excel to return an error value. Perhaps more difficult to detect is an Excel formula that has been entered correctly, but that has used the wrong formula. One way of checking the accuracy of the formulas is by using Excel's **audit** feature, which allows you to review the structure and behavior of the formulas in your worksheet.

For example, having viewed the contents of the Balance Sheet worksheet in the financial report workbook, Kevin notices that the total assets displayed in the range B21:D21 are lower than what he expected, given his prior experience with the company's financial records. He thinks that the wrong formula might have been used and asks you to check it out.

The Formula Auditing toolbar contains tools that graphically display the formulas used in your worksheet. You will use one of these tools to examine the formula that calculates the company's total assets. First you will display the Formula Auditing toolbar.

To display the Formula Auditing toolbar:

1. Click **Tools** on the menu bar, point to **Formula Auditing**, and then click **Show Formula Auditing Toolbar**. Excel displays the toolbar. See Figure 7-2.

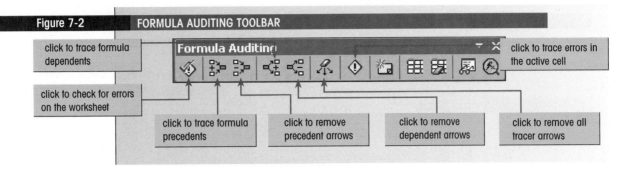

Figure 7-2 FORMULA AUDITING TOOLBAR

Several of the tools on the Formula Auditing toolbar display tracer arrows on your worksheet. A **tracer arrow** shows the relationship between the active cell and a related cell. There are two types of tracer arrows: one that displays precedent cells and one that displays dependent cells. **Precedent cells** are the cells that are used in the formula of the active cell. **Dependent cells** are the cells that use the value in the active cell in their formulas.

REFERENCE WINDOW **RW**

Tracing Precedent and Dependent Cells
- Select the cell that contains the formula that you want to trace.
- Click the Trace Precedents button to display tracer arrows pointing to the formula's precedent cells.
- Click the Trace Dependents button to display tracer arrows pointing to cells dependent on the formula's value.

Tracing Precedent Cells

To address Kevin's concern about the total assets displayed in the range B21:D21, you can start by tracing the cells that are used in the formula in cell B21. The value in cell B21 should be based on the total current assets in row 11, the marketable securities in row 12, the net computer equipment and improvements in row 17, and the other assets listed in rows 18 through 20. But is it? You will trace the cells used in the formulas in the range B21:D21.

To trace the precedent cells for the range B21:D21:

1. Click cell **B21**.
2. Click the **Trace Precedents** button 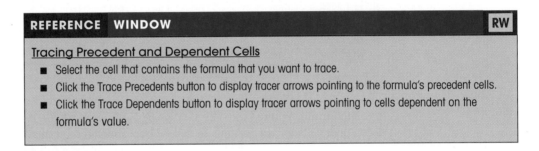 on the Formula Auditing toolbar. Excel displays tracer arrows that point from the precedent cells to the active cell.
3. Click cell **C21** and then click to display the tracer arrows that point from the precedent cells to cell C21, the active cell. Note that the tracer arrows for cell B21 are still displayed.
4. Click cell **D21** and then click to display the tracer arrows that point from the precedent cells to cell D21.
5. Click cell **B21** to make it the active cell again. Figure 7-3 shows the tracer arrows for all three cells.

Figure 7-3   PRECEDENT TRACER ARROWS

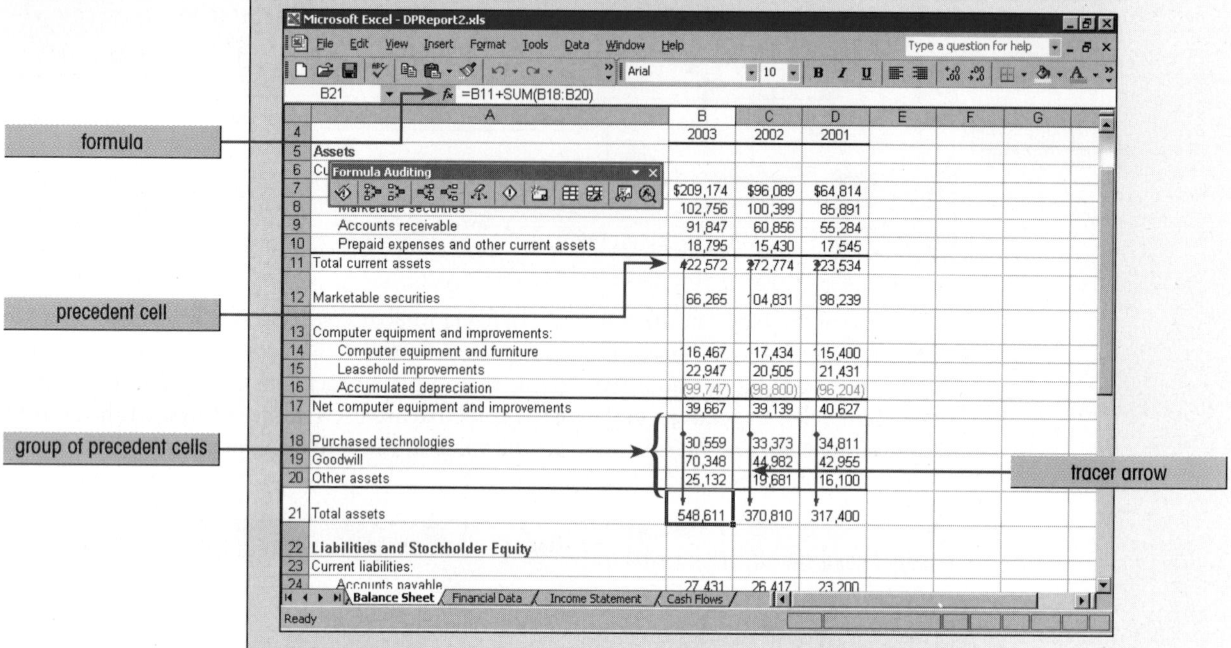

The formula entered into cell B21 is *=B11+SUM(B18:B20)*. As shown in Figure 7-3, the precedent cells for the formula in cell B21 are indicated by small solid blue circles, such as the one displayed in cell B11. The formula also contains a function that references a range of cells, that is (SUM(B18:B20), whose precedent cells are enclosed in a solid blue square. All of the precedent cells are connected by a blue tracer arrow that points to cell B21. As you view the tracer arrows, it is now obvious that the marketable securities in row 12 and the net computer equipment and improvements in row 17 are *not* included as precedent cells. These omissions may account for the fact that the total assets are lower than Kevin expected. You will add those cells to the formulas in the range B21:D21.

To revise the formulas in range B21:D21:

1. With cell B21 still selected, click in the Formula bar, change the formula to **=B11+SUM(B18:B20)+B12+B17**, and then press the **Enter** key. Note that the tracer arrows have disappeared, and the value of the total assets shown in cell B21 has increased to 654,543. This value is more in line with Kevin's expectations.

2. Click the **Remove All Arrows** button 🔏 on the Formula Auditing toolbar to remove all of the tracer arrows on the worksheet.

   You need to copy the revised formula to the other total asset cells.

3. Click cell **B21** and then drag the fill handle to the right, over the range **B21:D21**. The value of the total assets in cell C21 increases to 514,780, and the value in cell D21 increases to 456,266.

Tracer arrows are particularly helpful in more complicated formulas involving several ranges and multiple worksheets. In those cases, formula errors might not be so easily detected by examining the formula itself. Sometimes a graphical view is more helpful.

Tracing Dependent Cells

There are other locations in this workbook that might rely on the total assets values in range B21:D21. Now that you've modified the formula, you're interested in seeing how this might have affected other cells in the workbook. To find out, you will trace the dependent cells for cell B21.

To trace the dependent cells:

1. Click cell **B21** and then click the **Trace Dependents** button [icon] on the Formula Auditing toolbar. A tracer arrow appears pointing from cell B21 to a worksheet icon. See Figure 7-4. This worksheet icon means that a cell on a different worksheet is dependent on cell B21.

| Figure 7-4 | DEPENDENT TRACER ARROWS |

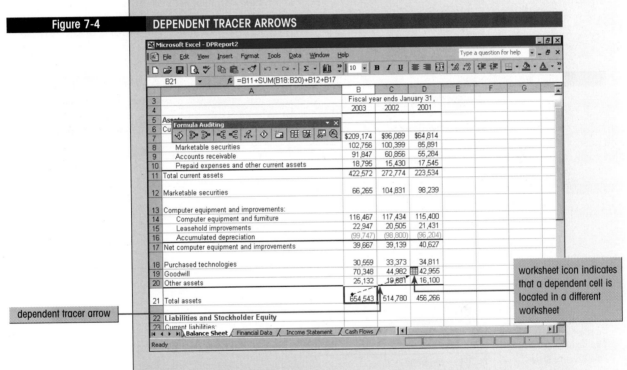

To determine the dependent cell, you need to open the Go To dialog box, which you can do by double-clicking the tracer arrow.

2. Move the pointer over the tracer arrow until the pointer changes to ⌖, and then double-click the **tracer arrow**. The Go To dialog box opens.

3. Click **'(DPReport2.xls)Financial Data'!$B$13** in the Go to list box. See Figure 7-5.

Figure 7-5   GO TO DIALOG BOX

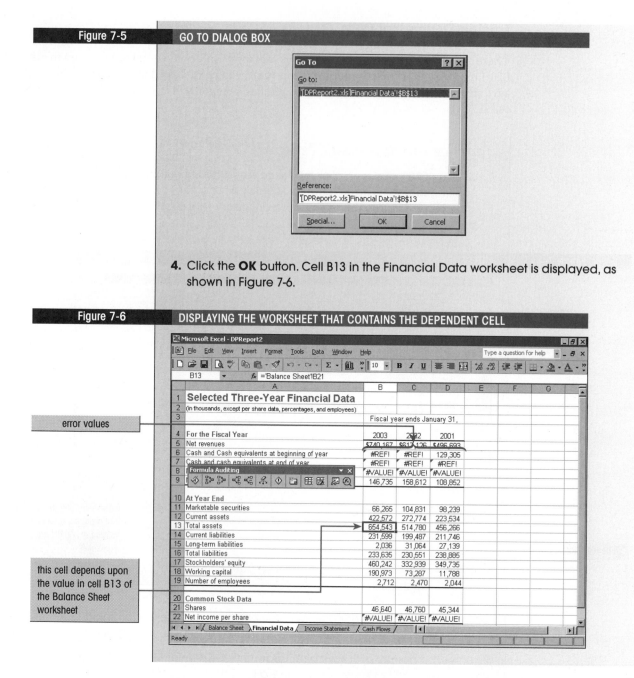

4. Click the **OK** button. Cell B13 in the Financial Data worksheet is displayed, as shown in Figure 7-6.

Figure 7-6   DISPLAYING THE WORKSHEET THAT CONTAINS THE DEPENDENT CELL

You've located the cell in the workbook that depends on the total assets value; however, in doing so, you've accessed a worksheet that seems to have several problems. Several of the cells display the #REF! or #VALUE! error value. What do these error values mean, and how do you fix them?

Tracing and Fixing Errors

When an error has been entered in a formula, Excel displays an error value to warn you of the problem. Figure 7-7 provides descriptions of several of the error values that might appear in your workbooks.

Figure 7-7	EXCEL ERROR VALUES

ERROR VALUES	SOURCE OF ERROR
#DIV/0!	The formula or function contains a number divided by zero.
#NAME?	Excel doesn't recognize text in the formula or function, such as when the name of an Excel function has been misspelled.
#N/A	A value is not available to a function or formula, which can occur when an invalid value is specified in the VLOOKUP function.
#NULL!	A formula or function requires that two cells ranges intersect, but they don't.
#NUM!	Invalid numbers are used in a formula or function, such as entering text in a function that requires a numeric value.
#REF!	A cell reference used in a formula or function is no longer valid, which can occur when cells used by the function have been deleted from the worksheet.
#VALUE!	The wrong type of argument has been used in a function or formula. This can occur when you supply a range of values to a function that requires a single value.

Excel also attempts to provide additional information about the source of the error. For example, Excel will indicate that you've attempted to divide a number by zero or that the formula is attempting to reference a cell that has been deleted. You can view this additional information by clicking the cell that contains the error. Try this now with the error value displayed in cell B6.

To view error information:

1. Click cell **B6**. An alert box ◈, which provides the additional information about the error value, appears to the left of cell B6.

2. Click the **alert box** ◈. A shortcut menu appears, providing different options for dealing with the error in the cell.

3. Click **Help on this error**. The Microsoft Excel Help window opens with information relating to the #REF! error value. See Figure 7-8. The Help window also provides some possible solutions for correcting the error.

Figure 7-8	HELP ON THE #REF ERROR

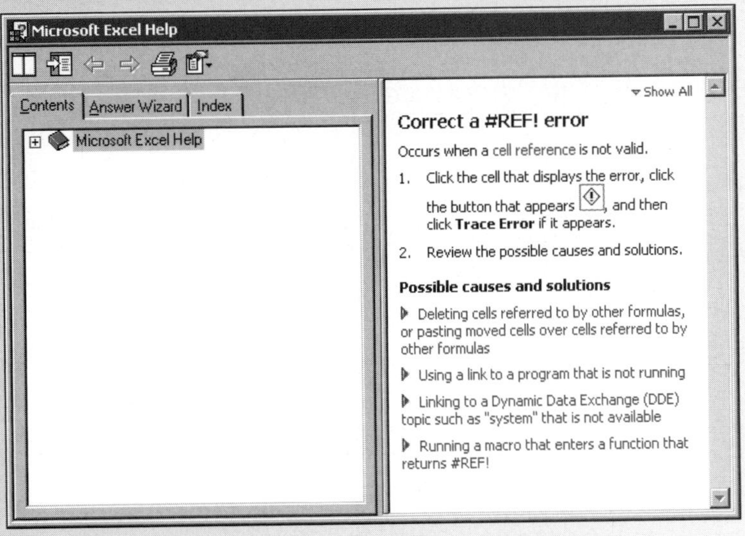

TROUBLE? Don't worry if the Help information appears on the Index page of the Help window. The information is the same.

4. Close the Help window.

One possible source of the error in cell B6 is that a cell that was being used by a formula somewhere in the worksheet has been deleted. When that happens, Excel returns the #REF! error value, and the error will propagate down through any workbook cells that are dependent upon the formula. What you need to do then is trace the error value in cell B6 back to its source. You can do that by repeatedly clicking the Trace Precedents button on the Formula Auditing toolbar as you move through the formula's precedents, but a much faster way is to use the Trace Error button.

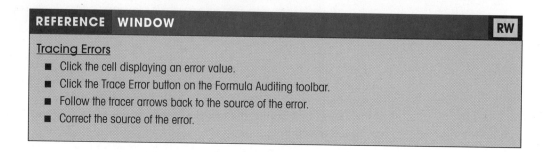

REFERENCE WINDOW   **RW**

Tracing Errors
- Click the cell displaying an error value.
- Click the Trace Error button on the Formula Auditing toolbar.
- Follow the tracer arrows back to the source of the error.
- Correct the source of the error.

You will trace the source of the error in cell B6 now.

To locate the source of the error in cell B6:

1. Verify that cell B6 is still the active cell and that the Formula Auditing toolbar is still visible.

2. Click the **Trace Error** button ⬦ on the Formula Auditing toolbar. A tracer arrow appears, pointing from cell B6 to a worksheet icon, which means that the source of this error value lies on a different worksheet.

3. Double-click the **tracer arrow** with ⬦, click **'(DPReport2.xls)!Cash Flows'!$B$5** in the Go to list box, and then click the **OK** button. Cell B5 in the Cash Flows worksheet is displayed.

TROUBLE? If the Go To dialog box does not open, click cell B6 again, hover the pointer over the tracer arrow until the pointer changes to ⬦, and then double-click the tracer arrow again.

4. Click ⬦ again. A series of red tracer arrows appears, tracing the error from cell B5 to cells C5, C6, D6, D7, and then finally to cell D38. See Figure 7-9.

Figure 7-9 | **TRACING THE #REF! ERROR**

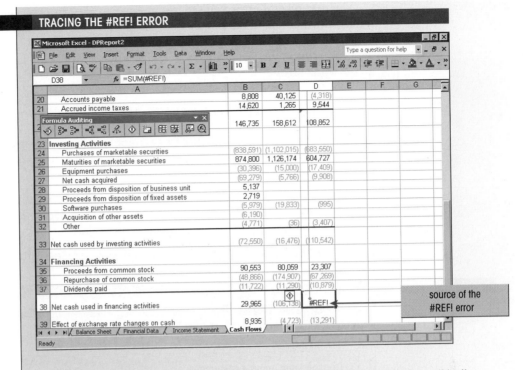

TROUBLE? To see the tracer arrows that begin at cell B5, you must scroll to the top of the worksheet. Be sure to scroll to the bottom of the worksheet before continuing.

Apparently the source of the error lies in cell D38 of the Cash Flows worksheet. The formula in the cell is *=SUM(#REF!)*, which indicates that the SUM function is attempting to use worksheet cells that were probably deleted at some point in the creation of the worksheet. Cell 38 should display the total net cash of the company's financing activities, which should be equal to the sum of the values in range D35:D37.

You will modify the formula so that it points to these cells.

To correct the error value:

1. If necessary, click cell **D38**, change the formula in cell D38 to **=SUM(D35:D37)**, and then press the **Enter** key. The error value disappears and is replaced with the value –54,841.

   Now check to see whether the error values from the Financial Data worksheet have been fixed.

2. Click the **Financial Data** tab. The #REF! error value in cell B6 has been replaced with the value 90,758. Although there are other error values in the worksheet, you can remove the tracer arrows that you just used to identify the source of the #REF! error value.

3. Click the **Remove All Arrows** button 🔏 on the Formula Auditing toolbar to remove the tracer arrows from the worksheet.

The next type of error you see in the Financial Data worksheet is the #VALUE! error value, which occurs in the ranges B8:D8 and B22:D22. This type of error occurs when an improper value is used as an argument in a formula. For example, a formula might call for a numeric value, but a text string is used instead. As before, you'll trace the error to its roots in the workbook.

To trace the #VALUE! error value:

1. Click cell **B8** in the Financial Data sheet, and then click the **Trace Error** button on the Formula Auditing toolbar. The source of the error is on another work-sheet, as indicated by the worksheet icon.

2. Double-click the **tracer arrow** with ↳, click **'(DPReport2.xls)Income Statement'!$B$18** in the Go to list box, and then click the **OK** button. Cell B18 in the Income Statement worksheet is displayed.

3. Click again. Excel traces the error to cell B14. See Figure 7-10.

| Figure 7-10 | TRACING THE #VALUE! ERROR |

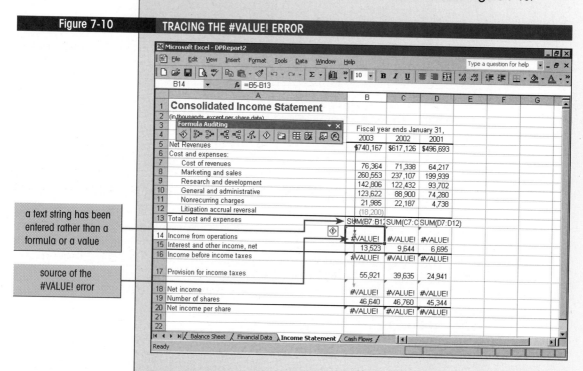

Cell B14 displays the operational income for Digital Products, which is calculated by subtracting the total costs and expenses in cell B13 from the net revenues in cell B4. However, a value has not been entered for the total costs and expenses in cell B13. Instead, the text string "SUM(B7:B12)" has been entered. The previous user has forgotten to enter an equal sign before the SUM function name in this cell and in the other cells in range B13:D13. Correct this mistake now.

4. Click cell **B13**, change the formula to **=SUM(B7:B12)**, and then click the **Enter** button on the Formula bar.

5. Drag the fill handle to the right over the range **B13:D13**. The #VALUE! error values is removed from all of the cells in the Income Statement worksheet.

6. Switch to the Financial Data worksheet. All of the error values have been removed from the Financial Data worksheet.

Not all mistakes in formulas result in error values. As you saw earlier, an incorrect formula can be entered that returns a value—just the wrong value. Most of the time mistakes such as these are difficult to detect; however, you can use the Error Checking button on the Formula Auditing toolbar. This option flags those cells in which there is reason to suspect that a mistake in the formula has been made.

REFERENCE WINDOW   **RW**

Locating Suspect Formulas
- Click the worksheet tab of the sheet you want to search for suspect formulas.
- Click the Error Checking button on the Formula Auditing toolbar.
- Use the options presented in the Error Checking dialog box to correct the suspect formula, or click the Next button to move on to the next suspect formula.
- Click the OK button.

Excel labels cells containing "suspect" formulas with a green triangle located in the cell's upper-left corner. You can also search for these cells using the Error Checking button on the Formula Auditing toolbar. To ensure that the worksheet does not include other suspect formulas, you will search the rest of the workbook for errors using the Error Checking button.

To search for errors in the workbook:

1. Click the **Error Checking** button ⬦ on the Formula Auditing toolbar. An Excel message box appears, indicating that the error check is complete for the entire sheet. No more errors have been detected on the Financial Data worksheet.

2. Click the **OK** button.

3. Click the **Income Statement** tab, click ⬦ , and then click the **OK** button when the Excel message dialog box appears indicating that no errors have been found.

4. Click the **Cash Flows** tab, and then click ⬦ . The Error Checking dialog box opens. This dialog box displays information relating to a possible error in cell D22, which calculates the total net cash provided by the operating activities. See Figure 7-11.

Figure 7-11   **CHECKING FOR ERRORS IN THE WORKSHEET**

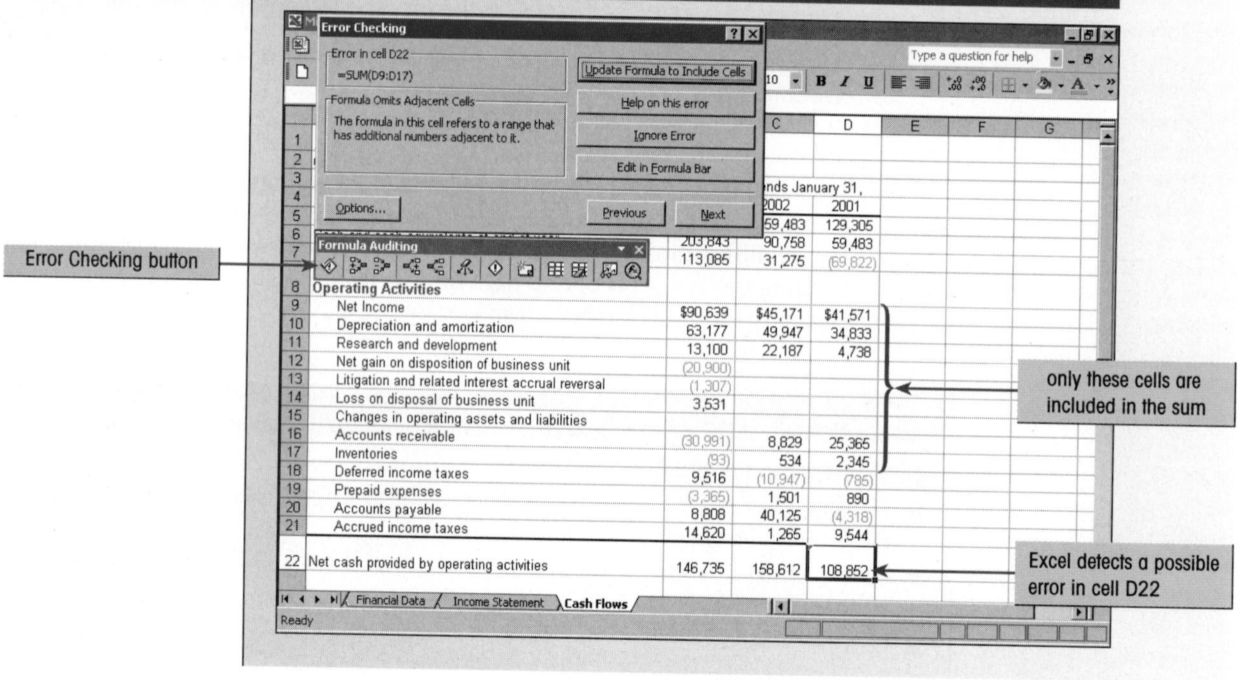

What is the problem? The formula in cell D22 applies the SUM function to the range D9:D17 and therefore ignores the values in the range D18:D21. When the SUM function is applied to a range that has additional numbers adjacent to it, Excel will flag the formula as a possible error. In this case, the SUM function should be applied to *all* of the operating income values in the range D9:D21. Rather than retyping the formula yourself, you can have Excel update the formula automatically.

To correct the error in the SUM function:

1. Click the **Update Formula to Include Cells** button in the Error Checking dialog box. Excel updates the formula, changing it to *=SUM(D9:D21)*.

   This is the only suspect formula in the worksheet.

2. Click the **OK** button to close the message box and the dialog box.

   Note that Excel did *not* flag cells B22 and C22, which calculate the total operating incomes for the years 2003 and 2002. Examine the formulas in those cells.

3. Click cell **B22** and then cell **C22**. Note that the formulas in those two cells are *=SUM(B9:B21)* and *=SUM(C9:C21)*. Excel has also updated the formulas in these cells as well.

By using the tracer arrow feature and the error checking feature, you can locate and resolve many of the errors in your workbook.

Viewing Worksheet Formulas

Excel's Formula Auditing tools often work on only one cell at a time. However, if you want to get an overall view of the formulas contained in a worksheet, you can view all the formulas by switching to Formula Auditing mode. In **Formula Auditing mode** Excel displays the formulas in each cell of the worksheet rather than the values.

To see the formulas in the Cash Flows worksheet, you will switch to Formula Auditing mode.

To display worksheet formulas:

1. Click **Tools** on the menu bar, point to **Formula Auditing**, and then click **Formula Auditing Mode**. The Cash Flows worksheet now displays each cell's formula.

2. Click the **right scroll arrow** on the horizontal scroll bar to display the formulas in cells B22, C22, and D22 as shown in Figure 7-12.

| Figure 7-12 | DISPLAYING FORMULAS IN THE WORKSHEET |

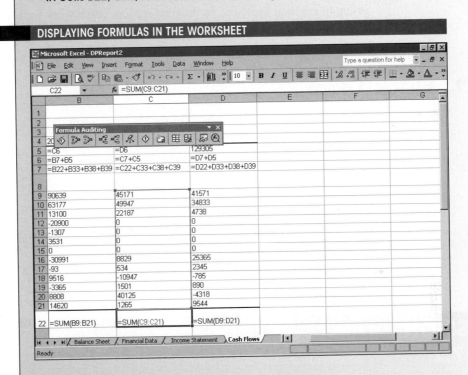

To switch back to normal mode, you can select the Formula Auditing Mode option again, or you can press and hold down the Ctrl key and then press the grave accent key (`); pressing this keyboard shortcut toggles back and forth between the two modes.

3. Press **Ctrl +** ` (grave accent key). Excel switches to normal mode.

TROUBLE? The grave accent key is usually located above the Tab key on your keyboard. Do not confuse this key with the apostrophe key (') located to the left of the Enter key.

You've completed your editing of the rough draft of the Digital Products' financial report, so you will close the Formula Auditing toolbar and the workbook, and then exit Excel.

To complete your work:

1. Click the **Close** button ☒ to close the Formula Auditing toolbar.

2. Switch to the Documentation worksheet, and then, if necessary, click cell **A1**.

3. Click the **Close Window** button ☒, and then click the **Yes** button when prompted to save your changes.

4. Exit Excel.

You discuss the edited workbook with Kevin, and he's satisfied that the formulas and text are free from error. However, he needs to share the workbook with other employees in his group to get their feedback. In the next session, you'll work with Kevin to set up this workbook to allow others to collaborate on it.

Session 7.1 QUICK CHECK

1. To check the spelling in *all* of the sheets in a workbook, what must you do first before running the spelling checker?

2. What are precedent cells? What are dependent cells?

3. What would cause Excel to display the #NAME? error value in a cell?

4. What is the fastest way of locating the source of an #REF! error value in a formula?

5. How does Excel indicate cells whose formulas are "suspect," but which do not necessarily return an error value?

6. How do you display all of the formulas in the worksheet?

SESSION 7.2

In this session, you'll attach comments to worksheet cells and share a workbook with other users. You'll see how Excel resolves conflicts between users editing the same workbook by tracking and reviewing changes made by other users. You'll also learn how to share a workbook through e-mail, and you'll review the many different options Excel provides for e-mailing your workbook. Finally, you'll merge two workbooks, comparing the differences between the two documents and arriving at a final version of the file.

Adding **Comments to a Workbook**

In the last session, you and Kevin completed your edit of the initial draft of Digital Products' financial report. You're now ready to share this document over the company network with three other members of your group: Anjali Mahanez, Brad Vukovich, and Sally Breen. A fourth member of your group, Karen Ziegler, is currently at an overseas conference and will not be back for a week. You'll e-mail a copy of the document to her after you receive feedback from the other members.

Kevin is concerned that the scope of the report is not broad enough. Currently the report only covers the last three years, but he has seen other reports in which a five-year history is reported. He wants you to add a comment to the workbook, asking the other members of his group whether the scope of the report should be expanded.

REFERENCE WINDOW   **RW**

Attaching a Comment
- Click the cell to which you want to attach a comment.
- Right-click the cell and then click Insert Comment on the shortcut menu (or click Insert and then click Comment).
- Type your comment into the comment box.

An Excel comment is a text box that is attached to a specific cell in the worksheet. In a collaborative document, comments from several different users could be attached to the same cell; therefore, the comment box will typically include the name of the user along with the text of the comment.

You'll add Kevin's comment to cell B6 of the Documentation sheet in the DPReport2 workbook.

To attach a comment to cell B6:

1. If you took a break at the end of the previous session, make sure Excel is running and the **DPReport2** workbook in the Tutorial.07\Tutorial folder on your Data Disk is open.

2. If necessary, display the Documentation sheet.

3. Right-click cell **B6** and then click **Insert Comment** on the shortcut menu. Excel opens a text box to the right of cell B6. Your user name should appear in bold at the top of the box. A small red triangle appears in the upper-right corner of the cell.

   TROUBLE? Depending on your Excel configuration, the user name might be yours, or the network administrator or technical support person may have set it to a different name.

4. Type **Should we increase the scope of this report to cover the previous five years?** in the text box. Selection handles appear around the comment box. Using the selection handles, you can increase the size of the box or move it to a new location on the worksheet.

   In its current location, the comment box obscures part of the information in cell B6. Try moving the text box further to the right and down.

5. Move the pointer over the border of the comment box until the pointer changes to ⬧, press and hold down the mouse button, and drag the selection handle down and to the right.

6. Release the mouse button. Figure 7-13 shows the current location of the comment box. Note that an arrow points from the text box to the cell B6, which contains the comment.

| Figure 7-13 | INSERTING A COMMENT INTO A CELL |

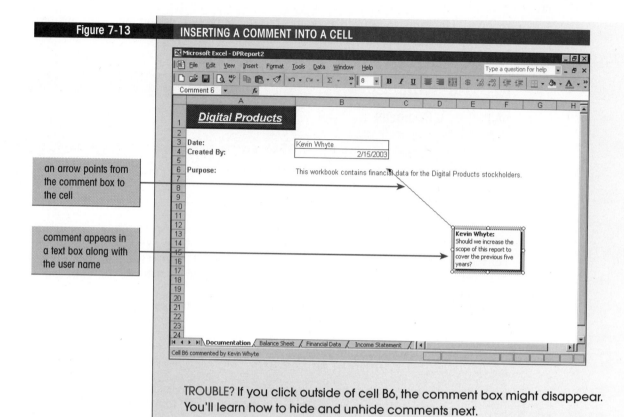

an arrow points from the comment box to the cell

comment appears in a text box along with the user name

TROUBLE? If you click outside of cell B6, the comment box might disappear. You'll learn how to hide and unhide comments next.

Comments can be distracting in a worksheet. To reduce the distraction, you can hide a comment. The comment box then will only appear when you hover the pointer over the cell containing the comment. The presence of a hidden comment will be indicated by the small red triangle located in the upper-right corner of the cell.

To hide and then redisplay the comment in cell B6:

1. Right-click cell **B6** and then click **Hide Comment** on the shortcut menu. The comment disappears; however, the small red triangle remains in the upper-left corner of the cell.

   TROUBLE? If the Hide Comment command does not appear on the shortcut menu, your version of Excel is already set up to hide comments automatically. If that is the case, click cell B6 and continue with the next step.

2. Hover the pointer over cell B6 to display its comment.

3. Move the pointer away from cell B6. The comment disappears.

4. To redisplay the comment, right-click cell **B6** and then click **Show Comment** on the shortcut menu.

By default, a comment box appears with a yellow background, and the font used is Arial. To format the comment box, you can click it to select it, and then double-click the selection border to open the Format Comment dialog box, which contains various formatting options. You can also open the Format Comment dialog box by right-clicking the comment box and selecting Format Comment or by clicking Format on the menu bar and then clicking Comment.

You can choose whether or not to have comments appear on the worksheet printout. By default, comments are not printed, but to change that you can open the Page Setup dialog box for the active worksheet and then click the Sheet tab. On the Sheet tab, you can click the Comments list arrow and then choose from one of three printing options:

- **None**: Suppresses the display of comments on the printout
- **At end of sheet**: Prints all of the comments on a separate sheet at the end of the printout of the worksheet
- **As displayed on sheet**: Prints all of the comments on the printout as they appear in the workbook window

At this point, Kevin does not need to print out the comment that you added to the Documentation sheet, but he'll remember this information for future tasks. Now that you've added Kevin's comment to the worksheet, you are ready to share the workbook with the other members of the group.

Creating a Shared Workbook

A **shared workbook** is a workbook that can be edited by more than one user. Excel allows for simultaneous editing, which can occur if the workbook has been placed in a network folder accessible to several network users. The editing could also be done sequentially, in which case, several users can access the workbook in turn and make changes.

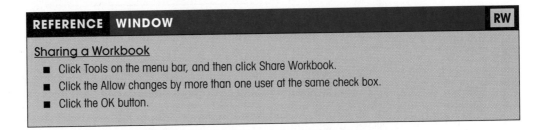

REFERENCE WINDOW   **RW**

Sharing a Workbook
- Click Tools on the menu bar, and then click Share Workbook.
- Click the Allow changes by more than one user at the same check box.
- Click the OK button.

Using a shared workbook is similar to using any workbook. You can enter numbers and text, edit cells, move date around a worksheet, insert new rows and columns, and perform other tasks. In a shared workbook, however, there are some features of Excel that aren't available. For example, you cannot delete worksheets or cell ranges. You also cannot insert a block of cells, or merge or split cells. Nor can you use the Drawing toolbar or insert or change charts.

Sharing a Workbook

Because the data displayed in the workbook comes from various sources, Kevin wants to make sure the information is correct and that nothing has been omitted or misrepresented. By sharing the workbook with other members of his group, Kevin will be able to gather feedback that might affect the information contained in the workbook.

To begin sharing the workbook:

1. Click **Tools** on the menu bar, and then click **Share Workbook**. The Share Workbook dialog box opens. See Figure 7-14.

Figure 7-14   SHARE WORKBOOK DIALOG BOX

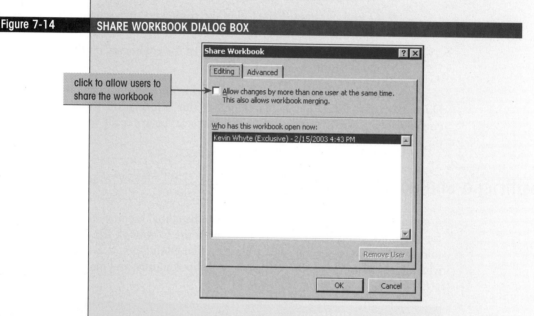

click to allow users to share the workbook

2. Click the **Allow changes by more than one user at the same time** check box to allow other members of the group simultaneous access to this workbook.

3. Click the **OK** button. A message box appears, indicating that the workbook will be saved in order to change its status to a shared document.

4. Click the **OK** button to save and share the workbook. The workbook is saved on the network. Note that the text "(Shared)" appears in the title bar.

Kevin notifies the other members of his group that the workbook is available on the network for review. He will monitor their access to the document by opening the same Share Workbook dialog box that he used to save the workbook as a shared workbook. For example, when Kevin selects the Share Workbook option on the Tools menu a second time, he might see a dialog box similar to the one shown in Figure 7-15.

| Figure 7-15 | SHARED WORKBOOK WITH TWO USERS |

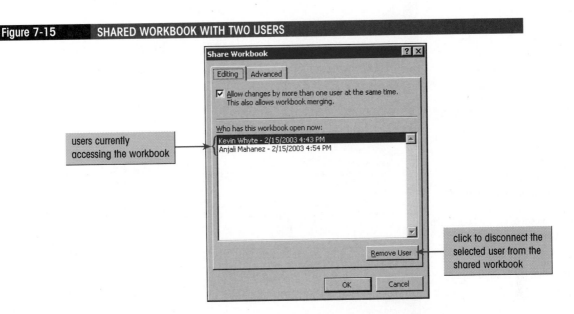

Apparently, Anjali has already responded to Kevin's message and has opened the workbook. So now there are two employees working simultaneously on the financial report: Kevin and Anjali. If both Kevin and Anjali have the workbook open at the same time, how does Excel manage the changes they might make?

Resolving Conflicts

As long as each person makes changes to different cells, Excel will automatically integrate these changes into the shared workbook and notify the users of the change. Consider the situation shown in Figure 7-16, in which Anjali edits the content of cell B7. She then saves and closes the document. Afterwards, Kevin saves his changes to the shared workbook. The action of saving the shared document forces Excel to display any changes made by other users and to attach a comment to the modified cells (in this case, cell B7). Note that Excel will automatically remove this comment the next time Kevin opens the workbook.

Figure 7-16   MODIFYING A SHARED WORKBOOK

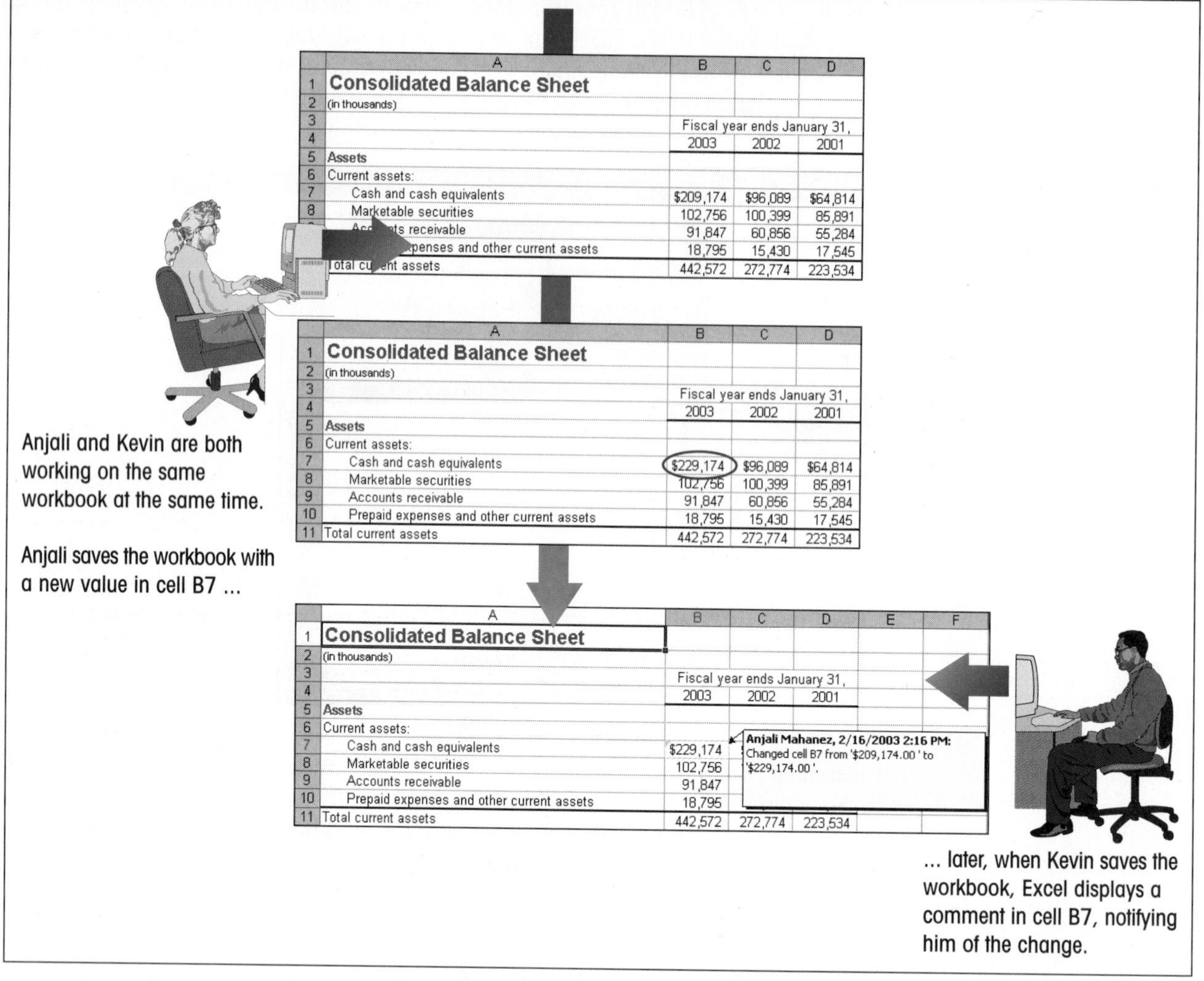

Anjali and Kevin are both working on the same workbook at the same time.

Anjali saves the workbook with a new value in cell B7 ...

... later, when Kevin saves the workbook, Excel displays a comment in cell B7, notifying him of the change.

A conflict can occur when users try to save different changes to the same cell. As shown in Figure 7-17, both Anjali and Kevin have the workbook open at the same time and are editing the contents of cell B7. Anjali saves her changes first. When Kevin tries to save his work, Excel notices a conflict in the value of cell B7 and displays the Resolve Conflicts dialog box. From this dialog box, Kevin can choose which edit to accept. If there are several conflicting cells, Kevin can go through the list, accepting some of Anjali's edits and rejecting others, or he can accept (or reject) them all at once.

Figure 7-17   **RESOLVING A CONFLICT IN A SHARED WORKBOOK**

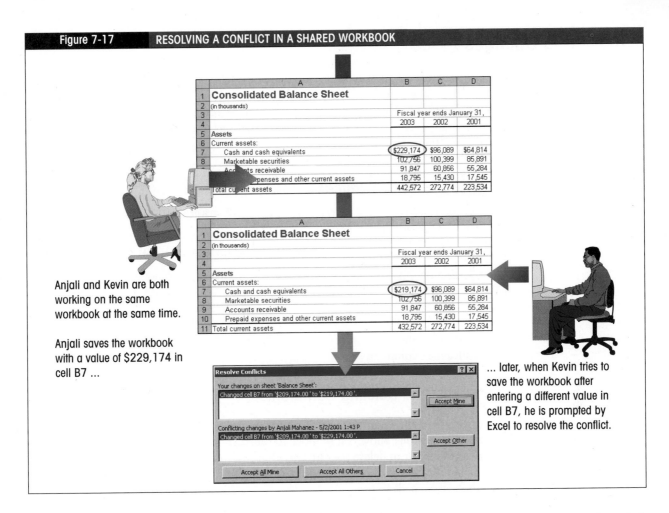

Anjali and Kevin are both working on the same workbook at the same time.

Anjali saves the workbook with a value of $229,174 in cell B7 ...

... later, when Kevin tries to save the workbook after entering a different value in cell B7, he is prompted by Excel to resolve the conflict.

All users have equal authority in deciding which changes are kept and which are discarded. The last user to save the document sees the Resolve Conflicts dialog box. However, rejected changes are stored in a **tracking log** to allow the users to go back and retrieve erroneously rejected changes. This feature is particularly useful when a large group is editing a document and more control over the final content is needed. In this financial report project, Kevin is the final authority, so he will need to review the tracking log before signing off on the report.

At this point, Kevin has no further work to do on the financial report. You can close his document and await the feedback from his colleagues.

To save your changes:

1. Click cell **A1** in the Documentation sheet.

2. Click the **Close Window** button ⊠.

3. Click the **Yes** button to save your changes.

Tracking **Changes**

A few days have passed. The other members of Kevin's group have had time to examine the contents of the workbook; they've inserted their own comments and made their own edits. Kevin returns to you with a new version of the workbook. He needs your help in reviewing and reconciling their edits. You will open the new version of the workbook, which has been saved as DPReport3.

To open the DPReport3 workbook:

1. Open the **DPReport3** workbook located in the Tutorial.07\Tutorial folder on your Data Disk.

2. Enter the date and your name in the Documentation sheet.

3. Save the workbook as **DPReport4** in the Tutorial.07\Tutorial folder on your Data Disk.

Before reviewing the changes that have been made to the document, you'll first review your colleague's comments.

Reviewing and Deleting Comments

To review all of the comments in a workbook, you can use the Reviewing toolbar, which contains buttons that allow you to move to the next or previous comment in the workbook, as well as to edit or to delete the currently selected comment.

You will display the Reviewing toolbar so you and Kevin can review the comments that the others have made.

To view your colleague's comments:

1. Click **View** on the menu bar, point to **Toolbars**, and then click **Reviewing**. The Reviewing toolbar is displayed.

   TROUBLE? The location of the Reviewing toolbar on your screen might be different. You can drag the toolbar to place it above the Formula bar, or you can drag it to a blank area of the workspace.

2. Click the **Next Comment** button 📝 on the Reviewing toolbar. Excel selects the first comment on the Documentation sheet, as shown in Figure 7-18.

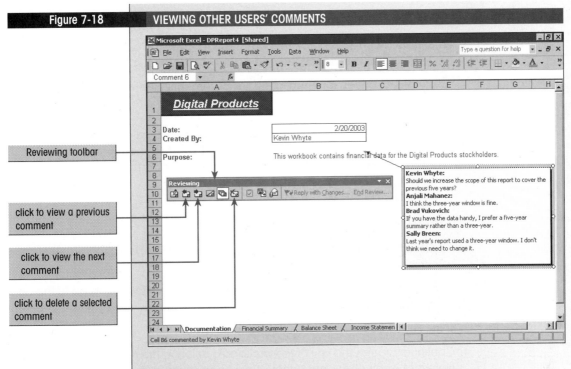

Figure 7-18   **VIEWING OTHER USERS' COMMENTS**

Reviewing toolbar

click to view a previous comment

click to view the next comment

click to delete a selected comment

> **TROUBLE?** If you click the comment box with your mouse, your user name will appear in the box, and Excel will wait for you to enter your own comments. If this happens, click cell B7 to deselect the comment box.

Recall that Kevin asked that you insert a comment into the workbook questioning whether the scope of the report should be expanded to cover the last five years. In the first comment, Kevin sees the response to his query. Anjali and Sally think that the three-year report is fine, whereas Brad would prefer a five-year report if the data is easily available.

You will continue to review the comments.

To continue reviewing the comments:

1. Click the **Next Comment** button 🔲 on the Reviewing toolbar. The next comment appears in cell A1 on the Financial Summary sheet. From this comment, you learn that Anjali has moved the Financial Report worksheet to the front and that Brad has renamed the worksheet.

2. Click 🔲. Excel jumps to the comment attached to cell A19. Anjali has a question about whether the number of employees reported on the worksheet includes part-time employees.

3. Continue to click 🖻, and read each comment.

When you reach the end of the comments, a message box appears, indicating that you have reached the end of the workbook.

4. Click the **OK** button to return to the first comment in the workbook.

After reviewing all of the comments, Kevin wants to remove them from the workbook because he no longer needs them. He has decided to leave the report coverage at three years. He can review the edits made by the other users without having to read their comments again.

To delete the comments:

1. Click the **Delete Comment** button 🖻 on the Reviewing toolbar to delete the selected comment.

2. Click the **Next Comment** button 🖻 on the Reviewing toolbar to go to the next comment in the workbook.

3. Click 🖻 to delete the second comment.

4. Continue through the rest of the workbook, deleting the remaining comments. Note that when all the comments have been deleted from the workbook the Next Comment button and the Delete Comment button are no longer available on the Reviewing toolbar.

5. Close the Reviewing toolbar when you're finished.

TROUBLE? If the Reviewing toolbar is floating, click its Close button 🗙. If the toolbar is anchored, click View on the menu bar, point to Toolbars, and then click Reviewing.

From reading the comments, Kevin has learned that the other users in his group have been editing the contents of some of the cells, deleting others, and moving and renaming worksheets. Although his colleagues have noted these changes in their comments, they might not have documented all of the changes they made. Kevin wants to be able to review everything his colleagues have done in the workbook.

Reviewing Changes

As noted earlier, Excel stores changes to a shared workbook in a tracking log. By default, the log will store changes in the workbook entered over the previous 30 days. Not all changes are tracked. Excel will not track changed sheet names, inserted or deleted worksheets, and format changes.

To review the changes that are tracked, you can have Excel highlight them. Highlighting a change displays a text box alongside the cell, indicating what change was made, who made it, and when. Highlight the changes made in the workbook so you can review each edit.

REFERENCE WINDOW   `RW`

<u>Tracking Changes to Cells</u>

- Open a shared workbook.
- Click Tools on the menu bar, point to Track Changes, and then click Highlight Changes.
- Click the list arrow for the When check box, and select the timeframe when the changes occurred that you want to track.
- Click the list arrow for the Who check box, and then select whose changes you want to view.
- Click the Where reference box and specify where in the workbook you want to review the changes.
- Click the Highlight Changes on screen check box to display the changed cells in the worksheet.
- Click the List changes on a new sheet check box to display a list of changed cells on a separate worksheet.
- Click the OK button.

To display all the changes that have been made to this shared workbook, you will turn on the track changes feature.

To highlight the changes in the shared workbook:

1. Click **Tools** on the menu, point to **Track Changes**, and then click **Highlight Changes**. The Highlight Changes dialog box opens.

   From this dialog box, you can select a time interval for the changes you want highlighted. You can choose to highlight: 1) changes created since the last time you saved the workbook, 2) all changes, 3) changes that you haven't reviewed yet, or 4) changes since a specified date. You can also review changes from a specified user or changes made in a specified section of the workbook. In this case, you'll review all the changes made by everyone but yourself.

2. Click the **list arrow** for the When check box, and then click **All**.

3. Click the **list arrow** for the Who check box, and then click **Everyone but Me**. Note that clicking the list arrow automatically selects the Who check box. Note that the Everyone but Me option refers to all users who have edited this document other than the user who currently has it open.

4. Verify that the Highlight changes on screen check box is selected and that the List changes on a new sheet check box is *not* selected. The completed dialog box appears in Figure 7-19.

Figure 7-19   **HIGHLIGHTING CHANGES**

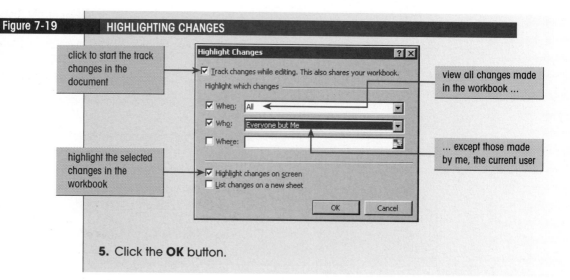

click to start the track changes in the document

view all changes made in the workbook ...

... except those made by me, the current user

highlight the selected changes in the workbook

5. Click the **OK** button.

Excel highlights the locations in the workbook that have been modified. Each cell that has been changed is displayed with a colored border. When you hover the pointer over the cell, a description of the change is displayed.

Kevin wants you to review all the changes beginning with the changes made to the Financial Summary sheet.

To review the changes made by other users:

1. Click the **Financial Summary** tab.

2. Hover the pointer over cell A11. A comment appears describing the change. See Figure 7-20.

Figure 7-20   **CHANGES IN THE WORKBOOK**

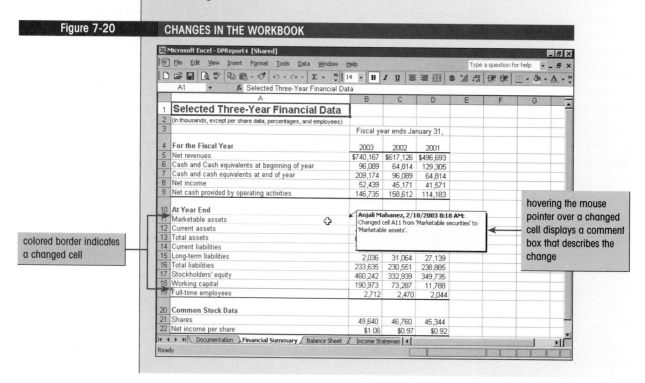

colored border indicates a changed cell

hovering the mouse pointer over a changed cell displays a comment box that describes the change

Examining all of the sheets in a workbook to look for changes might be a tiresome process, especially in large workbooks that contain many worksheets. Kevin asks whether there is a way of viewing the contents of the tracking log itself rather than having to switch to each sheet to look for the changes.

To make the process of reviewing changes in a workbook easier and more efficient, you can display the contents of the tracking log.

To show the tracking history:

1. Click **Tools** on the menu bar, point to **Track Changes**, and then click **Highlight Changes**. The Highlight Changes dialog box opens.

2. Click the **List changes on a new sheet** check box, and then click the **OK** button. The content of the tracking log appears in a new worksheet named "History." See Figure 7-21. The History worksheet displays each change in the order it was entered, along with the date and time it was made, who made the change, where it was made, and what kind of change it is. From viewing the contents of this sheet, Kevin can tell at a glance what kind of modifications have been made in the workbook.

| Figure 7-21 | HISTORY LIST DESCRIBING THE CHANGES MADE TO THE WORKBOOK |

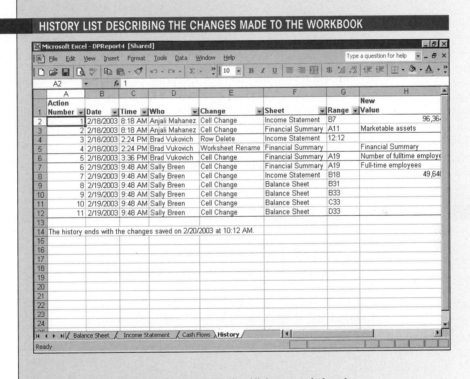

Action Number	Date	Time	Who	Change	Sheet	Range	New Value
1	2/18/2003	8:18 AM	Anjali Mahanez	Cell Change	Income Statement	B7	96,36
2	2/18/2003	8:18 AM	Anjali Mahanez	Cell Change	Financial Summary	A11	Marketable assets
3	2/18/2003	2:24 PM	Brad Vukovich	Row Delete	Income Statement	12:12	
4	2/18/2003	2:24 PM	Brad Vukovich	Worksheet Rename	Financial Summary		Financial Summary
5	2/18/2003	3:36 PM	Brad Vukovich	Cell Change	Financial Summary	A19	Number of fulltime employe
6	2/19/2003	9:48 AM	Sally Breen	Cell Change	Financial Summary	A19	Full-time employees
7	2/19/2003	9:48 AM	Sally Breen	Cell Change	Income Statement	B18	49,64(
8	2/19/2003	9:48 AM	Sally Breen	Cell Change	Balance Sheet	B31	
9	2/19/2003	9:48 AM	Sally Breen	Cell Change	Balance Sheet	B33	
10	2/19/2003	9:48 AM	Sally Breen	Cell Change	Balance Sheet	C33	
11	2/19/2003	9:48 AM	Sally Breen	Cell Change	Balance Sheet	D33	

The history ends with the changes saved on 2/20/2003 at 10:12 AM.

3. Review the different columns in the History worksheet.

Note that the History sheet will only exist for this Excel session. If you close the workbook, even saving your changes, the sheet will not appear the next time the workbook is opened.

Accepting and Rejecting Changes

After examining the contents of the History sheet, Kevin sees some changes that he might want to keep. Although he could reverse the changes by editing the workbook, he prefers to simply reject those changes that he doesn't approve of. Using the Accept or Reject Changes option of the Track Changes feature can save Kevin time and help him to maintain accuracy.

REFERENCE WINDOW   **RW**

Accepting and Rejecting Changes to Cells
- Open a shared workbook.
- Click Tools on the menu bar, point to Track Changes, and then click Accept or Reject Changes.
- Click the list arrow for the When check box, and then select the timeframe when the changes occurred that you want to review.
- Click the list arrow for the Who check box, and then select the person whose changes you want to review.
- Click the Where reference box and specify where in the workbook you want to review the changes.
- Click the OK button.

You will review the changes, accepting or rejecting them as needed.

To accept and reject changes to the workbook:

1. Click **Tools** on the menu bar, point to **Track Changes**, and then **Accept or Reject Changes**. The Select Changes to Accept or Reject dialog box opens. See Figure 7-22.

Figure 7-22	REVIEWING CHANGES

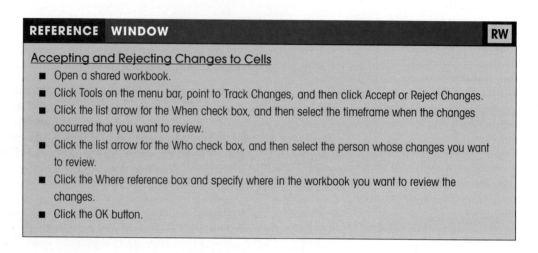

review all the changes that have not been previously reviewed ...

... except the changes made by me, the current user

You'll select those changes that have not yet been reviewed and limit the changes to only those created by users other than you.

2. Verify that your dialog box looks like the one shown in Figure 7-22, and then click the **OK** button. The Accept or Reject Changes dialog box opens, indicating that there are 11 changes made by others to this workbook, as shown in Figure 7-23.

Session 7.2

1. A shared workbook is a workbook that can be edited by more than one user. Shared workbooks have the word "[Shared]" displayed in the Excel title bar alongside the name of the workbook.

2. As long as each person makes changes to different cells, Excel will automatically integrate these changes into the shared workbook and notify the users of the change. If there is a conflict, Excel will display the Resolve Conflicts dialog box to the person who last attempts to save the workbook.

3. alongside each edited cell in a pop-up comment box or listed in a separate worksheet

4. the previous 30 days

5. Routing causes the workbook to move through a collection of users listed on a routing slip. When one recipient is finished with the workbook, it is then sent to the next person listed in the routing slip. For routing to work, all recipients must be running Microsoft Outlook.

6. The two workbooks must be copies of the same shared workbook. The workbooks must have different filenames. The workbooks must either have the same password or not be password-protected at all. Change tracking must be turned on for both workbooks from the time the copy is first made, and the tracking history must be kept from the time the copy is first made.

Session 7.3

1. HTML stands for Hypertext Markup Language, and it is the language used to format Web pages.

2. interactive Web pages, in which users can enter and edit data, and noninteractive Web pages, in which users can only view the contents of the workbook

3. Each time you attempt to save the workbook, Excel will prompt you to indicate whether you want to publish the new version to the Web page you created earlier.

4. Click the cell in which you want to insert the hyperlink, click Insert on the menu bar, and then click Hyperlink.

5. A ScreenTip provides additional information about the target of a hyperlink. A ScreenTip appears when the user hovers the mouse pointer over a hyperlink.

6. Right-click the cell, and then click Edit Hyperlink on the shortcut menu.

In this tutorial you will:

- Create validation rules for data entry

- Learn to protect the contents of worksheets and workbooks

- Create and use range names

- Learn about macro viruses and Excel's security features

- Create macros using the macro recorder

- Edit and print a macro using the Visual Basic Editor

- Assign a macro to a keyboard shortcut and a button

DEVELOPING AN EXCEL APPLICATION

Creating a Stock Reporter for Harris & Burton

CASE

Harris & Burton

Harris & Burton is a financial planning and investment firm located in Elkhorn, Indiana. Founded by Diane Harris and Kevin Burton, the company provides financial services to a large clientele mostly located in Indiana and Kentucky.

Nigel Turner is one of the financial planners employed by Harris & Burton. Nigel wants to create an Excel workbook that reports the activity of selected stocks. The report will contain a chart displaying the open, high, low, and close values of the stock, as well as the volume of shares traded. He wants the ability to quickly switch between reports of the stock's performance in the last 30, 60, or 90 days. He also wants to be able to insert the latest stock values into the report. Eventually, Nigel will be sharing this workbook with other people in the company, so he wants the workbook to be easy to work with.

Although many of these tasks can be accomplished using Excel in a traditional way, Nigel realizes that some people in the company are not always comfortable using Excel. Ideally, he would like a customized interface for this report that does not rely exclusively on Excel menus and toolbars.

In this tutorial, you will create an Excel application that will provide the stock-related information that Nigel wants.

SESSION 8.1

In this session, you'll plan and design an Excel application. You'll start by creating validation rules in order to ensure that correct data is entered into the application. Then you'll learn how to protect different parts of the workbook to prevent users from accessing and editing them.

Planning an Excel Application

Up to now, you've worked with Excel by using the toolbars, commands, and menus provided by the program. For most situations, this is fine. However, there are some cases in which you will want to create a customized interface, also called an Excel application, for your work. For example, rather than repeating a series of Excel commands each time you want to display your data in a specific way, you might find it more useful to assign all of those commands to a single menu item or toolbar button. Another important aspect of an Excel application is the ability to control where users are allowed to enter or edit data and what types of values they are allowed to enter.

Creating your own customized commands, menus, functions, and buttons is the essential idea behind an Excel application. There is a wide variety of Excel applications. An application can be so encompassing that it replaces almost the entire Excel interface with the application's own collection of menus, toolbars and commands, or the application can be less ambitious, simply augmenting the standard Excel interface by adding a special button or menu to perform a particular task.

Nigel has an Excel application in mind for his workbook. He has recorded the last 90 days worth of information on a particular stock, and he has generated a chart and a table of statistics describing the stock's performance. He wants you to create an Excel application that allows him to more easily enter new data and to view his data in different ways.

To open Nigel's workbook:

1. Start Excel and open the **Stock1** workbook located in the Tutorial.08\Tutorial folder on your Data Disk.

2. Enter the date and your name in the Documentation sheet.

3. Save the workbook as **Stock2** in the Tutorial.08\Tutorial folder on your Data Disk.

4. Review the contents of the workbook, and then return to the Reporter worksheet.

Aside from the Documentation sheet, there are two worksheets in the Stock2 workbook: Reporter and History Log, as shown in Figure 8-1. The Reporter worksheet displays a chart and table of statistics describing the performance of Maxwell Sports Inc., one of the stocks in Nigel's portfolio. The stock market data itself is stored in the range A1:F91 of the History Log worksheet, with the most recent values reported at the top of the table. Nigel has recorded information on the stock's daily open, high, low, and close values, as well as the volume of shares traded in millions.

Figure 8-1 | THE STOCK2 WORKBOOK

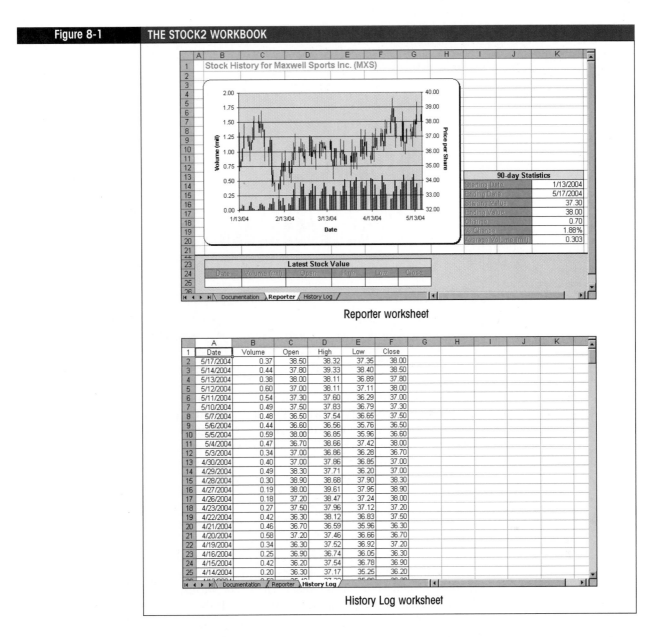

Reporter worksheet

History Log worksheet

Nigel describes the type of customized interface he wants you to create, shown in Figure 8-2. He wants to have the ability to view the stock history over the last 30, 60, or 90 days. To do this, he wants to be able to switch between reports by clicking one of three buttons located to the right of the stock history chart. As he receives the latest stock values, he wants to be able to enter those values into a range of cells at the bottom of the worksheet, and then, by clicking a button, transfer those values into the History Log sheet. Thus, clicking one of four buttons will do most of the work in this application, and there is little need for users to work with Excel's extensive system of menus and commands.

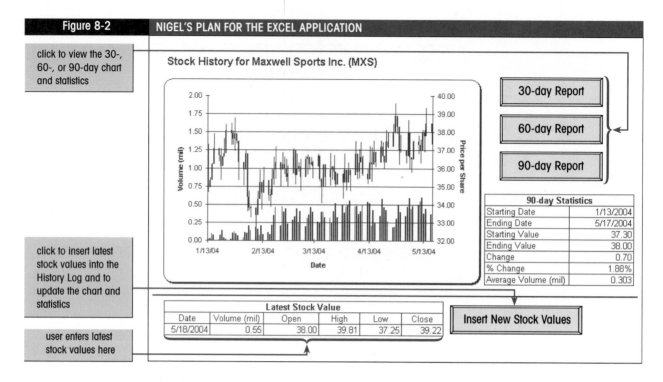

| Figure 8-2 | NIGEL'S PLAN FOR THE EXCEL APPLICATION |

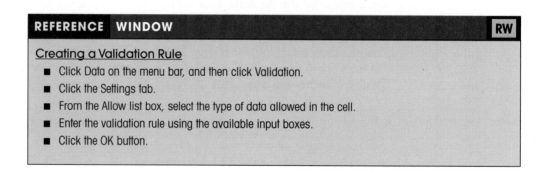

Nigel plans to share this application with other employees at the company. He's concerned that other users might unwittingly change essential parts of the workbooks, perhaps erasing an important value or formula. Therefore Nigel wants you to control what values users can enter into the workbook, and also control where they can enter those values.

You'll start work on Nigel's application by creating a series of validation checks, designed to prevent users from inserting erroneous data values.

Validating Data Entry

One way to ensure that correct data is entered into a cell or range is to use the Excel data validation feature, which restricts the data entry to follow a defined set of rules. You can specify the type of data (whole numbers, dates, time, or text) as well as a range of acceptable values (for instance, integers between 1 and 100). If the value entered by the user fails the validation check, Excel can display an error message, preventing the erroneous value from being stored. To assist the user in data entry, you can also display an input message specifying the type of data that can be entered in the cell.

REFERENCE WINDOW   RW

Creating a Validation Rule

- Click Data on the menu bar, and then click Validation.
- Click the Settings tab.
- From the Allow list box, select the type of data allowed in the cell.
- Enter the validation rule using the available input boxes.
- Click the OK button.

Specifying a Data Type and Acceptable Values

Nigel wants to restrict users to entering new values only in the range B25:G25 of the Reporter worksheet. He has three validation rules he wants you to add to the workbook. These are:

- The new date value in cell B25 must be greater than the previous ending date value stored in cell K15.
- The new opening value in cell D25 must be equal to the previous ending value stored in cell K17.
- The new closing value in cell G25 must fall between the high and low values in cells E25 and F25.

If users attempt to enter values that fail these validation rules, Nigel wants Excel to notify them of the problem and prevent the data from being stored in the cells.

To specify data types and the ranges of acceptable values:

1. Click cell **B25** in the Reporter worksheet.

2. Click **Data** on the menu bar, and then click **Validation**. The Data Validation dialog box opens. There are three tabs: Settings, Input Message, and Error Alert. You use the Settings tab to enter the validation rules for the active cell.

   In cell B25, you want users to enter a new date that is later than the date of the previous stock value. This date, identified as the Ending Date, is displayed in cell K15 of the Reporter worksheet.

3. Make sure that the Settings tab is displayed, click the **Allow** list arrow, and then click **Date**. The Data Validation dialog box expands to display the options that are specific to the Date setting you have selected.

4. Click the **Data** list arrow, and then click **greater than**. Note that the dialog box changes again to address the Data option that you selected.

5. Press the **Tab** key to move the insertion point to the Start date reference box, and then click cell **K15**. See Figure 8-3.

Figure 8-3	SETTING VALIDATION CRITERIA

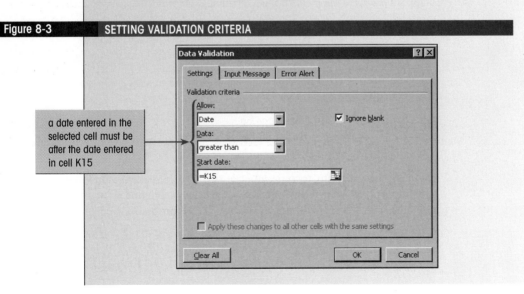

a date entered in the selected cell must be after the date entered in cell K15

TROUBLE? If necessary, move the Data Validation dialog box in order to see cell K15.

6. Click the **OK** button.

Next, enter the validation rule for cell D25, whose opening value must be equal to the value in cell K17 (which is the previous ending value).

7. Click cell **D25**, click **Data**, and then click **Validation**.

8. Click **Decimal** in the Allow list, click **equal to** in the Data list, press the **Tab** key, click cell **K17**, and then click the **OK** button.

Finally, enter the validation rule for cell G25, whose closing value should lie between the values in cell F25 (the low value) and cell E25 (the high value).

9. Click cell **G25**, click **Data**, and then click **Validation**.

10. Click **Decimal** in the Allow list box. Note that this time the dialog box displays a Minimum reference box and a Maximum reference box.

11. Make sure **between** is selected in the Data list box, press the **Tab** key, and then click cell **F25** as the minimum value.

12. Press the **Tab** key, click cell **E25** as the maximum value, and then click the **OK** button.

The options in the Allow list box dictate the types of values for which you can specify criteria. As you just saw, the Data Validation dialog box changes depending on the option you choose in the Allow list. Figure 8-4 provides the list of options and their descriptions.

Figure 8-4	OPTIONS IN THE ALLOW LIST BOX
ALLOW	**DESCRIPTION**
Any Value	Any value can be entered into the cell.
Whole Number	The cell will accept only integers. A validation rule can further specify the range of acceptable integers.
Decimal	The cell will accept any type of numeric value. A validation rule can further specify the range of acceptable values.
List	The cell will accept only values from a list. The list can be taken from a range of cells in the worksheet, or the list of values can be entered directly into the dialog box, with the values separated by commas.
Date	The cell will accept only dates. A validation rule can further specify the range of acceptable dates.
Time	The cell will accept only times. A validation rule can further specify the range of acceptable times.
Text Length	The cell will accept only text of a specified number of characters.
Custom	The validation rule will be based on an Excel logical formula.

An important point to remember is that the validation rules that you just entered only apply during data entry. If a cell already has an erroneous value in it when you create these validation rules, Excel will not notify you of the problem.

Specifying an Input Message

One way of reducing the chance of data entry error is to display an input message when a user clicks on the cell. The input message can provide additional information about the type of data expected for the cell. Input messages appear as ScreenTips next to the active cell.

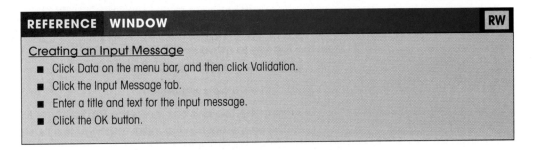

REFERENCE WINDOW **RW**

Creating an Input Message
- Click Data on the menu bar, and then click Validation.
- Click the Input Message tab.
- Enter a title and text for the input message.
- Click the OK button.

Create input messages now for all of the cells in the range B25:G25.

To create input messages for the cells:

1. Click cell **B25**, click **Data** on the menu bar, and then click **Validation**.

2. Click the **Input Message** tab.

3. Verify that the Show input message when cell is select check box is selected.

4. Click in the Title text box, and then type **Date**.

5. Press the **Tab** key and then type **Enter the date the stocks were traded.** in the Input message text box. Figure 8-5 shows the completed dialog box.

Figure 8-5   SPECIFYING AN INPUT MESSAGE FOR THE DATE VALUE

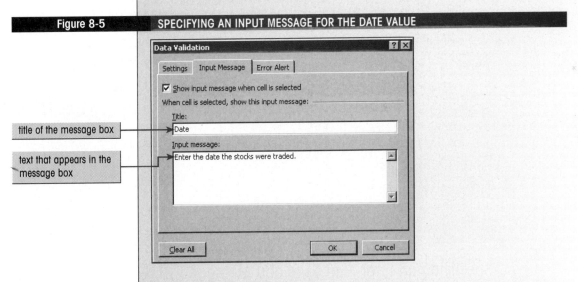

title of the message box

text that appears in the message box

6. Click the **OK** button. The input message you created appears next to cell C25. See Figure 8-6.

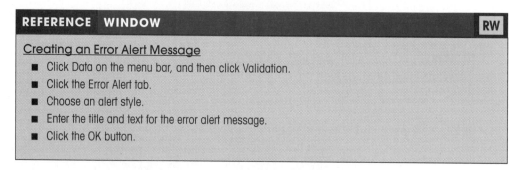

Figure 8-6   DISPLAYING THE DATE INPUT MESSAGE

input message title

input message text

7. Press the **Tab** key to move to cell C25. Note that the input message disappears when cell B25 is no longer the active cell.

8. Click **Data** and then click **Validation**.

9. Type **Volume** in the Title text box, press the **Tab** key, type **Enter the volume of shares traded (in millions).** in the Input message text box, and then click the **OK** button. The input message for cell C25 is displayed.

10. Press the **Tab** key to move to cell D25, and then enter the following input messages for the remaining cells in the range:

Cell D25: Title: **Open**	Input message:	**Enter the opening value of the stock.**	
Cell E25: Title: **High**	Input message:	**Enter the highest value of the stock for the specified date.**	
Cell F25: Title: **Low**	Input message:	**Enter the lowest value of the stock for the specified date.**	
Cell G25: Title: **Close**	Input message:	**Enter the closing value of the stock.**	

TROUBLE? If you make a mistake entering the input message, click the cell again, open the Data Validation dialog box, and then reenter the text correctly.

The input messages you've entered will make the worksheet easier to work with and will help minimize the chance of an employee entering an incorrect stock value.

REFERENCE WINDOW   **RW**

Creating an Error Alert Message
- Click Data on the menu bar, and then click Validation.
- Click the Error Alert tab.
- Choose an alert style.
- Enter the title and text for the error alert message.
- Click the OK button.

Specifying an Error Alert Style and Message

Nigel would still like Excel to display an error alert if data is entered that violates any of the three validation rules you specified above. Excel supports three types of error alerts, labeled as Stop, Warning, and Information. The style of the error alert determines what choices the user is presented with when an invalid entry is attempted. The most serious is the Stop alert, which prevents you from storing the data in the cell. Next in severity is the Warning alert, which, by default, rejects the invalid data, but allows you to override the rejection. The least severe is the Information alert, which, by default, accepts the invalid data, but still allows you to cancel the data entry.

Nigel wants you to use a Stop alert when a user attempts to violate the validation rules defined earlier.

To enter the error alert messages:

1. Click cell **B25**, click **Data** on the menu bar, and then click **Validation**.

2. Click the **Error Alert** tab.

3. Make sure **Stop** is displayed in the Style list box.

4. Click in the Title text box, type **Invalid Date**. This text will appear as the title in the alert message box.

5. Press the **Tab** key and then type **The date must be greater than the previous Ending Date shown in cell K15.** in the Error message list box. See Figure 8-7.

Figure 8-7	ERROR ALERT MESSAGE

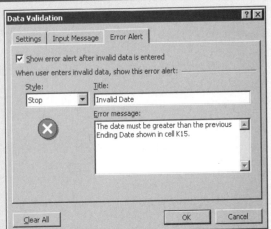

6. Click the **OK** button.

   Next, enter the error alert message for the validation rule you created for the stock's opening value.

7. Click cell **D25**, click **Data**, and then click **Validation**.

8. Type **Invalid Open Value** in the Title text box, press the **Tab** key, type **The Open value must be equal to the previous Ending Value shown in cell K17.** in the Error message list box, and then click the **OK** button.

   Finally, enter the error alert message for the validation rule for the closing stock value.

9. Click cell **G25**, click **Data**, and then click **Validation**.

10. Type **Invalid Close Value** in the Title text box, press the **Tab** key, type **The Close value must lie between the High value (E25) and the Low value (F25).** in the Error message list box, and then click the **OK** button.

Nigel has some new stock data to enter in the range B25:G25. You suggest that he could test the validation feature you've just created by initially entering incorrect values that violate the validation rules.

To test the data validation rules:

1. Click cell **B25**, type **5/17/2004**, and then press the **Tab** key. The Invalid Date message box opens, informing you that the date you entered must be greater than the date shown in cell K15 (in this case, that date is 5/17/2004).

2. Click the **Retry** button, type **5/18/2004** in cell B25, and then press the **Tab** key. Excel allows the new data to be stored in the cell.

3. Type **0.55** in cell C25, and then press the **Tab** key.

4. Type **38.5** in cell D25, and then press the **Tab** key. The Invalid Open Value message box opens, which indicates that the opening value must be equal to the value in cell K17.

5. Click the **Retry** button, type **38**, and then press the **Tab** key.

6. Type **39.5** in cell E25, and then press the **Tab** key.

7. Type **36** in cell F25, and then press the **Tab** key.

8. Type **40** in cell G25, and then press the **Tab** key. The Invalid Close Value message box appears, indicating that the closing value is not between the stock's high and low values for that day.

9. Click the **Retry** button, type **39**, and press the **Tab** key. Excel accepts the new stock data.

Nigel is pleased with the validation rules you've created. He can see how they will help to reduce the probability of incorrect data values being entered. The other way of controlling user error is to limit access to certain parts of the workbook.

Protecting a Worksheet and Workbook

When you **protect** a workbook, you control the ability users have to make changes to the file. For example, you can prevent users from changing all of the formulas in a worksheet, or you can keep users from deleting worksheets or inserting new ones. You can even keep users from viewing the formulas used in the workbook.

Nigel wants to protect the contents of the Reporter and History Log worksheets, prohibiting users from editing the contents of the cells, *except* for new stock values entered in the range B25:G25 of the Reporter worksheet. How can he protect some cells in the worksheet, but not others?

Locking and Unlocking Cells

Every cell in a workbook has a **locked** property that determines whether or not changes can be made to that cell. The locked property has no impact as long as the worksheet is unprotected; however, once you protect a worksheet, the locked property is enabled and controls whether or not the cell can be edited. By default, the locked property is turned on for each cell.

Before you protect a worksheet, you must first determine which cells you want to leave *unlocked*, so that they can be edited even when the worksheet is protected. In this case, those are the cells in the range B25:G25 of the Reporter worksheet.

To unlock the cells:

1. Select the range **B25:G25** in the Reporter worksheet.

2. Click **Format** on the menu bar, and then click **Cells**. The Format Cells dialog box opens.

3. Click the **Protection** tab, and then deselect the **Locked** check box, as shown in Figure 8-8.

| Figure 8-8 | UNLOCKING THE SELECTED CELLS |

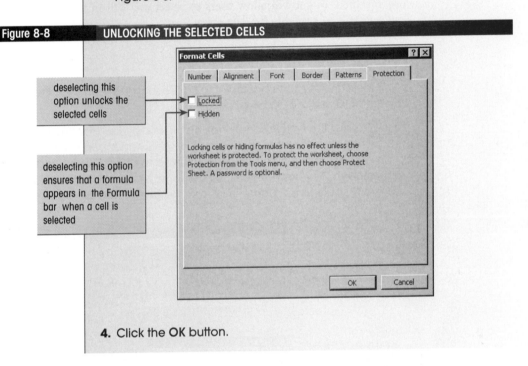

deselecting this option unlocks the selected cells

deselecting this option ensures that a formula appears in the Formula bar when a cell is selected

4. Click the **OK** button.

With the Locked check box deselected, the cells are no longer locked, and you can now proceed to protect the worksheet.

Protecting a Worksheet

As part of the process of protecting a worksheet, you specify which actions are still available to users once the sheet is protected. For example, you can allow users to insert new rows or columns into the sheet or to delete rows and columns. You can limit the user to selecting only unlocked cells or allow the user to select any cell in the sheet. The choices you make will be in force as long as the worksheet is protected.

A protected sheet can always be unprotected, but you can also require users to enter a password before the protection is removed. Unless you are working on confidential material, it's probably best to not specify a password.

Note of caution: Be sure to keep the password in a safe place and one to which you have easy access, because if you forget the password, there will be no way of removing the worksheet protection.

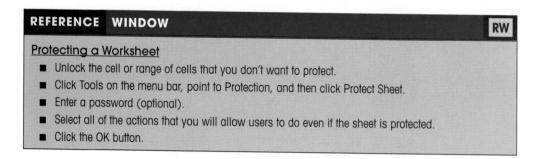

REFERENCE WINDOW **RW**

Protecting a Worksheet
- Unlock the cell or range of cells that you don't want to protect.
- Click Tools on the menu bar, point to Protection, and then click Protect Sheet.
- Enter a password (optional).
- Select all of the actions that you will allow users to do even if the sheet is protected.
- Click the OK button.

Nigel wants to protect the Reporter and History Log worksheets, but he doesn't want a password specified. Nigel will allow users to select any cell in those sheets, but only the unlocked cells will be available for data entry.

To enable worksheet protection:

1. Click **Tools** on the menu bar, point to **Protection**, and then click **Protect Sheet**. The Protect Sheet dialog box opens.

   You will leave the Password text box blank. However, below the Password text box is a list of actions that you can allow users to perform even if the sheet is protected. By default, users are only allowed to select locked and unlocked cells (though they cannot edit their contents.) This is all that Nigel wants his users to be able to do. Figure 8-9 shows the completed dialog box.

Figure 8-9	PROTECTING A WORKSHEET

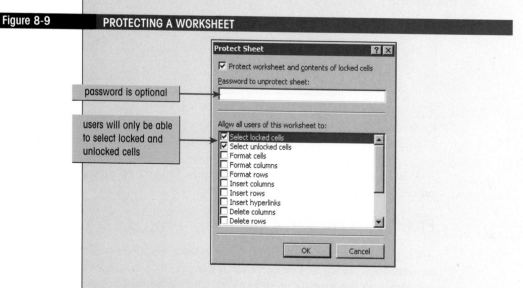

password is optional

users will only be able to select locked and unlocked cells

2. Click the **OK** button.

3. Click the **History Log** tab.

4. Click **Tools**, point to **Protection**, click **Protect Sheet**, and then click the **OK** button to accept the default set of user actions.

   Nigel wants to see what would happen if someone tried to edit one of the cells in the History Log sheet.

5. Click cell **A1** and press any letter on your keyboard. Excel displays a message box, indicating that the cell is protected and cannot be modified.

6. Click the **OK** button.

Protecting a Workbook

The contents of the two sheets can't be changed, but Nigel wonders whether the protection extends to the sheets themselves. Can someone rename or even delete a protected worksheet? The answer is "yes;" worksheet protection only applies to the contents of the sheet, not to the sheet itself. To keep the worksheets themselves from being modified, you will have to protect the workbook.

You can protect the structure and the windows of the workbook. Protecting the structure prohibits users from renaming, deleting, hiding, or inserting worksheets. Protecting the windows prohibits users from moving, resizing, closing, or hiding parts of the Excel window. The default is to protect only the structure of the workbook, not the windows used to display it.

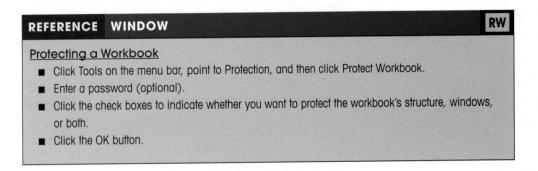

REFERENCE WINDOW   **RW**

Protecting a Workbook
- Click Tools on the menu bar, point to Protection, and then click Protect Workbook.
- Enter a password (optional).
- Click the check boxes to indicate whether you want to protect the workbook's structure, windows, or both.
- Click the OK button.

Nigel doesn't want users to be able to change the structure of the workbook, so you will set protection for the workbook structure, but not the window.

To enable workbook protection:

1. Click **Tools** on the menu bar, point to **Protection**, and then click **Protect Workbook**. The Protect Workbook dialog box opens, as shown in Figure 8-10.

| Figure 8-10 | PROTECTING A WORKBOOK |

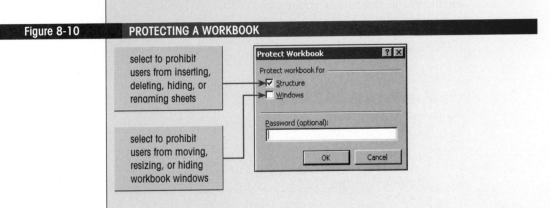

select to prohibit users from inserting, deleting, hiding, or renaming sheets

select to prohibit users from moving, resizing, or hiding workbook windows

2. Make sure the Structure check box is selected, and then click the **OK** button to protect the workbook, without specifying a password.

3. Right-click the **History Log** tab. Note that the Insert, Delete, Rename, and Move or Copy commands are all grayed out, indicating that the options that modify the worksheets are no longer available.

Unprotecting a Worksheet

Nigel is pleased with the different levels of protection that can be applied to the worksheet. At this point, you still have a lot of editing to do, so you'll turn off worksheet protection for now. Later on, when you've completed your modifications, you'll turn worksheet protection back on.

To disable worksheet protection:

1. Click **Tools** on the menu bar, point to **Protection**, and then click **Unprotect Sheet**.

2. Click the **Reporter** tab, click **Tools**, point to **Protection**, and then click **Unprotect Sheet**.

You've completed your work at this time on Nigel's application. Save and close the Stock2 workbook.

3. Click the **Save** button 🔳 on the Standard toolbar, and then click the **Close** button ☒ on the title bar to exit Excel.

The two worksheets in the Stock2 workbook are now unprotected. You do not have to unprotect the workbook, since Nigel does not foresee a need to insert, delete, or rename the sheets at this time.

Other Protection Options

In an environment where several users are collaborating on a document, you can specify which users are allowed to edit certain cells or ranges. Users granted this privilege can edit these cells, even if the cell is locked and the worksheet is protected.

To enable this level of protection, you select the Allow Users to Edit Ranges command from the Protection menu. This command opens a dialog box in which you can specify the ranges that are available to a specific group of users. Figure 8-11 displays a sample dialog box in which the range B25:G25 has been made available to other users on the system. Note that to enable this feature you must be running Windows 2000 or higher.

Figure 8-11	ALLOWING USERS TO EDIT RANGES

range that can be edited by users when the sheet is protected →

Allow Users to Edit Ranges

Ranges unlocked by a password when sheet is protected:

Title	Refers to cells
New Stock Values	$B$25:$G$25

New...
Modify...
Delete

Specify who may edit the range without a password:

click to specify which users can edit the range listed above →

Permissions...

☐ Paste permissions information into a new workbook

Protect Sheet...   OK   Cancel   Apply

A final option on the Protection menu is Protect and Share Workbook. This option enables workbook protection and also enables the workbook sharing, thus turning on Excel's collaboration tools.

You've completed your work in protecting Nigel's application from errors in data entry and edits. For more information on the collaboration tools in Excel see Tutorial 7.

In the next session, you'll start working on the main feature of the application—the ability to switch between a 30-, 60-, and 90-day stock report.

Session 8.1 QUICK CHECK

1. Name two features of an Excel application.

2. How do you turn on data validation for a specified cell?

3. How do you specify an input message for a cell?

4. Describe the three types of error alert messages that Excel can display when a user violates a validation rule.

5. What is a locked cell? Under what condition is the locked property enabled?

6. What is the difference between worksheet protection and workbook protection?

7. Can you rename a protected worksheet? Explain why or why not.

SESSION 8.2

In this session, you'll learn about range names. You'll learn how to create range names and apply them to specific cells and ranges in your workbook. You'll learn how to use range names in workbook formulas and charts. Finally, you'll learn how to edit the definition of a range name.

Working with Range Names

In Nigel's report, the following statistics are displayed in the range K14:K20 of the Reporter worksheet.

- The starting and ending date of the stock history
- The starting and ending values of the stock

- The actual change and percent change between the starting and ending values
- The average volume over the course of the stock history

These values are calculated from the data stored in the History Log worksheet. The first 31 rows of the History Log display the previous 30 days of activity, the first 61 rows cover the 60-day values, and finally, the entire 91 rows of the History Log record the values from the previous 90 days. Figure 8-12 lists the formulas used to calculate the statistics of the 90-day report.

Figure 8-12	FORMULAS USED IN THE REPORTER WORKSHEET	
REPORT VALUE	CELL	90-DAY REPORT FORMULAS
Starting Date	K14	=`History Log'!A9
Ending Date	K15	=`History Log'!A2
Starting Value	K16	=`History Log'!C91
Ending Value	K17	=`History Log'!F2
Change	K18	=K17-K16
% Change	K19	=K18/K16
Average Volume (mil)	K20	=AVERAGE(`History Log'!B2:B91)

The chart on the Reporter worksheet is also based on the values stored in the History Log worksheet. One way of switching between the 30-, 60-, and 90-day reports would be to change the cell reference in each formula in the worksheet along with the chart's data source. Another approach is to use range names.

Defining a Range Name

So far in Excel you have always referred to cells by their cell references, but you can also use a range name to do the same job. A **range name** has two parts: the name assigned to the range and the definition, which is the cell reference(s) associated with the range name. For example, if the range A1:A100 contains salary data for a list of 100 employees, you can create the range name "Salary" that points to the range containing the salary data. The Salary range name can then be used in place of the range reference. To calculate the average salary, you can use the formula =AVERAGE(A1:A100) or =AVERAGE(Salary).

Range names must begin with a letter or the underscore character (_). After the first letter, any character, letter, number, or special symbol—except hyphens and spaces—is acceptable. Range names can be up to 255 characters, although short, meaningful names of 5 to 15 characters are more practical.

There are several advantages to range names. A range name is more descriptive then a cell reference, making it easier for you to interpret your formulas. Also, if you change the definition of the range name, pointing it to a different range, the value of any formula using that range name will be updated automatically to reflect the new definition. The data source of any chart that uses that range name will be similarly updated. Using range names makes creating and defining a macro easier as well.

It is this feature of range names in which Nigel is interested. He proposes that you replace the cell references with range names. Then, to switch between the 30-, 60-, and 90-day report, you only have to edit the definitions of the range names rather than each formula. Figure 8-13 lists the range names you'll create for Nigel, along with their initial definitions.

Figure 8-13   **RANGE NAMES FOR THE STOCK2 WORKBOOK**

RANGE NAME	INITIAL DEFINITION
Date	'History Log'!A2:A91
Volume	'History Log'!B2:B91
Open	'History Log'!C2:C91
High	'History Log'!D2:D91
Low	'History Log'!E2:E91
Close	'History Log'!F2:F91
Starting_Date	'History Log'!A91
Starting_Value	'History Log'!C91

REFERENCE   WINDOW   **RW**

<u>Creating a Range Name</u>
- Select the range to which you want to assign a name.
- Type the range name into the Name box on the Formula bar
  or
- Click Insert on the menu bar, point to Name, click Define, enter the name of the range in the Names in Workbook text box, click the Add button, and then click the OK button.

To create names for ranges in an Excel list:
- Click Insert on the menu bar, point to Name and then click Create.
- Specify whether to create the ranges based on the first row, last row, first column, or last column in the list.
- Click the OK button.

Excel provides several ways of creating and defining range names. The most direct is to use the Name box located to the upper-left of the worksheet grid. Try using the Name box now to create the Starting_Date range name. The Starting_Date range name will point to the first, or oldest, date value in the report. For the 90-day report, this is the date in cell A91 of the History Log worksheet.

To create the Starting_Date range name using the Name box:

1. If you took a break after the last session, make sure Excel is running and the Stock2 workbook is open. Switch to the History Log worksheet, if necessary.

2. Press Ctrl + ↓ to move to cell A91 in the History Log worksheet. The starting date for the 90-day report is 1/13/2004.

3. Click in the Name box at the far left of the Formula bar. The cell reference A91 is automatically selected.

4. Type **Starting_Date** and then press the **Enter** key. See Figure 8-14.

Figure 8-14   **CREATING A RANGE NAME WITH THE NAME BOX**

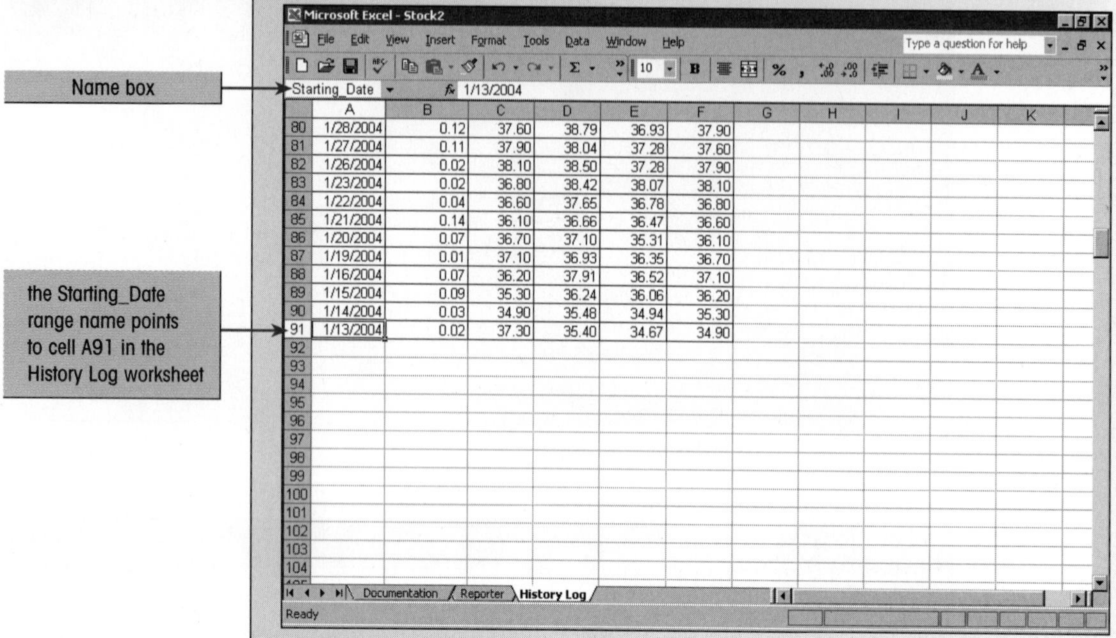

Name box

the Starting_Date
range name points
to cell A91 in the
History Log worksheet

	A	B	C	D	E	F	G	H	I	J	K
80	1/28/2004	0.12	37.60	38.79	36.93	37.90					
81	1/27/2004	0.11	37.90	38.04	37.28	37.60					
82	1/26/2004	0.02	38.10	38.50	37.28	37.90					
83	1/23/2004	0.02	36.80	38.42	38.07	38.10					
84	1/22/2004	0.04	36.60	37.65	36.78	36.80					
85	1/21/2004	0.14	36.10	36.66	36.47	36.60					
86	1/20/2004	0.07	36.70	37.10	35.31	36.10					
87	1/19/2004	0.01	37.10	36.93	36.35	36.70					
88	1/16/2004	0.07	36.20	37.91	36.52	37.10					
89	1/15/2004	0.09	35.30	36.24	36.06	36.20					
90	1/14/2004	0.03	34.90	35.48	34.94	35.30					
91	1/13/2004	0.02	37.30	35.40	34.67	34.90					

Starting_Date   ƒ 1/13/2004

Documentation / Reporter \ **History Log** /

The Name box, as the title implies, displays all of the range names in a workbook. If you want to jump to the location of a range name, you can select the name from the Name box, and the cell(s) referenced by the range name will be automatically selected. However, most of the work that you will do when creating and editing range names you will do using the Define Name dialog box. Open this dialog box now, and use it to create the Starting_Value range name. The Starting_Value range will point to the first, or oldest, stock value in the History Log worksheet. For the 90-day report, that value is stored in cell C91.

To create the Starting_Value range name using the Define Name dialog box:

1. Click cell **C91**.

2. Click **Insert** on the menu bar, point to **Name**, and then click **Define**. The Define Name dialog box opens, with a list of the range names already defined in the workbook. The cell reference of the active cell appears in the Refers to reference box.

   You will create a range name for the last value in the Open column, which is also the oldest stock value in the History Log.

3. Type **Starting_Value** in the Names in workbook text box. See Figure 8-15.

Figure 8-15	CREATING A RANGE NAME WITH THE DEFINE NAME DIALOG BOX

selected range name

range names in the workbook listed here

definition of selected range name

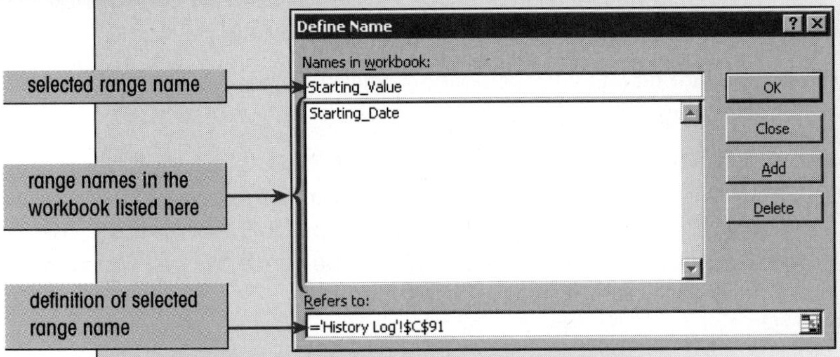

4. Click the **Add** button to add this range name to the list, and then click the **OK** button to close the dialog box.

If your data is organized in a list, you can quickly create range names for each column or row in the list by using the Create command on the Insert Name submenu. Excel will derive the range names based on the list's row or column labels. Any blanks or parentheses in the row or column labels will be changed to underscore characters (_) in the range names.

Create range names now for all of the stock values in the History Log worksheet.

To create range names based on the labels in the list:

1. Select the cell range **A1:F91**.

2. Click **Insert** on the menu bar, point to **Name**, and then click **Create**. The Create Names dialog box opens. From this dialog box you can create range names based on the labels entered into the top or bottom row of the list, or the left or right column of the list. By default, Excel will create range names based on the top row and left column labels.

3. Deselect the **Left column** check box. See Figure 8-16.

Figure 8-16	CREATING RANGE NAMES BASED ON A LIST

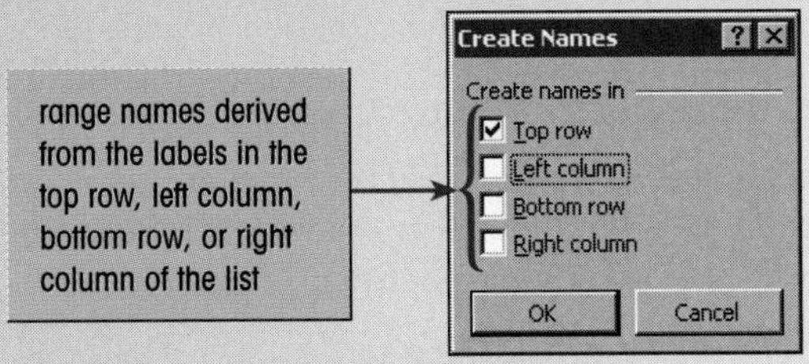

range names derived from the labels in the top row, left column, bottom row, or right column of the list

4. Click the **OK** button.

Excel creates range names from the labels in the first row of the list. To see the range names and their definitions, reopen the Define Name dialog box.

5. Click **Insert**, point to **Name**, and then click **Define**. There are now six additional range names in the workbook. Excel has derived these range names based on the labels in row 1 of the History Log worksheet.

   To learn how Excel has defined each of these new range names, you can click the range name from the list.

6. Click **Close** in the list of range names. The Close range name points to all of the closing values of the stock contained in the range F2:F91 of the History Log worksheet. See Figure 8-17. Note that the definition of the Close range name does not include the label in cell F1 because this cell was only used to derive the range name.

Figure 8-17	RANGE NAMES IN THE STOCK2 WORKBOOK

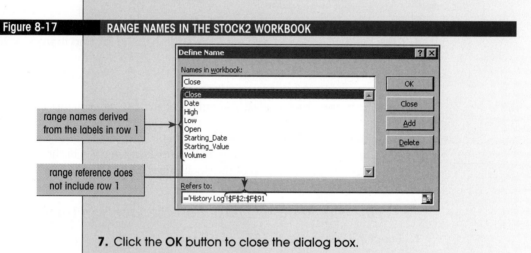

7. Click the **OK** button to close the dialog box.

Now that you've created all of the range names you need for the workbook, your next step will be to replace the cell references in the workbook with their corresponding range names.

Replacing Cell References with Range Names

Once you have created and defined the range names, you can use them in place of the cell references contained in the formulas and functions in a worksheet or workbook. You can also replace cell references used in the data series in a chart. Note that you can also replace all cell references with range names by clicking Insert on the menu bar, pointing to Name, and then clicking Apply. The limitation to this approach is that the formulas must be located on the same worksheet as the cells referenced by the range name. In the case of the stock report, the range names refer to cells on the History Log worksheet, whereas the formulas are all located on the Reporter sheet, so you cannot use this approach.

REFERENCE WINDOW   **RW**

<u>Replacing a Cell Reference with a Range Name</u>

- In a worksheet formula, replace the text for the cell reference with the text for the range name.

  or

- If the cell reference and range name definition both lie in the same worksheet, click Insert on the menu bar, point to Name, and then click Apply.
- Select the range names you want to apply from the Apply names list box, and click the OK button.

  or

- For cell references in charts, preface the range name with the name of the workbook, separated by an exclamation point (!).

There are two locations in the workbook in which you'll need to replace the cell reference with the range name: in the statistics section of the Reporter worksheet and in the data source for the embedded stock history chart.

To insert range names in the Reporter worksheet:

1. Switch to the Reporter worksheet.

2. Click cell **K14**. The current formula in this cell is = *'History Log'!A91*.

3. Replace the existing formula with the new formula **=Starting_Date**, and then press the **Enter** key.

4. Click cell **K16**, replace the formula with the new formula **=Starting_Value**, and then press the **Enter** key.

5. Click cell **K20**, replace the formula with the new formula **=AVERAGE(Volume)**, and then press the **Enter** key.

Now you'll replace the cell references in the embedded chart with range names. The syntax is slightly different in a chart. In the worksheet, you can simply type in the range name. However, in an embedded chart, a range name *must* be prefaced by the name of the workbook, regardless of what worksheet the range is located. For example, to reference the closing stock values in a chart, you cannot use *=Close*. Instead, you must use *=Stock2.xls!Close*.

The stock history chart displays the opening, closing, high, and low daily values of the stock. You need to replace these cell references, as well as the cell reference for the date, with the range names you created.

To insert range names in the chart's data series:

1. Click the embedded chart on the Reporter worksheet, click **Chart** on the menu bar, and then click **Source Data**. The Source Data dialog box opens.

2. If necessary, click the **Series** tab to display the list of data series in the chart.

3. Make sure **Volume** is displayed in the Series list box.

   First you'll replace the cell reference to the date values with the Date range name. In this chart, the date values are displayed on the chart's two x-axes.

4. Click the **Category (X) axis labels** reference box, and then replace the cell reference with the range name reference **=Stock2.xls!Date**. Note that you have included the workbook name.

   TROUBLE? The best way to replace the cell reference with the range name reference is to highlight the entire cell reference, press the Delete key on your keyboard, and then type the range name in the reference box.

5. Click the **Second category (X) axis labels** reference box, and replace the cell reference with the range name reference **=Stock2.xls!Date**. The date values for the chart data source now use the Date range name you specified.

   Now you'll replace the cell references for each of the five data series in the chart. The value for each series corresponds with the values from the History Log worksheet.

6. With Volume already selected in the Series list box, click the **Values** reference box, and then replace the cell reference with the range name reference **=Stock2.xls!Volume**. Figure 8-18 shows the revised Source Data dialog box.

Figure 8-18	USING RANGE NAMES IN A CHART

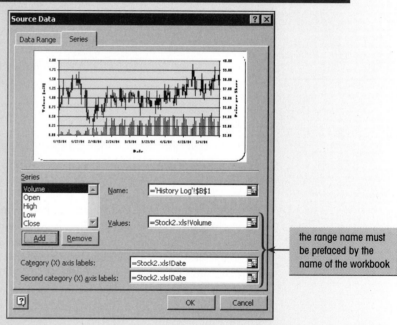

the range name must be prefaced by the name of the workbook

   TROUBLE? You don't have to change the reference in the Name box, because the cell reference points to the label contained in cell B1 of the History Log worksheet.

7. Click **Open** in the Series list box, and then replace the cell reference in the Values reference box with **=Stock2.xls!Open**.

   Continue to replace the cell references for the High, Low, and Close data series with their range name references.

8. Change the Values reference for the **High** data series to **=Stock2.xls!High**. Change the Values reference for the **Low** data series to **=Stock2.xls!Low**, and change the Values reference for the **Close** data series to **=Stock2.xls!Close**.

> TROUBLE? If you inadvertently close the Source Data dialog box by pressing the Enter key after typing a range name reference, just reopen the dialog box. The information you already entered will have been retained.

9. Click the **OK** button.

Changing a Range Name Definition

With all of the range names now in place, you're ready to test the range name feature. Nigel proposes that you switch to a 60-day report. Rather than editing the formulas and the chart, you can switch the report by changing the definitions of the eight range names so that they point to the last 60 days worth of stock market data (contained in the values up to row 61 in the History Log worksheet), rather than to the last 90 days.

To edit the range names definitions:

1. Click cell **A1** of the Reporter worksheet to deselect the chart.

2. Click **Insert** on the menu bar, point to **Name**, and then click **Define**. The Define Name dialog box opens.

3. Click **Close** in the list of range names, click in the Refers to reference box, and then change the cell reference to ='History Log'!$F$2:$F$61. Note that you need only change the number 9 to a 6 (that is, change from 90 days to 60 days).

4. Click the **Add** button.

> TROUBLE? If you pressed the Enter key by mistake, the Define Name dialog box closed. Reopen the dialog box, and then continue with Step 5.

5. Click **Date** in the list of range names, change its definition to ='History Log'!$A$2:$A$61, and then click the **Add** button.

6. Replace the definitions of the remaining six range names as follows, clicking the **Add** button each time:

High	='History Log'!$D$2:$D$61
Low	='History Log'!$E$2:$E$61
Open	='History Log'!$C$2:$C$61
Starting_Date	='History Log'!$A$61
Starting_Value	='History Log'!$C$61
Volume	='History Log'!$B$2:$B$61

> TROUBLE? If you make a mistake when changing a definition, do not click the Add button. Instead, click the range name again, type the new definition, and then click the Add button.

7. Click the **OK** button to close the Define Name dialog box.

8. Click cell **I13**, change the text to **60-day Statistics**, and press the **Enter** key. The Reporter worksheet now displays the 60-day statistics and chart. See Figure 8-19.

Figure 8-19	60-DAY REPORT

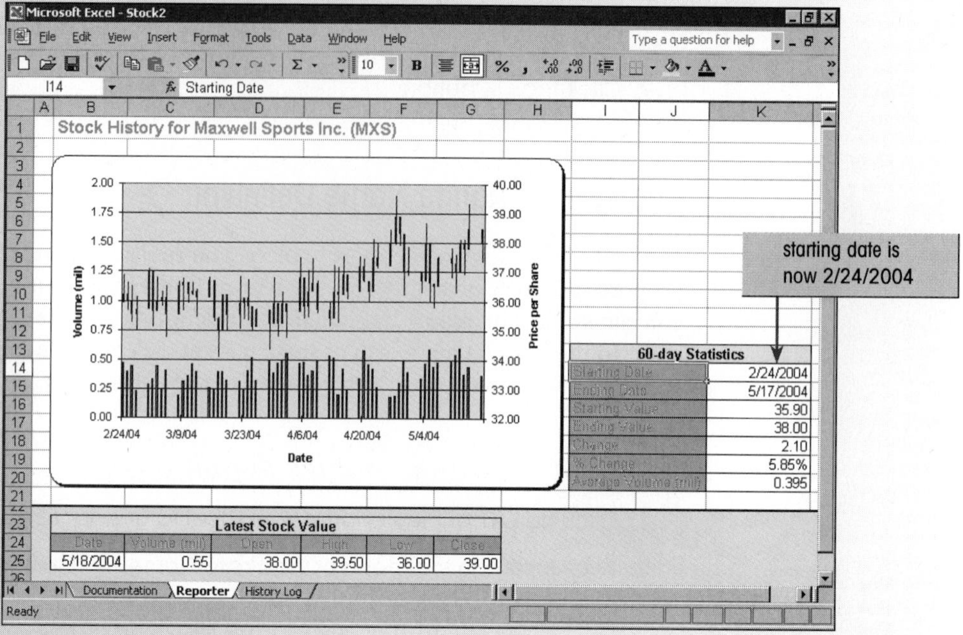

starting date is now 2/24/2004

You can save the workbook and then exit Excel.

9. Click the **Save** button 🖫 on the Standard toolbar to save your changes.

10. Click the **Close** button ✕ on the title bar.

Editing the range names has simplified the process of switching to a 60-day report, because you only have to work with a single dialog box, rather than several formulas and an embedded chart. However Nigel wonders whether that much has been gained, since there is still a lot of typing involved in switching all of the range name definitions. He wants this application to be fast and easy to use, and changing the range name definitions will be a cumbersome process for some users and prone to errors.

But you're not finished working with this Excel application, and in the next session, you'll learn how to save all of the keystrokes used in changing the range name definitions, and then you'll learn how to replay those keystrokes with a single keystroke or click of a button.

Session 8.2 QUICK CHECK

1. What is a range name? Give two advantages of using range names in your workbooks.

2. Describe three ways of creating a range name.

3. Which of the following (are) valid range names?
   a. Annual_Total
   b. 3rdQtr
   c. Annual total

4. To quickly go to the cell referenced by a range name, you can select the range name from the _____.

5. In the Report.xls workbook, the Sales range name refers to a list of sales figures stored in the range B2:B100. Currently the total sales figures are calculated with the formula =SUM(B2:B100). What would a formula using the range name look like?

6. The Report.xls workbook also contains a chart of sales data. What would a data source that uses the Sales range name look like?

SESSION 8.3

In this session, you'll complete the Excel application by recording a set of macros used to switch between the 30-, 60-, and 90-day reports. You'll also create a macro to insert new stock values into the History Log worksheet. You'll learn how to run these macros using both keyboard shortcuts and macro buttons. You'll also be introduced to the Visual Basic Editor, and finally, you'll learn how to edit and print macro code.

Working with Macros

At the end of the last session, you were able to present Nigel with a method of switching between the 30-, 60-, and 90-day reports by modifying range name definitions rather than formulas and charts. Nigel saw the value of using range names, but was concerned about the amount of retyping that users would be required to do. Nigel would like some way of recording those actions so that users can rerun the steps without having to do all of the retyping. You suggest using a macro. A **macro** is an action or set of actions used to automate tasks. For example, a macro can be created to print a worksheet, automatically insert a set of dates and values, or in Nigel's case, automatically change the definitions of a collection of range names. Macros carry out repetitive tasks more quickly than you can, and once the macro has been created, you don't have worry about mistakes that may occur from simple retyping errors.

Protecting Yourself Against Macro Viruses

In the last few years, many viruses have been attached as macros to documents created in Office programs, such as Excel. Unsuspecting users open these infected workbooks, and Excel automatically runs the attached virus-infected macro. For this reason, one must use caution when opening a workbook that has a macro attached to it. You should make sure that the workbook comes from a trusted source and that the macro was inserted by a colleague or friend.

Before you can start the process of creating macros for Nigel's application, you have to define how Excel will treat the macros it encounters in open workbooks. Excel provides two safeguards against macro viruses: digital certificates and security levels.

Working with Digital Certificates

A **digital certificate** is a file attachment that vouches for authenticity of the macro. You can obtain digital certificates from a commercial certification authority such as VeriSign Inc., or in some cases, from your system administrator. Each certificate should contain a **digital signature**, which confirms that the macro or document created by the signer has not been altered since the digital certificate was created. Your operating system stores a list of known and trusted digital certificates and signatures, so you can always be assured that the files you receive come from legitimate sources.

Macros should be signed and certified only after the file has been tested and is ready for distribution to other users, because whenever you modify a signed file, the digital signature is removed. Excel will treat a digital certificate lacking a digital signature as a possible macro virus. The combination of a valid digital certificate and signature ensures that the macro has been created by you and has not been altered by anyone else.

Setting the Security Level

You control how Excel handles suspect macros by setting Excel's **security level**. Excel supports three levels of security: high, medium, and low.

A high security level causes Excel to disable all macros either lacking a digital signature or containing an invalid digital signature. If the macro contains a valid signature from an unknown author, the user will be prompted as to whether or not to enable the macro. If the macro contains a valid signature from a known and trusted source, Excel will open the workbook and automatically enable the macro.

At a medium security level, Excel prompts the user as to whether or not to enable macros that lack a digital signature. Certificates with invalid signatures are still automatically disabled. Macros containing a valid signature are automatically enabled.

At the low security level, all macros are automatically enabled regardless of the status of the digital signature.

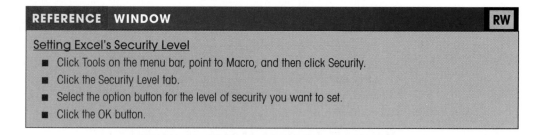

Nigel does not have access to a digital certificate, so he can't set Excel's security level to high. He does not want to set Excel's security level to low because he still wants some protection against macro viruses. Nigel suggests that you set the security level to medium, which will still allow him to open files containing macros, but may warn him of possible macro viruses.

To set Excel's security level:

1. If you took a break after the last session, make sure Excel is running. Note that you do not have to open a workbook. The security level works in conjunction with the Excel program itself.

2. Click **Tools** on the menu bar, point to **Macro**, and then click **Security**.

3. If necessary, click the **Security Level** tab.

4. Click the **Medium** option button, as shown in Figure 8-20, if necessary.

Figure 8-20	SETTING THE SECURITY LEVEL IN EXCEL

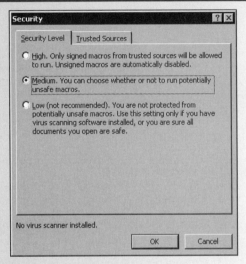

5. Click the **OK** button. Security for the Excel application has been set to medium. The next time you open a file that contains a macro lacking a digital signature, Excel will prompt you to disable or enable the macro.

Now that you've set Excel's security level, you are ready to begin creating Nigel's macros.

Recording **and Running a Macro**

You can create an Excel macro in one of two ways: You can use a macro recorder to record your keystrokes and mouse actions as you perform them, or you can write your own macros by entering a series of commands in the **Visual Basic for Applications (VBA)** programming language.

For new users, it's easiest to create a macro using the macro recorder. However, the recorder is limited to those actions you can perform from the keyboard or the Excel menus; thus for more sophisticated applications, writing the code directly into the macro application is a better choice.

For Nigel's application, the tasks you need to perform can all be done from the keyboard and the Excel menus. There are four macros you need to create: three that will be used to switch between the 30-, 60-, and 90-day reports, and the fourth will be used to enter new data into the History Log worksheet.

You'll start by recording the macro that displays the 30-day report. As with most complex projects, you need to plan your macro. Decide what you want to accomplish and the best way to go about it. If possible, you should practice the keystrokes or mouse actions before you actually record the macro. This may seem like extra work, but it reduces the chances of error when you actually record the macro.

REFERENCE WINDOW **RW**

Recording a Macro

- Click Tools on the menu bar, point to Macro, and then click Record New Macro.
- Enter a name for the macro, and specify the location in which you want to store the macro.
- Specify a shortcut key (optional).
- Enter a description of the macro (optional).
- Click the OK button to start the macro recorder.
- Perform the tasks you want the macro to automate.
- Click the Stop Recording button on the Stop Recording toolbar (or click Tools, point to Macro, and then click Stop Recording).

After discussing the macro with Nigel, you outline the actions you need to perform. These are:

1. Unprotect the Reporter worksheet.

2. Change the definition of each range name to point to the previous 30 days of stock market data.

3. Change the title in cell I13 to "30-day Statistics".

4. Set the protection for the Reporter worksheet again.

Note that the first and last actions involve turning off and on the worksheet protection. Recall that Nigel wants the workbook to be protected to keep other users from making changes to it. Currently the worksheets are not protected because in the last session you were still editing their contents, so you'll need to enable worksheet protection before recording the macro. There are other factors to consider when creating a macro.

Each macro must have a unique name. You can choose to create a shortcut key that will run the macro directly from the keyboard. You can provide a description of the macro that is being recorded. Finally, a macro needs to be stored somewhere. There are three options. By default, the macro is stored in the current workbook, making the macro available only to the workbook when it is open. Another option is to store the macro in the **Personal Macro workbook**. This is a hidden workbook opened whenever you start Excel, making the macro available anytime you use Excel. Finally, you can store the macro in a new workbook. Remember that the new workbook you create must be opened whenever you want to use the macro. For Nigel's application, you'll store the macro in the Stock2 workbook.

To begin the macro recorder:

1. If necessary, reopen the **Stock2** workbook, and switch to the Reporter worksheet.

2. Click **Tools** on the menu bar, point to **Protection**, and then click **Protect Sheet**.

3. Make sure that the ability to select locked and unlocked cells are the only options selected in the list box, and then click the **OK** button.

   Now you'll start the macro recorder.

4. Click **Tools** on the menu bar, point to **Macro**, and then click **Record New Macro**. Excel proposes a default name for the macro. The default name consists of the word "Macro" and a number one greater than the number of macros already recorded in the workbook in the current session.

   You need to change the default name to something that describes the purpose of the macro.

5. Type **Report30** in the Macro name text box, and then press the **Tab** key.

   Next you can specify a shortcut key combination to run the macro automatically from the keyboard. Nigel suggests that the Report30 macro be run whenever the user presses the Ctrl key plus the letter *a*.

6. Type **a** in the Shortcut key text box, and then press the **Tab** key twice. Note that "This Workbook" is the option displayed in the Store macro in list box.

   The final text box provides a space where you can enter a description of the macro. The default description indicates the date the macro is being recorded and the name of the macro author. Add an additional comment to this description.

7. Press the → key (or click at the of the default description within the Description text box), type **.** (a period) to end the statement, and then press the **Enter** key to start a new line.

8. Type **Generates a report of stock values for the last 30 days.** Figure 8-21 shows the completed Record Macro dialog box.

Figure 8-21	RECORDING THE REPORT30 MACRO

macro name → Macro name: Report30

user can press Ctrl + a to run the macro from the keyboard → Shortcut key: Ctrl+ a

Store macro in: This Workbook ← the macro will be stored as part of the Stock2 workbook

macro description → Description: Macro recorded 5/28/04 by Nigel Turner. Generates a report of stock values for the last 30 days.

9. Click the **OK** button to start recording the macro. A toolbar appears and the word "Recording" appears in the status bar.

   TROUBLE? Don't worry if the toolbar does not appear. It may have been closed in a previous Excel session.

You are now working in macro record mode. When Excel is in macro record mode, the Stop Recording toolbar appears in the workbook window. This toolbar contains two buttons: the Stop Recording button ■ and the Relative Reference button ▦. The Relative Reference button controls how Excel records the act of selecting a cell range in the worksheet. By default, the macro will select the same cells regardless of which cell is first selected because the macro records a selection using absolute cell references. If you want a macro to select cells regardless of the position of the active cell when you run the macro, set the macro recorder to record relative cell references. In this macro, you'll want to use the default absolute cell references, so you'll leave this button unchanged. Once you are finished recording your keystrokes, you will click the Stop Recording button.

You are now ready to record the actions of the Report30 macro. Every command and action you perform will be recorded and stored in the Report30 macro. For that reason it's very important that you follow the instructions below precisely. You'll start by removing the protection from the Reporter worksheet.

To record the Report30 macro:

1. Click **Tools** on the menu bar, point to **Protection**, and then click **Unprotect Sheet**.

   Now you'll change the definitions of all the range names so that they cover only the last 30 days of stock activity. You'll follow the same process you used in the last session when you changed the range names to refer to the previous 60 days.

2. Click **Insert** on the menu bar, point to **Name**, and then click **Define**.

3. Click **Close** in the list of range names, and then change the definition of the range name to ='History Log'!$F$2:$F$31. Note that you only have to change the number 6 to the number 3.

4. Click the **Add** button.

5. **Click** Date **in the list of range names, change its definition to** ='History Log'!$A$2:$A$31, and then click the **Add** button.

6. Replace the definitions of the remaining six range names as follows, clicking the **Add** button each time:

High	='History Log'!$D$2:$D$31
Low	='History Log'!$E$2:$E$31
Open	='History Log'!$C$2:$C$31
Starting_Date	='History Log'!$A$31
Starting_Value	='History Log'!$C$31
Volume	='History Log'!$B$2:$B$31

7. Click each range name to confirm that the definition now points to only the last 30 days of stock activity.

   TROUBLE? If any of the definitions are incorrect, click the range name in the list box, correct the definition, and then click the Add button.

8. Click the **OK** button to close the Define Name dialog box.

   Next you'll change the text of cell I13.

9. Click cell I13, type **30-day Statistics**, and then press the **Enter** key.

Finally, you'll reset the protection for the Reporter worksheet.

10. Click **Tools**, point to **Protection**, click **Protect Sheet**, and then click the **OK** button to enable worksheet protection.

11. Click the **Stop Recording** button on the Stop Recording toolbar to stop the macro recorder.

TROUBLE? If the Stop Recording toolbar does not appear on your screen, click Tools, point to Macro, and then click Stop Recording.

Figure 8-22 shows the 30-day report on the Maxwell Sports Inc. stock.

Figure 8-22	30-DAY REPORT

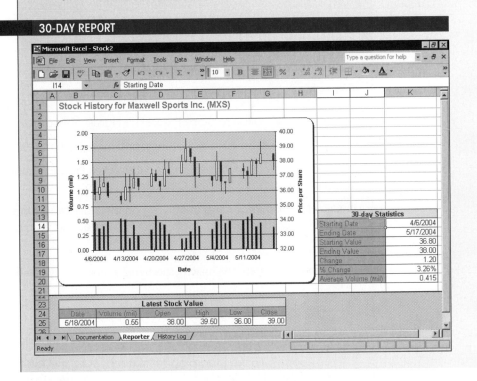

Next, you'll record the actions for the 60-day report. The steps will be the same, except that now you'll change the range name definitions to cover the last 60 days of stock activity. For this macro, you'll specify the Ctrl + b shortcut key.

To record the Report60 macro:

1. Click **Tools** on the menu bar, point to **Macro**, and then click **Record New Macro**.

2. Type **Report60** in the Macro name box, press the **Tab** key, type **b** in the Shortcut key text box, press the **Tab** key twice, and then click to position the insertion point at the end of the default description text.

3. Type **.** (a period) at the end of the description of the macro, press the **Enter** key, and type **Generates a report of stock values for the last 60 days.**, and then click the **OK** button.

4. Click **Tools**, point to **Protection**, and then click **Unprotect Sheet** to disable worksheet protection.

5. Click **Insert** on the menu bar, point to **Name**, and then click **Define** to open the Define Name dialog box.

6. Change the definitions of the eight range names as follows, clicking the **Add** button after each change:

Close	='History Log'!$F$2:$F$61
Date	='History Log'!$A$2:$A$61
High	='History Log'!$D$2:$D$61
Low	='History Log'!$E$2:$E$61
Open	='History Log'!$C$2:$C$61
Starting_Date	='History Log'!$A$61
Starting_Value	='History Log'!$C$61
Volume	='History Log'!$B$2:$B$61

7. Click the **OK** button to close the Define Name dialog box.

8. Click cell I13, type **60-day Statistics**, and then press the **Enter** key.

9. Click **Tools**, point to **Protection**, and then click **Protect Sheet** to open the Protect Sheet dialog box. Click the **OK** button.

10. Click the **Stop Recording** button ▣ on the Stop Recording toolbar to stop the macro recorder (or click Tools, point to Macro, and then click Stop Recording).

Finally, record the Report90 macro, specifying a shortcut key combination of Ctrl + c to run it.

To record the Report90 macro:

1. Click **Tools** on the menu bar, point to **Macro**, and then click **Record New Macro**.

2. Type **Report90** in the Macro name text box. Press the **Tab** key, and then type **c** in the Shortcut key text box. Press the **Tab** key twice. Append a period to the default description of the macro, press the **Enter** key, and then add the sentence **Generates a report of stock values for the last 90 days**. Click the OK button.

3. Click **Tools**, point to **Protection**, and then click **Unprotect Sheet** to disable worksheet protection.

4. Click **Insert** on the menu bar, point to **Name**, and then click **Define** to open the Define Name dialog box.

5. Change the definitions of the eight range names as follows, clicking the **Add** button after each change:

Close	='History Log'!$F$2:$F$91
Date	='History Log'!$A$2:$A$91
High	='History Log'!$D$2:$D$91
Low	='History Log'!$E$2:$E$91
Open	='History Log'!$C$2:$C$91
Starting_Date	='History Log'!$A$91
Starting_Value	='History Log'!$C$91
Volume	='History Log'!$B$2:$B$91

6. Click the **OK** button.

7. Click cell I13, type **90-day Statistics**, and then press the **Enter** key.

8. Click **Tools**, point to **Protection**, and then click **Protect Sheet**. Click the **OK** button to enable the worksheet protection.

9. Click the **Stop Recording** button ▣ on the Stop Recording toolbar to stop the macro recorder (or click Tools, point to Macro; and then click Stop Recording).

You've completed the recording of the three report macros now its time to test whether they work or not.

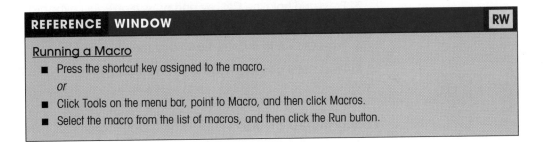

Running a Macro

There are two ways of running the report macros you created. One is to use the shortcut key you specified for each report; the other is to select the Run command in the Macro dialog box. You'll try both methods in the set of steps that follow.

To run the three report macros:

1. Click **Tools** on the menu bar, point to **Macro**, and then click **Macros**. The Macro dialog box opens, as shown in Figure 8-23. This dialog box lists all of the macros available to you in the current session. From here you can run a specific macro, or if you know the VBA programming language, you can edit the macro. You can also run the macro one step at a time, a useful feature if you're trying to fix a problem in your macro and need to slow it down to see where the problem occurs. You can also delete a macro if you discover that it is not working properly. At this point, you'll run the Report30 macro.

Figure 8-23   THE THREE REPORT MACROS

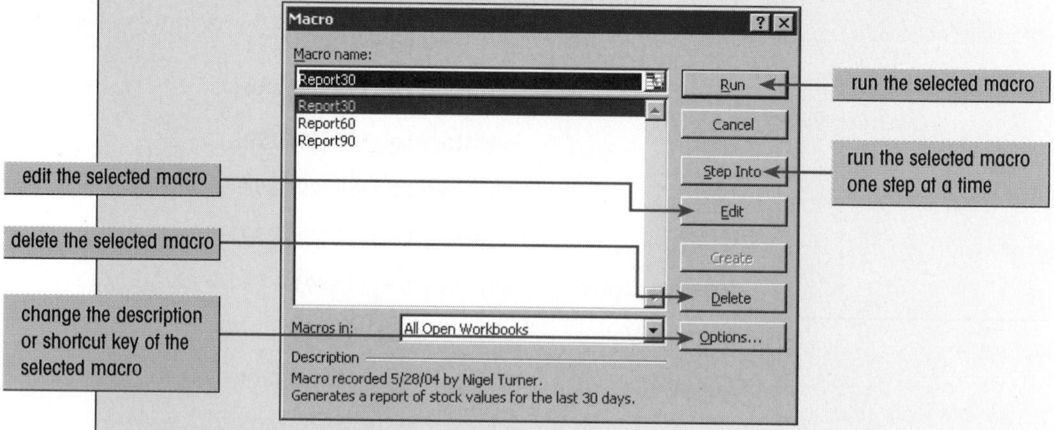

run the selected macro

run the selected macro one step at a time

edit the selected macro

delete the selected macro

change the description or shortcut key of the selected macro

2. Verify that **Report30** is highlighted in the list of macros, and then click the **Run** button. The Report30 macro runs, changing the statistics on the Reporter worksheet and updating the chart.

TROUBLE? If the Report30 macro did not run properly, you might have made a mistake in recording it. For now, continue with Step 3. You will learn how to test and fix your macro next in this session.

Now test the shortcut keys you specified for the other two macros. Recall that the Ctrl + a combination runs the 30-day report, the Ctrl + b combination runs the 60-day report, and the Ctrl + c combination displays the 90-day values.

3. Press and hold the **Ctrl** key and press **b** on your keyboard. The Report60 macro runs and the 60-day report is displayed with the updated chart.

4. Press **Ctrl + c** to display the 90-day report.

5. Press **Ctrl + a** to return to the 30-day report.

Fixing Macro Errors

Hopefully, all three of the macros you recorded worked correctly. If any of the macros did not work correctly, you can fix the macro. You will also find that sometimes a mistake is made in the macro recording that is not discovered until later. In either case, you have the following options for fixing an error that might have been created:

■ Rerecord the macro using the same macro name.

■ Delete the recorded macro, and then record the macro again.

■ Run the macro one step at a time in order to locate the source of the problem.

■ Edit the macro by accessing the VBA code in the Visual Basic Editor (requires your understanding VBA).

You can delete or edit the macro by opening the Macro dialog box (shown earlier in Figure 8-23), selecting the macro from the list, and then clicking the appropriate button. To rerecord the macro, simply restart the macro recorder, and enter the same macro name you used earlier. Excel will overwrite the previous version. If you have to reopen the Stock2 workbook, you will be prompted to enable the macros you've created. You should click the Enable Macros button to open the workbook and enable the macros.

Creating the NewData Macro

There is one more macro that you need to record. Earlier you typed the latest stock values into the Reporter worksheet, but these values were never added to the History Log sheet. The macro that you'll create will fix that problem. Nigel does not want this workbook to become too large as new stock values are added each day, so he has decided to limit the record to only the last 90 days. Thus, you will have to overwrite the oldest set of values as you insert the new ones. The actions of this macro will then be as follows:

1. Unprotect the History Log worksheet.

2. Copy the values in the range A2:F90 of the History Log worksheet.

3. Paste the values into the range A3:F91, thus deleting the oldest values in the list.

4. Copy the values in the range B25:G25 of the Reporter worksheet.

5. Paste the values into the range A2:F2 on the History Log worksheet, thus inserting the newest values at the top of the list.

6. Reset protection on the History Log worksheet.

7. Return to the Reporter worksheet.

Nigel wants you to name this new macro "NewData". You'll assign the shortcut key Ctrl + d. Because this macro will actually be changing values in the workbook, you'll save the file before running the macro. If you make a mistake, you can go back to the saved version and start over. Before you record the macro, you will enable worksheet protection again for the History Log sheet.

To record the NewData macro:

1. Click the **Save** button 🖫 on the Standard toolbar.

2. Click the **History Log** tab, click **Tools** on the menu bar, point to **Protection**, click **Protect Sheet**, and then click the **OK** button.

3. Click the **Reporter** tab, click **Tools** on the menu bar, point to **Macro**, and then click **Record New Macro**.

4. Type **NewData** in the Macro name box, press the **Tab** key, and then type the letter **d**. Press the **Tab** key twice, type **.** (a period), press the **Enter** key, type **Inserts new data into the History Log.**, and then click the **OK** button.

5. Click the **History Log** tab, click **Tools**, point to **Protection**, and then click **Unprotect Sheet** to remove the worksheet protection.

   Next you will copy the existing values in rows 2 through 90. You do not want to select row 91. When you paste the values, the oldest value (which is in row 91) will be deleted.

6. Select the range **A2:F90** (do *not* select row 91 of the worksheet).

7. Click the **Copy** button 🖺 on the Standard toolbar.

   Now you will paste the selection, beginning in row 3, moving all the values down one row.

8. Press the ↓ key to select cell A3, and then click the **Paste** button 📋 on the Standard toolbar.

Now you need to return to the Reporter worksheet so you can copy the new set of data values, which have been entered into the range B25:G25, but have not been entered into the History Log worksheet.

9. Click the **Reporter** tab, select the range **B25:G25**, and then click 📋.

To update the History Log with the latest stock values, you need to return to the History Log sheet and paste these new values in row 2.

10. Click the **History Log** tab, press the ↑ key to select cell A2, click 📋, and press the ↑ key to remove the selection.

Finally, enable worksheet protection and return to the Reporter worksheet.

11. Click **Tools**, point to **Protection**, click **Protect Sheet**, and then click the **OK** button.

12. Click the **Reporter** tab and click cell **A1** to remove the selection.

13. Click the **Stop Recording** button 🔲 on the Stop Recording toolbar (or click Stop Recording on the Tools Macro submenu). Figure 8-24 shows the new 30-day report with the latest data value inserted into the chart and statistics.

Figure 8-24	REPORTER WORKSHEET AFTER INSERTING THE NEW DATA VALUES

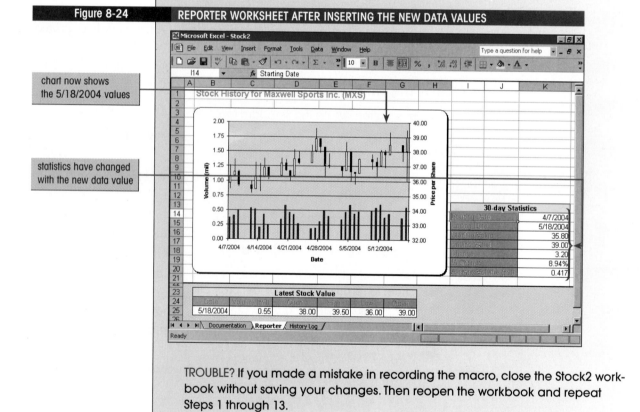

chart now shows the 5/18/2004 values

statistics have changed with the new data value

TROUBLE? If you made a mistake in recording the macro, close the Stock2 workbook without saving your changes. Then reopen the workbook and repeat Steps 1 through 13.

Nigel has some new stock market data to add to his worksheet. This is a good opportunity to test the NewData macro.

To test the NewData macro:

1. Click cell **B25**, type **5/19/2004**, and then press the **Tab** key.

2. Type **0.72** for the volume of shares traded, and then press the **Tab** key.

3. Enter an opening value for the stock of **39**, a high value of **39.5**, a low value of **36**, and a closing value of **36.8**. Make sure you press the Enter or Tab key after typing the closing value.

4. Press **Ctrl + d** to run the NewData macro, which inserts the new data into the History Log and updates the chart and statistics. See Figure 8-25.

Figure 8-25	REPORTER WORKSHEET AFTER INSERTING THE 5/19/2004 VALUES

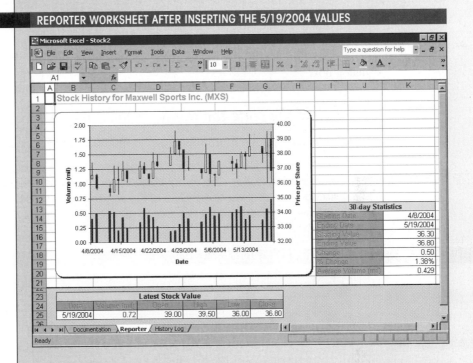

TROUBLE? If the macro fails to run correctly, close the Stock2 workbook without saving your changes. Reopen the Stock2 workbook and attempt to rerecord the NewData macro following the steps described earlier.

Nigel watches the operation of the NewData macro, and he's concerned about a flurry of activity that occurs when the macro is running as it switches from one worksheet to another, copying and pasting values. He thinks that this might be disconcerting to some users. Is there a way of hiding the actions of the macro as it runs through the recorded steps?

Working **with the Macro Editor**

You discuss Nigel's problem with Cindy Dean, who is a programmer at Harris & Burton. She tells you that there is no way of hiding the intermediate steps using only the macro recorder, but hiding steps can be done with two simple VBA commands. Even though you're not a VBA programmer and don't have the time to learn the language, you realize that this would be an opportunity to "peak under the hood" at Excel's macro capability, so you agree to try to edit the macro following Cindy's instructions.

REFERENCE   WINDOW   `RW`

Editing a Macro
- Click Tools on the menu bar, point to Macro, and then click Macros.
- Select the macro in the list, and then click the Edit button.
- Use the Visual Basic Editor to edit the macro code.
- To print the macro code, click File on the menu bar, click Print, select the item to print and other print-related options, and then click the OK button.
- Click File on the menu bar, and then click Close and Return to Microsoft Excel.

To view the code of the NewData macro, you need to open the **Visual Basic Editor**, a separate application that works with Excel and all of the Office products to edit and manage VBA code. Cindy tells you that you can access the Visual Basic Editor through the Macro dialog box.

To view the code for the NewData macro:

1. Click **Tools** on the menu bar, point to **Macro**, and then click **Macros**.

2. Verify that the **NewData** macro is highlighted in the list of macros, and then click the **Edit** button. The Visual Basic Editor opens as a separate program, consisting of several windows. One of the windows, the Code window, contains the VBA code generated by the macro recorder. See Figure 8-26.

Figure 8-26	**THE VISUAL BASIC EDITOR**

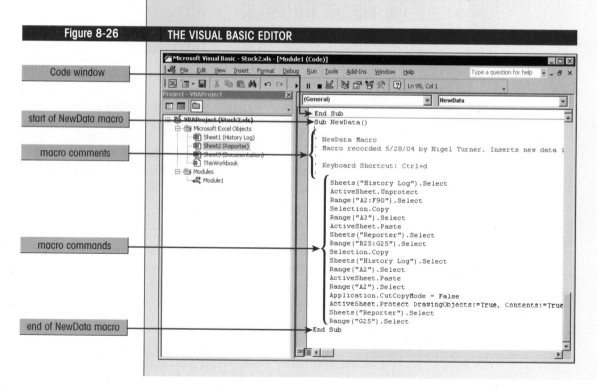

> **TROUBLE?** The number of windows and their content will vary depending on how your system is configured. At this point, you can ignore all other windows aside from the Code window. Also depending on how you recorded the macros and whether you had to close and reopen the Stock2 workbook in the process, you may see more than one module listed in the window at the left.
>
> **3.** If the Code window is not maximized in the editor, click the **Maximize** button ☐ on the Code window title bar.

Learning to interpret and write VBA code is a subject worthy of its own book. At this point, you'll just cover what you need to know to make Cindy's recommended changes.

Understanding the Structure of Macros

The VBA code shown in the Code window lists all of the actions you performed in recording the NewData macro. In VBA, macros are called **sub procedures**. Each sub procedure begins with the keyword "Sub" followed by the name of the sub procedure and a set of parentheses. In this example, the code begins with *Sub NewData()*, which provides the name of this sub procedure "NewData"—the same name you gave the macro. The parentheses are used if you want to include any arguments in the procedure. These arguments that pass information to the sub procedure have roughly the same purpose as the arguments used in an Excel function.

If you write your own VBA code, sub procedure arguments are an important part of the programming process, but they are not used when you create macros with the macro recorder.

Following the Sub NewData() statement, are **comments** about the macro, taken from the description you entered earlier in the Record New Macro dialog box. Note that each line appears in green and is prefaced with an apostrophe ('). This indicates that the line is a comment and does not include any actions that need to be performed by Excel.

After the comments, is the **body** of the macro, a listing of all of the commands performed by the NewData macro as written in the language of VBA. Your list of commands might look slightly different, depending on the exact actions you performed when recording the macro. Even though you might not know VBA, some of the commands are easy to interpret. Near the top of the NewData macro, you should see the command *Sheets("History Log").Select*, which is a command that tells Excel to select the History Log worksheet, making it the active sheet in the workbook. The next command *ActiveSheet.Unprotect* removes worksheet protection from the active sheet, in this case the History Log sheet. At the bottom of the macro, is the statement *End Sub*, which indicates the end of the NewData sub procedure.

A Code window can contain several sub procedures, with each procedure separated from the others by the Sub *ProcedureName*() statement at the beginning, and the *End Sub* statement at the end. Sub procedures are organized into **modules**. As shown in Figure 8-26, all of the macros that Nigel recorded have been stored in the Module1 module (your window may differ).

Writing a Macro Command

Cindy wants you to insert two commands into the NewData sub procedure to hide the actions of the macro as it runs. The first command, which needs to be inserted directly after the Sub NewData() statement, is *Application.ScreenUpdating = False*. This command turns *off* Excel's screen updating feature, keeping any actions that run in the macro from being displayed on the screen. The second command, which needs to be inserted directly before the End Sub statement is *Application.ScreenUpdating = True*. This command turns Excel's screen update feature back on, enabling the user to see the final results of the macro after it has completed running.

You have to copy these commands exactly. VBA will not be able to run a command if you mistype a word or omit part of the statement. The Visual Basic Editor does provide tools to assist you in writing error-free code. As you type a command, the editor will provide pop-up windows and text to help you insert the correct code. Try inserting these new commands now.

To insert the new commands into the macro:

1. Click the end of the Sub NewData () statement, and then press the **Enter** key. A new blank line appears under the statement.

2. Type **Application.** (make sure you include the period but do not insert a space in the command). The editor displays a list box with a selection of possible keywords you could type at this point in the command. You can either scroll down the list or continue typing the command yourself. You'll continue typing.

3. Type **ScreenUpdating=**. Note that as you type the command another list box appears, and once you type the equal sign, the editor prompts you with two possible choices: False or True.

4. Type **False** in order to turn off the screen updating feature of Excel, and then press the **Enter** key. Figure 8-27 shows the new command inserted into the sub procedure.

Figure 8-27	TURNING OFF SCREEN UPDATING IN THE NEWDATA MACRO

insert this line at the beginning of the macro →

```
Sub NewData()
Application.ScreenUpdating = False


'
' NewData Macro
' Macro recorded 5/28/04 by Nigel Turner. Inserts new data i
'
' Keyboard Shortcut: Ctrl+d
'
    Sheets("History Log").Select
```

Next you'll insert a command at the end of the sub procedure to turn screen updating back on.

5. If necessary, drag the Code window's **vertical scroll bar** down to view the end of the NewData sub procedure.

6. Click at the beginning of the End Sub statement to position the insertion point, and then press the **Enter** key. A new blank line appears above the End Sub statement.

7. Press the ↑ key to move the insertion point up into the new blank line.

8. Type **Application.ScreenUpdating=True** and then press the **Enter** key. Note that once again the editor displayed list boxes to assist you in typing the command. The new command appears as shown in Figure 8-28.

Figure 8-28	TURNING ON SCREEN UPDATING IN THE NEWDATA MACRO

insert this line at the end of the macro →

```
    Sheets("Reporter").Select
    Range("G25").Select
Application.ScreenUpdating = True

End Sub
```

Printing the Macro Code

As you learn more about VBA and writing your own programs, you will find it useful to document the code generated by the macro recorder. Cindy suggests that you print out the macro code for future reference.

To print the macro code:

1. Verify that the insertion point still appears in the Code window and that the Code window is active.

2. Click **File** on the menu bar, and then click **Print**. The Print – VBAProject dialog box opens.

   The editor gives two choices of items to print. One is the Current Project, which refers to all of the code in any module and any other features that might be involved in this collection of macros. Printing the project is usually done for Excel applications that involve more advanced features such as customized dialog boxes. The other choice, the default, is to print only those macros in the current module. To ensure that all of the macros in this application are printed, you will choose to print the current project.

3. Click the **Current Project** option button, and verify that the Code check box is selected.

4. If you need to send your output to a specific printer on your network, click the **Setup** button to select your printer and its settings; otherwise, click the **OK** button to send your output to the default printer.

   Now that you've viewed, edited, and printed the macro, you can close the Visual Basic Editor and return to Excel.

5. Click **File** on the menu bar, and then click **Close and Return to Microsoft Excel**. The Visual Basic Editor closes, and the Stock2 workbook is redisplayed.

If you want to return to the Visual Basic Editor, you can select one of the macros in the Macro dialog box and click the Edit button again, or you can click Tools on the menu bar, point to Macro, and then click Visual Basic Editor.

Nigel has a new set of data for you to enter. This time, you'll check to see whether your commands to turn off the screen updating feature makes the macro run more smoothly. Before running the macro, you should save your work so that if the macro runs incorrectly, you can go back to the previous version.

To test the screen updating command:

1. Click the **Save** button 📙 on the Standard toolbar.

2. Type **5/20/2004** in cell B25, and then press the **Tab** key.

3. Type **0.51** in cell B26, and then press the **Tab**.

4. Continue inserting the new stock values into the worksheet, typing **36.8** for the opening value, **37.9** for the high value, **36.2** for the low value, and **37.1** for the closing value.

5. Press **Ctrl + d**. The NewData macro runs, but this time the actions of the macro are hidden; only the final result is displayed.

Nigel is pleased with the change you've made to the macro. He thinks it runs more smoothly and will be less distracting to those who use this application.

Creating **Macro Buttons**

Another way to run a macro is to assign it to a button that is placed directly on the worksheet. Nigel wants you to add four macro buttons to the Reporter worksheet, one for each of the four macros you've created. Because the worksheet is still protected, you'll need to turn off the sheet protection before inserting the buttons.

REFERENCE WINDOW   **RW**

Creating a Macro Button

- Click View on the menu bar, point to Toolbars, and then click Forms.
- Click the Button tool on the Forms toolbar, and then click and drag the mouse pointer until the button is the size and shape you want.
- Release the mouse button. The button appears on the worksheet with a default label, and the Assign Macro dialog box opens.
- Select the macro you want to assign to the button. With the button still selected, type a new label.

Add the four buttons to the worksheet that will provide quick access to the macros.

To insert a button on the worksheet:

1. Click **Tools** on the menu bar, point to **Protection**, and then click **Unprotect Sheet**.

   To create the macro buttons, you have to display the Forms toolbar.

2. Click **View** on the menu bar, point to **Toolbars**, and then click **Forms**. The Forms toolbar appears, as shown in Figure 8-29. The Forms toolbar contains a variety of objects that can be placed on the worksheet. In this case, you'll work only with the Button tool. You'll have a chance to work with some of the other tools in the problems at the end of the tutorial.

Figure 8-29   **THE FORMS TOOLBAR**

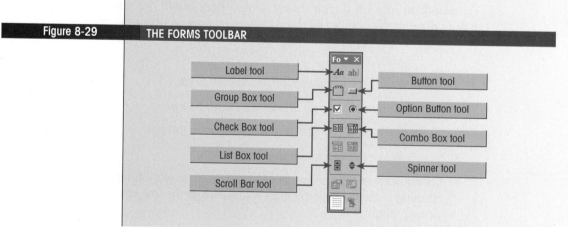

3. Click the **Button** tool [ ] on the Forms toolbar. As you move the pointer over the worksheet, the pointer changes to **+**.

4. Drag the pointer over the range **I4:J5**, and then release the mouse button. Excel places a button on the worksheet, and the Assign Macro dialog box opens. See Figure 8-30.

Figure 8-30 | **MACRO BUTTON AND THE ASSIGN MACRO DIALOG BOX**

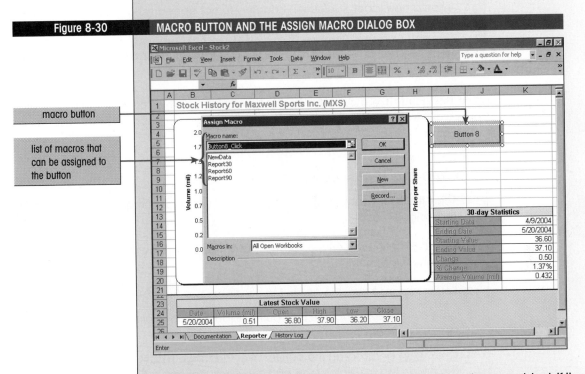

TROUBLE? Drawing a macro button is the same as drawing any object. If the button is not the exact size of the button in the figure, you can resize it after you change the label on the button. To resize the button, first select it by right-clicking the button, and then click and drag the selection handles to resize the button. To move the button, click the selection border (not on one of the selection handles), and drag the button to a new location.

When Excel creates the macro button, the Assign Macro dialog box automatically opens. From this dialog box, you can assign a macro to the button, or you can turn on the macro recorder to record a new macro. Nigel wants you to assign the Report30 macro to this new button.

To assign a button to the Report30 macro:

1. Click **Report30** in the list of macros, and then click the **OK** button.

Each macro button you create appears with a default label on it. The label on the button shown in Figure 8-30 is "Button 8" (the label on your screen might differ—the numbers are sequential). Nigel wants a more descriptive label to appear on the button.

2. With the selection handles still displayed around the button, type **30-day Report** (do not press the Enter key). The new label replaces the default label.

TROUBLE? If you do not see selection handles around the button, the button is not selected, and you will not be able to type a new label. To select the button, right-click anywhere within the button, and then click Edit Text on the shortcut menu. The insertion point appears within the button. From this point, you can insert a new label. If selection handles do not appear when you right-click the button, remove the protection from the worksheet and try again.

3. Click any cell in the worksheet to deselect the macro button.

At this point, if you click the 30-day Report button, the Report30 macro will run. Of course, the worksheet is already displaying the 30-day report, so you will add the other macro buttons first.

To add the remaining macro buttons:

1. Click the **Button** tool ▭ on the Forms toolbar, and then drag the pointer over the range I7:J8.

TROUBLE? If the tools on the Forms toolbar are grayed out, unprotect the Reporter worksheet.

2. Select **Report60** from the Assign Macro dialog box, and then click the **OK** button.

3. Type **60-day Report** for the new button label, and then click any cell to deselect the button.

4. Click ▭ again, drag the pointer over the range I10:J11, select **Report90** in the Assign Macro dialog box, click the **OK** button, type **90-day Report** for the button label, and then click any cell to deselect the button.

5. Click ▭ once again, drag the pointer over a rectangular region about three columns wide and three rows high to the right of cell G25, click **NewData** from the Assign Macro dialog box, and then click the **OK** button.

6. Type **Insert New Stock Values** as the new button label, and then click any cell in the worksheet to deselect the button. Figure 8-31 shows the Reporter worksheet with the four newly inserted macro buttons.

TROUBLE? If the macro buttons on your screen do not match the size and location of the buttons shown in the figure, you can click a button to select it, and then resize or reposition it on the worksheet.

Figure 8-31	MACRO BUTTONS IN THE STOCK2 WORKBOOK

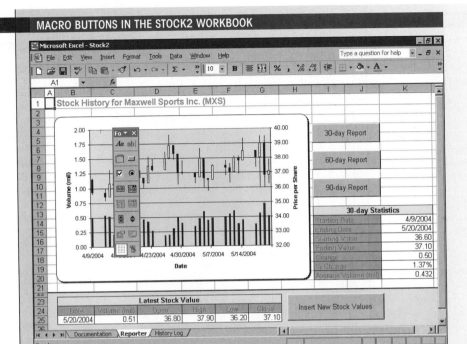

You no longer need the Forms toolbar, so you will close it, and then reset the worksheet protection.

7. Click the **Close** button ⊠ on the Forms toolbar.

8. Click **Tools** on the menu bar, point to **Protection**, and then **Protect Sheet**.

9. Click the **OK** button to enable the worksheet protection.

Now test the macro buttons to verify that they run the macros.

To test the macro buttons:

1. Click the **60-day Report** button to display the 60-day report chart and statistics.

2. Click the **90-day Report** button to display the 90-day report chart and statistics.

3. Click the **30-day Report** button to return to the 30-day display.

Nigel has one last set of values for you to enter. Use the new macro button to insert these values.

4. Click cell **B25**, type **5/21/2004**, and then press the **Tab** key.

5. Complete the rest of stock values as follows: the volume is **0.25**, the opening value is **37.1**, the high value is **38.3**, the low value is **35.1**, and the closing value is **36.9**.

6. Click the **Insert New Stock Values** button. Excel inserts the new stock values and updates the statistics and chart. See Figure 8-32.

Figure 8-32   FINAL FIGURES FOR THE STOCK REPORTER

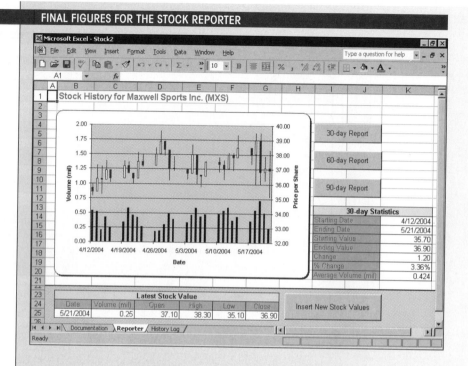

You've completed your work on the Excel application, so you can save and close the workbook and then exit Excel.

7. Click the **Save** button 🔲 on the Standard toolbar, and then click the **Close** button ☒ on the title bar.

Nigel is very pleased with the ease of the interface for the stock value workbook. He wants to study the Excel application some more and will get back to you with any other projects he needs to have done.

Session 8.3 QUICK CHECK

1. What are digital signatures? How do they protect you from macro viruses?

2. Discuss two ways of creating a macro.

3. What is VBA?

4. What are the three places you can store a macro?

5. How would you delete a macro?

6. How would you edit a macro?

7. In VBA, macros are called _____.

8. How would you insert a macro button into your worksheet?

REVIEW ASSIGNMENTS

Nigel is working on another Excel application. This application contains a chart displaying the closing value of a stock plotted against a date range. The workbook contains a list of closing values for four different stocks over the last 90 working days. Nigel wants users to have the ability to display any one of the four stocks in the chart. He also wants them to have the ability to control the date range displayed in the chart by specifying the starting and stopping date. This way, users can look at any time interval they want within the range of dates stored in the workbook.

You've been talking to Cindy about the problem. She says that you can't change the chart's date range by using the macro recorder, but she will write up a simple VBA program that you can use in the workbook. Your job will be to create the rest of the application. Figure 8-33 shows a preview of the application you'll create.

Figure 8-33

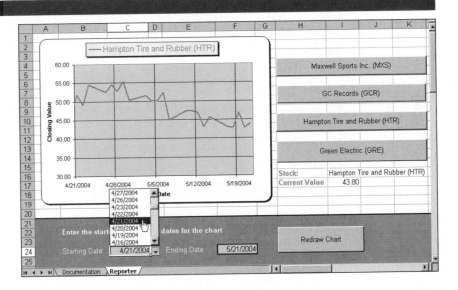

To complete this task:

1. Open the **Chart1** workbook located in the Tutorial.08\Review folder on your Data Disk. This workbook already contains a macro, so if Excel is set to a medium security level, enable the macro and open the workbook. If you have Excel set to a high security level, you will have to reduce the security level to open the workbook.

2. Enter the date and your name in the Documentation sheet. Save the workbook as **Chart2** in the Tutorial.08\Review folder on your Data Disk. Switch to the Reporter worksheet.

The Reporter worksheet contains the chart and all of the stock market data. The stock market data is entered in the range $O$1:$S$91. The four stock values are entered into the following ranges:

- Maxwell Sports $P$1:$P$91
- GC Records $Q$1:$Q$91
- Hampton Tire and Rubber $R$1:$R$91
- Green Electric $S$1:$S$91

The chart currently shows the data for Maxwell Sports.

3. Turn off the locked property for cells C24 and F24 so that users will be able to enter the starting and ending values for the chart in the worksheet.

Explore

4. Create a validation rule for cells C24 and F24 that allows users to select starting and ending dates from the list of dates stored in the range $O$2:$O$91. Verify that the In-cell dropdown check box is selected. Click cell C24 and then click cell F24 to verify that a list box containing dates appears when each cell is active.

5. Add Stop alerts to cells C24 and F24 with the title "Invalid Date" and the message "Choose a date from the drop-down list box."

6. Create the following range names using the definitions provided:

   - Date   =Reporter!$O$2:$O$91
   - Current_value   =Reporter!$P$2
   - Stock_values   =Reporter!$P$2:$P$91
   - Stock_name   =Reporter!$P$1

Explore

7. Select all of the cells in the worksheet. Click the Apply command on the Insert Name submenu, and then select all of the names in the Apply names list. Click the OK button to replace all cell references found in formulas in the selected cells with their corresponding range names. Click cell I16 and cell I17 to verify that the cell references in those cells have been replaced with range names.

8. Change the data source for the embedded chart so that the Name reference points to the Stock_name range name, the Values reference points to the Stock_values range name, and the Category (X) axis labels reference points to the Date range name.

9. Protect the worksheet, allowing users to select locked and unlocked cells. Do not specify a password.

10. Protect the structure of the workbook, but not the windows. Once again, do not specify a password.

Note: In the following steps, you'll be creating four macros. You should save your workbook before recording each macro. That way, if you make a mistake in recording the macro, you can open the saved file and try again.

11. Create a macro named "GCR" with the shortcut key combination Ctrl + b. The macro will display the stock values (found in the range $Q$1:$Q$91) and stock name of GC Records in the chart. Record the following steps to create GCR macro:

    a. Unprotect the worksheet.
    b. Change the definition of the Current_value range name to "=Reporter!$Q$2".
    c. Change the definition of the Stock_name range name to "=Reporter!$Q$1".
    d. Change the definition of the Stock_values range name to "=Reporter!$Q$2:$Q$91".
    e. Go to cell A1.
    f. Reset the worksheet protection.

12. After you turn off the macro recorder, press Ctrl + b to run the macro to verify that it works correctly. (*Note:* If the macro fails to work, close the workbook without saving your changes. Then reopen the workbook, and record the GCR macro again.)

13. Create a macro named "HTR" with the shortcut key combination Ctrl + c. This macro should display the stock values and stock name of Hampton Tire and Rubber in the chart. In this case, you'll follow the same procedure you used to create the GCR macro in Step 11, except that all of the cell references should now point to column R in the Reporter worksheet. Test the macro by pressing Ctrl + c.

14. Create a macro named "GRE", which displays the data for Green Electric, found in the range $S$1:$S$91 of the Reporter worksheet. Apply a shortcut key to this macro consisting of Ctrl + d. Once again, use the macro recorder and record the same steps you used to create the first two macros, except that all cell references must be to the values in column S in the Reporter worksheet. Test the macro after you're finished by pressing Ctrl + d.

15. Create a macro named "MXS", which displays the values in column B in the chart. Assign this macro the shortcut key Ctrl + a. Once again, record the same steps you used in creating the earlier macros, except that all cell references must point to the values in column P in the Reporter worksheet. Test the macro by pressing the shortcut key.

16. Unprotect the worksheet and create a macro button covering the range H4:K5. Assign the MXS macro to the button. Change the button's label to "Maxwell Sports Inc. (MXS)".

17. Create a macro button for the GCR macro, covering the range H7:K8, with the label "GC Records (GCR)". Create a macro button for the HTR macro, covering the range H10:K11, with the label "Hampton Tire and Rubber (HTR)". Create a macro button for the GRE macro, covering the range H13:K14, with the label "Green Electric (GRE)".

18. Click each button and verify that the macros change both the chart and the values in the range I16:I17.

19. Unprotect the worksheet again, and create a macro button assigned to Cindy's macro "Redraw_Chart" and position the button over the range H22:I24. Change the label of the button to "Redraw Chart". Protect the worksheet.

Explore ▷ 20. Click cell C24 and select 4/21/2004 in the list box. Click the Redraw Chart macro button, and verify that the chart now shows only the previous month of stock values.

Explore ▷ 21. Open the Macro dialog box, select the Redraw_Chart macro, and then click the Options button. Assign the shortcut key Ctrl + e to Cindy's macro.

22. With the Macro dialog box still open and with the Redraw_Chart macro selected, click the Edit button to access the Visual Basic Editor. Print the contents of the current module. Close the editor and return to Excel.

23. Print the contents of your workbook.

24. Save and close the workbook, and then exit Excel.

CASE PROBLEMS

Case 1. Creating a Retrieval Application for CarStats Reports CarStats Reports is a company that records statistics on old used cars. Belinda Stevenson works at CarStats and has asked you to help her create an Excel application to retrieve some car information from an old workbook that she has. The old workbook contains data on almost 400 cars that were manufactured from 1970 through 1982. Belinda wants to be able to specify the year and country of manufacture and have the application access her old workbook, retrieve the records matching her search criteria, and then copy and paste the records into the application. Belinda has formatted most of the workbook, but needs your help in programming the macro to retrieve this data, as well as inserting validation checks on the search criteria. She also wants to protect her application so that others cannot make changes to it.

In order to create this application, you will use the Advanced Filter feature of Excel. With an Advanced Filter, you can enter the filter criteria in a cell and then apply the criteria to a range of data. The data that matches the filter criteria can then be copied to a new location in the workbook containing the data to be filtered.

Figure 8-34 shows a preview of the finished application.

Figure 8-34

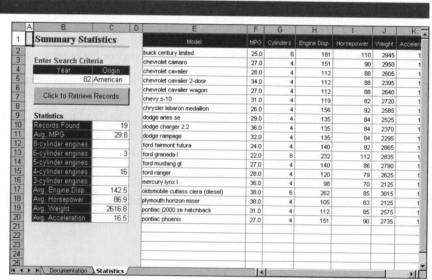

To complete this task:

1. Open the **CarStats1** workbook located in the Tutorial.08\Cases folder on your Data Disk. This workbook already contains a macro, so if Excel is set to a medium security level, enable the macro and open the workbook. If you have Excel set to a high security level, you will have to reduce the security level to open the workbook.

2. Enter the date and your name in the Documentation sheet. Save the workbook as **CarStats2** in the Tutorial.08\Cases folder on your Data Disk. Switch to the Statistics worksheet.

Explore

3. Create a validation rule for cell B5 that allows users to only select a value from a list of years. In the Source reference box, enter the numbers 70 through 82 separated by commas (no spaces). Make sure that the In-cell dropdown check box is selected. Create a Stop alert message with the title, "Invalid Year", and the message, "Choose a year from the drop-down list box."

Explore

4. Create a validation rule for cell C5 that allows users to only select values from a list. In the Source reference box, enter the words: American, European, and Japanese, separated by commas (no spaces). Create a Stop alert message with the title "Invalid Origin" and the message "Choose an origin from the drop-down list box."

5. Click cells B5 and C5 and verify that list boxes containing the values you specified appear when the cells are active.

6. Disable the Locked property for cells B5 and C5.

7. Protect the Statistics worksheet, allowing users only to select locked or unlocked cells. Protect the structure of the CarStats2 workbook. Do not specify a password.

Explore

8. Save the CarStats2 workbook, and then create a macro named "GetData" with the shortcut key Ctrl + f. This macro will retrieve data from the Car Data workbook and paste the data into the CarStats2 workbook. Record the following steps to the GetData macro:
   a. Unprotect the Statistics worksheet.
   b. Open the Car Data workbook from the Tutorial.08\Cases folder on your Data Disk.
   c. Open the Advanced Filter dialog box from the Data Filter submenu.
   d. Click the Copy to another location option button in the Advanced Filter dialog box, and then press the Tab key twice.
   e. With the insertion point in the Criteria range reference box, switch to the Statistics worksheet in the CarStats2 workbook, select the range B4:C5, and then press the Tab key.
   f. With the insertion point in the Copy to reference box, click cell K1 in the Data worksheet, and then click the OK button to close the Advanced Filter dialog box.
   g. Copy columns K through S of the Data worksheet.
   h. Return to the CarStats2 workbook, and select columns E through M.
   i. Click Edit on the menu bar, and then click Paste Special. Click the Values option button, and then click the OK button. Click cell A1 and then press the Esc key to remove the data from the paste buffer.
   j. Return to the Car Data workbook and close it without saving your changes.
   k. Reset protection on the Statistics worksheet.

9. To test the macro, click cell B5 and select "72" for the year. Click cell C5 and select "European" for the area of origin. Press Ctrl + f to run the GetData macro. When prompted to save changes to the Car Data workbook, click the No button. Verify that the macro retrieves five records from the Car Data workbook. (*Note*: If the macro fails to work, close the workbook without saving your changes, and then reopen the workbook and record the GetData macro again.)

   Belinda likes the macro, but does not like being prompted to save changes to the Car Data workbook. After discussing the issue with a programmer, you learn that this dialog box can be removed by making a simple change to the VBA code.

10. Save the workbook, and then open the GetData macro in the Visual Basic Editor.

Explore

11. At the bottom of the GetData() sub procedure, you will see the following command line *ActiveWindow.Close*. Click the end of this command line, and change the command to "ActiveWindow.Close False".

The programmer also points out that when you recorded the macro, it also recorded the exact path to the Car Data workbook. This means that you won't be able to move that workbook file. You can edit the macro, erasing the path information, and then the macro will look for the Car Data workbook in whatever folder the CarStats2 workbook file is located.

Explore

12. Locate the line *Workbooks.Open Filename:=* (which should be placed near the top of the sub procedure. Below (or next to) this line there should be the complete path and file-name of the Car Data workbook. Remove the path from the filename so that the text changes from *path \Car Data.xls* to simply *Car Data.xls*. (*Hint*: You can remove the path by selecting the path text with your pointer and pressing the Delete key.)

13. Print the contents of the current module, and then close the editor, returning to Excel.

14. Change the value of cell C5 in the Statistics worksheet to "American". Press Ctrl + f and verify that the GetData macro now runs without prompting you to save changes to the Car Data workbook. Eighteen records are retrieved from the workbook.

15. Unprotect the Statistics worksheet, and then insert a macro button roughly covering the range B6:C8. Assign the GetData macro to this button, and enter the label "Click to Retrieve Records". Reset protection on the worksheet.

16. Click the macro button to retrieve statistics on 1982 American cars.

17. Select the range A1:M21. Print the selected range (*not the entire worksheet*), using land-scape orientation. Add a footer to the page that displays your name and the date, aligned on the right.

18. Save and close the workbook. Exit Excel.

Case 2. Creating a Profit Analysis for Seattle Popcorn Seattle Popcorn is a small company located in Tacoma, Washington that produces a brand of gourmet popcorn favored by people in the Northwest. Steve Wilkes has developed a workbook that will allow him to perform a profit analysis for the company. Using this workbook, he can determine the break-even point for the company–the sales volume need so that revenues will match the monthly anticipated expenses. There are three factors in determining the break-even point: the sales price of each unit of Seattle Popcorn, the manufacturing cost to the company for each unit, and the fixed expenses (salaries, rent, insurance, and so on) that the company must pay each month. Steve wants to be able to explore a range of possible values for each of these factors.

- The sales price of each unit of Seattle Popcorn can vary from $5 to $15 in increments of $1.
- The manufacturing cost of each unit can vary from $5 to $15 in increments of $1.
- The fixed monthly expense for the company can vary from $15,000 to $30,000 in increments of $500.

Steve wants to interactively explore the company's break-even point. Rather than entering the values for the sales price of each unit, the manufacturing cost, and the monthly expenses, he wants to be able to set these values by clicking and dragging a scroll bar. He also wants to protect the contents of the workbook, so that someone else will not accidentally modify the formulas he has already entered. Figure 8-35 shows a preview of the application you'll create for Steve.

Figure 8-35

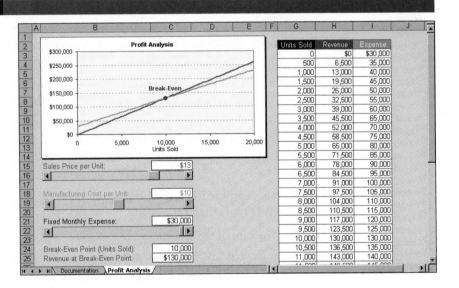

To complete this task:

1. Open the **Popcorn1** workbook located in the Tutorial.08\Cases folder on your Data Disk. Enter the date and your name in the Documentation sheet. Save the workbook as **Popcorn2** in the same folder. Switch to the Profit Analysis worksheet.

2. Disable the locked properties of cells C15, C18, and C21. Everything else in the worksheet should remain locked.

3. Create the following range names in the worksheet:

   - Price_per_Unit   ='Profit Analysis'!$C$15
   - Cost_per_Unit   ='Profit Analysis'!$C$18
   - Monthly_Expenses   ='Profit Analysis'!$C$21

Explore ▶ 4. Select all of the cells in the worksheet, and using the Apply command on the Insert Names submenu, replace all of the cell references to C15, C18, and C21 with the range names you just created.

Explore ▶ 5. Click the Scroll Bar tool on the Forms toolbar, and drag the pointer over the range B16:C16 to draw a scroll bar.

Explore ▶ 6. Right-click the scroll bar you created, and then click Format Control on the shortcut menu. Click the Control tab, and then set the ranges for the scroll bar so that the current value is 12, the minimum value is 5, the maximum value is 15, the incremental change value remains at 1, and the page change value is 5. Link the value of the scroll bar to cell C15. Click the OK button.

Explore ▶ 7. Click outside the scroll bar to deselect it. Click the scroll bar arrow to change the value in cell C15 to 15. The scroll bar should move to indicate the value entered in C15.

8. Create a scroll bar in the range B19:C19. Format the scroll bar so that the current value is 8, the minimum value is 5, the maximum value is 15, the incremental change value remains at 1, the page change value is 5, and the value of the scroll bar is linked to cell C18.

9. Create a scroll bar in the range B22:C22. Format the scroll bar so that the current value is 25,000, the minimum value is 15,000, the maximum value is 30,000, the incremental change value is 500, the page change value is 1000, and the value of the scroll bar is linked to cell C21.

10. Enable worksheet protection, preventing users from selecting or changing *anything* in the worksheet. Do *not* enter a password.

11. Protect the structure of the workbook. Do *not* enter a password.

12. Using the three scroll bars, enter the following values in the worksheet and to determine how many units must Seattle Popcorn sell each month in order to break even:

   - Sales Price = $13
   - Manufacturing Cost = $10
   - Monthly Expense = $30,000

13. Print the contents of the Profit Analysis worksheet on a single sheet of paper in portrait orientation.

14. Save and close the workbook, and then exit Excel.

Case 3. Creating a Sales Report for Trayle Bikes Trayle Bikes specializes in mountain bikes. Pat Boland works in the accounting office of Trayle Bikes. One of her jobs is to report regional sales data for the different Trayle Bikes models. Pat is interested in creating an Excel application to display pie charts for the four different sales regions, or for all sales regions combined.

Pat envisions a set of five option buttons placed on a worksheet. When one of the option buttons is clicked, the pie chart should change, displaying values from a different sales region. Pat has asked your help in creating this kind of application. The sales data and a pie chart have already been saved to a workbook. Your job will be to define the range names, record the macros, and create the option buttons needed for the application. Figure 8-36 shows a preview of the completed application.

Figure 8-36

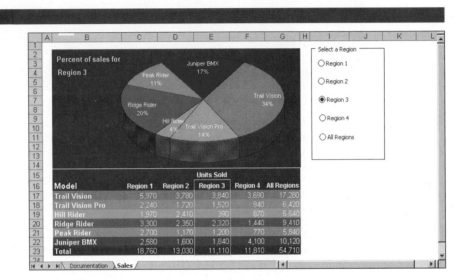

To complete this task:

1. Open the **MBikes1** workbook located in the Tutorial.08\Cases folder on your Data Disk. Enter the date and your name in the Documentation sheet. Save the workbook as **MBikes2** in the same folder. Switch to the Sales worksheet.

2. Create the range names shown in Figure 8-37.

Figure 8-37

RANGE NAME	DEFINITION
Name1	=Sales!$C$16
Name2	=Sales!$D$16
Name3	=Sales!$E$16
Name4	=Sales!$F$16
Name_All	=Sales!$G$16
Region1	=Sales!$C$17:$C$22
Region2	=Sales!$D$17:$D$22
Region3	=Sales!$E$17:$E$22
Region4	=Sales!$F$17:$F$22
Region_All	=Sales!$G$17:$G$22

Explore

3. Range names can refer to other range names. With this in mind, create two additional range names: Region_Name, which points to the Name1 range you just created, and Region_Values, which points to the Region1 range.

4. Edit the data source for the pie chart, changing the reference for the series name so that it points to the Region_Name range, and pointing the values reference so that it points to the Region_Values reference.

Explore

5. On the pie chart there is a label with the text "Region 1". Click the Region text label in the pie chart area, and then edit the cell reference so that it points to the Region_Name range rather than cell $C$16. (*Hint*: Use the same syntax that you used when you changed the chart's data source to point to the range names.)

6. Protect the worksheet and the structure of the workbook, preventing users from taking any action, including selecting locked *or* unlocked cells. Do *not* set any passwords. Save the workbook.

Note: In the following steps, you should save your workbook before recording each macro. After you stop recording, run the macro. If the macro does not run correctly, close the workbook without saving your changes. Then reopen the workbook, and record the macro again. Follow this procedure for each macro that you record.

7. Create a macro named "Region2". Record the following actions:
   a. Unprotect the Sales worksheet.
   b. Change the definition of the Region_Name range so that it points to the Name2 range.
   c. Change the definition of the Region_Values range so that it points to the Region2 range.
   d. Select the range C16:G23, and then remove all borders from the selected cells.
   e. Select the range D16:D23, and then apply a yellow outline border to the range.
   f. Click cell A1.
   g. Reset protection on the Sales worksheet.

8. Run the Region2 macro to verify that it works correctly. (*Note*: The macro will appear as *Module*.Region2 in the list of macros, where *Module* is the name of a module.) If the macro does not run correctly, close the MBikes2 workbook without saving your changes. Reopen the workbook and attempt to record the macro again.

9. Record the Region3 macro, using the same procedure that you followed in creating the Region2 macro, except that the Region_Name range name should point to the Name3 range, the Region_Values range name should point to Region3, and the yellow outline border should apply to the range E16:E23. Test the macro.

10. Create the Region4 macro in which the Region_Name range name points to Name4, the Region_Values range points to Region4, and the yellow outline border is applied to the range F16:F23. Test the macro.

11. Create the Region_All macro in which the Region_Name range name points to Name_All, the Region_Values range points to Region_All, and the yellow border is applied to the range G16:G23. Test the macro.

12. Create the Region1 macro in which the Region_Name range name points to Name1, the Region_Values range points to Region1, and a yellow border is applied to the range C16:C23. Test the macro.

Explore   13. Unprotect the worksheet and then, using the Group Box tool on the Forms toolbar, create a group box that is positioned over the range I2:J13. With the group box still selected, type "Select a Region" to change the group box's label. Click outside the group box to deselect it.

Explore   14. Using the Option Button tool on the Forms toolbar, create an option button that is positioned over the range I3:J3, but make sure that the object stays *within* the borders of the group box you just created. Do *not* let the borders of the option button fall outside of the group box border. With the option button still selected, type "Region 1" to change the option button's label. Click outside of the group box to deselect it.

Explore   15. Add the following option buttons in the indicated locations to the group box:

- Region 2 option button placed over the cell range I5:J5
- Region 3 option button placed over the cell range I7:J7
- Region 4 option button placed over the cell range I9:J9
- All Regions option button placed over the cell range I11:J11

Explore   16. Click each of the five options buttons and verify that when you click one option button, the others are automatically deselected. (*Note*: If more than one option button remains selected, it means that the borders of the option button fall outside of the group box border. You can right-click each option button to select it. If you click the selection border, you can adjust the positions or sizes of the option buttons so that they line up within the group box.)

Explore   17. Right-click the Region 1 option button, and then click Assign Macro on the shortcut menu. Select the Region1 macro from the macro list. Use the same procedure to assign the remaining option buttons to their corresponding macros.

18. Select the first 14 rows of the worksheet, and then change the fill color of the selected cells to white. Click cell A1 and then set the worksheet protection again.

19. Click each of the option buttons you created and verify that they run the correct macro, and update both the pie chart and the appearance of the table.

20. Print the code for the five macros you created.

21. Print the contents of the Sales worksheet in landscape mode. Add a footer that displays your name and the date in the lower-right corner of the page.

22. Save and close the workbook. Exit Excel.

Case 4. Creating a Data Entry Form for Homeware   Homeware is a company that sells specialized home cooking products. The company employs individuals to organize "Homeware Parties" in which the company's products are sold. Lisa Goodman is responsible for entering sales data from various Homeware Parties. She has asked your help in designing an Excel workbook to act as a data entry form. She has already created the workbook, but she needs your help in setting up data validation rules and in writing the macros to enter the data.

To complete this task:

1. Open the **HWSales1** workbook located in the Tutorial.08\Cases folder on your Data Disk. This workbook already contains a macro, so if Excel is set to a medium security level, enable the macro and open the workbook. If you have Excel set to a high security level, you will have to reduce the security level to open the workbook.

2. Enter your name and the date in the Documentation sheet. Save the workbook as **HWSales2** in the Tutorial.08\Cases folder on your Data Disk. Switch to the Sales Form worksheet.

3. Create the following validation rules for the Sales Forms. Create a validation rule that allows one of the five regions to be selected in the Sales Form worksheet. Create a validation rule that allows only the 12 product IDs listed in the worksheet to be entered. Create a validation rule that allows only positive numbers to be entered as the number of units sold. If users attempt to violate the validation rules, display a Stop alert message informing the users of the error and of the allowed range of values. Create an appropriate input message for cells C3, C4, and C7.

4. Prevent users from selecting any cell in the Sales Form worksheet other than cells C3, C4, and C7.

5. Have the product name and price automatically entered into the sales form. (*Hint*: Use a lookup function.) Automatically calculate the total sales for the order.

6. Protect all of the sheets in the workbook, except for the Documentation sheet.

7. Save the workbook, and then create a macro named "Add_Data" that does the following tasks (you will have to unprotect the worksheets and then reset the protection on the worksheets in the course of this macro):

   a. Inserts a new blank record in the second row of the Sales Record, shifting the rest of the records down

   b. Copies the values in range C3:C8 of the Sales Form worksheet into the new blank line (*Hint*: Paste only the transposed values; *do not include the formats* using the Paste Special command.)

   c. Refreshes the contents of the PivotTable displayed in the Sales Table worksheet to include the new data

   d. Clears the values in cells C3:C8 of the Sales Form worksheet

8. Assign the Add_Data macro to a button on the Sales Form worksheet named "Enter New Sales Information into the Sales Record".

9. Edit the Add_Data macro so that Excel does not display the action of the macro as it runs.

10. Create a macro named "View_Table" that displays the contents of the Sales Table worksheet. Create another macro named "View_Chart" that displays the sales chart. Finally, create a macro named "View_Form" that displays the Sales Form worksheet.

11. Add buttons to the Sales Form worksheet to run the View_Table and View_Chart macros. Label the buttons "View Sales Table" and "View Sales Chart".

12. Add a button labeled "Return to the Sales Form" to both the Sales Table worksheet and the Sales Chart sheet. Assign the View_Form macro to both buttons.

13. Test the data entry form by entering the following new records:
    Region =1, Product ID = CW, Units Sold = 5
    Region =3, Product ID = HR, Units Sold = 7
    Region =4, Product ID = OEG, Units Sold =3

14. Print the contents of the Sales Form and Sales Table worksheets.

15. Save and close the workbook, and then exit Excel.

INTERNET ASSIGNMENTS

Student Union

The purpose of the Internet Assignments is to challenge you to find information on the Internet that you can use to create effective spreadsheets. The actual assignments are updated and maintained on the Course Technology Web site. Log on to the Internet and use your Web browser to go to the Student Union on the New Perspectives Series site at **www.course.com/NewPerspectives/studentunion**. Click the Online Companions link, and then click the link for this text.

QUICK CHECK ANSWERS

Session 8.1

1. Excel menus and actions are replaced by customized menus and commands and the ability to control data entry.

2. Select the cell and then click Validation on the Data menu.

3. Select the cell. Open the Data Validation dialog box, select the Input Message tab, and then enter a title and text for the input message.

4. the Stop alert, which prevents the user from storing the data in the cell; the Warning alert, which, by default, rejects the invalid data, but allows the user to override the rejection; and the Information alert, which, by default, accepts the invalid data, but still allows the user to cancel the data entry.

5. A locked cell is one in which data entry is prohibited. The locked property is only enabled when the sheet is protected.

6. Worksheet protection controls the ability of the user to make changes to the cells within the worksheet. Workbook protection controls the users' ability to change the structure of the workbook (including worksheet names) and the format of the workbook window.

7. Yes, as long as the structure of the workbook is not protected.

Session 8.2

1. A range name is a name assigned to a cell or range and the definition of that cell or range. A range name is more descriptive than a cell or range reference, making it easier for you to interpret your formulas. If you change the definition of the range name, pointing it to a different range, the value of any formula using that range name will be updated automatically to reflect the new definition.

2. using the Name box, using the Define Name dialog box, and using the Create Names dialog box.

3. a. Annual_Total

4. Name box

5. =SUM(Sales)

6. =Report.xls!Sales

Session 8.3

1. A digital signature is an electronic signature on a digital certificate, which confirms that the macro or document created by the signer has not been altered since the digital certificate was created.

2. by using the macro recorder to record the exact keystrokes and commands that you want the macro to run, or by writing the macro code directly in the VBA macro language

3. Visual Basic for Applications—the macro language of all Microsoft Office applications.

4. in the current workbook, in a new workbook, or in a personal macro workbook that will be available whenever you use Excel

5. Click Tools, point to Macro, click Macros, select the macro from the list of macros, and then click the Delete button.

6. Click Tools, point to Macro, click Macros, select the macro from the list of macros, and then click the Edit button.

7. sub procedures

8. Unprotect the worksheet (if necessary) and display the Forms toolbar. Click the Button tool on the Forms toolbar, and then draw the button image on the worksheet. Assign a macro and label to the button.

New Perspectives on

MICROSOFT®
EXCEL 2002

Read This Before You Begin

To the Student

Data Disks

To complete the Level III tutorials, Review Assignments, and Case Problems, you need six Data Disks. Your instructor will either provide you with the Data Disks or ask you to make your own.

If you are making your own Data Disks, you will need **six** blank, formatted high-density disks. You will need to copy a set of files and/or folders from a file server, standalone computer, or the Web onto your disk. Your instructor will tell you which computer, drive letter, and folders contain the files you need. You could also download the files by going to www.course.com and following the instructions on the screen.

The information below shows you which folders go on your disks, so that you will have enough disk space to complete all the tutorials, Review Assignments, and Case Problems:

Data Disk 1

Write this on the disk label:
Data Disk 1: Excel 2002 Tutorials 9 and 10

Put these folders on the disk: Tutorial.09 and Tutorial.10

Data Disk 2

Write this on the disk label:
Data Disk 2: Excel 2002 Tutorial 11 (Tutorial)

Put this folder on the disk: Tutor11\Tutorial

Data Disk 3

Write this on the disk label:
Data Disk 3: Excel 2002 Tutorial 11 (Review and Cases)

Put these folders on the disk:
Tutor11\Review and Tutor11\Cases

Data Disk 4

Write this on the disk label:
Data Disk 4: Excel 2002 Tutorial 12

Put this folder on the disk: Tutorial.12

Data Disk 5

Write this on the disk label:
Data Disk 5: Excel 2002 Appendices 3 and 4

Put these folders on the disk: Appendix.03 and Appendix.04

Data Disk 6

Write this on the disk label:
Data Disk 6: Excel 2002 Additional Case Problems

Put this folder on the disk: AddCases

When you begin each tutorial, be sure you are using the correct Data Disk. Refer to the "File Finder" chart at the back of this text for more detailed information on which files are used in which tutorials. See the inside front or inside back cover of this book for more information on Data Disk files, or ask your instructor or technical support person for assistance.

Using Your Own Computer

If you are going to work through this book using your own computer, you need:

- **Computer System** Microsoft Windows 98, NT, 2000 Professional, or higher must be installed on your computer. This book assumes a typical installation of Microsoft Excel.

- **Data Disks** You will not be able to complete the tutorials or exercises in this book using your own computer until you have your Data Disks.

Visit Our World Wide Web Site

Additional materials designed especially for you are available on the World Wide Web.
Go to www.course.com/NewPerspectives.

To the Instructor

The Data Disk Files are available on the Instructor's Resource Kit for this title. Follow the instructions in the Help file on the CD-ROM to install the programs to your network or standalone computer. For information on creating Data Disks, see the "To the Student" section above.

EX 9.03

OBJECTIVES

In this tutorial you will:

- Examine cost-volume-profit relationships

- Learn the principles of multiple what-if analyses

- Use one-variable data tables to perform a what-if analysis

- Use two-variable data tables to perform a what-if analysis

- Learn how to create and use array formulas

- Create scenarios to perform what-if analyses

- Create a scenario summary report to save your conclusions

DATA
TABLES AND SCENARIO MANAGEMENT

Performing a Cost-Volume-Profit Analysis for Front Range Rafting

CASE

Front Range Rafting

Colorado's Front Range is a haven for outdoor enthusiasts. Visitors and residents can choose from skiing, mountain climbing, horseback riding, and many other pursuits. One of the most popular summertime activities is white-water rafting, and one of the favorite rafting spots is the Poudre River. Careful to ensure that the Poudre River's natural resources are not harmed from overuse, Colorado's Department of Natural Resources has limited the number of white-water rafting touring companies on this river to five.

Eddie Kaufmann, a rafting enthusiast since the age of twelve, is considering purchasing one of those five companies—Front Range Rafting. He has asked your help in determining the profitability of the enterprise. Eddie has some estimates on the average number of clients each year and the company's operating expenses, but he's unsure what the impact will be if the company has a down year or the operating expenses go up. With so many variables, Eddie feels overwhelmed in trying to determine the risk of buying the company. Eddie would like your help evaluating several possible financial scenarios for the future of Front Range Rafting.

SESSION 9.1

In this session, you'll examine the basic principles of cost-volume-profit analysis. You'll learn about data tables and how they can help you describe the relationship between cost, volume, and profits under different sets of circumstances. You'll learn about one- and two-variable data tables and how to create and display them. Finally, you'll learn about array formulas and the many ways of using array formulas in Excel.

Principle of Cost-Volume-Profit Relationships

One of Eddie's major tasks in deciding whether or not to purchase Front Range Rafting is to quantify the different factors that affect the company's profitability. For example, how many clients does the company need each season in order to break even? If Front Range Rafting can attract an average of five more clients each day, how much additional annual income will that generate, and how much additional overhead would be needed to accommodate more clients? How will increases in insurance costs affect the company's profitability?

You can find answers to questions like these by using cost-volume-profit analysis. **Cost-volume-profit (CVP) analysis** expresses the relationship between a company's expenses, its volume of business, and the resulting profit. CVP analysis is an important business decision-making tool because it quickly and easily predicts the effect of cutting overhead or raising prices on profit. Although volume and profit are straightforward terms, you should understand the types of expenses that are part of CVP calculations.

Types of Expenses

The first component of CVP analysis is cost, or expense. Most businesses have three types of expenses: variable, fixed, and mixed. **Variable expenses** change in direct proportion to the company's sales volume. For example, a company that produces shoes will have to spend more on raw materials if it wants to keep pace with rising sales. Front Range Rafting also has variable expenses. The company provides box lunches for each customer that it takes on a river tour, and the state Department of Resources also charges the company a usage tax based on the volume of river traffic created by its tours. Thus, the more clients the company takes on tours, the more money Eddie will have to spend to cover variable expenses.

Eddie tells you that the company spends $3 per client on box lunches and other amenities and $10 per client for usage fees. The line graph in Figure 9-1 shows Front Range Rafting's variable expenses for differing numbers of clients. As the number of customers increases (shown on the horizontal x-axis), so does the cost to the company. If Front Range Rafting can manage to attract 8,000 customers per season, it will cost the company over $100,000 in variable expenses.

Figure 9-1	CHART OF VARIABLE EXPENSES

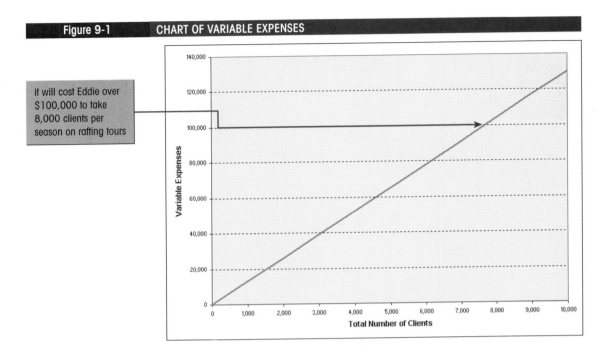

it will cost Eddie over $100,000 to take 8,000 clients per season on rafting tours

Eddie tells you that the standard fee for a white-water rafting tour on the Poudre River is around $60 per person. If you deduct the variable expense ($13) from that price, it appears that Eddie will make a profit of almost $47 each time he takes someone on a rafting trip. He won't, however, because he also has to pay for fixed expenses. A **fixed expense** is an expense that Eddie must pay regardless of the number of customers he has. For example, Eddie has to pay for the salaries and benefits for a team of six rafting guides and a support staff. He has to pay insurance and rent, and he has to spend money on maintenance and advertising. Eddie figures that the fixed expenses for Front Range Rafting will total $200,000 per year, and that's before he takes a single client on a rafting tour.

A third type of expense is **mixed expenses**, which are part variable and part fixed. For example, if the rafting company really takes off, Eddie may have to hire more guides or support staff. On the other hand, if the business is not performing well, Eddie may be forced to lay off some of his employees. At this point, Eddie is not considering any mixed expenses in his calculations.

By adding the variable and fixed expenses, Eddie can estimate the company's total expenses. The graph in Figure 9-2 shows Front Range Rafting's total expenses for a given number of customers per season.

Figure 9-2   **CHART OF TOTAL EXPENSES**

8,000 clients per season results in over $300,000 in total expenses

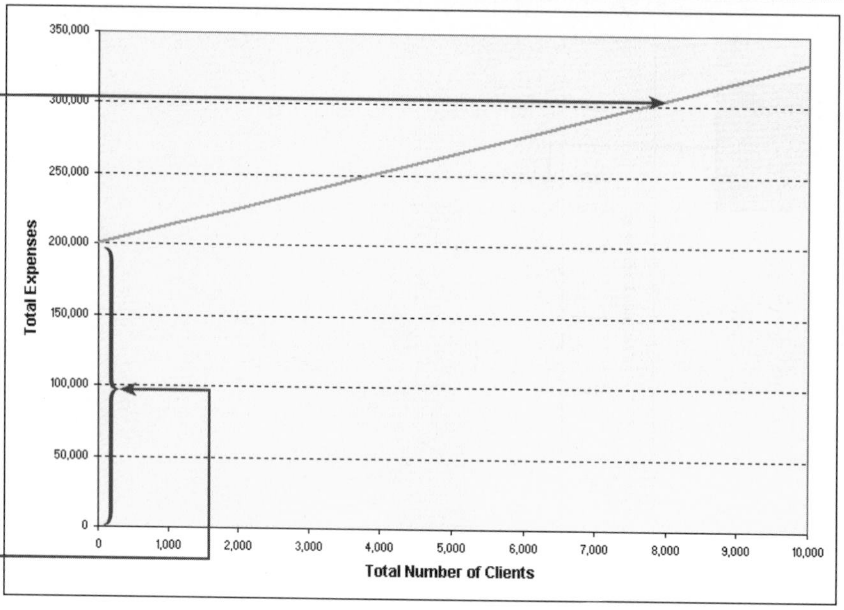

$200,000 in fixed expenses

If the company attracts 8,000 customers per season, the total expense would be over $300,000 of which $200,000 represents Eddie's fixed expenses and $100,000 represents variable expenses.

The Break-Even Point

Of course, as the company attracts more customers, it will bring in more revenue. As mentioned earlier, Front Range Rafting has charged each customer $60 for the Poudre River tour. Figure 9-3 shows the increase in revenue in relation to the increase in clientele.

Figure 9-3   **CHART OF REVENUE**

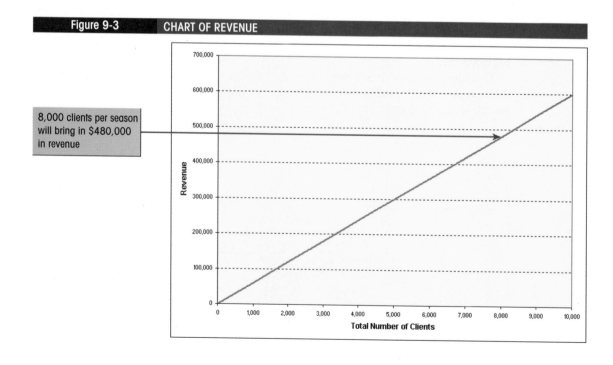

8,000 clients per season will bring in $480,000 in revenue

If Eddie can manage to attract 8,000 customers per season, Front Range Rafting will bring in $480,000 of revenue. As you saw in Figure 9-2, total expenses for 8,000 customers would be almost $300,000, which would mean a net income to the company of $180,000. That may, however, be an optimistic scenario. How many customers does Eddie need for his revenue to match his total expenses? The point where the revenue equals the expense is called the **break-even point**. For this reason, CVP analysis is sometimes called **break-even analysis**. Any money the company earns above the break-even point is called **operating income**, or **profit**.

You can present a break-even analysis by charting revenue and total expenses versus sales volume. The point at which the two lines cross is the break-even point. This type of chart is called a cost-volume-profit (CVP) chart. Figure 9-4 shows a typical CVP chart.

Figure 9-4	SAMPLE CVP CHART

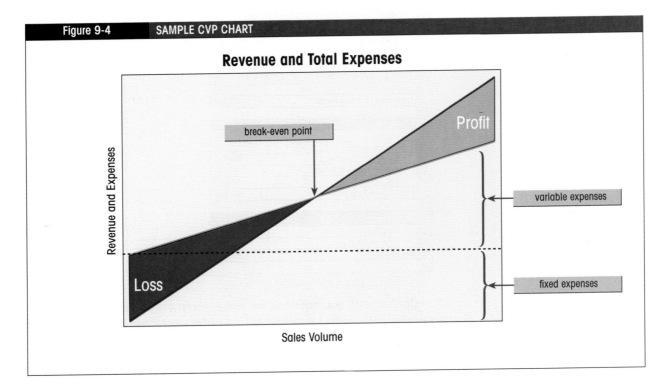

Using a chart like this, you can quickly determine the volume of sales necessary for a company to show a profit from a particular product or service.

Planning Income and Expenses at Front Range Rafting

Eddie wants to determine the number of customers per season that Front Range Rafting will need to attract to break even. To help you obtain this information, he has given you an income statement containing income and expense figures for a typical season. You will use these figures as the basis for a CVP analysis using Excel. The workbook is stored as Rafting1 on your Data Disk.

To open the Rafting1 workbook:

1. Start Excel and open the **Rafting1** workbook located in the Tutorial.09\Tutorial folder on your Data Disk.

2. Enter the date and your name in the Documentation sheet.

3. Save the workbook as **Rafting2** in the Tutorial.09\Tutorial folder on your Data Disk.

4. Switch to the Income Statement worksheet. See Figure 9-5.

Figure 9-5	INCOME STATEMENT FOR FRONT RANGE RAFTING

	A	B	C	D
1	Income Statement			
2				
3	Season Information			
4	Length of Season (days)	120		
5	Avg. Number of Clients (per day)	45		
6	Total Number of Clients	5,400		
7				
8	Revenue			
9	Fee per Client	60		
10	Total Revenue	$ 324,000		
11				
12	Variable Expenses			
13	Expense per Client	3		
14	River Usage Tax per Client	10		
15	Total Variable Expenses	$ 70,200		
16				
17	Fixed Expenses			
18	Insurance	10,000		
19	Maintenance	25,000		
20	Salary and Benefits	95,000		
21	Administrative & Advertising	35,000		
22	Est. Taxes	35,000		
23	Total Fixed Expenses	$ 200,000		
24				
25	Summary			
26	Total Revenue	324,000		
27	Total Expenses	270,200		
28	Net Income	$ 53,800		
29				

TROUBLE? Don't worry if you can't see the entire worksheet as shown in Figure 9-5. Your screen might hide the lower portion; the entire worksheet is shown here so you can see its entire contents.

The Income Statement worksheet contains the revenue, variable expenses, and fixed expenses for a typical season at Front Range Rafting. No mixed expenses are reported. As you can see in Figure 9-5, the touring season for Front Range Rafting lasts 120 days, and Eddie expects to average about 45 customers a day during the season. If each customer pays $60 for a rafting tour, the result will be $324,000 in total revenue over the course of a season. The variable expense for taking that many people on rafting tours will be $70,200; adding this variable expense to Eddie's fixed expense of $200,000 per year results in a total yearly expense of $324,000. Under this scenario, Eddie will make a profit of $53,800.

Eddie wonders what would happen to his profit margin if he increased his customer base from 45 to 50 customers per day.

To calculate profit assuming 50 customers per day:

1. Click cell **B5**.

2. Type **50** and press the **Enter** key. The revenue in cell B10 increases to $360,000, and the total profit in cell B28 changes to $82,000.

You show Eddie the new figures. He now wonders what the profit margins would be for a whole range of values, for example from 30 customers per day up to 60. You could calculate these values by entering each value separately into the workbook and then recording the resulting revenue and net income values in a table, but it would be more efficient if Excel would generate that table for you.

One-Variable **Data Tables**

One of the advantages of spreadsheets is that they enable you to quickly see how changing variables (items that can change), such as sales price or sales volume, can affect the value of a calculated figure, such as operating income. The ability to investigate different possibilities is called **what-if analysis**. You just performed a what-if analysis for Eddie, determining how the average number of customers per day affects his profit margin. But Eddie wants you to do a what-if analysis for a range of values. **Data tables** are a way of organizing and displaying the results of multiple what-if analyses. Excel supports two kinds of data tables: one-variable data tables and two-variable data tables.

There are two important elements involved in creating data tables: input cells and result cells. **Input cells** are the cells containing values you want to modify in a what-if analysis. **Result cells** are the cells containing the values that you want to examine.

In a **one-variable data table**, you can specify one input cell and any number of result cells. The possible values for the input cell are placed in the first row or column of the data table, and the corresponding values of the result cells are placed in the accompanying rows or columns. Figure 9-6 shows a one-variable data table created to determine the monthly payment and total cost of a mortgage for different interest rates.

| Figure 9-6 | A SAMPLE OF A ONE-VARIABLE DATA TABLE |

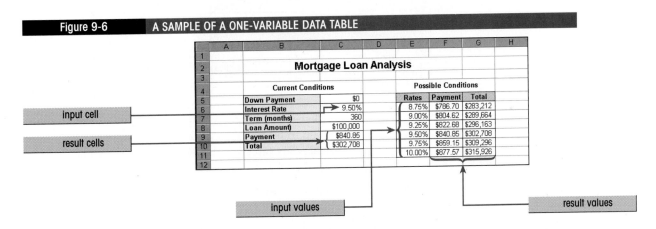

In this case, the interest rate in cell C6 is the input cell, and the values in the range E6:E11 comprise **input values**, that is, possible values for the input cell. Cells C9 and C10 are the result cells, and the values in the range F6:G11 are the **result values**. The results from six different what-if analyses are displayed in this single table. For example, you can quickly see that a 10% interest rate will result in an $877.57 monthly payment and a total mortgage cost of $315,926.

Now that you have seen what a one-variable data table looks like, you are ready to create your own for Eddie's workbook.

Creating a One-Variable Data Table

In the Income Statement worksheet, the input cell for the data table will be cell B5, the average number of clients per day that Eddie can expect to take on rafting tours, and the result cells will be cells B26 through B28, containing the company's total revenue, total expenses, and net income, as shown in Figure 9-7.

Figure 9-7   **INPUT CELL AND RESULT CELLS FOR RAFTING WORKBOOK**

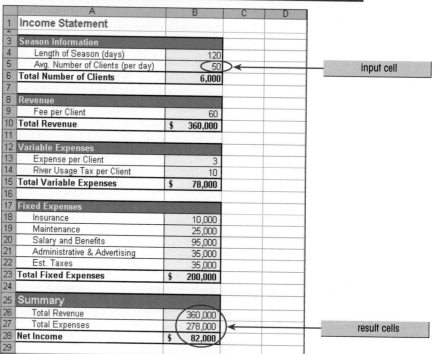

Eddie wants you to perform what-if analyses for a range of customer values, starting with 30 customers per day and going up to 60 customers per day in increments of 2 customers per day. To create the one-variable data table for this what-if analysis, you'll follow these general steps:

1. Enter a title for the column of input values and the titles for the three columns of result values.

2. Under the column titles, insert a row of formulas that reference the input cell and the three result cells. Thus, the first row of your table will display the current values of the input and result cells in your workbook.

3. Beneath the first title, insert the input values in the table's first column.

4. Select the entire table, and then use the Data Table command to automatically generate the three columns of result values.

REFERENCE WINDOW   **RW**

Creating a One-Variable Data Table

- Determine whether you want the values for the input cell to appear in the first row or first column of the table.
- Insert a formula that references the input cell in the upper-left cell of the table.
- If you want the input values in the first row, insert a formula that references the result cells in the first column of the table beneath the formula referencing the input cell. If you want input values in the first column, insert formulas referencing the result cells in the first row of the table to the right of the formula referencing the input cell.
- If you want the input values in the first row, insert the input values in the first row of the table. If you want the input values in the first column, insert the input values in the first column of the table.
- Select the table, click Data on the menu bar, and then click Table.
- Enter the cell reference for the input cell in the Row input cell reference box when input values are in the first row or in the Column input cell reference box when input values are in the first column, and then click the OK button.

You're ready to create the data table to address Eddie's questions. You'll place the table in the range D3:G20 of the Income Statement worksheet.

To begin creating the one-variable data table:

1. Click cell **D3** and then enter **Clients**.

2. Enter the remaining labels as follows:

   Cell E3: **Revenue**

   Cell F3: **Expenses**

   Cell G3: **Income**

3. Enter formulas that reference the Clients, Revenue, Expenses, and Income cells as follows:

   Cell D4: **=B5**

   Cell E4: **=B26**

   Cell F4: **=B27**

   Cell G4: **=B28**

With the column headings and formulas entered for the data table, you'll now enter a column of input values. You will place these values in the first column in range D5:D20.

To enter the input values:

1. Enter **30** in cell D5.

2. Enter **32** in cell D6.

3. Select the range **D5:D6**, and then drag the fill handle to extend the range to cell **D20**. After you release the mouse button, Excel fills the range with clients-per-day values ranging from 30 to 60 in increments of 2. See Figure 9-8.

Figure 9-8	ENTERING INPUT VALUES

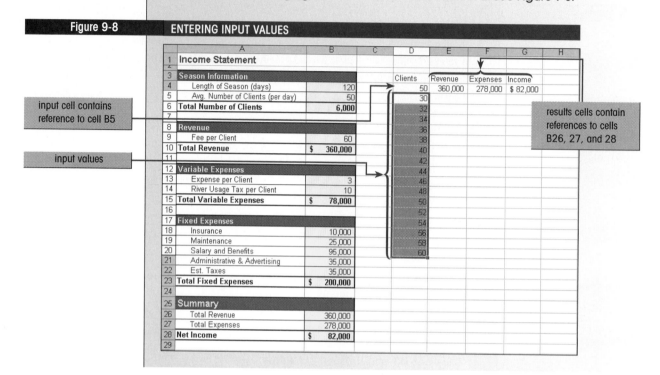

input cell contains reference to cell B5

input values

results cells contain references to cells B26, 27, and 28

	A	B	C	D	E	F	G	H
1	Income Statement							
2								
3	Season Information			Clients	Revenue	Expenses	Income	
4	Length of Season (days)	120		50	360,000	278,000	$ 82,000	
5	Avg. Number of Clients (per day)	50		30				
6	Total Number of Clients	6,000		32				
7				34				
8	Revenue			36				
9	Fee per Client	60		38				
10	Total Revenue	$ 360,000		40				
11				42				
12	Variable Expenses			44				
13	Expense per Client	3		46				
14	River Usage Tax per Client	10		48				
15	Total Variable Expenses	$ 78,000		50				
16				52				
17	Fixed Expenses			54				
18	Insurance	10,000		56				
19	Maintenance	25,000		58				
20	Salary and Benefits	95,000		60				
21	Administrative & Advertising	35,000						
22	Est. Taxes	35,000						
23	Total Fixed Expenses	$ 200,000						
24								
25	Summary							
26	Total Revenue	360,000						
27	Total Expenses	278,000						
28	Net Income	$ 82,000						
29								

The final step in creating the one-variable data table is to instruct Excel to fill the table with the result values. To do this, you select the range that contains the data table (excluding the column headings), and then you run Excel's Data Table command. You will also need to designate the input cell and indicate whether the input values are in row or column format. Because your input values are in a column, you will use the Column input cell option. If you had oriented the table so that the input values were in a single row, you would use the Row input cell option.

To complete the one-variable data table:

1. Select the range **D4:G20**, click **Data** on the menu bar, and then click **Table**. The Table dialog box opens. Now you'll specify that the input cell is cell B5 and that it is in column format.

2. Type **B5** in the Column input cell reference box. See Figure 9-9.

Figure 9-9	ENTERING THE LOCATION OF THE INPUT CELL

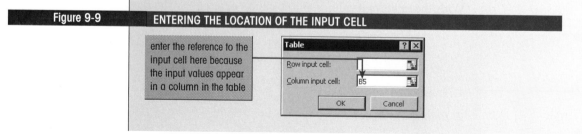

enter the reference to the input cell here because the input values appear in a column in the table

Table	? ☒
Row input cell:	
Column input cell:	B5
	OK Cancel

3. Click the **OK** button. Excel places the result values into the data table, as shown in Figure 9-10.

Figure 9-10

THE RESULTS VALUES FOR REVENUE, TOTAL EXPENSES, AND NET INCOME

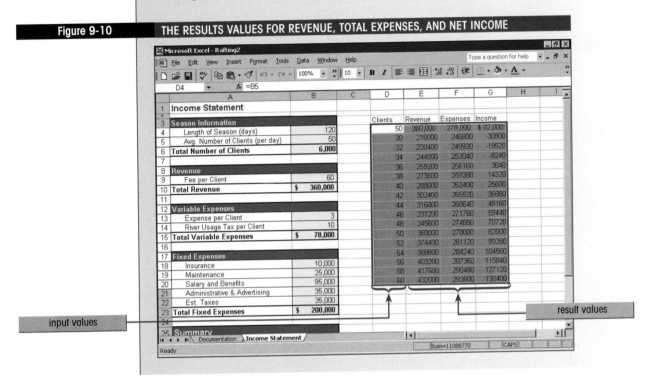

The table will be easier to interpret if you reformat the values using the Currency Style format.

To format the values in the table:

1. Select the range **E4:G20**, click **Format** on the menu bar, and then click **Cells**.

2. If necessary, click the **Number** tab.

3. Click **Number** in the Category list, reduce the number of decimal places to **0**, select the fourth option (that is, the number 1234.10 set in a red font surrounded by parentheses) for the negative numbers format, and then click the **OK** button.

4. Click cell **D3** to deselect the range. Figure 9-11 shows the formatted data table.

Figure 9-11   **FORMATTED DATA TABLE**

	A	B	C	D	E	F	G	H
1	Income Statement							
2								break-even point
3	Season Information			Clients	Revenue	Expenses	Income	
4	Length of Season (days)	120		50	360,000	278,000	82,000	
5	Avg. Number of Clients (per day)	50		30	216,000	246,800	(30,800)	
6	Total Number of Clients	6,000		32	230,400	249,920	(19,520)	
7				34	244,800	253,040	(8,240)	
8	Revenue			36	259,200	256,160	3,040	
9	Fee per Client	60		38	273,600	259,280	14,320	
10	Total Revenue	$ 360,000		40	288,000	262,400	25,600	
11				42	302,400	265,520	36,880	
12	Variable Expenses			44	316,800	268,640	48,160	
13	Expense per Client	3		46	331,200	271,760	59,440	
14	River Usage Tax per Client	10		48	345,600	274,880	70,720	
15	Total Variable Expenses	$ 78,000		50	360,000	278,000	82,000	
16				52	374,400	281,120	93,280	
17	Fixed Expenses			54	388,800	284,240	104,560	
18	Insurance	10,000		56	403,200	287,360	115,840	
19	Maintenance	25,000		58	417,600	290,480	127,120	
20	Salary and Benefits	95,000		60	432,000	293,600	138,400	
21	Administrative & Advertising	35,000						
22	Est. Taxes	35,000						
23	Total Fixed Expenses	$ 200,000						
24								
25	Summary							
26	Total Revenue	360,000						
27	Total Expenses	278,000						
28	Net Income	$ 82,000						
29								

Eddie wants to study the relationship between average number of clients per day and net income. With the data table you just created, you can explain the relationship to him. If Front Range Rafting averages 34 customers per day or less, Eddie will show a net loss. On the other hand, if he can attract 60 customers per day, the company will show a profit of $138,400. The break-even point lies somewhere between 34 and 36 customers per day because, at these levels, the operating income goes from a negative number to a positive number.

Charting a One-Variable Data Table

You could give Eddie a copy of the data table you have created, but the results will be much clearer if you include a CVP chart along with the table. The chart will give him a better picture of the relationship between the three variables. To create a CVP chart, you use an Excel scatter chart to chart the revenue and total expenses against the average number of customers per day.

To create the CVP chart:

1. Select the range **D3:F20**, click **Insert** on the menu bar, and then click **Chart**.

   TROUBLE?   If the Office Assistant appears, click the No, don't provide help now option button.

2. Click **XY (Scatter)** in the Chart type list box, and then click the **Scatter with data points connected by lines without markers** sub-type, as shown in Figure 9-12.

Figure 9-12	CREATING A CVP SCATTER CHART

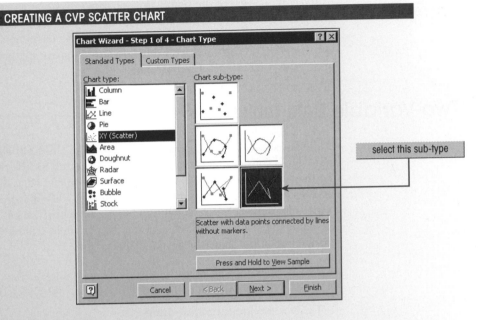

select this sub-type

3. Click the **Next** button twice so you can enter titles for the chart and the x-axis so that others will know how to interpret the chart.

4. Type **Cost-Volume-Profit** in the Chart title text box, and press the **Tab** key.

5. Type **Customers per Day** in the Value (X) Axis text box, and click the **Next** button. Now you'll specify that you want the chart placed on a separate sheet.

6. Click the **As new sheet** option button, and type **CVP Chart** in the As new sheet text box.

7. Click the **Finish** button. Figure 9-13 displays the completed chart. Note the chart appears on a new sheet.

Figure 9-13	THE COMPLETED CVP CHART

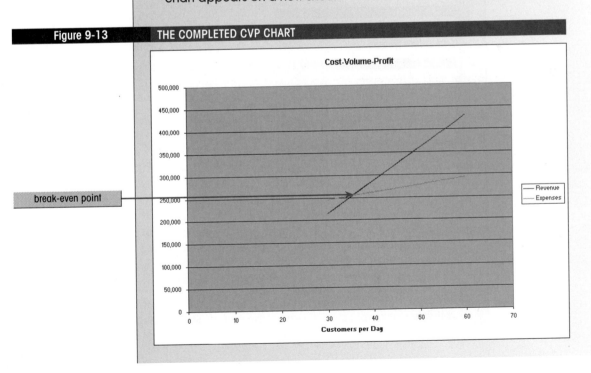

break-even point

Excel plots each of the points in your data table, connecting them with a line. The dark blue line represents revenue and the pink line represents expenses. The break-even point between revenue and expenses occurs at about 35 customers per day. With the data table and CVP chart, you can give Eddie a comprehensive picture of the impact of sales levels upon both total expenses and revenue.

Two-Variable Data Tables

Eddie has studied the figures you gave him from the CVP chart and the one-variable data table. He is considering changing the price structure for the rafting tours. To be more competitive with other rafting companies, Eddie wonders what the impact would be if he lowered his rates. He wants you to perform another what-if analysis.

Because data tables are dynamic, changes in the worksheet are automatically reflected in the data table values. You'll change the fee per client from $60 to $50 to see the effect this change has on the values in the data tables.

To view the effect of changing the rafting fee:

1. Click the **Income Statement** tab.

2. Enter **50** in cell B9. Figure 9-14 shows the updated worksheet and data table.

Figure 9-14   DATA TABLE ASSUMING A $50 RAFTING FEE

	A	B	C	D	E	F	G	H
1	Income Statement							
2								
3	Season Information			Clients	Revenue	Expenses	Income	
4	Length of Season (days)	120		50	300,000	278,000	22,000	
5	Avg. Number of Clients (per day)	50		30	180,000	246,800	(66,800)	
6	Total Number of Clients	6,000		32	192,000	249,920	(57,920)	
7				34	204,000	253,040	(49,040)	
8	Revenue			36	216,000	256,160	(40,160)	
9	Fee per Client	50		38	228,000	259,280	(31,280)	
10	Total Revenue	$ 300,000		40	240,000	262,400	(22,400)	
11				42	252,000	265,520	(13,520)	
12	Variable Expenses			44	264,000	268,640	(4,640)	
13	Expense per Client	3		46	276,000	271,760	4,240	
14	River Usage Tax per Client	10		48	288,000	274,880	13,120	
15	Total Variable Expenses	$ 78,000		50	300,000	278,000	22,000	
16				52	312,000	281,120	30,880	
17	Fixed Expenses			54	324,000	284,240	39,760	
18	Insurance	10,000		56	336,000	287,360	48,640	
19	Maintenance	25,000		58	348,000	290,480	57,520	
20	Salary and Benefits	95,000		60	360,000	293,600	66,400	
21	Administrative & Advertising	35,000						
22	Est. Taxes	35,000						
23	Total Fixed Expenses	$ 200,000						
24								
25	Summary							
26	Total Revenue	300,000						
27	Total Expenses	278,000						
28	Net Income	$ 22,000						
29								

break-even point

3. Switch to the CVP Chart sheet and view the results of the change you made in the rafting fee. The break-even point, where the Revenue and Expenses lines intersect, has moved to the right, indicating that Eddie would have to attract around 45 customers per day to break even at this new price.

4. Return to the Income Statement worksheet, and then enter **60** in cell B9. The one-variable data table and the rest of the worksheet now display their prior values.

Eddie's concerned that the break-even point for the $50 rafting fee is too high. He now would like you to perform what-if analyses for different combinations of rafting fees and clients-per-day values. He asks you to calculate the net income for rafting fees from $40 to $70 in increments of $5 and for clients-per-day values from 30 to 60 in increments of 2.

You can perform such a what-if analysis with a two-variable data table. As the name implies, a two-variable data table uses two input cells, but, unlike a one-variable data table, only the value of a single result cell is displayed. Figure 9-15 shows an example of a two-variable data table that calculates mortgage costs.

Figure 9-15	A SAMPLE TWO-VARIABLE DATA TABLE

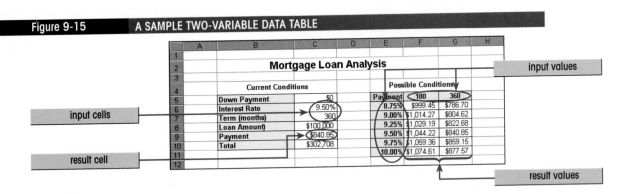

In this example, there are two input cells: cell C6, the interest rate, and cell C7, the number of months before the loan is repaid (180 or 360 months). Notice that the first row of the data table displays two possible values for the number of months before the loan is paid (180 and 360 months). The first column of the data table displays different possible interest rates (8.75% to 10% in increments of 0.25%). At the intersection of each interest rate and length of term, the table displays the required monthly payment. For example, a 180-month term at a 9.50% interest rate requires a monthly payment of $1,044.22 (cell F9).

Creating a Two-Variable Table

To create a two-variable data table for the new what-if analysis, you'll follow these general steps:

1. Create a column of different clients-per-day values from 30 to 60 in increments of 2.

2. Create a row of possible rafting fees from $40 to $70 in increments of $5.

3. In the upper-left corner of the table, insert a formula that references the result cell (net income).

4. Apply the Data Table command to the table you created to generate result values for each combination of customers per day and rafting fees.

REFERENCE WINDOW **RW**

Creating a Two-Variable Data Table

- In the upper-left cell of the table, insert a reference to the result cell.
- Beneath the upper-left cell, enter a column of input values for the table.
- To the right of the upper-left cell, fill in the row with the second set of input values.
- Select the table, click Data on the menu bar, and then click Table.
- In the Row input cell reference box, enter the input cell corresponding to the row of input values.
- In the Column input cell reference box, enter the input cell corresponding to the column of input values.
- Click the OK button.

You'll place the two-variable data table below the one-variable data table you just created. Because you are going to use the same range of input values for the clients per day, you can copy those values to the new table you are creating.

To enter the row and column headings for the two-variable data table:

1. Copy the range **D5:D20**, click cell **D24**, and click the **Paste** button 📋 on the Formatting toolbar.

   With the first set of input values in the table, you will enter the second set of input values, the range of rafting fees.

2. Type **$40** in cell E23 and press the **Tab** key, and then type **$45** in cell F23 and press the **Enter** key.

3. Select the range **E23:F23**, and then drag the fill handle to extend the range to **K23**. After you release the mouse button, Excel fills the range with unit prices ranging from $40 to $70 in increments of $5.

In two-variable tables, you must always place a reference to the result cell in the upper-left corner of the table at the intersection of the row values and the column values. In this case, you will place a formula in cell D23 referencing the company's net income.

Because placing that value in this location on your table might prove confusing to some users, you'll format the cell to hide the actual value. Instead of displaying the actual cell contents, you will format the cell so it displays the label "Customers," text that describes the values in the first column of the two-variable table.

To insert the reference to the result cell in the two-variable data table:

1. Click cell **D23**, type **=B28**, and then press the **Enter** key. The current net income appears.

   Now you'll format the cell to hide the actual value and instead display a heading for the Customers column.

2. Right-click cell **D23** and then click **Format Cells** on the shortcut menu. The Format Cells dialog box opens. You use this dialog box to assign standard formats to cell values. In this case, you'll use the Custom format to display a label in cell D23.

3. Click the **Number** tab if necessary, and then click **Custom** in the Category list box. Now you'll replace the default format code with a label.

4. Delete the format code displayed in the Type text box.

5. Type **"Customers"** (including the quotation marks) in the Type text box. See Figure 9-16.

Figure 9-16   **CREATING A CUSTOM FORMAT**

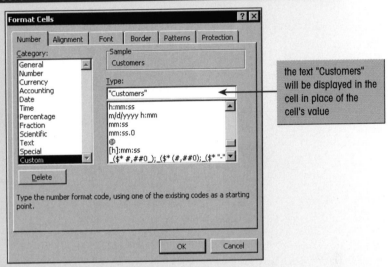

6. Click the **OK** button. The label "Customers" appears in cell D23, but the underlying formula entered in that cell remains intact, even if it is not visible.

   TROUBLE? If the text in cell D23 on your screen does not appear correctly, you may have forgotten to include the quotation marks. Repeat Steps 2 through 6.

   Now you'll enter a label centered above the row of possible rafting fees.

7. Enter **Rafting Fee** in cell E22, select the range **E22:K22**, and then click the **Merge and Center** button on the Formatting toolbar. The text is now centered above the range of possible rafting fees.

8. Click cell **D23**. Your two-variable table should now look like Figure 9-17.

Figure 9-17 | ROW AND COLUMN HEADINGS FOR THE TWO-VARIABLE DATA TABLE

cell D23 contains a formula referencing cell B28 but displays the text "Customers"

second set of input values: rafting fees

first set of input values: clients per day

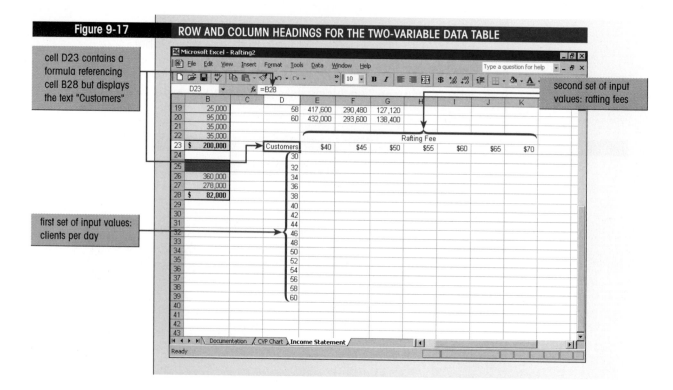

Now that you've set up the table, you can use the Data Table command to calculate and display operating income for each combination of rafting fees and customers. When creating a two-variable data table, you must identify the row input cell and the column input cell. The **row input cell** is the cell on which you base values placed in the first row of the data table. The first row of your data table contains rafting fees, so the row input cell is B9—the cell containing the fee that Front Range Rafting charges its customers. Similarly, the **column input cell** is the cell on which values placed in the first column of the data table are based. In this case, that would be cell B5, the average number of clients per day that Eddie can expect for his business.

To complete the two-variable table:

1. Select the range **D23:K39**, click **Data** on the menu bar, and then click **Table**. The Table dialog box opens.

2. Type **B9** in the Row input cell reference box to refer to the cell containing the rafting fee, and then press the **Tab** key.

3. Type **B5** in the Column input cell reference box to refer to the cell containing the average number of customers per day. See Figure 9-18.

Figure 9-18 | SPECIFYING ROW AND COLUMN INPUT CELLS

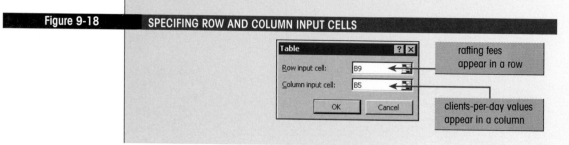

rafting fees appear in a row

clients-per-day values appear in a column

4. Click the **OK** button. Excel places the result values into the data table.

   Next you'll format the values in the table using the same currency format you used in the one-variable data table.

5. Click cell **G20** and then click the **Format Painter** button 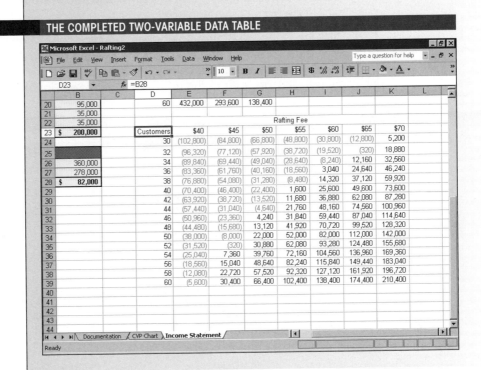 on the Standard toolbar.

6. Select the range **E24:K39** with the Format Painter pointer to format the values in the specified Number format.

7. Click **D23** to remove the selection. Figure 9-19 shows the completed two-variable data table.

Figure 9-19	THE COMPLETED TWO-VARIABLE DATA TABLE

	B	C	D	E	F	G	H	I	J	K	L
20	95,000		60	432,000	293,600	138,400					
21	35,000										
22	35,000					Rafting Fee					
23	$ 200,000		Customers	$40	$45	$50	$55	$60	$65	$70	
24			30	(102,800)	(84,800)	(66,800)	(48,800)	(30,800)	(12,800)	5,200	
25			32	(96,320)	(77,120)	(57,920)	(38,720)	(19,520)	(320)	18,880	
26	360,000		34	(89,840)	(69,440)	(49,040)	(28,640)	(8,240)	12,160	32,560	
27	278,000		36	(83,360)	(61,760)	(40,160)	(18,560)	3,040	24,640	46,240	
28	$ 82,000		38	(76,880)	(54,080)	(31,280)	(8,480)	14,320	37,120	59,920	
29			40	(70,400)	(46,400)	(22,400)	1,600	25,600	49,600	73,600	
30			42	(63,920)	(38,720)	(13,520)	11,680	36,880	62,080	87,280	
31			44	(57,440)	(31,040)	(4,640)	21,760	48,160	74,560	100,960	
32			46	(50,960)	(23,360)	4,240	31,840	59,440	87,040	114,640	
33			48	(44,480)	(15,680)	13,120	41,920	70,720	99,520	128,320	
34			50	(38,000)	(8,000)	22,000	52,000	82,000	112,000	142,000	
35			52	(31,520)	(320)	30,880	62,080	93,280	124,480	155,680	
36			54	(25,040)	7,360	39,760	72,160	104,560	136,960	169,360	
37			56	(18,560)	15,040	48,640	82,240	115,840	149,440	183,040	
38			58	(12,080)	22,720	57,520	92,320	127,120	161,920	196,720	
39			60	(5,600)	30,400	66,400	102,400	138,400	174,400	210,400	

Based on the results shown in Figure 9-19, Eddie has a better picture of the impact of rafting fees and customer traffic on his net income. For example, he knows that if he charges $55 a person, he will have to average at least 40 customers per day to show a profit. On the other hand, if the number of customers per day drops to 36, he will have to charge $60 a person to show any sort of profit.

Charting a Two-Variable Data Table

There are so many possible combinations of rafting fees and customer base to consider. Perhaps making a chart of these different combinations will simplify matters.

To begin creating the chart of the two-variable data table values:

1. Select the range **D24:K39**, click **Insert** on the menu bar, and then click **Chart**.

TROUBLE? Do not select the rafting fees in row 23 because Excel will interpret these values not as labels but as data values to be plotted. You'll add labels from within the Chart Wizard.

2. Click **XY (Scatter)** in the Chart type list, click the **Scatter with data points connected by lines without markers** sub-type, and then click the **Next** button. The second dialog box of the wizard opens.

Because of the structure of the two-variable table, you must manually insert the rafting fees into the chart's legend. You can do this by replacing the name of a series with a reference to the cell that contains the rafting fee.

3. Click the **Series** tab, verify that **Series1** is selected in the Series list box, and then click in the Name reference box.

4. Click the **Collapse Dialog Box** button 🔳, click cell **E23** on the Income Statement worksheet, and then click the **Expand Dialog Box** button 🔲. The absolute cell reference for cell E23 appears in the Name reference box, and the text "$40" appears as the name for Series1. See Figure 9-20.

Figure 9-20	SETTING UP THE SERIES TITLES

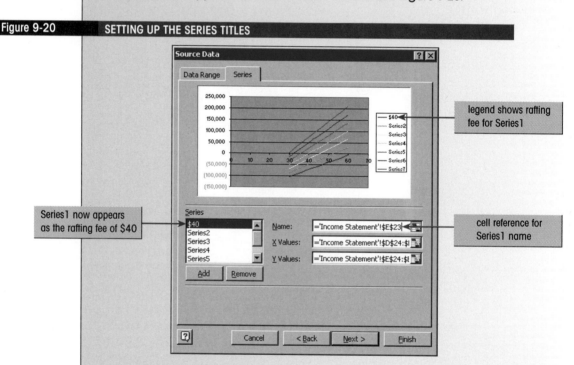

legend shows rafting fee for Series1

Series1 now appears as the rafting fee of $40

cell reference for Series1 name

TROUBLE? If you moved the Source Data dialog box and clicked cell E23, pressing the Enter key entered the cell reference in the Name reference box, but displayed the third wizard dialog box. Click the Back button to return to the Source Data dialog box.

Note that you could have typed the actual value of $40 into the Name reference box, but, by using the cell reference, you can change input values in the data table, and then both the chart and the chart legend will update automatically to reflect the new input values.

To replace each series name with the rafting fees:

1. Click **Series2** in the Series list box, click in the Name text box, click the **Collapse Dialog Box** button 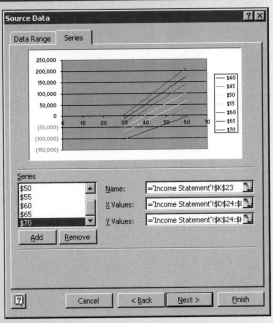, click cell **F23**, and then press the **Enter** key.

2. Using the same technique, replace each of the following series names with a cell reference:

   Series3 with cell reference **G23**

   Series4 with cell reference **H23**

   Series5 with cell reference **I23**

   Series6 with cell reference **J23**

   Series7 with cell reference **K23**

   The seven series should now have series names matching their rafting fees. See Figure 9-21.

Figure 9-21   **NEW LEGEND TEXT**

3. Click the **Next** button.

Complete the steps in the Chart Wizard by adding titles for the chart and axes and by placing the chart on its own sheet.

To complete the chart of two-variable table values:

1. Click in the Chart title text box, type **Revenue vs. Customers per Day**, and then press the **Tab** key.

2. In the Category (X) axis text box, type **Customers per Day** and then press the **Tab** key.

3. In the Value (Y) axis text box, type **Revenue** and click the **Next** button.

4. Click the **As new sheet** option button, type **Revenue vs. Customers**, and click the **Finish** button. Figure 9-22 displays the completed chart of revenue.

Figure 9-22   REVENUE UNDER DIFFERENT BUSINESS CONDITIONS

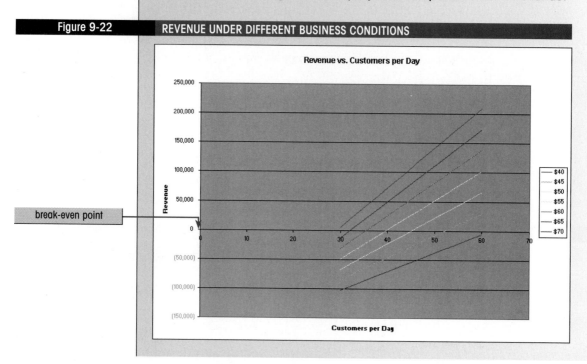

By viewing the chart, Eddie can quickly see how different rafting fees will affect the relationship between customers per day and net income. A value of zero on the vertical axis represents the break-even point. The $40 line doesn't cross zero, indicating that Eddie cannot make a profit by charging $40 per customer unless the company attracts an average of more than 60 customers per day. On the other hand, at $70 a person, Eddie will always show a profit (albeit a small one) with even as low as 30 customers per day.

Before closing this discussion of data tables, you may find it useful to understand how Excel creates a data table. You can do this by studying the underlying formulas involved.

To view the data table formula:

1. Click the **Income Statement** tab.

2. Click cell **E24**. The formula displayed in the Formula bar is {=TABLE(B9, B5)}. Note that the cell references B9 and B5 are the row and column input cells you specified earlier (see Figure 9-18).

3. Click cell **F24** and note that the formula for cell F24 is the same as the formula for cell E24.

If cells E24 and F24 have the same formula, why do they show different values, and why do the formulas have braces around them?

Using Array Formulas

The formulas you just examined are special examples of array formulas. An **array formula** is a formula that performs multiple calculations on one or more sets of values and then returns either a single value or multiple values. In the case of the data tables, Excel uses a special array function called TABLE to generate the table of values. Because the TABLE array formula returns multiple values, there is only one formula used in all of the cells in the data table. That is why the same formula appears to be entered into both E24 and F24.

Array formulas act on two or more sets of values known as **array arguments**, which refer to either cell ranges or collections of data values. In Figure 9-23, an array formula has been entered into cell B1 to calculate the total value of a stock portfolio. There are two array arguments. The first, B4:B11, refers to the price of each share of stock; the second, C4:C11, refers to the number of shares in the portfolio. By multiplying the first array argument by the second, the total value of the portfolio can be determined without having to calculate the value of each individual stock and then summing the results.

Array formulas are inserted in the same ways as regular formulas except that you press the keyboard combination Ctrl + Shift + Enter after typing the formula. Once you enter an array formula, Excel will enclose the formula in a set of braces, just like the ones you saw in cells E24 and F24. This is how you differentiate an array formula from a regular formula.

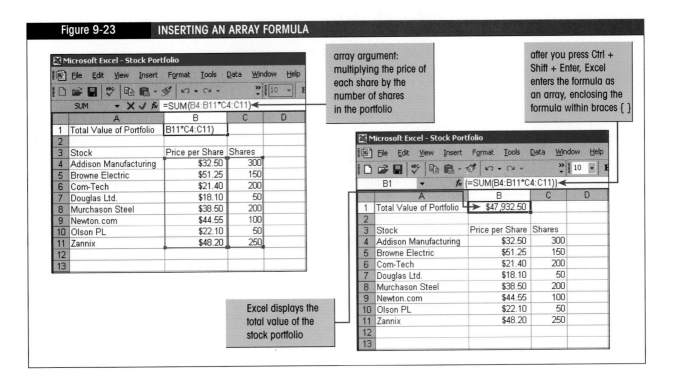

Figure 9-23   INSERTING AN ARRAY FORMULA

To create an array formula that displays several values, you must enter the formula into a selection of cells that has the same number of rows and columns as the array arguments have. One of the Excel functions that can be used to display multiple values (most do not) is the TREND function that can be used to forecast a straight-line trend of values. Figure 9-24 shows a sample workbook that uses the TREND function with array arguments to project the next seven values of a particular stock. Note that you must first select the range of cells that will contain the array formula and then enter the formula into the first cell in the range. Once again, you must press Ctrl + Shift + Enter (rather than the Enter key) when inserting the array formula.

Figure 9-24   USING AN ARRAY FORMULA FOR MULTIPLE VALUES

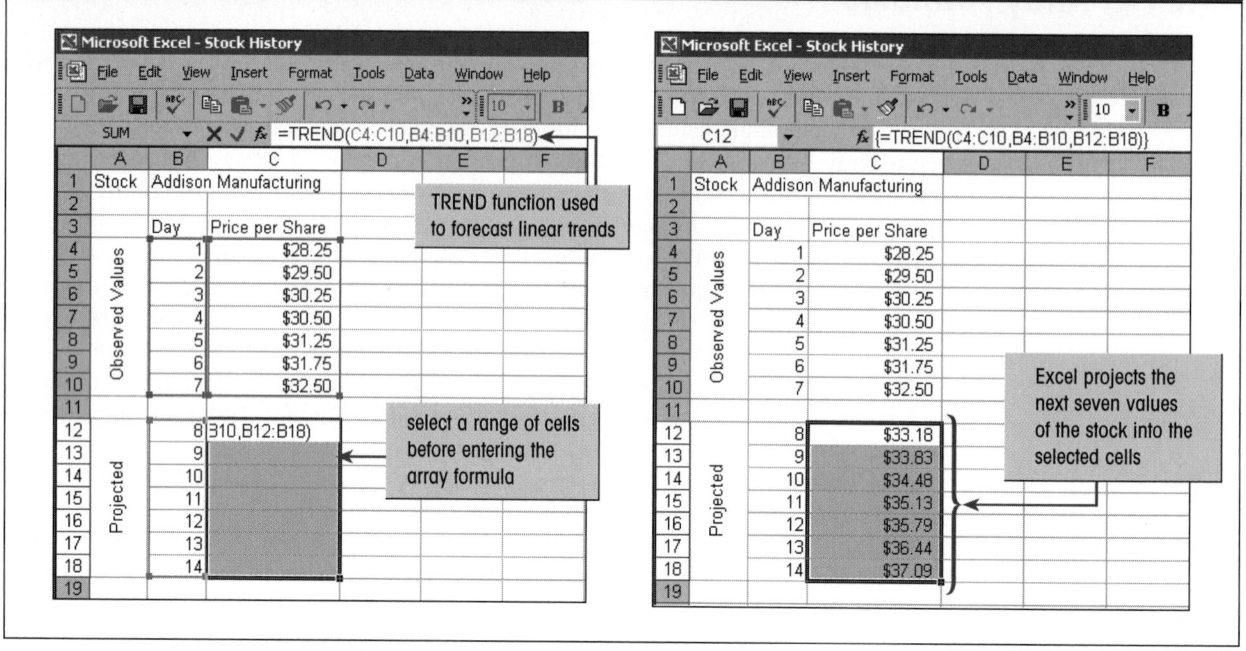

If you want to use constants in your arrays, place the constant values within a set of braces with each value separated by commas. For example, enter the values one through five as {1, 2, 3, 4, 5}.

With a better understanding of array formulas, you can see that array formulas are a useful feature of Excel, especially when you need to create a table of values, such as in a one-variable or two-variable data table. You are now ready to close the workbook.

> *To complete your work:*
>
> 1. Click the **Documentation** tab so this sheet appears when the next user opens this workbook.
>
> 2. Close the workbook, saving your changes.
>
> 3. Exit Excel.

Your analyses will help Eddie decide whether or not to purchase Front Range Rafting. He can see that a change in a few customers per day can make a big difference in the company's profitability. Eddie will take these figures and study them for a while.

Session 9.1 QUICK CHECK

1. What is a data table?
2. What is an input cell? What is a result cell?
3. What is a one-variable data table?
4. What is a two-variable data table?
5. How many result cells can you display with a one-variable data table? How many with a two-variable table?
6. What is an array formula?
7. What must you press after typing in an array formula in order for Excel to interpret it as an array?

SESSION 9.2

In this session, you'll use the Excel Scenario Manager to see the effect of changing several input cells on several result cells. You'll edit and save your scenarios and print scenario reports.

Using Scenario Manager

Eddie has looked over the what-if analyses you did for him. He would like to look at some more what-if analyses, changing other values in the worksheet to see what impact they would have on the company's net income. He has described four analyses that he wants you to investigate, as shown in Figure 9-25.

Figure 9-25	FOUR REVENUE AND EXPENSE OPTIONS			
REVENUE AND EXPENSE CATEGORIES	**AVERAGE SEASON**	**SLOW SEASON**	**BUSY SEASON**	**REDUCED PRICES**
Clients per Day (B5)	50	40	55	60
Fee per Client (B9)	60	60	60	45
Maintenance (B19)	25,000	25,000	30,000	20,000
Salary and Benefits (B20)	95,000	75,000	105,000	90,000
Administrative & Advertising (B21)	35,000	35,000	45,000	25,000
Est. Taxes (B22)	35,000	25,000	40,000	35,000

The **Average Season** option assumes the current revenue and expenses conditions at Front Range Rafting, with customers charged $60 per trip at an average of 50 customers per day. Eddie also wants to investigate a **Slow Season** option in which the average number of clients per day drops to 40, while expenses remain fixed except for salary and benefits. If Eddie spends more on advertising and benefits, this increase could lead to an increase in his customer base. Therefore, he has also written up a **Busy Season** option in which he increases the amount of money spent on advertising and salaries concurrent with increases in average number of clients per day and the fee per client. Finally, Eddie wants to investigate a **Reduced Prices** option in which he reduces his fees to $45 per trip along with slashing his expenses. Would he be able to break even if he can average 60 customers per day?

You quickly see that you can't generate such a report using a data table because Eddie has asked you to work with several input cells. To perform a what-if analysis with more than two input cells, you have to create scenarios. A **scenario** is a set of values entered into a worksheet that describes different situations, like the options that Eddie laid out in Figure 9-25. Instead of creating workbooks for each possible situation or entering values every time you want to perform a what-if analysis, you can set up these situations as scenarios using Excel's Scenario Manager. Once you have saved the scenarios, you can view them and work with them any time you want. You'll use Scenario Manager to create the four scenarios that Eddie has outlined for you.

Before using Scenario Manager, you should assign range names to all the input and result cells that you intend to use in your scenarios. As you'll see later, the range names will automatically appear in Scenario Manager's dialog boxes and reports. Though not a requirement, range names make it easier for you to work with your scenarios and for other people to understand your scenario reports.

To create range names for the values in the table:

1. If you took a break after the last session, start Excel and reopen the **Rafting2** workbook located in the Tutorial.09\Tutorial folder on your Data Disk.

2. Switch to the Income Statement worksheet, press **Ctrl + Home** if necessary to return to the top of the worksheet, and then select the nonadjacent range **A4:B5;A9:B9;A13:B14;A18:B22;A26:B28**.

   TROUBLE? To select nonadjacent ranges, select the first range, press and hold the Ctrl key, and then select the second range and so forth.

3. Click **Insert** on the menu bar, point to **Name**, and then click **Create**.

4. Make sure the Left column check box is the only check box selected, and then click the **OK** button.

5. Click cell **A1** to deselect the range.

Now that you have entered the range names in the workbook, you are ready to start defining the scenarios using Scenario Manager.

Defining Scenarios

To create the first scenario, you start Scenario Manager and enter a name for the scenario.

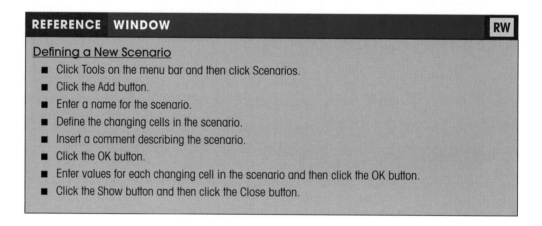

REFERENCE WINDOW   RW

Defining a New Scenario
- Click Tools on the menu bar and then click Scenarios.
- Click the Add button.
- Enter a name for the scenario.
- Define the changing cells in the scenario.
- Insert a comment describing the scenario.
- Click the OK button.
- Enter values for each changing cell in the scenario and then click the OK button.
- Click the Show button and then click the Close button.

You'll enter the Average Season scenario first.

To add the Average Season scenario to the workbook:

1. Click **Tools** on the menu bar, and then click **Scenarios**. The Scenario Manager dialog box opens. See Figure 9-26.

| Figure 9-26 | SCENARIO MANAGER DIALOG BOX |

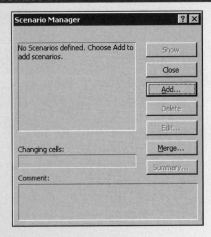

2. Click the **Add** button to add a new scenario to the workbook. The Add Scenario dialog box opens.

3. Type **Average Season** in the Scenario name text box, and then press the **Tab** key.

Next you'll specify the input cells you want to use for this scenario. Scenario Manager refers to input cells as **changing cells** because these are the worksheet cells containing values you want to change. Changing cells can be located anywhere on the worksheet. You can type in the names or locations of changing cells, but it's usually easier to select them with the mouse. To select nonadjacent changing cells, press and hold the Ctrl key as you click each cell. In each scenario, the values that will change are as follows:

- Cell B5: Clients per Day
- Cell B9: Fee per Client
- Cell B19: Maintenance
- Cell B20: Salary and Benefits
- Cell B21: Administrative and Advertising
- Cell B22: Estimated Taxes

To specify the input cells in the scenario:

1. Click in the Changing cells reference box, click the **Collapse Dialog Box** button, select the nonadjacent range **B5,B9,B19:B22** on the worksheet, and then click the **Expand Dialog Box** button.

2. Press the **Tab** key and then type **Projected profit assuming an average season.** in the Comment text box. See Figure 9-27.

Figure 9-27   **SPECIFING INPUT CELLS FOR THE AVERAGE SEASON SCENARIO**

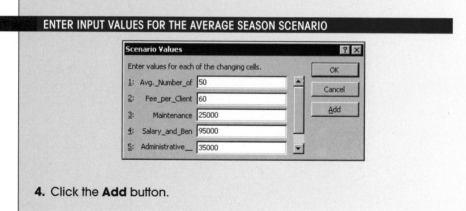

scenario name

input cells

scenario description

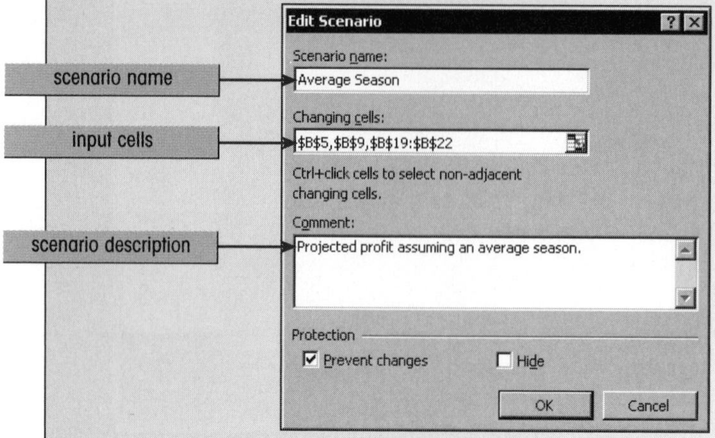

3. Click the **OK** button. The Scenario Values dialog box opens. So far, you've specified the location of the input cells; the next step is to specify values for each of the input cells. In this case, however, the Average Season scenario values represent the current values in the workbook, so you can accept the current figures as displayed in the Scenario Values dialog box. See Figure 9-28.

Figure 9-28   **ENTER INPUT VALUES FOR THE AVERAGE SEASON SCENARIO**

4. Click the **Add** button.

Note that in Figure 9-28, Excel displays part of the range name for each of the input cells in the scenario. This makes it easier for you to correctly enter scenario information. Note also that, because you clicked the Add button rather than the OK button, you are returned to the Add Scenario dialog box and can proceed to add Eddie's remaining scenarios.

To add the three remaining scenarios:

1. Type **Slow Season** in the Scenario name text box, and then press the **Tab** key twice.

2. Type **Projected profit assuming a slow season.** in the Comment text box, and then click the **OK** button.

3. Enter the following values for the Slow Season scenario in the Scenarios Values dialog box, pressing the Tab key to move from text box to text box:

Avg._Number_of box: **40**

Fee_per_Client box: **60**

Maintenance box: **25000**

Salary_and_Ben box: **75000**

Administrative_ box: **35000**

Est._Taxes box: **25000**

TROUBLE? If you press the Enter key instead of the Tab key, you are returned to the Scenario Manager dialog box. Make sure the Slow Season scenario is selected in the list box, click the Edit button, and then click the OK button to reopen the Scenario Values dialog box so you can enter the remaining values.

4. Click the **Add** button, type **Busy Season** as the scenario name, type **Projected profit assuming a busy season.** as the comment, and then click the **OK** button.

5. Enter the following values for the Busy Season scenario:

Avg._Number_of box: **55**

Fee_per_Client box: **60**

Maintenance box: **30000**

Salary_and_Ben box: **105000**

Administrative_ box: **45000**

Est._Taxes box: **40000**

6. Click the **Add** button, type **Reduced Prices** as the scenario name, type **Projected profit assuming a reduction in fees and expenses.** as the comment, and then click the **OK** button.

7. Enter the following values for the Busy Season scenario:

Avg._Number_of box **60**

Fee_per_Client box **45**

Maintenance box **20000**

Salary_and_Ben box **90000**

Administrative_ box **25000**

Est._Taxes box **35000**

8. Click the **OK** button. Figure 9-29 shows all four scenarios listed in the Scenario Manager dialog box.

Figure 9-29 THE FOUR SCENARIOS IN THE RAFTING2 WORKBOOK

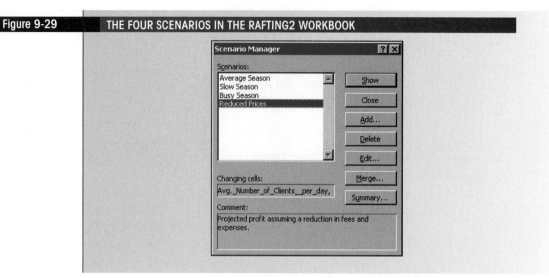

Your scenarios are entered and you are ready to view the effect of each scenario.

Viewing Scenarios

Now that you have entered the four scenarios, you can view the impact each scenario has on operating income by selecting the scenario and clicking the Show button or by double-clicking the scenario name.

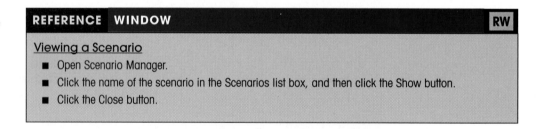

REFERENCE WINDOW   RW

Viewing a Scenario
- Open Scenario Manager.
- Click the name of the scenario in the Scenarios list box, and then click the Show button.
- Click the Close button.

You'll preview the effect of each scenario on the company's seasonal profit.

To view each scenario:

1. Click **Slow Season** in the Scenarios list box.

2. Click the **Show** button and then the **Close** button. Figure 9-30 shows the income statement for Front Range Rafting assuming a slow season with cutbacks in salaries and benefits and a reduced estimated tax.

Figure 9-30	INCOME STATEMENT FOR THE SLOW SEASON SCENARIO

	A	B	C
1	**Income Statement**		
3	**Season Information**		
4	Length of Season (days)	120	
5	Avg. Number of Clients (per day)	40	
6	**Total Number of Clients**	4,800	
7			
8	**Revenue**		
9	Fee per Client	60	
10	**Total Revenue**	$ 288,000	
11			
12	**Variable Expenses**		
13	Expense per Client	3	
14	River Usage Tax per Client	10	
15	**Total Variable Expenses**	$ 62,400	
16			
17	**Fixed Expenses**		
18	Insurance	10,000	
19	Maintenance	25,000	
20	Salary and Benefits	75,000	
21	Administrative & Advertising	35,000	
22	Est. Taxes	25,000	
23	**Total Fixed Expenses**	$ 170,000	
24			
25	**Summary**		
26	Total Revenue	288,000	
27	Total Expenses	232,400	
28	**Net Income**	$ 55,600	
29			

Excel has automatically changed the values in the six input cells. Eddie notices that under the Slow Season scenario, his net income would be $55,600. This is a drop from the $82,000 net income Eddie would expect under the Average Season scenario with which he was originally presented. Compare the net incomes resulting under those two scenarios with the net incomes resulting under the Busy Season and Reduced Prices scenarios.

To view the remaining scenarios:

1. Click **Tools** on the menu bar, and then click **Scenarios**.

2. Double-click **Busy Season** in the list of scenarios to show the scenario, and then click the **Close** button. In the Busy Season scenario, the net income shown in cell B28 would be $80,200.

3. Click **Tools**, click **Scenarios**, double-click **Reduced Prices**, and then click the **Close** button. The net income under the Reduced Prices scenario would be $50,400. Figure 9-31 shows the complete income statement for all four scenarios.

Figure 9-31   INCOME STATEMENT FOR THE FOUR SCENARIOS

average season

Income Statement	
Season Information	
Length of Season (days)	120
Avg. Number of Clients (per day)	50
Total Number of Clients	6,000
Revenue	
Fee per Client	60
Total Revenue	$ 360,000
Variable Expenses	
Expense per Client	3
River Usage Tax per Client	10
Total Variable Expenses	$ 78,000
Fixed Expenses	
Insurance	10,000
Maintenance	25,000
Salary and Benefits	95,000
Administrative & Advertising	35,000
Est. Taxes	35,000
Total Fixed Expenses	$ 200,000
Summary	
Total Revenue	360,000
Total Expenses	278,000
Net Income	$ 82,000

slow season

Income Statement	
Season Information	
Length of Season (days)	120
Avg. Number of Clients (per day)	40
Total Number of Clients	4,800
Revenue	
Fee per Client	60
Total Revenue	$ 288,000
Variable Expenses	
Expense per Client	3
River Usage Tax per Client	10
Total Variable Expenses	$ 62,400
Fixed Expenses	
Insurance	10,000
Maintenance	25,000
Salary and Benefits	75,000
Administrative & Advertising	35,000
Est. Taxes	25,000
Total Fixed Expenses	$ 170,000
Summary	
Total Revenue	288,000
Total Expenses	232,400
Net Income	$ 55,600

busy season

Income Statement	
Season Information	
Length of Season (days)	120
Avg. Number of Clients (per day)	55
Total Number of Clients	6,600
Revenue	
Fee per Client	60
Total Revenue	$ 396,000
Variable Expenses	
Expense per Client	3
River Usage Tax per Client	10
Total Variable Expenses	$ 85,800
Fixed Expenses	
Insurance	10,000
Maintenance	30,000
Salary and Benefits	105,000
Administrative & Advertising	45,000
Est. Taxes	40,000
Total Fixed Expenses	$ 230,000
Summary	
Total Revenue	396,000
Total Expenses	315,800
Net Income	$ 80,200

reduced season

Income Statement	
Season Information	
Length of Season (days)	120
Avg. Number of Clients (per day)	60
Total Number of Clients	7,200
Revenue	
Fee per Client	45
Total Revenue	$ 324,000
Variable Expenses	
Expense per Client	3
River Usage Tax per Client	10
Total Variable Expenses	$ 93,600
Fixed Expenses	
Insurance	10,000
Maintenance	20,000
Salary and Benefits	90,000
Administrative & Advertising	25,000
Est. Taxes	35,000
Total Fixed Expenses	$ 180,000
Summary	
Total Revenue	324,000
Total Expenses	273,600
Net Income	$ 50,400

As you look over the four scenarios, you can draw several conclusions. Both the Average Season and the Busy Season scenarios result in net income values of around $80,000, whereas the Slow Season and Reduced Prices values result in net incomes of around $50,000. However, Eddie has also assumed that he will be able to successfully cut costs in the Reduced Prices scenarios. It's quite possible that he will be unable to cut expenses as much as he hopes. It is also possible that expenses will not rise as much as he thinks in the Busy Season scenario and that he could expect an even higher profit margin.

You present the scenario results to Eddie, who evaluates the impact of each strategy on monthly operating income. After some thought, he wants you to modify the Reduced Prices scenario, this time assuming that the maintenance expenses will rise to $25,000 (from the assumed $20,000) and that the average number of customers per day will drop to 55 (from the previously assumed 60).

Editing Scenarios

Once you have created a scenario, it's easy to make changes so you can examine variations of given sets of assumptions. The scenario results will automatically update to reflect the new information.

Editing a Scenario
- Open Scenario Manager.
- Click the scenario name in the Scenarios list box, and click the Edit button.
- Enter a new cell range for the changing cells if necessary, and click the OK button.
- Enter new values for the changing cells, and then click the OK button.
- Click the Show button to show the results of the edited scenario, and then click the Close button.

You return to the worksheet to modify the scenario values in the Reduced Prices scenario.

To edit the Reduced Prices scenario:

1. Click **Tools** on the menu bar, and then click **Scenarios**.

2. Click **Reduced Prices** in the Scenarios list box (if necessary), and then click the **Edit** button.

3. Click the **OK** button to accept the range for the changing cells.

4. In the Avg._Number_of text box, type **55**, press the **Tab** key twice, type **25000** in the Maintenance text box, and then click the **OK** button.

5. Click the **Show** button and then click the **Close** button. The Income Statement showing the new values for the Reduced Prices scenario appears in Figure 9-32.

Figure 9-32 | NEW INCOME STATEMENT FOR THE REVISED REDUCED PRICES SCENARIO

	A	B	C
1	Income Statement		
2			
3	Season Information		
4	Length of Season (days)	120	
5	Avg. Number of Clients (per day)	55	
6	Total Number of Clients	6,600	
7			
8	Revenue		
9	Fee per Client	45	
10	Total Revenue	$ 297,000	
11			
12	Variable Expenses		
13	Expense per Client	3	
14	River Usage Tax per Client	10	
15	Total Variable Expenses	$ 85,800	
16			
17	Fixed Expenses		
18	Insurance	10,000	
19	Maintenance	25,000	
20	Salary and Benefits	90,000	
21	Administrative & Advertising	25,000	
22	Est. Taxes	35,000	
23	Total Fixed Expenses	$ 185,000	
24			
25	Summary		
26	Total Revenue	297,000	
27	Total Expenses	270,800	
28	Net Income	$ 26,200	
29			

The net income under this scenario drops to $26,200. From these results, Eddie is concerned that an unexpected increase in maintenance expenses coupled with smaller than expected customer traffic could reduce his net income by half.

Although the scenarios help you make important business decisions, you might find comparing the results of each scenario to be time consuming. Eddie wants to have a table of scenario values that he can hold in his hand and show to others. You could type the results of each scenario into a table for Eddie, or you can save yourself time by having Scenario Manager generate a formatted report automatically.

Creating a Scenario Summary Report

A scenario summary report is a useful tool for those making business decisions based on scenario results. Rather than listing all the cells on the Income Statement, the scenario summary report lists only the changing cells or input values and the result cells for each scenario. The report's tabular layout makes it easy to compare the results of each scenario, and the automatic formatting makes it useful for reports and meetings.

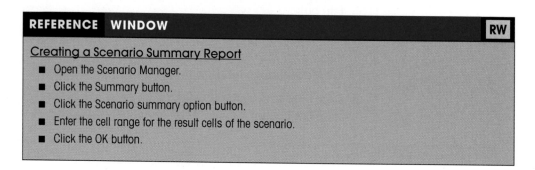

REFERENCE WINDOW **RW**

Creating a Scenario Summary Report
- Open the Scenario Manager.
- Click the Summary button.
- Click the Scenario summary option button.
- Enter the cell range for the result cells of the scenario.
- Click the OK button.

In creating the report, you can identify which cells are the result cells. Eddie is most interested in the following values:

- B26: Total Revenue
- B27: Total Expense
- B28: Net Income

Put these values along with the values of the input cells into your report.

To create the scenario summary report:

1. Click **Tools** on the menu bar, and then click **Scenarios**.

2. Click the **Summary** button. The Scenario Summary dialog box opens, allowing you to create a scenario summary report or a scenario pivottable report.

3. Verify that the Scenario summary option button is selected.

   Now enter the result cells containing the revenue, expenses, and net income.

4. Type **B26:B28** in the Result cells reference box. See Figure 9-33.

Figure 9-33	NEW INCOME STATEMENT FOR THE REVISED REDUCED PRICES SCENARIO

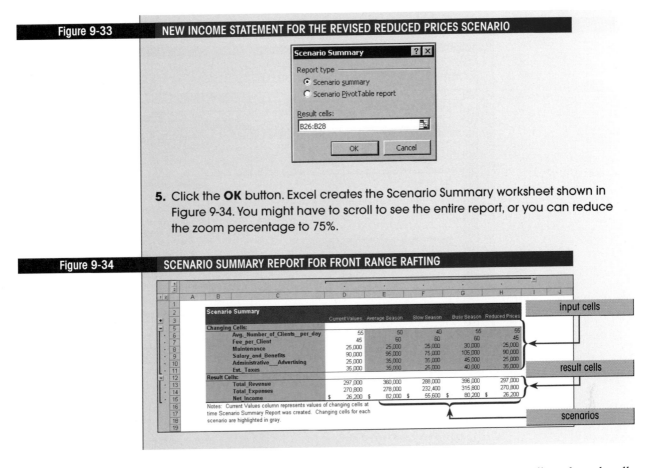

5. Click the **OK** button. Excel creates the Scenario Summary worksheet shown in Figure 9-34. You might have to scroll to see the entire report, or you can reduce the zoom percentage to 75%.

Figure 9-34	SCENARIO SUMMARY REPORT FOR FRONT RANGE RAFTING

The scenario summary report displays the values for the changing cells and result cells for each scenario. Each scenario is listed by name, and the current worksheet values are also displayed. As it did with the individual scenarios, Scenario Manager has labeled each cell using the range names you defined earlier. By creating range names, you've made the report easier for Eddie to interpret.

Creating a Scenario PivotTable Report

Another way of displaying the results of your scenarios is with a PivotTable report. As the name implies, a PivotTable report inserts each scenario as a pivot field in a PivotTable. You decide to summarize the four scenarios in a PivotTable and PivotChart.

To create a scenario PivotTable report:

1. Switch to the Income Statement worksheet.

2. Click **Tools** on the menu bar, click **Scenarios**, and then click the **Summary** button in the Scenario Manager dialog box.

3. Click the **Scenario PivotTable report** option button, and then click the **OK** button. Excel displays the PivotTable, as shown in Figure 9-35.

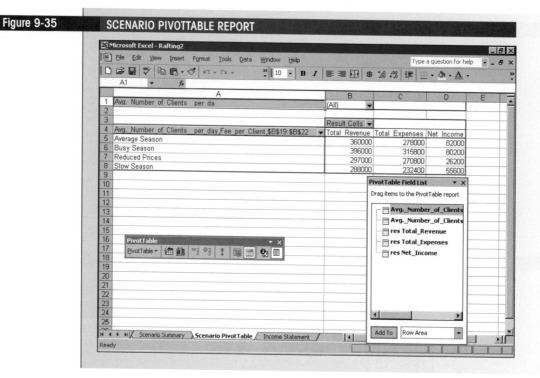

Figure 9-35   SCENARIO PIVOTTABLE REPORT

You can edit the table to make it easier to read and also use it to generate a chart of revenue, expenses, and net income.

To edit the scenario PivotTable report:

1. Right-click the **Avg._Number_of_Clients_per_day** field in cell A4, and then click **Field Settings** on the shortcut menu.

2. Change the text in the Name text box to **Scenarios**, and then click the **OK** button.

3. Drag the field button in cell A1 off the PivotTable, removing the field from the table.

4. Select the values in the range **B5:D8**, click **Format** on the menu bar, and then click **Cells**.

5. Click the **Number** tab if necessary, click **Currency** in the Category list, reduce the number of decimal places to **0**, select the fourth option in the Negative numbers list box, and then click the **OK** button.

6. Click cell **A1** to remove the selection from the table. Figure 9-36 shows the formatted PivotTable.

Figure 9-36   **FORMATTED PIVOTTABLE REPORT**

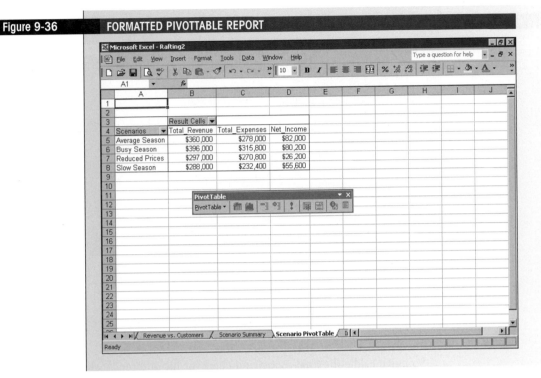

Finally, display the results of this table in a PivotChart.

To create a PivotChart:

1. Click cell **A3** to reselect the PivotTable, and then click the **Chart Wizard** button on the PivotTable toolbar. Excel displays the PivotTable data in a stacked column chart.

   Change the chart format to a clustered column chart.

2. Click **Chart** on the menu bar, and then click **Chart Type**.

3. Click the **Clustered Column** sub-type (first row, first column), and then click the **OK** button.

4. Close the PivotTable toolbar and the PivotTable Field List. Figure 9-37 shows the PivotChart.

Figure 9-37   **SCENARIO PIVOTCHART**

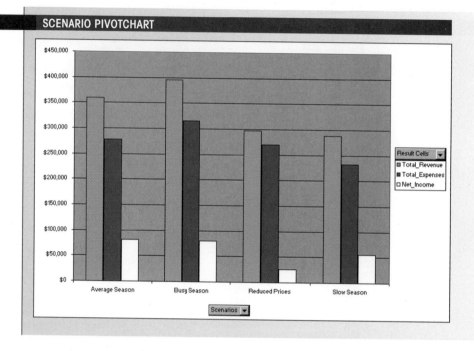

You give Eddie the final report and chart for his different scenarios. He will look it over and get back to you if he needs to explore any other scenarios. Based on your findings, you tell Eddie that he should be able to expect net income from the Front Range Rafting company of $50,000 to $80,000 per year. You also recommend that he not pursue the Reduced Prices scenarios because of the risk of substantially reduced profits.

Scenarios are a very useful feature of Excel. You can also use scenarios in situations involving multiple workbooks, where a scenario from one workbook can be merged into another workbook. In this way, several users can work on a common set of scenarios for different reports and analyses.

Session 9.2 QUICK | CHECK

1. What is an advantage of scenarios over data tables?

2. What should you do before starting Scenario Manager to make the reports you generate easier to interpret?

3. What are changing cells?

4. What are result cells? Where do you define result cells in Scenario Manager?

5. How do you display a scenario?

6. How do you create a scenario PivotTable report?

REVIEW ASSIGNMENTS

Eddie has received some more information about Front Range Rafting. He has learned that although the average season is 120 days, problems with weather sometimes reduce that value by up to 10 days. On the other hand, with an early spring, the rafting season can sometimes be extended up to 130 days. Eddie wants to explore the rafting company's profitability for seasons of different lengths. He also wants to use varying season lengths for different scenarios.

To complete this task:

1. Start Excel and open the **Season1** workbook located in the Tutorial.09\Review folder on your Data Disk. Enter the date and your name in the Documentation sheet. Save the workbook as **Season2** in the same folder. Switch to the Income Statement worksheet.

2. Create a one-variable data table to calculate the revenue, expenses, and net income for Front Range Rafting for lengths of seasons of 110 days to 130 days in increments of 2 days. Assuming that the company averages 45 clients per day at a fee of $60 per client, is there any danger of the company losing money during the season? Format the table so that it is easy to read.

3. Create a CVP chart of the values in the one-variable data table. Store the chart on a chart sheet named "CVP Chart". Enter "CVP Chart" as the chart title, "Length of Season" as the x-axis title, and "Revenues and Expenses" as the y-axis title.

4. Create a two-variable data table for the input cells, length of season, and average customers per day. Assume that the length of season can vary from 110 to 130 days (in increments of 2) and the average number of customers per day can vary from 30 to 60 (in increments of 5). Calculate the net income under all of these possibilities.

Explore
5. Given that Eddie can't control the weather or the number of clients, calculate the average net income value in the two-variable data table. Based on your calculations, what can he expect for a net income?

6. Format the two-variable data table so that it is easy to read. Use a custom format on the cell in the upper-left corner of the table so that it displays the text "Season". Format the average net income value.

7. Using the Name Create command, create names for values in column B based on the labels in column A (click the Yes button when you are prompted to replace the definition of Total Revenue).

8. Eddie wants to investigate three possible scenarios: a Lean Year scenario, a Full Year scenario, and an Average Year scenario. He has listed the parameters of the scenarios in Figure 9-38. Add these scenarios to the Season2 workbook.

Figure 9-38

REVENUE AND EXPENSE CATEGORIES	AVERAGE YEAR	LEAN YEAR	FULL YEAR
Length of Season (B4)	120	110	125
Clients per Day (B5)	50	40	55
Salary and Benefits (B20)	95,000	80,000	105,000
Est. Taxes (B22)	35,000	25,000	40,000

9. Create a scenario summary report of the three scenarios you created, reporting on the total revenue, total expenses, and net income under each scenario.

10. Edit the Full Year scenario, this time assuming that the length of season will be 130 days. Also edit the Lean Year scenario, changing the cost of salaries and benefits to $95,000. Redo the scenario summary report.

11. Create a scenario PivotTable report of the values from your second set of scenarios. Format the table so that it is easy to read. (*Hint*: To change the long field name in cell A4 to "Scenarios," use the Field Settings command on the shortcut menu.)

12. Create a PivotChart showing a clustered column chart of the net income, total expenses, and total revenue values.

13. Print your data tables, summary reports, and charts. Include a description of your findings and indicate to Eddie what range of income he could expect for different lengths of seasons and under different scenarios.

14. Save and close the workbook, and then exit Excel.

CASE PROBLEMS

Case 1. Calculating a Grading Curve at MidWest University Professor David Templeton teaches Math 220 at MidWest University. He is in the process of grading the results of the final exam. Professor Templeton uses a grading curve. Ideally, he would like to have exam grades distributed among his students according to following percentages:

- ■ F's   5%
- ■ D's   10%
- ■ C's   35%
- ■ B's   35%
- ■ A's   15%

He has given you his grading workbook. He would like you to investigate the grading scenarios listed in Figure 9-39 and report which of them falls closest to his ideal grade distribution.

Figure 9-39

GRADE	SCENARIO 1	SCENARIO 2	SCENARIO 3	SCENARIO 4	SCENARIO 5
F	0 – 49	0 – 50	0 – 55	0 – 50	0 – 50
D	50 – 69	51 – 65	56 – 72	51 – 60	51 – 61
C	70 – 79	66 – 75	73 – 82	61 – 70	62 – 74
B	80 – 89	76 – 85	83 – 92	71 – 80	75 – 84
A	90 – 100	86 – 100	93 – 100	81 – 100	85 – 100

The layout of the workbook has already been done for you. Your job will be to create a frequency table using the FREQUENCY array formula to calculate the total number of students assigned to each letter grade. You will also use a lookup table to assign each student his or her calculated grade. Finally, you will create a scenario report for each of the five scenarios, analyzing the distribution of grades under each scenario.

To complete this task:

1. Open the **Curve1** workbook located in the Tutorial.09\Cases folder on your Data Disk. Enter the date and your name in the Documentation sheet. Save the workbook as **Curve2** in the same folder. Switch to the Grades worksheet.

2. Enter the scores and grades from the first scenario into the range E3:E7. Note that, because of the way the FREQUENCY array formula operates, you should enter the *maximum* score associated with each grade into the table. As you enter the first scenario grades, the grade scale in the lookup table is automatically entered for you. You do not have to enter any values in the lookup table.

Explore

3. Use the array formula FREQUENCY to calculate the counts associated with each grade. Place the counts (the number of time each grade occurs) in the range G3:G7. (*Hint*: To insert the FREQUENCY array formula, first review Excel's online Help for information on the FREQUENCY function. Select the range G3:G7, and enter the FREQUENCY function using the range B2:B51 for the data_array parameter and range E3:E7 for the bins_array parameter. Press Ctrl + Shift + Enter to enter the FREQUENCY array function for all of the grade counts in the selected range.)

4. In the range H3:H7, calculate the percentage of students assigned each grade. (*Hint*: There are a total of 50 students in Professor Templeton's class.)

5. Use the VLOOKUP function to determine each student's grade in the range C2:C51. Figure 9-40 shows the completed worksheet for the first scenario.

Figure 9-40

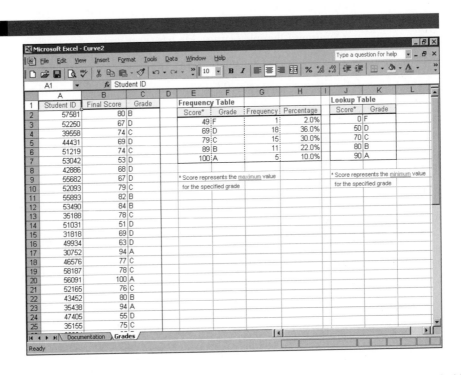

6. Assign the range names to cells in the Grades worksheet as shown in Figure 9-41.

Figure 9-41

CELL	RANGE NAME	CELL	RANGE NAME
E3	GradeF	H3	PercentF
E4	GradeD	H4	PercentD
E5	GradeC	H5	PercentC
E6	GradeB	H6	PercentB
E7	GradeA	H7	PercentA

7. Define the five scenarios described by Professor Templeton in the workbook. (*Hint*: Use the range E3:E7 as your input cells, and insert the *maximum* score for each grade.)

8. Create a scenario summary report, reporting on the percentage figures for each grade under each scenario.

9. Print the scenario summary report. Which scenario best matches the curve that Professor Templeton wants to apply to his grades?

10. View the contents of the Grades worksheet using the scenario you selected as the best. Print the contents of the Grades worksheet under this scenario.

11. Save and close the workbook, and then exit Excel.

Case 2. Sales Mix at Fine Prints, Inc. When a company sells more than one product, the company must produce and sell the right combination of products to maximize its profits. This combination is called the "sales mix" and is an important factor in determining CVP relationships. At Fine Prints, Inc., the manager, Mark Davis, is selling posters for the upcoming Summer Olympic Games. He has three styles of posters: regular, fine, and matted. Mark wants you to determine how the sales mix affects the cost-volume-profit relationship. At present, Mark produces and sells about 500 copies of the Olympics prints in the following proportions: 40% of the regular style, 30% of the fine style, and 30% of the matted style. Mark wants you to explore what would happen to the operating income and the break-even point if the sales mix were as follows:

- Current   Units Sold=500, Regular = 40%, Fine = 30%, Matted = 30%
- Even   Units Sold=500, Regular = 33.3%, Fine = 33.3%, Matted = 33.3%
- Regular   Units Sold=500, Regular = 50%, Fine = 25%, Matted = 25%
- Fine   Units Sold=500, Regular = 25%, Fine = 50%, Matted = 25%
- Matted   Units Sold=500, Regular = 25%, Fine = 25%, Matted = 50%

To complete this task:

1. Open the **Prints1** workbook located in the Tutorial.09\Cases folder on your Data Disk. Enter the date and your name in the Documentation sheet. Save the workbook as **Prints2** in the same folder. Switch to the Sales worksheet.

2. Assign the range name "Units_Sold" to cell C4, which contains the total number of the prints that have been sold. Use the Name Create command to create names for the Percent of Sales values found in the range D6:F6 of the Sales worksheet.

3. Using Scenario Manager, create the five scenarios listed above. The input cells in each scenario are the percent of sales values found in the D6:F6 range and the Units Sold value found in cell C4. Add a description for each scenario.

4. Use the Name Create command to create names for the outcome values in the range C20:C21.

5. Create a scenario summary report for the five scenarios. Include the net income and the break-even point in the scenario summary report.

6. Print the scenario summary report in landscape orientation.

7. Analyze the report. Which sales mix results in the highest net operating income and the lowest break-even point? Based on this, which of the three print types is the most profitable to the company?

Explore ➤ 8. Create a scenario PivotTable report of the net income that displays the Fine, Regular, and Matted scenarios. Format the PivotTable so that it is easy to read and interpret. Create a column PivotChart based on the PivotTable .

9. Save and close the workbook, and then exit Excel.

Case 3. Calculating the Present Value of an Investment When companies plan expenditures for upgrading equipment or adding new products, they hope that the expenditures will produce additional revenue and profit. Given that that they could invest their money elsewhere, companies need to determine if the income generated by capital improvements gives them a desirable rate of return on the investment. One way to evaluate the rate of return on an investment is to calculate the **present value** of the expenditure based on its anticipated earnings in the future. The present value expresses the worth of the investment in today's dollars. If the present value is greater than the initial investment, the investment is profitable. If not, the company may want to consider investing in other vehicles that are more likely to produce the desired rate of return.

You work with Allan Williams, owner of the Bread House Bakery. Allan has $50,000 to invest and is considering using it to upgrade the bakery's kitchen. The cost of the upgrade is $50,000. Allan expects that the new kitchen will result in increased efficiency and productivity, which will be worth about $15,000 a year for the next five years. Allan wants to know how this level of increased revenue compares with other investments that could yield returns of 10% to 16% a year. If the level is equal to or above the return rate of other investments, he will proceed with the renovation.

A workbook calculating the net present value of Allan's proposed kitchen upgrade has been created for you. The workbook shows the present value of upgrading the equipment, based on the assumptions that the renovation will increase revenue by $15,000 per year and that Allan would like to see at least a 12% return on his $50,000 investment. Allan wants you to use this workbook to calculate the value of upgrading the bakery for return rates other than 12%, such as rates between 10% and 16%.

Allan is also not sure that the upgrade will generate the type of extra revenue he is expecting. He wants you to calculate the present value of his investment assuming that the bakery upgrade yields the revenue shown in the following scenarios:

Low Initial Income

     Desired Rate of Return = 12%

     Year 1 = $5000

     Year 2 = $10,000

     Year 3 = $15,000

     Year 4 = $25,000

     Year 5 = $35,000

Early Income

  Desired Rate of Return = 12%

  Year 1 = $25,000

  Year 2 = $20,000

  Year 3 = $15,000

  Year 4 = $10,000

  Year 5 = $5000

Steady Growth Income

  Desired Rate of Return = 12%

  Year 1 = $10,000

  Year 2 = $12,000

  Year 3 = $14,000

  Year 4 = $16,000

  Year 5 = $20,000

To complete this task:

1. Open the **Bakery1** workbook located in the Tutorial.09\Cases folder on your Data Disk. Enter the date and your name in the Documentation sheet. Save the workbook as **Bakery2** in the same folder. Switch to the Present Value worksheet.

2. In the Present Value worksheet, create in the range F6:G13, a one-variable data table using the desired rate of return as the input cell and the net present value as the result cell. Use the following input values in the data table: 10%, 11%, 12%, 13%, 14%, 15%, and 16%. Label the data table appropriately, and then resize the columns.

3. Analyze the table and determine at what rate of return the investment in the equipment is no longer as profitable. In other words, under what conditions is the present value of the upgrade worth less than $50,000? If Allan can get a 16% yearly rate by investing his money elsewhere, should he do so?

4. Name cell B7 "Year_1", cell B8 "Year_2", and so forth through cell B11. Assign appropriate names to cells B4 and D14 as well.

5. Use Scenario Manager to create the three scenarios that Allan has outlined for you. Create a scenario summary report showing the net present value of the investment under each scenario. Do any of the scenarios show a negative net present value for the kitchen upgrade? What would you tell Allan regarding the value of the kitchen upgrade versus investing the $50,000 elsewhere? Are there some situations that Allan should watch out for given that he wants his upgrade to be financially successful?

6. Select the scenario that provided the highest net present value, and then display the scenario in the Present Value worksheet. Print the scenario summary report and the contents of the Present Value worksheet.

7. Save and close the workbook, and then exit Excel.

Case 4. Starting a Bed and Breakfast Steve and Linda Gonzales are considering opening a bed and breakfast in Port Supreme, Washington. They would like your help in analyzing what kind of customer base they would need to show a profit. Linda has outlined the following expenses for the bed and breakfast:

Variable Expense

Average cost of food per meal	$4
Average cost of room upkeep per customer	$1.50

Fixed Expenses

Est. Taxes	$15,000 per year
Insurance	$5,000 per year
Maintenance and Upkeep	$5000 per year
Food	$15,000 per year

Linda is trying to determine how much to charge per customer. She assumes that the bed and breakfast will serve about 500 customers per year and each customer will be provided with 3 meals. Her initial estimate also indicates that they would charge $140 per visit for a one-night stay at their bed and breakfast. Steve wants the bed and breakfast to show a net income of $60,000 per year in order for them to risk the venture. They would like your help in analyzing the situation.

To complete this task:

1. Create a workbook named **Inn** in the Tutorial.09\Cases folder on your Data Disk.

2. Insert a Documentation sheet with your name and the date the workbook was created. Include a purpose statement.

3. Create a worksheet named "Analysis" that contains Linda's initial revenue and expenses estimates.

4. Create a one-variable data table that calculates the total revenue, expenses, and net income for fees that range from $130 per person per night to $180 per person per night in increments of $5.

5. Create a two-variable data table for the same fees you calculated for the one-variable data table, and assume that the number of customers per year can vary from 400 to 700 in increments of 50. What combinations of total customers and fees yield the net income that the Gonzales are looking for?

6. Calculate the net income under the four scenarios listed in Figure 9-42.

Figure 9-42				
CATEGORIES	**SCENARIO 1**	**SCENARIO 2**	**SCENARIO 3**	**SCENARIO 4**
Customers per Year	500	500	600	600
Fee per Customer	$140.00	$160.00	$140.00	$160.00
Cost per Meal	$3.00	$4.00	$3.00	$4.00
Cost per Room	$1.50	$2.00	$1.50	$2.00
Food	$10,000.00	$15,000.00	$10,000.00	$15,000.00

7. Print the scenario summary report for the four scenarios.

8. Prepare a report for Steve and Linda indicating whether you believe that their venture will produce the net income they're looking for.

9. Save and close the workbook, and then exit Excel.

INTERNET ASSIGNMENTS

Student Union

The purpose of the Internet Assignments is to challenge you to find information on the Internet that you can use to create effective spreadsheets. The actual assignments are updated and maintained on the Course Technology Web site. Log on to the Internet and use your Web browser to go to the Student Union on the New Perspectives Series site at **www.course.com/NewPerspectives/studentunion**. Click the Online Companions link, and then click the link for this text.

QUICK | CHECK ANSWERS

Session 9.1

1. a table that shows the results of several what-if analyses

2. An input cell is the cell in the table containing the value you are interested in changing. The result cell is the cell containing the value you're interested in viewing.

3. a data table with a single column or row of input values and multiple result values

4. a data table with two input values and a single result value

5. You can display an unlimited number of result values with the one-variable data table, but only one result value with the two-variable data table.

6. a formula that performs multiple calculations on one or more sets of values and then returns either a single value or multiple values

7. Ctrl + Shift + Enter

Session 9.2

1. Scenarios enable you to perform what-if analyses using several input and result cells.

2. assign range names to the cells

3. cells containing values you are changing in the scenario

4. Result cells display the output values you're interested in. You define result cells when creating scenario summary reports.

5. Click Tools, click Scenarios, and then click the scenario name in the list of available scenarios.

6. Click the Summary button in the Scenario Manager dialog box, click the Scenario summary option button, enter the result cells range reference, and then click the OK button.

OBJECTIVES

In this tutorial you will:

- Formulate a problem

- Perform what-if analyses

- Try to solve a problem using trial and error

- Use Goal Seek to automate the trial-and-error process

- Use Solver to find the best solution

- Create an answer report

- Explore how to configure Solver to best work with your data

USING SOLVER FOR COMPLEX PROBLEMS

Determining the Optimal Product Mix for GrillRite Grills

CASE

GrillRite

GrillRite of Tucson, Arizona, is one of the biggest manufacturers of grills in the country. Dawn Li is a new product manager for GrillRite's southwest sales region. Her job is to manage the orders for stores in Arizona, New Mexico, and Nevada. It's spring, and Dawn has to prepare an order to be ready for the heavy early summer sales.

GrillRite makes four models of grills: the Standard model, the Deluxe model, the Dual model, and the Extended model. Dawn has to decide how many of each model to order for her stores. There are many factors involved in making up her order. She needs to order enough of each model to satisfy store demand. Each grill has to be assembled at a regional plant, so Dawn can only order models that require parts that are currently in stock. She can only order what the plant can produce. Finally, she has to order a mix of models that will maximize GrillRite's net income for the coming months. Some of the models have a higher profit margin than others.

Trying to balance all of these factors is a great challenge. Dawn has asked your help in putting together an order that will satisfy her customers, the plant managers, and her bosses.

SESSION 10.1

In this session, you will plan and create a grill order, perform a what-if analysis, seek a solution by trial and error, and use the Excel Goal Seek command. With the skills you learn in this session, you will be able to use Excel to find answers to questions by experimenting with different sets of financial conditions.

Optimizing Product Mix

You meet with Dawn Li to start work on her grill order. Your job will be to find the purchase order that maximizes GrillRite's profits while meeting consumer demand and satisfying the limitations of the production process. Dawn has already put together a workbook containing all of the factors you need for your work. You decide to examine this workbook to get a better grasp on the issues confronting her.

To open Dawn's workbook:

1. Start Excel and open the **Grill1** workbook located in the Tutorial.10\Tutorial folder on your Data Disk.

2. Enter the date and your name in the Documentation sheet.

3. Save the workbook as **Grill2** in the Tutorial.10\Tutorial folder on your Data Disk.

4. Switch to the Order worksheet.

There are two sections in the Order worksheet. The left section of the worksheet, shown in Figure 10-1, contains an income analysis of the four grill models: Standard, Deluxe, Dual, and Extended. Based on the cost of parts and assembly, you can see that the most expensive grill to produce is the Extended model at $203 per grill. The least expensive is the Standard model, which costs $106.50 per unit to produce. When GrillRite sells these grills, it sells the Extended model for $315 and the Standard model for $155. The prices of the other two models fall between these two. GrillRite also has fixed expenses of $30,000 that Dawn will have to account for when she determines the profitability of her order.

Figure 10-1   INCOME ANALYSIS FOR A GRILL ORDER

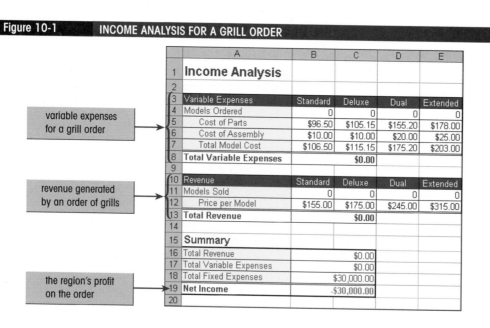

	A	B	C	D	E
1	**Income Analysis**				
2					
3	Variable Expenses	Standard	Deluxe	Dual	Extended
4	Models Ordered	0	0	0	0
5	Cost of Parts	$96.50	$105.15	$155.20	$178.00
6	Cost of Assembly	$10.00	$10.00	$20.00	$25.00
7	Total Model Cost	$106.50	$115.15	$175.20	$203.00
8	**Total Variable Expenses**		$0.00		
9					
10	Revenue	Standard	Deluxe	Dual	Extended
11	Models Sold	0	0	0	0
12	Price per Model	$155.00	$175.00	$245.00	$315.00
13	**Total Revenue**		$0.00		
14					
15	**Summary**				
16	Total Revenue		$0.00		
17	Total Variable Expenses		$0.00		
18	Total Fixed Expenses		$30,000.00		
19	**Net Income**		-$30,000.00		
20					

variable expenses for a grill order

revenue generated by an order of grills

the region's profit on the order

Dawn has already received requests for grills from various stores in her region. Any order she makes will need to include at least these quantities of grills:

- Standard model: 125 units
- Deluxe model: 100 units
- Dual model: 100 units
- Extended model: 75 units

When Dawn orders a grill, it has to be assembled at a regional plant. On the right side of the Order worksheet, Dawn has inserted the parts inventory data from the plant (see Figure 10-2). The first column of this table contains a list of the parts used in the assembly of the four grill models. The second column indicates how many of those parts are currently in stock. The third and fourth columns record how many parts will be required by Dawn's order and the number of parts remaining at the plant after Dawn's order has been fulfilled. The fifth column shows the cost of each part.

Figure 10-2   **GRILL PARTS INVENTORY**

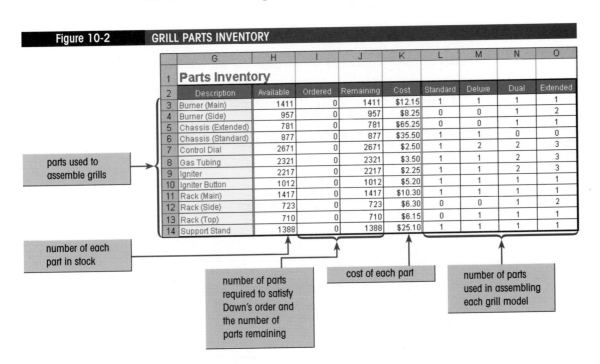

	G	H	I	J	K	L	M	N	O
1	**Parts Inventory**								
2	Description	Available	Ordered	Remaining	Cost	Standard	Deluxe	Dual	Extended
3	Burner (Main)	1411	0	1411	$12.15	1	1	1	1
4	Burner (Side)	957	0	957	$8.25	0	0	1	2
5	Chassis (Extended)	781	0	781	$65.25	0	0	1	1
6	Chassis (Standard)	877	0	877	$35.50	1	1	0	0
7	Control Dial	2671	0	2671	$2.50	1	2	2	3
8	Gas Tubing	2321	0	2321	$3.50	1	1	2	3
9	Igniter	2217	0	2217	$2.25	1	1	2	3
10	Igniter Button	1012	0	1012	$5.20	1	1	1	1
11	Rack (Main)	1417	0	1417	$10.30	1	1	1	1
12	Rack (Side)	723	0	723	$6.30	0	0	1	2
13	Rack (Top)	710	0	710	$6.15	0	1	1	1
14	Support Stand	1388	0	1388	$25.10	1	1	1	1

parts used to assemble grills

number of each part in stock

number of parts required to satisfy Dawn's order and the number of parts remaining

cost of each part

number of parts used in assembling each grill model

The remaining four columns indicate how many of each part is used in assembling the grills. For example, all four models use a single main burner; however, only the Dual and Extended models use a side burner. The Extended model requires two side burners, whereas the Dual model needs only one. Any grills that Dawn orders cannot use more parts than are currently available. For example, Dawn knows that she can't order more than 500 Extended grills because that would require 1000 side burners, and there are only 957 side burners in stock. There are twelve parts that go into assembling these grills, and, aside from the side burners, it's not immediately clear to Dawn what factors limit the number and type of grills she can order. Therefore, as you help Dawn put together her order, you need to meet the following requirements:

- Satisfy the stores that have already ordered grills.
- Order no more grills than can be assembled at the manufacturing plant.
- Maximize the company's profits.

What you need to do is help Dawn find the **optimal product mix**—the mix of products that satisfies customer and production constraints while at the same time maximizing profit. Optimizing product mix is a common problem in production and marketing.

Finding a Solution Using Trial and Error

Putting aside the issue of how to maximize GrillRite's net income, Dawn explains to you that she is not even sure that the plants have enough parts on hand to assemble grills to satisfy the stores. You explain to Dawn that one way of getting a handle on the problem is to start entering what seem to be reasonable values. This approach is called trial and error. Although it is unlikely that Dawn will find the optimal product mix, using this approach will give her a feeling for how all of these factors relate to each other.

You propose that you start by entering the minimum order necessary to confirm that there are enough parts at the plant to satisfy her stores.

To enter a grill order:

1. Click cell **B4**, type **125**, and then press the **Tab** key.

2. Continue entering the remaining orders by inserting **100** in cell C4, **100** in cell D4, and **75** in cell E4. Figure 10-3 shows the income analysis for this order.

Figure 10-3	INCOME ANALYSIS FOR DAWN'S MINIMUM ORDER

	A	B	C	D	E
1	**Income Analysis**				
2					
3	Variable Expenses	Standard	Deluxe	Dual	Extended
4	Models Ordered	125	100	100	75
5	Cost of Parts	$96.50	$105.15	$155.20	$178.00
6	Cost of Assembly	$10.00	$10.00	$20.00	$25.00
7	Total Model Cost	$106.50	$115.15	$175.20	$203.00
8	**Total Variable Expenses**		$57,572.50		
9					
10	Revenue	Standard	Deluxe	Dual	Extended
11	Models Sold	125	100	100	75
12	Price per Model	$155.00	$175.00	$245.00	$315.00
13	**Total Revenue**		$85,000.00		
14					
15	**Summary**				
16	Total Revenue		$85,000.00		
17	Total Variable Expenses		$57,572.50		
18	Total Fixed Expenses		$30,000.00		
19	**Net Income**		-$2,572.50		
20					

orders show a net loss for the company

The net income for the order would be –$2,572.50, representing a loss to GrillRite of over $2500, but that's okay because this represents the minimum order Dawn would make. A larger order will show a profit for the company. Her bigger concern is whether the plant can produce enough grills to match this minimum order.

3. If necessary, scroll to right to display the contents of the Parts Inventory table.

Figure 10-4	PARTS INVENTORY FOR DAWN'S MINMUM ORDER

Parts Inventory

	Description	Available	Ordered	Remaining	Cost	Standard	Deluxe	Dual	Extended
3	Burner (Main)	1411	400	1011	$12.15	1	1	1	1
4	Burner (Side)	957	250	707	$8.25	0	0	1	2
5	Chassis (Extended)	781	175	606	$65.25	0	0	1	1
6	Chassis (Standard)	877	225	652	$35.50	1	1	0	0
7	Control Dial	2671	750	1921	$2.50	1	2	2	3
8	Gas Tubing	2321	650	1671	$3.50	1	1	2	3
9	Igniter	2217	650	1567	$2.25	1	1	2	3
10	Igniter Button	1012	400	612	$5.20	1	1	1	1
11	Rack (Main)	1417	400	1017	$10.30	1	1	1	1
12	Rack (Side)	723	250	473	$6.30	0	0	1	2
13	Rack (Top)	710	275	435	$6.15	0	1	1	1
14	Support Stand	1388	400	988	$25.10	1	1	1	1

there are plenty of parts left in stock to assemble more grills

As shown in Figure 10-4, there are plenty of parts remaining at the plant. For example, there are over 1000 main burners left in stock. This means that Dawn can order still more grills. Buoyed by her success, Dawn asks you to increase the order by 150 units per model. Perhaps this order will result in a profit without exceeding the parts supply.

To change the order without exceeding the parts supply:

1. Click cell **B4** and then enter **275**.

2. Change the number of Deluxe grills in cell C4 to **250**, the number of Dual grills to **250**, and the number of Extended grills to **225**. Figure 10-5 shows GrillRite's income. With this scenario, the company shows a net profit of almost $41,000 if it can sell all of those grills.

Figure 10-5	INCOME WITH A LARGER ORDER

Income Analysis

	A	B	C	D	E
3	Variable Expenses	Standard	Deluxe	Dual	Extended
4	Models Ordered	275	250	250	225
5	Cost of Parts	$96.50	$105.15	$155.20	$178.00
6	Cost of Assembly	$10.00	$10.00	$20.00	$25.00
7	Total Model Cost	$106.50	$115.15	$175.20	$203.00
8	**Total Variable Expenses**	$147,550.00			
9					
10	Revenue	Standard	Deluxe	Dual	Extended
11	Models Sold	275	250	250	225
12	Price per Model	$155.00	$175.00	$245.00	$315.00
13	**Total Revenue**	$218,500.00			
14					
15	**Summary**				
16	Total Revenue	$218,500.00			
17	Total Variable Expenses	$147,550.00			
18	Total Fixed Expenses	$30,000.00			
19	**Net Income**	$40,950.00			
20					

the company's income has increased to over $40,000

Now you check the parts inventory to verify that the plant can meet Dawn's proposed order.

3. Scroll to the right of the worksheet to view the Parts Inventory table. See Figure 10-6. Unfortunately, Dawn's latest order exceeds the parts supply. Her order will require 15 more top racks than are currently available.

Figure 10-6	PARTS REQUIREMENTS FOR A LARGER ORDER

	G	H	I	J	K	L	M	N	O
1	**Parts Inventory**								
2	Description	Available	Ordered	Remaining	Cost	Standard	Deluxe	Dual	Extended
3	Burner (Main)	1411	1000	411	$12.15	1	1	1	1
4	Burner (Side)	957	700	257	$8.25	0	0	1	2
5	Chassis (Extended)	781	475	306	$65.25	0	0	1	1
6	Chassis (Standard)	877	525	352	$35.50	1	1	0	0
7	Control Dial	2671	1950	721	$2.50	1	2	2	3
8	Gas Tubing	2321	1700	621	$3.50	1	1	2	3
9	Igniter	2217	1700	517	$2.25	1	1	2	3
10	Igniter Button	1012	1000	12	$5.20	1	1	1	1
11	Rack (Main)	1417	1000	417	$10.30	1	1	1	1
12	Rack (Side)	723	700	23	$6.30	0	0	1	2
13	Rack (Top)	710	725	-15	$6.15	0	1	1	1
14	Support Stand	1388	1000	388	$25.10	1	1	1	1

the order will require 15 more top racks than are currently available

Dawn asks you to reduce the number of Extended grills by 15 so that her order will be in compliance with the plant's inventory.

4. Click cell **E4** and then change the number of Extended grills to **210**. Check the net income and then scroll to view the parts inventory numbers. The net income of the company drops to $39,270, but at least the order does not exceed the number of parts available.

With these changes, Dawn has an order that shows a profit of almost $40,000 without exceeding the inventory. Of course, she doesn't know whether this is the best product mix available. Dawn knows that she can't order any more grills that require a top rack because her current order uses up all of the top racks. However, the Standard model doesn't need a top rack, and there are plenty of parts left at the plant to make more Standard grills. Perhaps she should increase the number of Standard grills in her order.

At this point, Dawn could continue the trial-and-error method to learn how many more Standard grills she could order. She asks you whether there is a more efficient way of doing this.

Finding a Solution Using Goal Seek

One way to quickly and easily find solutions to product mix problems is to use Excel's Goal Seek analysis tool. **Goal Seek** automates the trial-and-error process by changing one cell in the worksheet in order to force another cell to show a specific value. Goal Seek uses a different approach from traditional what-if analysis, where you change *input values* in worksheet cells, and Excel uses these values to calculate *result values*. With Goal Seek, you specify the result values you want, and Excel changes the input values to produce them. Figure 10-7 illustrates the difference between a what-if analysis and a Goal Seek.

Figure 10-7   WHAT-IF ANALYSIS AND GOAL SEEK

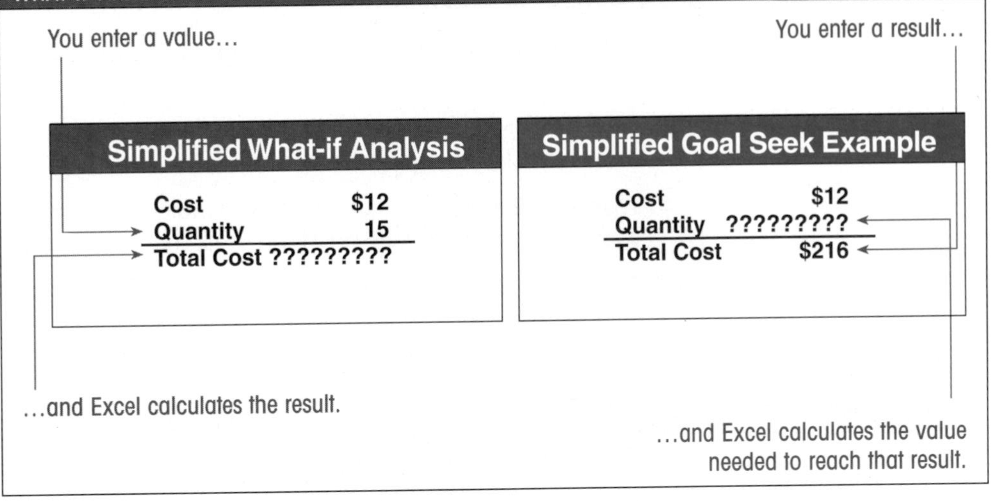

You enter a value...   You enter a result...

Simplified What-if Analysis	Simplified Goal Seek Example
Cost $12	Cost $12
Quantity 15	Quantity ?????????
Total Cost ?????????	Total Cost $216

...and Excel calculates the result.

...and Excel calculates the value
needed to reach that result.

In this example, suppose you want to purchase some audio CDs that cost $12 each. You can ask the what-if question, "*What* would it cost *if* I buy 15 CDs?" Figure 10-7 shows the result of this what-if analysis on the left. If you were to place this data in Excel, you would quickly write a formula to show that the cost of 15 CDs is $180.

Goal Seek takes a different approach: If you have $216 to spend, how many CDs can you purchase? You could use the Goal Seek capability to determine that the answer is 18. Unlike traditional what-if analysis, Goal Seek starts with the end result (the formula) and determines what value you should use to reach a desired answer.

REFERENCE WINDOW   **RW**

Using Goal Seek

- Set up the worksheet with labels, formulas, and values.
- Click Tools on the menu bar, and then click Goal Seek to open the Goal Seek dialog box.
- In the Set cell reference box, enter the location of the result cell.
- In the To value text box, enter the value that you want to see in the result cell.
- In the By changing cell reference box, enter the location of the changing cell.
- Click the OK button.

Dawn wants to know how many Standard grills she should order to increase the company's net income to $42,000. You explain to her that you can use Goal Seek to answer her question. To set up this Goal Seek, first you need to identify two cells in your worksheet: the result cell and the changing or input cell. The **result cell** is the cell containing your goal, which in this case is cell B19—the net income produced by the order. The **changing cell** is the cell whose value is changed in order to reach your goal. In this case, the changing cell is cell B4—the number of Standard grills.

What about the parts inventory? Excel will not consider this factor as it seeks a result for the problem. So after Excel solves the problem, you will need to manually confirm that the number of parts available has not been exceeded. You are ready to use Goal Seek to answer Dawn's questions.

To use Goal Seek to increase the net income to $42,000:

1. Click **Tools** on the menu bar, and then click **Goal Seek** to open the Goal Seek dialog box.

2. Enter **B19** in the Set cell reference box, and then press the **Tab** key. This reference is the location of the result cell.

3. Type **42000** in the To value text box to indicate that the net income in cell B19 should be set to $42,000, and then press the **Tab** key.

4. Type **B4** in the By changing cell reference box to indicate that Goal Seek should change the order quantity of Standard grills in cell B4 to arrive at the result. The dialog box should look like Figure 10-8.

Figure 10-8	COMPLETED GOAL SEEK DIALOG BOX

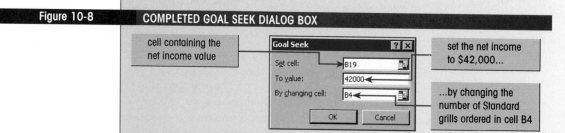

cell containing the net income value

set the net income to $42,000...

...by changing the number of Standard grills ordered in cell B4

5. Click the **OK** button to seek the goal. The Goal Seek Status dialog box, shown in Figure 10-9, indicates that Goal Seek has found a solution.

Figure 10-9	RESULTS OF THE GOAL SEEK

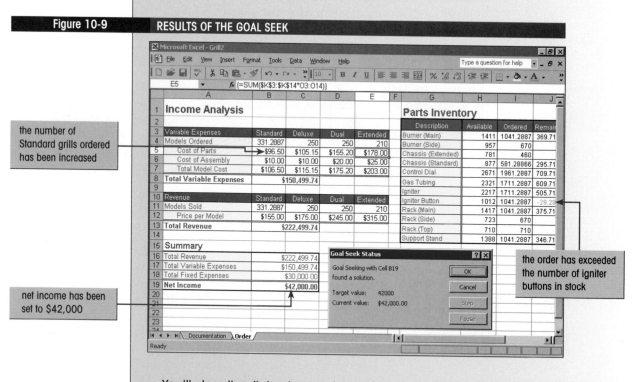

the number of Standard grills ordered has been increased

the order has exceeded the number of igniter buttons in stock

net income has been set to $42,000

You'll close the dialog box and examine the solution Goal Seek has entered on the worksheet.

6. Click the **OK** button.

Goal Seek determined that an order of around 331 Standard grills (Goal Seek cannot differentiate between integers and whole numbers, so it shows 331.2887 grills in cell B4) would result in a net income of exactly $42,000. However, this order would exceed the number of available igniter buttons by 29. To correct this problem, you will use the Goal Seek command to change the remaining amount of igniter buttons from –29 to 0 by altering the number of Standard grills ordered.

To set the number of igniter buttons to zero:

1. Click **Tools** on the menu bar, and then click **Goal Seek**.

2. Enter **J10** (the cell containing the remaining number of igniter buttons) in the Set cell reference box, and then press the **Tab** key.

3. Type **0** in the To value text box, and press the **Tab** key.

4. Enter **B4** in the By changing cell reference box, and then click the **OK** button twice. Excel sets the value in cell J7 to –1.82E–12.

   The Goal Seek command does not always result in the exact value of the number for which you are searching. You can correct this by typing in the exact integer value of the number of Standard grills to order in cell B4. The value displayed in cell B4 is 302.

5. Click cell **B4** and note that the value in the Formula bar is 302.000000000002. This is the little error that the Goal Seek command created, which you'll correct by retyping the value in cell B4, removing the extra decimals.

6. Type **302** and then press the **Enter** key. The number of igniter buttons remaining, shown in cell J10, is exactly 0, and the net income for the company drops to $40,579.50.

   You tell Dawn that an order of 302 Standard grills would result in a net income for GrillRite of over $40,000 without exceeding the parts supply. Using Goal Seek, you were able to arrive at a solution much quicker than using a trial-and-error approach, so you will save the changes that you have made and then exit the program.

7. Save the changes you have made to the workbook, and then close it.

8. Exit Excel.

Dawn now has a solution, but how does she know that it is the *best* solution? Goal Seek works very well in situations in which a single cell is being set to a value by changing the value of a single other cell. It does not work as well when several values in the workbook could be changed to arrive at the stated goal.

To Dawn it seems that there would be an almost infinite number of combinations of grill orders, some which might even provide more net income than the one that you arrived at, but how can she test them all to find the best combination of grills? In the next session, you'll learn how to use an Excel tool that can examine all of those combinations and arrive at a solution.

Session 10.1 QUICK CHECK

1. What is an optimal product mix?

2. Describe the trial-and-error process.

3. What is a limitation of the trial-and-error process?

4. Describe the difference between a what-if analysis and a Goal Seek.

5. Identify a typical business problem that you could solve using Goal Seek.

6. Define the terms changing cell and resulting cell.

7. Name the three components of the Goal Seek command.

SESSION 10.2

In this session, you'll use Solver to calculate the optimal product mix for Dawn's order. You'll learn how to create constraints so that any solution Excel calculates fulfills the conditions that Dawn requires. You'll summarize your results in an Answer report, and you'll also learn how to save and load Solver models. Finally, you'll study some of the properties of Solver in order to efficiently use Solver in the future.

Finding a Solution Using Solver

In the last session, you arrived at a solution that fulfilled the customer's orders, didn't exceed the parts inventory, and provided GrillRite a profit of over $40,000. Dawn is pleased with the results, but she knows that the solution was arrived at by trial and error. It's the "error" part that worries Dawn. How does she know $40,000 represents the highest net income she can attain? What if a better order exists that fulfills all of the conditions and provides the company an even higher profit? Dawn would like some assurance that she has come up with the best solution possible.

One way to do this is to use Solver. **Solver** is a program that searches for the optimal solution of a problem involving several variables. For example, Solver can be used to find the curve or line that best fits a set of data or to minimize production costs for a product or service. Dawn wants you to use Solver to maximize GrillRite's profits, but GrillRite's plant manager might use Solver to minimize the amount of unused parts at the plant, thus reducing his overhead.

There are three items or **parameters** that you must specify when using Solver: a target cell, the adjustable or changing cells, and the constraints that apply to your problem. You specify the target cell, changing cells, and constraints using the Solver Parameters dialog box. A **target cell** is a cell that you want to maximize, minimize, or change to a specific value, such as the total profit from the appliance order. In this case, the company's net income would be your target cell, which you would want to set to its maximum value. An **adjustable cell** is a cell that Excel changes to produce the desired result in the target cell. In Dawn's workbook this is the number of grills of each type to order. Finally, a **constraint** is a limit that is placed on the problem's solution. You've already had to deal with constraints in your trial-and-error analysis. One was that the orders could not exceed the available parts; the other was that the orders had to meet store demand.

Installing Solver

Solver is an example of an **add-in**, a customized program that adds commands and features to Microsoft Office programs like Excel. Because Solver is an "added" feature of Excel, it might not be installed on your computer. Before attempting to run Solver, you will want to check to see if it is installed.

To test whether Solver has been installed:

1. If you took a break at the end of the previous session, start Excel and reopen the **Grill2** workbook from the Tutorial.10\Tutorial folder on your Data Disk.

2. Click **Tools** on the menu bar to display the contents of the Tools menu.

3. Click the **arrows** at the bottom of the Tools menu to display all of the menu commands. If Solver has been installed and has been activated on your computer, you should see the menu displayed in Figure 10-10.

| Figure 10-10 | CONTENTS OF THE TOOLS MENU |

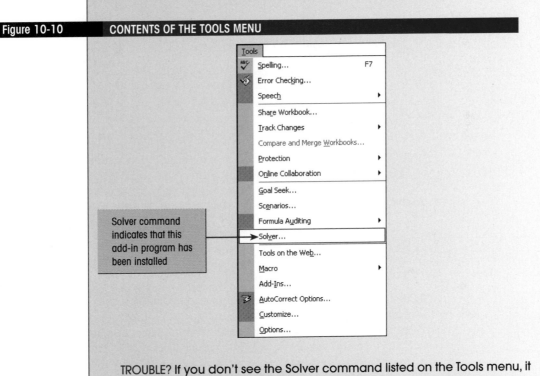

Solver command indicates that this add-in program has been installed

TROUBLE? If you don't see the Solver command listed on the Tools menu, it could be that Solver has not been installed or activated. You'll learn how to install and activate Solver next.

Note that if the Solver command appears on your Tools menu, you can proceed to the next section to learn how to use Solver; otherwise, continue with this section.

If Solver did not appear as a command on the Tools menu, the program either needs to be installed or activated. If you are working on a network, you might have to have your instructor or network administrator install Solver for you. If you are working on a stand-alone PC, you might have to install the program yourself using your Microsoft Office XP installation CD. However, Solver might be installed, just not activated. You should test for this possibility first.

To activate Solver:

1. If necessary, click **Tools** on the menu bar, and then click **Add-Ins**. The Add-Ins dialog box opens. See Figure 10-11. This dialog box displays the list of add-ins available in Excel. If an add-in is installed, its check box will be selected. The Solver add-in shown in Figure 10-11 has not been installed.

Figure 10-11	LIST OF AVAILABLE ADD-INS

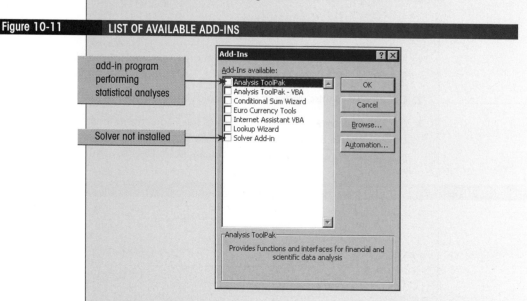

add-in program performing statistical analyses

Solver not installed

TROUBLE? Depending on which add-ins have been installed on your computer, your list of add-ins might differ from those shown in Figure 10-11.

2. Click the **Solver Add-in** check box, and then click the **OK** button.

If Solver has been installed, but not activated, the Add-Ins dialog box will simply close, and the Solver command will be added to the Tools menu. If Solver has not been installed yet, Excel will notify you of this fact. You should continue with the next step to install Solver.

3. To install Solver, click the **Yes** button, insert your Microsoft Office XP CD in your computer's CD drive, and then click the **OK** button. Your computer will then install and activate Solver. You will not have to install Solver again after this point.

Solver is only one of a collection of Excel add-ins. Other add-ins provide the ability to perform statistical analyses, calculate conditional sums, or connect easily to the Internet. You can also create your own add-in using the VBA (Visual Basic for Applications) macro language. The process of activating and installing add-ins follows the same process you used to install and activate the Solver add-in.

REFERENCE WINDOW   RW

Installing and Activating Add-Ins

- To activate an add-in, click Tools on the menu bar, click Add-Ins, and then click the check box for the add-in you want to activate.
- To install one of Excel's built-in add-ins, click Tools on the menu bar, click Add-Ins, click the check box for the add-in you want to install, and then follow the on-screen directions.
- To install an add-in from a third party, click Tools on the menu bar, click Add-Ins, click the Browse button, locate the drive and folder containing the add-in file, and then click the OK button to install and activate the add-in.
- To deactivate an add-in, click Tools on the menu bar, click Add-Ins, deselect the check box for the add-in you want to deactivate, and then click the OK button.

Setting Up Solver to Find a Solution

Now that you've activated Solver to work in Excel, you are ready to enter the information that Solver needs to find a solution that addresses your problem. The first step in the process is inserting the parameters for the Solver problem. You must specify any limitations.

REFERENCE WINDOW   RW

Using Solver

- Create a worksheet that contains the labels, values, and formulas for the problem you want to solve.
- Click Tools on the menu bar, and then click Solver to open the Solver Parameters dialog box.
- In the Set Target Cell reference box, enter the cell reference for the target cell, which is the cell you want to maximize, minimize, or set to a certain value.
- In the By Changing Cells reference box, list the cells that Excel can change to arrive at the solution.
- Click the Add button to add constraints that limit the changes Solver can make to the values in the cells.
- Click the Solve button to generate a solution.
- Click the OK button to return to the worksheet.

The first step in setting up your Solver model process is specifying the target cell (cell B19, the net income cell) and then changing cells (range B4:E4, the quantity of grills to order).

To specify the target cell and the changing cells:

1. Click **Tools** on the menu bar, and then click **Solver**. The Solver Parameters dialog box opens.

2. Type **B19** in the Set Target Cell reference box, and then press the **Tab** key.

TROUBLE? You can use the Collapse Dialog Box button 🔳 to select cells in the worksheet, and then click the Expand Dialog Box button 🔳 to return to the dialog box.

3. Verify that the Max option button is selected to indicate that you want Solver to calculate the maximum possible value for the target cell. In other words, you want Solver to return the highest net income that GrillRite can generate based on the best grill order.

4. Click in the By Changing Cells reference box, type **B4:E4**, and then press the **Tab** key.

Next you'll add a constraint, or limit, for the solution. Constraints are important because they ensure a realistic solution to your problem. For example, the more grills the company builds and sells, the greater is GrillRite's profit; therefore, to maximize profits, Dawn should just keep ordering grills without limit. But that's a ridiculous solution. Obviously the company can't sell more grills than it can build, so the first constraint you'll add will ensure that the number of grills ordered does not exceed the supply of available parts.

To insert the first constraint:

1. Click the **Add** button to open the Add Constraint dialog box.

   You want the parts ordered in the range I3:I14 to be less or equal to the parts available in the cell range H3:H14.

2. To select the range, click the **Collapse Dialog Box** button 🔳 for the Cell Reference box, drag the pointer down the range **I3:I14**, click the **Expand Dialog Box** button 🔳, and then press the **Tab** key.

3. Make sure the **<=** option is selected in the list box located in the middle of the Add Constraint dialog box, and then press the **Tab** key.

4. Click 🔳 for the Constraint reference box, drag the pointer down the range **H3:H14**, and then click 🔳. Figure 10-12 shows the completed Add Constraint dialog box.

Figure 10-12	ADD CONSTRAINT DIALOG BOX

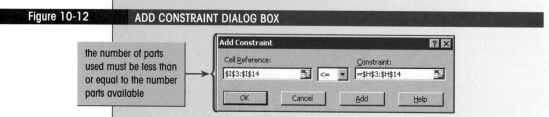

the number of parts used must be less than or equal to the number parts available

5. Click the **OK** button. Figure 10-13 shows the Solver Parameters dialog box.

Figure 10-13	SOLVER PARAMETERS DIALOG BOX

cell to maximize

cells whose values Solver will change

constraint to the Solver solution

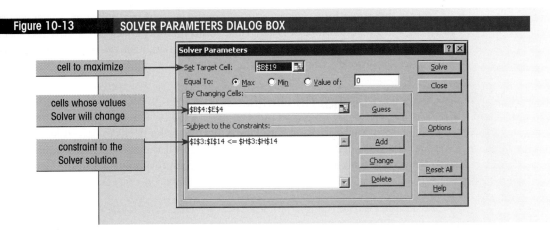

Now that you have specified the target cell, changing cells, and a constraint, you are ready to have Solver look for a solution to the problem.

To generate the solution using Solver:

1. Click the **Solve** button in the Solver Parameters dialog box. In the status bar, you can see Solver rapidly "trying out" solutions. After a short time, the Solver Results dialog box appears and displays the message that indicates Solver has found a solution that satisfies the constraints. See Figure 10-14.

Figure 10-14	INITIAL SOLVER SOLUTION

a negative number of Dual grills have been ordered

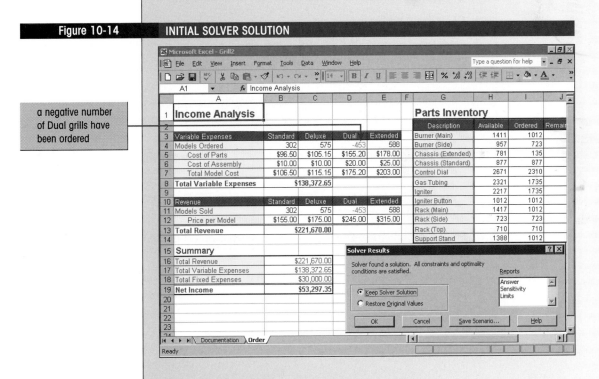

2. If necessary, drag the dialog box out of the way to view the values Solver has produced so far as a solution to the problem.

You see that something is clearly wrong. In the current trial solution, Solver recommends ordering a negative number of Dual grills. You remember that you have to also specify constraints that will ensure that the order will at least match the current store requests. You'll have to add additional constraints to the solution.

Inserting Additional Constraints

You recall from your discussion with Dawn that any order needs to have at least 125 Standard, 100 Deluxe, 100 Dual, and 75 Extended grills. You'll want to add these four constraints to your Solver solution, but first you should restore the previous values to the Order worksheet.

To restore the original values to the worksheet:

1. Click the **Restore Original Values** option button in the Solver Results dialog box. Rejecting the Solver solution restores the original values to the worksheet.

2. Click the **OK** button. Solver restores the original values to the worksheet.

Now add the four new constraints to the Solver parameters.

To add the new constraints to Solver:

1. Click **Tools** on the menu bar, and then click **Solver** to start Solver.

2. Click the **Add** button.

3. Enter the constraint **B4 >= 125** in the Add Constraint dialog box to require that at least 125 Standard grills will be ordered. Note that the Constraint parameter is a fixed number and not a cell reference.

4. Click the **Add** button. Clicking the Add button saves the constraint you just specified and keeps the Add Constraint dialog box open so you can add another constraint.

5. Enter the constraint **C4 >= 100** to ensure that the order will include at least 100 Deluxe grills, and then click the **Add** button.

6. Enter the constraint **D4 >= 100** to ensure that 100 Dual grills will be ordered, and then click the **Add** button.

7. Enter the constraint **E4 >= 75** to guarantee that the order will contain at least 75 Extended grills.

8. Click the **OK** button to save the fourth constraint and close the dialog box. The new constraints are listed in the Subject to the Constraints list box, as shown in Figure 10-15.

Figure 10-15	ADDING NEW CONSTRAINTS TO SOLVER

new constraints

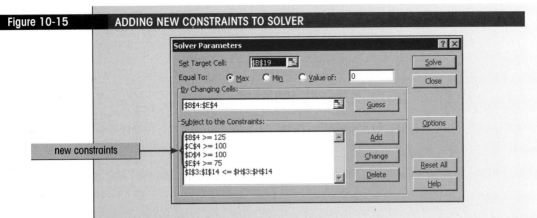

TROUBLE? If the constraints on your screen are not the same as those in Figure 10-15, you can edit the constraint: Click the constraint that you need to fix, click the Change button, adjust the values in the Change Constraint dialog box using the information in Steps 4, 5, 6, or 7, and then click the OK button. If you need to add a constraint, click the Add button. If you need to delete a constraint, click the constraint, and then click the Delete button.

9. Click the **Solve** button. The solution is shown in Figure 10-16.

Figure 10-16	SECOND SOLVER SOLUTION

order values are not integers

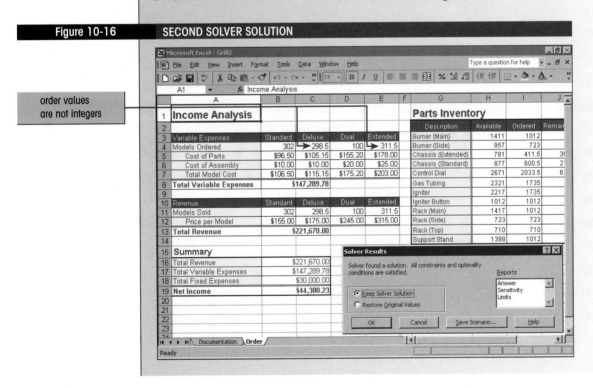

This solution is better. Solver did not order negative quantities, and it did order enough of each item to cover the customer requests. However, you notice yet another problem. Solver has ordered 298.5 Deluxe grills and 311.5 Extended grills. Because you can only order whole grills, you need another constraint to have Solver order only integer quantities.

Inserting an Integer Constraint

In addition to constraints based on values or on the contents of other cells, you can have Solver control the type of value displayed in the cell. You can specify that a cell contain only integers or only binary values (0 or 1). Integers are particularly important in a situation like Dawn's grill order, where you can't order part of an item. You might need to use a binary constraint when a cell indicates the presence or absence of an item. In this case, you'll add a constraint limiting the values in the range B4:E4 to only integers.

To specify integers in cells B4:E4:

1. Click the **Restore Original Values** option button, and then click the **OK** button.

2. Click **Tools** on the menu bar, and then click **Solver**.

3. Click the **Add** button in the Solver Parameters dialog box.

4. If necessary, move the Add Constraint dialog box, and then use your pointer to enter the range **B4:E4**, the cells containing order quantities for each appliance, in the Cell Reference box.

5. Click the **list arrow** in the middle of the dialog box, and then click **int**. The word "integer" appears in the Constraint reference box, as shown in Figure 10-17.

| Figure 10-17 | ADDING AN INTEGER CONSTRAINT |

6. Click the **OK** button.

   Now, run Solver with the new constraint.

7. Click the **Solve** button in the Solver Parameters dialog box. Solver returns a message stating that it has found a solution.

8. Click the **OK** button. Solver's solution, shown in Figure 10-18, presents the order values, and Figure 10-19 shows the effect of the order on the parts inventory.

Figure 10-18	FINAL SOLVER SOLUTION

	A	B	C	D	E
1	**Income Analysis**				
2					
3	Variable Expenses	Standard	Deluxe	Dual	Extended
4	Models Ordered	302	299	100	311
5	Cost of Parts	$96.50	$105.15	$155.20	$178.00
6	Cost of Assembly	$10.00	$10.00	$20.00	$25.00
7	Total Model Cost	$106.50	$115.15	$175.20	$203.00
8	**Total Variable Expenses**	$147,245.85			
9					
10	Revenue	Standard	Deluxe	Dual	Extended
11	Models Sold	302	299	100	311
12	Price per Model	$155.00	$175.00	$245.00	$315.00
13	**Total Revenue**	$221,600.00			
14					
15	**Summary**				
16	Total Revenue	$221,600.00			
17	Total Variable Expenses	$147,245.85			
18	Total Fixed Expenses	$30,000.00			
19	**Net Income**	$44,354.15			
20					

Figure 10-19	FINAL PARTS REMAINING IN THE INVENTORY

	G	H	I	J	K	L	M	N	O	P
1	**Parts Inventory**									
2	Description	Available	Ordered	Remaining	Cost	Standard	Deluxe	Dual	Extended	
3	Burner (Main)	1411	1012	399	$12.15	1	1	1	1	
4	Burner (Side)	957	722	235	$8.25	0	0	1	2	
5	Chassis (Extended)	781	411	370	$65.25	0	0	1	1	
6	Chassis (Standard)	877	601	276	$35.50	1	1	0	0	
7	Control Dial	2671	2033	638	$2.50	1	2	2	3	
8	Gas Tubing	2321	1734	587	$3.50	1	1	2	3	
9	Igniter	2217	1734	483	$2.25	1	1	2	3	
10	Igniter Button	1012	1012	0	$5.20	1	1	1	1	
11	Rack (Main)	1417	1012	405	$10.30	1	1	1	1	
12	Rack (Side)	723	722	1	$6.30	0	0	1	2	
13	Rack (Top)	710	710	0	$6.15	0	1	1	1	
14	Support Stand	1388	1012	376	$25.10	1	1	1	1	
15										

Solver indicates that Dawn should order 302 Standard grills, 299 Deluxe grills, 100 Dual grills, and 311 Extended grills. This solution provides the company $44,354.15 in net income ($4000 more than you were able to provide using the trial-and-error approach), satisfies the store orders, and does not exceed the supply of available parts. This solution uses up all of the igniter buttons and top racks available and leaves only one side rack.

Note that this might not be the ultimate solution because Solver tries a limited number of combinations in its search for a solution. There is a small chance that the best solution might not be found. However, given the amount of parts remaining in the warehouse and the amount of profit, you feel comfortable in telling Dawn that any other solution will not be much better.

When you find a solution using Solver, it's usually a good idea to include an analysis of the constraints and conditions by which Solver arrived at its solution. You can do this by creating an answer report.

Creating a Solver Answer Report

How do you evaluate and report the solution that Solver produced? Solver can create three different reports—an answer report, a sensitivity report, and a limits report. The **answer report** is the most useful of the three because it summarizes the results of a successful solution by displaying information about the target cell, changing cells, and constraints. This report includes the original and final values for the target and changing cells, as well as the constraint formulas. The **sensitivity** and **limits reports** are used primarily in science and engineering environments when the user wants to investigate the mathematical aspects of the Solver solution. These reports allow you to quantify the reliability of the solution. However, you can't use these reports when your problem contains integer constraints, so you can only create an answer report for your inventory solution.

As part of the written report you'll give Dawn about your analysis of the grill order, you will create an answer report, which will provide information on the process used to go from the original values to the final solution. To make sure that the answer report includes information on the entire process, you'll set the quantities to order back to their original values, and then you will solve the problem again and generate the answer report.

To create an answer report:

1. Change the values in the range **B4:E4** back to **0**.

2. Click **Tools** on the menu bar, and then click **Solver**. Your original parameters, changing cells, and constraints remain as you set them earlier.

3. Click the **Solve** button. The Solver Results dialog box appears.

   You can now create the answer report.

4. Click **Answer** in the Reports list box, and make sure the Keep Solver Solution option button is selected this time. See Figure 10-20.

Figure 10-20	CREATING AN ANSWER REPORT

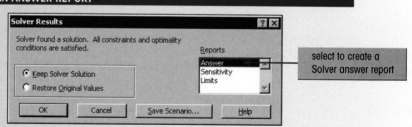

5. Click the **OK** button to save the answer report. After a few seconds, Solver places the answer report in a separate sheet called "Answer Report 1." The first time you create an answer report for a problem, Excel names it Answer Report 1. Excel calls the second report Answer Report 2, and so on.

6. Click the **Answer Report 1** tab. Figure 10-21 shows the answer report for the solution Solver just produced.

Figure 10-21   **THE ANSWER REPORT**

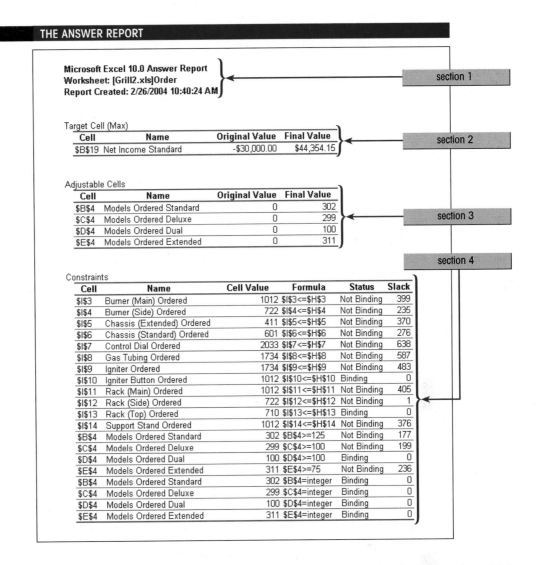

Microsoft Excel 10.0 Answer Report
Worksheet: [Grill2.xls]Order
Report Created: 2/26/2004 10:40:24 AM
                                                                        section 1

Target Cell (Max)

Cell	Name	Original Value	Final Value
$B$19	Net Income Standard	-$30,000.00	$44,354.15

                                                                        section 2

Adjustable Cells

Cell	Name	Original Value	Final Value
$B$4	Models Ordered Standard	0	302
$C$4	Models Ordered Deluxe	0	299
$D$4	Models Ordered Dual	0	100
$E$4	Models Ordered Extended	0	311

                                                                        section 3

                                                                        section 4

Constraints

Cell	Name	Cell Value	Formula	Status	Slack
$I$3	Burner (Main) Ordered	1012	$I$3<=$H$3	Not Binding	399
$I$4	Burner (Side) Ordered	722	$I$4<=$H$4	Not Binding	235
$I$5	Chassis (Extended) Ordered	411	$I$5<=$H$5	Not Binding	370
$I$6	Chassis (Standard) Ordered	601	$I$6<=$H$6	Not Binding	276
$I$7	Control Dial Ordered	2033	$I$7<=$H$7	Not Binding	638
$I$8	Gas Tubing Ordered	1734	$I$8<=$H$8	Not Binding	587
$I$9	Igniter Ordered	1734	$I$9<=$H$9	Not Binding	483
$I$10	Igniter Button Ordered	1012	$I$10<=$H$10	Binding	0
$I$11	Rack (Main) Ordered	1012	$I$11<=$H$11	Not Binding	405
$I$12	Rack (Side) Ordered	722	$I$12<=$H$12	Not Binding	1
$I$13	Rack (Top) Ordered	710	$I$13<=$H$13	Binding	0
$I$14	Support Stand Ordered	1012	$I$14<=$H$14	Not Binding	376
$B$4	Models Ordered Standard	302	$B$4>=125	Not Binding	177
$C$4	Models Ordered Deluxe	299	$C$4>=100	Not Binding	199
$D$4	Models Ordered Dual	100	$D$4>=100	Binding	0
$E$4	Models Ordered Extended	311	$E$4>=75	Not Binding	236
$B$4	Models Ordered Standard	302	$B$4=integer	Binding	0
$C$4	Models Ordered Deluxe	299	$C$4=integer	Binding	0
$D$4	Models Ordered Dual	100	$D$4=integer	Binding	0
$E$4	Models Ordered Extended	311	$E$4=integer	Binding	0

The answer report is divided into four sections. The first section includes titles, which indicate that this is an Excel answer report created from the Orders sheet in the Grill2 workbook created on the day and at the time specified. The second section displays information about the target cell, its location, the cell label, and the cell's original value and final values.

The third section displays information about the changing cells, which the report calls Adjustable Cells. This section of the report shows the location, column and row label, the original value, and the final value of each cell. The column and row labels from the worksheet are joined to form the cell name in the answer report. For example, on the worksheet, Models Ordered is the row label and Standard is the column label, so cell B4 is called Models Ordered Standard in the answer report.

The fourth section of the report displays information about the constraints. In addition to the location, name, and value of each constraint, this section shows the constraint formulas. The second column from the right shows the status of each constraint. The status of the cells in the range I3:I9 is listed as "Not Binding." **Not binding** means that these constraints were not limiting factors in the solution. The status of some of the other constraints is listed as "Binding." **Binding** means that the final value in these cells was equal to the constraint value. For example, the Igniter Button Order constraint was $I$10 <=$H$10. In the solution, all igniter buttons were used up, which is at the maximum limit of the constraint, so this was a binding constraint in the solution.

The last column on the right shows the slack for each constraint. The **slack** is the difference between the value in the cell and the value at the limit of the constraint. For example, the constraint for the number of Extended grills ordered in cell E4 was >=75. In the solution, the total number of Extended grills was 311, so the difference, or slack, is 236. Binding constraints always show a slack of 0. Constraints listed as not binding show the difference between the constraint limit and the final value.

Saving and Loading Solver Models

You show Dawn your solution and the answer report. She's very happy with your work, but she has another request to make. One of her supervisors has asked that she also determine the order that uses the plant's inventory most efficiently—leaving the fewest number of unused parts.

Dawn would like you to run this analysis, but she doesn't want to lose the work you've already done. In other words, she would like the workbook to have two Solver models: one that maximizes profits and the other that minimizes the unused inventory.

Rather than reentering the Solver parameters for each model, you can save the parameters into cells on the worksheet. Then, if you want to rerun a particular problem, you can reload the parameters from the worksheet cells without having to reformulate the problem. You decide to store the parameters for both models in empty cells on the Order worksheet. You'll start by saving the current Solver model. This command is available in the Solver Options dialog box.

To save the current Solver model:

1. Click the **Order** tab to return to the Order worksheet, click **Tools** on the menu bar, and then click **Solver**.

2. Click the **Options** button. Solver opens the Solver Options dialog box, shown in Figure 10-22. From this dialog box, you can control how Solver operates, and you can also save and load Solver models.

| Figure 10-22 | SOLVER OPTIONS DIALOG BOX |

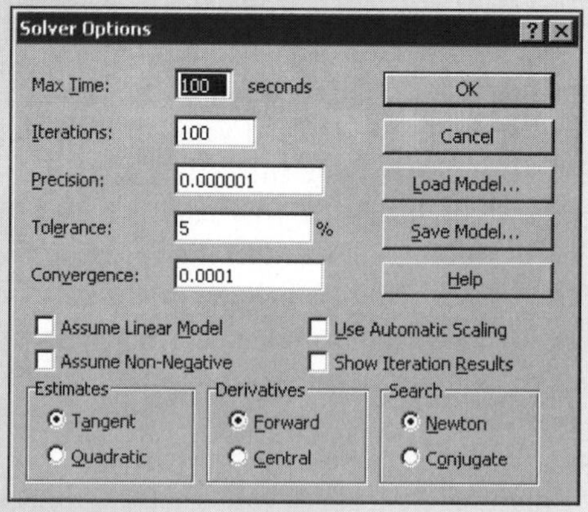

3. Click the **Save Model** button. Solver displays the Save Model dialog box, along with a suggested area on the worksheet to place the model information. See Figure 10-23.

| Figure 10-23 | SAVING A SOLVER MODEL |

suggested area for saving model information (the suggested area on your screen might differ)

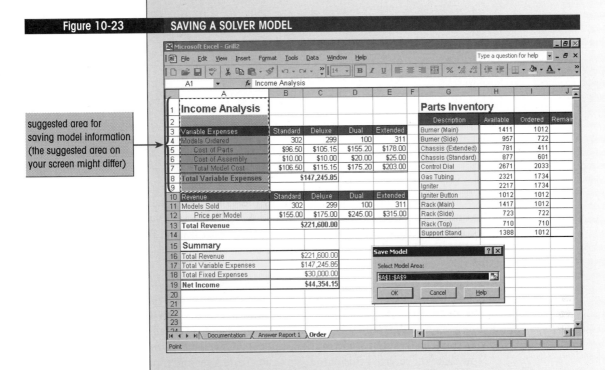

Sometimes the selected area will contain cells that you do not want overwritten, which is the case with the worksheet shown in Figure 10-23. You need to select a blank area of the worksheet that doesn't contain data that would be overwritten by Solver. In this case, you will choose an area below the Summary section of the worksheet.

4. Click cell **A22** and then click the **OK** button. Excel writes information on the Solver parameters into the worksheet.

5. Click the **Cancel** button and then click the **Close** button to close Solver.

6. Scroll down the worksheet to view the information written in column A, beginning with cell A22.

   You will enter a label that identifies the information in these cells as Solver parameters.

7. Click cell **A21**, type **Maximum Profit Model**, and then press the **Enter** key. See Figure 10-24.

Figure 10-24	SOLVER PARAMETERS AS THEY APPEAR IN THE WORKSHEET

15	Summary	
16	Total Revenue	$221,600.00
17	Total Variable Expenses	$147,245.85
18	Total Fixed Expenses	$30,000.00
19	Net Income	$44,354.15
20		
21	Maximum Profit Model	
22	$44,354.15	
23	4	
24	TRUE	
25	TRUE	
26	TRUE	
27	TRUE	
28	TRUE	
29	TRUE	
30	100	

Solver parameters saved in empty cells on the worksheet →

Documentation / Answer Report 1 \ Order /

Ready

The first parameter in cell A22 displays the value $44,354.15, which is the maximum profit under this model. The second cell, cell A23, displays the value 4, indicating the number of changing cells in the model. Note that the next several parameter cells display the value TRUE. Those cells correspond to the constraints in the model. The fact that they all display the value TRUE indicates that all of the values in the worksheet satisfy the constraints. If, at a later date, Dawn changes some of the values in this worksheet, violating one those constraints, this fact will be displayed in the Solver parameter cells. Thus, the cells can act as a visual check that all of the model's conditions are still being met as the worksheet is modified. The final parameter cell, A30, contains technical details about how Excel will run Solver. You'll learn about some of the technical details later in the tutorial.

Now that you've saved this model, you can create a second model to determine the order that will minimize the number of unused parts at the plant. The constraints for this model will be slightly different; instead of trying to satisfy the store orders, Dawn's supervisor only wants her to ensure that the order does not exceed the parts supply and that the number of grill models ordered is greater than or equal to zero. First you have to insert a cell to calculate the number of parts remaining, and then you can begin creating the model.

To minimize the number of unused parts:

1. Click cell **J15** and then enter the formula **=SUM(J3:J14)**. There are a total of 3770 unused parts after the current order.

   Now create a Solver model to minimize this value.

2. Click **Tools** on the menu bar, and then click **Solver**.

3. With the Set Target Cell reference box active, click cell **J15** and then press the **Tab** key.

4. Click the **Min** option button to indicate that this model will be used to minimize the value of cell J15.

   Next, you have to delete some of the constraints from the Maximum Profit model.

5. Click **$B$4 >= 125** in the list of constraints, and then click the **Delete** button.

6. Delete the following constraints: **$C$4 >= 100**, **$D$4 >= 100**, and **$E$4 >= 75**.

   Finally, you will add the constraint that all orders should be greater than or equal to zero.

7. Click the **Add** button to open the Add Constraint dialog box, select the range **B4:E4**, and then press the **Tab** key.

8. Click **>=** in the list box, type **0**, and then click the **OK** button. Figure 10-25 shows the Solver Parameters dialog box for the minimization model.

Figure 10-25   SOLVER MODEL TO MINIMIZE THE AMOUNT OF UNUSED PARTS

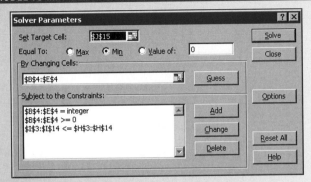

9. Click the **Solve** button. Solver calculates the solution shown in Figure 10-26.

Figure 10-26   SOLUTION TO THE MINIMIZATION PROBLEM

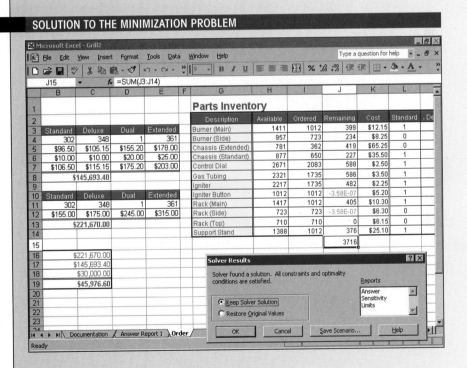

10. Click the **OK** button to keep Solver's solution.

The order that uses the parts in stock most efficiently contains 302 Standard grills, 348 Deluxe grills, 1 Dual grill, and 361 Extended grills. It will leave 3716 unused parts. Note that cells J10 and J12 display the value –3.58E–07, which is equal to –0.000000358 (practically zero). The reason why it is not exactly equal to zero is because of the way in which computers and Excel store decimal values. Sometimes it is not possible for Solver to find an exact solution, so it finds one within a defined tolerance.

Dawn can report to her supervisor that the best model will still leave 3716 unused parts, which is pretty close to the number of unused parts in her model that maximizes profit. Dawn asks you to save this model and reload the maximum profit model.

To save the model and reload the Maximum Profits model:

1. Click **Tools** on the menu bar, click **Solver**, click the **Options** button, and then click the **Save Model** button.

2. Click cell **A33** and then click the **OK** button. Excel places the parameters for this model in the range A33:A38.

3. Click the **Cancel** button and then click the **Close** button to return to the Order worksheet

4. Click cell **A32**, type **Minimum Parts Model**, and then press the **Enter** key.

5. Click cell **A21**, click the **Format Painter** button 🖌 on the Standard toolbar, and then click cell **A32**. Figure 10-27 shows the parameters for the two models you created. Next, reload the model to maximize GrillRite's profit.

Figure 10-27	PARAMETERS FOR THE TWO SAVED MODELS

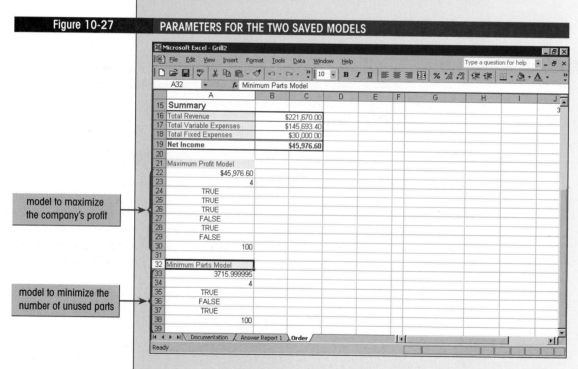

model to maximize the company's profit

model to minimize the number of unused parts

6. Click **Tools**, click **Solver**, and then click the **Options** button.

7. Click the **Load Model** button.

8. Select the range **A22:A30** containing the parameters for the Maximum Profit model, and then click the **OK** button. Solver asks whether you want to reset the previous Solver cell selections.

9. Click the **OK** button twice. The Solver Parameters dialog box should now display the parameters used to maximize the company's profit.

10. Click the **Solve** button and then click the **OK** button to run and save the Solver solution.

11. Click cell **A1** to return to the top of the Order worksheet.

The workbook now displays the results of the Maximum Profit model. If Dawn wants to return to the Minimize Parts model, she can easily do so by loading the model parameters from the worksheet.

Understanding **Solver**

Dawn greatly appreciates the work you've done on setting up the two models, but she is a bit concerned about the results of the Minimize Parts model. She wonders about the value of –0.000000358 that Solver determined for the number of unused parts and would like to know a bit more about the technical details of Solver. How does Solver determine when the solution it has calculated is the best one?

Working with the Iterative Process

Solver arrives at optimal solutions through an **iterative procedure**, which means that Solver starts with an initial solution (usually the original values inserted into the worksheet) and uses that as a basis to calculate a series of solutions. Each step, or iteration, in that series improves the solution until Solver reaches the point where one solution is no longer significantly better than the previous one. At that point, Solver will stop and indicate that it has found an answer.

From viewing the settings in the Solver Options dialog box (shown earlier in Figure 10-22), you learned a little of how Solver goes through this iterative process. The default length of time that Solver will spend on the iterative process is 100 seconds or 100 total iterations. If 100 seconds or 100 iterations have passed and Solver has not found a solution, it will indicate this fact with a dialog box. At that point you can have Solver continue the iterative process or stop the process without finding a solution. If Solver is taking too long to find a solution, you can halt the program at any time by pressing the Esc key. If you want to see the iterative process in action, click the Show Iteration Results check box, and Excel will pause after each iteration and show the intermediate solutions that it finds.

As noted earlier, Solver will stop the iterative process when one solution is not significantly better than the previous one tested, but what does "significantly better" mean? This is determined by the value in the Convergence text box. The default convergence value is 0.001, which means that if the change in the target cell between one solution and the next is less than or equal to 0.001, Solver will consider that it has converged to the solution. The lower the convergence value, the longer Solver will take to find a solution. On the other hand, if you are having problems with Solver failing to converge to any solution, you may want to try increasing the convergence value.

The Precision and Tolerance text boxes control how Solver handles constraints. For example, when you set a constraint such as "A2 = 500," you are specifying that the value of cell A2 must be equal to 500; but as you saw with the Minimize Parts model, it may not be possible to set a cell *exactly* equal to the constraint. In that case, Solver uses the Precision text box to determine when it is close enough. The default precision is 0.000001, which means that a value within 0.000001 of the constraint will be considered equal to the constraint. The tolerance value does the same thing, but it applies to integer constraints. The default value of 5 indicates that an integer constraint must be within 5% of the constraint's value. This is why Solver stopped when it did with the Minimize Parts model. Even though the number of unused parts wasn't exactly equal to zero, it was within the tolerance limit.

Working with Linear and Nonlinear Models

Solver models are divided into two classes: those that use linear functions and those that use nonlinear functions. A **linear function** is a function that can be written as the sum of a series of terms, with each term multiplied by a constant value. For example, the function $w = 14 + 25x - 37y + 108z$ is linear because it is written as a sum of the variables x, y, and z, with each variable multiplied by a constant. Many linear problems involve several combinations of linear functions.

A **nonlinear** problem is any problem that involves functions that cannot be written in a simple linear form. For example, the function $y = 1/sin(x)cos(y)tan(z)$ is nonlinear. The distinction between linear and nonlinear is important where Solver is concerned. Solver can quickly and easily solve linear functions. In fact, if you know that your problem is linear, you can greatly speed up Solver's process to find a solution by selecting the Assume Linear Model check box in the Solver Options dialog box. If Solver discovers the problem is actually nonlinear, it will notify you of this and solve it, if possible.

If your problem is nonlinear, you could run into several difficulties. Solver can display different solutions depending upon your worksheet's initial values. Solver may even fail to find a solution. For this reason, if you are using Solver with a nonlinear problem, you should try several different starting values in your worksheet and then choose the solution that produces the optimal value for the target cell.

Another way of dealing with the difficulties of nonlinear problems is to choose different arithmetic methods for Solver to arrive at a solution. The different arithmetic methods are listed in the Estimates, Derivatives, and Search sections of the Solver Options dialog box. Generally, these options are designed for more experienced users.

Now that you've studied a little bit of the inner workings of Solver, you are ready to close Excel, saving the final version of your workbook.

To save your changes:

1. Save your changes to the Grill2 workbook, and then close the workbook.

2. Exit Excel.

In this tutorial, you formulated a problem that had several parameters and constraints, and attempted to solve it using both trial and error and Solver. Solver proved to be the fastest and most effective way of solving this type of problem. You were also able to use Solver to calculate an order that minimized the number of unused parts and to save both models in the Order worksheet. You take the final report to Dawn. She's pleased that you were able to resolve her problem and show her one of Excel's more powerful tools.

Session 10.2 QUICK CHECK

1. What is an add-in?

2. What should you do if you do not want Solver to produce fractional numbers as the solution?

3. Define the following terms:

    a. not binding constraint

    b. binding constraint

    c. slack

4. How would you create several Solver models on a single worksheet?

5. What is the iterative procedure? If Solver fails to converge to a solution, suggest two ways of solving this problem.

6. What is a linear model? What are some advantages of using linear models with Solver?

7. What are some challenges associated with nonlinear models?

REVIEW ASSIGNMENTS

Dawn was very pleased with your assistance in finding a solution for her problem. She has come back to you with another problem. GrillRite is considering adding discounts on all of their grill models in order to increase sales. Marketing analysis of Dawn's sales region has indicated that for every 1% discount in the price of their grills, GrillRite will sell an extra 60 grills. Of course, reducing the price of the grills also reduces the company's profit margin, so at some point the discount will be so large that GrillRite will not show a profit no matter how many grills they sell.

Dawn has been asked to determine the optimal discount that will maximize GrillRite's net income in her region. Dawn can either apply the same discount to all four grill models, or she can apply different discounts to different models.

Dawn has created a workbook for you containing sales estimates for her region. Your job will be to determine what the best discount strategy will be for the company.

To complete this task:

1. Open the **Discount1** workbook located in the Tutorial.10\Review folder on your Data Disk. Enter the date and your name in the Documentation sheet. Save the workbook as **Discount2** in the same folder. Switch to the Standard Discount worksheet.

2. Dawn created the Standard Discount worksheet to calculate the company's net income when the same discount is applied to all four grill models. The discount value is stored in cell B4. Use the Goal Seek command to calculate what discount value would result in a net income of 0 for the company. This would represent the highest discount that GrillRite could offer and still show a profit. Does the value returned by the Goal Seek command seem reasonable? (*Hint*: How many additional models are sold under this discount? Is that value positive or negative?)

Explore   3. Change the discount value to 20.00%, and repeat the Goal Seek command you applied in Question 2. Did Excel calculate the same value? What does this tell you about the importance of initial values when using Goal Seek? Report your conclusions, and print the Standard Discount worksheet showing the discount value that you think is the highest discount that GrillRite can offer and still break even.

4. Using Solver, determine the standard discount that results in the highest net income for the company. Include the constraint that the discount must be greater than or equal to zero.

5. Set the discount value back to 0, and then use Solver to create an Answer report of the solution found. Name the Answer report worksheet "Standard Discount Report".

Explore

6. The assumption that sales will increase by 60 units for each 1% increase in the discount is just an assumption. It could be wrong. Calculate the amount of money that GrillRite would lose if there were no sales increase using the discount value you calculated in Question 4. (*Hint*: Perform a what-if analysis, using the discount value calculated by Solver but changing the increase in sales in cell B3 from 60 to 0; then compare the net income under this scenario to one in which the discount value in cell B4 is 0. Be sure to return the value in cell B3 to 60 after performing your analysis.)

7. Save your Solver model in the range A29:A32 of the Standard Discount worksheet. Add an appropriate label to cell A28.

8. Switch to the Discount by Model worksheet. In this worksheet, Dawn wants to apply a different discount to each of the four grill models. The discount values are stored in the range B10:E10. Use Solver to calculate the discounts that maximize GrillRite's net income. Constrain the discount values in the range B10:E10 to be zero or greater.

9. Set the discount values back to 0, and then create an answer report of the solution that Solver finds. Name the answer report worksheet "Discount by Model Report".

10. Save your Solver model in the range A28:A31 of the Discount by Model worksheet. Add an appropriate label to cell A27.

11. Compare the maximum profit under the standard discount approach to the approach that uses different discounts for different models. Which approach results in a higher net income?

12. Choose a discount strategy for Dawn, and write a report summarizing your conclusion.

13. Save and close the workbook, and then exit Excel.

CASE PROBLEMS

Case 1. Arranging a Work Schedule at the Lincoln Museum Curtis Lehman is the personnel director at the Lincoln Museum of Natural History. One of his jobs is to set up the work schedule for the museum attendants. There are 16 attendants employed at the museum; 14 are full-time employees and 2 are part-time. The museum needs 8 attendants to work at the museum each weekday and 11 attendants on the weekends. Curtis has to make sure that there are always enough attendants to fill the required slots.

Curtis is currently working on the attendant schedule for the second week in July. Because it's summer, many employees are making vacation plans, and Curtis has received several requests for time off. When Curtis sets up a schedule, he tries to accommodate all of the requests while at the same time meeting his obligation to the museum. It's an arduous task to arrange a schedule that pleases everyone. Curtis wonders whether he can use Excel to automatically generate a work schedule for him and has come to you for help. He has already created a workbook that contains the names of the attendants and their time-off requests. He needs you to determine which attendants will be working which days.

To complete this task:

1. Open the **Staff1** workbook located in the Tutorial.10\Cases folder on your Data Disk. Enter the date and your name in the Documentation sheet. Save the workbook as **Staff2** in the same folder. Switch to the Schedule worksheet.

Curtis indicates whether an employee is working on a given day by putting a 1 in the cell for the day. If the employee is not working that day, a 0 is entered. The Schedule worksheet calculates the total number of attendants working each day, the number required, and the total shortfall. The worksheet also calculates the total hours each employee works each week. A Notes column records the requests made by the attendants for time off.

Explore

2. Start Solver, and begin by setting the value of the target cell, the total shortfall of scheduled attendants versus needed attendants, equal to 0, and selecting the range B5:H20 as the changing cells.

3. Continue to set up the Solver model by inserting the following constraints:

    ■ The number of attendants scheduled to work each day must be equal to the number of attendants required.

Explore

    ■ The cells in the range B5:H20 must contain binary values.

    ■ Each full-time employee must work no more than 40 hours.

    ■ Each part-time employee must work no more than 24 hours.

Explore

4. Examine the Notes column, and then add constraints for each time-off request to the Solver model. (*Hint*: If an employee asks for a particular day of the week off, his value for that day should be constrained to 0.)

5. Run Solver and print the schedule that Solver calculates (it may take Solver at least a minute to arrive at a solution). Verify that all of the constraints have been satisfied, including each time-off request.

6. Save and close the workbook, and then exit Excel.

Case 2. Determining a Shipping Schedule for AutoMaze SuperStore Jon Whitney is a shipping manager at AutoMaze SuperStore, an up-and-coming auto parts supply store chain. He manages five stores located in Reston, Atlanta, Minneapolis, Denver, and Los Angeles, and four warehouses located in Richmond, Chicago, Dallas, and Sacramento. One of Jon's primary responsibilities is to ensure that parts from the warehouses reach the stores in a timely and cost-efficient manner.

Distance is an important facet in calculating overall shipping costs. Obviously it will be cheapest if each store can order the parts they need from the nearest warehouse, but that is not always possible. Sometimes a warehouse will run short of a particular item, and Jon will have to use a warehouse that is farther away, increasing shipping costs for the company.

Jon has asked your help in setting up a workbook that will allow him to determine a shipping strategy to get parts from the warehouses to the stores in the cheapest way, while ensuring that each store gets the parts it needs. Jon has already set up the workbook, but he needs your help in finding an optimal strategy.

To complete this task:

1. Open the **Auto1** workbook located in the Tutorial.10\Cases folder on your Data Disk. Enter the date and your name in the Documentation sheet. Save the workbook as **Auto2** in the same folder.

    Aside from the Documentation sheet, the Auto2 workbook contains four worksheets. The Shipping worksheet lists nine parts that have been requested by the five stores and the amount of each part currently in stock at the four warehouses. The Parts List worksheet displays how much it costs to ship each part per 100 miles. The Store Distances worksheet calculates the distance between each store and the four warehouses. The Shipping Costs worksheet calculates the cost of shipping the requested parts from the warehouses to the stores. You will be working mostly in the Shipping worksheet.

2. Switch to the Shipping worksheet.

The Shipping worksheet contains six tables. The first table displays the amount of parts in stock at the four warehouses. The second table displays the number of parts requested by each store. The third and fourth tables will be used to display how many parts from each warehouse are shipped to the five stores. The fifth table displays the remaining warehouse stock after the parts have been shipped, and the sixth table displays the total number of parts shipped to each of the five stores. At the bottom of the Shipping worksheet is the total cost of doing all of the shipping between the warehouses and the stores.

3. Set up Solver to minimize the total shipping cost by changing the number of parts sent from each warehouse to each store (*Hint*: Use the values in the third table in the range B29:U37 as your changing cells.)

4. Add the following constraints to the Solver model:

   ■ The number of parts shipped from the warehouses to the stores must be an integer.

   ■ The number of parts shipped from the warehouses to the stores must be greater than or equal to zero.

   ■ The number of each part requested by each store must be equal to the number of each part shipped to the store (*Hint*: Compare the values in the second and sixth tables.)

   ■ The number of parts remaining in stock at the warehouses after the shipments must be greater than or equal to zero.

Explore ▷ 5. Because this is a complex problem involving lots of constraining cells and changing cells, set the maximum number of iterations used by Solver to 200.

Explore ▷ 6. This is an example of a linear model. Use this information to increase Solver's efficiency at finding a solution, and then run Solver.

7. Save your model to the range A79:A85. Add a label to cell A78.

8. Jon has been hearing complaints that the Richmond warehouse has been running low in timing belts. Study this problem by observing where the two East coast stores, Reston and Atlanta, need to go to get their boxes of timing belts. Does your model indicate a problem with the Richmond warehouse?

9. Print the shipping schedule calculated by Solver. Be sure to set up the page so that it is easy to read and to interpret your printed schedule.

10. A new shipping company has approached AutoMaze offering discounted delivery. The Parts List worksheet contains a cell for entering a possible shipping discount. Using the shipping schedule you calculated with Solver along with Goal Seek, determine what discount would be needed to reduce the overall shipping cost to exactly $1,200. Report your results.

11. Save and close the workbook, and then exit Excel.

Case 3. Efficiently Using Advertising Dollars at Diskus Diskus is a small home-grown business that manufactures unique and unusual recreational games and toys. One of the latest creations is a "Hover Disk," which, according to the literature, combines the aerodynamic features of a flying disk, a boomerang, and a glider. Sales in a test market have been very encouraging for the four models of Hover Disks in production. Most of the advertising has been done by word-of-mouth. The founders of Diskus, Tim Blanchard and Steve Douglas, are interested in putting money into advertising the Hover Disks to a wider audience.

But how much money should they spend on advertising? They believe that there is an upper limit to the amount of Hover Disks that can be sold, no matter how much they spend advertising it. Tim Blanchard has put together a model, shown in Figure 10-28, in which sales increase with advertising dollars up to about 3000 additional units sold. After that point, any extra money spent on advertising would be wasted and would reduce the company's net income.

Figure 10-28

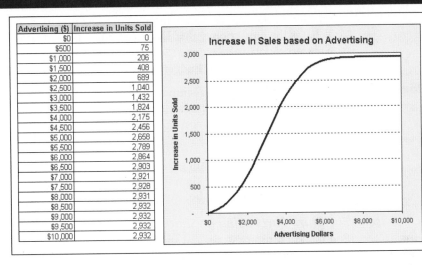

Advertising ($)	Increase in Units Sold
$0	0
$500	75
$1,000	206
$1,500	408
$2,000	689
$2,500	1,040
$3,000	1,432
$3,500	1,824
$4,000	2,175
$4,500	2,456
$5,000	2,658
$5,500	2,789
$6,000	2,864
$6,500	2,903
$7,000	2,921
$7,500	2,928
$8,000	2,931
$8,500	2,932
$9,000	2,932
$9,500	2,932
$10,000	2,932

Steve has asked you to evaluate the results from the test market and insert Tim's model into the mix. He would like to know how much money the company should spend on advertising to maximize its net income. He also wants to know how the advertising dollars should be divided among the four models of the Hover Disk.

To complete this task:

1. Open the **Disk1** workbook located in the Tutorial.10\Cases folder on your Data Disk. Enter the date and your name in the Documentation sheet. Save the workbook as **Disk2** in the same folder. Switch to the Income Statement worksheet.

2. Start Solver and calculate the maximum total net income for Diskus by changing the amount of money spent on advertising for the four Hover Disk models. Use the following constraints in your model:

   ■ The amount of money spent on advertising for each of the four models should be greater than or equal to zero.

   ■ The total amount spent on advertising should not exceed $15,000.

3. Run the model. Print your solution with the header "Solution with initial advertising values of 0" in the upper-right corner of your printout.

Explore

4. Steve's proposed relationship between sales and advertising is a nonlinear one. Mindful that Solver solutions for nonlinear problems can change based on the initial values in the worksheet, change the initial advertising dollars from $0 per Hover Disk model to $1000, and rerun Solver. Print your solution with the right-aligned header "Solution with initial advertising values of 1000". Compare the two solutions. Which solution resulted in the highest net income? How confident are you that this answer represents the optimal solution to the breakdown of advertising dollars for each Hover Disk model? What could you do to search for other solutions?

5. Save your Solver model to the range H2:H6. Insert the label "Advertising Budget = $15,000" in cell H1.

6. Steve is not sure that he wants to spend $15,000 on advertising. Create a new Solver model, this time assuming an advertising budget of no more than $10,000. Use the same initial worksheet values that you used in Step 4. Print the solution found by Solver. Save this model in the range H9:H13. Insert the label "Advertising Budget = $10,000" in cell H8.

7. Create a third model, this time assuming no limit to the amount that Diskus can spend on advertising. Use the same initial values that you used for the previous two models. What is the most money that Diskus can spend on advertising before it becomes counterproductive? Save the model into the range H16:H19. Insert the label "Unlimited Advertising Budget" into cell H15.

Explore

8. Reload the first model (assuming an advertising budget of no more than $15,000) into the Income Statement worksheet (click the OK button when asked to reset Solver's settings), and rerun Solver using the initial values you settled on earlier in Step 5.

9. Save and close the Disk2 workbook, and then exit Excel. Write a report describing any problems you had evaluating Tim's model. Also provide an estimate for Tim and Steve about how much money they should spend on advertising and what the best division of advertising funds would be.

Case 4. Furniture Purchasing at Southland Furniture Eve Bowman is the manager of Southland Furniture store, and she is planning a New Year's Day sale. The store has only 75 square feet of space available to display and stock this merchandise. During the sale, each folding table costs $5, retails for $11, and takes up two square feet of space. Each chair costs $4, retails for $9, and takes up one square foot of space. The maximum amount allocated for purchasing the tables and chairs for the sale is $280. Eve doesn't think she can sell more than 40 chairs, but the demand for tables is virtually unlimited. Eve has asked you to help her determine how many tables and chairs she should purchase in order to make the most profit.

To complete this task:

1. Create a workbook named **Sale**, and save it in the Tutorial.10\Cases folder on your Data Disk. Include a Documentation worksheet containing your name, the date, and the purpose of the workbook. Also include an Orders worksheet containing an income statement for Southland Furniture as well as an estimate on the amount of space that the folding tables and chairs will take up in the display area.

2. Determine the number of chairs and tables that Eve should set up to maximize the company's net income (assuming that each table and chair will be purchased). Include any constraints that you believe are necessary to solve this problem.

3. Create an answer report, detailing the parameters of the problem and the optimal solution.

4. Save your model to a blank area of the Orders worksheet.

5. Print your solution.

6. Save and close the workbook, and then exit Excel.

INTERNET ASSIGNMENTS

Student Union

The purpose of the Internet Assignments is to challenge you to find information on the Internet that you can use to create effective spreadsheets. The actual assignments are updated and maintained on the Course Technology Web site. Log on to the Internet and use your Web browser to go to the Student Union on the New Perspectives Series site at **www.course.com/NewPerspectives/studentunion**. Click the Online Companions link, and then click the link for this text.

QUICK CHECK ANSWERS

Session 10.1

1. mix of products that satisfies customer and production constraints while, at the same time, maximizes profit

2. hit-and-miss approach in which you try different values, attempting to find the optimal solution

3. With several variables to consider, you might never hit upon the best solution.

4. In a what-if analysis, you change the input cell to observe the value in the result cell. In a Goal Seek, you define a value you want to obtain for the result cell, and then you determine what value is required in the input cell.

5. One example is "How should I change the price of my product to maximize my profit?"

6. The changing cell is the cell in a Goal Seek that you want to modify. The result cell is the cell in a Goal Seek that contains the value you want to match.

7. the location of the changing cell, the location of the result cell, and the value you want to see in the result cell

Session 10.2

1. a customized program that adds commands and features to Microsoft Office programs such as Excel

2. Define an integer constraint on the target cell.

3. a) A not binding constraint is a constraint that is not a limiting factor in the Solver solution.

   b) A binding constraint is a limiting factor.

   c) Slack is the difference between the value of the constraining cell and the limiting value of the constraint.

4. Save the Solver parameters to different cells in the worksheet, and load each model that you want to run from the saved cells.

5. The iterative procedure starts with an initial solution and uses it as a basis to calculate a series of solutions. Each step, or iteration, in that series improves the solution until the point is reached where one solution is no longer significantly better than the previous one.

6. A linear model is based on a function that can be written as the sum of a series of terms, with each term multiplied by a constant value. Linear models are much easier to solve and do not run into problems with initial values.

7. Nonlinear models can be more difficult to solve. Sometimes Solver will not find a solution. Different initial values can result in different solutions returned by Solver.

OBJECTIVES

In this tutorial you will:

- Import data from a text file into an Excel workbook

- Retrieve data from a database using the Query Wizard

- Retrieve data from multiple database tables

- Retrieve data from a database into a PivotTable

- Retrieve stock market data from a Web page and the World Wide Web

- Use hyperlinks to view information on the World Wide Web

IMPORTING DATA INTO EXCEL

Working with a Stock Portfolio for Davis & Larson

CASE

Davis & Larson

Davis & Larson is a brokerage firm based in Chicago. Founded by Charles Davis and Maria Larson, the company has provided financial planning and investment services to Chicago-area corporations and individuals for the last 15 years. As part of its investment services business, the company advises clients on its investment portfolios, so it needs to have a variety of stock market information available at all times. Like all brokerage firms, the company is connected to many financial and investment information services. The investment counselors at the company must have access to current financial data and reports, but they also must be able to examine information on long-term trends in the market.

Some of this information comes from Excel workbooks, but other information is stored in specialized financial packages and statistical programs. In addition, the company maintains a database with detailed financial information about a variety of stocks, bonds, and funds. Company employees also have access to the Internet to receive up-to-the-minute market reports. Because much of the information that the counselors need comes from outside the company, they must retrieve information in order to analyze it and make decisions.

Kelly Watkins is an investment counselor at Davis & Larson. She wants you to help her manage the different types of data available to her as she works on the Sunrise Fund, one of the company's most important stock portfolios. Because Kelly prefers to work with financial data using Excel, she wants you to retrieve the data for her and place it into an Excel workbook.

SESSION 11.1

In this session, you'll use the Excel Text Import Wizard to retrieve data from a text file. You'll select columns of data for retrieval and specify the format of the incoming data. You'll learn about basic database concepts and about how to retrieve information from a database using the Query Wizard. Finally, you'll learn how to create retrieval criteria so you can retrieve only the information you want.

Planning Data Needs at Davis & Larson

In her job as an investment counselor at Davis & Larson, Kelly helps her clients plan their investment strategies. To do her job well, Kelly needs to look at the stock market from a variety of angles. She needs to examine long-term trends to help her clients understand the benefits of creating long-term investment strategies. She also needs to see market performance for recent months in order to analyze current trends. Finally, she needs to be able to assess the daily mood of the market by regularly viewing up-to-the-minute reports.

The information that Kelly needs to do her job comes from a variety of sources. As shown in Figure 11-1, long-term and historical stock information from the company's old record-keeping system has been retrieved from other financial software packages and placed in text files that are accessible to all counselors. The company stores its current market information in databases, which is where Kelly gets information on recent trends. Kelly can also access current market reports electronically from the Internet.

Figure 11-1   KELLY'S DATA SOURCES

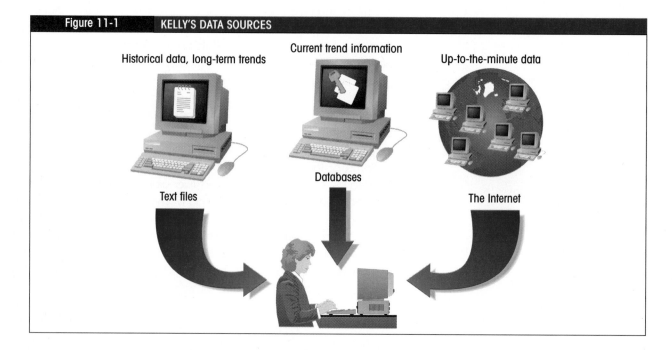

Historical data, long-term trends · Current trend information · Up-to-the-minute data

Text files · Databases · The Internet

Kelly is responsible for tracking the performance of one of the company's investment vehicles called the Sunrise Fund. The Sunrise Fund is composed of 21 different stocks on the New York Stock Exchange (NYSE), and it is one of Davis & Larson's oldest and most successful funds. Kelly would like to have a single Excel workbook that summarizes essential information about the Sunrise Fund. She wants the workbook to include historical information describing a) how the fund has performed over the past few years, b) more recent information on the fund's performance in the last year as well as the last few days, and c) up-to-the-minute reports on the fund's current status. To that end, Kelly has laid out the strategy for the workbook that she wants you to create, shown in Figure 11-2.

| Figure 11-2 | KELLY'S PLAN FOR THE SUNRISE FUND WORKBOOK |

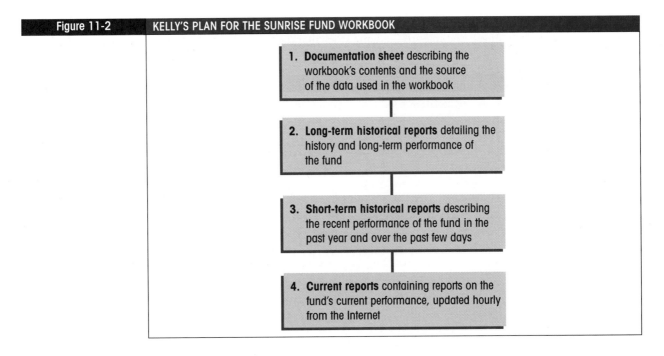

1. **Documentation sheet** describing the workbook's contents and the source of the data used in the workbook

2. **Long-term historical reports** detailing the history and long-term performance of the fund

3. **Short-term historical reports** describing the recent performance of the fund in the past year and over the past few days

4. **Current reports** containing reports on the fund's current performance, updated hourly from the Internet

Once she has the three types of report-related information in her Excel workbook, Kelly will use Excel tools to analyze the data.

Locating and organizing the different types of data Kelly wants in the workbook will be challenging because you will have to bring in data from three different sources. You quickly see that you're going to have to master the techniques of retrieving information from each of them. First, you'll begin by retrieving the long-term information, the Sunrise Fund's historical data, for Kelly. After talking with a few coworkers, you locate a text file containing daily values for the fund over the previous three years. You'll import this text file to Excel.

Working with Text Files

A **text file** contains only text and numbers without any formulas, graphics, special fonts, or formatted text that you would find in a file saved in a spreadsheet program format. Text files are one of the simplest and most widely used methods of storing data because most software programs can both save and retrieve data in a text file format. For example, Excel can open a text file into a worksheet, where you can then format it as you would any data. Excel can also save a workbook as a text file, preserving only the data, without any of the formats applied to it. In addition, many different types of computers can read text files. So, although text files contain only raw, unformatted data, they are very useful in situations where you want to share data across software applications and computer systems. There are several types of text file formats, which you'll learn about in the next section.

Text File Formats

Because a text file doesn't contain formatting codes to give it structure, there must be some other way of making it understandable to the program that reads it. If a text file contains only numbers, how will the importing program know where one group of values ends and another begins? When you import or create a text file, you have to know how that data is organized within the file. One way to structure text files is to use a **delimiter**, which is a symbol—usually a space, a comma, or a tab—that separates one column of data from another. Text that is separated by delimiters is called **delimited text**. Figure 11-3 shows three examples of the same stock market data delimited by spaces, commas, and tabs.

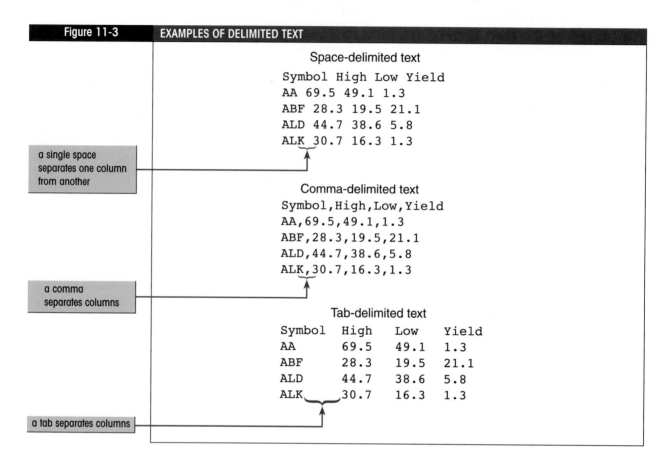

Figure 11-3	EXAMPLES OF DELIMITED TEXT

Space-delimited text

```
Symbol High Low Yield
AA 69.5 49.1 1.3
ABF 28.3 19.5 21.1
ALD 44.7 38.6 5.8
ALK 30.7 16.3 1.3
```

a single space separates one column from another

Comma-delimited text

```
Symbol,High,Low,Yield
AA,69.5,49.1,1.3
ABF,28.3,19.5,21.1
ALD,44.7,38.6,5.8
ALK,30.7,16.3,1.3
```

a comma separates columns

Tab-delimited text

```
Symbol    High    Low    Yield
AA        69.5    49.1   1.3
ABF       28.3    19.5   21.1
ALD       44.7    38.6   5.8
ALK       30.7    16.3   1.3
```

a tab separates columns

In each example there are four columns of data: Symbol, High, Low, and Yield. In the first example, a space separates the columns. The second example shows the same data, except that a comma separates each data column. In the third example, a tab separates the columns. As you can see, columns in delimited text files are not always vertically aligned as they would be in a spreadsheet, but this is not a problem for a program that can recognize the delimiter. A tab delimiter is often the best way of separating text columns because tab-delimited text can include spaces or commas within each column.

In addition to delimited text, you can also organize data with a fixed-width file. In a **fixed-width** text file, each column will start at a same location in the file. For example, the first column will start at the first space in the file, the second column will start at the 10th space, and so forth. Figure 11-4 shows columns arranged in a fixed-width format. As you can see, all the columns line up visually because each one must start at the same location.

Figure 11-4	AN EXAMPLE OF FIXED-WIDTH TEXT

```
Symbol    High    Low    Yield
AA        69.5    49.1   1.3
ABF       28.3    19.5   21.1
ALD       44.7    38.6   5.8
ALK       30.7    16.3   1.3
```

each column entry begins at the same point in the text file

When Excel opens a text file, the program automatically starts the **Text Import Wizard** to determine whether the data is in a fixed-width format or a delimited format—and if it's delimited, what delimiter is used. If necessary, you can also intervene and tell Excel how to interpret the text file.

REFERENCE WINDOW   **RW**

<u>Importing a Text File with the Text Import Wizard</u>
- Click File on the menu bar, and then click Open.
- In the Files of type list box, select Text Files.
- In the file list window, click the name of the text file you want to import, and then click the Open button.
- In the first step of the Text Import Wizard, select the Delimited or Fixed width data type option based on how the text is formatted, and then set the Start import at row value to the row where the data begins.
- In the second step of Text Import Wizard, do one of the following: If the text file is delimited, check the appropriate delimiter symbol, or, if the text file is fixed width, click, double-click, or drag the vertical column break lines to indicate where columns begin and end.
- In the third step of the Text Import Wizard, select a Column data format option that specifies the format for each incoming column, or click the Do not import Column (Skip) option button to omit a specific column from the import, and then click the Finish button.

Having seen some of the issues involved in using a text file, you are ready to import the file containing the Sunrise Fund's historical data.

Starting the Text Import Wizard

The text file that Kelly wants you to import into Excel is stored in the file named History.txt. The .txt filename extension identifies it as a text file. (Some other common text filename extensions are .dat, .prn, or .csv.) The person who gave you the text file didn't tell you anything about its structure, but you can easily determine that using the Text Import Wizard. You'll begin by opening the text file, which is similar to opening an Excel workbook, except that in the Open dialog box you need to tell Excel to display text filenames in the file list. By default, Excel will display only Excel workbooks unless you indicate you want to see other types of files.

To open the History text file:

1. Start Excel and make sure your Data Disk is in the appropriate drive.

2. Click **File** on the menu bar, and then click **Open**.

3. Using the Look in list box, locate the Tutor11\Tutorial folder on your Data Disk. Note that the folder name for this tutorial is slightly different from the names of the other folders. A folder name cannot include an extension, such as one used with the other folders in this book (the period followed by the number of the tutorial), because of the way in which the Microsoft Web Query tool functions.

   TROUBLE? Because of how Microsoft Query (a program you'll learn about later in this tutorial) handles folder names, the folder in this tutorial will be named Tutor11 instead of Tutorial.11.

4. Click the **Files of type** list arrow, and then click **Text Files**. The names of all text files in that folder now appear.

5. Click **History** and click the **Open** button. The Text Import Wizard automatically starts, as shown in Figure 11-5. In the Original data type pane, the Fixed width option button is already selected, indicating that Text Import Wizard has determined that the data is arranged in fixed-width format.

| Figure 11-5 | TEXT IMPORT WIZARD STEP 1 OF 3 |

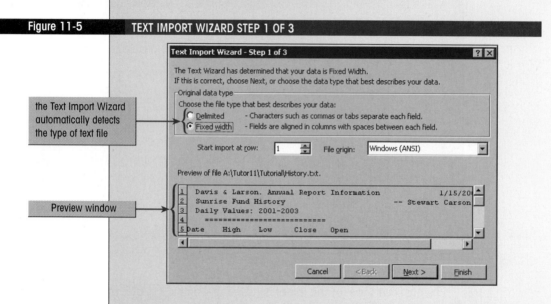

6. Scroll down the Preview window to view the data in the text file, and note that the data list doesn't actually begin until row 6 (or row 5 if you include the column titles).

There are five columns of data in the text file—Date, High, Low, Close, and Open—each corresponding to the date, the fund's high and low values on that date, and the fund's opening and closing values. The Preview window also shows that the first four lines, or rows, of the text file contain titles and lines describing the contents of the file. You want to import only the data, not the title lines, so you'll indicate the row at which you want to begin the import process, called the starting row.

Specifying the Starting Row

By default, the Text Import Wizard will start importing text with the first row of the file. Because you're only interested in retrieving the data and not the title lines, you will have the Text Import Wizard skip the first four lines of the file. You do this by specifying a new starting row for the import. You want it to start with the fifth row, which contains the labels for each column of numbers.

To specify the starting row or line number of the text file:

1. Click the **Start import at row** up arrow to change the value to **5**. The Preview window now displays only the labels for the columns and the data from the text file without the rows of descriptive text.

TROUBLE? Don't be concerned if the Preview window doesn't change quickly; it might take a few seconds before the window updates.

2. Click the **Next** button to display the second wizard dialog box. See Figure 11-6.

| Figure 11-6 | TEXT IMPORT WIZARD STEP 2 OF 3 |

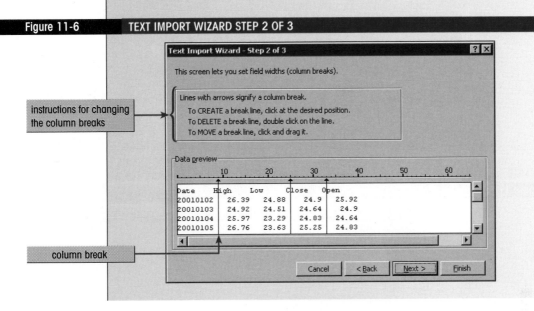

Having specified the starting row for the text file, you'll next indicate the starting and stopping points for each column.

Editing Column Breaks

For a fixed-width text file to import correctly into Excel, there must be some way for the Text Import Wizard to know where each column begins and ends. The point at which one column ends and another begins is called a **column break**. In a delimited file, the delimiter automatically determines the column break. In a fixed-width file, the wizard tries to determine the location of the column breaks for you and then places vertical lines in the Data preview window at its best guess at column locations. Sometimes the wizard's attempt to define the number and location of columns is not correct, so you should always check the Data preview window and edit the columns if necessary. Figure 11-6 shows the columns that the wizard has proposed for your text file. Unfortunately, the wizard has not inserted a column break between the High and the Low columns. In addition, some of the column breaks are in the wrong positions. The column break between the Date and High columns cuts the High column title in half, for example. Clearly, you'll have to revise the Text Import Wizard's choice of column breaks and their locations.

You insert a new column break by clicking the position in the Data preview window where you want the break to appear. If a break is in the wrong location, you click and drag it to a new location in the Data preview window. You can also delete an extra column break by double-clicking it. You'll use these techniques to modify the column breaks for the History text file.

To edit the Text Import Wizard's column breaks:

1. Click the vertical line between the Date and High columns, and drag it to the left so that it lies between the High column title and the values in the Date column.

2. Click the space between the High and Low columns to create a break there. Make sure the break does not intersect any values or text.

TROUBLE? If the vertical line you just created intersects the values or text, drag the line to the right so that it lies between the Low column title and the values in the High column.

3. Drag the vertical line between the Low and Close columns to the left so as not to cross over any values or text.

4. Drag the column break between the Close and Open columns to the left, making sure the vertical line does not intersect any values or text in either column. Figure 11-7 shows the Data preview window with the column breaks in the correct locations. When Excel imports this text file, the program will now place each column into a separate column in the worksheet.

| Figure 11-7 | REVISED COLUMN BREAKS |

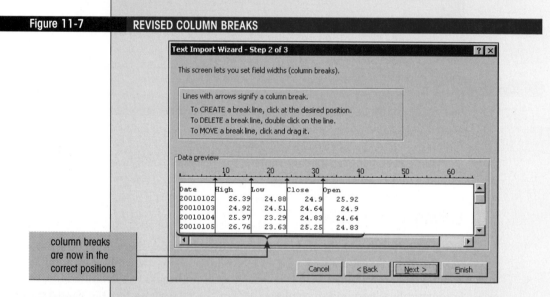

column breaks are now in the correct positions

5. Click the **Next** button to display the third dialog box of the Text Import Wizard. See Figure 11-8.

| Figure 11-8 | TEXT IMPORT WIZARD STEP 3 OF 3 |

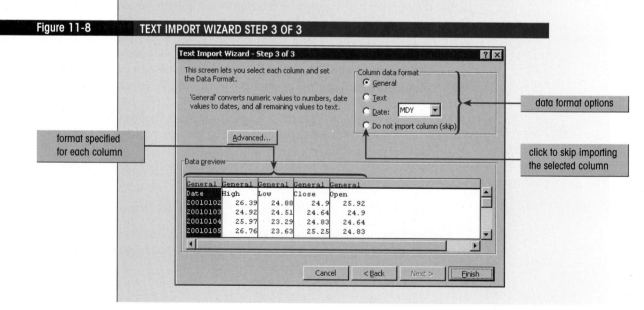

format specified for each column

data format options

click to skip importing the selected column

Now you'll tell Excel how you want to format each column of the incoming data.

Formatting and Trimming Incoming Data

The third and final step of the Text Import Wizard allows you to format the data in each column. Unless you specify a format, Excel will apply a General format to all columns, which means that the Import Wizard tries to determine which columns contain text, numbers, or dates.

If you're worried that the wizard will misinterpret the format of a column, you can specify the format yourself in this dialog box before the column is imported. In addition to specifying the data format, you can also indicate which columns you do not want to import at all. Eliminating columns is useful when there are only a few items you want to import from a large text file containing many columns.

As you look over the Data preview window shown in Figure 11-8, you note that the Date column displays the year first, followed by the month and the day with no separators. This is an unusual date format, so you'll want to make sure that the Text Import Wizard correctly interprets these values by applying a date format to these values, rather than the General format.

To reduce the amount of data in the workbook, you also decide not to import the daily opening value of the Sunrise Fund because the value is the same as the closing value from the previous day. You'll therefore only import the date and the high, low, and close values of the fund for each day.

To specify a Date format and remove the Open column:

1. Make sure that the first column is selected in the Data preview window. Now you'll assign the correct date format.

   TROUBLE? If the first column is not selected, click anywhere in the column to select it.

2. In the Column data format pane, click the **Date** option button.

3. Click the **Date** list arrow, and click **YMD** in the list of date formats. Although the data appears unchanged, the column heading changes from General to YMD, indicating that Excel will interpret the values in this column as dates formatted with the year followed by the month and day.

   Now you'll omit the Open column from the import because the open values are the same as the close values.

4. In the Data preview window, click anywhere in the **Open** column to select it, and then click the **Do not import column (skip)** option button in the Column data format pane. The column heading for the Open column changes to Skip Column, indicating that Excel will not import it.

5. Click the **Finish** button. Excel retrieves the data from the text file and places it into a new workbook. Note that Excel has already applied a date format to the data values in column A.

At this point the text file has been placed into a worksheet named "History," and the name of the workbook appears to be "History" as well. However, this workbook has not been saved. If you close the workbook now without saving it, it will revert back to the original text file format. You decide to rename the worksheet and save the file in Excel workbook format.

To rename the worksheet and save the workbook:

1. Double-click the **History** tab, and rename the worksheet as **Fund History**.

2. Click **File** on the menu bar, and then click **Save As**.

3. Click the **Save as type** list arrow, and then click **Microsoft Excel Workbook**.

4. Double-click the name in the File name text box, and then type **Sunrise1**.

5. Click the **Save** button.

Next, you will format the contents of the Fund History worksheet.

To format the worksheet:

1. Select the range **B2:D755**.

   TROUBLE? If you are having difficulty selecting this range, you can use the method described here. To select this large range quickly and easily, select the range B2:D2, and then press and hold the Shift key while you double-click the bottom border of the selected range with the pointer.

2. Click **Format** on the menu bar, click **Cells** to open the Format Cells dialog box, click the **Number** tab if necessary, click **Number** in the Category list, verify that the number of decimal places is set to **2**, and then click the **OK** button.

3. Increase the width of column A to **12** characters.

4. Select the column labels in the range **A1:D1**, click the **Bold** button **B** on the Formatting toolbar, and then click the **Center** button on the same toolbar.

5. Click cell **A1**. Figure 11-9 shows the formatted worksheet.

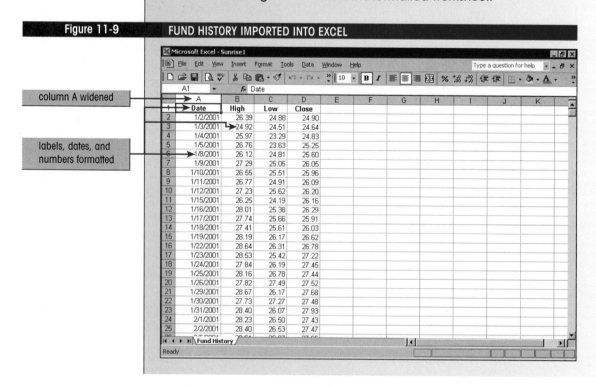

Figure 11-9   FUND HISTORY IMPORTED INTO EXCEL

column A widened

labels, dates, and numbers formatted

In addition to the fund values themselves, Kelly would like you to include a high-low-close chart in the workbook displaying the fund's recent history. You will select the Stock chart type, which is designed to compare the high, low, open, and close prices of a stock.

To create a high-low-close chart for the fund data:

1. Click **Insert** on the menu bar, and then click **Chart** to display the first Chart Wizard dialog box, which provides the options for choosing the chart type and sub-type you want to use.

2. Click **Stock** in the Chart type list, and, if necessary, click the **High-Low-Close** chart type, as shown in Figure 11-10.

Figure 11-10	CHOOSING A CUSTOM STOCK CHART

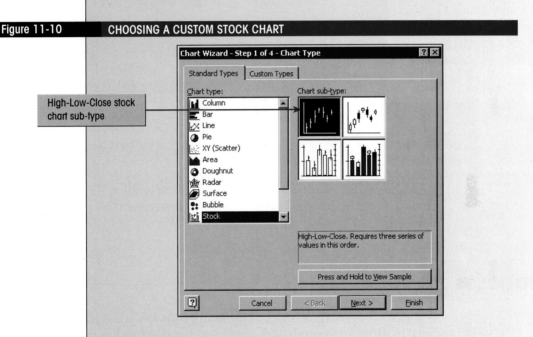

High-Low-Close stock chart sub-type

3. Click the **Next** button twice to open the third Chart Wizard dialog box.

4. Click the **Titles** tab if necessary, and enter the chart title as **Sunrise Fund: 2001 - 2003**, the x axis title as **Date**, and the y axis title as **Fund Value**.

5. Click the **Legend** tab, deselect the **Show legend** check box to remove the legend from the chart, and then click the **Next** button to display the fourth and final Chart Wizard dialog box.

6. Place the chart on a new chart sheet named **History Chart**, and then click the **Finish** button. Figure 11-11 shows the Sunrise Fund value from 2001 through 2003.

Figure 11-11   CHART OF THE FUND'S PERFORMANCE 2001–2003

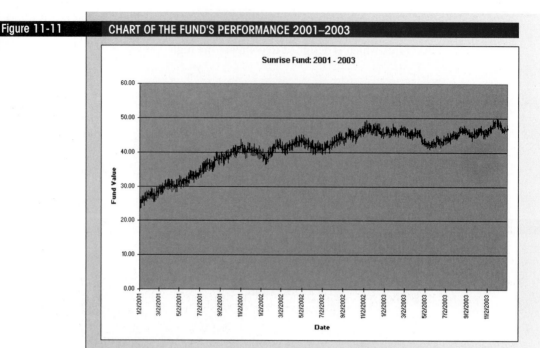

Kelly is pleased with the progress you've made in locating the text file, importing it into Excel, and charting the fund's history in a high-low-close chart. Now that she has the historical stock information she needs, she wants you to insert some current data from the company's databases.

Databases and Queries

As in many financial firms, much of the information Davis and Larson analysts work with is stored in databases. A **database** is a program that stores and retrieves large amounts of data and creates reports describing that data. There are many database programs available, including Microsoft Access, dBASE, Paradox, Oracle, and FoxPro. Excel can retrieve data from most database programs. At Davis and Larson, information on the stocks in the Sunrise Fund is stored in the Sunrise database, which was created in Access.

Databases contain information stored in the form of tables. A **table** is a collection of data that is stored in rows and columns. Figure 11-12 shows an example of one database table Kelly wants you to work with. Each column of the table, called a **field**, stores information about a specific characteristic of a person, place, or thing. In this example, the middle field, called the Company field, stores the names of the companies whose stock is part of the Sunrise portfolio. Each row of the table, called a **record**, displays the collection of characteristics of a particular person, place, or thing. The first record in the table in Figure 11-12 displays stock information for the Aluminum Company of America, which has the ticker symbol AA and belongs to the group of industrial stocks.

Figure 11-12   A DATABASE TABLE

Ticker Symbol	Company	Category
AA	Aluminum Company of America	INDUSTRIALS
ABF	Airborne Freight Corporation	TRANSPORTATION
AEP	American Electric Power Company, Inc.	UTILITIES
CRR	CONRAIL Inc.	TRANSPORTATION
CX	Centerior Energy Corporation	UTILITIES
ED	Consolidated Edison Company of New Y	UTILITIES
EK	Eastman Kodak Company	INDUSTRIALS
GM	General Motors Corporation	INDUSTRIALS
LUV	Southwest Airlines Co.	TRANSPORTATION
NMK	Niagara Mohawk Power Corporation	UTILITIES
R	Ryder System, Inc.	TRANSPORTATION
T	AT&T Corp.	INDUSTRIALS
TX	Texaco Inc.	INDUSTRIALS
UCM	Unicom Corporation	UTILITIES
UNP	Union Pacific Corporation	TRANSPORTATION

row or record

column or field

The Sunrise database has four tables: Company, Long Term Performance, Recent Performance, and Stock Info. Figure 11-13 describes the contents of each table.

Figure 11-13   SUNRISE DATABASE TABLE NAMES AND DESCRIPTIONS

TABLE NAME	DESCRIPTION
Company	Data about each company in the fund and the percentage of the fund that is allocated to purchasing stocks for that company
Long Term Performance	Summarizes the performance over the last 52 weeks for each stock, recording the high and low values over that period of time, and its volatility
Recent Performance	Daily high, low, closing, and volume values for each stock in the portfolio over the last five days
Stock Info	Description of each stock including the yield, dividend amount and date, earnings per share, and the number of outstanding shares

With several tables in a database, you need some way of relating information in one table to information in another. You relate tables to one another by using **common fields**, which are the fields that are the same in each table. As shown in Figure 11-14, both the Company table and the Stock Info table contain the Ticker Symbol field, so Ticker Symbol is a common field in this database.

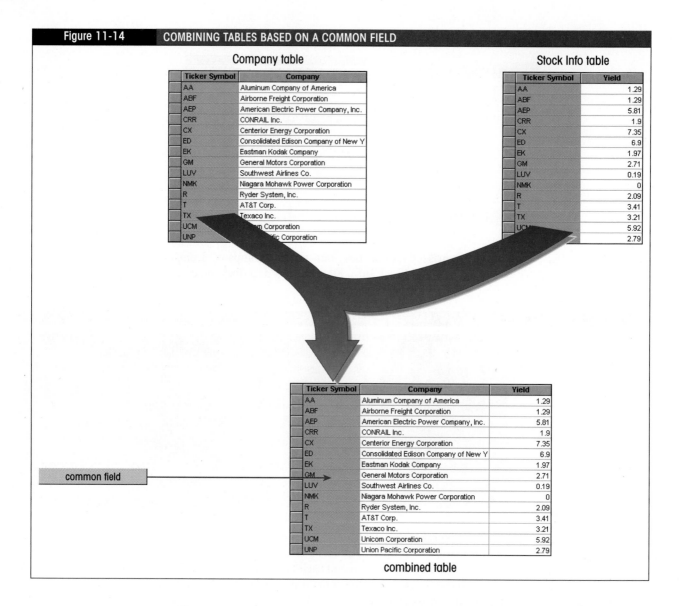

Figure 11-14   COMBINING TABLES BASED ON A COMMON FIELD

combined table

When you want to retrieve information from two tables, like the Company table and the Stock Info table, Excel matches the value of the ticker symbol in one table with the value of the ticker symbol in the other. Because the ticker symbol values match, you can create a new table that contains information about both the company and the stock itself. Without common fields, there would be no way of matching the company information from one table with the yield information from the other.

A large database can have many tables, and each table can have several fields and thousands of records, so you need a way to choose only the information that you most want to see. When you want to look only at specific information from a database, you create a query. A **query** is a question you ask about the data in the database. In response to your query, the database displays the records and fields that meet the requirements of your question. A query might ask something like, "What are the names of all the stocks in the portfolio, and what are their corresponding ticker symbols?" To answer this question, you would submit the query to the database in a form that the database can read. The database would then extract the relevant information and create a table of all the stocks and their symbols.

When you query a database, you might want to extract only specific records. In this case, your query would contain **criteria**, which are conditions you set to limit the number of records the database extracts. Excel then extracts only those records that match the specified conditions. For example, you might want to know the names and ticker symbols of only the top five performing stocks from the past three months. In submitting the query to the database, you would include this criteria to limit the information returned to only the top five performing stocks from that time period in the portfolio.

In a query, you can also specify how you want the data to appear. If you want the names and ticker symbols of the top ten performing stocks arranged alphabetically by ticker symbol, you can include that in your query definition.

Extracting just the information you need from a database to answer a particular question might seem like a daunting task, but Excel provides an add-in called the **Query Wizard** to simplify the task of creating and running your queries. You'll use the Query Wizard to extract data from Davis and Larson's database and to add the next set of worksheets to Kelly's Sunrise1 workbook.

Using the Query Wizard

Kelly next wants you to add a worksheet to the workbook that lists the stocks in the Sunrise Fund and describes their performance in the last year. As you'll remember from the worksheet plan, you can get this current trend information from the company database called Sunrise. You'll start the process of retrieving this information with the Query Wizard. Before doing that, you'll have to insert a new worksheet into the workbook.

> *To start retrieving data from an external source:*
>
> **1.** Insert a new worksheet at the beginning of the workbook, and then rename the worksheet as **Portfolio**.
>
> Now you are ready to start the process of retrieving the stock information into this worksheet.
>
> **2.** Click **Data** on the menu bar, point to **Import External Data**, and then click **New Database Query**. The Choose Data Source dialog box opens, as shown in Figure 11-15.
>
> TROUBLE? If Excel displays a dialog box indicating that Microsoft Query is not installed, click the Yes button to begin the installation. You will be instructed to insert your Microsoft Office XP Installation CD in your CD drive. After inserting the CD, click the OK button to start installing the add-in. If you are working on a network, your instructor or technical resource person might need to install Microsoft Query for you. For more information on add-ins, see the discussion on add-ins in Tutorial 10.

Figure 11-15	CHOOSE DATA SOURCE DIALOG BOX

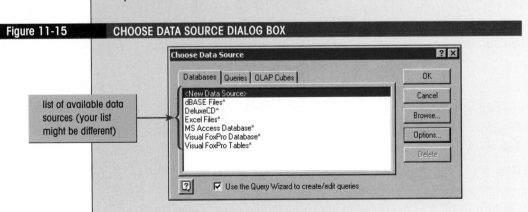

list of available data sources (your list might be different)

Connecting to a Data Source

A **data source** is any file that contains the data that you want to retrieve. Data sources can be databases, text files, or other Excel workbooks. Excel provides several data sources listed in Figure 11-15 (your list may differ), or you can define your own data source by clicking "<New Data Source>" from the list of databases. In this case, however, because you're trying to connect to a Microsoft Access database, you'll use the MS Access Database data source.

To connect to an Access data source:

1. Click **MS Access Database*** in the list of data sources, and then click the **OK** button. The Select Database dialog box opens.

2. Locate the Tutor11\Tutorial folder on your Data Disk if necessary, and then select the **Sunrise.mdb** database. See Figure 11-16.

Figure 11-16	LOCATION OF THE SUNRISE FUND DATABASE

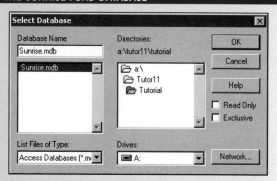

3. Click the **OK** button. Excel opens the Query Wizard – Choose Columns dialog box, shown in Figure 11-17.

Figure 11-17	TABLES IN THE SUNRISE DATABASE

Sunrise database tables

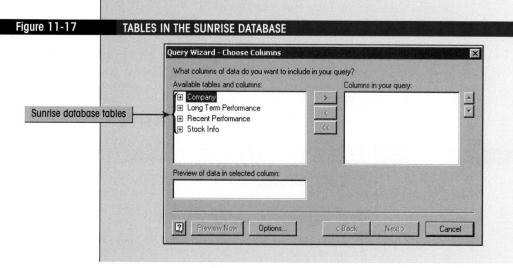

Choosing Tables and Columns

The next step in retrieving data from the Sunrise database is to choose the table and fields (columns) to include in the query. The Query Wizard lets you "peek" inside the database so that you can preview the structure of the database and its contents. You'll start by examining the fields in the Company table.

To view a list of the fields in the Company table:

1. Click the **plus sign** ⊞ in front of the Company table name. The Available tables and columns list box expands to display the columns (or fields) in the Company table. See Figure 11-18.

| Figure 11-18 | FIELDS IN THE COMPANY TABLE |

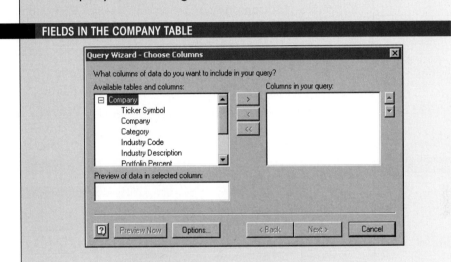

You're not sure what fields Kelly wants to place into the worksheet. You contact her and she indicates that she would like to include the ticker symbol, the company, and the portfolio percent from the Company table. The portfolio percent, you learn, is the percentage of the portfolio that is invested in each particular stock. Kelly also wants the Year High and Year Low fields from the Long Term Performance table so that she can tell what the high and low points in the previous year have been for each stock in the portfolio. Because the two tables share Ticker Symbol as a common field, you'll select data from both tables with the Query Wizard.

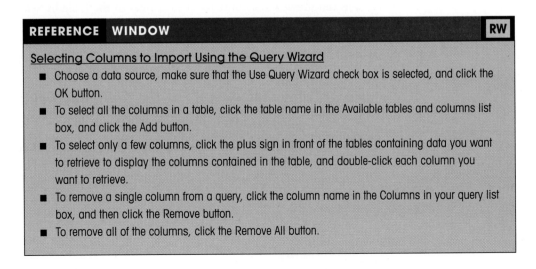

REFERENCE WINDOW **RW**

Selecting Columns to Import Using the Query Wizard
- Choose a data source, make sure that the Use Query Wizard check box is selected, and click the OK button.
- To select all the columns in a table, click the table name in the Available tables and columns list box, and click the Add button.
- To select only a few columns, click the plus sign in front of the tables containing data you want to retrieve to display the columns contained in the table, and double-click each column you want to retrieve.
- To remove a single column from a query, click the column name in the Columns in your query list box, and then click the Remove button.
- To remove all of the columns, click the Remove All button.

To select fields, you can click the field name and click the Add button, or you can simply double-click the field name, and Excel will automatically move it to the list of selected columns in your query.

To select the columns you want to import into Excel:

1. Click **Ticker Symbol** in the Available tables and columns list box, and then click the **Add** button ⯈ . Ticker Symbol moves to the Columns in your query list box, indicating that it will be included in your query.

    You'll continue selecting the remaining columns that Kelly wants to view by using the alternative method of double-clicking.

2. Double-click **Company** and then double-click **Portfolio Percent**. These columns now appear in the Columns in your query list box.

    Next, you'll open the Long Term Performance table and select the other fields you need.

3. Click the **plus box** ⊞ in front of the Long Term Performance table name.

4. Double-click **Year High** and then double-click **Year Low**. The five fields that Kelly wants should now be selected. See Figure 11-19.

Figure 11-19	FIELDS SELECTED FOR THE QUERY

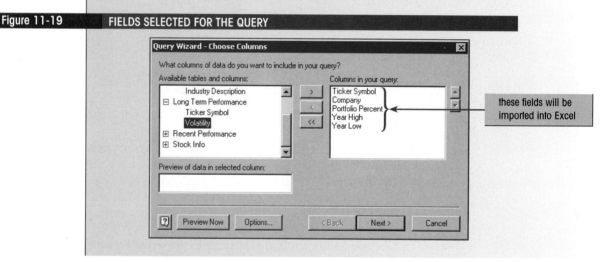

You can preview the contents of each field in the table by selecting it (either in the left pane or the right pane of the Choose Columns dialog box) and then by clicking the Preview Now button. You decide to preview the contents of the Company field to get an idea of the types of entries it contains.

To preview the contents of the Company field:

1. Click **Company** in the Columns in your query list box.

2. Click the **Preview Now** button. Some of the values in this column display in the Preview of data in selected column list box. See Figure 11-20.

Figure 11-20   **PREVIEWING THE COMPANY FIELD**

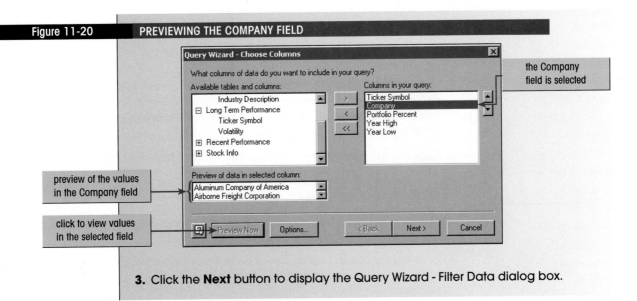

the Company field is selected

preview of the values in the Company field

click to view values in the selected field

3. Click the **Next** button to display the Query Wizard - Filter Data dialog box.

Now that you have selected the five columns for your Portfolio worksheet, you next have to determine whether to retrieve all of the records in the database or only records that satisfy particular criteria.

Filtering and Sorting Data

In discussing the issue with Kelly, she indicates that she would like you to retrieve information on all the stocks. However, she thinks there will be occasions in the future when she'll only want information on some of the stocks. You decide to examine the filtering capabilities of the Query Wizard to get familiar with them.

When you filter data, you specify which records you want to retrieve. In this query, you can filter the data to remove particular stocks or to retrieve only those stocks that perform at a certain level.

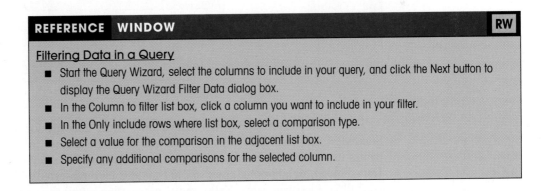

REFERENCE   WINDOW   **RW**

Filtering Data in a Query

- Start the Query Wizard, select the columns to include in your query, and click the Next button to display the Query Wizard Filter Data dialog box.
- In the Column to filter list box, click a column you want to include in your filter.
- In the Only include rows where list box, select a comparison type.
- Select a value for the comparison in the adjacent list box.
- Specify any additional comparisons for the selected column.

To see how the data filter works, you'll create a filter that will retrieve stock information only for stocks from the Eastman Kodak Company or from Southwest Airlines.

To create a filter:

1. Click **Company** in the Column to filter list box. On the right side of the Query Wizard - Filter Data dialog box, there are two columns of list boxes. The column on the left specifies the type of comparison you want to make in the filter, such as "equals," "greater than," or "less than." In the column on the right, you enter a value for the comparison. You'll use these two list boxes to have the query retrieve the Eastman Kodak stock.

2. Click the **list arrow** in the first row of the left column, and then click **equals**.

3. Click the **list arrow** in the first row of the right column, and then click **Eastman Kodak Company** in the list.

   Next, you'll add a second set of conditions so that the query includes either the Eastman Kodak Company *or* Southwest Airlines Co.

4. Click the **Or** option button. Now that you have completed the first row and indicated that you want to include another filter, the second row of list boxes becomes available.

5. Click the **list arrow** in the second row of the left column, and then click **equals**.

6. Click the **list arrow** in the right column of the second row, and then click **Southwest Airlines Co.** in the list. Figure 11-21 shows the completed Filter Data dialog box.

Figure 11-21	CREATING A DATA FILTER

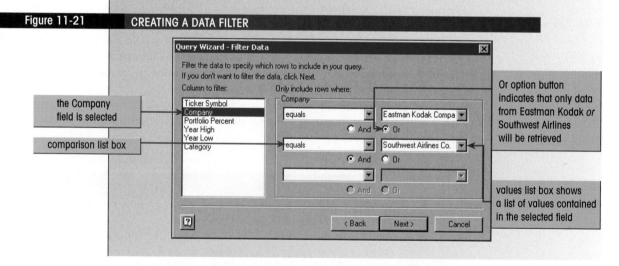

the Company field is selected

comparison list box

Or option button indicates that only data from Eastman Kodak *or* Southwest Airlines will be retrieved

values list box shows a list of values contained in the selected field

The filter you created will retrieve only those records for Eastman Kodak *or* for Southwest Airlines. The Query Wizard will not retrieve stock information for other companies in the Sunrise Fund. Although only three rows of criteria are shown in the Filter Data dialog box, additional rows would be added if you inserted additional requirements to your filter. However, since Kelly wants information on all the companies in the portfolio, you'll now remove the data filters you just created.

To remove the filter:

1. Click the comparison **list arrow** in the second row of the left column, and click the blank space at the top of the list (you might have to scroll up to see it).

2. Repeat Step 1 for the comparison list box in the first row. The filters are removed from the query.

3. Click the **Next** button to proceed to the next step of the Query Wizard.

So far, you've identified the fields you want to retrieve, and you've had a chance to filter out any records. In the last part of creating your query, you specify whether you want the data sorted in a particular order.

Sorting Data in a Query
- Start the Query Wizard, select columns to include in your query, define any filters you want to apply to the query, and then click the Next button to display the Sort Order dialog box.
- Click the Sort by list arrow, and then click the column by which you want to sort the retrieved data.
- Click the Ascending or Descending option button.
- Add extra levels to the sort by filling in the additional Sort by list boxes.

Kelly has indicated that she would like to have the portfolio displayed starting with the stocks in which the Sunrise Fund has the largest capital investment, and proceeding down to the stocks with the smallest capital investment. The Portfolio Percent field tells you how much of the fund is invested in each stock, so you should sort the data by the values in that field in descending order (from highest percentage to lowest).

To sort the data by company name:

1. Click the **Sort by** list arrow, and then click **Portfolio Percent**.

2. Click the **Descending** option button.

3. Click the **Next** button to display the final Query Wizard dialog box.

You have finished defining your query. You could run the query now and get the information that Kelly has requested, but you should first save your query.

Saving Your Queries

When you save a query, you are actually placing the query choices you've made into a file. You can open the file later and run the query, saving you the trouble of redefining it. You can also share the query with others who might want to extract the same type of information from the data source. Query files can be stored in any folder you choose. The default folder for queries is the Queries folder located on your computer's hard disk. Saving the query file to this folder has some advantages. If you are running Excel on a network, you can make the query file accessible to other network users. Also, query files in this folder will appear on the Queries tab of the Choose Data Source dialog box (see Figure 11-15), giving you quick and easy access to your saved queries. In this case, however, you'll save your query to your Data Disk because you may not have access to your Queries folder. After saving a query as a file, you automatically return to the last dialog box of the Query Wizard, where you can then retrieve the data from the database into your workbook.

REFERENCE WINDOW **RW**

Saving a Query
- Run the Query Wizard, completing all the dialog boxes and proceeding to the final Query Wizard dialog box.
- Click the Save Query button.
- Select a location for your query.
- Enter a name for the query, and click the Save button.
- Return to the Query Wizard, and retrieve the data from the query.

You decide to save your query with the name "Sunrise Portfolio" because it displays a list of stocks in the Sunrise Fund. Save this query to your Data Disk.

To save the query:

1. Click the **Save Query** button.

2. Open the Tutorial folder for Tutor11 on your Data Disk.

3. Select the text in the File name text box, and then type **Sunrise Portfolio** as the name of the saved query. The file type for query files is (*.dqy), meaning that your saved query files will have the .dqy extension.

4. Click the **Save** button.

Now that you have saved your query, you have three options. You can:

- Return (import) the data into your Excel workbook.
- Open the results of your query in Microsoft Query. Microsoft Query is an add-in included on your installation disk with several tools that allow you to create even more complex queries.
- Create an OLAP cube. **OLAP** (On-line Analytical Processing) is a way to organize large business databases. An OLAP cube organizes data so that reports summarizing results of your query are easier to create. An OLAP cube allows you to work with larger data sets than you would otherwise be able to in Excel. Data returned via an OLAP cube appears in the form of a PivotTable report, not as individual records.

You can learn more about these three options from Excel's online Help. Which one should you choose now? You don't need to refine the query at this point, so you don't need to open it in Microsoft Query. Moreover, you're interested in viewing individual records from the database and not a summary report; therefore, you won't be using this query to create an OLAP cube. Therefore, you'll choose the first option and simply import the data into the Sunrise Fund workbook.

To retrieve the data from the Sunrise database:

1. If necessary, click the **Return Data to Microsoft Excel** option button to select it.

2. Click the **Finish** button. The Import Data dialog box opens, in which you can select where you want to place the imported data.

3. Click cell **A3** in the Portfolio sheet to insert the retrieved data into the worksheet, starting at that cell. The cell reference, which includes the sheet name, appears in the Existing worksheet reference box.

   TROUBLE? If necessary, move the Import Data dialog box to the right so you can click cell A3.

4. Click the **OK** button. Excel retrieves the data from the Sunrise database and inserts it into the current worksheet. Excel also displays the External Data toolbar, which lets you perform several common tasks with your data; you'll use it in the next session. See Figure 11-22.

Figure 11-22   **PORTFOLIO DATA RETRIEVED INTO THE SUNRISE1 WORKBOOK**

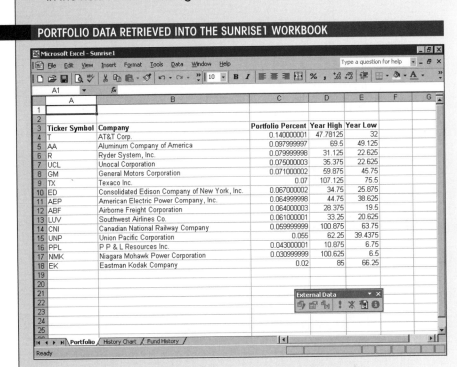

Before closing and saving your workbook, you should add a title and then format the portfolio information.

To format the Portfolio worksheet:

1. Type **Sunrise Fund Portfolio** in cell A1, format the text in 16-point boldface type, and then center it across the first five columns of the worksheet.

2. Apply the **Percent Style** format to the values in the Portfolio Percent column, and then display the percentages with **2** decimal places.

3. Apply the Comma Style format to the values in the Year High and Year Low columns, which will display the values to two decimal places.

4. Click cell **A1**. Figure 11-23 shows the formatted worksheet.

Figure 11-23   **FORMATTED PORTFOLIO DATA**

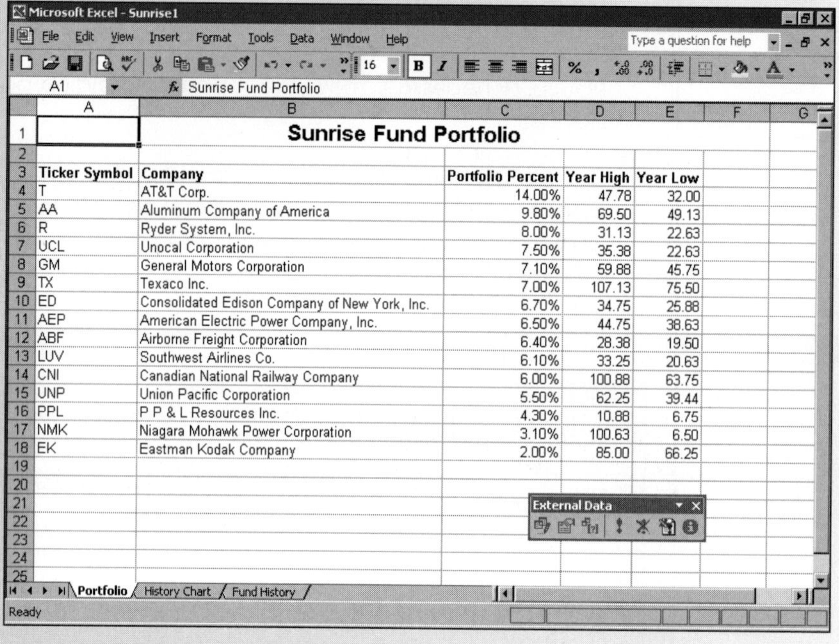

	A	B	C	D	E	F	G
1		Sunrise Fund Portfolio					
2							
3	Ticker Symbol	Company	Portfolio Percent	Year High	Year Low		
4	T	AT&T Corp.	14.00%	47.78	32.00		
5	AA	Aluminum Company of America	9.80%	69.50	49.13		
6	R	Ryder System, Inc.	8.00%	31.13	22.63		
7	UCL	Unocal Corporation	7.50%	35.38	22.63		
8	GM	General Motors Corporation	7.10%	59.88	45.75		
9	TX	Texaco Inc.	7.00%	107.13	75.50		
10	ED	Consolidated Edison Company of New York, Inc.	6.70%	34.75	25.88		
11	AEP	American Electric Power Company, Inc.	6.50%	44.75	38.63		
12	ABF	Airborne Freight Corporation	6.40%	28.38	19.50		
13	LUV	Southwest Airlines Co.	6.10%	33.25	20.63		
14	CNI	Canadian National Railway Company	6.00%	100.88	63.75		
15	UNP	Union Pacific Corporation	5.50%	62.25	39.44		
16	PPL	P P & L Resources Inc.	4.30%	10.88	6.75		
17	NMK	Niagara Mohawk Power Corporation	3.10%	100.63	6.50		
18	EK	Eastman Kodak Company	2.00%	85.00	66.25		

Looking at the contents of the portfolio, you can quickly see that 14% of the fund is invested in the AT&T Corporation and that the value of that stock has ranged from a high of 47.78 points to a low of 32 points. This worksheet will be very helpful to Kelly in working with the stocks in the Sunrise Fund portfolio.

Print the Portfolio worksheet, and then save and close your workbook.

To print and save the Sunrise Fund data:

1. Print the Portfolio worksheet.

2. Save and close the workbook, and then exit Excel.

You show Kelly the progress that you've made in importing the data from the company database. She wants to work with the newly imported Sunrise Fund Portfolio to see if it meets her needs.

In the next session, you'll add more current information about the Sunrise Fund stocks to your workbook. You'll learn how to refresh data, edit your queries, and control the way Excel retrieves data from its data sources. You'll then see how to import data into a PivotTable.

Session 11.1 QUICK CHECK

1. What is the difference between a fixed-width and a delimited text file?

2. Name three delimiters that can separate data in a delimited text file.

3. How do you insert column breaks when importing a text file using the Text Import Wizard?

4. Define the following terms:
   a. database
   b. table
   c. field
   d. record
   e. common field
5. What is a query?
6. What is a data source?
7. Once you've finished creating your query, describe the three options Excel provides you for using that query.

SESSION 11.2

In this session, you'll learn how to edit and rerun your queries to retrieve new data. You'll see how to modify the properties of your existing queries. Finally, you'll learn how to use a PivotTable to summarize the data in your database.

Working with External Data and Queries

In the last session, you learned two ways to bring data into Excel: by importing a text file and by importing data from a database. Importing data from a database has several advantages over importing from a text file. Using queries, you can control which records you import into your workbook. More importantly, by retrieving data from a database, you can easily refresh, or update, the data in your workbooks when the data source itself is updated.

Refreshing External Data

When you retrieved the portfolio data for Kelly in the last session, you did more than insert the data into the Excel workbook. By defining a data source, you also gave Excel information about where to go to find updated information for your workbook. Davis & Larson are constantly updating their databases, and it's important for Kelly to be able to view the most up-to-date information on the Sunrise Fund so that she can offer accurate and timely advice to her clients.

Excel allows you to keep your data current by refreshing the data in your queries. When you refresh a query, Excel retrieves the most current data from the data source, using the query definition you've already created.

REFERENCE WINDOW   RW

Refreshing External Data
- Click a cell in the range containing the external data, and click the Refresh button on the External Data toolbar.

  or
- If your workbook contains several external data ranges, click the Refresh All button on the External Data toolbar to refresh all the external data in the workbook.

You've explained the concept of refreshing data to Kelly. She wants you to show her how to refresh the information in the Sunrise Fund workbook so she can make sure she has the most current version of the database information. To refresh the imported data, you select a cell from the range containing the data and use the Refresh command.

To refresh the portfolio data:

1. If you took a break at the end of the last session, make sure Excel is running, and then open the **Sunrise1** workbook in the Tutor11\Tutorial folder on your Data Disk.

2. Click cell **A3** in the Portfolio worksheet. Although you've selected cell A3 here, you can select any cell in the data range when you refresh your data.

3. Click the **Refresh Data** button ⬇ on the External Data toolbar. Excel goes to the Sunrise database and retrieves the current information from the database back into the worksheet. The status bar shows that the data is being refreshed. The mode indicator on the status bar will return to Ready when the process is complete. Note that the contents of this workbook did not change because the Sunrise database has not been modified since you last saved the Sunrise Fund workbook.

TROUBLE? If the External Data toolbar is not visible, click View on the menu bar, point to Toolbars, and click External Data to display the toolbar.

Having seen how the refresh command works, Kelly wonders if there are any other ways to control how and when Excel refreshes external data.

Setting External Data Properties

Kelly likes the fact that she can refresh her external data so quickly and easily, but she has a couple of concerns. She worries that she might forget to refresh the data each time she opens her workbook and she prefers to have Excel automatically refresh the data. On the other hand, there are times when she wants some of her workbooks to contain a "snapshot" of the data as it exists at a particular moment in time. In that case, her needs are just the opposite—she doesn't want the data refreshed at all.

You can meet both of these requirements by modifying the properties of the query. By modifying the query properties, you can:

- Remove the underlying external data query, freezing the data so that it cannot be refreshed.

- Require that the user enter a password before the data is refreshed, thus keeping other users from updating the data without permission.

- Run the query in the background, so you can work on other portions of the workbook as you wait for the data to be retrieved; this is helpful if you are retrieving large amounts of data.

- Refresh the data automatically whenever the workbook is reopened or at specific intervals when the workbook is in use.

- Specify how new data from the external data source is added when the size of the external data range changes. You can insert new cells and delete unused cells, insert an entire row and clear unused cells, or replace existing cells with new data.
- Automatically copy formulas into adjacent columns, preserving them as the size of the external data range expands into new columns after refreshing.

As you can see, Excel gives you a great deal of flexibility as to how and when you refresh your external data.

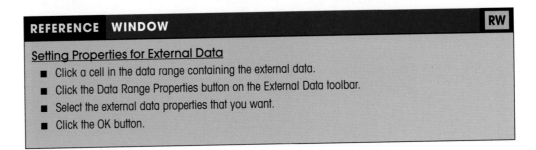

REFERENCE WINDOW   **RW**

<u>Setting Properties for External Data</u>
- Click a cell in the data range containing the external data.
- Click the Data Range Properties button on the External Data toolbar.
- Select the external data properties that you want.
- Click the OK button.

Because she frequently consults her database files as she advises her clients on stock market trends, Kelly decides that she would like to have the query refreshed automatically whenever she opens the Sunrise Fund workbook. You will set the properties for the workbook.

To set properties for the Industrial Stocks external data:

1. Click the **Data Range Properties** button 🖼 on the External Data toolbar.

2. Click the **Refresh data on file open** check box to select this option. Selecting this option automatically makes the Remove external data from worksheet before saving check box available. This option allows Excel to remove the data that you've retrieved from the workbook before closing the workbook. The advantage is that removing the data makes the size of the workbook relatively small when the workbook is not in use. Then, when you reopen the workbook, Excel automatically retrieves the data and puts it back in its proper place. You tell Kelly about this option, but she decides to keep the data in the workbook at all times because the amount data being retrieved is not very large.

   You could also select the Refresh every option in order to have the results of the query refreshed periodically when the workbook is opened. However, because this query retrieves historical data, it is unlikely that the database will be updated within the period of time that Kelly is working on it. So you'll leave this check box unselected.

   The completed External Data Range Properties dialog box should appear as shown in Figure 11-24.

Figure 11-24   **PROPERTIES OF THE SUNRISE PORTFOLIO QUERY**

query name

click to have Excel refresh the query at specified time intervals

click to have Excel refresh the query when it opens the workbook

properties that control how Excel formats the query data

External Data Range Properties   ? X

Name: Sunrise Portfolio

Query definition
☑ Save query definition
☑ Save password

Refresh control
☑ Enable background refresh
☐ Refresh every   60 ▲▼   minutes
☑ Refresh data on file open
☐ Remove external data from worksheet before saving

Data formatting and layout
☑ Include field names   ☑ Preserve column sort/filter/layout
☐ Include row numbers   ☑ Preserve cell formatting
☑ Adjust column width

If the number of rows in the data range changes upon refresh:
◉ Insert cells for new data, delete unused cells
○ Insert entire rows for new data, clear unused cells
○ Overwrite existing cells with new data, clear unused cells

☐ Fill down formulas in columns adjacent to data

[OK]   [Cancel]

properties that control how Excel inserts or removes rows of cells when the data source changes

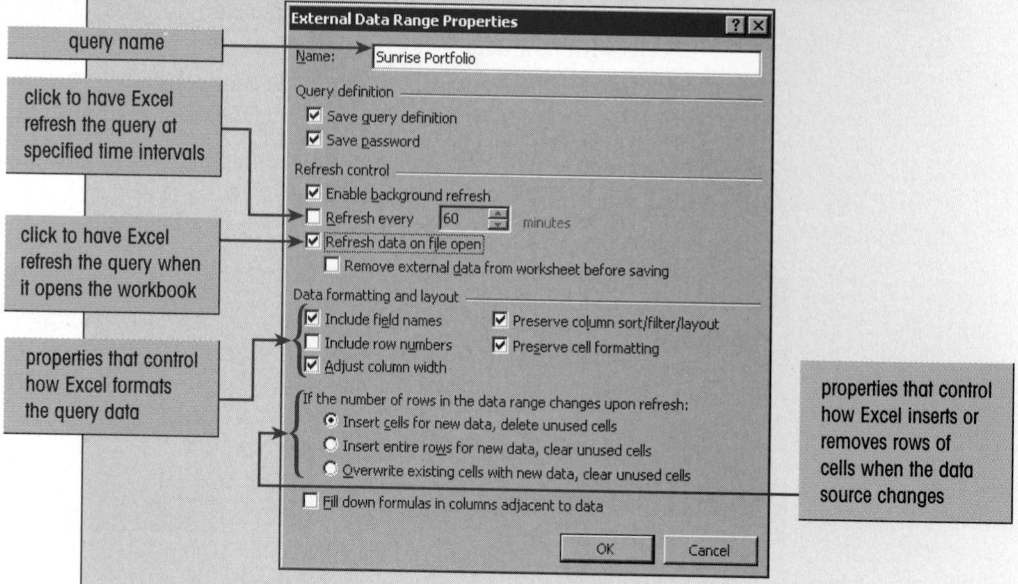

3. Click the **OK** button.

From now on, whenever Kelly opens this workbook, Excel will automatically refresh the data. Kelly now asks you how she can modify the query that you performed earlier, in case she needs to import additional information.

Editing a Query

Once you've created a query, you can go back and modify the query's definition using the Query Wizard. By editing the query, you can add new columns to your worksheet, change the sort order options, or specify a filter.

Kelly has reviewed the contents of the Portfolio worksheet. She would like you to include a field that determines whether the stock is an industrial, transportation, or utility stock in order to determine how the fund is distributed over these kinds of classifications. She also wants the data sorted by stock category and within each stock category by descending order of portfolio percentage. You can add the Category column to the Portfolio worksheet and modify the sort order by editing the query.

To edit the query:

1. Click the **Edit Query** button 🖼 on the External Data toolbar. The Query Wizard starts and displays the Query Wizard - Choose Columns dialog box. First, you'll add the Category column to the list of selected fields.

2. Click the **plus box** ⊞ in front of the Company table, and double-click **Category**. Category is added to the list of columns in the query. See Figure 11-25.

| Figure 11-25 | ADDING THE CATEGORY FIELD TO THE QUERY |

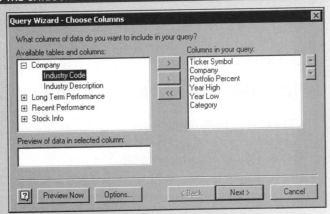

3. Click the **Next** button twice to go to the Query Wizard - Sort Order dialog box, where you'll enter the two sorting criteria.

4. Click the **Sort by** list arrow, click **Category**, and then click the **Ascending** option button.

5. Click the **Then by** list arrow, click **Portfolio Percent**, and then click the **Descending** option button.

6. Click the **Next** button and then click the **Finish** button to retrieve the data. Figure 11-26 displays the contents of the Portfolio worksheet with the newly added Category column and the sort order changed. Notice that the first category listed is INDUSTRIALS, and within INDUSTRIALS the Portfolio Percent column is ordered from highest to lowest.

| Figure 11-26 | THE REVISED QUERY |

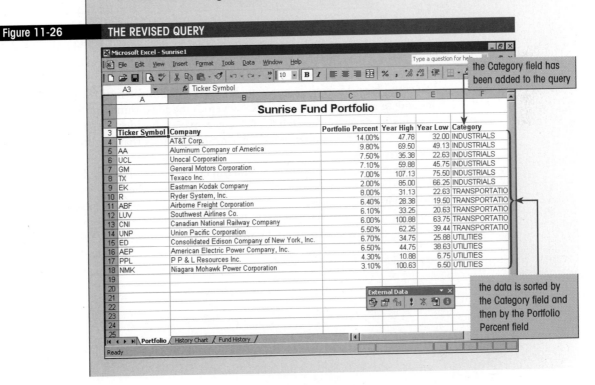

In reviewing the category values, you note that the fund is comprised of 15 stocks with 6 industrials, 5 transportation stocks, and 4 utilities. The fund is therefore fairly well balanced across the three categories. Kelly is satisfied with the appearance of the Portfolio worksheet. The next thing she wants you to insert into the workbook is the most recent performance of the 15 stocks in the Sunrise Fund.

Creating a PivotTable and PivotChart from External Data

The Recent Performance table in the Sunrise database contains a record of the last five days of stock data for each of the 15 stocks in the Sunrise Fund. Figure 11-27 shows the contents of the Recent Performance table.

Figure 11-27 THE RECENT PERFORMANCE TABLE IN THE SUNRISE DATABASE

Recent Performance : Table

Ticker Symbol	Date	Volume	High	Low	Closing
AA	02/04/2004	364300	68.75	68	68.25
AA	02/05/2004	412300	68.625	67.125	67.25
AA	02/06/2004	650100	67.25	66	66.75
AA	02/07/2004	891200	69.25	66.75	67.625
AA	02/10/2004	459500	68	66.625	66.625
ABF	02/04/2004	331300	28	27	27.25
ABF	02/05/2004	92600	27.375	27.125	27.25
ABF	02/06/2004	20000	27.125	26.75	26.875
ABF	02/07/2004	68800	27.125	26.625	27.125
ABF	02/10/2004	36200	27.375	27	27.25
AEP	02/04/2004	134100	41.625	41.125	41.25
AEP	02/05/2004	1481100	41.625	40.75	41.125
AEP	02/06/2004	1761000	40.875	40.5	40.625
AEP	02/07/2004	459300	41.375	40.75	41.375
AEP	02/10/2004	494100	41.75	41.25	41.75

Record: 1 of 75

Kelly wants to extract this data and place it in the Sunrise workbook. She also wants to chart this data, so that she can visually track each stock's recent history.

As you review the table, you wonder how best to display the results in the workbook. You could have 15 worksheets—one for each stock in the fund, displaying the table of values and an accompanying chart. Kelly vetoes the idea, thinking that it would be too cumbersome to navigate through 15 worksheet pages. Besides, she argues that at some point she wants to create similar workbooks for other funds that might have hundreds of stocks in their portfolios.

A second option occurs to you. You can create a PivotTable and PivotChart that will display market values from the past five days. By using the page feature of PivotTables and PivotCharts, you can include a list box that Kelly can use to display the values for only the stock that she is interested in. As Kelly clicks a different stock from the page's list box, a new table and chart will be created. Figure 11-28 shows a preview of what you intend to create.

Figure 11-28   **PIVOTTABLE AND PIVOTCHART YOU PLAN TO CREATE**

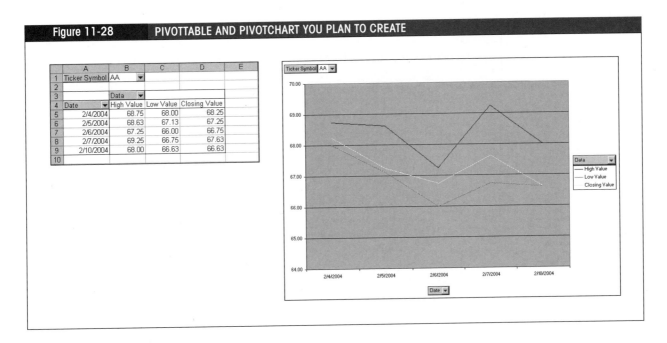

One advantage of this approach is that you can place the recent performance data on a single worksheet. A second advantage is that the PivotTable can use data that is stored in databases or other external files. This means that you won't have to insert the entire contents of the Recent Performance table to display recent performance values. You can let the PivotTable retrieve only those values for each stock when needed.

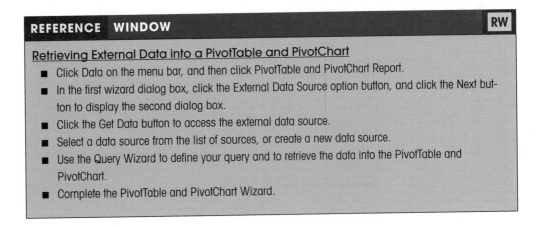

REFERENCE WINDOW   **RW**

Retrieving External Data into a PivotTable and PivotChart
- Click Data on the menu bar, and then click PivotTable and PivotChart Report.
- In the first wizard dialog box, click the External Data Source option button, and click the Next button to display the second dialog box.
- Click the Get Data button to access the external data source.
- Select a data source from the list of sources, or create a new data source.
- Use the Query Wizard to define your query and to retrieve the data into the PivotTable and PivotChart.
- Complete the PivotTable and PivotChart Wizard.

Start the PivotTable and PivotChart Wizard now.

To start creating the PivotTable and PivotChart:

1. Insert a new sheet after the Portfolio worksheet, and rename the new sheet as **Recent Results**.

2. Click **Data** on the menu bar, and click **PivotTable and PivotChart Report**. The first step of the PivotTable and PivotChart Wizard appears.

3. Click the **External data source** option button.

4. Click the **PivotChart report (with PivotTable report)** option button.

5. Click the **Next** button to move to the next step of the wizard.

6. Click the **Get Data** button to open the Choose Data Source dialog box.

7. Click **MS Access Database*** in the list of data sources, and click the **OK** button.

8. Select the **Sunrise.mdb** database from the Tutor11\Tutorial folder on your Data Disk, and click the **OK** button.

Now you indicate the columns that you want to include in the PivotTable. You want to retrieve the ticker symbol of each stock, the daily high and low of the stock, and the closing value. All these fields are located in the Recent Performance table. Once you've selected the columns for the table, you can go through the rest of the Query Wizard without specifying any filters or sorting. You're only interested in the complete and unfiltered recent performance data.

To enter the query for the PivotTable:

1. Click **Recent Performance** in the list of tables, and then click the **Add** button [>]. The columns in the Recent Performance table appear in the pane on the right side of the dialog box.

2. Click the **Next** button three times to reach the end of the Query Wizard.

3. Click the **Finish** button. You are returned to the second step of the PivotTable and PivotChart Wizard, and the comment "Data fields have been retrieved" now appears next to the Get Data button.

You're finished with the query, and the PivotTable Wizard has retrieved the data. You'll next design the layout for your PivotTable.

To design the PivotTable's layout:

1. Click the **Next** button to display the third step of the PivotTable and PivotChart Wizard.

2. Verify that the Exiting worksheet option button is selected, and then click cell **A1** so that the PivotTable will be inserted in a range starting at cell A1 in the current worksheet.

3. Click the **Layout** button. You will use the diagram to design the PivotTable.

4. Drag the **Ticker Symbol** field button to the Page area.

5. Drag the **Date** field button to the Row area.

6. Drag the **High**, **Low**, and **Closing** field buttons to the Data area. Figure 11-29 displays the layout of the PivotTable.

Figure 11-29   **LAYOUT OF THE PIVOTTABLE**

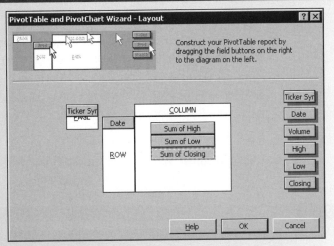

TROUBLE? If your layout does not match the one shown in Figure 11-29, drag the field buttons until their positions match those shown in the figure. If you inadvertently drag the wrong field button, drag it off the diagram to remove the field altogether.

Notice that the Data area labels read "Sum of" before the name of each field. This label is a little misleading because there is only one value of these items for each stock on each day, so the PivotTable will show a "sum" of only one record. Although the table will display individual volume and stock values, you should change these labels to avoid confusing others who might interpret them as the sum of many such values. You can also specify the format for these values at this time.

To change the labels and format the data values in the table:

1. Double-click the **Sum of High** field button. The PivotTable Field dialog box opens.

2. In the Name text box, change the name to **High Value**.

3. Click the **Number** button, click **Number** in the Category list, verify that the number of decimal places is set to **2**, and then click the **OK** button twice.

4. Rename the two remaining data values **Low Value** and **Closing Value**, and then format these fields with the Number format displayed with 2 decimal places.

5. Click the **OK** button to close the PivotTable Field dialog box. The third step of the wizard is redisplayed.

You're almost finished defining the PivotTable. You still have to set some of the options for the behavior of the PivotTable and PivotChart.

To define PivotTable and PivotChart options:

1. Click the **Options** button.

2. Deselect the **Grand totals for columns** and **Grand totals for rows** check boxes so that the PivotTable and PivotChart do not include grand totals.

3. Click the **Refresh on open** check box so that Excel will refresh the PivotTable and PivotChart whenever the "Sunrise1" workbook is open, retrieving the latest data from the company's database.

4. Click the **OK** button.

5. Click the **Finish** button. Excel creates the PivotTable and PivotChart on separate sheets. The PivotChart is shown in Figure 11-30.

Figure 11-30	INITIAL PIVOTCHART

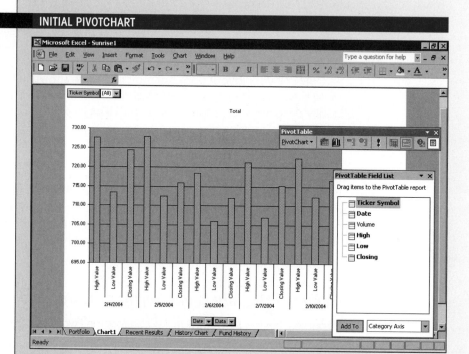

6. Click the **Recent Results** tab to view the PivotTable. Neither the chart nor table look as you expected. This is because you have to make one minor change to the layout of the PivotTable.

7. Drag the **Data** field button in cell B3 over to cell **C3**, and then release the mouse button. By moving the Data button, you change the orientation of the data results from rows to columns.

   Now return to the sheet with the PivotChart, and change the chart type from a column chart to a line chart.

8. Switch to the Chart1 sheet, click **Chart** on the menu bar, and then click **Chart Type**.

9. Click **Line** in the Chart type list, and then double-click the **Line. Displays trend over time or categories** chart sub-type (first row, first column on the left). See Figure 11-31 for the final version of the PivotTable and PivotChart.

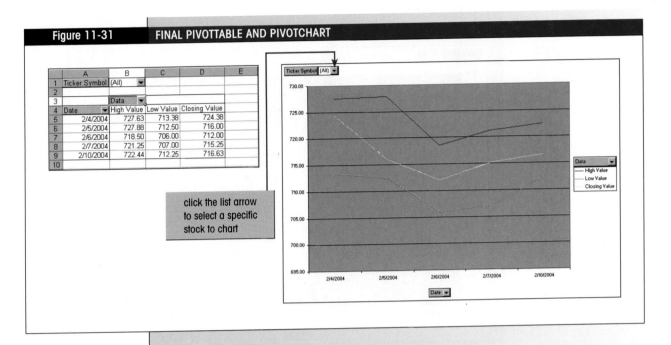

| Figure 11-31 | FINAL PIVOTTABLE AND PIVOTCHART |

10. Rename Chart1 sheet as **Recent Results Chart**.

The line chart gives you a quick view of each stock's low, high, and closing values. By default, the PivotTable and PivotChart show the sum of these values over all of the stocks in the portfolio. This display itself is not very useful; however, by clicking the Ticker Symbol list arrow, you can quickly view the daily values from the last five days for any individual stock in the portfolio. Try this now.

To use the PivotTable to display five days of market values for the Alcoa Aluminum stock:

1. Click the **Ticker Symbol** list arrow located in the upper-left corner of the chart.

2. Click **AA** (Alcoa Aluminum) in the list of stock symbols, and then click the **OK** button. The stock values for Alcoa Aluminum for the last five days appear, replacing the prior values in the PivotChart.

3. Click the **Ticker Symbol** list arrow again, select **GM**, and then click the **OK** button. Values for the General Motors stock replaces those for Aluminum Alcoa. See Figure 11-32.

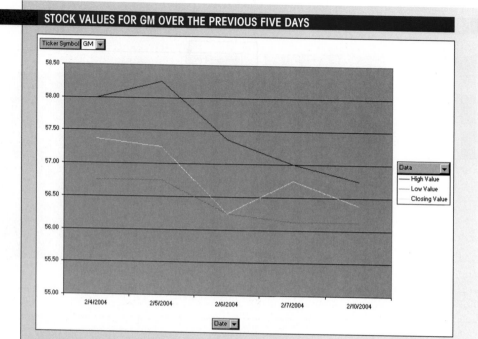

Figure 11-32   **STOCK VALUES FOR GM OVER THE PREVIOUS FIVE DAYS**

Note that as you change the PivotChart, the PivotTable automatically changes.

4. Click the **Recent Results** tab. The PivotTable displays the values for General Motors that you saw reflected in the PivotChart.

You show Kelly the latest version of the workbook for the Sunrise Fund. She likes working with the PivotTable and PivotChart to retrieve values from the Sunrise database quickly and easily. Kelly will experiment with the workbook and get back to you later with any changes she wants you to make. For now you can close the workbook.

To save the Sunrise Fund workbook:

1. Click cell **A1** in the Portfolio worksheet so that this is the first worksheet you'll see the next time you open the workbook.

2. Save and close the workbook, and then exit Excel.

In this session, you've learned some techniques to increase the power and flexibility of your database queries. You've seen how to control the properties of your query and how to edit them. You've used queries to create PivotTables to summarize data from your database. In the next session, you'll learn how to retrieve the most current data Kelly needs from the World Wide Web.

Session 11.2 QUICK CHECK

1. How do you refresh external data, and what does refreshing do?

2. How would you set up your external data so that it refreshes automatically whenever the workbook is opened?

3. How do you edit a query?

4. How do you create a PivotTable and PivotChart based on an external data source?

5. What is the advantage of using external data in a PivotTable rather than importing data into the workbook and creating a PivotTable from the imported data?

SESSION 11.3

In this session, you'll learn how to use create a query to retrieve data from a Web page. You'll also learn how to save a query. Finally, you'll learn how to retrieve data in real time from the World Wide Web and you'll study other tools for importing data in real time from other data sources.

Creating a Web Query

Davis & Larson has one other data source that Kelly can access—its Web site. On the company's Web site are Web pages that describe the various funds the company supports. There is a page for the Sunrise Fund that provides descriptive information about the fund such as the fund's manager, its inception date, and so forth. A preview of this page is shown in Figure 11-33.

Figure 11-33	SUNRISE FUND WEB PAGE

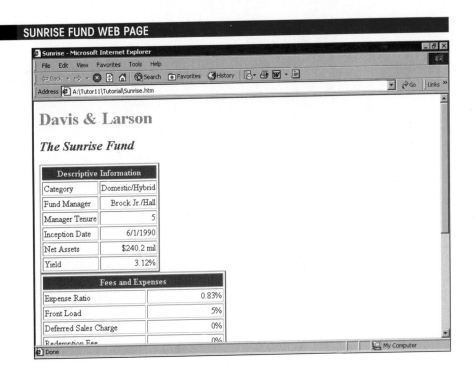

There are many ways to fulfill Kelly's request. You could copy and paste the data from the Web page into your workbook, for example, but Kelly would like to have the data automatically refreshed whenever she opens the file. The worksheet should be consistent with whatever information the company is putting out on its Web site.

To create a Web query, you need to know the URL of the Web page you're accessing. The **URL** (Uniform Resource Locator) is the address of the page. A copy of the Sunrise Fund's information Web page has been made available to you with the filename "Sunrise.htm." The URL for this Web page depends upon the location of your Data Disk. The general form of a URL for a file located on your computer will be

> file:///*drive:/path/filename*

where *drive* is the drive letter of the disk containing the file, *path* is the full pathname of the folder containing the file, and *filename* is the filename of the Web page. For example, if your Data Disk is in drive A and Sunrise.htm is located in the Tutor11\Tutorial folder, the URL will be as follows:

> file:///A:/Tutor11\Tutorial/Sunrise.htm

If you've placed Sunrise.htm in a different folder or in a different drive, you'll have to change the URL accordingly.

To create a Web query to import the contents of the Sunrise Web page:

1. If you took a break after the last session, make sure Excel is running, and open the **Sunrise1** workbook located in the Tutorial\Tutor11 on your Data Disk. Click the **Enable automatic refresh** button when prompted by Excel.

2. Create a new worksheet named **Sunrise Fund** at the beginning of your workbook, and make sure cell A1 is the active cell.

3. Click **Data** on the menu bar, point to **Import External Data**, and then click **New Web Query**.

   Depending on how Excel has been configured, your computer might attempt to connect to a default Web site or your home page. In Figure 11-34, Excel has attempted to connect to the MSN Web site.

Figure 11-34	OPENING A NEW WEB QUERY

enter the URL of the Web page you want to query

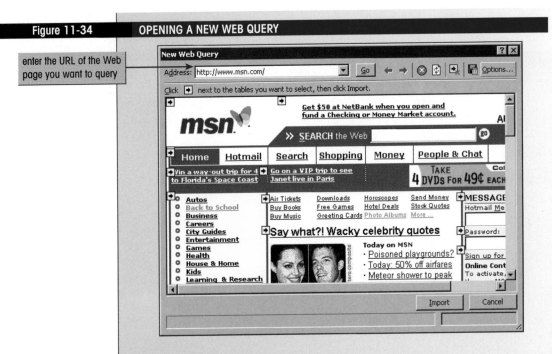

4. Type **file:///A:/Tutor11/Tutorial/Sunrise.htm** in the Address list box of the New Web Query dialog box, and then click the **Go** button. Excel accesses the Sunrise.htm file, as shown in Figure 11-35. Note that Excel has placed selection arrows ➡ next to the different parts of the page. You can choose which parts of the page to import by clicking each selection arrow. A selected part has its icon change from ➡ to ☑. If you click the first selection arrow on the page, the entire page will be selected. Kelly wants you to select all of the tables, but not the page title.

TROUBLE? If the Sunrise.htm Web page is located at a different URL on your computer or network, enter that URL instead. Contact your instructor or technical support person if you have problems entering the correct URL for the Sunrise.htm file.

Figure 11-35   SELECTING PARTS OF A WEB PAGE TO QUERY

URL of the
Sunrise Web page

selection arrow

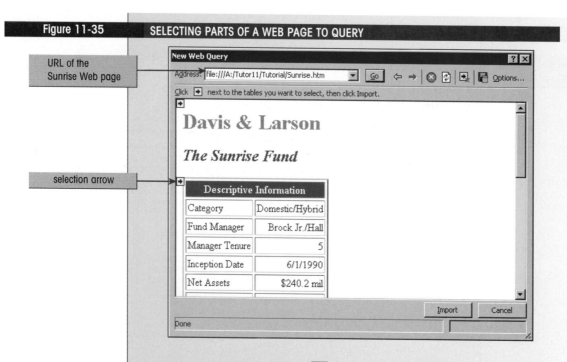

5. Click the **selection arrows** 🔁 next to the Descriptive Information table, the Fees and Expenses table, and the Projected Expenses for $1,000 Purchase table to select each table. Note that the selection arrow changes to a check mark to indicate the table has been selected.

6. Click the **Import** button.

7. Verify that the data will be put in cell A1 of the existing worksheet, and then click the **OK** button. Excel imports the data into the Sunrise Fund worksheet, as shown in Figure 11-36.

Figure 11-36   IMPORTING THE SUNRISE WEB PAGE

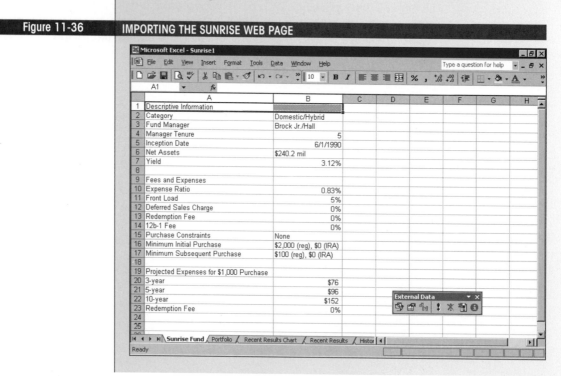

The data has been imported into Kelly's workbook and, as with other queries, can be automatically updated as the Web page changes.

Formatting a Web Query

Kelly wants you to format this information so that it resembles the Web page from which the data originated. You can have Excel retrieve the formatting as well as data, using one of three options: None (the default), Rich text formatting only, or Full HTML formatting.

The **Rich text formatting only** option retrieves the text along with simple formatting (such as boldface, italics, and color), but not advanced formatting such as hyperlinks or complicated table structures. The **Full HTML formatting** option retrieves all simple as well as advanced HTML formatting features including hyperlinks. Full HTML formatting will result in imported data that most closely resembles the appearance of the Web page. Kelly wants you to edit the Web query you just created to use Full HTML formatting.

> ### To apply Full HTML formatting to the Web query:
>
> **1.** Click the **Edit Query** button 🔄 on the External Data toolbar.
>
> **2.** Click the **Options** button in the Edit Web Query dialog box.
>
> **3.** Click the **Full HTML formatting** option button as shown in Figure 11-37.

Figure 11-37   **SETTING WEB QUERY OPTIONS**

> **4.** Click the **OK** button, and then click the **Import** button. Excel imports the Web data again, this time applying the HTML formatting codes used in the original Web page. See Figure 11-38.

Figure 11-38   WEB QUERY DATA USING HTML FORMATTING

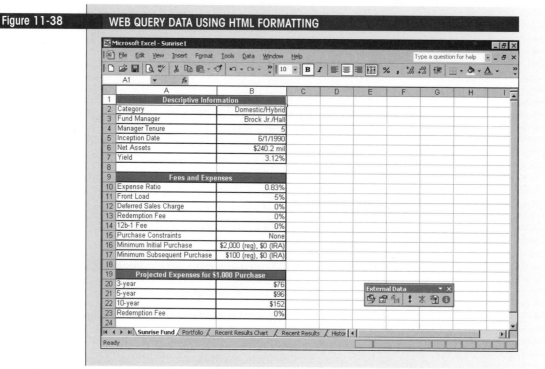

Saving a Web Query

Kelly appreciates your work in creating the Web query. She has other Excel workbooks in which she would like to place this information. Rather than copying the worksheet into those workbooks, she wants to save the query so that she can run it whenever she needs to in whatever workbook she chooses.

To save the Web query:

1. Click the **Edit Query** button on the External Data toolbar.

2. Click the **Save Query** button. By default, Excel saves Web queries in the Queries folder on your computer's hard disk.

3. Locate the Tutor11\Tutorial folder on your Data Disk, type **Sunrise Web Page** in the File name text box, and then click the **Save** button. Excel saves the query to a file on your Data Disk.

4. Click the **Cancel** button to close the Edit Web Query dialog box.

Now when Kelly wants to import the contents of the Sunrise Fund Web page, she can use the saved query file and her choice of what parts of the page to import and all of her formatting options will be automatically used.

Experienced Web page authors can also use the Extensible Markup Language (XML) in their Web queries. **XML** is a format used to deliver data from an application in a standard, consistent way. By redirecting a Web query to an XML data source, Web page authors can increase the reliability of the data exchange. To redirect a Web query to an XML data source, include the following namespace declaration in the opening HTML tag of the Web page:

<HTML xmlns:o="urn:schemas-microsoft-com:office:office">

and then in any TABLE tags in the HTML file, add the following attribute:

<TABLE ... o:WebQuerySourceHRef=<Italics On>source<Italics Off> ...>

where *source* is the data source to which you want to redirect the Web query. Note that you can create your own XML file from the data in your Excel workbook, by using the File Save As command from the Excel menu bar, and selecting XML Spreadsheet from the Save as type list box. Interested Web authors should see Excel's online Help for more information.

Retrieving Data from the World Wide Web

As you've seen, the files of Davis & Larson contain long-range historical data in text files and more recent data in databases and on the company's Web site, but sometimes Kelly needs even more current information. She would like to know how the stocks in the Sunrise portfolio are doing at this very moment. She can get that kind of information from the World Wide Web, where up-to-the-minute stock values are posted for online traders and brokers.

Kelly wants a Web query that retrieves that online data and imports it into her Excel workbook. To help her access data from the Web, Excel has supplied several Web query files. These files are similar to the query file you created and saved on your Data Disk, except that they define how to retrieve data from a page on the Web.

Kelly knows that there is a huge amount of stock information available on the Web, and she wants you to make her Sunrise Fund workbook capable of retrieving current values on all of the stocks in the Sunrise portfolio.

Retrieving Multiple Stock Quotes

There are 15 stocks in the Sunrise Fund, and Kelly wants to be able to view current information on all of them. One of the Web query files Excel supplies is the Microsoft Investor Stock Quotes query. It allows the user to enter up to 20 ticker symbols (abbreviations for the stock names used by the market), and then it retrieves current market values of those stocks and places the information into a table in the workbook. This seems to be just what Kelly wants, so you will begin by creating a worksheet for the values that will be imported from a Web query.

> *To insert a new worksheet in the Sunrise1 workbook:*
>
> **1.** Insert a new worksheet to the right of the Portfolio worksheet, and rename the new sheet **Current Values**.
>
> **2.** Make sure cell A1 is the active cell.

You'll place the Web query results in this worksheet.

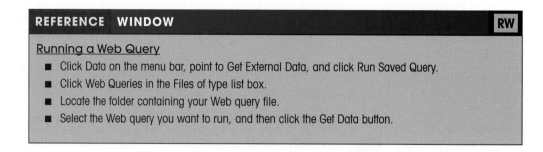

REFERENCE WINDOW **RW**

Running a Web Query
- Click Data on the menu bar, point to Get External Data, and click Run Saved Query.
- Click Web Queries in the Files of type list box.
- Locate the folder containing your Web query file.
- Select the Web query you want to run, and then click the Get Data button.

Using the worksheet you just created, you'll now run the Stock Quotes Web query.

To run the Stock Quotes Web query:

1. Click **Data** on the menu bar, point to **Import External Data**, and then click **Import Data**. The Select Data Source dialog box opens.

2. Click **Web Queries** in the Files of type list box. Excel displays the Web queries located in the My Data Sources folder. See Figure 11-39.

Figure 11-39	LIST OF SAVED QUERY FILES

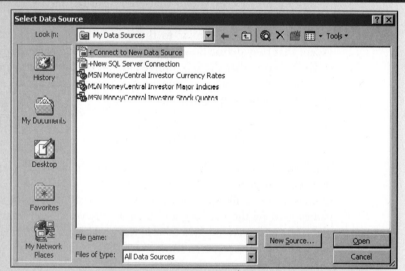

TROUBLE? Your list of Web queries might be different from the one shown in Figure 11-39.

3. Click the **MSN MoneyCentral Investor Stock Quotes** query, and then click the **Open** button. The Import Data dialog box opens, in which you can specify the parameters for your query. If you click the OK button now, Excel will then prompt you for the ticker symbols of the stocks you want to see. You can also have Excel retrieve the ticker symbols from a cell range in the workbook. Because you've already retrieved this information and placed it in the Portfolio worksheet, you'll choose that option and save yourself some typing.

4. Click the **Parameters** button. The Parameters dialog box opens.

5. Click the **Get the value from the following cell** option button.

Now you'll select the cell range containing the ticker symbols.

6. Click the **Collapse Dialog Box** button 📲, select the range **A4:A18** on the Portfolio worksheet, and then press the **Enter** key. The dialog box reappears with the cell reference entered.

7. Click the **OK** button twice to initiate your Web query. Depending on the speed of your Internet connection, it might take a few seconds or up to a minute to retrieve current stock quotes from the Web. Once you are connected and the query is processed, Excel displays the data in the table format shown in Figure 11-40.

| Figure 11-40 | STOCK QUOTES IMPORTED FROM THE WORLD WIDE WEB |

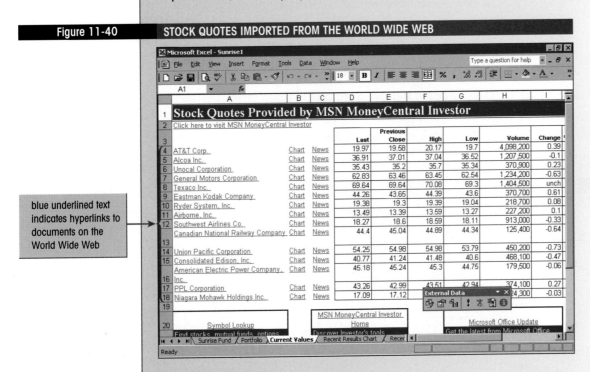

blue underlined text indicates hyperlinks to documents on the World Wide Web

TROUBLE? The values in your table will be different from the values shown in Figure 11-40 because you are retrieving stock values at a different point in time.

You show the results of the Web query to Kelly. Based on this information, she has a good idea how the stocks of the Sunrise Fund are doing at the moment. Kelly is happy that it is so easy to retrieve timely information from the Web into her Excel workbooks. You point out to her that the stock quotes returned from the Web query are twenty minutes old; paid subscribers to an investor service can receive up-to-the-minute stock information. She asks you how she would update stock quotes during a normal workday. You tell her she can refresh a Web query in much the same way she would refresh queries for data retrieved from the company's database.

Refreshing a Web Query

Kelly can easily refresh the information in her workbook at any time. When you direct Excel to refresh Web data, Excel reconnects to the Web page supplying the data. To show Kelly how this works, you decide to refresh the Multiple Stock Quotes query.

To refresh the Multiple Stock Quotes query:

1. Click the **Refresh** Data button 🔋 on the External Data toolbar.

2. If necessary, reconnect to the Internet. Excel retrieves the latest information on the stocks.

Another way of ensuring current stock results is to have Excel periodically refresh the stock quotes for you. You can set up this procedure through the Properties dialog box for the Web query. You decide to set up the query so that it automatically retrieves stock information every ten minutes when the workbook is open.

To set up Excel to periodically retrieve stock quotes:

1. Click the **Data Range Properties** button 🖾 on the External Data toolbar.

2. Click the **Refresh data on file open** check box so that Excel will automatically retrieve stock information when the workbook is initially opened.

3. If necessary, click the **Refresh every** check box, and then enter **10** in the minutes text box. See Figure 11-41.

Figure 11-41	SETTING THE REFRESH OPTION FOR A WEB QUERY

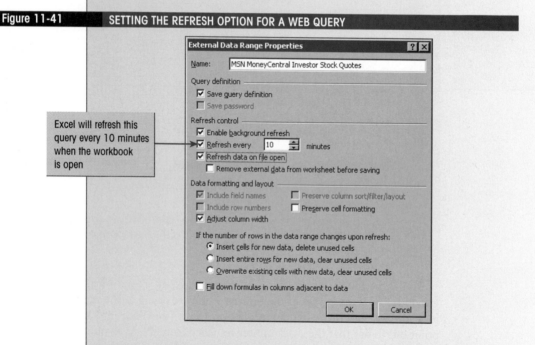

Excel will refresh this query every 10 minutes when the workbook is open

The workbook will now retrieve stock values every 10 minutes from the Microsoft Investor Web page. Please note that these stock values will be at least 20 minutes old. If you need to have real-time stock reports, you will have to pay for that service.

4. Click the **OK** button.

As you look over the Web page, you decide that the Web query has worked well in retrieving information from the page into the workbook. Kelly is pleased with the additional information that this query provides and that the information can be updated from the Web page.

Using Hyperlinks

In looking over the results of the Web query in the Current Values worksheet, Kelly notices that some of the text is underlined in blue. This text is a hyperlink to documents on the World Wide Web that contain additional information about the stocks in the portfolio. Clicking a hyperlink in a worksheet will activate her computer's Web browser to display the Web page associated with that entry. Kelly will find this feature useful when she wants more detailed information about a particular stock. She can even use a hyperlink to access the home page of each company listed in the fund. You decide to demonstrate this feature by activating the hyperlink associated with AT&T.

To activate a hyperlink:

1. Position your mouse pointer over the AT&T hyperlink in cell A4. The pointer changes to 🖑.

   TROUBLE? If the AT&T hyperlink does not appear in your table, choose a different hyperlink and continue with the remaining steps.

2. Click the mouse button. Excel starts your default Web browser and displays the Web page shown in Figure 11-42.

| Figure 11-42 | WEB PAGE FOR AT&T STOCK |

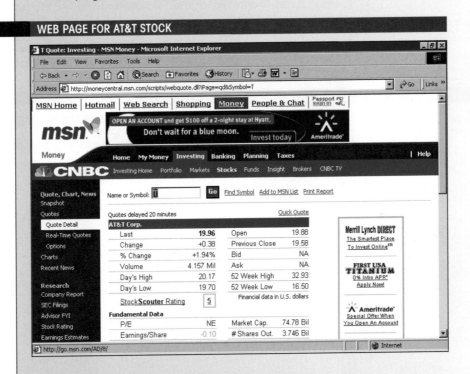

TROUBLE? The numeric values of the Web page you retrieve will be different from the one shown in Figure 11-42 because the figures change rapidly over time. Also, if you are using a different Web browser, such as Netscape Navigator, you might notice some other differences as well. If you can't get the links to work, ask your instructor or technical support person for assistance.

3. Click **File** on the menu bar, and click **Close** to close the Web browser.

> TROUBLE? If you are using a browser other than Internet Explorer, you might have to click File on the menu bar and then click Exit to close the browser and return to your workbook.

The Web page that you have linked to contains additional information about the stock along with links to other pages on the Web with even more information. Thus, the Sunrise Fund portfolio workbook contains important information in its own right, but it will also act as a gateway to additional data resources.

You've completed your job of retrieving data into Excel. You've seen how easy it is to retrieve data from text files using the Text Import Wizard and how flexible the Query Wizard is in allowing you to choose the records and fields you want to display. Using Web queries, you can retrieve information from Web pages and import up-to-the-minute stock information.

To complete the Sunrise Fund workbook, you should add a documentation sheet. The documentation sheet should include information about the source of all data in the workbook. This will help create an audit trail so that others who use your workbook can, if needed, go to the primary data sources.

To finish and save the workbook:

1. Insert a new worksheet named **Documentation** at the beginning of the workbook.

2. Enter the information shown in Figure 11-43 into the Documentation sheet. Enter the date and your name in cells B4 and B5 of the worksheet.

Figure 11-43 **DOCUMENTATION SHEET**

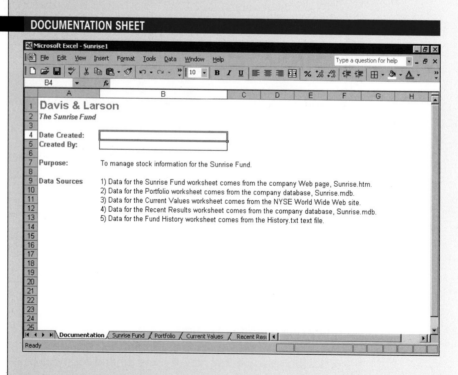

3. Save the completed workbook.

4. Close the workbook and then exit Excel.

You're finished with the Sunrise Fund workbook. Kelly appreciates the work you've done. By tapping into a variety of data sources, you've created a document for her that she can use to get current information on the fund as well as examine long-term and short-term data to look for important trends. She expects to find many ways to incorporate this wealth of new information into her daily work as an investment counselor at Davis and Larson.

Real-Time Data Acquisition

For Kelly's workbook, data was imported from three sources: text files, databases, and Web pages. For scientists and researchers, there is a fourth possible data source: real-time data values from measuring devices and scientific equipment. For example, a scientist might connect a computer to a temperature sensor and import temperature values at one-minute intervals directly into an Excel worksheet. In most cases, you will have to purchase an add-in to work between Excel and the device.

To facilitate the process of importing data from an external device, Excel provides the RTD function. The syntax of the RTD function is

RTD(*ProgID*, *server*, *topic1*, [*topic2*], [*topic3*], ...)

where *ProgID* is the program ID of the add-in that has been installed on the computer to retrieve the real-time data, *server* is the name of the server where the add-in is run (leave the *server* parameter blank if the add-in is being run on your computer), and *topic1*, *topic2*, and so forth are names that are assigned to the real-time data values. You can insert up to 28 different topics. Once you insert the RTD function into a cell, the value of the cell will display the latest value retrieved from the measuring device. One can also write a VBA macro to run the RTD function in a range of cells, recording the last several values from the measuring device.

By using the RTD function along with an add-in program, the scientist or researcher can save hours of time that would've been spent typing values into an Excel worksheet.

Session 11.3 QUICK CHECK

1. Describe how to import data from a table on a Web page.

2. What are the three options for formatting Web page data?

3. How would you retrieve financial information from the World Wide Web into your Excel workbook?

4. How current are the stock quotes retrieved from Excel's built-in Web queries?

5. What function would you use to retrieve real-time data from a measuring device attached to your computer?

REVIEW ASSIGNMENTS

Kelly has had a chance to work with some of the data you've retrieved for her. She wants you to create a new workbook that analyzes the performance of the stocks in the Sunrise database by the three NYSE categories: the industrials, the transportation stocks, and the utilities.

She has a text file that contains the daily indexes of these subgroups for the year 2003. First she wants you to import the text file into the Excel workbook. Then she would like you to create a table of yield and P/E ratio values for the stocks in the Sunrise database, sorted by category. Your next task will be to create a table and chart that displays the average closing values of the industrial, transportation, and utility stocks in the Sunrise Fund over the past five days. Kelly wants the data in a PivotTable in which she can click a Category list box and view the corresponding table and chart for that category (industrial, transportation, or utility). Finally, she would like a worksheet that displays a table of current Dow Jones Stock quote data retrieved from the Web.

To complete this task:

1. Use Excel to open the text file **NYA2003.txt** located in the Tutor11\Review folder on your Data Disk.

2. Using the Text Import Wizard, import the Date, Composite, Industrial, Transport, and Utility column. You should choose the fixed-width file type option, and the first four lines of the text file should be skipped. Import the Date column in YMD format. Do not import the Finance column.

3. Resize the columns on the sheet so you can view all of the data in the cells, and then rename the worksheet as "NYSE Index". Save the workbook as **Index1** in the Tutor11\Review folder on your Data Disk. Be sure to save the file in Excel workbook format.

4. Insert a new sheet named "Yield and PE Values" after the NYSE index worksheet. Use the Query Wizard to choose the following fields from the Microsoft Access database **Sunrise.mdb** located in the Tutor11\Review folder on your Data Disk:

   ■ Ticker Symbol and Category fields from the Company table
   ■ Yield and P/E Ratio fields from the Stock Info table

5. Within the Query Wizard, sort these values by the Category field in ascending order.

6. Save the query as **Index Query** to the Tutor11\Review folder of your Data Disk, and then return the data to cell A1 of the Yield and PE Values worksheet.

7. Edit the properties of the query you just created so that Excel refreshes the query whenever the workbook is opened.

8. Create a PivotTable and PivotChart in order to display the average closing value for each stock category over the last five days. Retrieve the following fields from the Sunrise.mdb database in the Tutor11\Review folder on your Data Disk:

   ■ The Category field from the Company table
   ■ The Date and Closing fields from the Recent Performance table

9. Lay out the PivotTable as follows:

   ■ In the Page area, display the Category field.
   ■ In the Row area, display the Date field.
   ■ In the Data area, insert the average Closing value.

10. Set up the query so that it refreshes when the workbook is opened. Do not display grand totals for the columns or rows of the PivotTable.

11. Format the PivotChart as a line chart, using the line sub-type.

12. Name the worksheet containing the PivotTable "Index Table" and the PivotChart sheet "Index Chart".

Explore 13. Insert a new worksheet named "Summary" at the beginning of your workbook. Create a Web query that accesses the **Summary.htm** file located in the Tutor11\Review folder on your Data Disk. Retrieve only the four tables located at the bottom of the page, and format them using rich text formatting. Place the imported data into cell A1 of the Summary worksheet.

14. Add a new sheet after the Summary sheet named "Dow Jones", and then using the Web query "MSN MoneyCentral Investor Major Indices," retrieve stock and category data from the Web and insert it into the Dow Jones worksheet starting in cell A1.

15. Add a documentation sheet to the beginning of your workbook, describing the source of the data used in the workbook. Include your name and the current date in the title sheet.

16. Print the entire workbook, save and close it, and then exit Excel.

CASE PROBLEMS

Case 1. Retrieving Product Information from DigiWorld DigiWorld is a computer store that specializes in digital cameras and scanners. Thomas Glenn, an employee of DigiWorld, would like to maintain an Excel workbook that displays data on the digital cameras the company sells. Information on the digital cameras has been saved in a text file that Thomas would like your help to import into Excel. The text file uses a delimited format in which one column is separated from another using the / character.

To complete this task:

1. Use Excel to locate the **DCList** text file located in the Tutor11\Cases folder on your Data Disk.

Explore 2. Open the text file using a delimited format, with the / (forward slash) character as the column delimiter. (*Hint*: Click the Other check box in the list of delimiters, and type "/" in the accompanying text box.) Do not import the Horizontal Resolution, Vertical Resolution, and the Shipping columns.

3. After importing the text file, resize the columns to allow you to view all of the data in each column. Rename the worksheet "Digital Cameras", and then save the file as **DCList2** in Excel workbook format in the Tutor11\Cases folder on your Data Disk.

4. Using the PivotTable and PivotChart Wizard, create a PivotTable on a new sheet, showing the average price of the digital cameras, broken down by the amount of memory in the camera and the manufacturer.

5. Name the sheet containing the PivotTable "Price Analysis".

6. Print the Price Analysis worksheet.

7. Insert a documentation sheet at the beginning of the workbook containing your name, the date, the purpose of the workbook, and a description of the data source used in your analysis.

8. Save and close the workbook, and then exit Excel.

Case 2. Retrieving Parts Information at EZ Net Robert Crawford has just started working as the parts inventory manager at EZ Net, one of the leading suppliers of computer network cards and devices. He's responsible for managing the parts inventory. The company uses an Access database to store information on the parts that it uses and the vendors that supply the parts.

The database, named EZNet, contains three tables: Orders, Parts, and Vendors. The Orders table records information on the parts orders the company places with vendors. The Parts table contains descriptive information on each part. The Vendors table records descriptive information on each vendor. Common fields link each table with another.

EZ Net purchases its parts from many different vendors. Robert wants to retrieve the contents of the three tables into an Excel workbook so that he can examine which vendors are responsible for which parts. He also wants to create a table that will tabulate the number of parts broken down by part number and vendor. He has asked you to help him perform these tasks.

To complete this task:

1. Open a blank workbook and import data from the **EZNet.mdb** Microsoft Access database located in the Tutor11\Cases folder on your Data Disk.

2. Using the Query Wizard, retrieve the contents of the Orders, Parts, and Vendors tables and place them in three separate worksheets in your workbooks. Name the three worksheets "Orders", "Parts", and "Vendors".

3. Add a fourth worksheet to your workbook named "Parts Summary."

4. Using the PivotTable and PivotChart Wizard, retrieve the following fields from the EZNet database into a PivotTable on the Parts Summary worksheet:

   ■ Quantity from the Orders table
   ■ Description from the Parts table
   ■ Name from the Vendors table

5. Save your query as **Vendor Query** to the Tutor11\Cases folder on your Data Disk.

6. Place the name of the vendor in the row section, the description of the part in the column section, and the sum of quantity in the data section of the table.

7. Write a paragraph analyzing the table you created. Which vendor supplies most of the parts to EZNet? Which one supplies the least?

8. Modify each query in the workbook so that it refreshes automatically whenever the workbook is opened.

9. Print the four worksheets in the workbook.

10. Add a documentation sheet describing the contents of the workbook and the source of the data. Include your name and the date in the sheet.

11. Save the workbook as **EZNet2** in the Tutor11\Cases folder on your Data Disk.

12. Close the workbook and then exit Excel.

Case 3. Creating a Currency Exchange Calculator Henry Sanchez is a financial consultant at Brooks & Beckman. He is working on an Excel workbook that will allow him to calculate money values in different currencies, based on the current exchange rate. He has already created the part of the workbook that performs the actual calculations, but he needs your help in determining the current exchange rate between U.S. dollars and foreign currencies. Henry is paying particular interest to the exchange rate between U.S. dollars and Italian Lira. Therefore, he also wants to insert the contents of a text file that has the last 120 days of exchange rate information into the workbook.

One of the built-in Web queries offered by Excel links to a Web page that displays current exchange rates. You'll use this query in order to complete Henry's workbook.

To complete this task:

1. Open the **Rates1** workbook located in the Tutor11\Cases folder on your Data Disk. Enter the current date and your name in the Documentation sheet. Save the workbook as **Rates2** in the same folder.

2. Insert a new worksheet at the end of the workbook, and rename the worksheet "Currency Rates".

Explore 3. Using the built-in Web query, "MSN MoneyCentral Investor Currency Rates," provided by Excel, retrieve the current exchange rates into the Currency Rates worksheet.

4. Change the properties of the Web query so that it refreshes every 10 minutes.

5. Switch to Currency Calculator worksheet.

6. In cell E6, use the VLOOKUP function to retrieve the exchange rate between the foreign currency listed in cell D5 and U.S. dollars. (*Hint*: Use the second column of values from the Web query displayed in the Currency Rates worksheet.) Multiply this exchange rate by the value in cell E5.

7. In cell E12, use the VLOOKUP function to retrieve the exchange rate between U.S. dollars and the foreign currency listed in cell D12. Multiply this rate by the value in cell E11.

8. Use the currency calculator to determine how much 15,000 Italian lira are worth in U.S. dollars and how much $1,000 is worth in Italian lira. Print your results.

9. Insert a new worksheet at the end of the workbook named "Lira Rate History".

Explore 10. Using the Import Data command from the Data submenu, locate the **LRate.txt** text file in the Tutor11\Cases folder on your Data Disk and import it into the Lira Rate History worksheet. Use a comma-delimited format for the import.

11. Create a column chart of the exchange rate history, storing the chart in a chart sheet named "History Chart". Print the History chart.

12. Save and close the workbook, and then exit Excel.

Case 4. Retrieving Sales Information at EuroArts   EuroArts, located in Ste. Genevieve, Missouri, sells reproductions of European art to American interior design companies and to homeowners by mail order. Jeanne Domremy is the finance manager who prepares quarterly reports on the company's products and sales. The company is interested in increasing its sales to the home market, so she's particularly interested in information on sales and products intended for home use. She has asked you to help retrieve some product and sales information from the company database into an Excel workbook.

The company data is stored in an Access database named Arts. The database has five tables: Products, Customer, Orders, Item, and Staff. Each table shares a common field with at least one other table in the database. The Products table stores information about products in the company's catalog. The Customer table records personal information about people who have bought products from EuroArt. The Orders table contains information about each order, including the date, who placed the order, and who recorded the transaction. The Item table records the items purchased in each order. Finally, the Staff table contains information about the sales personnel who take the orders.

Jeanne wants the following information:

■ What items in the current catalog are of interest to homeowners? She wants the list to include the catalog ID number, product category, product type, product description, and price. She wants the list sorted by descending order of price.

■ How many units have been sold recently, of what kind, and where? She wants a PivotTable that shows items sold by region versus product type.

To complete this task:

1. Open a blank workbook and start importing data from the Microsoft Access Arts.mdb database located in the Tutor11\Cases folder on your Data Disk.

2. Start the Query Wizard and start retrieving the necessary data from the Arts database.

3. Select all the fields in the Products table.

Explore ▶
4. In the Query Wizard's Filter Data dialog box, limit the query to only those records whose Location value equals Home or Multiple.

5. Sort the query in descending order of Item Price and retrieve the data.

6. Save the query as **Arts Query** in the Tutor11\Cases folder on your Data Disk.

7. Import the query data into a worksheet named "Products". Set up the query so that it is refreshed whenever the workbook is opened. Print the Products worksheet.

8. Add a Documentation sheet displaying the date, your name, the purpose of the workbook, and the data source of the query. Save the workbook as **Arts1** in the Tutor11\Cases folder on your Data Disk.

9. Open another blank workbook, and start the PivotTable and PivotChart Wizard to create a PivotTable.

10. Access the Arts data source and select the following fields from the following tables:
    - Order_ID# and Region from the Orders table
    - Item_ID# and Quantity from the Item table
    - Type from the Products table

11. Do not add any criteria to the query, but return to the wizard.

12. Place Region in the Column area of the table, Type in the Row area of the table, and Sum of Quantity in the Data area of the PivotTable.

13. Set up the query so that it refreshes whenever the workbook is opened.

14. Name the worksheet containing the PivotTable "Order Information".

15. Add a documentation sheet to the workbook displaying the date and your name and describing the contents of the workbook and the source of the data.

16. Print the worksheet containing the resulting PivotTable, and then save this workbook as **Arts2** in the Tutor11\Cases folder on your Data Disk.

17. Close the workbook, and then exit Excel.

INTERNET ASSIGNMENTS

Student Union

The purpose of the Internet Assignments is to challenge you to find information on the Internet that you can use to create effective spreadsheets. The actual assignments are updated and maintained on the Course Technology Web site. Log on to the Internet and use your Web browser to go to the Student Union on the New Perspectives Series site at **www.course.com/NewPerspectives/studentunion**. Click the Online Companions link, and then click the link for this text.

QUICK | CHECK ANSWERS

Session 11.1

1. A fixed-width text file places all columns in the same location in the file; a delimited text file uses a special character to separate columns.

2. space, comma, tab

3. Click the location in the Data preview window of the Text Import Wizard to indicate you want the column break to appear.

4. **a.** a program that stores and retrieves large amounts of data and creates reports describing the data

   b. a collection of data that is stored in rows and columns

   c. fields information about a specific characteristic for a particular person, place, or thing

   d. a row of the table that displays the collection of characteristics for a particular person, place, or thing

   e. a field that is shared by two or more tables and used to combine information from those tables

5. a question that is asked about the data in a database

6. A data source is any file that contains the data that you want to import into Excel.

7. Return (import) the data in an Excel workbook, open the results in Microsoft Query, or create an OLAP cube.

Session 11.2

1. Click the Refresh Data button on the External Data toolbar. Refreshing data causes Excel to go back to the data source and retrieve the data using the query you created.

2. With a cell selected in the data range containing the external data, click the Data Range Properties button on the External Data toolbar, and click the Refresh data on file open check box.

3. Click the Edit Query button on the External Data toolbar.

4. Start the PivotTable and PivotChart Wizard, and click the External data source option button in the first step.

5. It reduces the size of the workbook.

Session 11.3

1. Click Data, point to Import External Data, and then click New Web Query. Enter the URL of the Web page in the Address list box of the New Web Query dialog box and click the Go button. Click the yellow arrow that points to the table to select it. Click the Import button to import the table into the worksheet.

2. None, Rich text formatting only, and Full HTML formatting

3. Click Data, point to Import External Data, and then click Import Data. Choose one of the built-in Microsoft financial queries from the list, and click the Open button.

4. 20 minutes old

5. RTD function

OBJECTIVES

In this tutorial you will:

- Create macros using the macro recorder

- Assign a macro to a button

- View macro code in the Visual Basic Editor

- Learn about the features of the Visual Basic Editor

- Write a macro with the Visual Basic Editor

- Learn basic concepts and principles of the Visual Basic for Applications (VBA) programming language

- Write an interactive macro that asks the user for input

- Modify a macro so it responds to different user input

- Customize Excel's menu and toolbars

ENHANCING EXCEL WITH VISUAL BASIC FOR APPLICATIONS

Creating a Quality Control Application for Datalia Inc.

CASE

Datalia Inc.

Datalia Inc. is one of the country's leading manufacturers of infant-care products. One of these products is baby powder. Each bottle is filled automatically by a machine called a "filler." The weight of each bottle filled with powder should be 400 grams; however, because of random variation in the production process, the actual weight varies. Any bottle that weighs less than 360 grams will have to be rejected and run through the filler again. A bottle that weighs too much can be a problem as well. The excess powder will be irretrievably lost in the production process, costing the company money. Also, excess powder can spill into the filler resulting in mechanical problems later on. For this reason, any bottle that weighs more than 420 grams will have to be rejected.

Kemp Wilson is a quality control engineer for Datalia. Part of his job is to oversee the production process. He has approached you about creating an application to monitor the operations of the fillers and report those fillers with high failure rates. The application has to be very flexible and easy for others to use because Kemp intends on sharing it with the other quality control engineers. You suggest that he use Excel and the Visual Basic for Applications (VBA) programming language to build the application.

SESSION 12.1

In this session, you'll review how to create a macro using the Excel macro recorder. After creating the macro, you'll view the macro code in the Visual Basic Editor. You'll learn about some of the features of the editor, and you'll use it to create additional macros based on the one that you recorded.

Starting an Excel Application

You meet with Kemp to discuss the application he wants you to create. Kemp has sampled bottle weights from five fillers, labeled A, B, C, D, and E, taken at random during the 1:00–5:00 a.m. shift. He has placed the data along with charts and statistics into an Excel workbook that he wants you to examine.

To open Kemp's workbook:

1. Start Excel and open the **Datalia1** workbook located in the Tutorial.12\Tutorial folder on your Data Disk.

2. Enter the date and your name in the Documentation sheet.

3. Save the workbook as **Datalia2** in the Tutorial.12\Tutorial folder on your Data Disk.

4. Study the contents of each worksheet in the workbook, and then return to the Control Panel worksheet.

Besides the Documentation sheet, the Datalia workbook contains five worksheets labeled Control Panel, Statistics, Time Chart, Histogram, and Raw Data, the contents of which are described below:

- ■ The **Control Panel** worksheet displays the current status of a selected filler. If the filler has not produced any bottles heavier than 420 grams or lighter than 360 grams, the filler is said to be "in control;" otherwise, the worksheet will display the text, "Control Violations." The worksheet also contains buttons designed to display the contents of other worksheets in the workbook and to choose a filler to view.

- ■ The **Statistics** worksheet contains statistics describing the samples taken from a selected filler.

- ■ The **Time Chart** worksheet displays the bottle weights taken from a selected filler over the 4-hour shift. Two dotted red lines indicate the minimum and maximum acceptable bottle weights.

- ■ The **Histogram** worksheet displays a column chart showing the distribution of bottle weights from a selected filler over the 4-hour shift. The left-most column counts those bottles that are too light, while the right-most column counts those bottles that are too heavy.

- ■ The **Raw Data** worksheet displays bottle weights from all five filler samples.

Kemp wants this workbook to be easy for even non-Excel users to operate. To do this, he created the Control Panel worksheet shown in Figure 12-1. The worksheet contains five macro buttons (for a discussion on creating and using macro buttons, see Tutorial 8). The first four of the macro buttons are labeled Statistics, Time Chart, Histogram, and Data.

Kemp wants you to create macros for these buttons to display the corresponding worksheets in the workbook. Each of the worksheets has its own button labeled, "Return to the Control Panel," which the user can click to return to the Control Panel worksheet. The fifth button on the Control Panel worksheet, labeled "Choose a Filler," will be used to select one of the five fillers in Kemp's sample. By using the buttons in the Control Panel worksheet, users who are not familiar with Excel can still access the main features of the application without using Excel commands.

Figure 12-1	KEMP'S PROPOSED APPLICATION

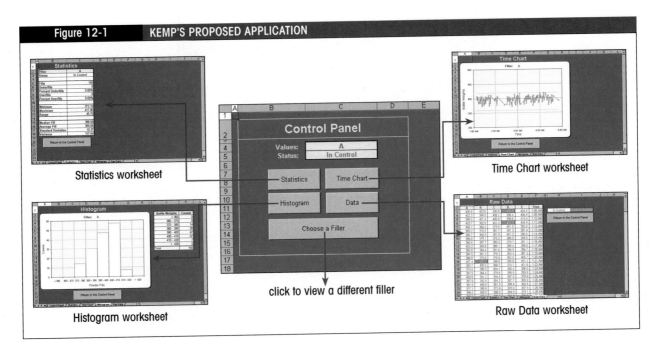

Statistics worksheet

Time Chart worksheet

Histogram worksheet

click to view a different filler

Raw Data worksheet

The fastest way to create macros is to use the Excel macro recorder (also discussed previously in Tutorial 8). Once a macro has been recorded, you can edit the macro to make it more suitable for Kemp's needs. The first macro you'll record will display the contents of the Statistics worksheet. You'll name the macro "Statistics."

To record the Statistics macro:

1. Click **Tools** on the menu bar, point to **Macro**, and click **Record New Macro**.

2. Type **Statistics** in the Macro name text box, and make sure that **This Workbook** is selected in the Store macro in list box because this macro will only be used in the current workbook.

   Now add a description of the macro.

3. In the Description text box, replace the existing text with **This macro displays the contents of the Statistics worksheet**. See Figure 12-2 for the completed Record Macro dialog box.

Figure 12-2   RECORD MACRO DIALOG BOX

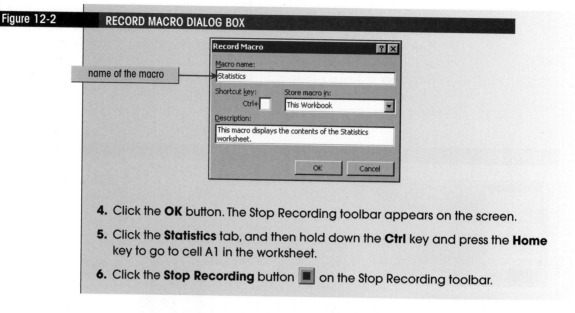

name of the macro

4. Click the **OK** button. The Stop Recording toolbar appears on the screen.

5. Click the **Statistics** tab, and then hold down the **Ctrl** key and press the **Home** key to go to cell A1 in the worksheet.

6. Click the **Stop Recording** button ■ on the Stop Recording toolbar.

Before going further with the macro, you will run it and verify that it works correctly.

To test the Statistics macro:

1. Click cell **C2** in the Statistics worksheet.

2. Click the **Control Panel** tab.

3. Click **Tools** on the menu bar, point to **Macro**, and click **Macros** to open the Macro dialog box.

4. Make sure that **Statistics** is selected in the Macro name list box, and click the **Run** button. The Statistics worksheet appears in the document window with cell A1 now selected.

TROUBLE? If the Statistics macro does not display the Statistics worksheet with cell A1 selected, reopen the Macro dialog box, click Statistics in the Macro name list box, and then click the Delete button to delete the macro. Then use the macro recorder to record the macro again.

Having created and tested your first macro in this workbook, you are ready to examine the macro code to evaluate how it works and use it as a foundation for writing your own macro code. Recall that Excel macros are written in a programming language called Visual Basic for Applications (VBA). VBA is the common language used by all Microsoft Office XP programs, so as you learn how to use VBA in Excel, you can apply your knowledge to Word, PowerPoint, Access, and other Office XP products.

Starting **the Visual Basic Editor**

To edit the VBA program you've created with the macro recorder, you need to use the Visual Basic Editor. You can open the Visual Basic Editor by selecting this command on the Macro submenu or by editing a macro you've created using the macro recorder.

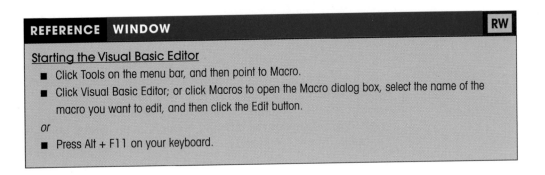

REFERENCE WINDOW   **RW**

Starting the Visual Basic Editor
- Click Tools on the menu bar, and then point to Macro.
- Click Visual Basic Editor; or click Macros to open the Macro dialog box, select the name of the macro you want to edit, and then click the Edit button.

or

- Press Alt + F11 on your keyboard.

You'll edit the Statistics macro, which will automatically open the Visual Basic editor.

To start the Visual Basic Editor:

1. Click **Tools** on the menu bar, point to **Macro**, and click **Macros**.

2. Make sure **Statistics** is selected in the Macro name list box, and click the **Edit** button. The Visual Basic Editor opens. See Figure 12-3.

Figure 12-3	VISUAL BASIC EDITOR

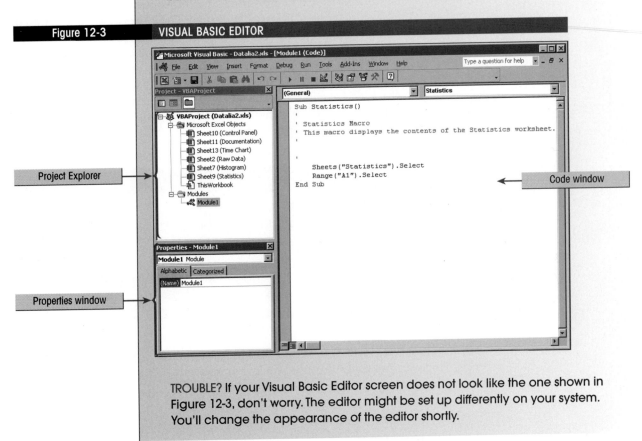

TROUBLE? If your Visual Basic Editor screen does not look like the one shown in Figure 12-3, don't worry. The editor might be set up differently on your system. You'll change the appearance of the editor shortly.

Before you begin studying the code of the Statistics macro, take a moment to become familiar with the main features of Visual Basic Editor.

Elements of the Visual Basic Editor

When the Visual Basic Editor opens, it usually displays three windows: the Project Explorer, the Properties window, and the Code window. You can use these windows to look at the structure and content of your workbooks, as well as any macros you've created. You might see other windows, depending on how the editor was installed on your system. To start learning about the different features of the editor, you'll begin with a clean slate by closing these windows and reopening them one at a time.

To clear the Visual Basic Editor window:

1. Click the **Close** button ☒ on each window in Visual Basic Editor window.

The Visual Basic Editor window is now empty.

The Project Explorer

One important use of the Visual Basic Editor is to manage your projects. A **project** is a collection of macros, worksheets, data entry forms, and other items that make up the customized application you're trying to create. The **Project Explorer** is a window in the editor that displays a hierarchical list of all currently opened projects and their contents.

The Project Explorer window is **dockable**, meaning that you can drag it to the edge of the screen, and the window will always remain on top, above other windows. Docking a window is useful when you want the contents of that window to always remain in view, but this can be a drawback if the window is taking up valuable screen space. The alternative is to not dock the window, so it floats free within the Visual Basic Editor. You can resize or minimize the window as you would other windows.

REFERENCE WINDOW   **RW**

Viewing Windows in the Visual Basic Editor

- Click View on the menu bar, and then click the name of the window you want to view.
- To float a window within the Visual Basic Editor, right-click the window's title bar, and then click Dockable on the shortcut menu.
- To dock a window within the Visual Basic Editor, click Tools on the menu bar, click Options, click the Docking tab, and then click to select the check box corresponding to the window you want to dock.

To begin working with your Visual Basic project, you'll display the contents of the Project Explorer. You'll also float the window to make it easier to view the other windows that you'll soon open.

To view and undock the Project Explorer:

1. Click **View** on the menu bar, and then click **Project Explorer**. The Project Explorer window opens, with Project - VBAProject in its title bar.

2. Right-click the title bar of the Project Explorer window, and then click **Dockable** on the shortcut menu.

3. If you don't see a shortcut menu when you right-click the title bar, Project Explorer is already undocked, and you can continue with the tutorial. Figure 12-4 shows the contents of the undocked Project Explorer window.

| Figure 12-4 | PROJECT EXPLORER WINDOW |

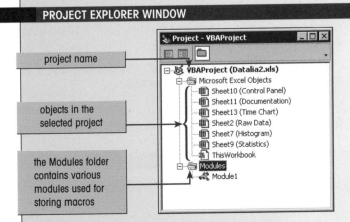

project name

objects in the selected project

the Modules folder contains various modules used for storing macros

TROUBLE? Depending on what other workbooks or Excel add-ins you might have opened, your Project Explorer window might look different than the one shown in Figure 12-4.

Like Windows Explorer, Project Explorer allows you to view your project components hierarchically. At the top of the hierarchy is the project itself. Each project is identified by the ⬛ icon followed by the project name and the filename in parentheses. The default project name given to new projects is "VBAProject." You might see other projects listed in Project Explorer including projects for Excel add-ins such as Solver. Within each project are various items called objects. An **object** is an element of a custom application, such as a worksheet, macro, or workbook. In VBA, just about anything can be an object, including a project. As shown in Figure 12-4, some of the objects listed for the Datalia2 workbook include each of the worksheets and an object called "ThisWorkbook," which actually refers to the Datalia2 workbook itself.

| REFERENCE WINDOW | RW |

Changing the Name of a Project

- Make sure the Project Explorer window is the active window within the Visual Basic Editor.
- Click Tools on the menu bar, and then click *Project_Name* Properties, where *Project_Name* is the current name of your project.
- On the General tab, enter a new name in the Project Name text box.
- Enter a description of the project in the Project Description text box (optional).
- Click the OK button.

Because the default name for your project, "VBAProject," isn't very descriptive, you'll change it to something more informative for future users of the workbook. You will change the name and enter a description of the project in the Project Properties dialog box.

To change the name of your project and add a description:

1. Click the title bar of the Project Explorer window to make it the active window if necessary.

2. Click **Tools** on the menu bar, and then click **VBAProject Properties**. Because project names cannot include spaces, you'll use an underscore to separate the words in the name.

3. Click the **General** tab if necessary, type **Datalia_Baby_Powder** in the Project Name text box, and then press the **Tab** key.

4. In the Project Description text box, type **Application to review baby powder quality control data.** See Figure 12-5.

Figure 12-5   PROPERTIES OF A VBA PROJECT

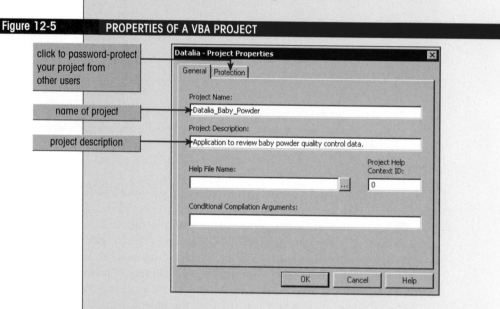

5. Click the **OK** button. Project Explorer displays the new project name.

You've changed the name and description of your project, but to change characteristics of other objects, you will need to use one of the other Visual Basic windows—the Properties window.

The Properties Window

When you entered the name and description of your project, you were actually modifying two of its properties. A **property** is an attribute of an object that defines one of its characteristics, such as its name, size, color, or location on the screen. All objects have properties. You can view a list of properties for any object in the **Properties window**. Try displaying the Properties window now for the Datalia_Baby_Powder project.

To view the Properties window:

1. Click **Datalia_Baby_Powder** in Project Explorer.

2. Click **View** on the menu bar, and then click **Properties Window**. The Properties window opens.

3. If the window is docked, right-click the title bar of the Properties window, and then click **Dockable** on the shortcut menu. The Properties window undocks from the menu bar and appears as a window in the Visual Basic Editor display area. See Figure 12-6.

Figure 12-6	PROPERTIES WINDOW FOR THE DATALIA_BABY_POWDER PROJECT

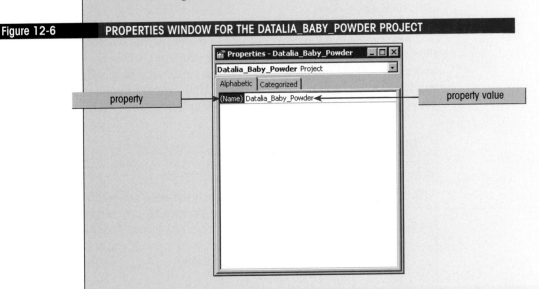

property

property value

TROUBLE? If you don't see a shortcut menu when you right-click the title bar, the Properties window is already undocked, and you can continue with the tutorial.

The Properties window displays each property in the left column and the property's value in the right column. To view the list of properties in alphabetic order and by category, you can click the Alphabetic and Categorized tabs at the top of the window. In Figure 12-6, there is only one property listed, the Name property, which has the value "Datalia_Baby_Powder."

To see how the Properties window works for objects other than projects, you decide to change the name of the Raw Data worksheet in the Datalia2 workbook to "Sample Data." You could do this from within Excel, but changing the name from within VBA, will give you some practice with the Project Explorer and the Properties window.

To change the name of the Raw Data worksheet:

1. Click **Sheet2 (Raw Data)** in the Project Explorer. The contents of the Properties window immediately change to show a list of properties for the Raw Data worksheet.

2. Click the **Alphabetic** tab in the Properties window if necessary. There are two columns: one contains the "(Name)" of the property and the other contains the values associated with the property.

3. Locate and then click the **Name** property (listed before the ScrollArea property), and then select the property value **Raw Data**.

TROUBLE? If the Properties window is small, you might have to scroll down the window to locate the Name property, or you can resize the window so more of the properties are visible.

4. Type **Sample Data** and then press the **Enter** key. The name of the worksheet displayed in the Project Explorer window changes to Sample Data. The next time you return to the Datalia2 workbook, you will find that the worksheet name has been changed there as well.

There can be many properties listed in the Properties window. The meaning of some of them will be very clear (such as the Name property), whereas others will not be as readily understandable. If you need more information about a particular property in the Property window, you can use Visual Basic online Help. You'll use online Help now to learn more about one of the properties of the Main Menu worksheet.

To view information on a property:

1. Click **StandardWidth** in the list of properties.

2. Press the **F1** key. The Microsoft Visual Basic Help window, shown in Figure 12-7, opens with the information that the StandardWidth property returns or sets the standard (default) width of all the columns in the worksheet. So, if you want to change the default width of the columns in the Sample Data worksheet, you would change the value for this property.

Figure 12-7   HELP FILE ON THE STANDARDWIDTH PROPERTY

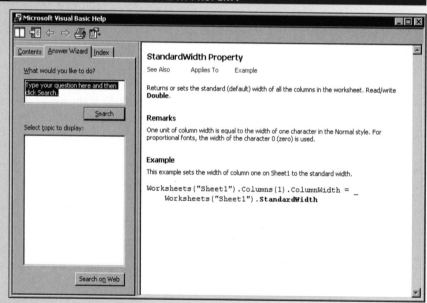

TROUBLE? If the Visual Basic Editor fails to display the Help topic, the Visual Basic Help files might not be installed. See your instructor or technical support person for assistance.

3. Click the **Close** button to close the Visual Basic Help window.

In general, if you are not sure what a VBA button, command, or object does, you can get information on it by selecting it and pressing the F1 key. You can display online Help either when you are in the Properties window or when you're writing or reviewing VBA code.

Modules

When you viewed your project in Project Explorer, you might have noticed the folder at the bottom of the object list called Modules. A **module** is a collection of VBA macros. A project might contain several different modules, with each module containing macros that accomplish a common set of tasks. For example, you might group all the macros that handle printing tasks in one module and the macros that format worksheets in another. When you recorded the Statistics macro, the Visual Basic Editor placed the macro in a new module with the default name "Module 1."

You can give your module a name that better describes the type of macros it will contain. You decide to change the name of Module1 to "Sheet_Macros" because the macros in this module will be used to display different worksheets in the workbook.

To change the name of the macro module:

1. Click **Module1** in Project Explorer.

2. Click the Properties window title bar to make the window active.

3. Double-click **Module1** in the (Name) row, type **Sheet_Macros**, and then press the **Enter** key. The name of the module in the Project Explorer window and the Properties window changes to Sheet_Macros. See Figure 12-8.

Figure 12-8	CHANGING THE NAME OF A PROJECT MODULE

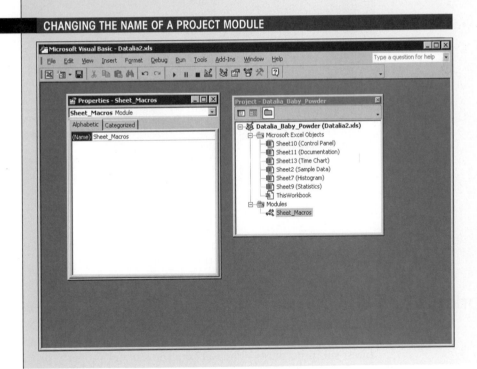

To review the contents of the Statistics macro, you need to open the third window of the Visual Basic Editor, the Code window.

The Code Window

When you want to view the contents of the macros in your project modules, you use the Code window. The **Code window** displays the VBA macro code associated with any item in the Project Explorer. You saw the Code window when you first opened the Visual Basic Editor. You'll reopen it now.

To view the Code window:

1. Click **View** on the menu bar, and click **Code**.

Figure 12-9 shows the contents of the Code window for the Sheet_Macros module.

Figure 12-9	VIEWING THE CODE WINDOW

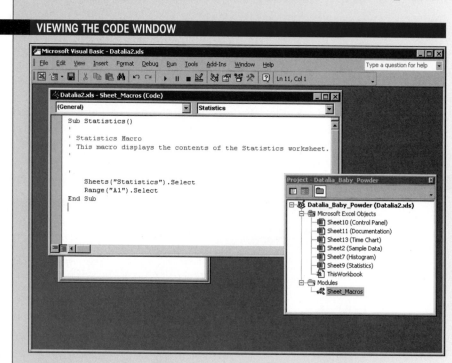

The Code window displays the lines of VBA code that make up your Statistics macro. Let's examine the structure of this code first.

Working **with Visual Basic Sub Procedures**

A macro in Visual Basic is called a **procedure**. Visual Basic supports three kinds of procedures: sub procedures, function procedures, and property procedures. A **sub procedure** performs an action on your project or workbook, such as formatting a cell or displaying a chart. A **function procedure** calculates a value. Function procedures are often used to create customized functions that can be entered into worksheet cells. A **property procedure** is a more advanced subject, used when you want to create customized properties for the objects in your project.

Because your project deals with displaying different worksheets within the Datalia workbook, you'll be create only sub procedures–not function procedures or property procedures.

Introducing Sub Procedures

In order to write a sub procedure, you'll have to know a few basic rules of VBA syntax. **Syntax** refers to the set of rules specifying how you must enter certain commands so that VBA will interpret them correctly, much like the grammatical syntax rules that make our sentences understandable to others. If you use improper syntax, Excel will not be able to run your macro, or it might run it incorrectly. The general syntax for a VBA sub procedure is:

```
Sub Procedure_Name(parameters)
      VBA commands and comments
End Sub
```

where *Procedure_Name* is the name of the macro and *parameters* are values passed to the sub procedure that control the operation of the macro. For example, the macro you created with the macro recorder has the sub procedure name "Statistics." Note that there are no parameter values for the Statistics sub procedure, but the parentheses are required anyway.

After the Sub Procedure_Name line, you enter either commands that perform certain tasks or comments that document the procedure's use. The End Sub command is always the last line in a sub procedure and tells Excel to stop running the macro. To see an example of a sub procedure, look at the Statistics macro you created earlier.

Figure 12-10	CODE OF THE STATISTICS MACRO

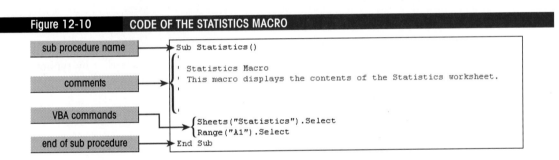

Figure 12-10 shows the VBA code for the Statistics macro. Below the name of the sub procedure, Excel has inserted the comments you entered earlier in the Record Macro dialog box (see Figure 12-2). **Comments** are statements that describe the behavior of the procedure. Comments begin with an apostrophe (') and are usually displayed by the editor in green text. After the comments, the procedure lists the VBA commands needed to first select the Statistics worksheet and then to select cell A1 on that worksheet. The End Sub line signals the end of the Statistics macro.

If you want more information about sub procedures or about any of the commands in the Statistics macro, you can open online Help the same way you did earlier in the Properties window.

To view additional information about sub procedures:

1. Select the word **Sub** in the first line of the Statistics macro.

2. Press the **F1** key. The Help window opens with additional information on sub procedures and the Sub statement.

3. Click the **Close** button ✕ to close the Help window.

You can use this method to interpret many of the commands and statements you'll see in the Code window. Simply select a word from the command and press the F1 key to bring up the corresponding help window.

Now that you are familiar with the structure of your Statistics sub procedure, you'll use it to create another macro for the Datalia2 workbook.

Creating a Sub Procedure Using Copy and Paste

The Statistics macro you created displays the Statistics worksheet, but you need macros to display other sheets in the workbook. You could use the macro recorder to create these other sub procedures, but because that code will be very similar to the Statistics sub procedure, you will save yourself the trouble by copying the macro code. You'll start by creating a sub procedure, called Time_Chart, that displays the Time Chart worksheet.

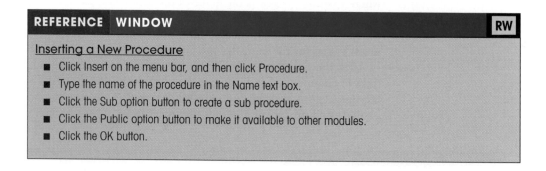

REFERENCE WINDOW   **RW**

Inserting a New Procedure
- Click Insert on the menu bar, and then click Procedure.
- Type the name of the procedure in the Name text box.
- Click the Sub option button to create a sub procedure.
- Click the Public option button to make it available to other modules.
- Click the OK button.

New sub procedures can be entered into the Code window either by typing the VBA commands directly or by using the Insert Procedure command.

To begin creating a new procedure:

1. If necessary, click the title bar of the Code window to activate it.

2. Click **Insert** on the menu bar, and then click **Procedure**. The Add Procedure dialog box opens, in which you'll enter the name and type of procedure you're creating.

3. Type **Time_Chart** in the Name text box to assign a title to the macro. See Figure 12-11.

Figure 12-11   ADD PROCEDURE DIALOG BOX

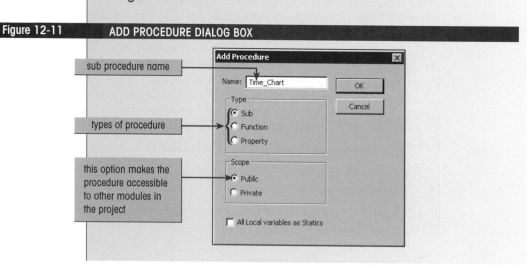

4. Make sure that the **Sub** and **Public** option buttons are selected. A public sub procedure is one that will be accessible to all modules in this project.

5. Click the **OK** button. See Figure 12-12. The Code window displays the beginning and ending lines of the new sub procedure. A horizontal line separates the new procedure from the first one. The first line of code indicates that the macro is public and then shows the name you gave the macro in the Add Procedure dialog box. The Statistics procedure is also public, even though the text "Public" is not shown. All procedures are considered public unless prefixed with the term "Private."

Figure 12-12	INSERTING A NEW SUB PROCEDURE

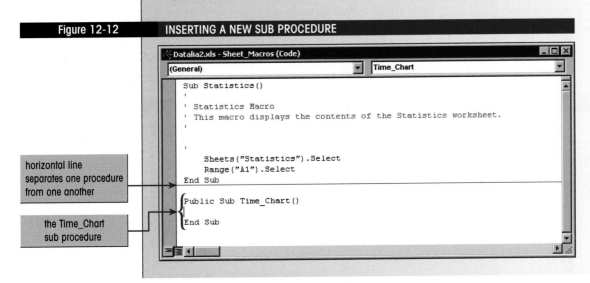

horizontal line separates one procedure from one another

the Time_Chart sub procedure

With the new procedure created, you are ready to copy the VBA code from the Statistics Sub Procedure into the Time_Chart Sub Procedure. You add, delete, and replace text in the Code window the same way you do in any text editor. Note that, if you had not already recorded the Statistics macro, you would have to enter the codes yourself. Using copy and paste will save you some time.

To copy and paste the VBA code:

1. Scroll up the Code window until you can see the entire Statistics macro.

  TROUBLE? You might want to enlarge the Code window to make it easier to view, copy, and paste the VBA code.

2. Position the insertion point to the right of the first apostrophe located under the Sub Statistics ( ) line of code.

3. Select the lines beginning with the first apostrophe down through the Range("A1") line. Do not include either the Sub Statistics ( ) or the End Sub line in your selection.

4. Click the **Copy** button 🖺 on the toolbar.

5. Scroll down and click the blank line in the middle of the Time_Chart sub procedure.

6. Click the **Paste** button 🖺 on the toolbar. The VBA code is pasted into the Time_Chart sub procedure.

Your next task is to replace the occurrences of "Statistics" with "Time Chart." You can do this by selecting the old text and typing over it with the new text, or you can use the editor's Replace command to replace all the occurrences at once.

To replace text in the Time_Chart sub procedure:

1. Click **Edit** on the menu bar, and then click **Replace**.

2. Type **Statistics** in the Find What list box, and then press the **Tab** key.

3. Type **Time Chart** in the Replace With list box.

4. In the Search section, click the **Current Procedure** option button to replace only the occurrences of the word "Statistics" in the current procedure (not in the entire module or project). See Figure 12-13.

Figure 12-13	REPLACE DIALOG BOX

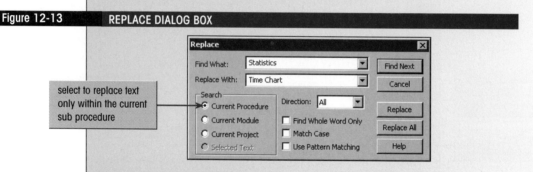

select to replace text only within the current sub procedure

5. Click the **Replace All** button. Excel indicates that three occurrences of the text "Statistics" have been replaced.

6. Click the **OK** button and then click the **Cancel** button. Figure 12-14 displays the Time_Chart sub procedure after the text replacement.

Figure 12-14	COMPLETED TIME_CHART SUB PROCEDURE

```
Public Sub Time_Chart()
'
' Time Chart Macro
' This macro displays the contents of the Time Chart worksheet.
'


'
    Sheets("Time Chart").Select
    Range("A1").Select

End Sub
```

Running a Sub Procedure

Using copy, paste, find, and replace, you've created a new procedure in the Datalia_Baby_Powder project. Because you've replaced the name "Statistics" with "Time Chart," this new procedure should display the contents of the Time Chart worksheet when you run it. You could test this macro by returning to the Datalia2 workbook and running it there, or you can run it from within the Visual Basic Editor.

To run the Time_Chart sub procedure:

1. With the insertion point still within the Time_Chart sub procedure, click **Run** on the menu bar, and then click **Run Sub/UserForm**. The Visual Basic Editor runs whatever macro is currently displayed in the Code Window, in this case, the Time_Chart sub procedure.

    Test whether the macro was run correctly by returning to the Datalia2 workbook.

2. Click the **Microsoft Excel – Datalia2** program button on the taskbar. The Time Chart worksheet should now be displayed with cell A1 selected.

3. Return to the Visual Basic Editor by clicking the **Microsoft Visual Basic – Datalia2** program button on your Windows taskbar.

    TROUBLE? Depending on the number of program buttons on the taskbar, the complete program title might not be displayed.

Note that you can also run the selected sub procedure by pressing the F5 key or by pressing the Run Sub/UserForm button on the Visual Basic Editor's Standard toolbar.

Use the copy and paste technique to create macros to display the remaining worksheets in the Datalia2 workbook:

To create the remaining sub procedures:

1. With the Code window active, click **Insert** on the menu bar, and then click **Procedure**.

2. Type **Histogram** in the Name text box, and then click the **OK** button. The insertion point appears in the middle of the Histogram sub procedure.

3. Click the **Paste** button 📋 on the Standard toolbar to paste the macro code for the Statistics macro into the newly created Histogram sub procedure.

4. Click **Edit** on the menu bar, click **Replace**, make sure **Statistics** appears in the Find What list box, press the **Tab** key and type **Histogram** in the Replace With list box, make sure that the Current Procedure option button is selected, and then click the **Replace All** button. The Visual Basic Editor replaces three occurrences of the word "Statistics."

5. Click the **OK** button and then click the **Cancel** button.

6. Click **Insert**, click **Procedure**, type **Sample_Data** as the new sub procedure name, and then click the **OK** button.

7. Click 📋 to paste the Statistics macro code into the Sample_Data sub procedure.

8. Click **Edit**, click **Replace**, and then replace all occurrences of the word "Statistics" in the sub procedure with **Sample Data**.

    You will create a sub procedure to display the contents of the Control Panel worksheet.

9. Insert a new sub procedure into the Code Window named **Control_Panel**, and then click 📋 to paste the Statistics macro code into the sub procedure.

10. Replace all occurrences of the word "Statistics" in the Control_Panel sub procedure with the text **Control Panel**.

TROUBLE? If you make a mistake replacing the text, you can click the Undo button [↶] on the toolbar to reverse the action.

Now that you've created the five sub procedures to display various worksheets in the Datalia2 workbook, you can return to Excel and assign those macros to the different macro buttons in the workbook.

To assign the sub procedures to macro buttons:

1. Click **File** on the menu bar, and then click **Close and Return to Microsoft Excel**.

2. Click the **Control Panel** tab.

3. Right-click the **Statistics** macro button, and then click **Assign Macro** on the shortcut menu. This macro button will be used to display the contents of the Statistics worksheet.

4. Click **Statistics** in the list of macro names in the Assign Macro dialog box. See Figure 12-15.

Figure 12-15	ASSIGNING THE STATISTICS MACRO TO A MACRO BUTTON

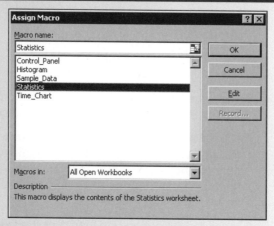

5. Click the **OK** button, click outside of the Statistics macro button to deselect it, and then click it again. The Statistics worksheet appears.

Now you will assign the Control_Panel macro to the Return to the Control Panel macro button.

6. Right-click the **Return to the Control Panel** button, click **Assign Macro** on the shortcut menu, click **Control_Panel** in the list of macros, and then click the **OK** button.

7. Click outside of the Return to the Control Panel macro button to deselect it, and then click the button again. You are returned to the Control Panel worksheet.

8. Using the same process, assign the appropriate macros to the Time Chart, Histogram, and Data macro buttons on the Control Panel worksheet.

TROUBLE? Do not worry about the Choose a Filler macro button. You'll assign a macro to that button in the next session.

9. On the Time Chart, Histogram, and Sample Data worksheets, assign the Control_Panel macro to the Return to the Control Panel macro button.

10. Test the macro buttons in the workbook, verifying that by clicking the buttons you can jump to different sheets in the workbook.

At this point, you've created macros to switch between sheets in the workbook, but the workbook only shows the quality control data for filler A. You will save your changes for now.

To save your changes:

1. Return to the Documentation sheet so that the next time you open this worksheet, this sheet is displayed.

2. Click cell **B3**, and save and close the workbook.

3. Exit Excel.

In the next session, you'll create a macro that will allow you to switch to any of the five fillers in Kemp's sample, and, in the process, you'll learn how to write and interpret VBA sub procedures.

Session 12.1 QUICK CHECK

1. Describe what each of the following is used for:
   a. Project Explorer
   b. Properties window
   c. Code window

2. Define the following terms:
   a. project
   b. object
   c. property
   d. module
   e. syntax

3. How would you get help on a particular property listed in the Properties window?

4. What are the three types of procedures in VBA?

5. Describe the syntax of a sub procedure.

6. Why would a project contain several modules?

SESSION 12.2

In this session, you'll learn about the fundamentals of the Visual Basic for Applications programming language. You'll learn how to use the Visual Basic Editor to enter VBA code without errors. Finally, you'll learn how to create a macro that prompts the user for input and then uses that information to determine which tasks the macro will perform.

Introducing **Visual Basic for Applications**

You've completed the first stage of Kemp's application by creating macros that allow users to easily move between sheets in the workbook. The next macro you'll create will allow users to view quality-control data for different fillers. To do this, you have to learn a little more about the Visual Basic for Applications programming language. Whole books are devoted to the study of VBA; the discussion that follows is designed to give you an overview and a starting point for some of the concepts involved in writing a VBA program.

Objects

VBA is an **object-oriented programming language**, in which tasks are performed by manipulating objects. An Excel object can be almost anything, from a single cell, to an entire worksheet, to the Excel application itself. Figure 12-16 describes some of the important Excel objects available to you in your VBA programs.

Figure 12-16	OBJECTS AND THEIR VBA OBJECT NAMES

EXCEL OBJECT	DESCRIPTION
Range	A cell in a worksheet
Name	A range name in a workbook
Chart	A chart in the workbook (either embedded within a worksheet or stored as a chart sheet)
ChartObject	A chart embedded within a worksheet
Worksheet	A worksheet in a workbook
Workbook	A Excel workbook
VBAProject	A VBA project
Application	The Excel application itself

Objects are often grouped into collections, which are themselves objects, called **collection objects**. For example, a sheet in a workbook is an object, but also the collection of all the sheets in a workbook is an object. To refer to a specific object in a collection, you use the following syntax:

object_collection(*id*)

where *object_collection* is the name of the object collection and *id* is either a name or number that identifies an individual object in the collection. For example, one of the object collections is Sheets, which refers to all of the sheets in a particular workbook. If Kemp wanted you to write a VBA code that references the Control Panel worksheet—the second sheet in the workbook—you could refer to the worksheet as either Sheets("Control Panel") or Sheets(2). Figure 12-17 provides other examples of VBA code that make use of object collections.

Figure 12-17   OBJECT COLLECTIONS

VBA CODE	DESCRIPTION
Range("A1:B10")	The collection of cells in the cell range, A1:B10
Names("FillerA")	The FillerA range name
ChartObjects(3)	The third embedded chart in a worksheet
Charts(3)	The third chart sheet in a workbook
Sheets("Sample Data")	The Sample Data worksheet
Workbooks("Datalia2")	The Datalia2 workbook
Windows(2)	The second open Excel workbook window

VBA organizes all of these objects and object collections in a hierarchy going from the Excel application itself down to the individual cells of a workbook. This hierarchy is often referred to as the **Excel Object Model**. Figure 12-18 shows a small portion of the Excel Object Model. You can view the complete listing of the hierarchy using the online Help available in the Visual Basic Editor.

Figure 12-18   A PORTION OF THE EXCEL OBJECT MODEL

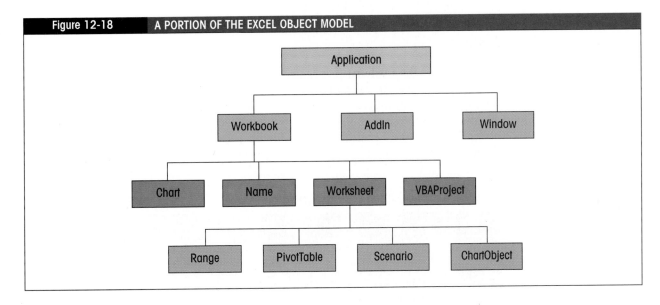

Sometimes you will have to refer to an object by indicating its place within the Excel Object Model. The general syntax for doing this is as follows:

   object1.object2.object3

where *object1* is an object at the upper level of the hierarchy, *object2* is next in line, and *object3* is at the lower level in the hierarchy. For example, if your VBA code needs to reference cell A1 in the Statistics worksheet of the Datalia2 workbook, the reference would be

   Workbooks("Datalia2").Sheets("Statistics").Range("A1")

going from an upper level in the Excel Object Model (workbooks) all the way down to an individual cell.

It can be complicated to always have to worry about an object's place in the Excel Object Model, so VBA provides special object names to refer directly to certain objects. One such name is "ActiveSheet," which refers to whatever worksheet is currently being displayed in the workbook. Figure 12-19 lists some of these special object names and their meanings.

Figure 12-19	SPECIAL OBJECT NAMES

SPECIAL OBJECT NAME	DESCRIPTION
ActiveCell	The currently selected cell
ActiveChart	The currently selected chart
ActiveSheet	The currently selected sheet
ActiveWindow	The currently selected window
ActiveWorkbook	The current workbook
ThisCell	The cell from which a custom function is being run
ThisWorkbook	The workbook containing the macro code that is currently running

Once you have a way of referring to an object in your workbook, you'll usually want to affect a change to that object. This is done in two ways: by modifying the object's properties or by applying a method to the object.

Properties

Properties are the attributes that characterize the object. A cell will have several properties, for example, such as the value or formula contained in the cell, the formatting applied to the cell's appearance, or the text of the comment that might be attached to the cell. Using VBA, you can change the value of such properties to change the content or appearance of the object. Some of the Excel objects and the properties associated with them are shown in Figure 12-20.

Figure 12-20	OBJECTS AND THEIR PROPERTIES	

OBJECT	PROPERTIES	DESCRIPTION
Range	Address	The cell reference of the range
	Comment	A comment attached to the cell
	Formula	The formula entered into the cell
	Value	The value of the cell
Name	RefersTo	The cell(s) to which a range name refers
	Value	The value of the cell referred to by the range name
Worksheet	Name	The name of the worksheet
	Visible	Whether the worksheet is visible or hidden
Chart	ChartTitle	The text of the chart's title
	ChartType	The type of the chart
	HasLegend	Whether the chart has a legend or not
Workbook	HasPassword	Whether the workbook has a password or not
	Name	The name of the workbook
	Path	The folder and drive in which the workbook has been stored
	Saved	Whether the workbook has been saved or not

This list is only a small sample of the vast number of objects and properties available to you in your VBA programs. Literally, every aspect of every object in Excel can be expressed in terms of an object property.

REFERENCE WINDOW   **RW**

Changing an Object's Property
■ Enter the following VBA command:
object.property = expression
where *object* is the object name, *property* is the name of the property, and *expression* is a value, text, or function that you want to assign to the property.

To change the property of an object using VBA, the command should take the following form:

   object.property = expression

where *object* is the object name, *property* is the name of the property, and *expression* is a value that you want to assign to the property. For example, if you want to change the value of cell A2 to "395," you would use the command *Range("A2").Value = 395*. Figure 12-21 shows three other examples of VBA statements that use this syntax.

| Figure 12-21 | CHANGING A PROPERTY USING VBA |

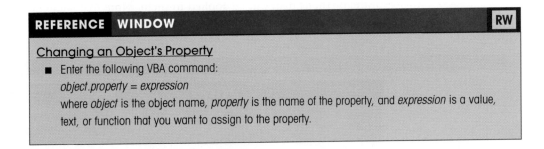

VBA CODE	DESCRIPTION
ActiveCell.Value = 23	Changes the value of the active cell to 23
Range("A5").Formula = "SUM(A1:A4)"	Changes the formula of cell A1 to sum up the values in the range A1:A4
Worksheets("Raw Data").Name = "Sample Data"	Changes the name of the "Raw Data" worksheet to "Sample Data"
ActiveWorkbook.Password = "powder"	Changes the password of the current workbook to "powder"
Application.StatusBar = "Running macro ..."	Displays the text, "Running macro ..." in Excel's status bar

Note that the third example from Figure 12-21 changes the Name property of the Raw Data worksheet object to "Sample Data." You did this in the last session when you changed the name of the worksheet using the Properties window. This is how you would write the command to do the same thing in VBA.

You can also use an object property statement to turn a property on or off, as in the following VBA command:

   Sheets("Documentation").Visible = False

This command hides the Documentation worksheet from the user by making the Visible property "False" (that is, hidden). To make the worksheet visible again, you would use this command:

   Sheets("Title Sheet").Visible = True

Now you will learn how to use methods to alter Excel objects.

Methods

A **method** is an action that can be performed on an object, such as closing a workbook or printing the contents of a worksheet. Figure 12-22 lists a few of the Excel objects and some of the methods than can be applied to them. Note that some methods do not require any parameters.

Figure 12-22	OBJECTS AND THEIR METHODS	

OBJECT	METHODS	DESCRIPTION
Range	Clear	Clears all formulas and values in the range
	Copy	Copies values of the range into the Clipboard
	Merge	Merges the cells in the range
Worksheet	Delete	Deletes the worksheet
	Select	Selects (and displays) the worksheet
Workbook	Close	Closes the workbook
	Protect	Protects the workbook
	Save	Saves the workbook
Chart	Copy	Copies the chart
	Select	Selects the chart
	Delete	Deletes the chart
Charts	Select	Selects chart sheets in the workbook
Worksheets	Select	Selects worksheets in the workbook

REFERENCE WINDOW	RW

Applying a Method to an Object

■ Enter the VBA command:

    object.method(value1, value2, ...)

    where *object* is the name of the object, *method* is a method that is associated with that object, and *value1, value2,* and so forth, are parameter values used by the method.

or

    object.method parameter1:= value1 parameter2:= value2 ...

    where *parameter1* and *parameter2* are the names of parameters associated with the method, and *value1* and *value2* (and so forth) are the values assigned to those parameters.

VBA supports two forms for applying a method to an object. One is:

    object.method(value1, value2, ...)

where *object* is the name of the object, *method* is a method that can applied to the object, and *value1, value2,* and so forth are the parameter values required by the method. Note that some methods do not require any parameter values. Figure 12-23 shows some examples of VBA code using this format.

Figure 12-23   APPLYING A METHOD USING VBA

VBA CODE	DESCRIPTION
Range("A1:B10").Clear	Clears the contents of the range A1:B10
Range("A1").AddComment("Total Assets")	Adds the comment "Total Assets" to cell A1
Range("A1").Select	Selects cell A1, making it the active cell
Sheets("Statistics").Select	Selects and displays the Statistics worksheet
ActiveSheet.Delete	Deletes the currently active sheet
Workbooks("Datalia1").SaveAs("Datalia2")	Saves the Datalia2 workbook with the filename "Datalia2"
ActiveWorkbook.Save	Saves the current workbook
ActiveWorkbook.Protect("powder")	Protects the current workbook, using the password "powder"

Some methods have a long list of parameters, so VBA also provides a form where the parameters and their values are explicitly indicated. The syntax for this form is

object.method parameter1:= value1 parameter2:= value2 ...

where *parameter1* and *parameter2* are the names of parameters associated with the method, and *value1* and *value2* are the values assigned to those parameters (there can be dozens of parameters and values). Figure 12-24 displays a collection of VBA commands that use this form to apply methods to objects.

Figure 12-24   INTERPRETING THE STATISTICS SUB PROCEDURE

VBA CODE	INTERPRETATION
Sub Statistics()	Sets the name of the sub procedure as "Statistics"
Sheets("Statistics").Select	Using the Select method, selects the Statistics worksheet object
Range("A1").Select	Using the Select method, selects the A1 range object
End Sub	Indicates the end of the sub procedure

With what you've learned about how VBA works with objects, properties, and methods, you can interpret the Statistics sub procedure you created in the last session in terms of objects, properties, and methods. See Figure 12-25.

Figure 12-25   SPECIFYING PARAMETERS IN A VBA METHOD

VBA CODE	DESCRIPTION
Range("A1").Copy Destination:= Range("A5")	Copies the contents of cell A1 into cell A5
Range ("A1").AddComment Text:="Total Assets"	Adds the comment "Total Assets" to cell A1
Sheets("Sheet 1").Move After:=Sheets("Sheet 3")	Moves the Sheet 1 worksheet after Sheet 3
ActiveWorkbook.SaveAs Filename:="Datalia2"	Saves the active workbook as "Datalia2"
ActiveWorkbook.Protect Password:= "powder"	Protects the current workbook, using the password "powder"

Variables

A **variable** is a named element in a program that can be used to store and retrieve information. Every variable is identified by a unique **variable name**. For example, you could create a variable named "Filler_Name" and use it to store the name of the filler currently displayed in the Datalia2 workbook. Variables can also store objects. A variable named "WBook" could be used to store the Datalia2 workbook itself. Case is important. VBA does make a distinction between a variable named "WBook" and one named "wbook."

The VBA syntax for storing a value or text string in a variable is

   variable = expression

where *variable* is the variable name and *expression* is a value or text string. If you want to store an object in a variable, the syntax is

   Set *variable = object_reference*

where *object_reference* is a VBA object reference, such as Sheets("Statistics"). Figure 12-26 shows a few sample VBA statements that use variables.

Figure 12-26	SETTING THE VALUE OF A VBA VARIABLE

VBA CODE	DESCRIPTION
Bottle = 395	Stores the value, 395, in the Bottle variable
Company = "Datalia Inc."	Stores the text string "Datalia Inc." in the Company variable
Bottle = Worksheets("Sample Data").Range("A2").Value	Stores whatever value is entered in cell A2 of the Sample Data worksheet in the Bottle variable
Set WSheet = Sheets("Statistics")	Points the WSheet variable to the Statistics worksheet
Set WBook = Workbooks("Datalia2")	Points the WBook variable to the Datalia2 workbook

Once you've created a variable and assigned it to a value, text string, or object, you can use it your VBA program. For example, in the Statistics sub procedure, you could create a variable named "SheetName" that stores the name of a sheet you want to select. The revised sub procedure might look as follows:

```
Sub SelectSheet()
     SheetName = "Statistics"
     Sheets(SheetName).Select
     Range("A1").Select
End Sub
```

Compare this code to the one shown earlier in Figure 12-25. By revising the value of the SheetName variable in the first line of this sub procedure, the SelectSheet macro can select any sheet in the workbook.

You've finished reviewing some of the basic concepts of the VBA programming language. Now you'll use these principles to create a sub procedure in which you can display the quality control data for any filler in Kemp's sample.

Creating a Program to Switch Fillers

To create a program to switch the display from one filler to another, you first have to understand how Kemp has organized the data in the Datalia2 workbook. Kemp has assigned range names to the sample data values he has collected and stored in the Sample Data worksheet (for a discussion of range names, see Tutorial 8). All of the charts and statistics displayed in the Datalia2 workbook are based on range names rather than cell references. Figure 12-27 lists all of the range names in the Datalia2 workbook.

Figure 12-27	RANGE NAMES IN THE DATALIA2 WORKBOOK	

RANGE NAME	DEFINITION	DESCRIPTION
Filler	=FillerA	The name of the currently selected filler machine
FillerA	='Sample Data'!$A$2	The name of filler machine A
FillerB	='Sample Data'!$B$2	The name of filler machine B
FillerC	='Sample Data'!$C$2	The name of filler machine C
FillerD	='Sample Data'!$D$2	The name of filler machine D
FillerE	='Sample Data'!$E$2	The name of filler machine E
Values	=ValuesA	Powder values from the currently selected filler
ValuesA	='Sample Data'!$A$3:$A$157	Powder values from FillerA
ValuesB	='Sample Data'!$B$3:$B$157	Powder values from FillerB
ValuesC	='Sample Data'!$C$3:$C$157	Powder values from FillerC
ValuesD	='Sample Data'!$D$3:$D$157	Powder values from FillerD
ValuesE	='Sample Data'!$E$3:$E$157	Powder values from FillerE
Time	='Sample Data'!$F$3:$F$157	The time each sample was drawn

The range A2:E2 of the Sample Data worksheet contains the letter designations of the five filler machines. Each of these cells has been assigned a range name. For example, the FillerA range name points to cell A2, which displays the letter A. Whichever of these five fillers is currently displayed in the workbook's charts and statistics is assigned the range name Filler. The current definition of the Filler range name is "=FillerA," which means that it points to the FillerA range (cell A2 of the Sample Data worksheet).

Similarly, the range names ValuesA, ValuesB, ValuesC, ValuesD, and ValuesE point to the sample values of the five fillers, and the range name, Values, points to the sample values of the currently selected filler. The time the bottle samples were drawn is stored in the Time range name.

If Kemp wants to switch the display in the workbook from one filler to another, he simply has to change the definition of the Filler and Values range names. For example, to switch to the filler B, he should change the definition of the Filler range name from "=FillerA" to "=FillerB" and change the definition of Values from "=ValuesA" to "=ValuesB." Once he does this, all of the charts and statistics will display data on filler B instead of filler A.

Kemp also wants to be able to automate this process because other users might not be familiar with range names or know how to use them. Instead of using the Define Range Names dialog box, he would like to have Excel prompt the user for the filler to be displayed and then have Excel automatically switch to the filler indicated by the user. You can create such a dialog box using VBA. First, you'll create the structure of the program using the macro recorder.

To record the macro:

1. If you took a break after the previous session, make sure Excel is running, and then open the **Datalia2** workbook located in the Tutorial.12\Tutorial folder on your Data Disk. Click the **Enable Macros** button if warned by Excel about the presence of macros in the workbook.

2. Click **Tools** on the menu bar, point to **Macro**, and then click **Record New Macro**.

3. Type **Choose_Filler** in the Macro name text box, replace the default description text with **Choose a filler to display.** , and then click the **OK** button.

4. Click **Insert** on the menu bar, point to **Name**, and then click **Define**.

5. Click **Filler** in the Names in the workbook list box, click in the Refers to reference box and change the definition from =FillerA to **=FillerB**, and then click the **Add** button.

6. Click **Values** in the list of range names, change the definition in the Refers to reference box from =ValuesA to **=ValuesB**, and then click the **OK** button.

7. Click the **Stop Recording** button ▣ on the Stop Recording toolbar.

   TROUBLE? If the Stop Recording toolbar is not visible on your screen, click Tools, point to Macro, and then click Stop Recording.

   Now check to see whether the workbook displays data on Filler B instead of Filler A.

8. Click the **Control Panel** tab. The Control Panel worksheet should now display "B" in the Values filler box with the text "Control Violations" in the Status filler box, indicating that filler B has either overfilled or underfilled some bottles.

9. Click the **Statistics**, **Time Chart**, and **Histogram** buttons to view the contents of those worksheets. Verify that they display statistics and charts for Filler B. Return to the Control Panel worksheet.

Next, you will view the contents of the macro you created in the Visual Basic Editor.

To view the Choose_Filler macro:

1. Click **Tools** on the menu bar, point to **Macro**, and then click **Macros**.

2. Make sure **Choose_Filler** is currently selected in the list of macros, and then click the **Edit** button. The macro code appears in the Code window of the Visual Basic Editor, as shown in Figure 12-28.

Figure 12-28	THE CHOOSE_FILLER SUB PROCEDURE

VBA command to add the Filler range name to the active workbook

VBA command to add the Values range name to the active workbook

```
Sub Choose_Filler()
'
' Choose_Filler Macro
' Choose a filler to display.
'


    ActiveWorkbook.Names.Add Name:="Filler", RefersToR1C1:="=FillerB"
    ActiveWorkbook.Names.Add Name:="Values", RefersToR1C1:="=ValuesB"
End Sub
```

Editing the Choose_Filler Macro

The Choose_Filler macro consists of two lines. The first line uses the Add method to add a new range name definition to the active workbook (Datalia2). The Name parameter indicates that this new definition will have the name "Filler," and the RefersToR1C1 parameter indicates that the new range name will refer to the range "=FillerB"—that is the cell containing the name of Filler B. Similarly, the second line of the program uses the Add method again to add a new definition of the Values range name, referring to the range "=ValuesB."

What if you wanted to change this program so that it displays the bottle weights from Filler C? You could edit the code, changing "FillerB" and "ValuesB" to "FillerC" and "ValuesC," but a more general approach would be to create a variable named "Source" that stores the letter of the bottle filler you want to display.

To create the Source variable:

1. Click the end of the last blank comment line, and then press the **Enter** key to open a blank line above the VBA command to add the Filler range name.

2. Type **Source = "C"** .

Next, you'll use the Source variable to change the cell references of the two range names. Currently, the Filler range name is given the reference "=FillerB." You'll replace this value with the expression:

"=Filler" & Source

The & (ampersand) symbol is used to combine two text strings into a single text string. Because Source has a value of "C," the value of "=Filler" & Source would be "=FillerC." Similarly, the reference for the second range name should be changed from "=ValuesB" to "=Values" & Source.

To use the Source variable:

1. Click the end of the command to add the Filler range name.

2. Change the text string "=FillerB" to **"=Filler" & Source**, and then press the ↓ key on your keyboard.

   TROUBLE? As you type the text string, the editor will display a pop-up description box that provides the syntax of the function. Pressing the ↓ key closes the box.

3. Change the text string "=ValuesB" to **"=Values" & Source**, and then press the ↓ key again. Figure 12-29 shows the revised text of the Choose_Filler macro.

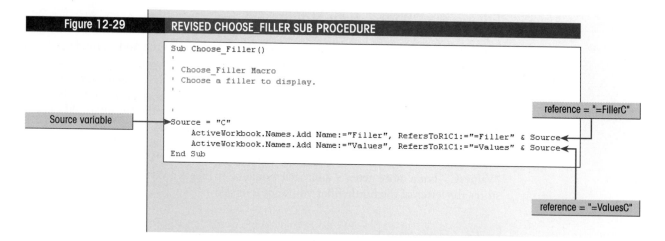

Figure 12-29 **REVISED CHOOSE_FILLER SUB PROCEDURE**

```
Sub Choose_Filler()
'
' Choose_Filler Macro
' Choose a filler to display.
'

'
Source = "C"
    ActiveWorkbook.Names.Add Name:="Filler", RefersToR1C1:="=Filler" & Source
    ActiveWorkbook.Names.Add Name:="Values", RefersToR1C1:="=Values" & Source
End Sub
```

Source variable

reference = "=FillerC"

reference = "=ValuesC"

Test the revised Choose_Filler macro in the Datalia2 workbook without closing the editor.

To test the Choose_Filler macro:

1. Click the **Microsoft Excel Datalia2** program button on the taskbar.

2. Right-click the **Choose a Filler** macro button on the Control Panel worksheet, and then click **Assign Macro**.

3. Click **Choose_Filler** in the list of macros, and then click the **OK** button.

4. Click outside the Choose a Filler macro button to deselect it, and then click it again to run the Choose_Filler macro. Excel runs the macro, now displaying the results for Filler C, which shows no control violations.

5. View the rest of the workbook using the Control Panel macro buttons, and then return to the Control Panel sheet.

Retrieving **Information from the User**

The macro works, but now you need to find some way of prompting users for the value of the Source variable rather than entering it directly into the VBA code. You can do this using the InputBox command. The syntax of the command is

$$variable = \text{InputBox}(Prompt, Title)$$

where *variable* is a variable whose value is set based on whatever the user enters into the input box, *Prompt* is the message you want to appear in the input box, and *Title* is the text that appears in the title bar of the input box. For example, the following VBA code

Payment = InputBox("Enter your monthly payment", "Mortgage Analysis")

will produce the input box shown in Figure 12-30.

Figure 12-30   **INPUTBOX FUNCTION**

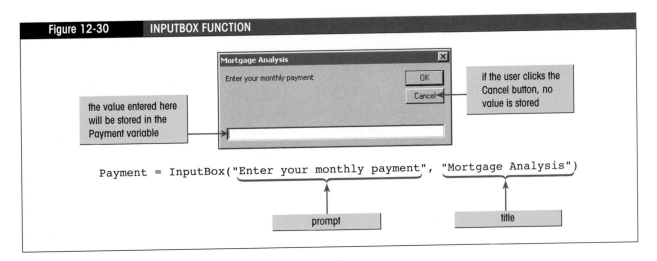

In this example that concerns mortgage payments, the results from the input box will be stored in a variable named "Payment."

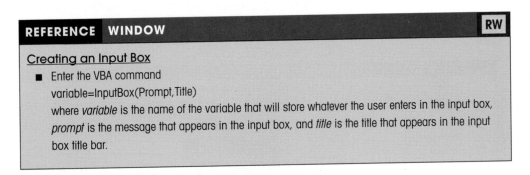

REFERENCE WINDOW   **RW**

Creating an Input Box

- Enter the VBA command
  variable=InputBox(Prompt,Title)
  where *variable* is the name of the variable that will store whatever the user enters in the input box, *prompt* is the message that appears in the input box, and *title* is the title that appears in the input box title bar.

You'll create a similar input box to allow users to input the value of the Source variable you just created.

To insert the InputBox function:

1. Press **Alt + F11** to return to the Visual Basic Editor.

2. Change the Source = "C" line of code to **Source = InputBox("Enter a filler (A – E)", "Specify Bottle Filler")**. See Figure 12-31.

Figure 12-31   **REVISED CHOOSE_FILLER MACRO**

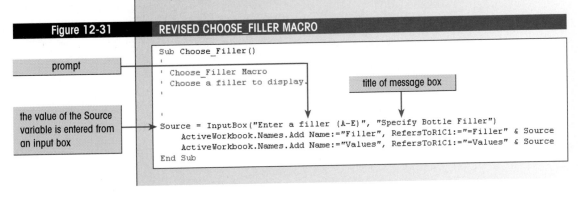

Now test the InputBox function by using it to display the sample values for filler D.

To test the InputBox function:

1. Click the **Microsoft Excel - Datalia2** program button on the taskbar to return to Excel.

2. Click the **Choose a Filler** button on the Control Panel worksheet. Excel displays the Specify Bottle Filler input box shown in Figure 12-32.

Figure 12-32   SPECIFY BOTTLE FILLER INPUT BOX

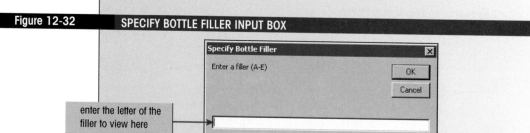

enter the letter of the filler to view here

3. Type **d** in the input box, and then click the **OK** button. Excel displays the quality control status of filler D. See Figure 12-33. Because range names are not case sensitive, you can type either an uppercase or lowercase d.

Figure 12-33   STATUS OF FILLER D

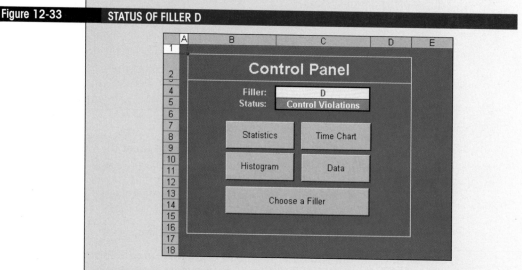

4. Click the Control Panel macro buttons to view the statistics and charts describing the operation of Filler D, and then return to the Control Panel worksheet.

You're finished working on the Choose_Filler macro for now. Save the Datalia 2 workbook.

To save your changes:

1. Return to the Documentation sheet, and make sure cell B3 is the active cell.

2. Save and close the workbook. Exit Excel

Using the VBA, you have been able to create a macro that will help Kemp monitor the operations of the fillers. The input box will be a great help to the quality control engineers who need to work with filler-related data. In the next session, you'll learn how to create procedures called control structures that "make decisions" based on the type of information the user enters.

Session 12.2 QUICK CHECK

1. Define the following terms:
   a. object-oriented programming language
   b. collection object
   c. method
   d. parameter
   e. variable

2. What VBA command would you enter to change the name of the Histogram worksheet to "Histogram Chart"? (*Hint*: The object name is Sheets("Histogram"), and the name of the worksheet is contained in the Name property.)

3. What VBA command would you enter to select the Histogram worksheet?

4. What VBA command would you enter to store the name of the active worksheet in a variable named "Sheetname"?

5. What VBA command would you enter to display an input box containing the prompt "Enter your last name", the text "Log In" in the title bar, and then save whatever the user entered into a variable named "Lastname"?

SESSION 12.3

In this session, you'll learn about control structures that cause your macros to operate differently under different conditions. You'll learn how to create message boxes that provide directions for your users. Finally, you'll learn how to modify the toolbars and menus used by Excel and how to protect your workbook from unauthorized changes.

Introducing Control Structures

You've shown Kemp the Datalia2 workbook that you completed in the last session. He was very impressed. He clicked on the Choose a Filler button and was able to quickly bring up information on any of the five fillers in his sample. Unfortunately, he has also found two problems. Once he mistakenly typed F in the input box, and Excel displayed the dialog shown in Figure 12-34.

Figure 12-34   THE CONTROL PANEL AFTER KEMP MAKES HIS TYPING MISTAKE

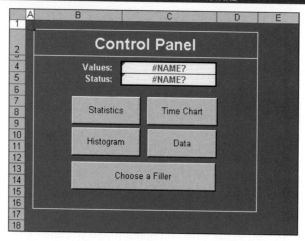

He quickly realized that the Choose_Filler macro would not accept any entry other than a letter from A to E. Later on, he mistakenly typed F again. However, instead of clicking the OK button in the input box, he clicked the Cancel button, but Excel displayed the same results.

What happened? The #NAME? error value means that Excel cannot find the range name that is used in the formula. When Kemp typed the letter F into the input box, the Choose_Filler macro attempted to assign the Filler and Values range names to the cell references "=FillerF" and "=ValuesF." But because there are no such range names in the Datalia2 workbook, Excel had to display the #NAME? error value for those formulas in the workbook that use either the Filler or Values range name.

Similarly, when Kemp clicked the Cancel button, *no* value was assigned to the Source variable in the Choose_Filler macro, so once again the definitions of Filler and Values range names were not properly changed.

You explain this to Kemp, and he understands the problem. He's concerned that other users who are not familiar with Excel will be confused if and when this happens to them. He would like you to modify the Choose_Filler macro somehow to handle this problem.

To do this, you have to create a control structure. A **control structure** is a series of commands that evaluates conditions in your program and then directs the program to perform certain actions based on the status of those conditions. Figure 12-35 shows the kind of control structure that Kemp has in mind for the Choose_Filler macro.

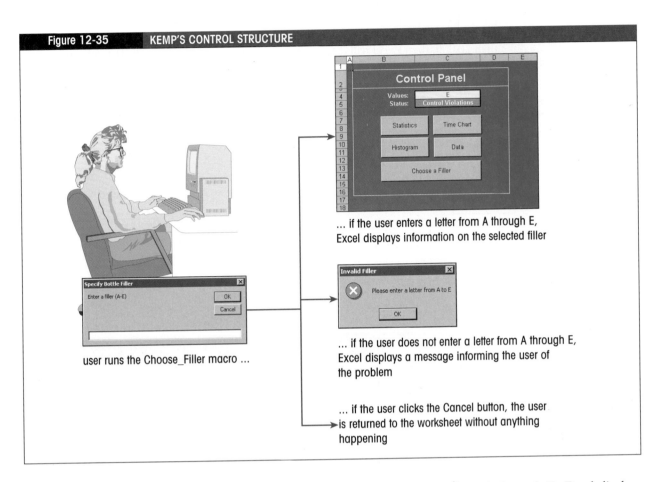

Figure 12-35   KEMP'S CONTROL STRUCTURE

Control Panel

Values: E
Status: Control Violations

Statistics   Time Chart

Histogram   Data

Choose a Filler

... if the user enters a letter from A through E, Excel displays information on the selected filler

Invalid Filler

Please enter a letter from A to E

OK

... if the user does not enter a letter from A through E, Excel displays a message informing the user of the problem

Specify Bottle Filler

Enter a filler (A-E)

OK
Cancel

user runs the Choose_Filler macro ...

... if the user clicks the Cancel button, the user is returned to the worksheet without anything happening

In this control structure, if the user enters a letter from A through E, Excel displays information on the selected filler. However, if the user does not enter a letter from A through E, the program displays a message telling the user what the acceptable entries are. If the user clicks the Cancel button instead of entering a filler letter, the input box closes without doing anything, and the user is returned to the Control Panel worksheet.

To adjust your macro to handle all three of these situations, you'll need to create a VBA If-Then-Else control structure.

Using the If-Then-Else Control Structure

The most commonly used control structure in VBA is the If-Then-Else control structure. In this structure, a condition is evaluated. One set of commands is run if the condition is true and a different set if the condition is false. The syntax for an If-Then-Else control structure is

```
If Condition Then
      Commands if the condition is true
Else
      Commands if the condition is false
End If
```

where *Condition* is a VBA expression that is either true or false. If the condition is true, then the first set of commands is run; otherwise, the second set of commands is run. Figure 12-36 shows an example of an If-Then-Else control structure that might be used in a VBA program to evaluate the conditions of a loan. This macro has two possible outcomes based on whether the user has more than $20,000 in savings or not. If the value of the Savings variable is greater than 20,000, then Excel will display the text "Loan Approved" in cell B10; otherwise, the text string "Loan Denied" is displayed.

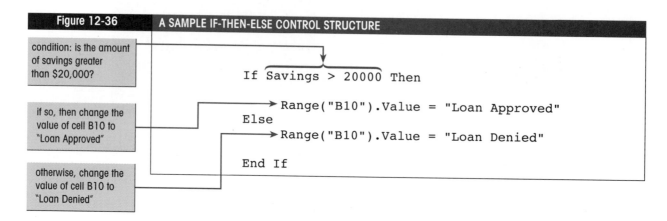

Figure 12-36   A SAMPLE IF-THEN-ELSE CONTROL STRUCTURE

condition: is the amount of savings greater than $20,000?

if so, then change the value of cell B10 to "Loan Approved"

otherwise, change the value of cell B10 to "Loan Denied"

```
If Savings > 20000 Then
        Range("B10").Value = "Loan Approved"
    Else
        Range("B10").Value = "Loan Denied"

    End If
```

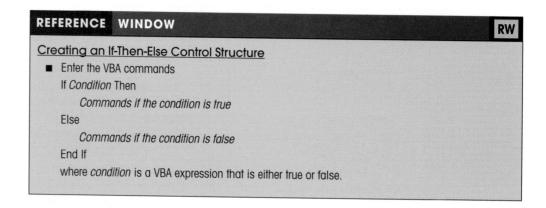

REFERENCE WINDOW   **RW**

Creating an If-Then-Else Control Structure
- Enter the VBA commands
  If *Condition* Then
      Commands if the condition is true
  Else
      Commands if the condition is false
  End If
  where *condition* is a VBA expression that is either true or false.

If your control structure has more than two possible outcomes, you will have to use an If-Then-ElseIf control structure. The syntax for this control structure in VBA is

If *Condition1* Then

    Commands if Condition1 is true

ElseIf *Condition2* Then

    Commands if Condition2 is true

ElseIf *Condition3* Then

    Commands if Condition3 is true

Else

    Commands if none of the conditions are true

End If

where *Condition1*, *Condition2*, *Condition3*, and so forth are expressions that represent three distinct conditions. One can specify an unlimited number of conditions.

Figure 12-37 shows an example of VBA code using multiple conditions in a control structure that evaluates whether or not a user qualifies for a loan. In this example, there are three conditions: 1) the person applying for the loan could have more than $20,000 in savings, 2) she could have between $15,000 and $20,000, or 3) she could have less than $15,000. Based on which of these conditions is true, the text "Loan Approved," "Loan Pending," or "Loan Denied" will be entered into cell B10.

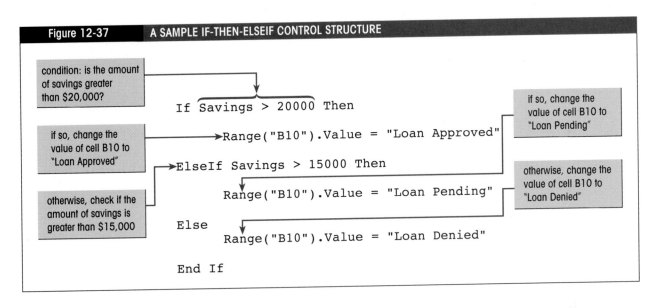

Figure 12-37   A SAMPLE IF-THEN-ELSEIF CONTROL STRUCTURE

condition: is the amount of savings greater than $20,000?

if so, change the value of cell B10 to "Loan Approved"

otherwise, check if the amount of savings is greater than $15,000

if so, change the value of cell B10 to "Loan Pending"

otherwise, change the value of cell B10 to "Loan Denied"

```
If Savings > 20000 Then
        Range("B10").Value = "Loan Approved"
ElseIf Savings > 15000 Then
        Range("B10").Value = "Loan Pending"
Else
        Range("B10").Value = "Loan Denied"

End If
```

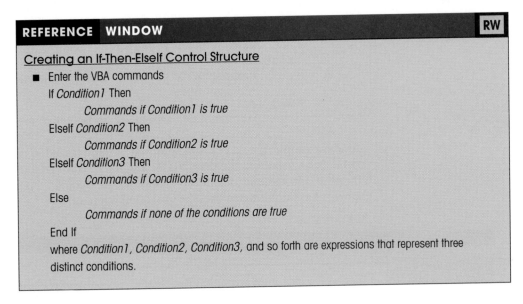

REFERENCE WINDOW   RW

Creating an If-Then-Elself Control Structure

- Enter the VBA commands
    If *Condition1* Then
            Commands if Condition1 is true
    Elself *Condition2* Then
            Commands if Condition2 is true
    Elself *Condition3* Then
            Commands if Condition3 is true
    Else
            Commands if none of the conditions are true
    End If
    where *Condition1, Condition2, Condition3,* and so forth are expressions that represent three distinct conditions.

Comparison and Logical Operators

To determine whether the expression used in the condition is true or false, the expression needs to contain a comparison operator. A **comparison operator** is a symbol used to compare one value with another. You saw one such example in Figure 12-36 and Figure 12-37, in which the > (greater than) sign was used in the expression determining whether the value of the Savings variable was less than 20000. There are other operators you can use in your conditional expressions. Figure 12-38 shows some of the comparison operators you'll frequently use in your VBA control structures.

Figure 12-38	COMPARISON OPERATORS	
COMPARISON OPERATOR		**DESCRIPTION**
>		Greater than
<		Less than
>=		Greater than or equal to
<=		Less than or equal to
=		Equal to
<>		Not equal to
is		Compares whether one object is the same as another

Another type of operator that you'll use in writing conditions for your control structures are logical operators. **Logical operators** are used to combine expressions within a condition. The most commonly used logical operators are the And and Or operators. You use the And operator when you want both expressions to be true before the procedure acts upon them, whereas the Or operator requires only one of the expressions to be true. Figure 12-39 shows an example of a condition that uses the And logical operator.

Figure 12-39	CONDITION USING THE AND OPERATOR

condition using the logical And operator to combine two expressions

```
If Savings > 20000 And Credit = "Good" Then

        Range("B10").Value = "Loan Approved"
Else
        Range("B10").Value = "Loan Denied"

    End If
```

In this example, the text "Loan Approved" will be placed in cell B10 only if the Savings variable has a value greater than 20,000 *and* the Credit variable has the value "GOOD." Otherwise, the value placed in cell B10 is "Loan Denied." Figure 12-40 shows a similar example of a condition that uses the Or logical operator.

Figure 12-40	CONDITION USING THE OR OPERATOR

condition using the logical Or operator to combine two expressions

```
If Savings > 20000 Or Equity = 10000 Then

        Range("B10").Value = "Loan Approved"
Else
        Range("B10").Value = "Loan Denied"

    End If
```

In this example, the loan is approved if either the Savings variable is greater than 20,000 *or* the value of the equity in a home mortgage is greater than 10,000.

As you continue to learn VBA, you'll discover that it supports other control structures. These include the For-Next control structure, which allows you to repeat a series of commands a set number of times, and the Do-While control structure, which repeats a series of commands as long as a particular condition is true.

Writing an If-Then-ElseIf Control Structure

You are ready to write a control structure needed to make the Choose_Filler macro work under all possible conditions. Before you start revising the macro, review the various conditions that you have to account for in the macro and how those conditions relate to the value of the Source variable. The three possible conditions are the following:

- The user enters a valid filler name (the Source variable equals A, B, C, D, or E).
- The user enters an invalid filler name (the Source variable does not equal A, B, C, D, or E).
- The user clicks the Cancel button (the Source variable has no value).

Because you have three conditions to account for, you will have to include an If-Then-ElseIf control structure. Also, you'll have to account for the fact that the first condition (that the user enters a valid name) has five valid answers, and, therefore, that condition will need to contain several expressions linked with the OR operator.

One thing you will have to be careful about is case distinctions. You need to make sure that your control structure works for both uppercase and lowercase letters. You could make the first condition test for 10 valid filler names (testing for both uppercase and lowercase versions of the letters A through E), but that might be too cumbersome. Instead, you will use VBA's UCase function to convert whatever the user enters into the input box to uppercase letters. Then you would only have to test for five letters (uppercase only).

Now you will start editing the Choose_Filler macro to specify the conditions necessary for the macro to work properly.

To edit the Choose_Filler macro:

1. If you took a break after the previous session, make sure Excel is running and open the **Datalia2** workbook located in the Tutorial.12\Tutorial folder on your Data Disk. Enable the macros in the workbook if prompted by Excel.

2. Click **Tools** on the menu bar, point to **Macro**, and click **Macros**.

3. If necessary, click **Choose_Filler** in the Macro name list box, and click the **Edit** button.

   The Visual Basic Editor opens with the Code window displaying the Choose_Filler sub procedure.

The first line you'll add to the macro will convert the text string entered by the user to all uppercase letters. You will then enter the first condition to test whether the user has entered an A, B, C, D, or E.

To enter the first condition in the If-Then-ElseIf control structure:

1. Click the end of the line containing the InputBox function, and press the **Enter** key to open a new blank line.

2. Type **Source=UCase(Source)** and then press the **Enter** key. This indicates that any text string entered into the Source variable will be converted to uppercase letters.

   Now enter the condition that checks whether the Source variable has one of the five allowable values.

3. Type **If Source="A" or Source="B" or Source="C" or Source="D" or Source="E" Then**.

After the IF statement that you just entered, the next two lines add the new definitions for the Filler and Values range name; but this will only happen if the user enters a letter A through E. In the next part of the control structure, you'll account for the two remaining possibilities: the user has entered an invalid filler name in the input box, or, by clicking the Cancel box, has not entered any value. You'll first determine whether a value was entered into the input box, and if so, an error message will display that an incorrect filler name was entered.

To enter the second condition in the If-Then-ElseIf control structure:

1. Click the beginning of the End Sub line, press the **Enter** key, and then press the ↑ key to move the insertion point into the new blank line.

2. Type **ElseIf Source <>"" Then** and then press the **Enter** key. This is the second condition. Assuming that the user did not enter an A, B, C, D, or E, the condition tests whether the Source variable is "not equal to" nothing. In other words, as long as something was entered into the input box, this condition will be true.

   Although you don't know how to display an error message at this point, you will enter a comment statement as a placeholder for this outcome.

3. Type **'Display an error message** and then press the **Enter** key. You'll replace the comment with a VBA command later on.

The only remaining possibility is that the user has entered nothing at all, which would occur if the Cancel button on the input box has been clicked. If this happens, you want the macro to do nothing, so you simply end the If-Then-ElseIf structure without entering any commands for this condition.

To finish the If-Then-ElseIf control structure:

1. Type **End If** and then press the ↓ key. Figure 12-41 displays the Choose_Filler macro at this point in time.

| Figure 12-41 | THE CHOOSE_FILLER CONTROL STRUCTURE |

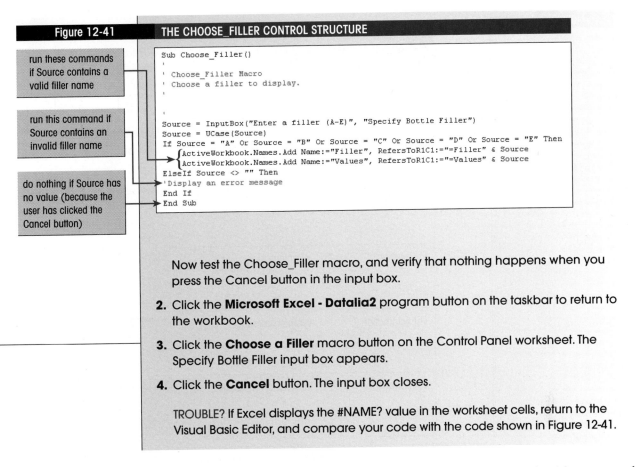

run these commands if Source contains a valid filler name

run this command if Source contains an invalid filler name

do nothing if Source has no value (because the user has clicked the Cancel button)

```
Sub Choose_Filler()
'
' Choose_Filler Macro
' Choose a filler to display.
'
'
'
Source = InputBox("Enter a filler (A-E)", "Specify Bottle Filler")
Source = UCase(Source)
If Source = "A" Or Source = "B" Or Source = "C" Or Source = "D" Or Source = "E" Then
    ActiveWorkbook.Names.Add Name:="Filler", RefersToR1C1:="=Filler" & Source
    ActiveWorkbook.Names.Add Name:="Values", RefersToR1C1:="=Values" & Source
ElseIf Source <> "" Then
'Display an error message
End If
End Sub
```

Now test the Choose_Filler macro, and verify that nothing happens when you press the Cancel button in the input box.

2. Click the **Microsoft Excel - Datalia2** program button on the taskbar to return to the workbook.

3. Click the **Choose a Filler** macro button on the Control Panel worksheet. The Specify Bottle Filler input box appears.

4. Click the **Cancel** button. The input box closes.

TROUBLE? If Excel displays the #NAME? value in the worksheet cells, return to the Visual Basic Editor, and compare your code with the code shown in Figure 12-41.

Your next step is to replace the error message comment in the macro code with a command to display an error message in a dialog box when the user enters an incorrect filler.

Creating a Message Box

To create a message box, you use the MsgBox function, which is similar to the InputBox function you used in the last session, except that MsgBox function does not contain a text box for the user to enter values. You would use a message box for situations where you simply want to send the user a message. The syntax for the MsgBox function is

MsgBox *Prompt, Buttons, Title*

As in the InputBox function, *Prompt* is the message in the dialog box, and *Title* is the text that appears in the title bar. The *Buttons* parameter specifies the kind of buttons that appear in the message box, as well as the style of the message box itself. There are several options you can choose for the Buttons parameter, a few of which are described in Figure 12-42.

Figure 12-42   **VALUES OF THE BUTTON PARAMETER**

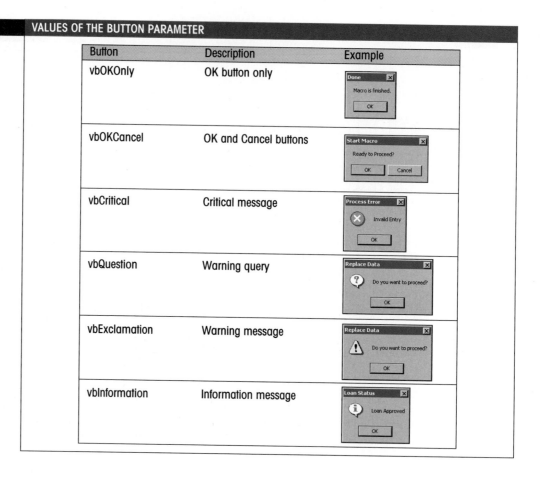

Button	Description	Example
vbOKOnly	OK button only	
vbOKCancel	OK and Cancel buttons	
vbCritical	Critical message	
vbQuestion	Warning query	
vbExclamation	Warning message	
vbInformation	Information message	

Some button styles merely inform, some ask a question, and others provide an alert to a problem of some kind. You don't have to learn the names of these different buttons and message styles; the Visual Basic Editor will display a description box as you enter the MsgBox function.

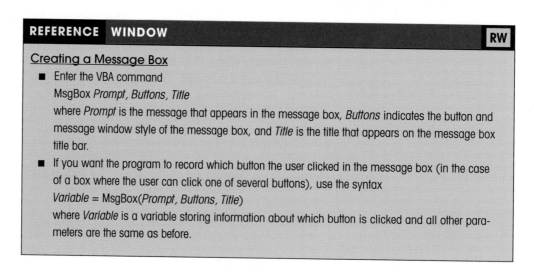

REFERENCE WINDOW   **RW**

Creating a Message Box

- Enter the VBA command

  MsgBox *Prompt, Buttons, Title*

  where *Prompt* is the message that appears in the message box, *Buttons* indicates the button and message window style of the message box, and *Title* is the title that appears on the message box title bar.

- If you want the program to record which button the user clicked in the message box (in the case of a box where the user can click one of several buttons), use the syntax

  Variable = MsgBox(*Prompt, Buttons, Title*)

  where *Variable* is a variable storing information about which button is clicked and all other parameters are the same as before.

Now that you've seen the syntax of the MsgBox function, you can use it in the Choose_Filler macro. Because the message box will be reporting an error on the part of the user, you'll use the vbCritical button style to indicate this fact.

To enter the MsgBox function:

1. Press **Alt + F11** to return to the Visual Basic Editor.

2. Select the comment line you entered as a placeholder in the previous set of steps, and then press the **Delete** key, leaving a blank line in its place.

3. With the insertion point at the beginning of the blank line, press the **Tab** key and type **MsgBox**, and then press the **spacebar**. The Visual Basic Editor displays the syntax for the MsgBox function, with the word "Prompt" bolded.

   TROUBLE? If the insertion point is not at the beginning of a blank line, press the Enter key and then press the ↑ key. The blank line should appear above the End If line.

   You'll first enter the prompt or message that you want to show the user.

4. Type **"Please enter a letter from A to E.",** . After typing the comma, the editor displays a pop-up list box showing all the possible button styles.

5. Double-click **vbCritical** in the list, and then type **,** (another comma).

   The next parameter you need to enter is the text for the message box title bar.

6. Type **"Invalid Filler"** and then press the ↓ key. The completed macro is shown in Figure 12-43

   TROUBLE? If you see an error message, study Figure 12-43 and try retyping the MsgBox command to match the command shown in the figure.

Figure 12-43	COMPLETED CHOOSE_FILLER MACRO

```
Sub Choose_Filler()
'
' Choose_Filler Macro
' Choose a filler to display.
'
'
'
Source = InputBox("Enter a filler (A-E)", "Specify Bottle Filler")
Source = UCase(Source)
If Source = "A" Or Source = "B" Or Source = "C" Or Source = "D" Or Source = "E" Then
    ActiveWorkbook.Names.Add Name:="Filler", RefersToR1C1:="=Filler" & Source
    ActiveWorkbook.Names.Add Name:="Values", RefersToR1C1:="=Values" & Source
ElseIf Source <> "" Then
    MsgBox "Please enter a letter from A to E.", vbCritical, "Invalid Filler"
End If
End Sub
```

MsgBox function ⟶

Now test your macro to verify that it displays a message box when an invalid filler is entered.

7. Click **File** on the menu bar, and then click **Close and Return to Microsoft Excel** to close the Visual Basic Editor and return to the Datalia2 workbook.

8. Click the **Choose a Filler** button on the Control Panel worksheet.

9. Type **f** in the Specify Bottle Filler input box, and then click the **OK** button. Excel displays the message box shown in Figure 12-44.

| Figure 12-44 | INVALID FILLER MESSAGE BOX |

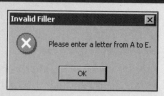

10. Click the **OK** button. You are returned to the Control Panel worksheet.

TROUBLE? If your macro does not work properly, return to the Visual Basic Editor and compare the macro code shown in Figure 12-43 with the code in your Choose_Filler macro.

The macro now appears to work properly. You contact Kemp to show him the new features of the macro and to ask him if there are any more changes he wants you to make.

Creating **Customized Toolbars and Menus**

Kemp has studied the Datalia2 workbook. He's pleased with how easy it is to switch between one filler and another and how the Choose_Filler macro keeps users from entering invalid data. Kemp does have one suggestion. He notices that, whenever he wants to switch between the Statistics, Time Chart, and Histogram worksheets or to choose a different filler, he has to return to the Control Panel worksheet first. Kemp wants to be able to move between these sheets in a single step.

You explain that you could copy all of the macro buttons on the Control Panel worksheet to each of the other sheets in the workbook, but Kemp worries that this will make those other sheets seem too congested. Kemp wonders if you can create a toolbar or menu for those macros that would be accessible from any sheet in the workbook.

Customizing Toolbars and Menus

You tell Kemp that Excel provides users with a wealth of menus and toolbars, useful for almost any situation. However, users do have the ability to customize these menus and toolbars to meet their own needs or to create entirely new menus and toolbars.

One important point, though: the changes you make to Excel's menus and toolbars affect the entire Excel working environment, not just the workbook or worksheet that is currently opened. Any user who works with Excel after you do will confront the modifications you have made. For that reason, you'll make changes to the menu and toolbars for now, but then you'll restore them to their original form before you close Excel. This will allow other Excel users who might be working on different workbooks to work with the default Excel settings.

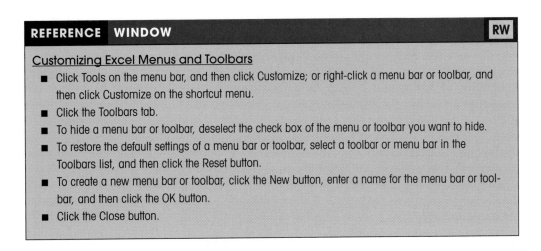

Customizing Excel Menus and Toolbars

- Click Tools on the menu bar, and then click Customize; or right-click a menu bar or toolbar, and then click Customize on the shortcut menu.
- Click the Toolbars tab.
- To hide a menu bar or toolbar, deselect the check box of the menu or toolbar you want to hide.
- To restore the default settings of a menu bar or toolbar, select a toolbar or menu bar in the Toolbars list, and then click the Reset button.
- To create a new menu bar or toolbar, click the New button, enter a name for the menu bar or toolbar, and then click the OK button.
- Click the Close button.

You explain to Kemp that you can create a new toolbar that will contain the buttons for each of the quality control macros that you have created for the Datalia2 workbook.

To create a new toolbar named "QC Tools":

1. Click **Tools** on the menu bar, and then click **Customize**. The Customize dialog box opens.

2. Click the **Toolbars** tab if necessary.

3. Click the **New** button. The New Toolbar dialog box opens.

4. Type **QC Tools** in the Toolbar name text box. See Figure 12-45.

| Figure 12-45 | CUSTOMIZE AND NEW TOOLBAR DIALOG BOXES |

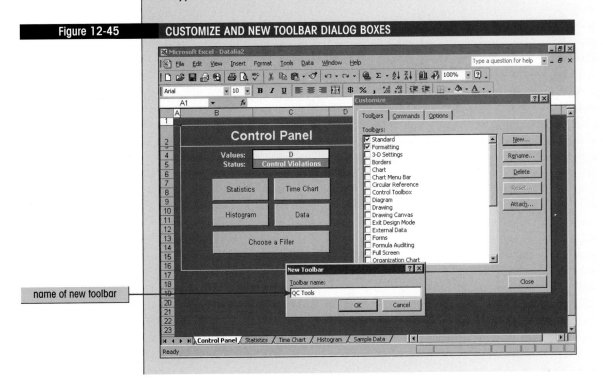

name of new toolbar

5. Click the **OK** button. The new QC Tools toolbar appears.

TROUBLE? If the new toolbar is hidden by the Customize dialog box, drag the dialog box so the toolbar is visible. The new toolbar will be very small because there are not buttons on the toolbar yet.

Your next task is to add the macro buttons to the toolbar.

Inserting a Button or Menu Command

To insert a button or menu command, you drag a command from the Customize dialog box to the toolbar or menu. The Customize dialog box contains a list of all Excel commands and menus and also provides access to the macros you've created.

REFERENCE WINDOW   **RW**

<u>Adding to a Menu or Toolbar</u>
- Open the Customize dialog box, and click the Commands tab.
- To add an existing menu item or button to the menu bar or toolbar, locate the category that contains the menu item or button, and drag it to the menu bar or toolbar.

or
- To create a new item based on a macro, locate the Macros category in the Categories list box, and then drag the Custom Menu Item or Custom Button option to the menu bar or toolbar.

You will create a toolbar button for the Choose_Filler macro on the new toolbar.

To create a toolbar button for the Choose_Filler macro:

1. With the Customize dialog box still open, click the **Commands** tab. The commands available to you are displayed in the Commands list box on the right side of the dialog box. Commands are organized into categories, many of which correspond to the various menus on the original Excel menu bar. You will create toolbar buttons based on your macros.

2. Scroll down the Categories list box, and then click **Macros**. See Figure 12-46.

Figure 12-46 COMMANDS TAB

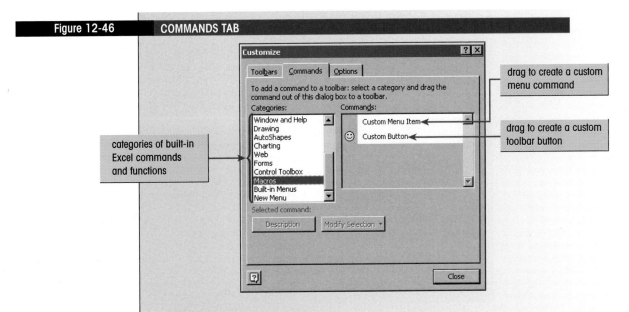

categories of built-in Excel commands and functions

drag to create a custom menu command

drag to create a custom toolbar button

Your macro can be added to a menu bar or toolbar in one of two ways: as a menu item or as a button. Both will operate in the same way. In this case, you'll create a button.

3. Drag **Custom Button** from the Commands list to the empty QC Tools toolbar you just created.

Move the QC Tools toolbar if necessary so it is visible. The QC Tools toolbar should now have a single smiley face button, shown in Figure 12-47.

Figure 12-47 CREATING A CUSTOM TOOLBAR BUTTON

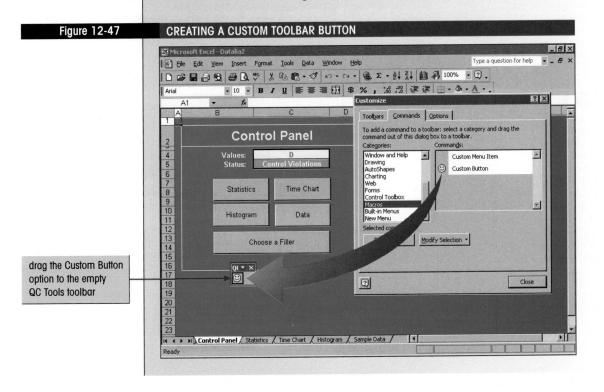

drag the Custom Button option to the empty QC Tools toolbar

At this point, the button is not associated with any macro or menu command. Nor is the default smiley face icon necessarily helpful for the other quality control engineers at Datalia. You'll fix both of those problems by editing the properties of the toolbar button.

Editing a Menu Item or Button

Editing the properties of a menu item or toolbar button enables you to change the name of the item or button, select an image for the item, and choose to display the image with or without text.

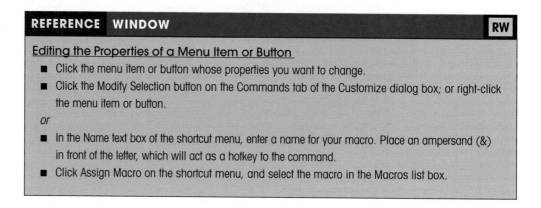

REFERENCE WINDOW   **RW**

Editing the Properties of a Menu Item or Button

- Click the menu item or button whose properties you want to change.
- Click the Modify Selection button on the Commands tab of the Customize dialog box; or right-click the menu item or button.

or

- In the Name text box of the shortcut menu, enter a name for your macro. Place an ampersand (&) in front of the letter, which will act as a hotkey to the command.
- Click Assign Macro on the shortcut menu, and select the macro in the Macros list box.

Kemp wants you assign the Choose_Filler macro to this first toolbar button. He also wants you to change the button image to something that resembles a filler, and he wants you to display the text "Choose a Filler" next to the button icon, so that there is no doubt about what the button does.

To edit the toolbar button:

1. With the new button still selected on the toolbar, click the **Modify Selection** button on the Commands tab of the Customize dialog box. A menu appears that lists the options that you can use to edit the properties of the selected toolbar button. See Figure 12-48.

| Figure 12-48 | MODIFYING A TOOLBAR BUTTON |

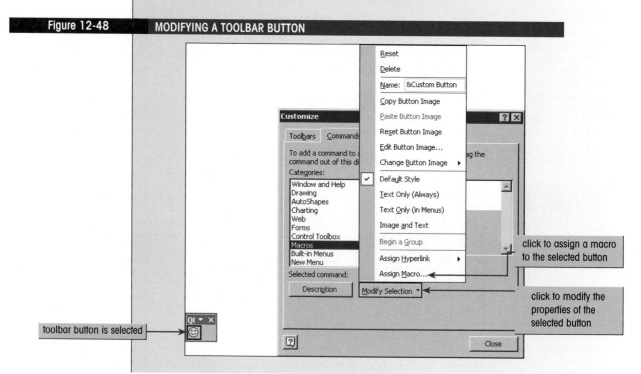

2. Click **Assign Macro** to open the Assign Macro dialog box.

3. Click **Choose_Filler** in the list of macros, and then click the **OK** button.

Next, you will change the button's icon to something resembling a filler.

4. Right-click the smiley button on the QC Tools toolbar, and then point to **Change Button Image** on the shortcut menu. A palette of icons appears.

5. Point to the icon in the first row and fourth column from the left of the palette. See Figure 12-49.

Figure 12-49	CHANGING A BUTTON IMAGE

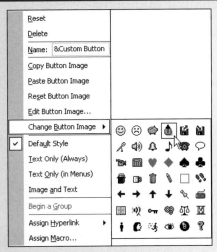

6. Click to select the icon. The selected icon replaces the smiley face image on the toolbar button.

Next, you will change the text associated with the new button and then display that text on the QC Tools toolbar. The default text associated with a new button is "&Custom Button." The ampersand (&) symbol indicates that the letter that follows acts as a hotkey. For example, you can access Excel's File menu by pressing the keyboard combination Alt + F, in which the letter F is the hotkey. The default hotkey for a new toolbar button is the letter C. You can change the default hotkey by typing the ampersand symbol in front of a different letter.

In this case, you will not change the hotkey letter, but you will change the label of this new button to "Choose a Filler" and display the text with the icon on the toolbar.

To edit and display the toolbar button text:

1. Right-click the **filler** button 🔘 on the QC Tools toolbar, and then click in the Name box that appears on the shortcut menu.

2. Edit the default text to read **&Choose a Filler**. Note that the hotkey letter is "C."

3. Click **Image and Text** on the shortcut menu to show both the button image and the button text. Figure 12-50 shows the revised QC Tools toolbar. Note that the letter "C" is underlined, a visual indicator that C acts as the hotkey in this toolbar command.

Figure 12-50   **CHOOSE A FILLER BUTTON**

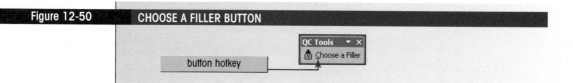

Thus far, you have created a new toolbar and added a button to it. Now you will use the same process to add a menu item to the toolbar. You can use the same process because Excel makes no distinction between toolbar buttons and menu items.

Inserting a Submenu

Toolbars and menus can also contain submenus, useful for separating one group of menus from another or for ensuring that a list of commands doesn't become too long and unwieldy. Kemp wants the QC Tools toolbar to contain buttons for displaying the various sheets in the workbook. You will place all of these buttons on a submenu named "Display," which you will create first.

To create a submenu for the macros:

1. Click **New Menu** in the Categories list.

2. Drag **New Menu** from the Commands list to the QC Tools toolbar, placing the item to the right of the **Choose a Filler** button. See Figure 12-51.

Figure 12-51   **CREATING A MENU ITEM**

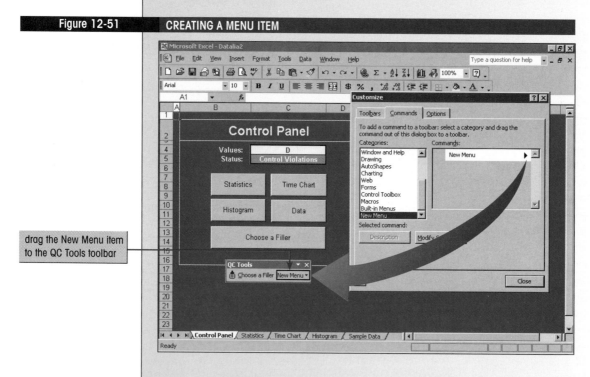

drag the New Menu item to the QC Tools toolbar

3. Right-click **New Menu** on the QC Tools toolbar, and then click in the Name text box on the shortcut menu.

4. Delete the default text, type **&Display**, and then press the **Enter** key. The label for the menu item is now "Display."

Now you'll add toolbar buttons for the remaining macros and place the buttons on the Display submenu.

To create buttons from the remaining macros and place them on the submenu:

1. Click **Macros** in the Categories list.

2. Drag **Custom Button** from the Commands list and position it over the QC Tools toolbar until a blank submenu appears under the Display menu.

3. Release your mouse button to drop the Custom Button image onto the blank submenu. See Figure 12-52.

Figure 12-52	ADDING A TOOLBAR BUTTON ON A SUBMENU

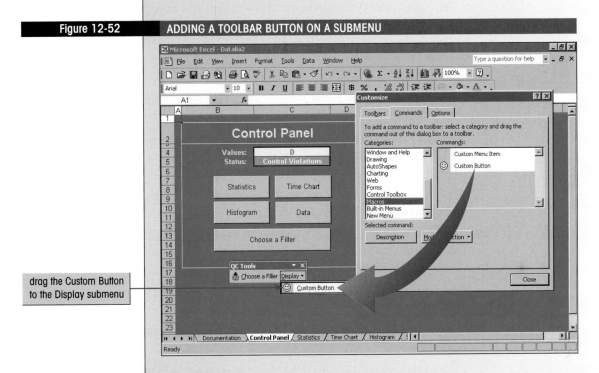

drag the Custom Button to the Display submenu

TROUBLE? If the Custom Button appears on the toolbar as a button, you might not have waited long enough for the Display submenu to appear. Drag the Custom Button off the toolbar, and then repeat Steps 2 and 3, making sure you wait for a blank submenu to appear before releasing your mouse button.

Now assign the Statistics macro to this new button.

4. Right-click the smiley face button icon, click in the Name text box on the short-cut menu, replace the default text with **&Statistics**, click **Assign Macro** on the shortcut menu, click **Statistics** in the list of macros, and then click the **OK** button. Note that the hotkey for the Statistics macro is S.

5. Using the same steps, create the following buttons, placing each of them on the QC Tools toolbar: the **&Time Chart** button assigned to **Time_Chart** macro, the **&Histogram** button assigned to the **Histogram** macro, and the **Data** button assigned to the **Sample_Data** macro. Figure 12-53 shows the completed Display submenu. Note that the hotkey for the Sample Data macro is A, the second letter in the button label.

Figure 12-53   CONTENTS OF THE DISPLAY SUBMENU

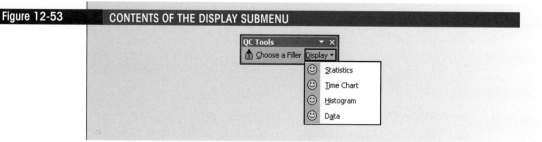

Kemp stops by to see your work in progress. He doesn't like the smiley face button icons. He looks through the list of other button images, but he doesn't see one that he likes there either. You explain that you can edit the button image to create your own customized icon, but that can be a time-consuming task. Another option is to copy an icon from another button or menu item. Kemp sees several icons that he likes and asks you to copy those to the buttons in the Display submenu.

To copy and paste new images to the buttons on the Display submenu:

1. Make sure the Customize dialog box is still open. Note that the Customize dialog box must be open for you to copy and paste selected images to the buttons on the Display submenu.

2. Click **Insert** on the menu bar, right-click **Function**, and then click **Copy Button Image** on the shortcut menu.

3. Click the **Display** submenu on the QC Tools toolbar, right-click **Statistics**, and then click **Paste Button Image** on the shortcut menu. Excel pastes the *fx* image into the Statistics button.

   Now you will copy the Chart button image to the Time Chart macro option on the Display submenu.

4. Click **Insert** on the menu bar, right-click **Chart**, and then click **Copy Button Image**.

5. Click the **Display** submenu, right-click **Time Chart**, and then click **Paste Button Image**.

   You will apply the same image to the Histogram button.

6. Right-click the **Histogram** button on the Display submenu, and then click **Paste Button Image**.

   Finally, you will copy the ▦ from the View menu.

7. Click **View** on the menu bar, right-click **Normal**, and then click **Copy Button Image**.

8. Click the **Display** submenu, right-click **Data**, and then click **Paste Button Image**. Figure 12-54 displays the completed Display menu.

Figure 12-54	FINAL QC TOOLS TOOLBAR

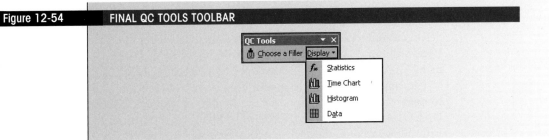

Now test the QC Tools toolbar.

To test the QC Tools toolbar:

1. Click the **Close** button on the Customize dialog box.

2. Click the **Choose a Filler** button on the QC Tools toolbar, type **e** in the input box, and then click the **OK** button to switch to filler E.

3. Click **Display** on the QC Tools toolbar, and then click **Time Chart** to view the time chart for filler E. See Figure 12-55.

Figure 12-55	TIME CHART FOR FILLER E

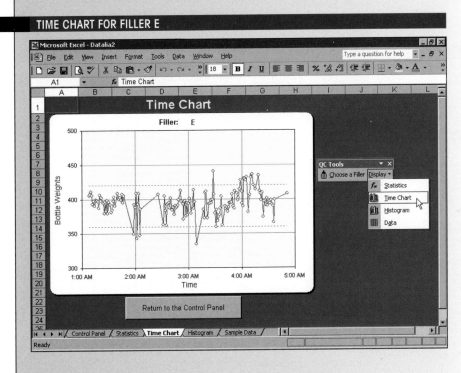

4. Click the remaining buttons in the QC Tools toolbar to verify that they work properly.

Attaching a Toolbar or Menu to a Workbook

Having created a custom toolbar, you might be wondering how it relates to built-in toolbars. A custom toolbar becomes part of the list of toolbars available to Excel. Even after you close the Datalia2 workbook, the QC Tools toolbar will still be displayed in any subsequent workbooks that you open. This can be a bit confusing to other users because the macros used in the toolbar only work with the Datalia2 workbook. It might be useful to unload and delete custom toolbars when the workbooks that rely on them are closed; but unfortunately, Excel will not do this automatically. You can write VBA code to do this automatically, and many VBA programmers use that approach when designing custom applications.

Customized toolbars and menus can also be attached to a workbook, which forces Excel to open the workbook whenever the toolbar or menu is displayed. However, if the workbook is subsequently closed, Excel will still display the custom toolbar, rather than closing it with the workbook. Nevertheless, Kemp would like you to attach the QC Tools toolbar to the Datalia2 workbook.

To attach a toolbar to a workbook:

1. Click **Tools** on the menu bar, and then click **Customize**.

2. Click the **Toolbars** tab.

3. Scroll down the Toolbars list, and then click **QC Tools**.

4. Click the **Attach** button. The Attach Toolbars dialog box opens. Any custom toolbar available in Excel appears in this dialog box.

5. Click **QC Tools** in the Custom toolbars list, and then click the **Copy >>** button. Excel attaches the QC Tools toolbar to the Datalia2 workbook. See Figure 12-56.

| Figure 12-56 | ATTACHING A TOOLBAR TO A WORKBOOK |

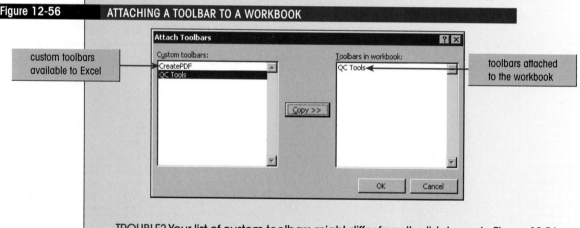

custom toolbars available to Excel

toolbars attached to the workbook

TROUBLE? Your list of custom toolbars might differ from the list shown in Figure 12-56.

6. Click the **OK** button, and then click the **Close** button.

The QC Tools toolbar works just as Kemp had hoped it would. Next, he wants you to modify the appearance of Excel's menus and worksheets. Kemp does not want the other elements of Excel to distract users, so he wants to only display the Datalia2 workbook, the QC Tools toolbar, and only a few of the other Excel screen elements.

Customizing Excel Screen Elements

Excel's screen elements fall into two general categories: those that are part of the Excel workbook window and those that are part of the worksheet. The difference is important. When you hide screen elements that are part of the workbook window, those elements will be hidden in *all* Excel workbooks that you open, whereas screen elements that are part of the worksheet will be hidden in that worksheet only. Other worksheets and workbooks will be unaffected. Figure 12-57 displays the screen elements that you'll hide and to which category they belong.

Figure 12-57	EXCEL SCREEN ELEMENTS

SCREEN ELEMENT	PART OF THE...
Formula bar	Workbook window
Horizontal and vertical scrollbars	Worksheet
Row and column headers	Worksheet
Sheet tabs	Worksheet
Startup Task Pane	Workbook window
Status bar	Workbook window
Toolbars	Workbook window
Worksheet gridlines	Worksheet

You can hide these elements using Excel's Options dialog box. The Options dialog box contains a list of features that you can modify to control how Excel behaves on your system. You'll use it now to determine what Excel displays and what it hides. First, though, you'll group your worksheets, so that when you hide screen elements that are part of individual worksheets, these changes will be reflected in all of the sheets in the group.

To hide elements of the Excel window:

1. Click the **Control Panel** tab, and then group the worksheets from the Control Panel to the Sample Data sheet. The color of the grouped worksheet tabs changes to white, and the text ("Group") appears in the title bar.

   TROUBLE? To group worksheets, click the first sheet in the group, press and hold the Shift key, and then click the last sheet that you want to include in the group.

2. Click **Tools** on the menu bar, and then click **Options**. The Options dialog box opens.

3. If necessary, click the **View** tab. This tab contains a list of the screen elements that you can choose to hide. Note that some of these elements are associated with the Excel workbook window and will be hidden in all Excel workbooks, and some apply only to those sheets that you've just grouped.

4. Deselect the following elements by clicking the appropriate check boxes: **Startup Task Pane, Formula bar, Status bar, Gridlines, Row & column headers, Horizontal scroll bar**, and **Sheet tabs**. See Figure 12-58.

Figure 12-58   OPTIONS DIALOG BOX

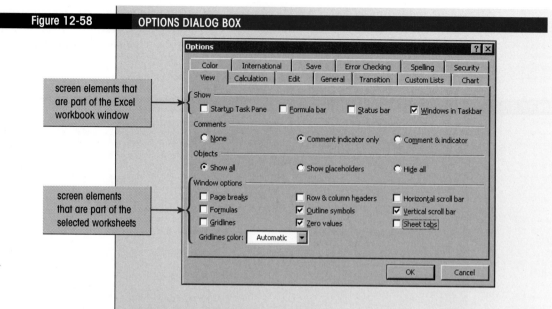

screen elements that
are part of the Excel
workbook window

screen elements
that are part of the
selected worksheets

5. Click the **OK** button.

6. Click **View** on the menu bar, point to **Toolbars**, and then deselect all of the toolbars in the list *except* the QC Tools toolbar. The view of your workbook is changed with several of Excel's screen elements now hidden from the user.

You've managed to hide several elements of the screen, and now the users will only see the contents of each worksheet and the Excel menu. If users want to move from one worksheet to another, they'll have to use the buttons you've created. As a final task, Kemp wants you to edit the contents of the Excel menu bar.

Editing Built-In Toolbars and Menus

All of the techniques that you've used to edit the contents of the QC Tools toolbar can be used on Excel's own built-in toolbars and menus. Kemp would like you to simplify the Excel interface for other users, who may be confused by the many menus and commands that Excel offers. Instead, he would like the main menu bar to only display the File menu. Don't worry; you'll restore the menu bar later.

To remove the other menus from the main menu bar:

1. Click **Tools** on the menu bar, and then click **Customize**.

2. Click **Help** on the menu bar.

3. Drag **Help** off the menu bar onto the display area so that the pointer changes to ▧.

4. Release the mouse button. The Help menu is now removed from the menu bar.

5. Continue removing the remaining menus from the menu bar, except for the File menu.

6. Click the **Close** button in the Customize dialog box. Figure 12-59 shows the final appearance of the Excel workbook with all screen elements hidden or removed except for the File menu and the QC Tools toolbar.

Figure 12-59	THE FINAL VERSION OF KEMP'S APPLICATION

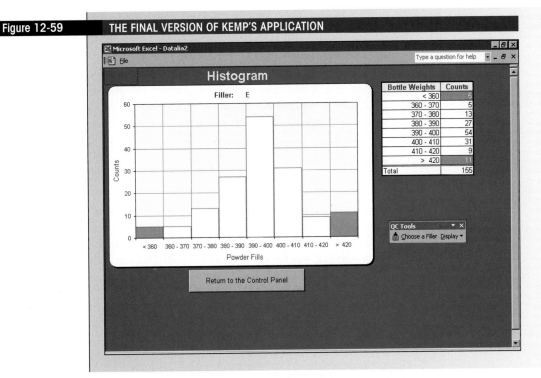

You show Kemp the Excel screen, and he's pleased with the plain, simple look. He tells you to go ahead and restore Excel to its former appearance.

Resetting Built-In Menus and Toolbars

You can reset the menu bar using the same Customize dialog box you used to modify it in the first place. You'll also restore the Standard and Formatting toolbar that you hid earlier.

To restore the Excel menu bar and other toolbars:

1. Right-click the **Excel menu bar**, and then click **Customize** on the shortcut menu.

2. Make sure the **Toolbars** tab is selected.

3. Click the **Standard** and the **Formatting** check boxes in the Toolbars list box.

4. Scroll down the list and make sure the Worksheet Menu Bar check box is selected, and then click the **Reset** button.

5. Click the **OK** button when prompted to reset the changes you've made.

6. Click the **Close** button.

Now restore the other screen elements.

To restore the other screen elements:

1. Click **Tools** on menu bar, and then click **Options**.

2. Click the **View** tab, and then select the **Startup Task Pane**, **Formula bar**, and **Status bar** check boxes to restore these screen elements. You do not have to restore the other screen elements because they are native to each individual worksheet and will not affect the appearance of other, unrelated, workbooks or worksheets.

3. Click the **OK** button.

If you want to return the customized menu bar you created, you'll have to go through the editing process again. You can also use the Customize dialog box to create your own menu or toolbar that will be attached to the workbook or use VBA to automate the process of editing the Excel menu bar; but those are more advanced topics. You can finish your work.

To finish your work:

1. Click the **Return to the Control Panel** button to return to the Control Panel worksheet, if necessary.

2. Close the Datalia2 workbook, saving your changes.

As part of your cleanup, you should also delete the QC Tools toolbar so that it doesn't appear in other, unrelated Excel workbooks. Don't worry, since you attached the toolbar to the Datalia2 workbook, it will reappear the next time you open that file.

To delete the QC Tools toolbar:

1. Click **Tools** on the menu bar, and then click **Customize**.

2. If necessary, click the **Toolbars** tab.

3. Scroll down the list of toolbars, and then click **QC Tools**.

4. Click the **Delete** button, and then click the **OK** button.

5. Click the **Close** button.

6. Exit Excel.

Kemp is very pleased with the job you've done and looks forward to using your workbook with new quality control data. He feels that your Excel workbook is user friendly and that it will help other users find the information they want easily, even if they aren't familiar with Excel.

Session 12.3 QUICK | CHECK

1. What is a control structure, and why might you need one in your VBA procedure?

2. Define the terms comparison operator and logical operator.

3. What is the syntax of the If-Then-Else control structure?

4. What control structure would you use if you had multiple conditions from which to choose?

5. What is the syntax of the MsgBox function?

6. What command would you enter to display a message box with the following elements: the text "File Status" in the title bar, the message "File Saved," and a single OK button in the dialog box.

REVIEW ASSIGNMENTS

Kemp has come up with a new version of his workbook for which he wants you to create macros. In this version, he has placed the time charts and histogram charts for each of the five fillers on separate chart sheets. Also, the Statistics worksheet now displays statistics on all five fillers.

Kemp wants you to create a custom toolbar to allow users to select different sheets to view. As before, you'll create an input box in which users can enter a letter from A through E (for fillers A through E). Any macros you create should verify that the user has entered a valid value.

To complete this task:

1. Open the **Powder1** workbook located in the Tutorial.12\Review folder on your Data Disk. Enter the date and your name in the Documentation sheet. Save the workbook as **Powder2** in the same folder.

2. Start the Visual Basic Editor and display the Properties window and Project Explorer. (*Hint*: If necessary, restore the Properties window so you can see the Project Explorer.)

3. Change the name of the Powder project from VBAProject to "QC_Report", and enter "Quality Report for Datalia Fillers" as the project description.

Explore   4. Using the Insert menu on the VBA Editor's menu bar, insert a new Module folder into the QC_Report project (do *not* insert a Class Module).

Explore   5. Within the Module1 module, insert a VBA sub procedure named "Show_Statistics", which first selects the Statistics worksheet and then selects cell A1.

6. Create a second sub procedure named "Show_Data", which selects the Sample Data worksheet and then selects cell A1.

Explore   7. Create a sub procedure named "Show_Histogram" that performs the following tasks:

   ■ Displays an input box with the message "What filler do you wish to view?" and the title "Display Histogram" to prompt users to enter the value of the variable named "Filler".

   ■ Changes the value of the Filler variable to uppercase letters.

- If Filler equals "A", "B", "C", "D," or "E," selects the Histogram sheet for the selected filler. (*Hint*: All Histogram sheets have the name "Histogram *filler*," where *filler* is a letter from A to E. Use the ampersand to add the value of the Filler variable to the text string "Histogram" in order to select the correct sheet from the workbook.)

- Else, if Filler is not equal to a missing value, displays a message box with the text "Please enter a letter from A through E" and with the title of the message box "Invalid Filler". Use the vbInformation button type.

8. Create a sub procedure named "Show_Time_Chart" similar to the Show_Histogram sub procedure, except that the new sub procedure should display the Time Chart sheet rather than the Histogram sheet.

Explore

9. Return to the Powder2 workbook, and then create a custom toolbar named "QC Report". The QC Report toolbar should contain the following:

- A command button named "&Show Statistics" assigned to the Show_Statistics macro; the button should display both the text and the "eye" button image (taken from the palette of button images on the Change Button Image menu).

- A command button named "Show &Data" assigned to the Show_Data macro; format the button to display both the text and the "eye" button image.

- A menu item named "&Charts".

- A command button named "&Histogram" placed on the Charts submenu; the Histogram button should be assigned to the Show_Histogram macro and have a chart image (copied from the Chart command on the Insert menu).

- A command button named "&Time Chart" placed on the Charts menu, assigned to the Show_Time_Chart macro; the button should also display a chart image.

10. Attach the QC Report toolbar to the Powder2 workbook.

11. Test the macro buttons in the QC Report toolbar, and verify that the proper sheets are displayed for each button and that the input box properly tests for valid filler names.

12. Group the Statistics worksheet through the Sample Data worksheet. Hide the sheet tabs and the row and column headers for the worksheet group.

13. Save your changes to the Powder2 workbook, and then close the workbook.

14. Delete the QC Report toolbar before exiting Excel.

CASE PROBLEMS

Case 1. Creating a Stock Reporter for Davis & Larson Lee Ellis is a broker at the investment firm of Davis & Larson. She is tracking the behavior of 24 different stocks in a customer's portfolio. She has placed data on those stocks in a workbook named "Sdata." The information on each stock has been placed in 24 different worksheets with each sheet named with the stock's symbol. For example, stock information on the Goodyear Tire and Rubber has been placed in worksheet named "GT" because that is the company's symbol on the New York Stock Exchange. In addition, Lee has recorded the last five days worth of closing prices for each of the 24 stocks and placed that information in a worksheet named "Last Five Days."

Because working with a file that has 25 worksheets can be cumbersome, Lee has created a second workbook named "SReport1," which she can use to display summary information on a single stock. Currently, the workbook displays information on Aluminum Company of America (stock symbol AA). All of the stock values in the workbook are linked to source data in the SData workbook. If Lee wants to display information on a different stock, she has to use Excel's Find and Replace command to replace the text "AA" in a selected range with the text of the stock symbol she wants to view. The updated formulas will then display information on the new stock.

Lee would like to automate this process. She has added a drop-down list box that displays 24 stock symbols. She wants to be able to select a stock from the list and have Excel automatically perform the Find and Replace command, replacing the current stock data with data from the stock selected in the list box. Figure 12-60 shows a preview of the workbook that Lee has asked you to create.

Figure 12-60

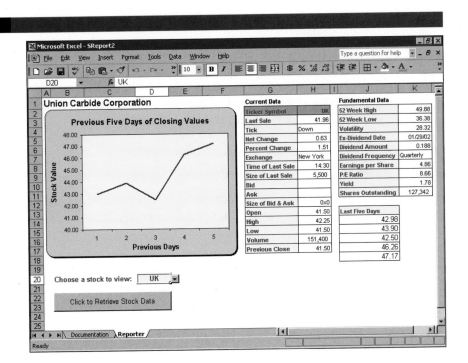

To complete this task:

1. Open the **SReport1** workbook located in the Tutorial.12\Cases folder on your Data Disk. Update the data source (SData workbook) linked to this workbook. Enter the date and your name in the Documentation sheet. Save the workbook as **SReport2** in the same folder. Switch to the Reporter worksheet.

   All of the values in the range A1:K18 of the Reporter worksheet are actually formulas, linked to the contents of the SData workbook. Cell H2 contains the stock symbol of the current viewed stock (AA). Cell D20 contains the stock symbol of the stock that Lee wants to view (in this case, IBM).

Lee wants the Click to Retrieve Stock Data macro button to automatically replace all occurrences of the text string "AA" with the text string "IBM" in the cell range A1:K18. The syntax for performing the Replace method on a range is

```
Range.Replace OldText, NewText
```

where *range* is a VBA object for a range of values, *OldText* is the text to be replaced, and *NewText* is the new text string. Lee also wants the Excel status bar to display information on data transfer. The syntax for changing the text of the Excel status bar is

```
Application.StatusBar = StatusBarText
```

where *StatusBarText* is the text you want displayed in the status bar. To return the status bar back to its default text, set *StatusBarText* to the value false.

2. Using the right-click method, assign a new macro named "Retrieve_Stock", and then open the Visual Basic Editor. (*Hint*: Click the New button in the Assign Macro dialog box.)

Explore ▶ 3. Insert the following commands (in the following order) into the Retrieve_Stock sub procedure:

   a. Create a variable named "OldStock" and set it equal to the value of cell H2.
   b. Create a variable named "NewStock" and set it equal to the value of cell D20.
   c. Change the text of the status bar to "Retrieving data on *NewStock* ...," where *NewStock* is the value of the NewStock variable. (*Hint*: Use the ampersand symbol (&) to place the value of the NewStock variable into the text of the status bar.)
   d. Replace all occurrences of "OldStock" with "NewStock" in the cell range A1:K18.
   e. Set the value of the status bar back to false.

4. Close the Visual Basic Editor and return to the SReport2 workbook.

Explore ▶ 5. Change the View options of the Reporter worksheet, hiding the sheet's gridlines. Also, do not display zero values in the worksheet.

6. Test the Retrieve_Stock macro by replacing all occurrences of "AA" with "IBM" to retrieve information on IBM stock; then, using the drop-down list box, retrieve stock information on Union Carbide (UK). (*Hint*: Make sure cell D20 is selected.)

7. Print the contents of the Reporter worksheet.

8. Save and close the workbook, and exit Excel.

Case 2. Creating an Order Entry Form for Maxwell Scientific   Karen Rosinski is a distributor for Maxwell Scientific, a company that specializes in science materials for educators. She is maintaining an inventory list in an Excel workbook. She would like to design an application to make it easier for her to enter new orders. The application should allow her to enter the order information in an Excel form, paste that information into an order history list in a separate worksheet, and then update the inventory list to reflect the new order. She has asked your help in writing a VBA program to automate this task.

To automate this task, you'll have to work with the WorksheetFunction property of the Application object. The WorksheetFunction property enables you to use Excel functions within your VBA programs. The syntax of the property is

   Variable = Application.WorksheetFunction.*function*(*parameters*)

where *Variable* is a VBA variable that will store the value of the function, *function* is the name of an Excel function, and *parameters* are the parameters required by the function. For example, to calculate the sum of the values in the range A1:A10, you would enter the formula *SUM(A1:A10)* in your Excel workbook. To do the same thing in a VBA macro, you would enter the command

Total = Application.WorksheetFunction.Sum(Range("A1:A10"))

which stores the sum of the values in a variable named "Total". Note that you have to use the VBA range object in the parameter list, *not* simply the text "A1:A10".

To complete this task:

1. Open the **Maxwell1** workbook located in the Tutorial.12\Cases folder on your Data Disk. Enter the date and your name in the Documentation sheet. Save the workbook as **Maxwell2** in the same folder. Switch to the Order Form worksheet.

2. Enter the order shown in Figure 12-61 into the form.

Figure 12-61

ITEMS TO ORDER		SEND TO:	
Order ID	R2	Name:	Alan Wilkes
Stock ID	M0507	School Name:	Lincoln High
Items to Order	20	Address:	55 Hampton Rd. Grovefield, CA 90215

3. Record the following steps in a macro named "Insert_Order":
   a. Go to the Submitted Orders worksheet.
   b. Select the third row of the worksheet, and insert a new row, pushing the current order down to the fourth row.
   c. Return to the Order Form worksheet, and copy the range C4:C11.
   d. Switch to the Submitted Orders worksheet, select cell A3, open the Paste Special dialog (from the Edit menu), click the Values option button, click the Transpose check box, and then click the OK button to paste the transposed values into the worksheet.
   e. Return to the Order Form worksheet, and copy the range C14:C19.
   f. Return to the Submitted Orders worksheet, select cell I3, and using the Paste Special dialog box, paste the transposed values into the worksheet.
   g. Click cell A1 on the Submitted Orders worksheet, and then return to the Order Form worksheet.
   h. Clear the contents of cells C4, C5, C8, and C14:C19.
   i. Click cell C4.

Explore   4. Open the Visual Basic Editor by editing the Insert_Order macro.

5. After the VBA comments in the Insert_Order sub procedure, but *before* the commands generated by the macro recorder, insert the commands that will:
   a. Store the value of cell C6 in a variable named "Item" (this is the name of the item ordered by the user).
   b. Store the value of cell C8 in a variable named "Ordered" (this is the quantity of the order).
   c. Use the VLOOKUP function along with the WorksheetFunction property of the Application object to determine the amount of the ordered item currently remaining in stock. (*Hint*: The lookup_value parameter should be Range("C5"), the table_array parameter should be Range("Inventory"), the col_index_num parameter should be 6, and the range_lookup parameter should be set to false.) Store this value in a variable named "Instock".

d. Create a variable named "Remaining" that is equal to the Instock variable minus the Ordered variable (this variable represents how much of the item will be now remaining if the order is processed).

Explore

6. Insert the following control structure into the Insert_Order sub procedure:

- If the value of the Remaining variable is greater than or equal to zero, then run the commands generated by the macro recorder (the commands that paste the order into the Submitted Orders worksheet), and display the message "You have *Remaining Item* remaining in stock." where *Remaining* and *Item* are the values of the Remaining and Item variables. The title of the message box should be "Order Entered." Use the vbInformation button style.

- Otherwise, do *not* run the commands generated by the macro recorder because there are not enough items in stock to cover the order. Instead, display the message "There are only *Instock Item* in stock." where *Instock* is the value of the Instock variable and *Item* is the value of the Item variable. The message box title should be "Order Rejected". Use the vbCritical button style.

7. Return to the Maxwell2 workbook, and then assign the Insert_Order macro to the macro button on the Order Form worksheet.

8. Save the Maxwell2 workbook.

9. Test the Insert_Order macro by submitting the orders, shown in Figure 12-62, into the workbook. Does the macro correctly indicate that the third order will exceed the quantity of lens kits available? Resubmit the order, ordering as many items as there are in stock. (Note: If your macro fails to work correctly, reopen the saved version of the Maxwell2 workbook and rewrite the macro.)

Figure 12-62

ITEMS TO ORDER			SEND TO:	
Order ID	R3		Name:	Debbie Larson
Stock ID	E1029		School Name:	King Middle School
Items to Order	34		Address:	14 West Wilson
				Erin, CA 90321
Order ID	R4		Name:	Cindy Grant
Stock ID	01003		School Name:	Tori High School
Items to Order	25		Address:	25 School Rd.
				Engleton, CA 90155
Order ID	R5		Name:	Kevin Li
Stock ID	01003		School Name:	Lawton High School
Items to Order	19		Address:	29 Oak Ave.
				Lawton, CA 92011

10. Once the macro works correctly, save your changes to the Maxwell2 workbook. Close the workbook and then exit Excel.

Case 3. Creating a Custom Function for Stock Valuation Luis Sanchez manages funds at Columbia Securities, a brokerage firm in Newport, Iowa. One aspect of Luis's job is to determine the risk factor associated with various stocks and funds. He has many tools at his disposal. One important mathematical function that he uses is the Capital Asset Pricing Model, or CAPM. The CAPM formula is

$$CAPM = R_F + B(R_M - R_F)$$

where R_F is the rate of return on a safe investment, such as a treasury bond, R_M is the rate of a return on a market benchmark, such as the S & P 500, and B (called "beta") is the risk factor that measures the behavior of a stock relative to the behavior of the market benchmark. A beta value greater than 1 indicates a stock that shows greater fluctuation in value (and hence greater risk) relative to the market benchmark. A stock with a beta value of 3 is said to be three times more risky than the overall market.

If Louis is examining a stock that has a beta value of 1.5 and knows that a safe investment like a treasury bond has a 5% rate of return, and the overall market is providing a 7.5% rate of return, the rate of return for the stock should be $0.05 + 1.5(0.075 - 0.05) = 0.0875$ or 8.75%. If Luis doesn't feel that the stock will attain this level of return, he might recommend against investing in it because of the increased risk compared to the market benchmark.

Luis feels that the CAPM formula is useful and wishes that Excel had included it in its list of financial functions. He has asked you for help in creating his own function.

To create a customized function, you must create a function procedure in VBA. The syntax for a function procedure is

```
Function function_name(parameters)
    VBA commands
    function_name = expression
End Function
```

where *function_name* is the name of the custom function, and *parameters* is a list of parameters (separated by commas) required by the function. Note that *function_name* is listed twice: once in the Function statement that starts the function procedure and then again when it is assigned a value by a VBA *expression*. Luis wants you to create a customized function whose *function_name* is CAPM and which will have three parameters labeled: RF, Beta, and RM.

To complete this task:

1. Open the **CAPM1** workbook located in the Tutorial.12\Cases folder on your Data Disk. Enter the date and your name in the Documentation sheet. Save the workbook as **CAPM2** in the same folder.

2. Open the Visual Basic Editor, and then change the name of the CAPM2 project from "VBAProject" to "Risk_Analysis".

3. Insert a new module in the Risk_Analysis module named "Functions".

Explore 4. Use the Insert Procedure command to insert a public function procedure named "CAPM".

Explore 5. Add the following parameters to the CAPM function procedure: RF, Beta, and RM.

Explore 6. Insert a line into the CAPM function procedure to calculate the value of the CAPM function.

7. Exit the VBA Editor and return to the Stocks worksheet in the CAPM2 workbook.

Explore 8. Use the Insert Function command to enter the CAPM function into cell J2 on the Stocks worksheet. Look for the function in the User Defined category of the functions displayed in the Insert Function dialog box.

9. Fill the CAPM function into the rest of the stock values in the range J2:J23.

10. Sort the stock in order of descending CAPM values. Are there any stocks whose CAPM values indicate a lower rate of return than the risk-free treasury bonds?

11. Print the contents of the Stocks worksheet.

12. Save and close the workbook and then exit Excel.

Case 4. Creating a Documentation Sheet Macro Sally Crawford works at BG Software, a company that produces educational software for children. Sally uses Excel workbooks to track product plans, schedules, marketing, and sales. Sally knows that documentation sheets are an important element of an Excel workbook. They allow others who look at the workbook to quickly see its purpose and contents. The steps Sally takes to create the documentation sheets are always the same from workbook to workbook. She could save herself time if she had a macro that automated the process of creating the sheet. Figure 12-63 shows the general format of Sally's documentation sheet.

Figure 12-63

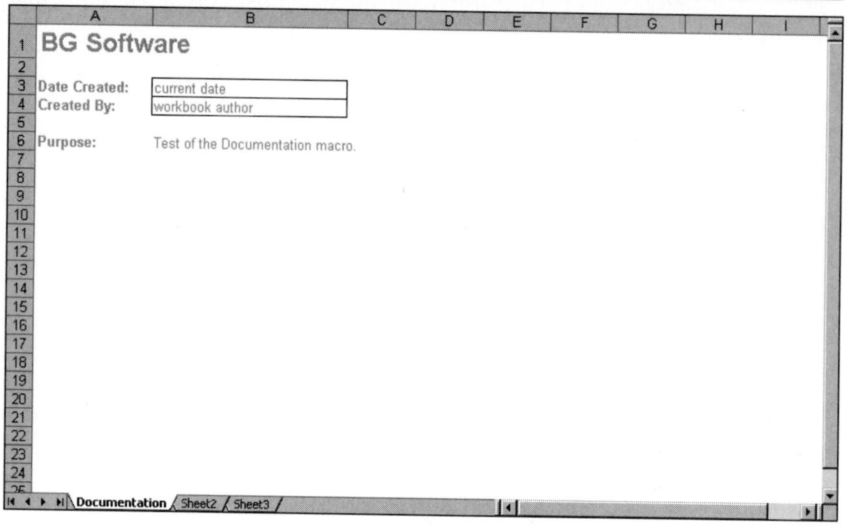

The contents of cells B3, B4, and B6 vary from workbook to workbook. To enter this information, Sally wants the macro to either prompt for the information or get the information from the workbook's properties. Sally has asked you to create the macro for her.

To complete this task:

1. Start Excel and create a new workbook named **BG** in the Tutorial.12\Cases folder on your Data Disk.

2. Use the macro recorder to create a macro named "Documentation" that renames the Sheet1 worksheet as "Documentation" and formats the sheet as shown in Figure 12-63. Enter the default text from Figure 12-63 in cells B3, B4, and B6 to act as placeholders for the text that you want to place into the sheet.

Explore   3. Edit the Documentation macro using the Visual Basic Editor, replacing the references to Sheets("Sheet 1") with the ActiveSheet object.

Explore   4. Create a variable named "DateCreated" that is equal to the VBA DATE function. (*Hint*: Look up information on the Date function using the VBA Editor's online Help.)

Explore   5. Create a variable named "Author" that is equal to the UserName property of the Application object.

6. Create a variable named "Purpose" whose value is entered by the user via an input box.

Explore   7. Replace the placeholder text that you inserted into cells B3, B4, and B6 with the values of the DateCreated, Author, and Purpose variables.

8. Return to the BG workbook. Delete the Documentation sheet and run the Documentation macro on the active worksheet, verifying that the macro properly renames the current sheet as the new Documentation sheet in the workbook.

9. Attach a toolbar to the workbook named "Utilities", containing a macro button named "&Format as a Documentation Sheet", assigned to the Documentation macro. Assign an appropriate button image to the toolbar button.

10. Save and close the BG workbook, and then delete the Utilities toolbar before exiting Excel.

INTERNET ASSIGNMENTS

Student Union

The purpose of the Internet Assignments is to challenge you to find information on the Internet that you can use to create effective spreadsheets. The actual assignments are updated and maintained on the Course Technology Web site. Log on to the Internet and use your Web browser to go to the Student Union on the New Perspectives Series site at **www.course.com/NewPerspectives/studentunion**. Click the Online Companions link, and then click the link for this text.

QUICK CHECK ANSWERS

Session 12.1

1. a) The Project Explorer gives a hierarchical view of the objects in your project.
   b) The Properties window gives you a view of the properties of the individual objects.
   c) The Code window displays the VBA code for your project's macros.

2. a) a collection of macros, worksheets, forms for data entry, and other items that make up the customized application you're trying to create
   b) an element of an application, such as a worksheet, cell, chart, form, or report
   c) an attribute of an object that defines one of its characteristics, such as its name, size, color, or location on the screen
   d) a collection of macros
   e) the set of rules specifying how you must enter certain commands

3. Select the property and press the F1 key.

4. sub, function, and property

5. Sub *Procedure_Name (parameters)*
   Visual Basic Commands
   End Sub

6. to organize macros based on their content and purpose

Session 12.2

1. a) a programming language that performs tasks by manipulating objects
   b) an object that is composed of a group of other objects
   c) an action that can be performed on a object
   d) a piece of information that controls how the method or function is used
   e) a named element in a program that can be used to store and retrieve information

2. Sheets("Histogram").Name="Histogram Chart"

3. Sheets("Histogram").Select

4. Sheetname = ActiveSheet.Name

5. Lastname = InputBox("Enter your last name", "Log In")

Session 12.3

1. A control structure is a series of commands that evaluates conditions in your program and then directs the program to perform certain actions based on the status of those conditions. Control structures are necessary for macros that need to perform different actions for different conditions.

2. A comparison operator is a word or symbol that is used to compare values or expressions within a condition. A logical operator is used to combine conditions within an expression.

3. If *condition* Then

     VBA commands if the condition is true

Else

     VBA commands if the condition is false

End If

4. If-Then-ElseIf control structure

5. MsgBox *Prompt, Button, Title*

6. MsgBox "Filed Saved", vbOKOnly, "File Status"

In this case you will:

- Create a template worksheet

- Format a worksheet to improve its appearance

- Enhance a worksheet with varied fonts and borders

- Create data validation based on a list of numbers

- Protect worksheet cells

- Use TODAY, IF and VLOOKUP functions

- Create a print macro

SALES INVOICING FOR ISLAND DREAMZ SHOPPE

CASE

Island Dreamz Shoppe

Like many entrepreneurs, Nicole Richardson discovered the old-fashioned way to make money: choose something you like to do, keep costs low and quality high, and make teamwork a priority. This principle led to the success of her Island Dreamz Shoppe, a gift gallery featuring crafts of artists from the Caribbean whose jewelry, paintings, and embroidered giftware capture the spirit of the islands.

Since the gallery opened two years ago, business has been brisk. Responding to requests from many of her customers, Nicole expanded her business to include mail orders. When customers visit the Shoppe, Nicole gives them a catalog to take home. Many customers find it more convenient to order items after they return home than to cram extra gifts into an already overstuffed suitcase.

On a good day, Nicole receives about a dozen phone calls from customers who want to place orders. With so few calls, she doesn't need a full-blown order-entry system, but she would like to automate her invoice preparation. She decides to create an Excel template for her sales invoices. After she creates the template, all she needs to do is enter data for each order and print the invoice.

Nicole recently completed a paper invoice for an order from Rachel Nottingham, shown in Figure AC-1. Using this invoice as a model for the labels, formulas, and format that she wants to use in her template worksheet, Nicole prepares her planning analysis sheet (Figure AC-2). The calculations she needs in the template include the current date, the unit price of each item ordered times the quantity ordered (the extended price), the total amount for all items, the sales tax, the shipping cost, and the total amount of the order.

Figure AC-1 | **ISLAND DREAMZ SHOPPE SALES INVOICE**

Island Dreamz Shoppe
1001 Anchor Cove
Montego Bay, Jamaica, B.W.I.

Date	24-Nov-04
Invoice No	1097

Name: Rachel Nottingham
Address: 2741 Landsdowne Road
City: Victoria, BC   Postal Code: V8R 3P6
Country: Canada

Item #	Description	Quantity	Unit Price	Extended Price
21	Summer Beach Scene	3	$25.00	$75.00
27	Sea Scape Watch	2	36.00	72.00
47	Spanish Ducat Key Chain	1	12.00	12.00
63	Raindrop Crew Neck T-shirt	2	14.00	28.00
67	Stone-washed Twill Jacket	3	54.00	162.00

	Total Sale	$349.00
	Sales Tax	24.43
	Shipping	25.00

Payment Method	
	Check
	Visa
X	MasterCard
	Discover
	American Express

TOTAL $398.43

Credit Card #	4799123456789000	Expiration	03/2006

Thank you for your order!

Figure AC-2 | **NICOLE'S PLANNING ANALYSIS SHEET**

Planning Analysis Sheet

My goal:
Develop a template worksheet for preparing sales invoices

What results do I want to see?
A sales invoice for each order

What information do I need?
Customer name and address
Item number and quantity to be shipped
Lookup description in product table ❶
Lookup unit price for item in product table ❷
Method of payment

What calculations will I perform?
1. Extended price ❸ = quantity * unit price
2. Total sale ❹ = sum of extended price
3. Sales tax ❺ = total sale * 7%
4. Shipping ❻ = if total sale is less than $200 then $15, otherwise $25
5. Total ❼ = total sale + sales tax + shipping

Using the original paper invoice and her planning analysis sheet, Nicole sketches the template she wants to create using Excel (Figure AC-3). For each item ordered, she wants to enter the item number, description, quantity, and unit price, and she wants Excel to perform the required calculations. (The circled numbers are guides to help you relate Nicole's sketch.)

Figure AC-3	NICOLE'S SKETCH OF HER TEMPLATE WORKSHEET

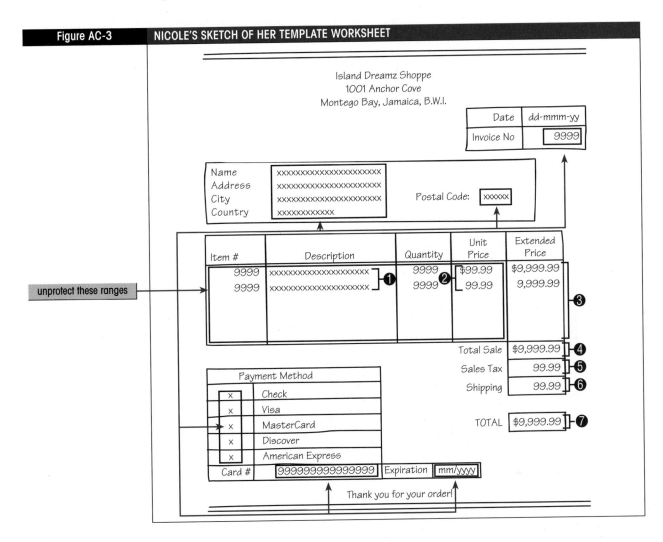

Nicole also sketches a table that lists the items Island Dreamz sells, as shown in Figure AC-4. The table includes the number, description, and unit price of each product.

Figure AC-4	ISLAND DREAMZ PRODUCT TABLE

Item #	Description	Unit Price
21	Summer Beach Scene	25.00
27	Sea Scape Watch	36.00
31	Victorian Walking Stick	28.00
47	Spanish Ducat Key Chain	12.00
63	Raindrop Crew Neck T-shirt	14.00
67	Stone-washed Twill Jacket	54.00
68	Island Can Coolers	6.00

Nicole has asked you to help her create the invoice worksheet.

To complete this task:

1. Start Excel, create a workbook named **Dreamz**, and then save it in the AddCases folder on your Data Disk. Rename the first sheet "Documentation" and then enter the name of the company at the top of the worksheet, and then enter the date, your name, and a statement that briefly describes the purpose of the workbook in the rows below the company name.

2. Rename the Sheet2 as "Invoice", and then begin creating the sales invoice by inserting the invoice labels, corresponding to placement of the labels as shown in Figure AC-3 (your sheet does not have to match Nicole's sketch exactly). Adjust column widths as necessary.

3. Enter the calculations specified in Figure AC-2 in the worksheet. Use the TODAY function to enter the current date in the appropriate location in the invoice.

4. Format the cells as shown in Figure AC-1. Note that the first cell in the Unit Price and Extended Price columns is formatted differently than the rest of the cells in those columns.

5. Add fonts and borders as shown in Figure AC-1 (try to match the figure as near as possible). Add any color combinations that you think enhance the readability and appearance of the invoice.

6. Add data validation to the cells in the Item # column so that users can only enter numbers from the following list: 21, 27, 31, 47, 63, 67, and 68.

7. Rename Sheet3 as "Product". Create a product table that contains the product information shown in Figure AC-4. Excluding the column titles, give this table the range name "Products". Print a copy of this worksheet.

Explore

8. Nicole wants Excel to automatically look up the description and unit price in the product table when an item number is entered in the worksheet. Use the VLOOKUP function to determine the description and unit price values in the invoice sheet based on what item number the user enters.

Explore

9. The invoice will show #N/A values for the description, quantity and extended price columns, if no item number is entered. Correct this problem by modifying the formulas in these columns using an IF function so that if no item number is entered (that is, the item number = ""), then the value in these columns are blank (that is, ""); otherwise the values are calculated as before.

10. Unlock those cells in which data is entered (but not cells containing formulas or text), and then protect the Invoice worksheet, allowing users only to select unlocked cells.

11. Test the operation of the worksheet by entering data for the order shown in Figure AC-1. Note how the values in the Extended Price column are calculated automatically as you enter the data.

12. Write a macro named "Print_Invoice" that prints the Invoice worksheet. Add a button labeled "Print" to the bottom of the Invoice worksheet to run the macro.

13. Save your changes to the Dreamz workbook.

14. Delete the data for Rachel's order.

15. Save the file as an Excel template named **Invoice** to the AddCases folder on your Data Disk.

OBJECTIVES

In this case you will:

- Create and use a multiple sheet workbook

- Enhance worksheets with formatting

- Consolidate worksheet data

- Create charts from summary data

- Create macros for displaying sheets and charts

- Edit your macros so they prompt the user for information and check user input

- Create a custom toolbar and add macro buttons

- Save a worksheet in HTML and XML format

PERFORMANCE REPORTING FOR BIODECK, INC.

CASE

Biodeck, Inc.

Biodeck, Inc. is a leading firm in the medical technology field. The company develops and manufactures catheters and other products that are used as alternatives to traditional surgery. As described by CEO Peter Nicholas: "We were one of the first companies to articulate the concept of less invasive procedures." Less invasive procedures are possible because current medical imaging techniques let physicians see inside the body and manipulate instruments through a natural opening or a tiny incision. Biodeck aggressively markets its products for these medical procedures. For example, a traditional coronary bypass operation often costs $50,000 to $70,000, including the hospital stay and weeks of recovery time. By contrast, clearing a clogged artery with one of Biodeck's catheters, which is inserted under the skin of a patient's arm, takes just a few hours and costs around $12,000.

Although many of Biodeck's products are expensive relative to the cost of a scalpel, they enable a patient to leave the hospital much sooner and avoid huge hospital bills. For this reason, Biodeck's products are popular and sales continue to increase rapidly.

Willow Shire joined Biodeck last year as a junior accountant. Her responsibilities include preparing the quarterly performance report that consolidates the financial results from four sales sections: Northwest, Southeast, Midwest, and Southwest. She also needs to add an interface to the workbook to make it easier to view reports for each sales sector and the overall total. Finally, she would like to be able to post a summary report on Biodeck's Web site. Willow has asked for your help with this project.

To complete this task:

1. Open the **Biodeck1** workbook located in the AddCases folder on your Data Disk. Enter the date and your name in the Documentation sheet. Save the workbook as **Biodeck2** in the same folder.

2. Add a consolidation sheet named "All" after the Documentation sheet. Insert formulas in the consolidation worksheet that add all of the sectors' results to determine the over-all total.

3. Enhance the appearance of the five accounting worksheets with special formatting, colors, and borders. The design of the worksheets is up to you.

4. Print a copy of the consolidation sheet.

5. Insert a worksheet named "Earnings" (before the All sheet) that displays the operating earnings for each sector by quarter for the entire year. Insert a column heading titled Total and display the total overall earnings by sector for the year. Then insert a row heading titled "Total" and display the total quarterly earnings for the year. Format the worksheet to match or complement the format of the other worksheets.

6. Create a chart sheet containing a clustered column chart that compares the operating earnings for each sector by quarter. Add appropriate titles to the chart. Name the chart sheet "Column Chart".

7. Create a chart sheet containing a pie chart that compares the operating earnings for the year (the value in the Total column from the Earnings worksheet) for the four sectors. Add only a chart title. Name the chart sheet "Pie Chart".

8. Print copies of the Earnings worksheet and the two chart sheets.

9. Create a macro that displays the All worksheet, selecting cell A1. Name the macro Show_Report.

10. Edit the macro in the Visual Basic Editor so that the macro prompts the user for the name of the sheet to view (indicating that he or she can select "All", "Northwest", "Southeast", "Midwest", or "Southwest") and then displays that worksheet. Include an If-Then-Else control structure to detect errors. If the user enters an incorrect name, the macro should display a message box informing the user of the error.

11. Create a second macro named Show_Chart that displays one of the two charts in the workbook. Include the necessary code to prompt the user for the name of the chart and to check the user's input, informing the user of any errors.

12. Print the VBA code for the macros you created.

13. Return to the Biodeck2 workbook. Create a custom toolbar named "Biotools" that contains buttons for both the Show_Chart and Show_Report macros. The design of the buttons is up to you, but the buttons must display the labels, "Show &Chart" and "Show &Report", respectively. Attach the Biotools toolbar to the workbook.

14. Save your changes to the Biodeck2 workbook.

15. Save the All worksheet as a noninteractive Web page with the file name, **Summary.htm** and the page title "Biodeck Summary Report".

Explore

16. Willow has been asked to make the date in the All worksheet available to other users as an XML spreadsheet. Save the contents of the All worksheet in XML spreadsheet format with the filename **Biodata** in the AddCases folder on your Data Disk.

17. Close your files, delete the Biotools custom toolbar, and then exit Excel.

OBJECTIVES

In this case you will:

- Create a query data source

- Retrieve data from a data source with a query

- Edit the properties of a query

- Create a PivotTable and PivotChart using external data

- Save a worksheet as a Web page

NEGOTIATING
SALARIES FOR THE NATIONAL BASKETBALL ASSOCIATION

CASE

National Basketball Association

When Dr. James Naismith nailed a peach basket to a pole, he could not possibly have envisioned the popularity of the sport that he founded. Since those early days of peach baskets and volleyballs, basketball has become one of the most popular sports in the world—especially in America.

The National Basketball Association (NBA) is home to some of the world's greatest athletes. The popularity of the NBA soared in the 1980s, thanks to players like Michael Jordan, Julius Erving, "Magic" Johnson, and Larry Bird. This popularity resulted in larger attendance at games, larger television viewing audiences, and an increase in advertising sponsorships that, in turn, led to increased player salaries. While growing up, Troy Jackson wanted to be a professional basketball player. However, during his senior year of college, Troy had reconstructive knee surgery, ending his chances of ever playing competitive basketball. But Troy was still determined to make it to the NBA one way or another. Upon graduation, he was offered a job in the NBA head offices in New York, working on the staff of the commissioner.

The commissioner and his staff are concerned with the large number of player salaries being decided through arbitration. Salary arbitration is the process of negotiating a contract when both sides cannot agree to a specific dollar amount. The arbitration process is conducted through an independent third party who listens to arguments from both sides and then makes a final determination about the terms of the contract. During the past several years, the number of contracts decided through arbitration has more than tripled. To help the NBA head office understand what has been happening in the arbitration process, Troy suggests viewing the results in an Excel workbook.

The commissioner agrees that this would be useful in overseeing salaries being decided through arbitration. The arbitration data has been placed in an Access database. Retrieve that data and analyze it.

To complete this task:

1. Start Excel and then create a workbook named **NBA** and save it in the AddCases folder on your Data Disk. Rename the first sheet "Documentation", and then enter the date, your name, and the purpose of the workbook. Rename the second worksheet as "Player List".

2. Create a database query using the Microsoft (MS) Access database **Players** located in the AddCases folder on your Data Disk. The query should retrieve the last and first names of each player from the Player table, the player's position from the Position table, the player's team from the Team table, and the bid that the player settled for from the Bids table. Have the query sort the retrieved data in descending order of the settled bid.

3. Save the query with the filename **Settle** in the AddCases folder on your Data Disk.

4. Retrieve the data from the query into cell A1 of the Player List worksheet. Print the player list.

5. Edit the properties of the query so that its data is automatically refreshed whenever the workbook is opened.

6. Create a PivotTable and PivotChart report, retrieving the following fields' data from the MS Access Players database: Player Bid, Team Bid, and Settle from the Bids table; PID, PosID, and TeamID from the Player table; Position from the Position table; and Team from the Team table.

7. Place the Team field in the Page area of the PivotTable, the Position field in the Row area, and the averages of the Player Bid, Team Bid, and Settle Bid in the Data area. Format these averages using the Currency format style, with zero decimal places.

8. Set up the PivotTable so that it refreshes whenever the workbook is opened.

9. Place the PivotTable on a worksheet named "Bid Table" and the chart on a chart sheet named "Bid Chart". If necessary, move these sheets after the Player List sheet.

Explore   10. Format the PivotTable using the Report 6 AutoFormat.

11. Calculate the average percentage increase of the settled bid over the original team offer. Display the percentage to two decimal places. For which position is the percent increase the largest?

12. Change the Bid Chart type to Clustered Column. Add a chart title of "Comparison of Player, Team, and Settled Bids" and the title "Bids" to the *y*-axis. Remove all gridlines from the chart. Place the legend at the bottom of the chart.

13. Group the Player List, Bid Table, and Bid Chart sheets. Format the printed output of these sheets so each sheet prints out in landscape orientation. Put your name and the date in the right section of the header. Put the text "NBA Salaries", the name of the workbook, and the name of the worksheet in the right section of the footer. Center the contents of the sheet both horizontally and vertically on the page.

14. Print the contents of the NBA workbook, and save the changes you have made to the workbook.

15. The commissioner would also like to have a copy of the PivotTable to place on the association's internal office Web site. Save the Bid Table worksheet as a noninteractive Web Page named **Arbitrate.htm**. Set the page title as "Salary Arbitration".

16. View the Arbitrate Web page in your browser and print it from there.

17. Close your browser, and then close the workbook before exiting Excel.

OBJECTIVES

In this case you will:

- Merge several workbooks

- Review and track changes made to a workbook

- Create a Solver model to maximize a company's net income

- Save and load different Solver models

- Save a Solver solution as a scenario

- Create scenario summary report

- Add a comment to a worksheet cell

ANALYZING PRODUCT MIX FOR STARDUST TELESCOPES

CASE

StarDust Telescopes

StarDust Telescopes of Denver is one of the leading manufacturers in the world of amateur class telescopes. Jan Fienberg works for StarDust Telescopes in the accounting department. The three most successful products created by StarDust are the StarDust4, StarDust6, and StarDust8 scope. Each week Jan has to create a report analyzing the company's current sales and income on these three products. She gets her information from many different sources. Her colleague, Steve Sanchez, maintains information on the number of scope orders each week from the domestic, European, and Pacific Rim customers. Albert Kohler keeps tabs on the current inventory of parts for the company's products and the price of production. Lisa Pearse, a fellow accountant, has information on the company's expenses.

Each person records their information in an Excel workbook, which Jan needs to merge together into a single workbook, that gives her a complete picture on how many products have been ordered, how many parts are in stock, and what the company's income and expenses are. She also needs to reconcile any differences in the values entered by her colleagues.

Brad Fewes, Jan's supervisor, would also like Jan to calculate the order that maximizes the company's profits while still meeting the requirements of the customers and the limitations of the items in stock. Brad would like Jan to include a report of her analysis.

Brad is also considering dropping the price of the StarDust8 telescope. He would like Jan to find out how reducing the price of this telescope will affect the company's net revenue and net income. Jan has asked your help in doing this analysis and creating this report.

To complete this task:

1. Start Excel and then open the **Scope1** workbook located in the AddCases folder on your Data Disk. On the Documentation sheet, enter the date, your name, and a statement describing the purpose of the workbook. Save the workbook as **Scope2** in the same folder.

2. Merge the Scope2 workbook with the **Albert**, **Lisa**, and **Steve** workbooks, all located in the AddCases folder.

3. Switch to the Order worksheet, and review the changes made to the workbook made by everyone, except yourself. Both Lisa Pearse and Albert Kohl have entered values for the cost of assembly in the range B8:D8. Accept Lisa Pearse's changes over Albert Kohl's. Accept the rest of the changes made by the Jan's colleagues.

4. Display the History worksheet showing all of the changes that Lisa Pearse made to the workbook. Print the History worksheet.

5. Remove workbook sharing from the Scope2 workbook.

6. Brad wants to determine the domestic order that Jan can put together that will maximize the company's profits. The conditions for this solution are:
    a. Only the values in the range B4:D4 can change.
    b. The values in the range B4:D4 must be integers.
    c. The number of domestic StarDust4 telescopes ordered must be 225 or greater, the number of domestic StarDust6 telescopes must be 150 or greater, and the number of domestic StarDust8 telescopes must be 100 or greater.
    d. The number of each telescope part remaining must be greater than or equal to zero.

Explore

7. Save the solution you discover as a scenario named "Domestic Sales".

8. Insert the text "Domestic" in cell A30, and then save your Solver model in the range A31:A38.

9. Print the range A1:D23 of the Order worksheet. Display the text "Domestic Sales Solution" in the left section of the header. Include your name and the date in the right section of the footer.

10. Brad also wants Jan to investigate a different model in which domestic and international sales are varied to maximize profits. The conditions for this solution are:
    a. Only the values in the cell range B4:D6 can change.
    b. The values in the range B4:D6 must be integers.
    c. The value of cell B4 must be 200 or greater, cell C4 must be 150 or greater, and cell D4 must be 100 or greater. The values in the range B5:B6 must be 85 or greater. The values in the range C5:C6 must be 80 or greater. Finally, the values in the range D5:D6 must be 65 or greater.
    d. The number of each telescope part remaining must be greater than or equal to zero.

11. Save the solution you discover as a scenario named "International Sales".

12. Type "International" in cell B30, and then save the current Solver model in the range B31:B41.

13. Print the range A1:D23 of the Order worksheet. Display the text "International Sales Solution" in the left section of the header. Include your name and the date in the right section of the footer.

14. Reload the Domestic model and rerun the Solver solution.

15. Create range names for the values in the range B20:B23 based on the labels stored in the range A20:A23.

16. Display a scenario summary report for the two scenarios you created, using the values in the range B20:B23 as the result cells. Compare the number of telescopes ordered for domestic consumption under the two scenarios.

17. Brad is considering changing the price of the StarDust8 telescope to $799.95, $819.95, $849.95, or $869.95. Create a one-variable data table showing the total revenue and net income under each of these scenarios.

18. How much will dropping the price of the StartDust8 telescope to $799.95 cost the company, assuming the Domestic Sales scenario? Report this fact by attaching a comment to cell D16 on the Order worksheet. Format the comment so that it is always visible on the worksheet.

19. Close the Scope2 workbook, saving your changes. Exit Excel.

OBJECTIVES

In this appendix you will:

- Review Excel's logical functions

- Create a nested IF function

- Calculate a conditional count

- Calculate a conditional sum

WORKING WITH LOGICAL FUNCTIONS

Recording Employee Financial Data

Branco, Inc.

Maria Alba is a new financial officer for Branco, Inc., a regional superstore for kitchen wares. One of Maria's jobs will be to record and summarize employee information, including the total cost of employee salaries and benefits. She will also keep track of employee enrollment in the various health plans offered by the company.

Maria has asked your help in inserting functions that will calculate how much the company spends for each employee's 401(k) retirement account and their health plan. She also wants the workbook to automatically sum up the total cost to the company for these benefits. To calculate these values, you'll have to use Excel's extensive library of logical functions.

SESSION A1.1

In this session, you'll study Excel's collection of logical functions. You'll learn how to use the AND function, and you'll also learn how to nest one IF function inside another IF function. Finally, you'll use the SUMIF and COUNTIF functions to calculate sums and counts based on search criteria.

Working with Logical Functions

You and Maria meet to discuss Branco's benefits program. There are two aspects of the benefits package that Maria is concerned about: the company's 401(k) savings plan and the company's health package. The 401(k) plan matches eligible employee's contributions dollar for dollar, up to 3% of the employee's salary. The company supports two health plans: a family plan that costs the company $5000 per employee and an individual plan that costs $4000 for each employee. An employee could also opt out of the health plan if he or she has coverage elsewhere.

Maria has created a workbook that contains descriptive data on each employee. You will open this workbook now and review the employee information.

To open Maria's workbook:

1. Start Excel and open the **Branco1** workbook located in the Appendix.01\Tutorial folder on your Data Disk.

2. Enter the date and your name in the Documentation sheet.

3. Save the workbook as **Branco2** in the Appendix.01\Tutorial folder on your Data Disk.

4. Review the contents of the workbook, and then switch to the Employee Data worksheet.

There are two sheets on which Maria needs your help. The Employee Data worksheet contains the employee data. Maria has recorded the employee's name and employment status (FT for full-time, PT for part-time, or CN for paid consultant). The worksheet also lists the employee's salary, the number of years the employee has been with Branco, and the type of health plan for which the employee has signed up (F for family, I for individual, or N for none). Maria needs you to add functions to this worksheet to calculate the 401(k) and health plan cost for each employee. Once you calculate those values, Maria wants to summarize that information on the Employee Summary worksheet, so she can report the total impact of the benefits package on the company.

Using the AND Function

You'll first work on creating a function to calculate the company's 401(k) contribution for each employee. To be eligible, an employee must a full-time worker with at least one year of job experience. Maria has outlined the eligibility conditions in the flowchart shown in Figure A-1.

| Figure A1-1 | FLOWCHART SHOWING EMPLOYEE ELIGIBILITY FOR THE 401(K) PLAN |

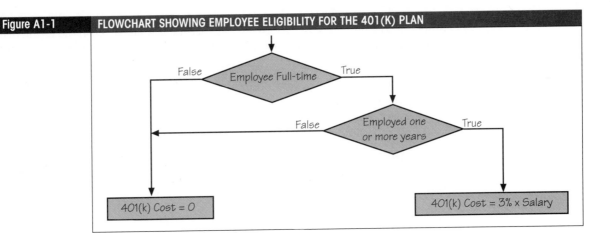

In Tutorial 2, you worked with the IF function to calculate values for a loan payment schedule. Recall that the IF function has the syntax

`=IF(`*`logical_test,value_if_true,value_if_false`*`)`

where *logical_test* is an expression that can be either true or false, *value_if_true* is the value returned by the function if the expression is true, and *value_if_false* is the value returned if the expression is false. For example, the IF function

`=IF(A2="FT","Full-time","Part-time")`

returns the text string "*Full-time*" if cell A2 contains the text "*FT*"; otherwise the formula will return the text string "*Part-time*".

This approach won't work for the 401(k) plan because there are *two* conditions that must be evaluated, not one. Instead you must include Excel's AND function. The syntax of the AND function is

`=AND(`*`logical condition1,[logical condition2],...`*`)`

where *logical condition1* and *logical condition2* are expressions that can be either true or false. If both of the logical conditions are true, the AND function returns the logical value, TRUE; otherwise the function returns the logical value, FALSE. Note that you can include additional logical conditions, but they all must be true for the AND function to return a true value.

Excel also supports the OR function that returns a true value if only one of multiple logical conditions is true and the NOT function that reverses the logical value of an expression. Figure A1-2 summarizes the syntax of the AND, OR, and NOT functions.

| Figure A1-2 | EXCEL'S LOGICAL FUNCTIONS |

FUNCTION	DESCRIPTION
AND(*logical condition1,[logical condition2],...*)	Returns the value TRUE if all arguments are true; returns FALSE if one or more arguments is false
FALSE()	Returns the value FALSE
IF(*logical_test,value_if_true,value_if_false*)	Returns *value_if_true* if the *logical_test* argument is true; returns the *value_if_false* if the *logical_test* argument is false
NOT(*logical*)	Returns the value TRUE if *logical* is false; returns the value FALSE if *logical* is true
OR(*logical condition1,[logical condition2],...*)	Returns the value TRUE if at least one argument is true; returns FALSE if all arguments are false
TRUE()	Returns the value TRUE

In the Employee Data worksheet, job status is stored in column B, and years employed is stored in column D. If you want to test whether the first employee in the list fulfills the eligibility requirements, you would use the AND function as follows: `AND(B2="FT",D2>=1)`

If the employee works full-time (B2="FT ") and has worked more one or more years (D2 >=1), then the AND function returns the logical value TRUE; otherwise the function returns the value FALSE.

However, to determine whether the first employee is eligible and also to calculate the amount of the 401(k) contribution, you insert the AND function within an IF function as follows:

`=IF(AND(B2="FT",D2>= 1),E2*0.03,0)`

If the employee is eligible, this function will return the value of the employee's salary in cell E2 multiplied by 0.03. For any other condition, the formula will return the value 0. Enter this formula now for the first employee in Maria's list.

To enter the logical function:

1. Click cell **F2**.

2. Type **=IF(AND(B2="FT",D2>=1),E2*0.03,0)** and press the **Enter** key. The value 0 appears in the cell because both conditions of the logical test have not been met for the first employee. Although the employee is full-time, the number of years worked is less than 1.

   Copy this formula into the remaining cells in the column.

3. Click cell **F2** and then drag the fill handle down over the range **F2:F103**.

4. Scroll back up the worksheet window, and then click cell **A1**. Figure A1-3 shows the 401(k) contributions for the first 23 employees in Maria's list.

| Figure A1-3 | 401(K) COSTS |

Next you'll calculate the health plan cost for each employee.

Creating Nested IF Functions

At Branco, every employee, except for paid consultants, are eligible for the company's health plan. There are two health plans: the Family plan (F) that costs the company $5000 per employee, or the Individual plan (I) that costs Branco $4000. Maria displays the logic for determining health plan costs in Figure A1-4.

Figure A1-4	FLOWCHART SHOWING HEALTH INSURANCE OPTIONS

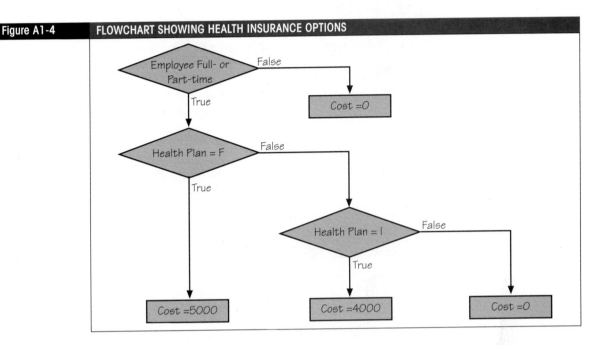

To convert this flowchart into an Excel function, you will work from the bottom upwards. This will have the same effect as creating the function from the inside out. First, you will create a statement that determines whether or not the first employee in Maria's list is enrolled in the individual (I) health plan. If so, the cost to company is $4000; otherwise the cost is zero. This is a simple IF function, and the formula will appear as:

```
IF(C2="I",4000,0)
```

Next, you will move up the flowchart. The employee could also have enrolled in family plan (F) at a cost of $5000 to Branco. To account for this situation, you will *nest* the first IF function inside of a second as follows:

```
IF(C2="F",5000,IF(C2="I",4000,0))
```

So if the first employee is enrolled in the family plan, the cost is $5000; otherwise Excel tests whether the employee is enrolled in either individual plan for $4000 or no plan at all.

You are not done with the flowchart yet. You still have to determine whether the employee is eligible for the health plan in the first place. The health plan is only available for full-time or part-time employees. You can nest the two IF functions inside of yet a third IF function to test whether the first employee is eligible. The complete function is:

```
=IF(OR(B2="FT",B2="PT"),IF(C2="F",5000,IF(C2="I",4000,0)),0)
```

So if the employee is eligible, Excel tests to see how much the health plan will cost the company; otherwise the cost is zero. Note that this function uses the OR function to determine whether the employee is eligible. Cell B2 must be equal to "FT" *or* "PT" for the OR function to return the logical value TRUE. Add this function to column G of the Employee Data worksheet.

To insert the nested IF function:

1. Click cell **G2** in the Employee Data worksheet, type **=IF(OR(B2="FT",B2="PT"), IF(C2="F", 5000, IF(C2="I",4000,0)),0)** and press the **Enter** key. There are several layers of parentheses in this function. You can keep track of the layer that you're in by viewing the color of the parentheses. The outermost layer is colored black, the next layer is green, and the innermost layer has purple-colored parentheses.

   Now copy the formula for the rest of the employees in the list.

2. Click cell **G2** and then drag the fill handle down over the range **G2:G103**.

3. Scroll back up the worksheet window, and click cell **A1**. Figure A1-5 shows the health costs for the first 23 employees in the list.

Figure A1-5	HEALTH PLAN COSTS

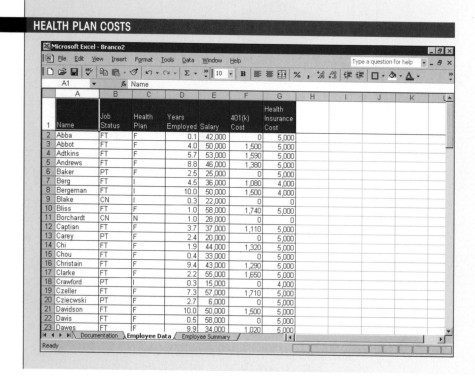

You've completed your work in calculating the cost of benefits for each employee. Next Maria wants you to summarize these results in the Employee Summary worksheet.

Calculating **Conditional Counts and Sums**

Excel provides the COUNT function to calculate counts and the SUM function to calculates sums. In some situations, you may want to calculate a conditional count or sum; that is, counting or summing values for only those cells that meet a particular condition. Maria wants you to add this feature to her workbook. She wants to be able to calculate the cost of salaries and benefits for full-time and part-time employees. She would also like to find out how many employees have signed up for the family or individual health plan and to calculate the total cost of each of those plans.

Using the COUNTIF Function

You can calculate conditional counts using the COUNTIF function. The syntax of the COUNTIF function is =COUNTIF(*range,criteria*)

where *range* is the range of cells that you want to count and *criteria* is an expression that defines which cells are to be counted. For example, Maria wants to know how many people are employed full-time at Branco. The job status information is stored in column B of the Employee Data worksheet. To count the number of full-time employees, she could use the formula =COUNTIF('Employee Data'!B:B,"FT") and Excel will count all of cells in column B (that is B:B) of the Employee Data worksheet that contain the text "FT". Note that because FT is a text string, you need to enclose it within a set of quotation marks. Use this function now in the Employee Summary worksheet.

To insert the COUNTIF function:

1. Click the **Employee Summary** tab.

2. Click cell **C4**, type the formula **=COUNTIF('Employee Data'!B:B,"FT")**, and then press the **Enter** key. Excel returns the value 71, indicating the company employees 71 full-time workers.

   Now add the formulas that calculate the number of part-time employees (PT) and the number of paid consultants (CN).

3. In cell C5, type the formula **=COUNTIF('Employee Data'!B:B,"PT")**, press the **Enter** key, and then enter the formula **=COUNTIF('Employee Data'!B:B,"CN")** in cell C6. There are 25 part-time employees and 6 paid consultants.

4. In cell C7, click the **AutoSum** button Σ ▾ on the Standard toolbar, and then press the **Enter** key to calculate the total number of employees at the company. There are a total of 102 people employed at Branco.

Next, calculate the total number of employees enrolled in the different health plans. Remember that the health plan information is stored in column C of the Employee Data worksheet.

To count the number receiving each benefit:

1. Click cell **C10**, type the formula **=COUNTIF('Employee Data'!C:C, "F")**, and then press the **Enter** key. Sixty-five employees have signed up for the family health plan.

   Now calculate the number of employees who have signed up for the individual plan (I) or for no plan at all (N).

2. In cell C11, type the formula **=COUNTIF('Employee Data'!C:C, "I")**, press the **Enter** key, and then enter the formula **=COUNTIF('Employee Data'!C:C, "N")** in cell C12. Twenty-six employees are on the individual plan, and 11 employees are not enrolled in any company-sponsored plan.

   As a check, calculate the total number of employees under the different health plan options.

3. In cell C13, click the **AutoSum** button Σ ▾ on the Standard toolbar, and then press the **Enter** key to calculate the total number of employees in the company, which is 102.

Finally, Maria wants to know how many employees are participating in the 401(k) plan. There is no column in the Employee Data worksheet that directly indicates this, but you can get at this information another way. Any employee receiving the 401(k) benefit will have a value greater than 0 in column F of the Employee Data worksheet. The criteria in the COUNTIF function can use the same comparison operators you use in Excel's IF function. So to count the number of employees matching this condition, you'll use the formula

```
=COUNTIF('Employee Data'!F:F,">0")
```

where ">0" is the criteria and counts the number of cells in column F whose values are greater than zero. Note that you have to enclose the criteria within a set of double quotation marks.

To count the number of employees receiving 401(k) benefits:

1. Click cell **C16**.

2. Type the formula **=COUNTIF('Employee Data'!F:F,">0")** and press the **Enter** key. Branco supplies 401(k) benefits for 65 employees. See Figure A1-6.

Figure A1-6	CALCULATING CONDITIONAL COUNTS

Now that Maria knows the number of people receiving various benefits, she needs to calculate the total cost of each benefit.

Using the SUMIF Function

The SUMIF function is the counterpart to the COUNTIF function. It calculates a sum based on a given criterion. The syntax of the SUMIF function is

```
=IF(range,criteria,[sum_range])
```

where *range* is the range of cells that you want to apply a specified *criteria* towards. The *sum_range* argument is the range of cells that you actually want to sum. For data that is organized in a list, the cells in *sum_range* are summed only if their corresponding cells in the specified *range* match the *criteria*. If you omit the *sum_range* argument, Excel will sum up the values specified in the *range* argument.

For example, Maria wants to calculate the total salaries paid out to full-time (FT) employees. Job status is recorded in column B of the Employee Data worksheet. Salary data is stored in column E. The formula to calculate this value would be

```
=SUMIF('Employee Data'!B:B,"FT",'Employee Data'!E:E)
```

Any employee whose job status is "FT" will have their salary value added to the total. You will insert this function into the Employee Summary sheet.

To insert the SUMIF function:

1. Click cell **F4**, type the formula **=SUMIF('Employee Data'!B:B,"FT", 'Employee Data'!E:E)**, and press the **Enter** key. Excel displays the value 3,496,000—the total amount paid out in full-time salaries.

   Calculate the total salaries for part-time (PT) employees and paid consultants (CN).

2. In cell F5, enter the formula **=SUMIF('Employee Data'!B:B,"PT",'Employee Data'!E:E)**, and then enter the formula **=SUMIF('Employee Data'!B:B,"CN", 'Employee Data'!E:E)** in cell F6. Branco spends $342,000 per year on part-time workers and $171,000 per year on paid consultants.

   Now calculate the total cost of all salaries.

3. Click cell **F7**, click the **AutoSum** button $\boxed{\Sigma \cdot}$ on the Standard toolbar, and then press the **Enter** key. The total cost of salaries is $4,009,000.

Next, Maria wants you to calculate the total cost of each health plan. Recall that health costs have been stored in column G of the Employee Data worksheet.

To calculate the cost of the different health plans:

1. Click cell **F10**, enter the formula **=SUMIF('Employee Data'!C:C,"F",'Employee Data'!G:G)**. Branco spends $325,000 per year on the family (F) health plan.

2. In cell F11, enter the formula **=SUMIF('Employee Data'!C:C,"I",'Employee Data'!G:G)**, and then enter the formula, **=SUMIF('Employee Data'!C:C,"N", 'Employee Data'!G:G)** in cell F12. The company has spent $100,000 on the individual health plan.

   Maria also wants you to calculate the total health care costs.

3. Click cell **F13**, click the **AutoSum** button $\boxed{\Sigma \cdot}$ on the Standard toolbar, and then press the **Enter** key. The total cost to the company is $425,000.

   Finally, you'll calculate the total cost of the 401(k) plan. In this case, it's simply the sum of values in column F of the Employee Data worksheet.

4. Click cell **C17**, enter the formula **=SUM('Employee Data'!F:F)**. Figure A1-7 shows the completed Employee Summary sheet.

Figure A1-7	CALCULATING CONDITIONAL SUMS

	A	B	C	D	E	F	G	H	I
1		**Employee Summary**							
2									
3		**Employees**			**Salaries**				
4		Full-Time	71		Full-Time	3,496,000			
5		Part-Time	25		Part-Time	342,000			
6		Consultants	6		Consultants	171,000			
7		**Total**	102		**Total**	4,009,000			
8									
9		**Health Insurance**			**Health Insurance Cost**				
10		Plan F	65		Plan F	325,000			
11		Plan I	26		Plan I	100,000			
12		None	11		None	0			
13		**Total**	102		**Total**	425,000			
14									
15		**401 (k) Cost**							
16		Number of Participants	65						
17		Total Cost	96,570						
18									

You can close your work and exit Excel.

5. Click the **Close** button ☒ on the title bar, and then click the **Yes** button when prompted to save your changes.

Maria looks over the work you've done. She's very pleased with the workbook. You inform her that as she enters new employees or edits the information on old ones, the values displayed in the Employee Summary worksheet will be automatically updated.

REVIEW ASSIGNMENTS

Maria has another workbook that she needs your help on. This workbook tracks the amount of vacation time and family leave used by each employee in the company. Maria needs to calculate how much vacation and family leave each employee is eligible for, and then subtract the amount they've already used from that amount. She also wants to calculate the total number of vacation and family leave days used by all employees, as well as the total number of days remaining. Here are the eligibility requirements for the different vacation and family leave plans:

For vacation:

- 17 days for full-time employees who have worked more than 5 years
- 12 days for full-time employees who have worked more than 1 year
- 7 days for full-time employees who have worked less than 1 year or for part-time employees who have worked more than 3 years

For family leave:

- 5 days for full-time employees who have worked more than 1 year
- 3 days for full-time employees who have worked less than 1 year or for part-time employees who have worked more than 2 years

Use these eligibility requirements to calculate the available vacation and family leave time for each employee.

To complete this task:

1. Open the **Leave1** workbook located in the Appendix.01\Review folder on your Data Disk. Enter the date and your name in the Documentation sheet. Save the workbook as **Leave2** in the same folder. Switch to the Employee Data worksheet.

2. In column D, create a nested IF statement to determine the number of vacation days each employee is eligible for based on the employee's job status in column B and on the number of years employed in column C.

3. Subtract the amount of vacation used from the available vacation time, displaying the remaining vacation time in column F for all employees.

4. In column G, create a nested IF statement to calculate each employee's total family leave time. (*Hint*: Use the AND and OR functions.)

5. To determine the remaining family time, subtract the used portion of the family leave from their total family leave and display the results in column I.

6. Switch to the Leave Summary worksheet. Use the COUNTIF function to calculate the total number of employees eligible for the different vacation leave and family leave plans. (*Hint*: An employee who is eligible for the 17-day vacation leave will have the value 17 in column D of the Employee Data worksheet).

7. Calculate the total number of employees in cells C8 and C14 by summing up the employees on each leave plan.

8. Calculate the total number of leave days per plan and overall in ranges D4:D8 and D11:D14.

9. Use the SUMIF function to calculate the number of vacation and family leave days already used by employee under each plan.

10. Calculate the total number of vacation and family leave days remaining in cells F4:F8 and F11:F14.

11. Save your changes, and then print the entire workbook.

12. Close the workbook and exit Excel.

CASE PROBLEMS

Case 1. Entering Purchase Orders at C-World   Linda Klaussen needs your help in designing an Excel workbook to enter purchase order information. She has already entered the product information on C-World's line of modems. She wants you to insert a lookup function to lookup data from the product table. The company also supports three shipping options that vary in price. She wants the purchase order sheet to be able to calculate the total cost of the order including the type of shipping the customer requests.

To complete this task:

1. Open the **Modem1** workbook located in the Appendix.01\Cases folder on your Data Disk. Enter the date and your name in the Documentation sheet. Save the workbook as **Modem2** in the same folder. Switch to the Purchase Order worksheet.

2. Product ID numbers will be entered in cell B5. Create a lookup function to display the product type in cell C7, the model name in cell C8, and the price in cell C13. Product information is displayed in the Product List worksheet. Review the material in Tutorial 6 on creating lookup functions, if necessary.

Explore
3. When no product ID number is entered in cell B5, cells C7, C8, and C13, display the #N/A error value. Linda wants these cells to display a blank value instead. Use an IF function along with the ISNA() function to first test whether the lookup functions you created in Step 2 display the #N/A value, if so then display a blank value, " "; otherwise display the results of the lookup function.

4. Cell B11 contains the three shipping options supported by C-World. Standard shipping costs $5.50, Express shipping costs $7.50, and Overnight shipping costs $10.50. Use an IF statement to insert the costs of the shipping into cell B14; if no shipping option is selected, display a blank value in cell B14.

5. Display the total cost of the product and shipping in cell B16. If the sum equals 0, display a blank value in the cell.

6. Test the worksheet using a product ID number of 1050 and the Express shipping option. How much is the total cost of the order? Print the resulting worksheet.

7. Save and close the workbook, and then exit Excel.

Case 2. Displaying Home Data for Glenwood Realty Tim Derkson is a realtor with Glenwood Realty. He has created a workbook containing data on homes in the Glenwood market. He has asked for your help in designing a worksheet that will display summary information on the homes he has entered. He has already formatted the sheet, but needs you to insert the correct formulas.

To complete this task:

1. Open the **Housing1** workbook located in the Appendix.01\Cases folder on your Data Disk. Enter the date and your name in the Documentation sheet. Save the workbook as **Housing2** in the same folder. Switch to the Home Summary worksheet.

   Tim has stored the housing data in the Home Data worksheet. He wants to use the Home Summary worksheet to search for information about the homes. There are two categories of homes that Tim is interested in: those in the upscale NE Sector of Glenwood and those on corner lots. In cells C3 and C12, he has created drop-down lists from which he can select the values "Yes", "No", or "Total". A value of "Yes" implies a house in the NE Sector (or on a corner lot), whereas a value of "No" indicates a house not in the NE Sector (or not on a corner lot). The value "Total" indicates all of the homes in the workbook.

2. In cell C4, create a function to count the number of houses listed in the Home Data worksheet. If a value of "Yes" is displayed in cell C3, count the number of NE Sector houses. If a value of "No" is shown in cell C3, count the number of non-NE Sector houses. If a value of "Total" is displayed, count the total number of houses. (*Hint:* You can use any numeric column in the Home Data worksheet as the basis for your count.)

Explore 3. In cells C5 through C8, calculate the average price, square footage, age, and annual taxes for the houses in the Home Data worksheet. Once again, the average will be based on the value chosen in cell C3: limiting the average to only the NE Sector houses, or non-NE Sector houses, or all of the houses that Tim has recorded. (*Hint:* To calculate the average value for either NE Sector or non-NE Sector houses, use the SUMIF function, divided by the count displayed in cell C4.)

4. Repeat Steps 2 and 3 for the values in cells C13 through C17, this time basing your calculations on whether the house is on a corner lot or not.

5. Click the drop-down list boxes in cells C3 and C12 and verify that the calculations in the table reflect the criteria chosen for each cell.

6. Display the count and average values for houses that are in the NE sector and for houses that are on a corner lot.

7. Insert a footer with your name and date on separate lines in the lower-right corner of the Home Summary worksheet. Save your changes, and print the Home Summary worksheet.

8. Close the workbook and then exit Excel.

OBJECTIVES

In this appendix you will:

- Learn about methods of integration using Office XP programs

- Link an Excel worksheet to a Word document

- Update a linked object

- Embed an object

- Modify an embedded object

INTEGRATING EXCEL WITH OTHER WINDOWS PROGRAMS

Creating Integrated Documents for The Lighthouse

CASE

The Lighthouse

The Lighthouse is a charitable organization providing shelter, meal programs, and educational opportunities for the people of rural central Pennsylvania. Beth Purcell is the financial director of The Lighthouse. Each year, she sends out a financial report to the organization's supporters and contributors. Beth stores the financial data in an Excel workbook, and she uses Microsoft Word to create the report. Beth wants to be able to copy the Excel data and paste it directly into the Word document. She also wants to learn how to tie the two documents together, so that if she updates the financial information in the Excel workbook, the report in the Word document will be automatically updated as well.

In this appendix, your task is to help Beth integrate her Excel data into her Word document and link the documents so the data in the report is automatically updated each time Beth modifies the workbook.

SESSION A2.1

In this session, you'll learn how to create a compound document by linking and embedding Excel cells and charts into a Word document. You'll learn about some of the concepts behind linking and embedding, and you'll study various techniques of sharing data between Office applications.

Methods of Integration

Excel is part of a suite of programs called Microsoft Office XP. In addition to Excel, the Office programs include Word, a word-processing program; Access, a database entry and management program; PowerPoint, presentations and slide shows program; Outlook, a personal information manager; FrontPage, a program for creating Web pages; and Publisher, a program for creating desk top publishing projects. All of these programs share a common interface and can read each other file formats.

Occasionally you will need to create a document that relies on information from more than one application. This type of document is called a **compound document**. Compound documents are usually created from two or more documents. The **source document** (or documents) contains the source of the information to be shared. The **destination document** is the document (or documents) that will display the information from the various source document or documents. Compound documents are easy to create in Office because of the tight integration of the Office applications. At The Lighthouse, Beth needs to create a letter using Word that incorporates information from an Excel workbook that contains financial data.

There are three ways to copy data between Windows applications: pasting, linking, and embedding. Each of these techniques can be used to create a compound document. Figure A2-1 describes each of these methods, and provides examples of when each method would be appropriate to use.

Figure A2-1	COMPARISON OF METHODS OF INTEGRATING INFORMATION	
METHOD OF SHARING	**DESCRIPTION**	**USE WHEN**
Copying and pasting	Places a copy of the information in a document	You want to exchange the data between the two documents only once, and it doesn't matter if the data changes.
Linking	Displays an object in the destination document but doesn't store it there—only the location of the source document is stored in the destination document	You want to use the same data in more than one document, and you need to ensure that the data will be current and identical in each document. Any changes you make to the source document will be reflected in the destination document(s).
Embedding	Displays and stores an object in the destination document	You want the source data to become a permanent part of the destination document, or the source data will no longer be available to the destination document. Any changes you make to either the destination document or the source document will not affect the other.

Pasting Data

You can **paste** an object, such as a range of cells or a chart, from one program to another, using Windows' copy and paste features. Once you paste an object from the source document into the destination document, that data is now part of the destination document. The pasted data is static, having no connection to the source document. If you want to change the pasted data, you must do so in the destination document. For example, a range of cells pasted into a Word document can only be edited from within the Word document. Any changes made in the original Excel workbook will have no impact on the Word document. For this reason, pasting is only used for one-time exchanges of information.

Object Linking and Embedding

If you want to create a live connection between two documents, so that changes in the source document will be automatically reflected in the destination document, you must use object linking and embedding. **Object Linking and Embedding** (or **OLE**) refers to the technology that allows you to copy and paste objects, such as graphic files, cell ranges, or charts, so that information about the application that create the object is included along with the object itself.

The objects are inserted into the destination document as either linked objects or embedded objects. A **linked object** is actually a separate file that is linked to the source document. If you make a change to the source document, the linked object can be automatically updated to reflect the change. An **embedded object** is information that is stored in the source document and inserted directly into the destination document. Once embedded, the object becomes part of the destination document. In the case of Office applications, embedded objects carry along their menus and toolbars. This means you can edit an Excel chart embedded in a Word document using the same tools and menu commands that are available to you in Excel. Embedded objects have no link to the source document, so that changes made to the embedded object are not reflected in the source.

Thus, the main difference between linked and embedded objects lies in how the data is stored and how it is updated after being inserted in the destination document. Figure A2-2 illustrates the difference between linking and embedding.

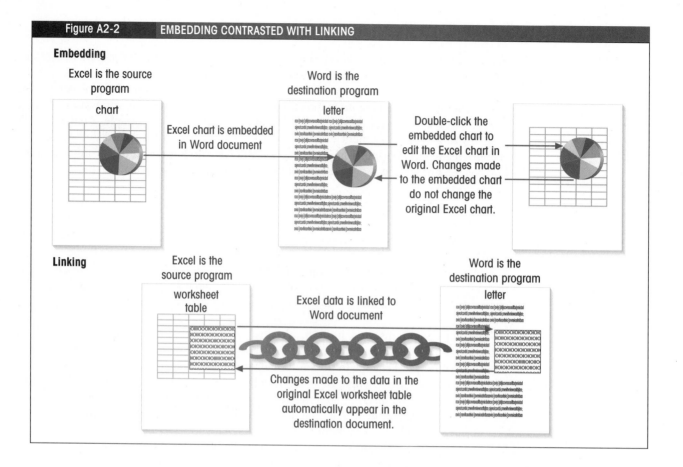

Figure A2-2   **EMBEDDING CONTRASTED WITH LINKING**

Linking an Excel Worksheet to a Word Document

Beth needs you to paste the financial data stored in her Excel workbook into a letter she has been composing for The Lighthouse's supporters. She is still working on the details of the financial report, and she might have to edit some of the values in the workbook. Rather than repasting the data each time she modifies the report, Beth wants you to create a link between her Excel workbook and her Word document, so that any changes she makes to the workbook are automatically reflected in the letter.

To open Beth's two files:

1. Start Excel and open the **LHouse1** workbook located in the Appendix.02\Tutorial folder on your Data Disk. Enter your name and the date in the Documentation sheet. Save the workbook as **LHouse2** in the same folder on your Data Disk.

2. Click the **Start** button on the taskbar, point to **Programs**, and then click **Microsoft Word** to start the Word program.

3. Open the **Letter1** document stored in the Appendix.02\Tutorial folder on your Data Disk.

4. Click **File** on the menu bar, and then click **Save As**, and save the document as **Letter2** in the Appendix.02\Tutorial folder.

5. Return to the **LHouse2** workbook, and switch to the Financial Summary worksheet shown in Figure A2-3.

| Figure A2-3 | THE LHOUSE2 WORKBOOK |

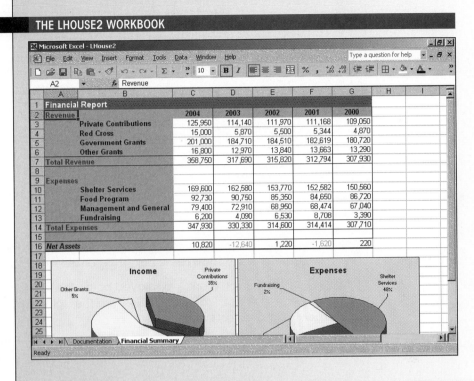

TROUBLE? If move between the programs, click the appropriate program button on the taskbar.

The financial data that Beth wants to display in her letter is stored in the range A2:G16 of the Financial Summary worksheet. To transfer that data, first you'll copy it and then you paste it as a link in the Word document.

To copy and paste the worksheet data:

1. Select the range **A2:G16**, and click the **Copy** button 🖺 on the Excel Standard toolbar.

2. Return to the **Letter2** document in your Word program. Figure A2-4 shows the content of the Letter2 file as it appears in Word.

| Figure A2-4 | THE LETTERS2 DOCUMENT |

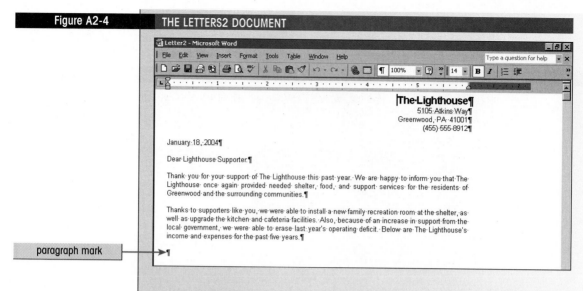

paragraph mark

TROUBLE? If your document does not show paragraph marks at the end of each paragraph, click the **Show/Hide** button ¶ on the Word Standard toolbar.

3. Click the paragraph mark ¶ displayed below the letter's second paragraph (below the sentence that reads "Below are The Lighthouse's income and expenses for the past five years").

4. Click **Edit** on the menu bar and then click **Paste Special**. The Paste Special dialog box opens. See Figure A2-5.

| Figure A2-5 | PASTE SPECIAL DIALOG BOX |

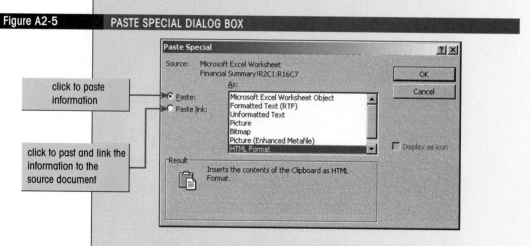

click to paste information

click to past and link the information to the source document

The Paste link option in the Paste Special dialog box allows you to paste information using several different formats. The default format is to insert the data as a Word table using the HTML formatting language. You could also paste Beth's data as a graphic image, as unformatted text, or as an embedded worksheet object. To create a link to the data in the LHouse2 workbook, you will click the Paste link option button. This will create the link that Beth wants so she can keep the data in each document in sync.

5. Verify that **HTML Format** is the selected format in the As list box. Click the **Paste link** option button. Click the **OK** button to paste Beth's financial data into her letter. The financial report is pasted into the letter as shown in Figure A2-6.

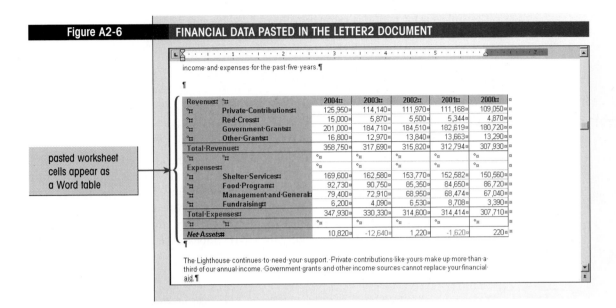

Figure A2-6 | FINANCIAL DATA PASTED IN THE LETTER2 DOCUMENT

pasted worksheet
cells appear as
a Word table

income and expenses for the past five years.

Revenue:		2004:	2003:	2002:	2001:	2000:
	Private Contributions:	125,950	114,140	111,970	111,168	109,050
	Red Cross:	15,000	5,870	5,500	5,344	4,870
	Government Grants:	201,000	184,710	184,510	182,619	180,720
	Other Grants:	16,800	12,970	13,840	13,663	13,290
Total Revenue:		358,750	317,690	315,820	312,794	307,930
Expenses:						
	Shelter Services:	169,600	162,580	153,770	152,582	150,560
	Food Program:	92,730	90,750	85,350	84,650	86,720
	Management and General:	79,400	72,910	68,950	68,474	67,040
	Fundraising:	6,200	4,090	6,530	8,708	3,390
Total Expenses:		347,930	330,330	314,600	314,414	307,710
Net Assets:		10,820	-12,640	1,220	-1,620	220

The Lighthouse continues to need your support. Private contributions like yours make up more than a
third of our annual income. Government grants and other income sources cannot replace your financial
aid.

The financial data is inserted into the Word document as a table. You can edit and format
this table using any of Word's formatting features.

Updating a Linked Object

Links between different programs work the same way as links between Excel workbooks. As
described in Tutorial 6, linked information will be updated under the following circumstances:

- The destination program will prompt you to update the link with the source
  document when you initially open the destination document.

- If both the destination and source documents are open, the link will be automatically updated whenever the information in the source document is changed.

- If only the destination document is open, you can manually update the link
  at any time by clicking Links on the Edit menu, selecting the link, and then
  clicking the Update Now button.

Beth has finished reviewing the financial summary in the LHouse2 workbook. She finds
a data entry error in the report. A $15,000 Red Cross contribution to The Lighthouse has
been entered, when the amount should've been only $5000. This is an excellent opportunity
for you to test the ability to update linked data without having to paste the data again.

To update the linked information:

1. Switch to the **LHouse2** workbook in Excel. Press the **Esc** key to remove the
   selection border around the range A2:G16.

2. Click cell **C4**, type **5,000** and press the **Enter** key to insert the correct value for
   the Red Cross contribution.

3. Switch to the **Letter2** document in Word. Note that the value of the Red Cross
   contribution has automatically changed, reflecting the current value in the
   LHouse2 workbook.

The linked information is automatically updated because both the source and destination documents are open. If this were not the case, you might have to open the Edit Links dialog box in the destination document to manually update the link. All of the Office applications use the same Edit Links dialog box to manage linked objects. You can refer to Tutorial 6 to learn more about managing linked data.

Embedding an Object

Beth also wants the letter to include a pie chart detailing the source of The Lighthouse's income. The pie chart is displayed in the LHouse2 workbook. Beth is now confident that the financial summary is correct and that no further edits are needed. So she doesn't want to create a link between her letter and the workbook's chart. Instead she would like to embed the chart in her letter. This will allow her to use Excel's chart editing tools from within her Word document, if she chooses to modify the chart's appearance before printing the letter.

To embed an Excel chart in a Word document:

1. Switch to the **LHouse2** workbook in Excel. Scroll down the Financial Summary worksheet window so the charts are completely visible, and click the **Income** chart.

2. Click the **Copy** button on the Excel Standard toolbar.

3. Switch to the **Letter2** document in Word.

4. Click the paragraph mark ¶ displayed above the letter's last paragraph (above the sentence that reads "If you would like to learn more about The Lighthouse, ...").

5. Click **Edit** on the menu bar, and then click **Paste Special**. The Paste Special dialog box opens, but this time displays different format options in the As list box.

   You have two format options for charts from which to choose: one is to paste the chart as an Excel chart object; the other is to paste the chart as a graphic. Beth wants to have the ability to use Excel's chart editing tools, so you'll choose the first option.

6. Verify that **Microsoft Excel Chart Object** is the selected format and that the Paste option button (*not* the Paste link option button) is selected. Click the **OK** button. Excel pastes the chart as an embedded object into the letter. See Figure A2-7.

Figure A2-7   **CHART EMBEDDED IN THE LETTER2 DOCUMENT**

The Lighthouse continues to need your support. Private contributions like yours make up more than a third of our annual income. Government grants and other income sources cannot replace your financial aid. ¶

Income

Private Contributions 36%

Other Grants 5%

Government Grants 58%

Red Cross 1%

If you would like to learn more about The Lighthouse, please feel free to call us at (455) 555-8912, or visit The Lighthouse offices at 5105 Atkins Way in Greenwood. ¶

Modifying **an Embedded Object**

After viewing the contents of the chart, Beth decides that she would like to change the chart's title from "Income" to "Income for 2004". She can do this by editing the chart from within Word. Recall that when you make changes to an embedded object, those changes will not be reflected in the object in the source document.

To edit the embedded chart:

1. Double-click the embedded chart in the Letter2 document. A thick border appears around the chart, and the Excel Chart menu appears in the Word menu bar. See Figure A2-8. Notice that the embedded object appears within an Excel workbook. You can now edit this object in place using Excel's chart editing commands. Thus, you have access to all of the Excel features while within Word.

| Figure A2-8 | EMBEDDED CHART SELECTED FOR EDITING |

Chart menu appears when the embedded chart is selected

thick border indicates the chart is selected

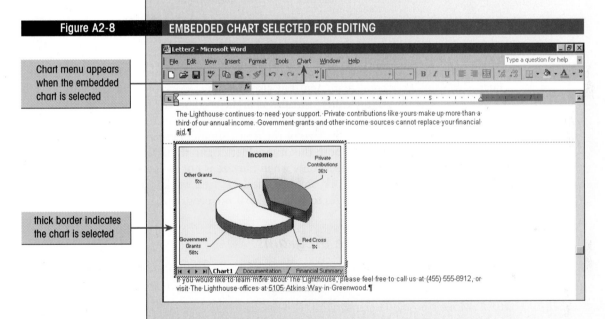

2. Click **Chart** on the menu bar, and then click **Chart Options**. Word opens the Chart Options dialog box.

3. If necessary, click the **Titles** tab, click in the Chart title text box, type **Income for 2004** as the new title, and then click the **OK** button. The chart title is changed.

4. Click outside of the chart to deselect it. The Chart menu disappears from the Word menu bar. See Figure A2-9.

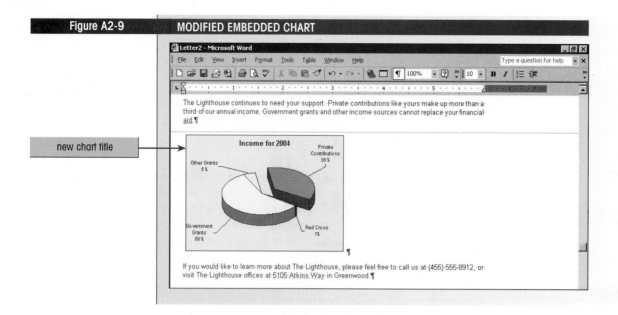

Figure A2-9   **MODIFIED EMBEDDED CHART**

new chart title

You may have noticed in Figure A2-8 that the embedded object included not just the chart sheet for the income statement but also the other worksheets in the workbook. You could've selected one of the other worksheets in the workbook and display that information in place of the chart. This fact also relates to one of the disadvantages of embedded objects: they tend to greatly increase the size of the destination document. The Letter2 document now contains the contents of both the original letter and the LHouse2 workbook. For this reason, you should embed objects only when file size is not an issue.

Beth has completed her work on both the LHouse2 workbook and the Letter2 document. You can save your changes to both and exit the programs.

To close and exit the programs:

1. Click the **Close** button ⊠ on the Word title bar, and then click the **Yes** button when prompted to save your changes.

2. Make sure the **LHouse2** workbook is displayed in Excel.

3. Click the **Close** button ⊠ on the Excel title bar, and then click the **Yes** button when prompted to save your changes.

Beth is very pleased with the ease of sharing information between Excel and other Windows programs. This is a technique that she will use often in her position as financial directory. She'll contact you again when she needs to do this kind of work in the future.

REVIEW ASSIGNMENTS

Beth is working on another letter that she needs your help on. She is writing a letter to the state government reporting on shelter and meal program use at The Lighthouse. She has this data in an Excel workbook and needs to incorporate the data into the letter she is composing in Word. Because the report will also include projections for the upcoming year, which she might be modifying, Beth wants to create a link between the information in the Excel workbook and the document in Word. She also wants to embed a chart in the Word document. She has asked for your help in linking the two documents.

To complete this task:

1. Start Excel and then open the **Use1** workbook located in the Appendix.02\Review folder on your Data Disk. Enter the date and your name in the Documentation sheet. Save the workbook as **Use2** in the same folder.

2. Start Word and then open the **Request1** Word document located in the Appendix.02\Review folder. Save the workbook as **Request2** in the same folder.

3. Copy the range A1:G8 in the Shelter Usage sheet of the Use2 workbook.

Explore 4. Paste the selected range as a link in Picture format below the first paragraph of Beth's letter.

5. Beth has discovered that the number of client days in the domestic abuse shelter in December of 2004 was actually 75, not 72. Make this change in the Use2 workbook and verify that the picture in the Request2 document is automatically updated.

6. Copy the Projected Usage chart from the Shelter Usage worksheet, and embed the chart below the second paragraph in Beth's letter (do not link the chart.)

7. Edit the embedded chart, changing the background color of the plot area from light yellow to white.

8. Save your changes to the Request2 and Use2 files, print the letter, and then close both programs.

CASE PROBLEMS

Explore **Case 1. Creating a Slide Show for Omicron.com** Howard Laarsen works in sales for Omicron.com, a multinational company that specializes in power and network solutions. He is preparing a slide show for an upcoming sales conference, and he wants to link some of the slides in the show to financial information contained in an Excel workbook. He has asked your help in creating a compound document combining both an Excel worksheet and a PowerPoint slide show.

To complete this task:

1. Start Excel and then open the **Omicron1** workbook located in the Appendix.02\Cases folder on your Data Disk. Enter the date and your name in the Documentation sheet. Save the workbook as **Omicron2** in the same folder.

2. Start PowerPoint and then open the **Show1** PowerPoint presentation located in the Appendix.02\Cases folder. Save the workbook as **Show2** in the same folder.

3. Copy the range A1:B9 in the Fast Facts worksheet and paste (but don't link) the selection into the fourth slide in the presentation as device independent bitmap. Select the table and drag the resizing handles to enlarge the table to fit the space available in the slide.

4. Paste the cell range A1:F22 of the Highlights worksheet as a linked worksheet object into the fifth slide of the presentation. Change the dividends paid per common share value in cell B16 from 0.50 to 0.52, and then verify that the table in the presentation is automatically updated.

5. Paste the revenue chart as an embedded chart object into the sixth slide of the presentation.

6. Change the chart type of the embedded chart to a clustered bar chart with a 3-D visual effect.

7. Save your changes to the Show2 presentation and the Omicron2 workbook. Print the contents of the Show2 presentation. Close both programs.

Case 2. Inserting Word Objects into a Financial Report Kurt Walters works as an accountant for Phoenix Software. He has been asked to create an Excel workbook containing the company's income statement, cash flow statement and balance sheet for the previous three years. Kurt wants to include some documentation in the workbook providing background details on the figures in his report. Such background details have already been entered into several Word documents. Kurt wants to embed these Word documents directly into his Excel workbook. He would like the documents to appear as icons, so that users can double-click the icons to view the document contents if they want. Kurt has asked for your help integrating the two documents. You can embed Word documents in your Excel workbooks using the Object command on the Excel Insert menu.

To complete this task:

1. Open the **Phoenix1** workbook located in the Appendix.02\Cases folder on your Data Disk. Enter the date and your name in the Documentation sheet. Save the workbook as **Phoenix2** in the same folder. Switch to the Balance Sheet worksheet and make cell E7 the active cell.

Explore   2. Open the Object dialog box, and then click the Create from File tab. Click the Browse button and then locate the **Accounting.doc** Word file that is stored in the Appendix.02\Cases folder on your Data Disk. Click the Insert button.

Explore   3. Click the Display as icon check box.

4. Click the Change icon button, and change the caption for the icon to "Accounting".

Explore   5. Double-click the Accounting icon that you just created and verify that it opens a Word document displaying a description of various accounting terms used in the Balance Sheet worksheet.

6. Close the Accounting document.

7. Embed the following documents as icons:

   ■ **Expenses.doc** in cell E8 of the Income Statement worksheet. Change the caption for the icon to "Expenses".

   ■ **Investment.doc** in cell E15 of the Income Statement worksheet. Change the caption for the icon to "Investment".

   ■ **Earnings.doc** in cell E22 of the Income Statement worksheet. Change the caption for the icon to "Earnings".

8. Verify that the icons open the correct documents. Close each document after it opens.

9. Save your changes to the workbook. Close both programs.

In this tutorial you will:

- Learn to create custom formats for numbers, text, and dates

- Work with custom formats for different conditions

CREATING CUSTOM FORMATS

Formatting Stock Market Data

CASE

Midland Clinic

Doctor Susan Simpson is a research physician at Midland Clinic. One of her areas of research involves low birth weight babies (less than 3.5 pounds) who have been admitted to the clinic's neonatal intensive care unit. Dr. Simpson is comparing the results of two different feeding regimens for these babies in order to determine which is the most effective in promoting weight gain. The two regimens, labeled "Standard" and "Test", use either the standard feeding regimen or a new test regimen.

Dr. Simpson has been recording data for the study in an Excel workbook. She would like to format the workbook to make it easier to read and interpret the study's results. She has asked for your help in designing custom formats specific to her workbook's needs.

SESSION A3.1

In this session, you'll use format codes to create custom formats for numbers, text, and dates. You'll also learn how to create conditional formats that change the cell's format based on the cell's value.

Using Format Codes

Dr. Simpson has recorded the data for her study in a workbook named Midland1. Open that workbook now.

To open Dr. Simpson's workbook:

1. Start Excel and open the **Midland1** workbook located in the Appendix.03\Tutorial folder on your Data Disk.

2. Enter your name and the date in the Documentation sheet.

3. Save the workbook as **Midland2** in the Appendix.03\Tutorial folder on your Data Disk.

4. Switch to the Clinical Data worksheet shown in Figure A3-1.

Figure A3-1   THE MIDLAND2 WORKBOOK

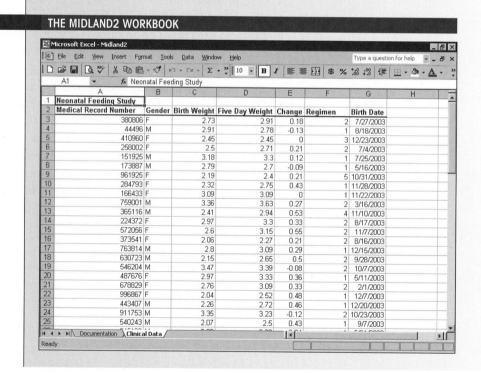

Dr. Simpson has recorded each infant's medical record number, gender, birth weight, five-day weight, and change in weight over the first five days in the neonatal ICU. She has also recorded an ID number indicating the infant's feeding regimen. A value of 1 indicates that the infant was enrolled in the Standard feeding regimen, and a value of 2 indicates enrollment in the Test regimen. Any other value in this column tells Dr. Simpson that the infant was fed following neither the Standard nor Test regimen. Finally, she has recorded each infant's date of birth. Currently, Dr. Simpson hasn't applied any formatting to her data. She wants you to correct this and outlines the formats she wants applied to her data:

■ The 6-digit medical record number values in column A are actually the combinations of two 3-digit insurance codes. Dr. Simpson wants a dash (-) to be placed between the first set of 3-digit numbers and the second so that the value 380806 appears as 380-806.

■ Weight values in columns C and D are recorded in pounds. Dr. Simpson would like these values displayed to two decimal place accuracy with the abbreviation "lbs." to be appended to each weight value in those columns so that the value 2.7 appears as "2.70 lbs."

■ The change in weight values in column E should appear in a red font if the infant lost weight during the study and blue if the infant gained weight, and if the infant's weight was unchanged, the cell should display the text "No Change" in a black font.

■ The regimen ID numbers should be formatted to display the following: "Standard" if the regimen value is 1, "Test" if the regimen is 2, and "Other" for any other value.

■ The birth date should be displayed with the name of the month, followed by the date and year (for example, 9/25/2003 should be displayed as September 25, 2003).

Excel supplies a generous collection of format and styles to improve the appearance and readability of your documents. However, there are no formats and styles to accommodate all of Dr. Simpson's requests. To format the workbook as she would like, you will have to create your own formats, called **custom formats**. Custom formats are created using **format codes**, a series of symbols that describe exactly how Excel should display a number, date, time, or text string. Format codes can be used to display text strings and spaces, determine how many decimal places to display in a cell, and even determine the color of the text in the cell.

Working with Numeric Codes

Each number is composed of digits. In displaying these digits, Excel makes special note of **insignificant zeros**, which are those zeros whose omission from the number does not change the number's value. For example, the number 203.00 contains two insignificant zeros to the right of the decimal point because omitting them does not change the number's value. One could also write this value as 0203.00 (though one usually doesn't), so there are actually insignificant zeros to the left of the left-most visible digit. To format a value, Excels uses special placeholders to represent individual digits. There are three types of placeholders: #, 0, and ?. Excel interprets each placeholder as follows:

■ # displays only significant digits and does not display insignificant zeros

■ 0 (zero) displays insignificant zeros as well as significant digits

■ ? replaces insignificant zeros with spaces on either side of the decimal point so that the decimal points align when formatted with a fixed-width font, such as Courier

A custom format can use combinations of these placeholders. For example, the custom format #.00 displays the value 8.9 as "8.90". If a value has more digits than placeholders in the custom format, Excel will round the value to match the number of placeholders. Thus, the value 8.938 formatted with the custom format #.## will be displayed as "8.94". Figure A3-2 shows how the same series of numbers would be displayed using different custom number formats.

Figure A3-2 — DIGIT PLACEHOLDERS

VALUE IN CELL	#.##	CUSTOM FORMATS 0.00	?.??	#.#0
0.57	.57	0.57	.57	.57
123.4	123.4	123.40	123.4	123.40
3.45	3.45	3.45	3.45	3.45
7.891	7.89	7.89	7.89	7.89
5.248	5.25	5.25	5.25	5.25

In addition to digit placeholders, Excel's number formats also include separators, such as the decimal point separator (.), thousands separator (,), and fraction separator (/). You've already seen examples of how the decimal point separator can be used in a custom format. The thousands separator can be used to separate the number in groups of one thousand, but it can also be used to scale a number by a multiple of one thousand.

The fraction separator displays decimal values as fractions. The general syntax is *placeholder/placeholder* where *placeholder* is one or more of the custom format placeholders discussed above. Excel will then display the fraction that best approximates the decimal value. You can also specify the denominator for the fraction to convert the decimals to halves, quarters, and so forth. Figure A3-3 provides examples of the thousands separator and the fraction separator.

Figure A3-3 — THOUSANDS SEPARATOR AND FRACTION SEPARATOR

VALUE	CUSTOM FORMAT	APPEARANCE
12000	#,###	12,000
12000	#,	12
12200000	0.0,,	12.2
5.4	# #/#	5 2/5
5.4	#/#	27/5
5.4	# #/25	5 10/25

Finally, the E and % format codes can be used to display the data value in either scientific notation or as a percentage. Figure A3-4 shows how these format codes can be used to format values.

Figure A3-4 — SCIENTIFIC AND PERCENT NOTATION

VALUE	CUSTOM FORMAT	APPEARANCE
12000	0.00E+00	1.20E+04
0.00012	0.00E+00	1.20E-04
0.2	0.00%	20.00%
0.2	#%	20%

All of the numeric format codes can be combined in a single custom format, providing the user with great control of the data's appearance. If you don't specify a numeric code for your data values, Excel will automatically insert the format code, **General**, which applies a general numeric format to the data values. The General format display hides all insignificant zeros.

Working with Text Codes

Excel also supplies formatting codes to work with text entries. To display a text string in the cell, enclose the text string in quotation marks ("") within the custom format. For example, the format #.00 "in." will display the value 2.54 as "2.54 in.". The following characters will be displayed without requiring any quotation marks: $ - + / () : ! & ~ {} = <> and the space character.

Recall that Dr. Simpson wanted all of the medical record numbers from column A displayed with a dash separating the first three numbers from the last three. You can display the data this way using the custom format: 000-000. Note that the dash acts as a text character, separating the two sets of digits.

To format the medical record numbers:

1. Select the range **A3:A77**.

2. Click **Format** on the menu bar, click **Cells**, and then click the **Number** tab if necessary.

3. Click **Custom** in the Category list box.

4. Type **000-000** in the Type text box. See Figure A3-5.

Figure A3-5	CREATING A CUSTOM FORMAT

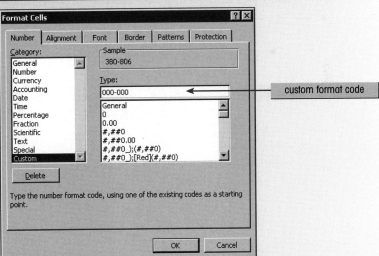

5. Click the **OK** button. Excel displays the values in column A using the dash divider. See Figure A3-6.

Figure A3-6	APPLYING A CUSTOM FORMAT

	A	B	C	D	E	F	G	H
1	Neonatal Feeding Study							
2	Medical Record Number	Gender	Birth Weight	Five Day Weight	Change	Regimen	Birth Date	
3	380-806	F	2.73	2.91	0.18	2	7/27/2003	
4	044-496	M	2.91	2.78	-0.13	1	8/18/2003	
5	410-960	F	2.45	2.45	0	3	12/23/2003	
6	258-002	F	2.5	2.71	0.21	2	7/4/2003	
7	151-925	M	3.18	3.3	0.12	1	7/25/2003	
8	173-887	M	2.79	2.7	-0.09	1	5/16/2003	
9	961-925	F	2.19	2.4	0.21	5	10/31/2003	
10	284-793	F	2.32	2.75	0.43	1	11/28/2003	
11	166-433	F	3.09	3.09	0	1	11/22/2003	
12	759-001	M	3.36	3.63	0.27	2	3/16/2003	
13	365-116	M	2.41	2.94	0.53	4	11/10/2003	
14	224-372	F	2.97	3.3	0.33	2	8/17/2003	
15	572-056	F	2.6	3.15	0.55	2	11/7/2003	
16	373-541	F	2.06	2.27	0.21	2	8/16/2003	
17	763-814	M	2.8	3.09	0.29	1	12/15/2003	
18	630-723	M	2.15	2.65	0.5	2	9/28/2003	
19	546-204	M	3.47	3.39	-0.08	2	10/7/2003	
20	487-676	F	2.97	3.33	0.36	1	5/11/2003	
21	678-829	F	2.76	3.09	0.33	2	2/1/2003	
22	996-867	F	2.04	2.52	0.48	1	12/7/2003	
23	443-407	M	2.26	2.72	0.46	1	12/20/2003	
24	911-753	M	3.35	3.23	-0.12	2	10/23/2003	
25	540-243	M	2.07	2.5	0.43	1	9/7/2003	

custom format applied to the values in column A

Documentation / Clinical Data

Next, Dr. Simpson wants the weight values in column C and D to be displayed with two decimal point accuracy and with the text "lbs." The format you'll use to display values this way is #.00 "lbs."

To format the weight values in columns C and D:

1. Select the range **C3:D77**.

2. Click **Format** on the menu bar, and then click **Cells**.

3. Click **Custom** in the Category list box, type **#.00 "lbs."** in the Type text box, and then click the **OK** button. Figure A3-7 shows the formatted weight values.

Figure A3-7	DISPLAYING TEXT IN A CUSTOM FORMAT

	A	B	C	D	E	F	G	H
1	Neonatal Feeding Study							
2	Medical Record Number	Gender	Birth Weight	Five Day Weight	Change	Regimen	Birth Date	
3	380-806	F	2.73 lbs.	2.91 lbs.	0.18	2	7/27/2003	
4	044-496	M	2.91 lbs.	2.78 lbs.	-0.13	1	8/18/2003	
5	410-960	F	2.45 lbs.	2.45 lbs.	0	3	12/23/2003	
6	258-002	F	2.50 lbs.	2.71 lbs.	0.21	2	7/4/2003	
7	151-925	M	3.18 lbs.	3.30 lbs.	0.12	1	7/25/2003	
8	173-887	M	2.79 lbs.	2.70 lbs.	-0.09	1	5/16/2003	
9	961-925	F	2.19 lbs.	2.40 lbs.	0.21	5	10/31/2003	
10	284-793	F	2.32 lbs.	2.75 lbs.	0.43	1	11/28/2003	
11	166-433	F	3.09 lbs.	3.09 lbs.	0	1	11/22/2003	
12	759-001	M	3.36 lbs.	3.63 lbs.	0.27	2	3/16/2003	
13	365-116	M	2.41 lbs.	2.94 lbs.	0.53	4	11/10/2003	
14	224-372	F	2.97 lbs.	3.30 lbs.	0.33	2	8/17/2003	
15	572-056	F	2.60 lbs.	3.15 lbs	0.55	2	11/7/2003	
16	373-541	F	2.06 lbs.	2.27 lbs.	0.21	2	8/16/2003	
17	763-814	M	2.80 lbs.	3.09 lbs.	0.29	1	12/15/2003	
18	630-723	M	2.15 lbs.	2.65 lbs.	0.5	2	9/28/2003	
19	546-204	M	3.47 lbs.	3.39 lbs.	-0.08	2	10/7/2003	
20	487-676	F	2.97 lbs.	3.33 lbs.	0.36	1	5/11/2003	
21	678-829	F	2.76 lbs.	3.09 lbs.	0.33	2	2/1/2003	
22	996-867	F	2.04 lbs.	2.52 lbs.	0.48	1	12/7/2003	
23	443-407	M	2.26 lbs.	2.72 lbs.	0.46	1	12/20/2003	
24	911-753	M	3.35 lbs.	3.23 lbs.	-0.12	2	10/23/2003	
25	540-243	M	2.07 lbs.	2.50 lbs.	0.43	1	9/7/2003	

Documentation / Clinical Data

Figure A3-8 describes some of the other text codes you can use in your custom formats. These include the ability to repeat characters and to specify exactly where text entered by the user will appear in the cell.

Figure A3-8	TEXT FORMAT CODES			
CODE	**DESCRIPTION**	**VALUE**	**CUSTOM FORMAT**	**DISPLAYED AS**
"text"	Displays the entry within quotation marks as text	325	### "Dollars"	**325 Dollar**
*	Repeats the character following the asterisk enough times to fill the cell	128	*0	00000000
@	Indicates where user input text will appear	Simpson	"Dr." @	Dr. Simpson
\	Displays the character following the back slash as text	325	###\@	325@
$-+/():!&~{}=<>	Displays character as shown	000-00-000	06742113	067-42-113
[color]	Displays characters in the cell in the indicated *color*	325	[Blue]###	325

As indicated in Figure A3-8, you can also specify the color of the characters in the cell. The syntax is [*color*], where color is black, blue, cyan, green, magenta, red, white, or yellow.

Using **Conditional Formats**

Excel recognizes four possibilities for a cell's value. A cell can have a positive value, a negative value, a zero, or a text string. For this reason, each custom format can be divided into four sections, separated by semicolons, specifying the format for positive values, negative values, zeros, and text strings. The general structure of the custom format is:

positive format; *negative format*; *zero format*; *text format*

If you specify only two sections, the first format is applied to positive numbers and zeros; the second format is applied to negative numbers. If you specify only one section, the format is used for all numbers. If you skip a section, you still need to include the semicolon for that section.

You'll take advantage of this structure to format the weight change values in column E of Dr. Simpson's worksheet. Dr. Simpson wants the values to appear in a red font if the weight change is negative, blue if the weight change is positive, and if the infant's weight change is zero, the cell should display the text "No Change" in a black font. You will use the following custom format:

[Blue]#0.00;[Red]-#0.00;"No Change"

Note that, if you do not specify a color, the text will appear in the default font color, which is black in this case.

To insert the conditional format:

1. Select the range **E3:E77**.

2. Click **Format** on the menu bar, and then click **Cells**.

3. Click **Custom** in the Category list box.

4. In the Type text box, type **[Blue]#0.00;(Red)-#0.00;"No Change"**. See Figure A3-9.

Figure A3-9	CREATING A CONDITIONAL FORMAT

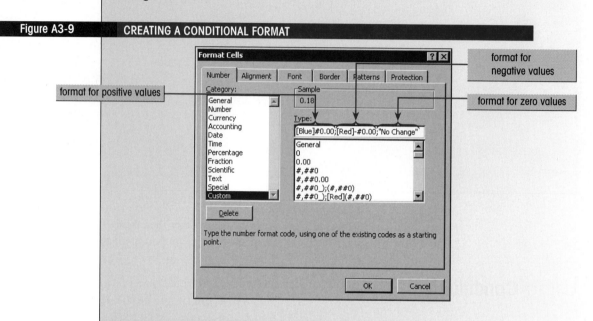

5. Click the **OK** button.

6. Enlarge column E to **10** characters. Figure A3-10 shows the formatted weight change values.

Figure A3-10	APPLYING A CONDITIONAL FORMAT

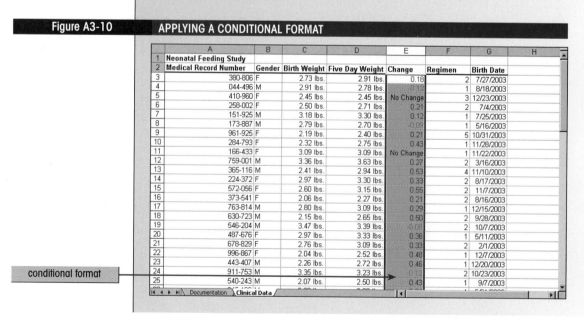

Sometimes you will want to apply a conditional format to entries other than positive, negative, or zero values. If that is the case, you can create a custom format by specifying the condition. The syntax for creating a custom format is

Format1[Condition1];Format2[Condition2];Default Format

where *Condition1* and *Condition2* are expressions that define certain conditions, and *Format1* and *Format2* are format codes applied when those conditions are true. The *Default Format* is applied when neither *Condition1* nor *Condition2* is true. For example, the following custom format

[Red][<100];[Blue][>200];[Black]

will display the cell's value in red if the value is less than 100, blue if the value is greater than 200, and black if neither of those conditions is true. You can only supply two conditions, and those conditions can only involve numeric comparisons.

Dr. Simpson wants the values in the Regimen column to display the text "Standard" for values of 1, "Test" for values of 2, and "Other" for all other values. The custom format to do this would be as follows:

"Standard"[=1];"Test"[=2];"Other"

Note that the values themselves are not changed, only what Excel displays in the cell.

To apply the condition format to the regimen values:

1. Select the range **F3:F77**.

2. Click **Format** on the menu bar, and then click **Cells**.

3. Click **Custom** in the Category list box.

4. Type **"Standard"(=1);"Test"(=2);"Other"** in the Type text box. See Figure A3-11.

Figure A3-11	CONDITIONAL FORMAT TO TEST FOR VALUE

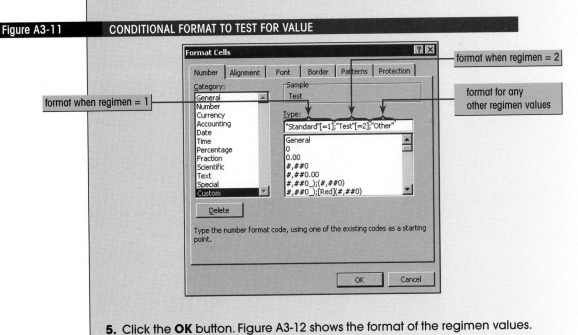

5. Click the **OK** button. Figure A3-12 shows the format of the regimen values.

Figure A3-12 | APPLYING A CONDITIONAL FORMAT

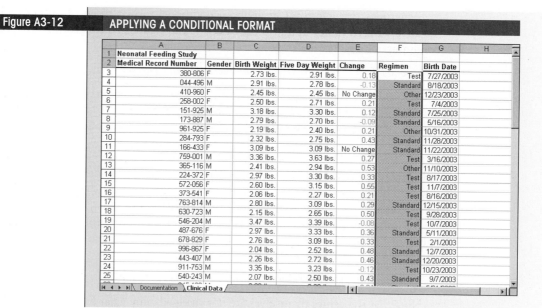

One last change is needed: changing the format of the date values in the last column.

Formatting Dates

When dates, times, or both are displayed in a workbook, you'll most likely use one of Excel's predefined date and time formats to display them in readable format. Although the predefined time and date formats are usually fine, you can also create your own custom date formats. Figure A3-13 illustrates the format codes used for dates and times.

Figure A3-13 | FORMAT CODES FOR DATES AND TIMES

SYMBOL	TO DISPLAY
m	Months as 1–12
mm	Months as 01–12
mmm	Months as Jan–Dec
mmmm	Months as January–December
d	Days as 1–31
dd	Days as 01–31
ddd	Days as Sun–Sat
dddd	Days as Sunday–Saturday
yy	Years as 00–99
yyyy	Years as 1900–9999
h	Hours as 1–24
mm	Minutes as 01–60 (when mm immediately follows h signifies minutes; otherwise, months)
ss	Seconds as 01–60

Dr. Simpson would like the date values in the last column to be displayed with the name of the month, followed by the date and year (for example, September 14, 2003). The format code to do this is *mmmm d, yyyy*.

Apply this format to the birth date values in column G.

To apply a date format:

1. Select the range **G3:G77**.

2. Click **Format** on the menu bar, and then click **Cells**.

3. Click **Custom** in the Category list box.

4. Type **mmmm d, yyyy** in the Type text box, and then click the **OK** button.

5. Click cell **A1**. Figure A3-14 shows the final formatted version of the Clinical Data worksheet.

Figure A3-14   FORMATTED MIDLAND2 WORKBOOK

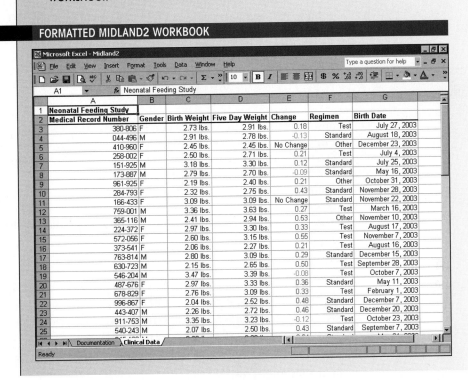

Once you create a custom format, it is stored in the workbook, and you can apply the custom format to any other cell range in the workbook. However, the format can only be used in the workbook in which it was created. If Dr. Simpson wants to use the formats you created in the Midland2 workbook elsewhere, she will have to reenter the custom format codes.

To complete your work:

1. Save your changes to the Midland2 workbook.

2. Close the workbook and exit Excel.

Dr. Simpson appreciates the work you've done for her. She will contact you again if she needs any more help with custom formats.

Session A3.1 QUICK | CHECK

1. What custom format would you enter to display the value .2 as "0.20"?

2. What custom format would you use to display the value 0.15 as a fraction?

3. What custom format would you enter to display the value 12 as "12 years"?

4. What custom format would you use to display the text "Standard" in a green colored font?

5. What custom format would you enter to display the text string "low" if the cell's value is less than 0, "high" if the value is greater than 0, and "no change" if the value is 0?

6. What custom format would you enter to display the text string "low" if the cell's value is less than 50, "high" if the value is 50 or greater?

7. What custom format would you use to display dates showing the day of the week, month, day, and year (for example, "Monday, September 20, 2004")?

REVIEW ASSIGNMENTS

Dr. Simpson's continues to enter data on her study. She has a new workbook for you to format. In this workbook, she recorded data on the 20-day weight gain for infants in her study. She would like to have some way of highlighting those infants who have gained more than 1 pound during the course of the study. She has also divided the study into two groups: those who have been fed with a low caloric formula and those who have been fed with a formula high in calories. These are entered into her workbook with the identification values: 0 (low cal) and 1 (high cal). She wants you to display the text string "low cal" or "high cal" in place of those ID values.

To complete this task:

1. Open the **Study1** workbook located in the Appendix.03\Review folder on your Data Disk. Enter the date and your name in the Documentation sheet. Save the workbook as **Study2** in the same folder. Switch to the Study Data worksheet.

2. Format the medical record numbers in column A so that a blank space separates the first three digits from the second three. Be sure that all insignificant zeros are displayed, including leading zeros.

Explore   3. Display the prefix "Dr." before each of the doctor's names in column B.

4. Format the weight values in columns D and E displaying two insignificant zeros to the right of the decimal point and one insignificant zero to the left. Display the text "lbs.", appended to each value.

Explore   5. Create a custom format for the values in the Change column so that the values equal to or greater than 1 are displayed in a blue font and values less than 1 are displayed in red. The values themselves should be displayed with two insignificant zeros to the right of the decimal point and one insignificant zero to the left.

6. Create a custom format for the values in Formula column, displaying the text "low cal" for a value of zero and "high cal" for a value of one.

7. Format the dates as *day-month-year* where *day* is the day of the month, *month* is the name of the month, and *year* is the four-digit year (for example, 27-July-2003).

8. Save your changes and close the workbook. Exit Excel.

CASE PROBLEMS

Case 1. Formatting Employee Data for BG Software Richard Lee is an accountant for BG Software. He has recorded employee data on an Excel workbook and asked your help in formatting the data. One of the things he wants you to do is format the salary data so that the actual salary figures are not visible on the worksheet. He also wants you to format social security numbers and information on each employee's choice of health plan and retirement plan.

To complete this task:

1. Open the **BG1** workbook located in the Appendix.03\Cases folder on your Data Disk. Enter the date and your name in the Documentation sheet. Save the workbook as **BG2** in the same folder. Switch to the Employees worksheet.

2. Format the values in the SSN column as social security numbers (for example, 113-20-9889).

Explore

3. Hide the values in the Salary column by creating a custom format that repeatedly displays a decimal point that fills up the entire cell.

4. Create a custom format in column C that displays the text "<5 years" for values that are less than 5 and ">= 5 years" for values that are equal to five or greater.

5. In column D, create a custom format that displays the text "Single" for the value 0 and "Family" for a value of 1.

6. In column E, create a custom format that displays the text "Standard" for the value 0 and "Extended" for a value of 1.

7. Save the workbook and then close it. Exit Excel.

Case 2. Formatting Golf Scores at DigiGolf DigiGolf is a golf store that maintains a database of golf scores of its customers in order to calculate their handicap. Alan Witt is an employee at DigiGolf. He is storing scores in an Excel workbook and would like your help in formatting the scores.

To complete this task:

1. Open the **Golf1** workbook located in the Appendix.03\Cases folder on your Data Disk. Enter the date and your name in the Documentation sheet. Save the workbook as **Golf2** in the same folder. Switch to the Score worksheet.

2. In row 5, Alan has recorded the score shot by John Krusk for each hole at the Hawk's Hill golf course. Format the score for the holes so that scores are displayed in red if less than par, blue if greater than par, and black if otherwise. (*Hint*: You will have to create a separate custom format for the par 3, 4, and 5 holes.)

3. In row 6, Alan has calculated the current total score through each hole. If the current score is 0, display the text "E", and if the score is greater than 0, display a plus sign (+) in front of the score (for example, +3).

Explore

4. Display the values in cells B15 and B16 as fractions with a denominator of 18 (for example, 9/18).

5. Save your changes to the workbook and then close it. Exit Excel.

QUICK | CHECK ANSWERS

Session A3.1

1. 0.00
2. ## / ## or 00/00 or ??/??
3. # "year" or #0 "years"
4. [Green]
5. "high";"low";"no change"
6. "low"[<50];"high"[>=50]
7. dddd, mmmm d, yyyy

In this tutorial you will:

- Learn about different ways Excel can create Web pages

- Learn about interactive and noninteractive Web pages

- Create a Web page based on a PivotTable

- Edit a PivotTable from within a Web page

- Export a PivotTable from the Web to an Excel workbook

SAVING PIVOTTABLES IN HTML FORMAT

Creating Interactive PivotTables for the Web

CASE

GP Golf Gloves

GP Golf is a manufacturer of golf apparel located in Argyle, Maine. The company's specialty is golf gloves. They sell three brands: the Regular glove, the Pro glove, and the SoftGrip glove. Each of these gloves comes in four sizes: small, medium, large and extra large. GP Golf creates separate versions of its gloves for women and men and for right handers and left handers.

The company has created an Excel workbook that contains monthly sales figures for each model, size and version of its gloves. Peter Boyle, the director of sales, would like to make this information easily available to his sales staff. The company has recently installed an Intranet in order to facilitate the sharing of documents and information among its employees. Peter has asked you to help him in placing his workbook on the Intranet.

You and Peter discuss the issue with the network group and are told that documents on the company's Intranet must be saved in HTML format—the standard format for Web pages. Peter objects, feeling that this would remove the workbook's functionality. Unable to convince them to change their policy, Peter asks you to find out whether Excel can create Web pages that will preserve some of the features of workbooks.

SESSION A4.1

In this session, you'll learn about the different ways Excel workbooks can be exported as Web pages. You'll learn how to create a Web page containing an interactive PivotTable. You'll have a chance to work with the PivotTable and learn how to perform many of the same operations in your Web browser that you perform from within Excel.

Saving Workbooks as Web Pages

Excel provides many different possibilities for creating Web pages based on your Excel workbook. These pages fall into two main categories: noninteractive and interactive. A **noninteractive Web page** contains the data from the workbook and some of the formatting, but it does not allow users to work with the data as they would from within Excel. Creating a noninteractive Web page is like creating a "snapshot" of the data in the workbook. Every time the workbook changes, it has to be resaved to the Web page, or else the page will be out of date.

An alternative is to create an **interactive Web page** that preserves some (but not all) of the workbook's functionality. When you publish your workbook in an interactive format, users can still do the following:

- Enter data
- Format data
- Enter formulas and functions
- Sort and filter a data list

If your interactive Web page contains data from an external data source, which may be the case when you create a PivotTable or chart, the user can refresh the page to retrieve the most current data. Thus there is no need to resave the workbook whenever new data is entered.

With all of these advantages, you might wonder why you would ever want to save your Web page in a noninteractive format. One reason could be that you want your page to be only a snapshot of the workbook at a specific moment in time (for example, when you want to display annual report information). Also, although interactive Web pages can be powerful, their features are not necessarily going to be supported by every type and version of Web browser. You might create a fancy Web page only to discover that your users lack the ability to view and use it. Thus, before publishing your workbook on the Web, you need to understand the needs and capabilities of your audience.

Excel provides three ways of producing interactive Web pages: pages with spreadsheet functionality, pages with interactive PivotTables, and pages with interactive charts.

Web Pages with Spreadsheet Functionality

A Web page with **spreadsheet functionality** works like an Excel spreadsheet. The spreadsheet appears within the Web page along with several Excel tools. With these tools users can sort and filter the data, format cells, insert functions and copy, cut and paste data. Figure A4-1 shows a worksheet you might create for GP Golf to analyze cost, volume and profit for the SoftGrip model. Figure A4-2 shows the same worksheet as it would appear on the Web page with spreadsheet functionality.

Figure A4-1	AN EXCEL WORKSHEET

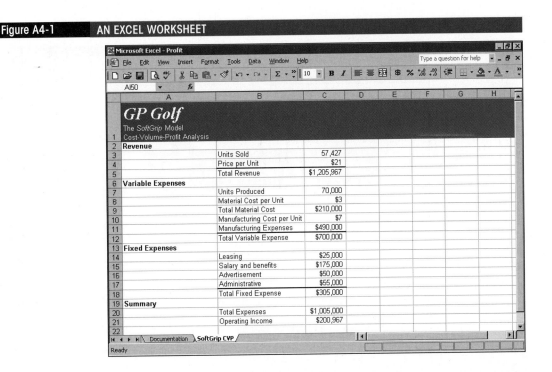

Figure A4-2	A WEB PAGE WITH SPREADSHEET FUNCTIONALITY

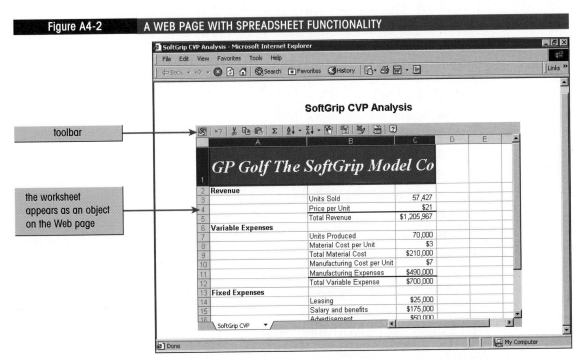

Though it may appear that the worksheet is an embedded object on the Web page, that's not the case. Any changes that a user makes to the page will not be reflected in the original workbook (though changes to the originally workbook will be reflected in the Web page). This leaves the user free to perform several what-if analyses on the data without having to worry about changing the source workbook. In this example, a user on GP Golf's intranet could use the Web page to explore the effects on SoftGrip's total revenue if the price were dropped to $20 per unit (see Figure A4-3).

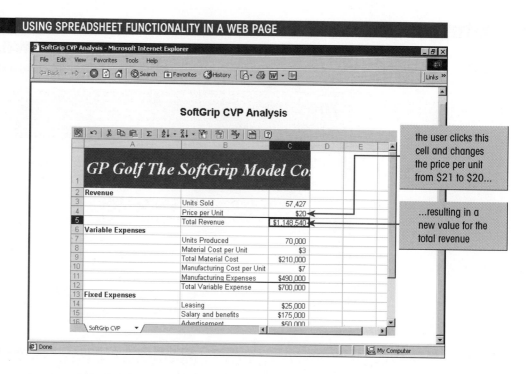

Figure A4-3   USING SPREADSHEET FUNCTIONALITY IN A WEB PAGE

Some formatting elements will not be transferred to your Web page. Among those features that will be lost when saving the worksheet to the Web are:

- Pattern fills
- Dotted or broken borders
- Graphics
- Named cells or ranges
- Drawing object layers
- Wrapped text within a cell
- Multiple fonts within a cell
- Conditional formatting
- Outlining
- Cell comments

There are other features, such as auditing, that are not available on the Web page. Review the online Help for a complete list of features and formatting that are changed or removed when creating a Web page with spreadsheet functionality.

Web Pages with PivotTable Lists

The Web version of a PivotTable is called a **PivotTable list**. PivotTable lists can be published with or without PivotTable functionality. **PivotTable functionality** allows the user to perform basic tasks like data filtering; but more importantly it enables the PivotTable list to be connected with the source data. The user can refresh the Web page at any time and be assured that the most current data is displayed in the PivotTable. A PivotTable list without PivotTable functionality behaves like a worksheet saved with spreadsheet functionality. You can work with the PivotTable, but the table is not connected to the data source. There are differences between the appearance of a PivotTable list and an Excel PivotTable. Figure A4-4 and Figure A4-5 show the same PivotTable viewed from within Excel and from within the Web browser.

Figure A4-4 | **AN EXCEL PIVOTTABLE**

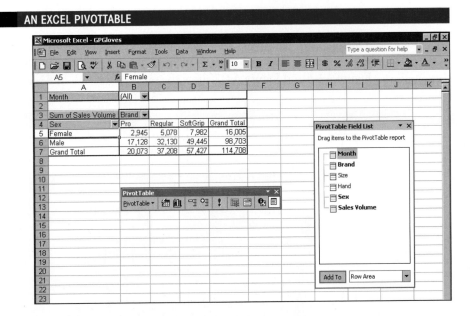

Figure A4-5 | **AN EXCEL PIVOTTABLE**

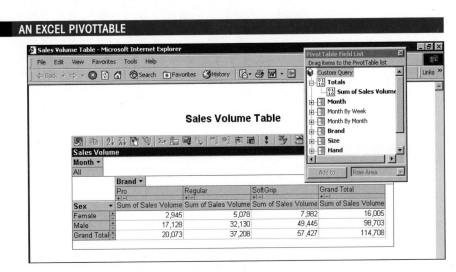

As with Excel's PivotTables, you can move fields around to alter the view of the table. You can also expand the table to view the underlying data. There are several features that Excel does not export to a PivotTable list. These include:

■ Calculated fields and items

■ Custom calculations and subtotals

■ Character and cell formatting

■ Custom sort orders

■ Background refresh of the data

■ The ability to change the table's data source

You are also limited in your choice of summary functions. The PivotTable list can display the sum, minimum, maximum or count of data field. You cannot, for example, display the average of a data field.

Web Pages with Interactive Charts

The final way of creating an interactive Web page is with an interactive chart. The **interactive chart** is a Web page that displays an Excel chart that the user can update and modify. Figure A4-6 and Figure A4-7 show the same chart both in Excel and on the Web.

Figure A4-6	AN EXCEL CHART

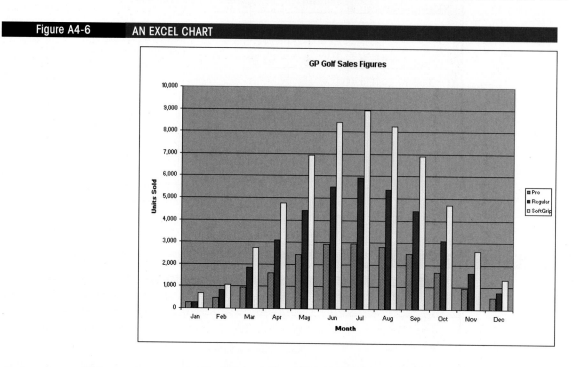

Figure A4-7	AN INTERACTIVE WEB CHART

the chart can be viewed but not edited or moved

the data table is displayed on the Web page below the chart

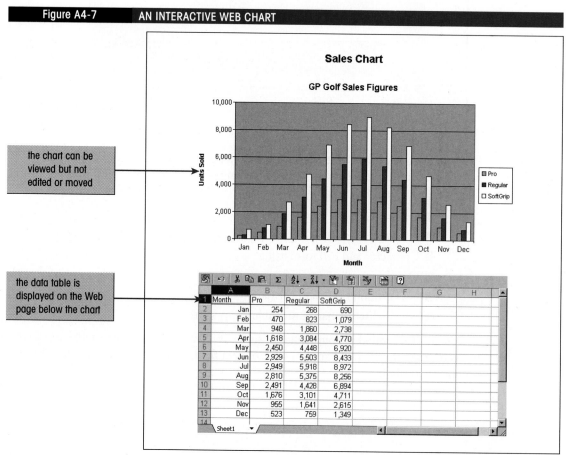

Note that the Web page includes the data for the chart. You can't change the chart's appearance, but you can change the data that the chart is based on. The data table is another example of a Web object with spreadsheet functionality. You can sort, filter and edit the data in this table, and your changes will be reflected in the chart. The chart and the data table are not connected to the original workbook, so any changes you make to the Web page are not reflected in the workbook, and if the workbook is changed, you'll have to republish its contents if you want the Web page to be current.

Many of the Excel features are not retained when you convert a chart to an interactive Web page. Among those features which are lost are:

- 3-D and surface chart types
- High-low lines, series lines, trend lines, and error bars
- Shadows, semitransparent fills, and auto-scale fonts
- Customized positioning and sizing of chart objects
- Drawing objects, text boxes, and pictures placed on the chart

If you want to edit the size and position of the chart within the Web page, you have to edit the page using an HTML editor such as Front Page Express.

Creating an Interactive PivotTable

Having reviewed some of the material on interactive components, you return to Peter with your information. Peter feels that he only needs to create a Web page containing a PivotTable list. This will provide his sales staff with quick access to the most current sales data and give them most of the functionality of an Excel PivotTable. He asks you to create such a Web page for him to review.

To open Peter's workbook:

1. Start Excel and open the **GP1** workbook located in the Appendix.04\Tutorial folder on your Data Disk.

2. Enter your name and the date in the Documentation sheet.

3. Save the workbook as **GP2** in the Appendix.04\Tutorial folder on your Data Disk.

4. Switch to the Sales Table worksheet shown in Figure A4-8.

| Figure A4-8 | THE GP2 WORKBOOK |

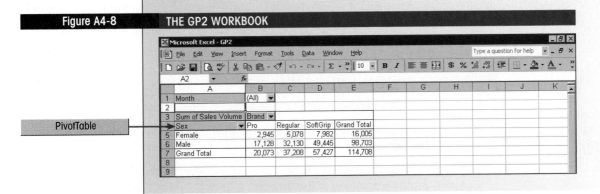

To convert this PivotTable to an interactive PivotTable list, you first use Excel's File Save As command, specifying Web Page as the file type.

To start creating the interactive PivotTable list:

1. Click **File** on the menu bar, wait for the File menu to expand, and then click **Save as Web Page**. The Save As dialog box opens.

2. Click the **Publish** button. The Publish as Web Page dialog box opens, as shown in Figure A4-9. Note that the default filename for the Web page is "Page.htm." You can change the filename to something more descriptive, which you will do shortly.

Figure A4-9 **PUBLISH AS WEB PAGE DIALOG BOX**

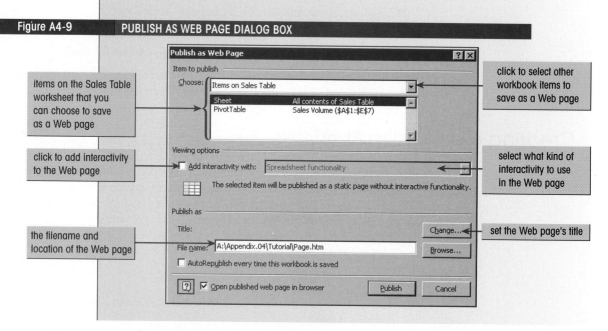

items on the Sales Table worksheet that you can choose to save as a Web page

click to select other workbook items to save as a Web page

click to add interactivity to the Web page

select what kind of interactivity to use in the Web page

the filename and location of the Web page

set the Web page's title

From this dialog box, you can specify which part of the current workbook you want to save as a Web page. As you can see from Figure A4-9, you could save the entire Sales Table worksheet or just the PivotTable on that worksheet. (To select other items in the GP2 workbook, you click the Choose list arrow.) You can also specify whether the Web page will be interactive or not, and if so, whether it employs Spreadsheet functionality or PivotTable functionality. You can also enter a title and filename for the Web page. You have all the options you need to create the Web page Peter envisions.

To enter options for the Web page:

1. Verify that **Items on Sales Table** is selected in the Choose list box.

2. Select **PivotTable** from the list of items so that only the PivotTable is published as the Web page.

3. Click the **Add interactivity with** check box, and verify that **PivotTable functionality** is selected in the list box.

4. Click the **Change** button to open the Set Title dialog box, type **GP Golf Sales Figures** as the Web page title, and then click the **OK** button.

5. Change the default Web page filename "Page.htm" to **Glove_Sales.html**, located in the Tutorial folder of Appendix.04.

TROUBLE? You can save Web page files with either the ".html" or ".htm" file extension. Web browsers will recognize either extension.

6. Verify that the Open published web page in browser check box is selected, so that your browser will open your Web page automatically after you save it. Figure A4-10 shows the completed dialog box.

Figure A4-10	COMPLETED PUBLISH AS WEB PAGE DIALOG BOX

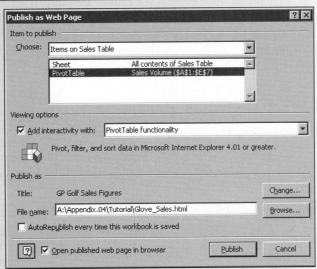

7. Click the **Publish** button. Figure A4-11 displays the completed Web page.

Figure A4-11	INTERACTIVE PIVOTTABLE WEB PAGE

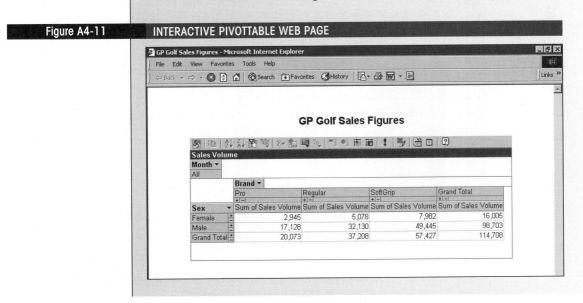

Working with an Interactive PivotTable

Now that you've created your PivotTable list, you'll find that it operates like an Excel PivotTable. You'll discover several important differences as well. You can manipulate the placement and type of fields. You can format the table's values and labels, and you can hide certain elements of the table. You'll start by working with the table's fields.

Modifying PivotTable Fields

This particular PivotTable has 4 areas: a Page area containing the Month field, a Row area containing the Sex field, a Column area displaying the Brand field and the Data area displaying the sum of the Sales Volume field for each combination of the other three fields. As with an Excel PivotTable, you move these fields around. Try this now by moving the Month field to the Row area of the table.

To move the Month field:

1. Click the **Month** field button, and then move it down to the left of the Sex field button.

2. Release the mouse button. The new PivotTable, shown in Figure A4-12, now shows a Row area that has both the Month and the Sex field.

Figure A4-12	PIVOTTABLE WITH THE MONTH FIELD MOVED TO THE ROW AREA

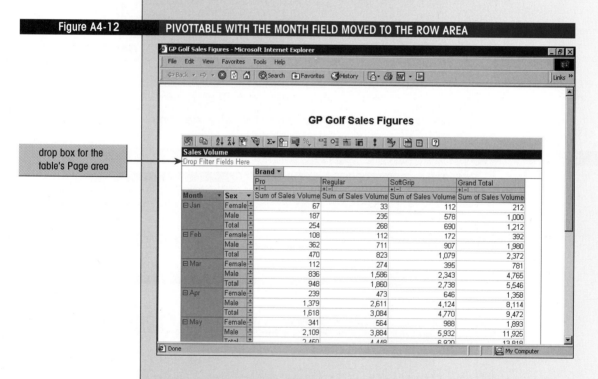

drop box for the table's Page area

3. Drag the **Month** field back to the Page area of the table (which appears with the label "Drop Filter Fields Here"), and then release the mouse button. The PivotTable is restored to its original appearance.

To display only a few levels of a field, you can select those levels from the field's drop-down checkbox–just as you would with a PivotTable in Excel. Try this now by changing the table so that it displays sales figures for only the SoftGrip glove.

To display only the SoftGrip sales figures:

1. Click the **Brand** drop-down list arrow.

2. Deselect the **Pro** and **Regular** check boxes, as shown in Figure A4-13.

| Figure A4-13 | REMOVING THE PRO AND REGULAR BRANDS FROM THE PIVOTTABLE |

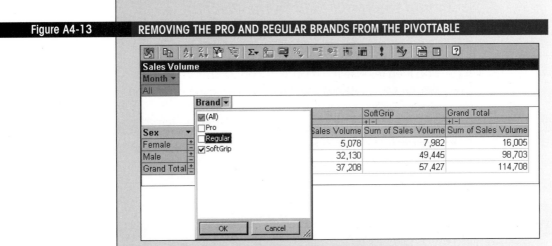

3. Click the **OK** button. The PivotTable now displays only the sales results for the SoftGrip brand.

4. Click the **Brand** drop-down list arrow again.

5. Click the **(All)** check box, and then click the **OK** button to restore the table.

If you want to remove a field, drag its button off of the table.

To remove the Sex field from the table:

1. Click the **Sex** field button.

2. Drag the field button to an empty spot on the Web page and release the mouse button. The Sex field is removed from the table. See Figure A4-14.

| Figure A4-14 | PIVOTTABLE WITH THE SEX FIELD REMOVED |

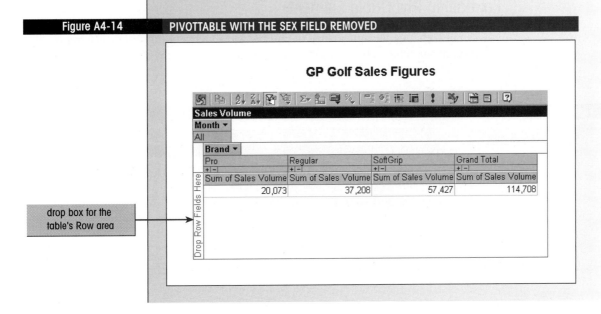

drop box for the table's Row area

If you want to add a new field to the table, you must first display the table's field list. You ask Peter about this, and he tells you that he would like to see the sales figures broken down between right-hand and left-hand sales. This information requires the use of the Hand field.

To add the Hand field to the PivotTable:

1. Click the **Field List** button [image] on the PivotTable toolbar.

2. Drag the **Hand** field from the PivotTable Field List to the Row area drop box, and then release the mouse button. As shown in Figure A4-15, the table now displays sales figures broken down by brand and hand.

Figure A4-15	ADDING THE HAND FIELD TO THE PIVOTTABLE

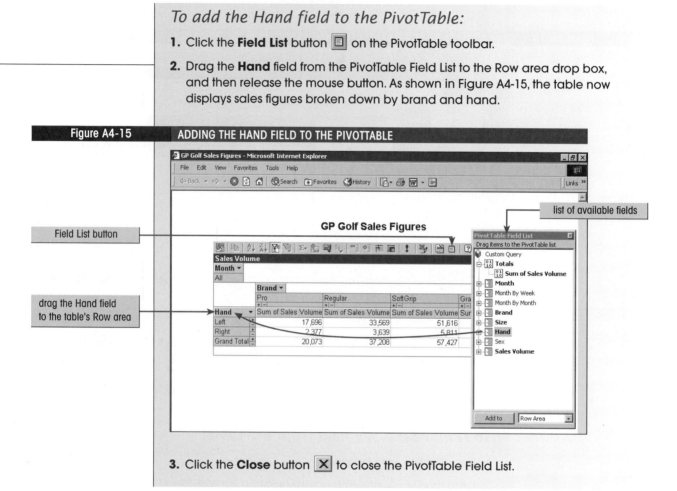

3. Click the **Close** button [X] to close the PivotTable Field List.

Formatting PivotTable Elements

You can also change the appearance of your PivotTable by hiding and displaying the different parts of the table. These include the title bar, toolbar, expand indicators and the drop areas or drop boxes. See Figure A4-16.

Figure A4-16	PIVOTTABLE ELEMENTS

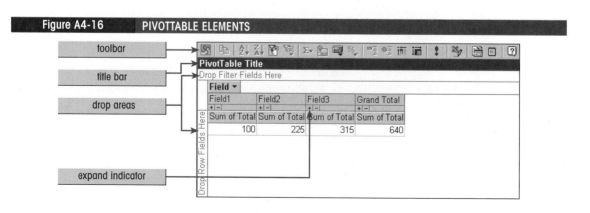

To view or hide these elements, you need to use the Commands and Options dialog box, which gives you complete control over the appearance of all elements of your PivotTable. Open the dialog box now and use it to hide the PivotTable's title bar.

To hide the title bar:

1. Click the **Commands and Options** button 🖼 on the PivotTable toolbar. The Commands and Options dialog box opens.

2. Click the **Behavior** tab.

3. Deselect the **Title bar** check box. See Figure A4-17.

| Figure A4-17 | COMMANDS AND OPTIONS DIALOG BOX |

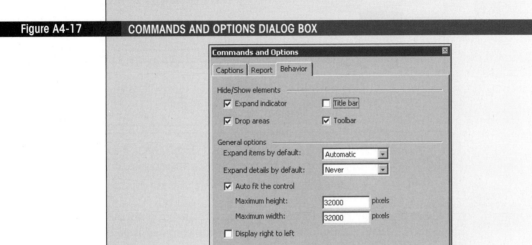

As you select different items in the PivotTable, the Commands and Options dialog box displays a different set of tabs from which you can further modify the appearance of the PivotTable. For example, you can use the Commands and Options dialog box to format the appearance of values and labels in the table. To see how this works, you decide to format the labels of the PivotTable to display yellow text on a solid blue background.

To format the PivotTable labels:

1. With the Commands and Options dialog box still open, click the **Hand** field button in the PivotTable. The options in the dialog box change.

2. Click the **Format** tab to display a collection of formatting options.

3. In the Text format pane, click the **list arrow** for the Font Color button 🅰, and then click the **Yellow** square (sixth row, fourth column from the left) in the color palette.

4. In the Cell format pane, click the **list arrow** for the Fill Color button 🖌, and then click the **Blue** square (second row, third column) in the color palette. Figure A4-18 displays the revised PivotTable.

Figure A4-18	FORMATTING PIVOTTABLE FIELDS

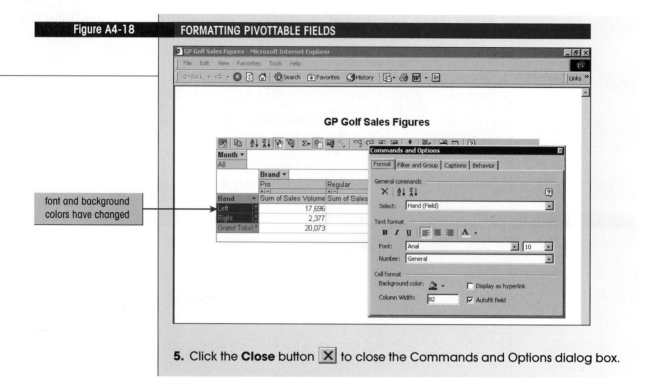

font and background colors have changed

5. Click the **Close** button ☒ to close the Commands and Options dialog box.

There are many other formatting options available with the Commands and Options dialog box. Many of these commands mirror the commands you've already worked with in your Excel workbooks. You may wonder what permanent effect these changes have had on the Web page. The answer is none. When you change the layout of the PivotTable or format the appearance of one or more PivotTable elements, those changes are present only for the time you're viewing the page. If you close your browser and reopen the page, it returns to its original state. Also, if someone else opens the Web page, they won't see any of your changes either. The changes you make to that page affect your browser only and only for that period of time that you're viewing the page.

Exporting a PivotTable to Excel

If you want to save your PivotTable in a more permanent format, you can export it back to Excel. The changed PivotTable won't replace the original table; rather a new workbook will be created containing the new PivotTable along with the underlying source data.

To export your PivotTable to Excel:

1. Click the **Export to Microsoft Excel** button 🔄 on the PivotTable toolbar. Excel opens a new workbook similar to the one shown in Figure A4-19 containing the PivotTable with your revised formatting. Note that the workbook contains two worksheets: Sheet1 contains the PivotTable and Sheet2 contains the underlying data values.

Figure A4-19	**EXPORTING THE WEB PIVOTTABLE TO EXCEL**

Excel automatically generates a new filename

PivotTable retains the formatting and layout of the Web page's PivotTable

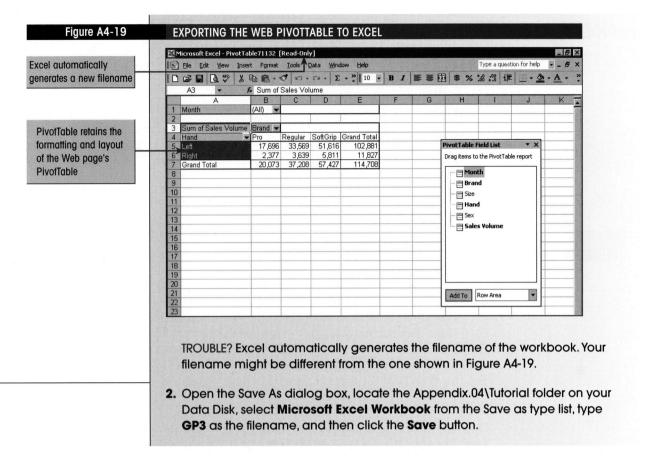

TROUBLE? Excel automatically generates the filename of the workbook. Your filename might be different from the one shown in Figure A4-19.

2. Open the Save As dialog box, locate the Appendix.04\Tutorial folder on your Data Disk, select **Microsoft Excel Workbook** from the Save as type list, type **GP3** as the filename, and then click the **Save** button.

You've completed your work on PivotTables and the Web. You can save and close your programs now.

To finish your work:

1. Close the GP2 and GP3 workbooks.

2. Close your Web browser.

The process of exporting the PivotTable to an Excel workbook will be useful to people in the Sales group. They'll be able to view sales data on the company's Intranet, and if they want, they can easily export that information to Excel for further work. Peter is pleased with what you've shown him about PivotTables and the Web. He'll look over your work and present the page you've created to the network group for their approval.

Session A4.1 Quick Check

1. What is the difference between an interactive and noninteractive Web page?

2. What is spreadsheet functionality?

3. What is a PivotTable list?

4. What is PivotTable functionality?

5. What are some limitations in creating an interactive chart for the Web? Can you edit the chart you create?

REVIEW ASSIGNMENTS

Peter has worked some more with the PivotTable Web page you created. He's very enthusiastic about it and would like to see you do the same thing for GP Golf's line of golf shoes. GP Golf makes three styles of shoes: the American, the Fairway, and the Standard models. Shoes come in two types: soft spikes and hard spikes. There are also different models for men and women. He has stored the sales data in an Excel workbook that contains a PivotTable that he wants you to export to a Web page. Like the page you created earlier, this PivotTable list should utilize PivotTable functionality.

To complete this task:

1. Open the **Shoes1** workbook located in the Appendix.04\Review folder on your Data Disk. Enter the date and your name in the Documentation sheet. Save the workbook as **Shoes2** in the same folder. Switch to the Shoe Sales Table worksheet.

2. Publish the PivotTable located on the Shoe Sales Table worksheet as an interactive Web page with the filename **GP_Shoes.html** located in the Appendix.04\Review folder on your Data Disk. Use PivotTable functionality in the Web page. Set "GP Golf Shoe Sales" as the title of the page.

3. Print the initial version of the Web page.

4. Add the Month field to the Page area of the PivotTable and have the PivotTable display sales data for only the month of April. (*Hint*: Deselect the (All) option, and then select just the month whose sales data you want to display.)

5. Add the Gender field to the Row area of the table so that values of the Spikes field are nested within the Gender field.

6. Hide the title bar area in the PivotTable.

7. Print the revised version of the Web page.

8. Export the PivotTable to Excel. Insert a Documentation sheet containing your name and the date. Save the workbook as **Shoes3.xls** in the Appendix.04\Review folder on your Data Disk. Be sure to save the file in Microsoft Excel Workbook format, and *not* as a Web page.

9. Close your workbooks and Web browser. Exit Excel.

CASE PROBLEMS

Case 1. Creating an Interactive Spreadsheet for Davis Blades Davis Blades is a leading manufacturer of roller blades. One of their most popular models is the Professional. Anne Costello, a sales analyst at Davis Blades, is examining the cost-volume-profit relationship of sales of the Professional for her region. She's preparing for an online sales conference over the Web and wants to create a Web page containing her CVP analysis. Because there will be different scenarios discussed at the online meeting, Anne would like a Web page to provide interactivity for the participants, allowing them to change her assumptions online and view the results. You tell Anne that you can create such a Web page using Excel and utilizing Spreadsheet functionality.

To complete this task:

1. Open the **Davis1** workbook located in the Appendix.04\Cases folder on your Data Disk. Enter the date and your name in the Documentation sheet. Save the workbook as **Davis2** in the same folder. Switch to the CVP Data worksheet.

Explore 2. Save the contents of the CVP Data worksheet as an interactive Web page using Spreadsheet functionality. The Web page filename should be **Davis_CVP.html** and should be stored in the Appendix.04\Cases folder on your Data Disk. Give the Web page the title "Davis Blades CVP Analysis". Print the Web page.

Explore 3. On the resulting Web page, change the number of units produced and sold from 1200 to 1500 units. What effect does this have on the operating income? (*Hint*: Use the vertical scroll bar to view the entire worksheet data.)

4. Format the background color of the cells in the first row of the spreadsheet, changing the color from green to red. Change the color of the text in cells A2 and A3 to red.

Explore 5. Hide the column and row headers, the title bar, the cell gridlines and the toolbar. (*Hint*: Look in the Sheet and Workbook tabs of the Commands and Options dialog box.)

6. Print the resulting Web page and close the Web browser.

7. Close your workbooks and Web browser. Exit Excel.

Case 2. Creating an Interactive Chart for the Bread Bakery It's time for the stockholders meeting for the Bread Bakery, a company specializing in finely baked breads. Your supervisor, David Keyes, would like to have some of the sales figures available on the Web for the stockholders before the convention. He's saved the information in a workbook and wants you to save the chart included in that workbook to the Web. He wants the chart to be interactive, rather than static.

To complete this task:

1. Open the **Bread1** workbook located in the Appendix.04\Cases folder on your Data Disk. Enter the date and your name in the Documentation sheet. Save the workbook as **Bread2** in the same folder. Switch to the Sales Chart worksheet.

Explore 2. Save the chart as a Web page with Chart functionality named **Sales_Chart.html** in the Appendix.04\Cases folder on your Data Disk. Give the Web page the title "Bread Bakery Sales".

3. Print the resulting Web page as it appears in your Web browser.

4. Edit the data table on the Web page using the AutoSum formula, and calculate the total sales for each brand of bread, for each quarter, and for all sales over the entire year. Print the Web page.

5. Filter the data table so that it displays the sales only for the third and fourth quarters. Print the Web page.

6. Hide the following elements in the data table: the toolbar, gridlines, title bar, row headers, and column headers. Print the resulting Web page.

7. Close your workbooks and Web browser. Exit Excel.

Session A4.1 QUICK CHECK

Session A4.1

1. A noninteractive Web page contains data from a workbook and some formatting, but does not allow the user to work with the data. An interactive Web page does allow the user to work with the data and perform some of the tasks of a spreadsheet.

2. the capability of a Web page to work like an Excel worksheet (in a limited fashion)

3. a Web version of the PivotTable with some of the features of an Excel PivotTable

4. the capability of a Web page to work like an Excel PivotTable, including the ability to link to a data source and refresh the appearance of the table with current data

5. Several features of the chart are lost when exported to the Web. You cannot edit the chart or format it.

INDEX

X

TASK REFERENCE

TASK	PAGE #	RECOMMENDED METHOD/NOTES
3-D cell reference, create	EX 6.08	When entering a function into a worksheet cell, select a sheet or sheet range, select a cell range within the selected sheet(s)
Absolute reference, change to relative	EX 2.14	Edit the formula, deleting the $ before the column and row references; or press F4 to switch between absolute, relative, and mixed references
Action, redo	EX 1.33	Click ⟳
Action, undo	EX 1.32	Click ⟲
Actions, redo several	EX 1.33	Click the list arrow for ⟳ ▾, select the action(s) to redo
Actions, undo several	EX 1.32	Click the list arrow for ⟲ ▾, select the action(s) to undo
Add-in, install and activate	EX 10.13	See Reference Window: Installing and Activating Add-Ins
Array formula, create	EX 9.23	Type the array formula into a cell or range of cells, press Ctrl + Shift + Enter after typing the formula
Auto Fill, copy formulas	EX 2.16	See Reference Window: Copying Formulas Using Auto Fill
Auto Fill, create series	EX 2.18	Select the range, drag the fill handle down, release mouse button, click ⊞, click the option button to complete series
AutoFilter	EX 5.19	See Reference Window: Filtering a List with AutoFilter
AutoFilter, custom	EX 5.21	Click any cell in the list, click Data, point to Filter, click AutoFilter, click the list arrow in the column that contains data you want to filter, click Custom, enter criteria in Custom AutoFilter dialog box, click OK
AutoFormat, apply	EX 3.31	Select the range, click Format, click AutoFormat, select an AutoFormat design, click OK
AutoShape, add text to	EX 4.37	See Reference Window: Inserting Text into an AutoShape
AutoShape, insert, reshape, resize, and rotate	EX 4.35	See Reference Window: Inserting an AutoShape
AutoSum, apply	EX 2.25	Click the cell in which you want the final value to appear, click the list arrow for Σ ▾, select the AutoSum function to apply
Background color, apply	EX 3.18	Select the range, click the list arrow for ▾, select a color square in the color palette
Background pattern, apply	EX 3.18	Open the Format Cells dialog box, click the Patterns tab, click the Pattern list arrow, click a pattern in the pattern gallery, click OK
Border, create	EX 3.15	Click the list arrow for ▾, select a border in the border gallery
Border, draw	EX 3.16	Click the list arrow for ▾, click, draw the border using the Pencil tool
Cell, clear contents of	EX 1.27	Click Edit, click Clear; or press Delete
Cell, edit	EX 1.31	See Reference Window: Editing a Cell
Cells, delete from worksheet	EX 1.27	Select the cell or range, click Edit, click Delete, select a delete option, click OK; or select the cell or range, right-click the selection, click Delete, select a delete option, click OK

TASK	PAGE #	RECOMMENDED METHOD/NOTES
Cells, insert into worksheet	EX 1.26	See Reference Window: Inserting New Cells into a Worksheet
Cells, merge	EX 3.21	Select the adjacent cells, open the Format Cells dialog box, click the Alignment tab, select the Merge check box, click OK
Cells, merge and center	EX 3.21	Select the adjacent cells, click
Cells, unlock	EX 8.11	Click Format, click Cells, click the Protection tab, deselect the Locked check box, click OK
Chart, add data label	EX 4.21	Select a data marker(s) or data series, click Chart, click Chart Options, click the Data Labels tab, select the data label type, click OK
Chart, add gridline	EX 4.10	Select the chart, click Chart, click Chart Options, click the Gridlines tab, click the check box for the gridline option you want to select, click OK
Chart, add, remove, revise data series	EX 4.18	See Reference Window: Editing a Chart's Data Source
Chart, change 3-D elevation	EX 4.34	Select a 3-D chart, click Chart, click 3-D View, enter the elevation value or click the Elevation Up or Elevation Down button, click OK
Chart, change location	EX 4.21	Select the chart, click Chart, click Location, specify the new location
Chart, change scale	EX 4.31	Double-click a value on the y-axis, enter the minimum and maximum values for the scale, click OK
Chart, change to 3-D	EX 4.32	Select the chart, click Chart, click Chart Type, select a 3-D sub-type, click OK
Chart, create with Chart Wizard	EX 4.04	See Reference Window: Creating a Chart with the Chart Wizard
Chart, format data marker	EX 4.27	Double-click the data marker, select the formatting options using the tabs in the Format Data Series dialog box
Chart, move	EX 4.12	Select the chart, move the pointer over the chart area, drag the chart to its new location, release the mouse button
Chart, resize	EX 4.13	Select the chart, move the pointer over a selection handle, drag the handle to resize the chart, release the mouse button
Chart, select	EX 4.12	Move the pointer over a blank area of the chart, and then click
Chart, update	EX 4.14	Enter new values for the chart's data source and the chart is automatically updated
Chart, use background image in	EX 4.29	Double-click the plot area, click the Patterns tab, click the Fill Effects, click the Picture tab, click Select Picture, locate and select the background image file, click Insert, click OK twice
Chart axis title, add or edit	EX 4.21	Select the chart, click Chart, click Chart Options, click the Titles tab, click in the Category (X) axis text box and type the text for the title, click in the Values (Y) axis text box and type the text for the title, click OK
Chart data markers, change fill color	EX 4.27	Double-click the data marker, click the Patterns tab, click Fill Effects, click the Gradient tab, select the color and related color options, click OK

TASK	PAGE #	RECOMMENDED METHOD/NOTES
Chart text, format	EX 4.23	Select the chart label, click a button on the Formatting toolbar; or double-click the chart label, select the formatting options using the tabs in the Format Data Label dialog box
Chart text, insert new unattached	EX 4.25	See Reference Window: Inserting Unattached Text into a Chart
Chart title, add or edit	EX 4.21	Select the chart, click Chart, click Chart Options, click the Titles tab, click in the Chart title text box and type the text for title, click OK
Chart Wizard, start	EX 4.04	Click [icon]
Code window, open	EX 12.07	See Reference Window: Viewing Windows in the Visual Basic Editor
Column, change width	EX 1.30	See Reference Window: Changing Column Width
Column, delete from worksheet	EX 1.27	Select the column, click Edit, click Delete; or select the column, right-click the selection, click Delete
Column, hide	EX 3.22	Select the headings for the columns you want to hide, right-click the selection, click Hide
Column, insert into worksheet	EX 1.30	See Reference Window: Inserting New Cells into a Worksheet
Column, repeat in printout	EX 3.38	Open the Page Setup dialog box, click the Sheet tab, click the Column to repeat at left box, click the column that contains the information you want repeated, click OK
Column, select	EX 1.19	Click the heading of the column you want to select. To select more than one column, press and hold the Ctrl key and click each individual column heading. To select a range of columns, click the first column heading in the range, press and hold the Shift key and click the last column in the range.
Column, unhide	EX 3.23	Select the column headings left and right of the hidden columns, right-click the selection, click Unhide
Comment, add	EX 7.17	See Reference Window: Attaching a Comment
Comment, format	EX 7.19	Right-click the border of the comment box, click Format Comment (or click Format, click Comment), select the formatting options you want to apply, click OK
Comment, hide	EX 7.18	Right-click the cell containing the comment, click Hide Comment
Copy, across worksheets	EX 6.09	Select a worksheet group, select the sheet in the group containing the data you want to copy, click Edit, point to Fill, and click Across Worksheets, specify whether you want to copy all of the selected cell or just the contents or format, click OK
Counts, create conditional	EX A1.06	Use the COUNTIF function
Custom format, create	EX A3.05	Open the Format Cells dialog box, click the Number tab, click Custom, enter the format code in the Type text box, click OK
Customize dialog box, open	EX 12.45	Click Tools, click Customize

TASK	PAGE #	RECOMMENDED METHOD/NOTES
Data, create a validation rule	EX 8.04	See Reference Window: Creating a Validation Rule
Data, create an error alert message	EX 8.08	See Reference Window: Creating an Error Alert Message
Data, create an input message	EX 8.07	See Reference Window: Creating an Input Message
Data, trim and format imported	EX 11.09	Begin importing the text file; in the Import Text Wizard – Step 3 of 3, use the options available to trim and format the data
Data form, add record	EX 5.14	See Reference Window: Adding a Record Using a Data Form
Data form, delete record	EX 5.17	See Reference Window: Deleting a Record Using a Data Form
Data form, search	EX 5.16	Click any cell in list, click Data, click Form, click Criteria, enter criteria, click Find Next
Date, insert current	EX 2.28	Insert the TODAY() or NOW() function
Dates, fill in with Auto Fill	EX 2.19	Select the cell containing the initial date, drag the fill handle to fill in the rest of the dates, click 🖼, select the option to fill in days, weekdays, months, or years
Delimited text file, import	EX 11.07	Begin to import the text file; in the Text Import Wizard - Step 2 of 3, click the Delimited option button, specify the delimiter
Drawing toolbar, display	EX 4.35	Click View, point to Toolbars, click Drawing; or click 🖫
Excel, exit	EX 1.19	Click File, click Exit; or click ☒
Excel, start	EX 1.05	Click Start, point to Programs, click Microsoft Excel
Find command, use	EX 5.09	Click Edit, click Find, enter the text to search for in the Find what list box, click Find All to display a list box of all cells matching the search criteria, click Find Next to go to the next cell that matches the search criteria
Fixed-width text file, create, remove column break in	EX 11.08	Begin to import the text file; in the Preview window in the Text Import move, Wizard - Step 2 of 3, click the location where you want to create a column, drag an existing line to a new location to move a column break, drag an existing line beyond the Preview window
Fixed-width text file, import	EX 11.06	Begin to import that text file; in the Text Import Wizard - Step 1 of 3, click the Fixed width option button
Font, change color	EX 3.10	Click the list arrow for 🇦▾, select a color in the color palette
Font, change size	EX 3.09	Click the list arrow for 10 ▾, click a size
Font, change style	EX 3.10	Select the text, click **B**, *I*, or U
Font, change typeface	EX 3.09	Click the list arrow for Arial ▾, click a font
Format, apply currency style, percent style, or comma style	EX 3.03	Click 💲, click %, or click 🔹; or open the Format Cells dialog box, click the Number tab, select a style, specify style-related options, click OK
Format, apply to several worksheets at once	EX 6.05	Group worksheets to be formatted, apply formatting commands, ungroup sheets after formatting

TASK	PAGE #	RECOMMENDED METHOD/NOTES
Format, clear	EX 3.25	Click Edit, point to Clear, click Formats
Format, conditional	EX 5.23	See Reference Window: Applying Conditional Formatting to Cells
Format, copy using fill handle	EX 3.07	Select the cell or range that contains the formatting you want to copy, drag the fill handle down, click [icon], click the Fill Formatting Only option button
Format, copy using Format Painter	EX 3.06	Select the cell or range that contains the formatting you want to copy, click [icon], drag the pointer over the cell or range to apply the formatting
Format, decrease decimal places	EX 3.03	Click [icon]
Format, find and replace	EX 3.26	See Reference Window: Finding and Replacing a Format
Format, increase decimal places	EX 3.05	Click [icon]
Format Cells dialog box, open	EX 3.07	Click Format, click Cells
Formula, copy	EX 2.12	See Reference Window: Copying and Pasting a Cell or Range
Formula, copy with Auto Fill	EX 2.16	See Reference Window: Copying Formulas Using Auto Fill
Formula, enter using keyboard	EX 1.23	See Reference Window: Entering a Formula
Formula, enter using mouse	EX 1.23	See Reference Window: Entering a Formula
Formulas, audit	EX 7.04	Click Tools, point to Formula Auditing, click Show Formula Auditing Toolbar, use available buttons to audit formulas
Formulas, enter into several worksheets at once	EX 6.04	Group worksheets, enter the formulas into the appropriate cells
Formulas, locate suspect	EX 7.13	See Reference Window: Locating Suspect Formulas
Formulas, trace errors	EX 7.10	See Reference Window: Tracing Errors
Formulas, trace precedent and dependent cells	EX 7.05	See Reference Window: Tracing Precedent and Dependent Cells
Formulas, view	EX 7.15	Click Tools, point to Formula Auditing, click Formula Auditing Mode; or press Ctrl + grave accent key (`) to toggle between the formula viewing and normal modes
Function, insert	EX 2.06	See Reference Window: Inserting a Function
Functions, create logical	EX A1.02	Use the IF, AND, OR, and NOT functions
Goal Seek, use	EX 10.07	See Reference Window: Using Goal Seek
Header/footer, create	EX 3.35	Open the Page Setup dialog box, click the Header/Footer tab, click the list arrow for the Header button or the Footer button, select an available header or footer, click OK

TASK	PAGE #	RECOMMENDED METHOD/NOTES
Header/footer, create custom	EX 3.36	Open the Page Setup dialog box, click the Header/Footer tab, click the Custom Header or Customer Footer button, complete the header/footer related boxes, click OK
Hyperlink, edit	EX 7.47	Right-click the cell containing the hyperlink, click Edit Hyperlink
Hyperlink, insert	EX 7.45	See Reference Window: Inserting a Hyperlink

If-Then-Else control structure, VBA syntax for creating	EX 12.35	If <Condition> Then
		   <Visual Basic Statements>
		Else
		   <Visual Basic Statements>
		End If

If-Then-Elself control structure, VBA syntax for creating	EX 12.36	If <Condition> Then
		   <Visual Basic Statements>
		Elself <Condition 2> Then
		   <Visual Basic Statements>
		Elself <Condition 3> Then
		   <Visual Basic Statements>
		Else
		   <Visual Basic Statements>
		End If

Input box, VBA syntax for creating	EX 12.30	Variable = InputBox(Prompt,Title)
Link, break	EX 6.31	Click Edit, click Links, select the link you want to break, click Break Link, click Break Links, click Close
Link, change source	EX 6.31	Click Edit, click Links, select the link whose source you want to change, click Change Source
Link, create to another Office XP program	EX A2.05	Select a chart or cell range in an Excel workbook, click [icon], switch to the other Office XP program, click Edit, click Paste Special, click the Paste link option button, click OK
Link, create to another workbook	EX 6.25	Click the cell in the destination file, type =, switch to the source file, click the cell that contains the data you want to link, complete the formula
Link, update	EX 6.31	Click Edit, click Links, select the link to update, click Update Values
Links, view list of	EX 6.31	Click Edit, click Links
List, create	EX 5.05	Enter field names in the top row of the list, enter the same type of data in each column of the list (the list should be separated from any other worksheet data by at least one blank row and one blank column)
List, display in outline view	EX 5.28	Click Data, click Subtotals, select a subtotals structure for the list, click the outline buttons located to the left of the worksheet window to hide and display outline levels

TASK	PAGE #	RECOMMENDED METHOD/NOTES
Lookup Table, create	EX 6.32	Create a table in a worksheet, insert compare values in the first row or column of the table, insert values to be retrieved in the rows or columns that follow
Lookup Table, use functions for	EX 6.34	Enter the VLOOKUP or HLOOKUP function in the active cell
Macro, edit	EX 12.39	Click Tools, point to Macro, click Macros, click the name of the macro name you want to edit, click Edit
Macro, record	EX 8.28	See Reference Window: Recording a Macro
Macro, run	EX 8.33	See Reference Window: Running a Macro
Macro, set security level for	EX 8.26	See Reference Window: Setting Excel's Security Level
Macro button, create	EX 8.42	See Reference Window: Creating a Macro Button
Macro code, print	EX 8.41	Click Tools, point to Macro, click Macros, select the macro whose code you want to print, click Edit, click File, click Print, select the Current Project option button, select the Code check box, click OK
Menu, add a toolbar button or menu item	EX 12.46	See Reference Window: Adding to a Menu or Toolbar
Menu, assign a macro to	EX 12.46	Display the menu, open the Customize dialog box, click the Commands tab, click Modify Selection, click Assign Macro, select the macro that you want to assign, click OK
Menu, customize	EX 12.45	See Reference Window: Customizing Excel Menus and Toolbars
Menu, copy and paste image	EX 12.52	Display the menu, open the Customize dialog box, click the Commands tab, click Insert, right-click the menu item or button whose image you want to copy, click Copy Button Image, right-click the menu to which you want to copy the image, click Paste Button Image
Menu item, edit properties of	EX 12.48	See Reference Window: Editing the Properties of a Menu Item or Toolbar Button
Menu item, remove	EX 12.56	Display the menu or toolbar, open the Customize dialog box, drag the menu item off the menu
Menu, restore	EX 12.57	Open the Customize dialog box, click the Toolbars tab, select the menu in the Toolbars list, click Reset
Message box, VBA syntax for creating	EX 12.41	MsgBox Prompt, Buttons, Title
Method, VBA syntax for applying	EX 12.24	Object.Method (Value1, Value2,...)
One-variable data table, create	EX 9.09	See Reference Window: Creating a One-Variable Data Table
Page, change orientation	EX 3.35	Open the Page Setup dialog box, click the Page tab, click the Landscape or Portrait option button

TASK REFERENCE

TASK	PAGE #	RECOMMENDED METHOD/NOTES
Page, set margins	EX 3.34	Open the Page Setup dialog box, click the Margins tab, specify the width of the margins, click OK
Page break, insert	EX 3.37	Click the cell below where you want the page break to appear, click Insert, click Page Break
Page Setup dialog box, open	EX 3.33	Click File, click Page Setup; or click the Setup button on the Print Preview toolbar
Pie chart, create	EX 4.14	Select the row or column of data values to be charted, click ▦, select Pie in the list of chart types, select a sub-type, complete the remaining Chart Wizard dialog boxes
Pie chart, explode piece(s)	EX 4.17	See Reference Window: Creating an Exploded Pie Chart
Pie chart, rotate	EX 4.16	Double-click the pie in the pie chart, click the Options tab, enter a new value in the Angle of first slice box, click OK
PivotChart, create	EX 5.45	Click any cell inside the PivotTable, click ▦ on the PivotTable toolbar, complete the Chart Wizard dialog boxes
PivotChart, retrieve external data for	EX 11.31	See Reference Window: Retrieving External Data for a PivotTable or PivotChart
PivotTable and PivotChart Wizard, start	EX 11.31	Click Data, click PivotTable and PivotChart Report
PivotTable, add a field	EX 5.40	Select the PivotTable, select a field in the PivotTable Field List, drag the field to the location on the table that where you want it to appear
PivotTable, add a page view	EX 5.41	Click and drag a pivot field to the area labeled Drop Page Fields Here
PivotTable, change layout	EX 5.38	Click a field button on the PivotTable, drag the field button to a new location in the table
PivotTable, create	EX 5.31	Select any cell in the list, click Data, click PivotTable and PivotChart Report, identify source, location, layout of data, and placement of the pivot table
PivotTable, create for the Web	EX A4.09	Select the worksheet containing the PivotTable, click File, click Save as Web Page, click Publish, select the PivotTable in the Choose list, click the Add Interactivity check box, select PivotTable functionality in the corresponding list box, click Publish
PivotTable, format numbers	EX 5.37	Click the PivotTable, click the ▦ on the PivotTable toolbar, select an AutoFormat, click OK; or click the PivotTable, use the buttons on the Formatting toolbar
PivotTable, hide a field item	EX 5.43	Click the list arrow for the field button, deselect the check box for the field item you want to hide
PivotTable, refresh	EX 5.44	Click ▦ on the PivotTable toolbar
PivotTable, remove a field	EX 5.42	Click the field button, drag it to an area outside of the table
PivotTable, retrieve external data for	EX 11.31	See Reference Window: Retrieving External Data for a PivotTable or PivotChart

TASK	PAGE #	RECOMMENDED METHOD/NOTES
PivotTable, sort	EX 5.39	Click a cell in the PivotTable that contains the field you want to sort, click Data, click Sort, specify how you want to sort the field, click OK; or click the cell that contains the field you want to sort, click ▤ or ▤
PivotTable, sort by multiple fields	EX 5.39	Click a cell in the PivotTable that contains the field you want to sort, click Data, click Sort, specify how you want to sort each field, click OK
PivotTable, specify a layout	EX 5.34	See Reference Window: Laying Out the PivotTable on the Worksheet
Print area, define	EX 3.37	Select the range, click File, point to Print Area, click Set Print Area
Print Preview, open	EX 3.32	Click ▤
Project, change name of	EX 12.07	See Reference Window: Changing the Name of a Project
Project Explorer, open	EX 12.06	See Reference Window: Viewing Windows in the Visual Basic Editor
Properties, change with the Properties window	EX 12.09	Select an object in Project Explorer, open the Properties window, select a property in the Alphabetic list, enter a new value for the property, press Enter
Properties window, open	EX 12.06	See Reference Window: Viewing Windows in the Visual Basic Editor
Property, VBA syntax for changing	EX 12.23	Object.Property =Expression
Query, edit	EX 11.28	Click a cell in the external data range, click ▤ on the External Data toolbar, use the options in the Query Wizard to edit the query
Query, filter data in	EX 11.19	See Reference Window: Filtering Data in a Query
Query, refresh	EX 11.25	See Reference Window: Refreshing External Data
Query, save	EX 11.22	See Reference Window: Saving a Query
Query, select columns (or fields) for	EX 11.17	See Reference Window: Selecting Columns to Import Using the Query Wizard
Query, set properties for	EX 11.27	See Reference Window: Setting Properties for External Data
Query, sort data for	EX 11.21	See Reference Window: Sorting Data in a Query
Query Wizard, start	EX 11.15	Click Data, point to Import External Data, click New Database Query, select the data source, select the Use the Query Wizard to create/edit queried check box, click OK
Range, copy	EX 1.18	Select the cell or range, press and hold the Ctrl key and drag the selection to the new location, release the mouse button and Ctrl
Range, move	EX 1.18	Select the cell or range, drag the selection to the new location, release the mouse button
Range, select adjacent	EX 1.16	See Reference Window: Selecting Adjacent or Nonadjacent Ranges of Cells
Range, select nonadjacent	EX 1.16	See Reference Window: Selecting Adjacent or Nonadjacent Ranges of Cells
Range name, create	EX 8.17	See Reference Window: Creating a Range Name

TASK	PAGE #	RECOMMENDED METHOD/NOTES
Range name, create from a list	EX 8.19	Place the range names in the first or last row or the first or last column of the list, select the list, click Insert, point to Name, click Create, specify whether to create the range names based on the first row, last row, first column, or last column in the list, click OK
Range name, edit	EX 8.21	Click Insert, point to Name, click Define, select the range name you want to edit, change the cell reference in the Refers to reference box, click Add
Range name, replace cell reference with	EX 8.21	See Reference Window: Replacing a Cell Reference with a Range Name
Relative reference, change to absolute	EX 2.14	Type $ before the column and row references; or press F4 to insert $
Review, accept and reject changes for	EX 7.30	See Reference Window: Accepting and Rejecting Changes to Cells
Review, route a workbook for	EX 7.33	See Reference Window: Mailing a Workbook
Review, track changes for	EX 7.27	See Reference Window: Tracking Changes to Cells
Review, view comments for	EX 7.24	Click View, point to Toolbars, click Reviewing, click [icon] to view the next comment in the workbook
Row, change height	EX 1.30	Move the pointer over the row heading border until the pointer changes to ✛, click and drag the border to increase or decrease the height of the row
Row, delete from worksheet	EX 1.27	Select the row, click Edit, click Delete; or select the row, right-click the selection, click Delete
Row, hide	EX 3.22	Select the headings for the rows you want to hide, right-click the selection, click Hide
Row, insert into worksheet	EX 1.30	See Reference Window: Inserting New Cells into a Worksheet
Row, repeat in printout	EX 3.38	Open the Page Setup dialog box, click the Sheet tab, click the Row to repeat at top box, click the row that contains the information
Row, select	EX 1.19	Click the heading of the row you want to select. To select more than one row, press and hold the Ctrl key and click each individual row heading. To select a range of rows, click the first row heading in the range, press and hold the Shift key and click the last row in the range
Row, unhide	EX 3.23	Select the rows headings above and below the hidden rows, right-click the selection, click Unhide
Row and column, freeze	EX 5.06	Select a cell below and right of row or column you want to freeze, click Window, click Freeze Panes
Row and column, unfreeze	EX 5.06	Select a cell below and right of row or column you want to freeze, click Window, click Unfreeze Panes
Scenario, create	EX 9.26	See Reference Window: Defining a New Scenario
Scenario, edit	EX 9.33	See Reference Window: Editing a Scenario
Scenario, view	EX 9.30	See Reference Window: Viewing a Scenario

TASK	PAGE #	RECOMMENDED METHOD/NOTES
Scenario Manager, open	EX 9.26	Click Tools, click Scenarios
Scenario PivotTable report, create	EX 9.35	Open the Scenario Manager, click Summary, click the Scenario PivotTable report option button, click OK
Scenario summary report, create	EX 9.34	See Reference Window: Creating a Scenario Summary Report
Sheet tab, format	EX 3.25	Right-click the sheet tab, click Tab Color, select a color in the color palette
Solver, add a constraint to	EX 10.14	Start Solver, click Add, specify the conditions of the constraint, click Add to add another constraint or click OK
Solver, add an integer constraint to	EX 10.18	Start Solver, click Add, specify the conditions of the constraint using INT in the list of constraints
Solver, create an answer report	EX 10.20	Start Solver, click Solve, click Answer, select the Keep Solver Solution option button, click OK
Solver, load model	EX 10.26	Start Solver, click Options, click Load Model, select the cell range containing the model parameters, click OK three times
Solver, save model	EX 10.22	Start Solver, click Options, click Save Model, specify the cell in which to store the model parameters, click OK, click Cancel, click Close
Solver, set options for	EX 10.22	Start Solver, click Options
Solver, set target cell for	EX 10.13	Start Solver, specify the cell reference for target cell, whether Solver should minimize, maximize, or set cell to a specific value
Solver, start and use	EX 10.14	See Reference Window: Using Solver
Sort, more than one sort field	EX 5.12	See Reference Window: Sorting a List Using More Than One Sort Field
Sort, single field	EX 5.11	Select any cell in column you want to sort by, click ⬆ or ⬇
Spelling, check	EX 7.03	See Reference Window: Checking a Workbook for Spelling Errors
Style, apply	EX 3.29	Select the range, click Format, click Style, select a style, click OK
Style, create	EX 3.29	Select the cell that contains the formatting you want to use as the basis of the new style, click Format, click Style, type a name for the style, click Modify, specify format options using the Format Cells dialog box, click OK twice
Style, modify	EX 3.30	Select the range, click Format, click Style, click Modify, change style attributes, click OK
Sub procedure, insert	EX 12.14	See Reference Window: Inserting a New Procedure
Sub procedure, VBA syntax for	EX 12.13	Sub Procedure_Name(Parameters) VBA Commands and Comments End Sub
Submenu, add new to menu or toolbar	EX 12.50	Open the Customize dialog box, click the Commands tab, click New Menu, drag the New Menu item to the menu or toolbar
Subtotals, insert	EX 5.26	See Reference Window: Calculating Subtotals in a List

TASK	PAGE #	RECOMMENDED METHOD/NOTES
Sum, create conditional	EX A1.06	Use the SUMIF function
Template, create	EX 6.16	See Reference Window: Saving a Workbook as a Template
Template, open	EX 6.14	See Reference Window: Opening a Workbook Based on a Template
Text, align within a cell	EX 3.11	Click [icon], click [icon], click [icon], click [icon], or click [icon]; or open the Format Cells dialog box, click the Alignment tab, select a text alignment option, click OK
Text, change indent	EX 3.11	Click [icon] or [icon]
Text, enter into cell	EX 1.20	Click the cell, type the text entry, press Enter
Text, replace	EX 5.09	Click Edit, click Replace, enter the text to be replaced in the Find what list box, enter the replacement value in the Replace with list box, click Replace All or Replace
Text, wrap in cell	EX 3.13	Open the Format Cells dialog box, click the Alignment tab, select the Text wrap check box, click OK
Text file, import	EX 11.05	Click File, click Open, select Text Files in Files of type list box, locate and select the text file you want to import, click Open, complete the steps of the Text Import Wizard
Text file, remove columns from	EX 11.08	Begin to import the text file; in the Text Import Wizard - Step 3 of 3 dialog box, click anywhere in the column, click the Do not import column (skip) option button
Text file, specify the starting row for	EX 11.06	Begin to import the text file; in the Text Import Wizard - Step 1 of 3 dialog box, change the value displayed in the Start import at row list box
Text Import Wizard, start	EX 11.05	Open any text file from within Excel
Toolbar, add a toolbar button or menu item	EX 12.46	See Reference Window: Adding to a Menu or Toolbar
Toolbar, customize	EX 12.45	See Reference Window: Customizing Excel Menus and Toolbars
Toolbar button, assign an image to custom	EX 12.52	Display the custom toolbar button, open the Customize dialog box, right-click the toolbar button, click Change Button Image, select an image from the icon palette
Toolbar button, assign a macro to	EX 12.48	Display the toolbar button, open the Customize dialog box, click the Commands tab, click Modify Selection, click Assign Macro, select the macro that you want to assign, click OK
Toolbar button, copy and paste image	EX 12.52	Display the toolbar button, open the Customize dialog box, click the and Commands tab, click Insert, right-click a button or menu item whose image you want to copy, click Copy Button Image, right-click the button or menu item to which you want to copy the image, click Paste Button Image
Toolbar button, display text on a custom	EX 12.49	Display the custom toolbar button, open the Customize dialog box, right-click the toolbar button, click in the Name box, edit the text and include & to indicate the hot key, click Image and Text

TASK	PAGE #	RECOMMENDED METHOD/NOTES
Toolbar button, edit properties of	EX 12.48	See Reference Window: Editing the Properties of a Menu Item or Toolbar Button
Toolbar button, remove	EX 12.56	Display the toolbar or menu, open the Customize dialog box, drag the button off the toolbar or menu
Toolbar, create new	EX 12.44	Open the Customize dialog box, click the Toolbars tab, click New, type the name of the new toolbar, click OK
Two-variable data table, create	EX 9.16	See Reference Window: Creating a Two-Variable Data Table
VBA, insert a command	EX 8.40	Open the Visual Basic Editor, display the macro in the Code window, click the end of a VBA command, press Enter, type the new command, click File, click Close and Return to Microsoft Excel
Visual Basic Editor, open	EX 8.41	Click Tools, point to Macro, click Visual Basic Editor (or press Alt + F11); or click Tools, point to Macro, click Macros, select a macro, click Edit
Web options, define	EX 7.47	Click Tools, click Options, click the General tab, click Web Options, select the Web-related options that you want to define, click OK
Web page, create	EX 7.41	See Reference Window: Saving a Workbook as a Web Page
Web query, create	EX 11.38	Click Data, point to Import External Data, click New Web Query, enter the name of the Web query, click Go, specify the conditions for importing the data
Web query, refresh	EX 11.46	Click a cell in the external data range, click [icon] on the External Data toolbar
Web query, run	EX 11.44	See Reference Window: Running a Web Query
Web query, save	EX 11.42	[icon] on the External Data toolbar, [icon] on the External Data toolbar
Workbook, create based on an existing file	EX 6.20	Click File, click New, click Choose workbook in the New from existing workbook section of the Task Pane, select the file on which to base the new workbook, click Create New
Workbook, mail	EX 7.33	See Reference Window: Mailing a Workbook
Workbook, open	EX 1.12	Click [icon] (or click File and click Open or click the Workbook link in the Task Pane), locate the drive and folder that contains the workbook, click the filename, click Open (or double-click the workbook filename in the Task Pane)
Workbook, print	EX 1.36	Click [icon]; or click File, click Print, select printer and print-related options, click OK
Workbook, protect	EX 8.13	See Reference Window: Protecting a Workbook
Workbook, remove sharing from	EX 7.36	Click Tools, click Share Workbook, deselect the Allow changes by more than one user at the same time check box, click OK, click Yes
Workbook, save for first time	EX 1.14	Click [icon] (or click File, click Save or Save As), locate the folder and drive in which to store the file, type a filename, click Save

TASK	PAGE #	RECOMMENDED METHOD/NOTES
Workbook, save in a different format	EX 1.14	See Reference Window: Saving a Workbook in a Different Format
Workbook, save to update	EX 1.14	Click 🖫; or click File, click Save
Workbook, save with new name	EX 1.14	Click File, click Save As, locate the folder and drive in which to store the file, type a filename, click Save
Workbook, share	EX 7.19	See Reference Window: Sharing a Workbook
Workbook, unprotect	EX 8.14	Clicks Tools, point to Protection, click Unprotect Workbook
Workbooks, merge	EX 7.34	See Reference Window: Merging Workbooks
Worksheet, add background image	EX 3.23	See Reference Window: Adding a Background Image to the Worksheet
Worksheet, change zoom setting	EX 5.07	Click View, click Zoom, enter the zoom setting or select a zoom setting option button, click OK
Worksheet, copy	EX 1.35	See Reference Window: Moving or Copying a Worksheet
Worksheet, delete	EX 1.33	Click the sheet tab, click Edit, click Delete Sheet; or right-click the sheet tab, click Delete
Worksheet, insert	EX 1.34	Click Insert, click Worksheet; or right-click a sheet tab, click Insert, click Worksheet icon, click Insert
Worksheet, move	EX 1.35	See Reference Window: Moving or Copying a Worksheet
Worksheet, protect	EX 8.14	See Reference Window: Protecting a Worksheet
Worksheet, rename	EX 1.35	Double-click the sheet tab that you want to rename, type a new name, press Enter
Worksheet screen elements, hide	EX 12.53	Click Tools, click Options, deselect the check boxes for the screen elements you want to hide, click OK
Worksheet screen elements, restore	EX 12.53	Click Tools, click Options, select the check boxes for the screen elements you want to restore, click OK
Worksheet, unprotect	EX 8.12	Click Tools, point to Protection, click Unprotect Sheet
Worksheets, group	EX 6.03	See Reference Window: Grouping and Ungrouping Worksheets
Worksheets, move between	EX 1.11	Click the sheet tab for the worksheet you want to view; or click one of the tab scrolling buttons, click the sheet tab
Worksheets, ungroup	EX 6.06	Right-click any worksheet tab in the group, click Ungroup Sheets; or click the tab of a worksheet outside of the group
Workspace, create	EX 6.38	Open all workbooks to be placed in the workspace, click File, Save Workspace, enter a name for the workspace, click Save
Workspace, open	EX 6.38	Click File, click Open, select the workspace file, click Open, click Update if prompted to update any links contained in the files

Core Standardized Coding Number	Certification Skill Activity Activity	Tutorial Pages	End-of-Tutorial Practice End-of-Tutorial Pages	Exercise	Step Number
Ex2002-1 Ex2002-1-1	**Working with Cells and Cell Data** Insert, delete, and move cells	1.18	1.38 1.39 1.39	Review Assignment Case Problem 1 Case Problem 2	7 2 4–5
		1.26–1.28	1.38	Review Assignment	4
Ex2002-1-2	Enter and edit cell data including text, numbers, and formulas	1.20–1.25, 1.31	1.38 1.39	Review Assignment Case Problem 1	3–6,10 3,5–8, 11,15
			1.39,1.40	Case Problem 2	3,7–10, 14
			1.40–1.41 1.41,1.42	Case Problem 3 Case Problem 4	3–6 2,3,5,7
Ex2002-1-3	Check spelling	7.02–7.04	7.49 7.52 7.53	Review Assignment Case Problem 3 Case Problem 4	2 5 4
Ex2002-1-4	Find and replace cell data and formats	3.25–3.27			
		5.09–5.10	5.50	Case Problem 2	5
Ex2002-1-5	Work with a subset of data by filtering lists	5.18–5.20	5.48 5.50	Review Assignment Case Problem 2	8,10 10
Ex2002-2 Ex2002-2-1	**Managing Workbooks** Manage workbook files and folders	1.12–1.14	1.38 1.39 1.39 1.40	Review Assignment Case Problem 1 Case Problem 2 Case Problem 3	1 1 1 1
Ex2002-2-2	Create workbooks using templates	6.14–6.16			
Ex2002-2-3	Save workbooks using different names and file formats	1.12–1.15	1.38 1.39 1.39 1.40 1.41	Review Assignment Case Problem 1 Case Problem 2 Case Problem 3 Case Problem 4	2 1 1 1 1
Ex2002-3 Ex2002-3-1	**Formatting and Printing Worksheets** Apply and modify cell formats	3.03–3.14	3.41	Review Assignment	4,6,7, 9–17
			3.42 3.43 3.44 3.45	Case Problem 1 Case Problem 2 Case Problem 3 Case Problem 4	4 3–8 3–8 6
Ex2002-3-2	Modify row and column settings	1.26–1.28	1.40	Case Problem 2	2
		3.22–3.23			
		5.06–5.07	5.49 5.50 5.51 5.52	Case Problem 1 Case Problem 2 Case Problem 3 Case Problem 4	3 4 4 3

Standardized Coding Number	Certification Skill Activity		Tutorial Pages	End-of-Tutorial Practice		
	Activity			End-of-Tutorial Pages	Exercise	Step Number
Ex2002-3-3	Modify row and column formats		1.29–1.30	1.38	Review Assignment	8,11
				1.39	Case Problem 1	4,12
				1.40	Case Problem 2	6,15
				1.41	Case Problem 4	4
			3.11–3.14	3.44	Review Assignment	4
					Case Problem 3	4
Ex2002-3-4	Apply styles		3.28–3.31	3.42	Case Problem 1	5
Ex2002-3-5	Use automated tools to format worksheets		3.31–3.32	3.41	Review Assignment	5
				6.38	Review Assignment	7
				6.40	Case Problem 1	6
				6.40	Case Problem 2	5
Ex2002-3-6	Modify Page Setup options for worksheets		3.33–3.39	3.41	Review Assignment	19
				3.42	Case Problem 1	6
				3.43	Case Problem 2	9,12
				3.44	Case Problem 3	10
Ex2002-3-7	Preview and print worksheets and workbooks		1.36	1.38	Review Assignment	14
				1.39	Case Problem 1	14
				1.40	Case Problem 2	16
				1.41	Case Problem 3	7
				1.42	Case Problem 4	6,8
			3.32–3.33	3.34	Case Problem 2	13
			3.37	3.41, 3.42	Review Assignment	18,22
				3.43	Case Problem 2	10,13
				3.44	Case Problem 3	9,12
				3.46	Case Problem 4	9
			4.38–4.40	4.43	Review Assignment	13,14
				4.45	Case Problem 2	13
				4.45	Case Problem 3	15
Ex2002-4	**Modifying Workbooks**					
Ex2002-4-1	Insert and delete worksheets		1.33–1.34	1.38	Review Assignment	9,13
				1.39	Case Problem 1	10,13
				1.40	Case Problem 2	12,13
				1.42	Case Problem 4	3,4
Ex2002-4-2	Modify worksheet names and positions		1.35	1.38	Review Assignment	9,12
				1.39	Case Problem 1	9,10
				1.40	Case Problem 2	11,13
				1.41	Case Problem 4	3
			3.24–3.25			
Ex2002-4-3	Use 3-D references		6.06–6.08, 6.22–6.25	6.38	Review Assignment	4,6
				6.39,6.40	Case Problem 1	2,5
				6.40	Case Problem 2	4
				6.41	Case Problem 3	2,4
				6.41,6.42	Case Problem 4	3,7

Standardized Coding Number	Certification Skill Activity		Tutorial Pages	End-of-Tutorial Practice		
		Activity		End-of-Tutorial Pages	Exercise	Step Number
Ex2002-5	**Creating and Revising Formulas**					
Ex2002-5-1	Create and revise formulas		2.03–2.20	2.30–2.31	Review Assignment	5–10, 13,14
				2.31–2.32	Case Problem 1	5,6,7,8
				2.34	Case Problem 2	4,6
				2.35	Case Problem 3	11
Ex2002-5-2	Use statistical, date and time, in formulas		2.03–2.29	2.30,2.31	Review Assignment	3,6–8, 14–15
				2.31–2.32	Case Problem 1	4–7
				2.33	Case Problem 1	5–7
				2.34–2.35	Case Problem 3	4,6, 8–10
				2.36	Case Problem 4	5
				5.48	Review Assignment	8
				5.50	Case Problem 2	10
				5.51	Case Problem 3	3
Ex2002-6	**Creating and Modifying Graphics**					
Ex2002-6-1	Create, modify, position and print charts		4.03–4.35	4.42–4.43	Review Assignment	4–9
				4.43–4.44	Case Problem 1	3–12
				4.44	Case Problem 2	3–10
				4.45	Case Problem 3	4–11
				4.47	Case Problem 4	2–8
Ex2002-6-2	Create, modify and position graphics		4.35–4.40	4.43	Review Assignment	10–12
				4.45	Case Problem 3	12–13
Ex2002-7	**Workgroup Collaboration**					
Ex2002-7-1	Convert worksheets into web pages		7.36–7.44	7.50	Review Assignment	14–15
				7.51	Case Problem 1	8
				7.51–7.52	Case Problem 2	7–9
				7.53	Case Problem 3	8
				7.54	Case Problem 4	6
Ex2002-7-2	Create hyperlinks		7.44–7.47	7.50	Review Assignment	13
				7.50–7.51	Case Problem 1	6–7
				7.51	Case Problem 2	6
				7.53	Case Problem 3	9
Ex2002-7-3	View and edit comments		7.16–7.19	7.49,7.50	Review Assignment	5,9,10
				7.52	Case Problem 3	7
				7.53	Case Problem 4	5

Expert Standardized Coding Number	Certification Skill Activity Activity	Tutorial Pages	End-of-Tutorial Practice		
			End-of-Tutorial Pages	Exercise	Step Number
Ex2002e-1 Ex2002e-1-1	**Importing and Exporting Data** Import data to Excel	11.05–11.09	11.50–11.51 11.51 11.52 11.53 11.54 A2.13	Review Assignment Case Problem 1 Case Problem 2 Case Problem 3 Case Problem 4 Case Problem 2	4–14 2–7 2–10 3–10 3–7 2–6
Ex2002e-1-2	Export data from Excel	A2.04–A2.08	A2.11 A2.12	Review Assignment Case Problem 1	2–6 2–5
Ex2002e-1-3	Publish worksheets and workbooks to the Web	7.38–7.44 A4.09–A4.11	7.50 7.50 7.51 7.53 7.53 A4.18 A4.19 A4.19	Review Assignment Case Problem 1 Case Problem 2 Case Problem 3 Case Problem 4 Review Assignment Case Problem 1 Case Problem 2	14–15 8 7–9 8 6 2 2 2
Ex2002e-2 Ex2002e-2-1	**Managing Workbooks** Create, edit, and apply templates	6.13–6.22	6.40 6.41 6.42	Review Assignment Case Problem 1 Case Problem 2	11 10 9
Ex2002e-2-2	Create workspaces	6.37–6.39	6.44	Case Problem 4	10
Ex2002e-2-3	Use Data Consolidation	6.08–6.11	6.40 6.41 6.42 6.43	Review Assignment Case Problem 1 Case Problem 2 Case Problem 3	4 2 4 2
Ex2002e-3 Ex2002e-3-1	**Formatting Numbers** Create and apply custom number formats	9-16–9.17 A3.03–A3.09	9.39 A3.12–A3.13 A3.13 A3.13–A3.14	Review Assignment Review Assignment Case Problem 1 Case Problem 2	6 2–7 2–6 2–4
Ex2002e-3-2	Use conditional formats	5.22–5.25	5.48 5.49 5.50 5.51 5.52	Review Assignment Case Problem 1 Case Problem 2 Case Problem 3 Case Problem 4	9 6 8 7 7
Ex2002e-4 Ex2002e-4-1	**Working with Ranges** Use named ranges in formulas	8.15–8.24 12.27–12.31	8.48 8.53 8.55	Review Assignment Case Problem 2 Case Problem 3	6–8 3–4 2–5

Standardized Coding Number	Certification Skill Activity — Activity	Tutorial Pages	End-of-Tutorial Practice		
			End-of-Tutorial Pages	Exercise	Step Number
Ex2002e-4-2	Use Lookup and Reference functions	6.32–6.37	6.40	Review Assignment	6
			6.41	Case Problem 1	5
			6.43	Case Problem 3	4,5
			6.44	Case Problem 4	3,7
			8.56	Case Problem 4	5
			12.62	Case Problem 2	3
Ex2002e-5	**Customizing Excel**				
Ex2002e-5-1	Customize toolbars and menus	12.44–12.54	12.60	Review Assignment	9–11
Ex2002e-5-2	Create, edit, and run macros	8.27–8.46	8.48	Review Assignment	11–22
			8.51	Case Problem 1	8–12
			8.53	Case Problem 2	7–12
			8.56	Case Problem 4	7–10
		12.03–12.04; 12.12–12.19; 12.28–12.31; 12.39–12.43	12.59	Review Assignment	4–7
			12.62	Case Problem 1	2–5
			12.63–12.64	Case Problem 2	4–7
			12.65	Case Problem 3	3–9
			12.66	Case Problem 4	2–7
Ex2002e-6	**Auditing Worksheets**				
Ex2002e-6-1	Audit formulas	7.04–7.08	7.49	Review Assignment	3
			7.50	Case Problem 1	5
Ex2002e-6-2	Locate and resolve errors	7.08–7.16	7.49	Review Assignment	4
			7.50	Case Problem 1	5
			7.52	Case Problem 3	6
Ex2002e-6-3	Identify dependencies in formulas	7.08–7.16	7.49	Review Assignment	3
			7.50	Case Problem 1	5
Ex2002e-7	**Summarizing Data**				
Ex2002e-7-1	Use subtotals with lists and ranges	5.25–5.28	5.48	Review Assignment	7
			5.49	Case Problem 1	5
			5.50	Case Problem 2	9
			5.51	Case Problem	8–9
Ex2002e-7-2	Define and apply filters	5.20–5.21	5.50	Case Problem 2	6
			5.51	Case Problem 3	6
Ex2002e-7-3	Add group and outline criteria to ranges	5.28–5.29	5.48	Review Assignment	12
			5.51	Case Problem 3	10
Ex2002e-7-4	Use data validation	8.04–8.10	8.48	Review Assignment	4
			8.50	Case Problem 1	3–4
			8.56	Case Problem 4	3

Standardized Coding Number	Certification Skill Activity		Tutorial Pages	End-of-Tutorial Practice			
	Activity			End-of-Tutorial Pages	Exercise	Step Number	
Ex2002e-7-5	Retrieve external data and create queries		11.12–11.32	11.50–11.51	Review Assignment	4–16	
				11.51	Case Problem 1	2–7	
				11.52	Case Problem 2	2–10	
				11.53	Case Problem 3	3–10	
				11.54	Case Problem 4	3–7	
Ex2002e-7-6	Create Extensible Markup Language (XML) Web queries		11.13-11.22	11.50	Review Assignment	4–6	
				11.52	Case Problem 2	2–5	
				11.54	Case Problem 4	2–6	
Ex2002e-8	**Analyzing Data**						
Ex2002e-8-1	Create PivotTables, PivotCharts, and PivotTable/PivotChart Reports		5.31–5.47	5.48	Review Assignment	11–14	
				5.49	Case Problem 1	10–11	
				5.50	Case Problem 2	11	
				5.51	Case Problem 3	10–11	
				5.52	Case Problem 4	8–9, 11–13	
			9.35–9.38	9.40	Review Assignment	11	
				9.43	Case Problem 2	8	
			A4.05–4.10	A4.18	Review Assignment	2	
Ex2002e-8-2	Forecast values with what-if analysis		9.23–9.24	9.41	Case Problem 1	3	
Ex2002e-8-3	Create and display scenarios		9.22–9.32	9.39	Review Assignment	8–12	
				9.40–9.42	Case Problem 1	7–9	
				9.42–9.43	Case Problem 2	3–7	
				9.43–9.44	Case Problem 3	5–6	
				9.44–9.46	Case Problem 4	6–7	
Ex2002e-9	**Workgroup Collaboration**						
Ex2002e-9-1	Modify passwords, protections, and properties		8.10–8.15	8.48	Review Assignment	9,10	
				8.51	Case Problem 1	7,15	
				8.53	Case Problem 2	10–11	
				8.55	Case Problem 3	6	
				8.57	Case Problem 4	4,6	
Ex2002e-9-2	Create a shared workbook		7.19–7.23	7.49	Review Assignment	6,11	
				7.51	Case Problem 2	5	
				7.52	Case Problem 3	4	
				7.53	Case Problem 4	1,4	
Ex2002e-9-3	Track, accept and reject changes to workbooks		7.24–7.32	7.50	Review Assignment	8	
				7.50	Case Problem 1	3	
				7.51	Case Problem 2	4,5	
				7.52	Case Problem 3	2,3	
Ex2002e-9-4	Merge workbooks		7.34–7.36	7.50	Case Problem 1	2	
				7.51	Case Problem 2	2	
				7.53	Case Problem 4	2	

Excel 2002 Level I File Finder

Location in Tutorial	Name and Location of Data File	Student Saves File As...	Student Creates New File
Tutorial 1			
Session 1.1	Tutorial.01\Tutorial\Lawn1.xls	Tutorial.01\Tutorial\Lawn2.xls	
Session 1.2	(Continued from Session 1.1)		
Review Assignments	Tutorial.01\Review\Income1.xls	Tutorial.01\Review\Income2.xls	
Case Problem 1	Tutorial.01\Cases\CFlow1.xls	Tutorial.01\Cases\CFlow2.xls	
Case Problem 2	Tutorial.01\Cases\Balance1.xls	Tutorial.01\Cases\Balance2.xls	
Case Problem 3	Tutorial.01\Cases\Site1.xls	Tutorial.01\Cases\Site2.xls	
Case Problem 4			Tutorial.01\Cases\CashCounter.xls
Tutorial 2			
Session 2.1	Tutorial.02\Tutorial\Loan1.xls	Tutorial.02\Tutorial\Loan2.xls	
Session 2.2	(Continued from Session 2.1)		
Review Assignments	Tutorial.02\Review\Mort1.xls	Tutorial.02\Review\Mort2.xls	
Case Problem 1	Tutorial.02\Cases\School1.xls	Tutorial.02\Cases\School2.xls	
Case Problem 2	Tutorial.02\Cases\Sonic1.xls	Tutorial.02\Cases\Sonic2.xls	
Case Problem 3	Tutorial.02\Cases\Leland1.xls	Tutorial.02\Cases\Leland2.xls	
Case Problem 4			Tutorial.02\Cases\JrCol.xls
Tutorial 3			
Session 3.1	Tutorial.03\Tutorial\Sales1.xls	Tutorial.03\Tutorial\Sales2.xls	
Session 3.2	(Continued from Session 3.1)		
Review Assignments	Tutorial.03\Review\Region1.xls	Tutorial.03\Review\Region2.xls	
Case Problem 1	Tutorial.03\Cases\Running1.xls	Tutorial.03\Cases\Running2.xls	
Case Problem 2	Tutorial.03\Cases\WBus1.xls	Tutorial.03\Cases\WBus2.xls	
Case Problem 3	Tutorial.03\Cases\Blades1.xls	Tutorial.03\Cases\Blades2.xls	
Case Problem 4			Tutorial.03\Cases\Payroll.xls
Tutorial 4			
Session 4.1	Tutorial.04\Tutorial\Vega1.xls	Tutorial.04\Tutorial\Vega2.xls	
Session 4.2	(Continued from Session 4.1)		
Review Assignments	Tutorial.04\Review\VegaUSA1.xls	Tutorial.04\Review\VegaUSA2.xls	
Case Problem 1	Tutorial.04\Cases\CIC1.xls	Tutorial.04\Cases\CIC2.xls	
Case Problem 2	Tutorial.04\Cases\Powder1.xls	Tutorial.04\Cases\Powder2.xls	
Case Problem 3	Tutorial.04\Cases\Pixal1.xls	Tutorial.04\Cases\Pixal2.xls	
Case Problem 4			Tutorial.04\Cases\ BCancer.xls

Excel 2002 Level II File Finder

Location in Tutorial	Name and Location of Data File	Student Saves File As...	Student Creates New File
Tutorial 5			
Session 5.1	Tutorial.05\Tutorial\Vehicles.xls	Tutorial.05\Tutorial\Vehicle Data.xls	
Session 5.2	(Continued from Session 5.1)		
Session 5.3	(Continued from Session 5.2)		
Review Assignments	Tutorial.05\Review\VehicleData1.xls	Tutorial.05\Review\VehicleData2.xls	
Case Problem 1	Tutorial.05\Cases\Teahouse1.xls	Tutorial.05\Cases\Teahouse2.xls	
Case Problem 2	Tutorial.05\Cases\Faculty1.xls	Tutorial.05\Cases\Faculty2.xls	
Case Problem 3	Tutorial.05\Cases\Receivables1.xls	Tutorial.05\Cases\Receivables2.xls	
Case Problem 4	Tutorial.05\Cases\GourmetSales1.xls	Tutorial.05\Cases\GourmetSales2.xls	

Excel 2002 Level II File Finder (continued)

Location in Tutorial	Name and Location of Data File	Student Saves File As...	Student Creates New File
Tutorial 6			
Session 6.1	Tutorial.06\Tutorial\LBC1.xls	Tutorial.06\Tutorial\LBC2003.xls	
Session 6.2	(Continued from Session 6.1)	Tutorial.06\Tutorial\LBC Cash Flow.xlt	
Session 6.3	Tutorial.06\Tutorial\LBC2000.xls Tutorial.06\Tutorial\LBC2001.xls Tutorial.06\Tutorial\LBC2002.xls Tutorial.06\Tutorial\LBCSum1.xls Tutorial.06\Tutorial\LBCSum2.xls	Tutorial.06\Tutorial\Choir Files.xlw	
Review Assignments	Tutorial.06\Review\Contrib1.xls Tutorial.06\Review\CList.xls	Tutorial.06\Review\Contrib2003.xls	Tutorial.06\Review\ Contribution Record.xlt
Case Problem 1	Tutorial.06\Cases\Grade1.xls Tutorial.06\Cases\GRange1.xls	Tutorial.06\Cases\Grade2.xls Tutorial.06\Cases\GRange2.xls	Tutorial.06\Cases\Grading Template.xlt
Case Problem 2	Tutorial.06\Cases\Refrig1.xls	Tutorial.06\Cases\Refrig2.xls	Tutorial.06\Cases\ Refrigerator Sales.xlt
Case Problem 3	Tutorial.06\Cases\Kitchen1.xls	Tutorial.06\Cases\Kitchen2.xls	
Case Problem 4	Tutorial.06\Cases\Bike1.xls Tutorial.06\Cases\Bike2.xls Tutorial.06\Cases\Bike3.xls	Tutorial.06\Cases\North.xls Tutorial.06\Cases\South.xls Tutorial.06\Cases\Southwest.xls	Tutorial.06\Cases\Tour Bike Reports.xls Tutorial.06\Cases\Tour Bike Files.xls
Tutorial 7			
Session 7.1	Tutorial.07\Tutorial\DPReport1.xls	Tutorial.07\Tutorial\DPReport2.xls	
Session 7.2	Tutorial.07\Tutorial\DPReport3.xls Tutorial.07\Tutorial\DPReport5.xl Tutorial.07\Tutorial\Karen1.xls	Tutorial.07\Tutorial\DPReport4.xls Tutorial.07\Tutorial\DPReport6.xls	
Session 7.3	Tutorial.07\Tutorial\DPReport6.xls Tutorial.07\Tutorial\Meeting.htm	Tutorial.07\Tutorial\FReport2003.htm	
Review Assignments	Tutorial.07\Review\Project1.xls Tutorial.07\Review\Project2.xls Tutorial.07\Review\Stockholders.htm	Tutorial.07\Review\Project2.xls Tutorial.07\Review\Project4.xls	Tutorial.07\Review\Project.htm
Case Problem 1	Tutorial.07\Cases\SynApps1.xls Tutorial.07\Cases\Burdett.xls Tutorial.07\Cases\Chavla.xls Tutorial.07\Cases\Cooke.xls Tutorial.07\Cases\Schmidt.xls	Tutorial.07\Cases\SynApps2.xls	Tutorial.07\Cases\SynApps.htm Tutorial.07\Cases\SynApps_files\ filelist.xml Tutorial.07\Cases\SynApps_files\ sheet001.htm Tutorial.07\Cases\SynApps_files\ sheet002.htm Tutorial.07\Cases\SynApps_files\ sheet003.htm Tutorial.07\Cases\SynApps_files\ stylesheet.css Tutorial.07\Cases\SynApps_files\ tabstrip.htm
Case Problem 2	Tutorial.07\Cases\CWorld1.xls Tutorial.07\Cases\NewModem.xls Tutorial.07\Cases\NewPrice.xls Tutorial.07\Cases\CHome.htm	Tutorial.07\Cases\CWorld2.xls	Tutorial.07\Cases\Modems.htm
Case Problem 3	Tutorial.07\Cases\Imageon1.xls	Tutorial.07\Cases\Imageon2.xls	Tutorial.07\Cases\Summary.htm Tutorial.07\Cases\Earnings.htm Tutorial.07\Cases\Assets.htm Tutorial.07\Cases\Liabilities.htm Tutorial.07\Cases\Report.htm

Excel 2002 Level II File Finder (continued)

Location in Tutorial	Name and Location of Data File	Student Saves File As...	Student Creates New File
Case Problem 4	Tutorial.07\Cases\Cutler1.xls Tutorial.07\Cases\Erdahl.xls Tutorial.07\Cases\Hung.xls Tutorial.07\Cases\Nolan.xls	Tutorial.07\Cases\Cutler2.xls	Tutorial.07\Cases\Cutler.htm Tutorial.07\Cases\Cutler_files\chart001.htm Tutorial.07\Cases\Cutler_files\chart002.htm Tutorial.07\Cases\Cutler_files\filelist.xml Tutorial.07\Cases\Cutler_files\image001.gif Tutorial.07\Cases\Cutler_files\image002.gif Tutorial.07\Cases\Cutler_files\sheet001.htm Tutorial.07\Cases\Cutler_files\sheet002.htm Tutorial.07\Cases\Cutler_files\sheet003.htm Tutorial.07\Cases\Cutler_files\stylesheet.css Tutorial.07\Cases\Cutler_files\tabstrip.htm
Tutorial 8 Session 8.1	Tutorial.08\Tutorial\Stock1.xls	Tutorial.08\Tutorial\Stock2.xls	
Session 8.2	(Continued from Session 8.1)		
Session 8.3	(Continued from Session 8.2)		
Review Assignments	Tutorial.08\Review\Chart1.xls	Tutorial.08\Review\Chart2.xls	
Case Problem 1	Tutorial.08\Cases\CarStats1.xls Tutorial.08\Cases\Car Data.xls	Tutorial.08\Cases\CarStats2.xls	
Case Problem 2	Tutorial.08\Cases\Popcorn1.xls	Tutorial.08\Cases\Popcorn2.xls	
Case Problem 3	Tutorial.08\Cases\MBikes1.xls	Tutorial.08\Cases\MBikes2.xls	
Case Problem 4	Tutorial.08\Cases\HWSales1.xls	Tutorial.08\Cases\HWSales2.xls	

Excel 2002 Level III File Finder

Location in Tutorial	Name and Location of Data File	Student Saves File As...	Student Creates New File
Tutorial 9 Session 9.1	Tutorial.09\Tutorial\Rafting1.xls	Tutorial.09\Tutorial\Rafting2.xls	
Session 9.2	(Continued from Session 9.1)		
Review Assignments	Tutorial.09\Review\Season1.xls	Tutorial.09\Review\Season2.xls	
Case Problem 1	Tutorial.09\Cases\Curve1.xls	Tutorial.09\Cases\Curve2.xls	
Case Problem 2	Tutorial.09\Cases\Prints1.xls	Tutorial.09\Cases\Prints2.xls	
Case Problem 3	Tutorial.09\Cases\Bakery1.xls	Tutorial.09\Cases\Bakery2.xls	
Case Problem 4			Tutorial.09\Cases\Inn.xls
Tutorial 10 Session 10.1	Tutorial.10\Tutorial\Grill1.xls	Tutorial.10\Tutorial\Grill2.xls	
Session 10.2	(Continued from Session 10.1)		
Review Assignments	Tutorial.10\Review\Discount1.xls	Tutorial.10\Review\Discount2.xls	
Case Problem 1	Tutorial.10\Cases\Staff1.xls	Tutorial.10\Cases\Staff2.xls	
Case Problem 2	Tutorial.10\Cases\Auto1.xls	Tutorial.10\Cases\Auto2.xls	
Case Problem 3	Tutorial.10\Cases\Disk1.xls	Tutorial.10\Cases\Disk2.xls	
Case Problem 4			Tutorial.10\Cases\Sale.xls

Excel 2002 Level III File Finder (continued)

Location in Tutorial	Name and Location of Data File	Student Saves File As...	Student Creates New File
Tutorial 11			
Session 11.1	Tutor11\Tutorial\History.txt Tutor11\Tutorial\Sunrise.mdb	Tutor11\Tutorial\Sunrise1.xls	Tutor11\Tutorial\Sunrise Portfolio.dqy
Session 11.2	(Continued from Session 11.1)		
Session 11.3	Tutor11\Tutorial\Sunrise.htm		Tutor11\Tutorial\Sunrise Web Page.htm
Review Assignments	Tutor11\Review\ NYA2003.txt Tutor11\Review\Sunrise.mdb Tutor11\Review\Summary.htm	Tutor11\Review\Index1.xls	Tutor11\Review\Index Query.htm
Case Problem 1	Tutor11\Cases\DCList.txt	Tutor11\Cases\DCList2.xls	
Case Problem 2	Tutor11\Cases\ EZNet.mdb	Tutor11\Cases\EZNet2.xls	Tutor11\Cases\Vendor Query.dqy
Case Problem 3	Tutor11\Cases\Rates1.xls	Tutor11\Cases\Rates2.xls Tutor11\Cases\LRates.txt	
Case Problem 4	Tutor11\Cases\Arts.mdb		Tutor11\Cases\Arts Query.dgy Tutor11\Cases\Arts1.xls Tutor11\Cases\Arts2.xls
Tutorial 12			
Session 12.1	Tutorial.12\Tutorial\Datalia1.xls	Tutorial.12\Tutorial\Datalia2.xls	
Session 12.2	(Continued from Session 12.1)		
Session 12.3	(Continued from Session 12.2)		
Review Assignments	Tutorial.12\Review\Powder1.xls	Tutorial.12\Review\Powder2.xls	
Case Problem 1	Tutorial.12\Cases\SReport1.xls Tutorial.12\Cases\SData.xlz	Tutorial.12\Cases\SReport2.xls	
Case Problem 2	Tutorial.12\Cases\Maxwell1.xls	Tutorial.12\Cases\Maxwell2.xls	
Case Problem 3	Tutorial.12\Cases\CAPM1.xls	Tutorial.12\Cases\CAPM2.xls	
Case Problem 4			Tutorial.12\Cases\BG.xls
Appendix 1			
Session A1.1	Appendix.01\Tutorial\Branco1.xls	Appendix.01\Tutorial\Branco2.xls	
Review Assignments	Appendix.01\Review\Leave1.xls	Appendix.01\Review\Leave2.xls	
Case Problem 1	Appendix.01\Cases\Modem1.xls	Appendix.01\Cases\Modem2.xls	
Case Problem 2	Appendix.01\Cases\Housing1.xls	Appendix.01\Cases\Housing2.xls	
Appendix 2			
Session A2.1	Appendix.02\Tutorial\LHouse1.xls Appendix.02\Tutorial\Letter1.doc	Appendix.02\Tutorial\LHouse2.xls Appendix.02\Tutorial\Letter2.doc	
Review Assignments	sszAppendix.02\Review\Use1.xls Appendix.02\Review\Request1.doc	Appendix.02\Review\Use2.xls Appendix.02\Review\Request2.doc	
Case Problem 1	Appendix.02\Cases\Omicron1.xls Appendix.02\Cases\Show1.ppt	Appendix.02\Cases\Omicron2.xls Appendix.02\Cases\Show2.ppt	
Case Problem 2	Appendix.02\Cases\Phoenix1.xls Appendix.02\Cases\Accounting.doc Appendix.02\Cases\Earnings.doc Appendix.02\Cases\Expenses.doc Appendix.02\Cases\Investment.doc	Appendix.02\Cases\Phoenix2.xls	
Appendix 3			
Session A3.1	Appendix.03\Tutorial\Midland1.xls	Appendix.03\Tutorial\Midland2.xls	
Review Assignments	Appendix.03\Review\Study1.xls	Appendix.03\Review\Study2.xls	
Case Problem 1	Appendix.03\Cases\BG1.xls	Appendix.03\Cases\BG2.xls	
Case Problem 2	Appendix.03\Cases\Golf1.xls	Appendix.03\Cases\Golf2.xls	

Excel 2002 Level III File Finder (continued)

Location in Tutorial	Name and Location of Data File	Student Saves File As...	Student Creates New File
Appendix 4 Session A4.1	Appendix.04\Tutorial\GP1.xls	Appendix.04\Tutorial\GP2.xls	Appendix.04\Tutorial\Glove_Sales.html Appendix.04\Tutorial\Glove_Sales\filelist.xml Appendix.04\Tutorial\Glove_Sales\GP2-27905-cache001.xml Appendix.04\Tutorial\GP3.xls
Review Assignments	Appendix.04\Review\Shoes1.xls	Appendix.04\Review\Shoes2.xls	Appendix.04\Tutorial\GP_Shoes.html Appendix.04\Tutorial\GP_Shoes\filelist.xml Appendix.04\Tutorial\GP_Shoes\Shoes2-17897-cache001.xml Appendix.04\Review\Shoe3.xls
Case Problem 1	Appendix.04\Cases\Davis1.xls	Appendix.04\Cases\Davis2.xls	Appendix.04\Cases\Davis_CVP.html
Case Problem 2	Appendix.04\Cases\Bread1.xls	Appendix.04\Cases\Bread2.xls	Appendix.04\Cases\Sales_Chart.html

Note: GIF and XML files will have different filenames for different users.